Triathlon Training with Power

Triathlon Training with Power

Chris Myers and Hunter Allen

cognella®
PRESS

I dedicate this book to my wife and son, Irina and Alex. Thank you for believing in me and the support on this endeavor. Honey, we did it!

I want to thank Hunter for the mentorship on teaching me the art of coaching. Also, I want to thank Steve Palladino for the late-night talks on run training.

Chris Myers

This book is dedicated to all those amazing people that have helped me along the path. I stand on the shoulders of giants. Most of all, thank you to my family for supporting my dreams.

Hunter Allen

Contents

Part II: Training Plans 141

Preface

This book is designed to introduce you to power and how to utilize it across all three sports of triathlon. We wrote this book integrating the most up-to-date scientific research and training techniques for exercise physiology and power theory. This book is the first of its kind to integrate power theory for all three sports in triathlon. The sport of cycling has used power training techniques for the past two decades. In more recent years, running has adopted this type of training. Now, swimming has the capability to utilize power to enhance training.

You will learn how to conduct field testing and apply those results to create personalized power training zones and accurately target training intervals that work on your specific strengths and limiters. You will be introduced to the advanced performance metrics a power meter provides in order to analyze your training and racing performance. Finally, you will be able to see how to create a comprehensive training program from the provided case studies and detailed training plans.

Introduction

Triathlon: More data than ever!

In cycling, power meters have been ubiquitous as aero bars. Professionals and serious hobby cyclists alike have used them. Initially embraced by Masters riders, "early tech adopters," and engineers, power meters eventually "trickled up" to the pro ranks. Power meter software's advent, turned power meters into a proper training tool instead of just a fancy bike toy. The watershed book by Hunter Allen and Dr. Andrew R. Coggan, PhD *Training and Racing with a Power Meter* laid out the power training principles and gave millions of serious cyclists a road map to use power meters quickly and effectively.

A Brief History

Power meters for cycling first came on the market with the SRM power meter from Germany, with famed cyclist Greg Lemond using one as early as 1994 in races. It wasn't until around 1997, when the PowerTap hub became more and more available, that regular riders could afford to purchase one of these new-fangled training devices. Mysterious, hard to interpret, and fussy, the power meters and the data coming from them were not earth-shattering. Many "squiggly" lines and numbers were being downloaded from these devices (when they worked), and no one knew how to analyze them, nor were there even metrics created to give them a reference to understand. In 2000, the first-ever power meter conference was held by USA Cycling, and the teachers at this conference all complained about the same thing, "there is no good software to analyze this data." The co-author of this book, Hunter Allen, and his client, Kevin Williams, attended the conference, and they soon begin developing the first-ever comprehensive power meter software originally called CyclingPeaks.

Along with Dr. Coggan, this team also produced most of the power meter metrics in use today and is known throughout the world. CyclingPeaks merged with a company called "Training Bible" created by Joe and Dirk Friel, along with Gear Fisher, to better automate Joe's Annual Training Plan from his book, *The Cyclist's Training Bible.* TrainingPeaks software was born and continues to lead the power analysis software game today.

In 2006, Hunter and Dr. Coggan authored the book *Training and Racing with a Power Meter.* This became a best-seller among cycling training books and is now in its 3rd edition, printed in 8 languages with over 250,000 copies sold. Their book laid out the steps to train with a power meter clearly and concisely, and you will learn more about these steps throughout this book. Concepts such as Functional Threshold Power, Training Stress Score, Power Profiling, and more have become the language all cyclists use when speaking about power training. Triathletes also began embracing these concepts and asking tough questions about how best to use a power meter in triathlon. How should you pace an Ironman in terms of the percentage of functional threshold power to hold? What about pacing an Olympic Distance event? How does creating power play a role in triathlon, and what cadence is best to maximize your power output and limited energy? Initially, there was a lack of data in triathlon as not many triathletes were using power meters, much less sharing the data. That changed, and pacing strategies were developed based on wattage output. Sophisticated training routines were created to maximize training time and to better train for the demands of triathlon.

We have learned a tremendous amount about using a bike power meter in triathlon, and we share these hard-won lessons throughout this book. As power meters for bikes became more and more common, many triathletes asked about running and swimming. Recently, technology has started to catch up to swimming and a great example of this is the Form Goggles. These goggles provide you will real-time data on your heart rate and pace. The next step is power in the pool. While on the running side, carbon fiber sole shoes and the growth of carbon fiber sole running shoes has contributed greatly to improving pace. These light-weight shoes are stiff and the material properties of carbon fiber help to increase the forward momentum of the running ... thus making you faster! But, was there something that could be done from a tech standpoint to capture running and swimming data? Could there be a power meter for running? How would you ever measure swimming beside a simple stopwatch? Power meters have been developed for running and dryland training for swimming. You will learn more about these in later chapters. The most popular power meter is running is called the "Stryd." It can measure wattage, pace, and a host of other metrics, which we will explain in detail in the chapter on running. This device, along with another one called, "Run-Scribe" has opened the eyes of many a running coach, their athletes, and the triathletes that have used them. Increasing your power and reducing your vertical oscillation are just two of the impressive metrics that you will improve after reading this book. Running is no longer just throwing on a pair of shoes and shorts and heading out the door. You can now track all your running data, upload it to analysis software and learn if you are executing your workout correctly or not. Swimming remains a challenge to measure in the water, but using the Vasa Swim Trainer during dryland training has been equally eye-opening. The data generated by your swim training is very exciting. The amount of power generated by your arms is easily measured and translated to the water so that you continue to improve your swim leg. Swimming with a power meter is like having someone assessing your swim mechanics during your entire workout! You can see if you are maximizing the force potential of your swim stroke or not. We will discuss how to analyze the data and how to apply it to your swim training. The swim is a challenge for many triathletes. Using the elemental power training principles will help you define your training zones, your specific strengths and weaknesses in your stroke, and give you critical information to reduce your swim time.

Why should I use a power meter?

As coaches, we believe that understanding the "why" behind your workouts, training plan, and hard work is a powerful motivator. When you know why you are doing a specific set of running drills, such as "turnovers or pick-ups," which will help you reduce your vertical oscillation, you will be more willing to complete those drills correctly and effectively. When you are fatigued after multiple hard training days, and your training plan has you doing five hill repeats to improve your functional threshold power, you might question why you are doing those hill repeats. However, when you know that riding at your functional threshold power will make your bike leg faster and give you a better chance of success, then you are more likely to push yourself in each of those hills and possibly even do a sixth one. Why should you train with a data acquisition device like a running power meter? What will it tell you? How does using a power meter relates to your current metrics like your heart rate or GPS pace? What are you doing with that data, and do you need it? Consider these answers to the "why."

1. **Training with a power meter gives you a complete record of your effort.** It records every second of your training and racing. Know how much time you've spent in your power training zones. In your post-analysis, you can highlight areas of interest, intervals (whether they are hills or flats), and pace for review by you and your coach, and you can learn from your pacing efforts in every length triathlon.
2. **Add real meaning to your heart rate monitoring.** Heart monitoring alone does not tell you how your actual performance is improving; it just means how fast your heart is pumping. A power meter measures your work rate (power) and analyzes your efficiency by allowing you to compare heart rate data to power output to your cadence on the bike and run and finally to your speed and pace.
3. **Track your fitness changes.** Know with certainty if your fitness is improving and when you have reached a new PR. Avoid non-functional overreaching and overtraining syndrome by tracking your Training Stress Score and Intensity Factor levels.
4. **Analyze your race!** Want a subjective viewpoint on your use of energy in the race? Did you pace yourself correctly? A power meter can help you better analyze your event. You can easily see when you burned a match and used too much energy in parts of the course that you should not have. By looking back on the data, you can replay the race in your head and see exactly what it took to climb the hill in the middle of the course and whether you created power correctly.
5. **Pinpoint your strengths and weaknesses.** Do your Impact G's increase when you reduce your pace below an 8 min/mile pace? Do you produce less power when your cadence drops below 80 rpm? If you have to do 105% of your functional

threshold power for more than 3 minutes, will you still be able to hit your target wattage for the rest of the event? What is your stamina? Can you maintain close to your functional threshold power for the entire half ironman?

6. **Improve your interaction with your coach!** If you have a coach, your coach will likely want to know precisely what you are doing for your entire training and racing time. It brings you and your coach closer together! Your coach can use this data to improve your training plan to push yourself to the limit but avoid the dreaded nonfunctional overreaching. Your coach can instantly see what you are doing in races, training, and rides and make suggestions for further improvements. A power meter doesn't lie!
7. **Achieve your physical potential!** When you train with a power meter, it allows you to concentrate on the workload and provide that extra motivation to improve your efforts. For example, if you make a 5-minute effort and watch your average watts drop near the end of the effort, you'll pick it up just another notch to achieve your 5-minute wattage goal.
8. **Test your position and aerodynamics.** Your body position is the single most significant factor in determining your speed while riding at a specific power output. Why risk the disadvantage of a poor position when measuring your aerodynamics and discovering your fastest position?
9. **Pace your efforts.** It allows you to pace your effort better in your events, interval workouts, hill climbs, and long training rides. When you know your functional threshold power, you can learn the exact percentage that you should pace yourself for every length triathlon, so you will see that you went as hard as you could go and still had enough for a PR in the run.
10. **Use as a mobile testing lab!** A power meter allows you to test every month to quantitatively see what areas you have improved on and what still needs work. Training is testing. Testing is training.
11. **Enhance your indoor training.** With the advent of smart trainers and online virtual riding, you can use your indoor trainer to the fullest extent. Highly focus your intervals in just the exact wattage zone for optimal improvement.
12. **Coordinate your sports nutrition for best performance.** Knowing how much work (in kJ) you do in training allows you to plan your post-exercise meals to the kcal. You will recover faster and be able to train harder sooner.
13. **Plan, control, and execute your training like the pros.** Train efficiently so that your best fitness peaks at your goal events. Every top triathlon performance has been aided by the use of power meter training technology.

We know that you will take the knowledge in this book and use the power training principles to improve whichever area needs the most help. We recognize that you will better understand your training zones and more accurately train in the correct energy system so that you will be prepared for the next event. The application of the principles in this book will make you more focused in your intervals and motivated to achieve even more. We know this book will make you a better and faster triathlete and help you achieve your athletic goals!

Part 1

Using Power Meters in Triathlon

Chapter 1

SPLASH! Swimming and Training with Pace

Many triathletes consider swimming to be the hardest sport as it is the most difficult to develop and the first to detrain. Swimming performance is considered difficult to train and maintain due to the complex biomechanics involved with developing propulsion and reducing drag. Often, triathletes swim with training partners or U.S. Masters' Swim (USMS) clubs, which provide a great avenue for triathletes to maintain and improve their swim performance. Now, with the advent of technology, swim training can be more individualized. This allows the individual athlete to tailor the training program to their training needs. In this chapter, we will discuss how to determine your swimming power zones, how to apply them, and how to perform post-workout analysis. There are many aspects to swimming that determine your fastest swimming speed and as triathletes, it's important to have a good understanding of both how to increase your pace and also the "why" behind this new power-based training you will be doing. Before we dig into the "why" you need to change your thinking around your swimming, we believe it's important to learn the key action items you will need to take immediately to make your swimming pace even faster. Pacing in endurance sports and in triathlon is one of the most basic fundamental skills you must possess in order to complete an event successfully. We have all seen it too often: The newbie going out too fast in the first 300 yards of the swim only to have to slow down and do breast-stroke or sidestroke for a while in order to recover. Learning how to pace yourself in triathlon begins early in your process of becoming a triathlete and that pacing must change for each length of event in which you might compete. The pace that you maintain in a sprint triathlon is very different than pacing in your first long distance 140.6 event. You pace everything in triathlon from each of your three sports to fluid intake, to your nutrition, to your training days and even your recovery weeks. Pacing is absolutely the first place you need to start on your journey as a triathlete, and it's something that even the most experienced pros still need to work on and hone their skills in order to create that perfect race.

Swim Pacing Method

Swimmers and triathletes train to manipulate their anatomy and biomechanics to better leverage the physics of swimming to go faster. But how do athletes do this? These next sections are important for you to read carefully, re-read, and clearly understand as you will need to take action in the pool in order to find your pace. We recommend you bring this book with you to the pool, so that you can refer to it as needed. The following methods are not complicated, but will require some work on your part, and not just in the pool. The great thing about learning your swimming pace is that you will already be one step closer to training even more intelligently and cutting minutes off your time in the next triathlon. Traditionally, swim training is based on laps and a timer. The interval is based on how fast you can complete the set distance. For example, a traditional description of a swim workout looks like this:

Warm up: 200 free, 200 kick (100 front crawl/100 back), 100 pull with paddles, 100 drill (Tarzan)

Pre-set: 12 × 50 with 15 sec. rest
Odds = Kick
Evens = Non-freestyle stroke

Main set:
4 × 200 free (on the 4:00)
2 × 50 kick with 15s rest
4 × 100 breast (on the 2:00)
2 × 50 kick with 15s rest
8 × 50 free (on the 1:45)
2 × 50 kick with 15s rest

Cool down: 200 easy (stroke of choice)

The athlete kept the time of his length of time per lap via the clock on the wall or a swim watch with lap timing. This style of training leaves little for the athlete to know if they are swimming in a specific training zone. This type of training is designed for team training sessions. It is not individualized. This is still how many swimming clubs continue to train. It is an excellent approach for training multiple athletes across different swimming lanes. However, it does not address the strengths and limiters of the individual athlete. A system exists to overcome this limitation.

Swimming Critical Velocity (V_{cr})

V_{cr} in swimming is an important concept for you to understand and be able to use. Wakayoshi et al. defines it as the swimming velocity over a very long period of time without exhaustion." Typically, it is accepted that 1500 m is the maximal distance to maintain true threshold efforts. V_{cr} is also called your "Threshold Pace," and we'll use the two terms interchangeably throughout the rest of the book. In 1992, Wakayoshi et al. proposed a linear regression model based on maximal effort in swimming tests of differing distances (one above threshold; i.e., 200 m, and one just at or below threshold; i.e., 400 m or 500 m) would correspond with lactate threshold (2, 3). A third interval at 1000 m can be performed to better determine V_{cr}. However, this change to protocol was not proposed by Wakayoshi et al. This change was added later. Wakayoshi et al. demonstrated this method, along with the correct percentages, could provide the individual swimmer with personalized training zones (2, 3). This is what you are about to do: Test your baseline fitness. We all need to understand where our current fitness is in order to correctly establish our training zones and then also to quantify our improvements. If you don't know where you were 8 weeks ago, and you train hard for 8 weeks and then test yourself, you won't really know if you have improved or not. We suggest that at a minimum, you should test yourself every 8 weeks, as our body adapts and improves in generally 8 week cycles. It's fine to test every 4 weeks if you like, but know that you might or might not see improvements at the 4 week test, as this depends largely on your own commitment and ability to improve, along with the training phase you are in as the year progresses.

V_{cr} Testing Protocol

The best aspect about this protocol is that it can be performed in any pool length (i.e., meters or yards). In this case example, we will assume the pool length is in meters. This V_{cr} protocol takes place over two different test days. This is done to prevent undue fatigue from confounding your performance. With these types of tests, you want to be as rested as possible. So, to ensure enough rest, perform the follow tests at least two days apart from each other.

Test Day #1:

Warm up: 200 m at an easy pace

Pre-set:

Pull: 200 m (100 m follow-through drill/ 100 m fingertip drill)

Kick: 100 m (kick on back, no board)

Main set #1: **1 × 400 m timed**. Swim as hard as you can, but do not start out too hard to where you cannot finish the test, or you slow down significantly. Follow with 5–10 min active and passive rest and then move to MS2.

Main set #2: **1 × 200 m timed**, swim as hard as you can for the 200 m

CD: 200 m easy

TEST DAY #2:

Warm up: 200 m free

Pre-set:

200 m kick

100 m pull

100 m drill (choice)

Main set #1: 12 × 50 with 15 sec. rest
Odds = Kick
Evens = Non-free swim

Main set #2: **1 × 1000 m timed.** Swim as hard as you can, but do not start out too hard to where you cannot finish the test or you slow down significantly.

CD: 200 m easy

Special items to record during your testing include the following:

1. 1000 m, 400 m, and 200 m times (in seconds).
2. 200 m must be faster than 400 m time. This is necessary, or you will not be able to perform the calculation properly.
3. Stroke rate (SR). You can get this metric from your swim watch or have someone count the number of strokes it takes you to complete one length of the pool.
4. The V_{cr} test can be performed with only the 200 m and 400 m times, but the 1000 m (or 1500 m) test makes the threshold pace calculation more accurate.

How to Calculate Your V_{cr}

To better discuss how to calculate $V_{cr,}$ let us use an example. On test day, long-course triathlete Flynn performed his test in a 50-m pool. He performed the initial test protocol as outline for Test Day #1. During his first attempt at the test, his results were as follows:

200 m time = 120 sec
400 m time = 235 sec

After the test, Fynn sat down to analyze his results and found them invalid due to the limitation of the test. The 200 m time needs to be faster than the 400-m time. This result is determined by multiplying the 200 m result by 2. In Flynn's case, he found the following:

Test #1 results:
200 m time = 3:05 = 185 sec
400 m time = 6:08 = 368 sec

185 sec × 2 = 370 sec = **more than** the 400-m time of 268 sec = **invalid test**

So, based on this result, Flynn needed to redo his V_{cr} test.

Three days later, Flynn performed a second iteration of the V_{cr} test. The new results were as follows:

200 m time = 3:00 = 180 sec
400 m time = 6:08 = 368 sec

180 sec × 2 = 360 sec = **less than** the 400 m time of 368 sec = **valid test**

Since Flynn's new V_{cr} results were valid, he decided to perform the 1000 m portion of the V_{cr} test. Knowing he needed to be well rested to perform test protocol #2, he waited 48 hrs before performing the test. Flynn performed test protocol #2 in the same pool. His result was as follows:

1000 m = 14:00 = 840 sec

It is important to note, at the time this chapter was writing, no published research stated any quality control guidelines for 1000 m as explained for the 200 m and 400 m results. Based on this knowledge, Flynn knew he was able to calculate his V_{cr}. He calculated his V_{cr} utilizing the following methodology:

$$V_{cr} = \frac{(1000\ m - 400\ m - 200\ m)}{(1000\ m\ time - 400.m\ time - 200\ m\ time)}$$

Tested times:

200 m = 3:00 = 180 sec
400 m = 6:08 = 368 sec
1000 m = 14:00 = 840 sec

$$V_{cr} = \frac{(1000\ m - 400\ m - 200\ m)}{(840\ sec - 368\ sec - 180\ sec)}$$

$$V_{cr} = \frac{400}{292} = 1.37 \text{ meters / second}$$

Threshold pace = 100 m / 1.37 m/s = 73 s / 100 m = **1:13 min/100 m**

Figure 1.1 details Flynn's results in a graphical format. All three results fall into a linear pattern. Looking for this pattern is another avenue to determine the validity of the test results. Based on this his calculation and checks for test result validity, Flynn determined his V_{cr} was 1:13 min/100 m or 1.37 m/s. This V_{cr} result now allows him to calculate his personalized training zones.

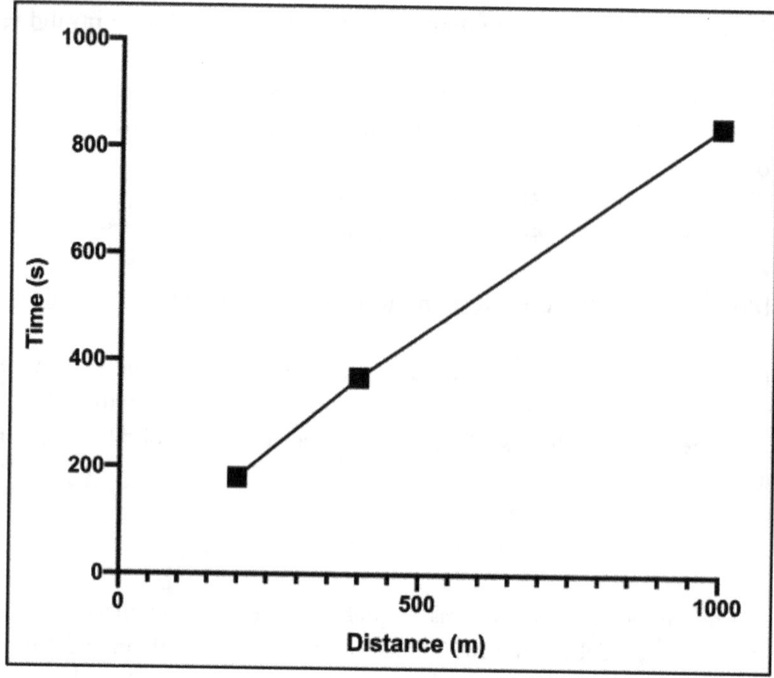

FIGURE 1.1 Graphic representation of Flynn's V_{cr} 200 m, 400 m, and 1000 m results.

Wakayoshi et al. presented creating pacing zones the following way (1):
Training zones (% of V_{cr}):

1. Zone 1: 75–80%
2. Zone 2: 80–90%
3. Zone 3: 90–100%
4. Zone 4: 100%
5. Zone 5: 100–110%
6. Zone 6: >110%

Utilizing the methodology presented by Wakayoshi et al., Flynn's swim training zones are as follows:

V_{cr} = 1.37 m/s = 1:37 min/100 m

1. Zone 1: 75–80%
   i. 75% = 1.03 m/s = 100 m / 1.03 m/s = 97s / 100 m = **1:37 min/100**
   ii. 80% = 1.10 m/s = 100 m / 1.10 m/s = 91s / 100 m = **1:31 min/100**
2. Zone 2: 81–90%
   i. 81% = 1.11 m/s = 100 m / 1.11 m/s = 98s / 100 m = **1:38 min/100**
   ii. 90% = 1.23 m/s = 100 m / 1.23 m/s = 81s / 100 m = **1:21 min/100**

3. Zone 3: 91–100%
   i. 91% = 1.24 m/s = 100 m / 1.24 m/s = 80s / 100 m = **1:20 min/100**
   ii. 99% = 1.36 m/s = 100 m / 1.36 m/s = 74s / 100 m = **1:14 min/100**
4. Zone 4: 100% = 100 m / 1.37 m/s = 73 s / 100 m = **1:13 min/100 m**
5. Zone 5: 100–110%
   i. 101% = 1.38 m/s = 100 m / 1.24 m/s = 72s / 100 m = **1:12 min/100**
   ii. 110% = 1.50 m/s = 100 m / 1.50 m/s = 67s / 100 m = **1:07 min/100**

Ultimately, the V_{cr} gives athletes individualized swimming training zones. This strategy allows you to tailor specific workouts to your target strengths and limiters. Furthermore, this approach allows the athlete to control the intensity to better plan a periodized training strategy. With all of this being said, the V_{cr} does have its limitations.

Conclusion

Swimming is as much technique as it is fitness. The more you can reduce drag in the water, the faster you will become. When it comes to stroke correction, the athlete needs a third party to provide feedback. The V_{cr} method does not provide biomechanical feedback. However, the lack of feedback is changed with the advent of swimming power meters which we discuss in the next chapter.

References

1. Ginn, E. (1993). *Critical speed and training intensities for swimming.* National Sports Research Centre.
2. Wakayoshi, K., Yoshida, T., Udo, M., Kasai, T., Moritani, T., Mutoh, Y., & Miyashita, M. (1992). A simple method for determining critical speed as swimming fatigue threshold in competitive swimming. *International Journal of Sports Medicine*, 13(5), 367–371. https://doi.org/10.1055/s-2007-1021282.
3. Wakayoshi, K., Yoshida, T., Udo, M., Harada, T., Moritani, T., Mutoh, Y., & Miyashita, M. (1993). Does critical swimming velocity represent exercise intensity at maximal lactate steady state? *European Journal of Applied Physiology and Occupation Physiology, 66*, 90–95. http://www.ncbi.nlm.nih.gov/pubmed/8425518.

Chapter 2

FREE-STYLE and POWER! Swimming and Training with Power

Swimming with Power

Swimmers in the past have used the simple stopwatch on the pool wall in order to quantify their improvements and one cannot fault this method. It is simple, easy to understand and something that any triathlete can do. However, triathletes, especially have longed for a tool to better help them understand their swimming. A difficult aspect with improving swimming is "feeling" the water. This aspect of swimming is often described as feeling the water during the catch and pull phases of the stroke cycle. Coaches provide drills such as sculling drills to improve this feeling. These drills are tried and true methods; however, they do not provide tangible feedback. The advent of swimming power technology solves this dilemma.

Technology has improved to the point that swimming power meters are becoming available to improve the quality of swim training. At the time of this writing, two swimming power meters are on the market: the Vasa SwimErg and the SmartPaddle.

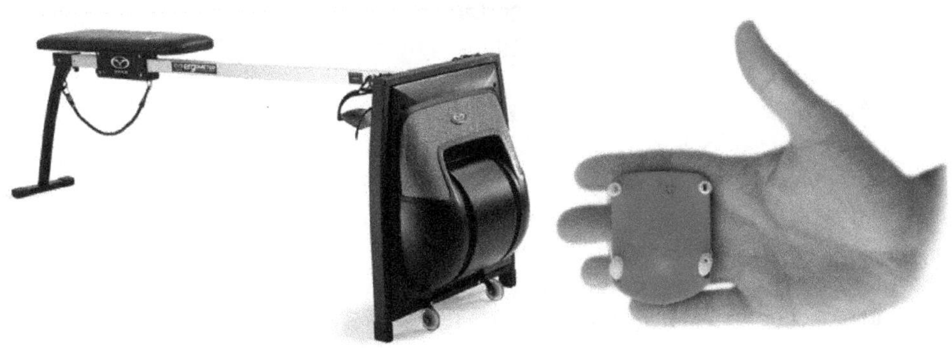

FIGURE 2.1 Vasa SwimErg (left) and SmartPaddle (right).

The Vasa SwimErg (Vasa, Essex Junction, VT) is a dry-side training ergometer, as shown in Figure 2.1. The system allows the athlete to work on their catch, pull, and push segments of the front quadrant portion of the freestyle swim stroke. The system has a built-in power meter that allows the athlete to work within your individualized training zones. You can pair this system with any smartwatch that utilizes Bluetooth and see your power in real time. Also, you can see your power output on the Vasa's display. This allows you to pace yourself utilizing power during your workouts. However, the system has one primary limitation. The system does not work in the water; it is a dry-side training aid. With this being said, the strength and endurance built from using this system does translate well to swimming in the pool and open water.

The SmartPaddle (Trainesense Ltd) is a force meter that is utilized in the water, as depicted in Figure 2.1. It measures the force generated by the hand in the water during the swim stroke. This system is not a power meter since it only reads the force of lift (F_L); the F_L is discussed in more detail in the next chapter. The system is held by the fingers similar to a fingertip paddle. This is the appropriate place for the force meter since the hand and forearm generate about 80% of the propulsion during the catch and pull phases (7, 8). Furthermore, the forces recorded by this device and the accompanied analysis software, allow the athlete to perform post-workout analysis. The insights gained from the analysis provide the athlete with feedback on the swim stroke and insights on how to make adjustments refinements for better efficiency. The limitation to this system is the athlete cannot see the force produced during the swim workout; however, the post-workout analysis is a powerful tool that provides analytics improve one's swim stroke.

With both systems, a standardized testing protocol needs to be used. At the time this book was written, no scientific articles were found that investigated how to use a power meter for swimming. However, we do have scientifically proven power-based protocols that can be used. Power theory for cycling and running has been used with great success. Biomechanically speaking, power application to swimming is similar to cycling given how the anatomy of the arm and shoulder works through the stroke cycle. In order to do this, you will need to swim for your maximal sustainable time for about 20 minutes. Similar protocols, that are backed by scientific research exist for cycling and running (1, 3). These protocols, discussed in cycling and running sections, are referred to as 20-minute threshold tests. The difficulty with this type of testing in swimming is knowing how long one is actually swimming. In order to perform a time check, the athlete needs to stop and look at a clock. To eliminate this limitation, the triathlete should use a distance that can be covered in 20 minutes.

The Australian Institute of Sport (AIS) suggests that triathletes perform a 1000 m swimming time trial to determine individualistic threshold pacing (6). The limitation to this test is, in most cases, swimming 1000 m can be done in under 15 minutes (6). This is much shorter than the accepted 20-minute test. For example, the AIS demonstrated that male and female elite and under 23 triathletes can finish the test in 12:24 to 13:28 (6). Performing a 1500 m time trial is a better option. For many age group triathletes, a 1500 m swimming time trial takes about 20–25 minutes to complete. The effort and time to swim 1500 m is similar to the running and cycling tests and agree with what Wakayoshi et al. defined for V_{cr}. This why the 1500 m swim test is the best option to perform the swimming functional threshold test.

The Swimming FTP (sFTP) Test

As with any test, you will need to ensure you are well rested, hydrated, and properly fueled beforehand. The test can be performed in a long- or short-course pool. However, the long course set up is better because it provides less turns and more steady state information. The following sFTP field testing protocol is different than described for V_{cr}. However, the duration is very similar to a cycling FTP test. The average triathlete can swim 1500 m in about 20 to 23 minutes. Due to this, a distance metric is provided over a duration metric. The following is the 1500 m sFTP test:

Warm up: 200 meters free/easy

Pre-set:

1 × 100 meters with paddles, focus on a smooth stroke
1 × 100 kick, no fins
1 × 100 kick with fins

Main set: Swim for 1500 m. You want your pace to be strong and consistent throughout the entire test. Ensure your swimming watch/computer is counting pace and strokes as well. If possible, capture your heart rate during the swim.

Cool down: 200 meters free/easy

Calculating Swimming FTP and Training Zones

To create your swimming power zones, you will need to calculate you swimming FTP (sFTP). This is done by taking the normalized power (NP) from the 1500 m time trial. Normalized Power "is the adjusted (normalized) average power" that "represents the physiological cost" if an uneven power output had been consistent (1, 2). You are encouraged to use the NP over the average power (AP) due to the turns in the pool. Most power-based analytical programs will take out the drops in power, especially those that would occur with turning in a swimming pool.

No matter the metric you use (NP or AP), you will want to take 92% to 95% of the 1500 m swim test. Dr. Myers created a coefficient system based on an athlete's experience and swimming fitness. This system takes into account your fitness level. Field data and his experience training triathletes and swimmers has demonstrated performance can fade over the 1500 m distance and is highly dependent on the athlete's fitness and experience level (4). The less experienced a triathlete/swimmer is in performing a long, steady-state effort, the less consistent the performance will be. Additionally, significant physiological differences exist between a beginner and an experienced triathlete swimmer. These coefficients take into account these variables. By using the correct coefficient, you will better determine your swimming FTP. The coefficients are as follows:

Experience Percentage
92%: New or inexperienced to distance swimming
93%: Some experience with distance swimming
94%: Experienced with distance swimming
95%: Very experienced with distance swimming

To better understand this, an example can be used. The triathlete, Flynn, bought a Vasa SwimErg. Just like the individualized training zones he determined during his V_{cr} testing, he wants to create individualized power training zones.

Utilizing the 1500 m swimming threshold test, Flynn had a NP of 105 W. He considered himself an experienced swimmer and used the 94% coefficient. Flynn calculated his sFTP utilizing the following equation:

$$\text{sFTP} = 1500 \text{ m power} \times \text{experience percentage}$$

So, for his test, Flynn's calculated his sFTP as

$$\text{sFTP} = 105 \text{ W} \times .94 = 99 \text{ W}$$

With the sFTP number of 99 W, Flynn utilized Dr. Coggan's classic power training levels to create personalized training zones similar to those used for V_{cr} zones.

The following power zones are based on Dr. Andy Coggan's work (2) and are discussed more in-depth in the next chapter.

COGGAN CLASSIC POWER LEVELS

LEVEL	DESCRIPTION	PERCENT
1	Active recovery	56% or less
2	Endurance	56% to 76%
3	Tempo	76% to 91%
4	Threshold	91% to 106%
5	$VO_{2\,Max}$	106% to 121%
6	Anaerobic capacity	121% or more

So, Flynn's power training zones from the calculated sFTP of 99 W are as follows:

COGGAN CLASSIC POWER LEVELS

LEVEL	DESCRIPTION	PERCENT	POWER RANGE	SUGGESTED DISTANCE
1	Active recovery	56% or less	< 55 W	Easy end/recovery
2	Endurance	56% to 76%	56–75 W	4000 m-plus
3	Tempo	76% to 91%	75–90 W	1500–4000 m
4	Threshold	91% to 106%	90–105 W	400–1500 m
5	$VO_{2\,Max}$	106% to 121%	105–120 W	100–400 m
6	Anaerobic capacity	121% or more	> 120 W	< 100 m

The creation of individualized swimming power zones will help in customizing workouts to target an athlete's swimming strengths and limitations. Additionally, the athlete can swim within the proper training zones tailored to target the correct metabolic system. This targeted approach helps to maximize training when an athlete is very limited on training time. An example workout utilizing power is as follows:

2-2-1 Efforts

Warm-up: 10 minutes working at endurance (power Z2, HR Z2, RPE 2–3)

Main Set: Repeat 8×:
– 2 min at steady effort or IRONMAN 70.3© swim pace at tempo (power Z3, HR Z3, RPE 4–5)
– 2 min hard or Olympic swim pace at threshold (power Z4, HR Z4, RPE 5–6)
– 1 min easy or recovery effort active recovery (power Z1, HR Z1, RPE 1–2)

Cool-down: 5 minutes easy active recovery (power Z1, HR Z1, RPE 1–2)

If the triathlete, Flynn, from the example were to use the same workout utilizing his individualized power swimming training zones, the workout would be as follows:

2–2–1 Efforts

Warm-up: 10 minutes working at endurance (56–75 W)

Main set: Repeat 8×:
– 2 min at steady effort or IRONMAN 70.3© swim pace at tempo (75–90 W)
– 2 min hard or Olympic swim pace at threshold (90–105 W)
– 1 min easy or recovery effort active recovery (< 55 W)

Cool-down: 5 minutes easy active recovery (< 55 W)

More importantly, these zones help make post-swim analysis more powerful.

Depending on the analysis program you utilize for post-workout analysis, you will be able to identify some of the following:

1. How fatigue affects your power output
2. How the differences in hand position increase or decrease your power output
3. How delays in the stroke cycle affect power output and propulsion
4. Accurate workout Training Stress Score (TSS) for overall training program progression

Note: Training Stress Score (TSS) is a composite number that takes into account the duration and intensity of a workout to arrive at a single estimate of the overall training load and physiological stress created by that training session. It is conceptually modeled after the heart rate-based training impulse. By definition, one hour spent at Functional Threshold Power (FTP) is equal to 100 points (1, 2).

An important aspect to consider with swimming power is why it is substantially lower than running and cycling power. This is due to the muscles involved and the environment. Remember, the muscles involved with the freestyle front quadrant mechanics are much smaller and less in number than running and cycling. The leg muscles are naturally bigger and can produce much more force (5). Additionally, swimming in water produces less force than running or cycling on concrete and dirt. These are the primary reasons for the power differences between swimming and the other two sports.

Conclusion

Advances in technology have brought power to swimming. Training with power will change the way you perform and analyze your swimming program. Power provides you with a multitude of analytical tools to improve your stroke and efficiency. Up to this point, we have provided you with advance power training tools for to apply power theory to your training program. In the next chapter, we will discuss the biomechanics and physics of free-style swimming and how it relates to power.

References

1. Allen, H., & Cheung, S. (2012). *Cutting-edge cycling.* Human Kinetics.
2. Allen, H., Coggan, A., & McGregor, S. (2019). *Training and racing with a power meter* (3rd ed.). VeloPress.
3. Coggan, A. *Training and racing with a power meter: An introduction.* VeloPress.
4. Newsome, P. S., & Young, A. (2012). *Swim smooth: The complete coaching programme for swimmers and triathletes.* Wiley.
5. Powers, S. K., & Howley, E. T. (2011). *Exercise physiology: Theory and application to fitness and performance* (8th ed.) McGraw-Hill.
6. Tanner, R. K., & Gore, C. J. (2013). *Physiological tests for elite athletes* (2nd ed.) Human Kinetics.
7. Toussaint, H. M. (1990). Differences in propelling efficiency between competitive and triathlon swimmers. *Medicine and Science in Sports and Exercise*, 22(3), 409–415.
8. Toussaint, H. M., Roos, P. E., & Kolmogorov, S. (2004). The determination of drag in front crawl swimming. *Journal of Biomechanics*, *37(11)*, 1655–1663. https://doi.org/10.1016/j.jbiomech.2004.02.020

Image Credits

Chapter 3

The FLOW of Swimming

Free-style Biomechanics and Physics of Swimming with Power

Basic Swimming Biomechanics

Now, that you have learned the most important steps of improving your swimming pace, it is important to clearly understand the different phases of the actual swim stroke so that you can continue to improve this biomechanical aspect of your swim. The front crawl (i.e., freestyle) stroke (shown in Figure 3.1) is a whole-body activity that requires a swimmer to use almost every muscle in the human body. The front quadrant arm mechanics of the freestyle swim stroke are arguably the most important element to going faster. Your hand, as it goes through the catch and pull phases, generates about 80% of the propulsion for forward movement (13, 16, 24, 25). Additional propulsion and buoyancy are created by the kicking motion (rear quadrant). The front quadrant portion of the front crawl stroke is broken into five phases: (a) entry and stretch, (b) catch, (c) pull (downsweep), (d) push (upsweep), and (e) overwater recovery (9, 19).

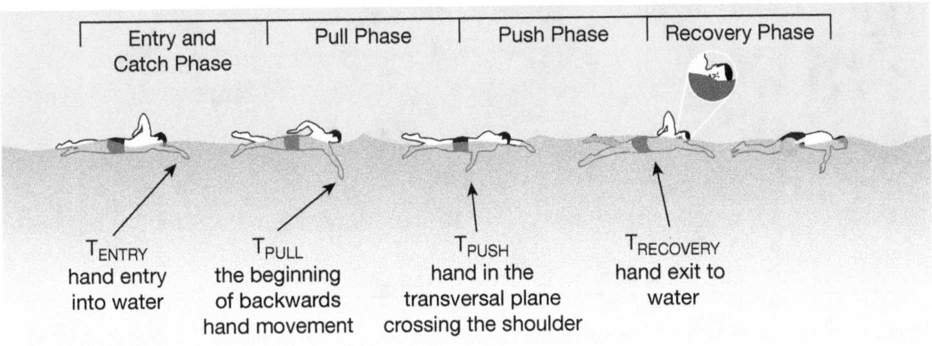

FIGURE 3.1 *(Continued)*

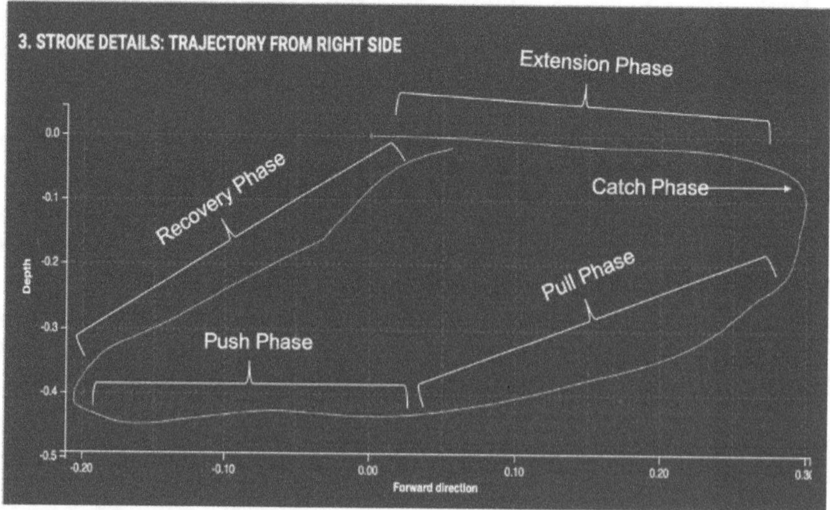

FIGURE 3.1 The top figure demonstrates the arm stroke phases in front crawl. The bottom figure depicts how the stroke cycle is measured by the SmartPaddle swim trainer. The yellow line demonstrates the trajectory of the right arm during the five phases of the stroke cycle.

A: Entry and Stretch Phase

During this phase, the arm is about to enter the water. This is considered the start of the stroke cycle. The arm is raised above the head and aligned slightly inside the shoulder. As the hand and arm enter the water, the arm begins to extend fully outward, as shown in Figure 3.2.

FIGURE 3.2 The stretch phase from the left arm during a single stroke.

B. Catch Phase

The catch phase begins after full extension of the arm. As the arm begins to pull downward, this action creates a "high elbow," as shown in Figure 3.3. The high elbow technique creates full usage of the hand and arm surface area to create maximum propulsion. The catch phase is arguably the most important element of front quadrant mechanics. Without maximizing the surface area of your arm, you significantly reduce your ability to create propulsion. We will dive into the "why" later in this chapter.

FIGURE 3.3 The catch phase from the left arm during a single stroke.

C. Pull Phase (Downsweep)

The pull phase starts immediately after the catch and as you begin the downward motion of pulling your arm backward towards your hips as shown in Figure 3.4. During the downward sweeping stroke, the arm creates a curvilinear motion that causes the shoulder, the wrist, and the hand to naturally turn outward (9, 16). This portion of the swim stroke produces the majority of the propulsion to move you forward, as shown in Figure 3.5. When the arm reaches the perpendicular position to the pool floor, the arm will begin to rotate upward. This point in the cycle denotes the end of the pull phase and the begin of the push phase.

FIGURE 3.4 The pull phase from the left arm during a single stroke.

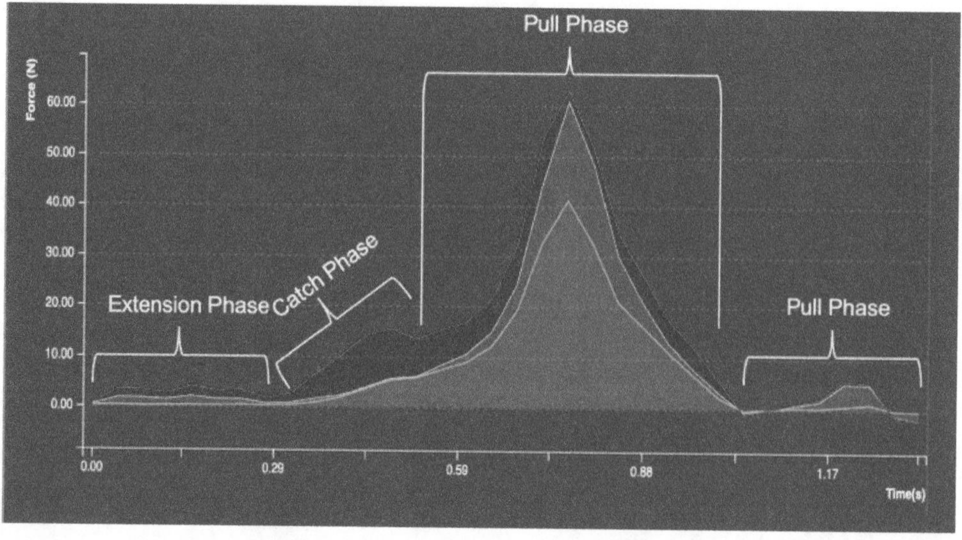

FIGURE 3.5 This figure depicts the amount of force (N) generated per each element of the stroke cycle. As shown, the catch phase begins the force generation where the majority of the propulsion is created during the pull phase. With a proper swim stroke, more propulsion can be created during the push phase, as depicted in this figure.

D. Push Phase (Upsweep)

This phase begins as the arm reaches the deepest part of the sweep, typically near your hips, and begins swinging upward (9, 16). As the arm pushes toward the rear of the body, the elbow begins to extend, "pushing" the hand backward toward the hip, as shown in Figure 3.6. This portion of the swim stroke provides a small amount of propulsion and transitions the arm for the recovery phase.

FIGURE 3.6 The beginning (left) and end (right) of the push phase.

E. Overwater Recovery Phase

This phase begins as the arm reaches the maximum extension at the end of the push phase. The arm exits the water and begins moving forward toward the head. Simultaneously, the elbow flexes 90 degrees or greater. Your fingertips should glide over the top of the water. This phase ends when the hand reenters the water allowing the stroke cycle to begin again.

The Physics Behind Freestyle Swimming Propulsion

Ultimately, athletic performance is measured on how fast the triathlete goes. Swimming velocity is calculated by using the following equation:

$$SV = SR \times SL$$

(equation 1)

Where:
SV = swim velocity
SR = stroke rate
SL = stroke length

Stroke rate (SR) = (# of strokes completed) / (Period of time or distance)
(Equation 2)

Swim velocity, SR, and SL are easily measured with current wearable technology (e.g., Garmin Forerunner 945, Fenix Series, or other smartwatches).

SR is one metric used to determine a swimmer's strength and endurance (15). Any changes in SR help determine an athlete's strength or weakness. However, SR is not a very reliable means to determine a swimmer's performance. A better way to measure performance is through power.

Traditionally, a cycling power meter utilizes torque and pedaling cadence to measure power (2, 3). The equation for power in cycling is as follows:

$$P = \text{cadence} \times \text{torque}$$

(Equation 3)

Where:
P = power (W)
cadence = rotations per minute (rpm)
τ = torque (Nm)

Power for swimming can be measure in a similar fashion. The main difference is the SR is substituted for the pedaling cadence. With this substitution, Equation 3 is transformed for swimming as follows:

$$P = SR \times \tau$$
(Equation 4)

Where:
P = power (W)
SR = stroke rate
τ = torque (Nm)

A better way to assess a swimmer's performance is to measure the force of lift (F_L) generated by each limb during the swimming stroke. In order to do this, one needs to understand the basic physics of swimming.

As started earlier, the catch phase is arguably the most important aspect of the freestyle front quadrant mechanics. The arm action during this phase creates the surface area needed to maximize propulsion during the pull phase. As shown in Figure 3.5, the pull phase produces the majority of the force for propulsion. This force is the F_L in Newtons (N).

An accurate way to measure the forces created by a swimmer's hand and arm during the freestyle swim stroke has eluded scientists, coaches, and athletes for decades (1). The characteristics of swimming are strongly rooted in fluid dynamics, kinematic physics, and human biomechanics (8). The proper measurement of a swimmer's F_L can give the coaches and the swimmers a powerful metric to improve stroke efficiency and strength.

The hand and forearm produce the preponderance of F_L for propulsion. The more cross-sectional surface area the hand and the arm can create, the more F_L is created. Studies, such as ones conducted by Bixler and Toussaint, have attempted to use computer modeling to calculate the optimal hand and finger positioning to generate the maximal amount of force. Elements such as finger spread, hand, and forearm angles all affect the amount of surface exposed changing the coefficient of drag (C_D) and F_L created, as shown in Figure 3.7. The more the F_L overcomes C_D, the faster the athlete moves through the water (6, 14, 17, 18, 26). The F_L translates to the propulsion for the swimmer through consistently changing around the axis of the shoulder (22).

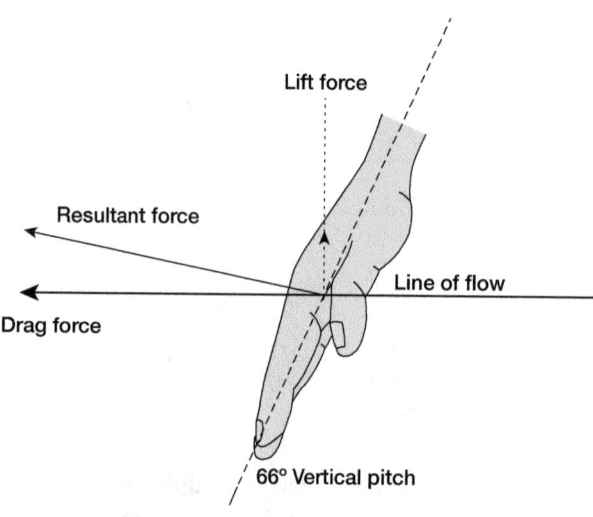

FIGURE 3.7 Forces acted on the hand during the stroke cycle.

Figures 3.1–3.6 show the front quadrant mechanics of the freestyle stroke are not static but dynamic. The swimmer's forward momentum is created by the rhythmic rotation of the arms. The resultant force of the axial rotation of the arms around the shoulder through the water with F_L creates torque. It's this resultant force that produces the majority of the forward propulsion an athlete experiences while doing the freestyle swim stroke (22).

Torque, by definition, is often referred to as a rotational force, and for swimmers produced perpendicularly to F_L. We briefly go into torque because it allows the coach and the athlete to view the rotation of the arms as crankset on the bike. Most cycling power meters measure power at the site of pedaling, which occurs with the crankset, as explained in Chapter 3. The circular motion of pedaling is similar to that of the arm cycle with freestyle swimming. The arms rotate around the shoulder joint. Cycling power meters utilize the rotational motion of pedaling to measure torque and then to calculate power. The same principle applies to swimming. The torque measured through the rotational movement of the arms while swimming is utilized to calculate the power generated during front-crawl swimming (Equation 4).

This information is great to know, but how does it ultimately fit into the phases of the front-crawl stroke cycle? Well, maximal F_L is created as the arm comes through the catch and pull phases of the stroke in a clockwise manner. Similar to cycling, the maximal torque is produced between the 1 o'clock to 5 o'clock positions. The same is true for the front crawl. This causes a forward directed motion of the body (12). One of the aspects to consider is the concept of active drag. The forward momentum through water creates the force known as active drag (F_D). F_L and F_D are always perpendicular to one another, as shown in Figure 3.7. As the swimmer's arm swings through the water, the vector magnitude of F_L and F_D are consistently changing. The magnitude of these forces are dependent on the angle (i.e., angle θ or angle of attack) the hand and forearm move through these phases, which creates the surface area to generate these forces (5). This relationship makes F_L and F_D interdependent.

During the catch phase, the largest amount of surface area of the hand and forearm are created, which allows for the greatest amount of F_L to be generated during the pull phase. As the hand and arm move through the water, a pocket of low pressure is created behind it. Since the hand and arm are nonstreamlined, and we want a large cross-sectional area, the water is unable to move around the hand in a streamline manner. This creates swirling motion around the hand (this can be seen in Figure 3.4 as the triathlete's right arm moves through the pull phase). Just behind the hand is the area of low pressure. This low pressure with the build-up of higher pressure on the front side of the hand increases the F_D (21). This phenomenon creates the F_D perpendicular to the F_L. Ultimately, the resultant force (as determined by Newton's second and third laws) is about 45° to either force (Figure 3.7). This resultant force determines the direction the triathlete moves through the water. This resultant force is at its greatest between the 1 o'clock to 5 o'clock angle θ positions of the catch and pull phases due to maximization of the cross-sectional area of the arm and hand. A more in-depth way to look at the relationship between these forces is to use the hydrodynamic formula for calculating F_L and F_D (21).

$$F_L = [(1/2)(\rho v^2)]*[(C_L)(A)] \qquad \text{(Equation 5)}$$

Where

F_L = Force of lift (N)

C_L = Coefficient of lift

A = Surface area of arm (m^2)

v = Velocity (m/s)

ρ = Density of water (kg/m^3)

$$F_D = [(1/2)(\rho v^2)]*[(C_D)(A)] \qquad \text{(Equation 6)}$$

Where
F_D = Force of drag (N)
C_D= Coefficient of drag
A = Surface area of arm (m^2)
v = Velocity (m/s)
ρ = Density of water (kg/m^3)

Equation 5 and 6 is used to calculate F_L and F_D, respectively. The coefficients of lift and drag (named C_L and C_D respectively) are derived via testing conducted by Toussaint in the late 1980s (25) in steady flow conditions. This equation is dependent on the surface area of the swimmer's hand and assuming the fingers are together (20, 24).

$$F = \iint p\,ds \qquad \text{(Equation 7)}$$

Where
p = Pressure
ds = Derivative of surface area (m^2)

Additionally, the surface area is dependent on the angle the hand and forearm sweep through the water. This is known as the "angle of attack," which is represented as "θ" (6). Given this analysis of the swimmer's forearm, one can address lift and drag in a two-dimensional (2D) way, whereas the arm is a three-dimensional (3D) object. Since water is an incompressible liquid, the vector sum of forces on the swimmer's hand and forearm can be visualized and calculated in 2D. In viewing the force vectors in this manner, they are the summed frontal surface area (10, 11). Due to this, Toussaint was able to calculate the drag coefficient (C_D) for freestyle swimming.

Toussaint stated calculation of force is dependent on the coefficient of drag (25). Drag is calculated using the following equation:

$$D = Kv^2$$
(Equation 8)

Where
D = Drag
K = Constant
v = Velocity (m/s)

Toussaint hypothesized that directly calculating the drag coefficient could be computed at a maximum velocity given the state of today's technology and understanding of fluid dynamics. The constant K changes with each individual. It takes into consideration the surface area of the swimmer's body that is in contact with the water. However, through research and active testing on front crawl swimmers, Toussaint was able to redefine Equation 8 further (25):

$$D = Av^n$$
(Equation 9)

Where
D = Drag
v = Velocity (m/s)
A = Area
n = Parameters used in the power function algorithm

The terms "A" and "n" were defined using the Levenberg–Marquardt algorithm, also known as the least squares method in using the computer program Matlab (25). The formula to calculate C_D is primarily used for aircraft. Additionally, these numbers are dependent on the Reynolds number, which typically ranges from 2×10^6 to 4×10^6 (25). Using this information along with the Matlab program, Toussaint was able to measure the values of the drag coefficient on the swimmer's arm and hand.

Up to this point, we discussed the relationship between all the forces generated by the arm as it moves in a circular pattern through the water. The relationship between these forces generates the forward propulsion to move through the water. Ultimately, for measuring power while swimming, the calculation of torque is the most important. Torque is the component necessary to calculate power (Equation 4). By measuring F_L and F_D, torque can be calculated.

The vector equation for torque (τ) is as follows:

$$\tau = R \times F$$
(Equation 10)

Where
τ = Torque vector (Nm)
R = Moment arm (m)
F = Resultant force vector of F_L and F_D (N)

The aspect of Equation 10 and natural arm movment in a circular motion around the shoulder joint allows swimming power to be calculated in the same fashion as cycling power. Remember, the torque generated by the moment arm, which is the swimmer's arm and hand, centers around the shoulder. This gives the swimmer the forward momentum in the water. In other terms, the shoulder, arm, and hand can be viewed as a bike crank. The shoulder is the bottom bracket, the arm the crank, and the hand is the pedal.

All this information presented about the differing forces and their relationships is to lay the foundation for your understanding how power theory can be applied to swimming. Looking at the front quadrant mechanics similar to those as the pedaling mechanics allows for the basic power equation to be utilized. The classic power equation, placed in swimming terms, is as follows:

$$P = SR \times \tau$$
(Equation 4)

It is this equation that allows us to have power as a metric to utilize in swimming.

A Note on Stroke Rate and Stroke Length

In the previous chapters, we discussed SR as metric to record during threshold testing. This is an important metric if you are using power. The stroke rate directly affects how much propulsion is created. The current hypothesis is the faster the SR, the less muscular power needed to generate power. In referring back to Equation 1 for swim velocity:

$$SV = SR \times SL$$

If the athlete keeps the SL consistent and increases the SR, then the swim velocity will increase. The same is true for swimming power generation. The power equation for swimming (Equation 3) is as follows:

$$P = SR \times \tau$$

Now, if we substitute the components of torque mentioned in Equation 10, the full swimming power equation is as follows:

$$P = SR \times (R \times F)$$

Where
P = power (W)
SR = stroke rate (strokes per minute)
R = Moment arm (m)
F = Resultant force vector of F_L and F_D (N)

Unlike cycling, a swimmer can change his SR and SL. The SL can be directly substituted for R using the following equation:

$$P = SR \times (SL \times F)$$

Where
P = Power (W)
SR = Stroke rate (strokes per minute)
SL = Stroke length ~ Moment arm (m)
F = Resultant force vector of F_L and F_D (N)
(Equation 11)

By being able to affect your SR and SL, this shows how dynamic measuring power is in the water. To better look how SR affects power, let's assume you are able to keep the same SL throughout the stroke cycle as you change your SR. Similar to cycling, if one keeps the torque the same and increases the SR (pedal cadence in cycling), the athlete's power will increase. Another great characteristic of a high SR is the ability to keep a consistent momentum, especially in open water events.

As shown earlier in this chapter, swimmers and triathletes are always fighting drag while swimming. During each stroke, the athlete begins to slow down after the apex of the power generation portion of the pull phase. The slower the SR is, the more energy (i.e., more power) is needed to overcome drag to maintain speed. However, at a higher SR, the less energy (i.e., less power) is used typically to maintain speed since less time exists between pull cycles to allow drag to slow the athlete down. This aspect will be analyzed in the case studies found in the next chapter. It is suggested the optimal SR is about 90 strokes/minute (4, 7, 19). This is true especially for professional triathletes and swimmers. However, it is hard for time-crunched triathletes to achieve this SR. Additionally, AIS has shown elite male and female triathletes tend to have a SR of 39 during the 1000 m time trial (23). Typically, if a triathlete can get their SR into the low 50s or higher, which we call the SR "sweet spot", the athlete is placing oneself in a good position to reduce the effects of drag and increase efficiency (19).

The issue with very high SRs, is most triathletes and swimmer reduce their SL. The length of the stroke is reduced in order complete the stroke cycle faster. If the SL decreases, the resultant F vector, as shown in Equation 11, will decrease. Again, with speaking with the differing SRs in the previous paragraph, we were assuming the SL did not change. So, if the SL decreases with the higher SR, the triathlete will need to produce more force to maintain power. This is why finding the "sweet spot" for your SR. You do not want to sacrifice your SL for a very high SR. You want to ensure are able to maximize the entire length of your entry, catch, pull, and push phases of your stroke cycle. This is why for most triathletes and swimmers, the SR "sweet spot" is in the low 50s strokes per minute range.

Conclusion

The biomechanics and physics of free-style swimming is very dynamic. In this chapter, we laid out the biomechanics of free-style swimming and the foundational physics for power in swimming. Understanding these foundational concepts is important to help you analyze your swimming power data and interpret the results. We will show you how to do this analysis in the next chapter.

References

1. Akis, T., & Orcan, Y. Experimental and analytical investigation of the mechanics of crawl stroke swimming. *Mechanics Research Communications*, 31(2), 243–261.
2. Allen, H., & Cheung, S. (2012). *Cutting-edge cycling*. Human Kinetics.
3. Allen, H., Coggan, A., & McGregor, S. (2019). *Training and racing with a power meter* (3rd ed.). VeloPress.
4. Barbosa, T. M., Bragada, J. A., Reis, V. M., Marinho, D. A., Carvalho, C., & Silva, A. J. (2010). Energetics and biomechanics as determining factors of swimming performance: Updating the state of the art. *Journal of Science and Medicine in Sport*, 13(2), 262–269.
5. Berger, M. A. M., Hollander, A. P., & De Groot, G. (1999). Determining propulsive force in front crawl swimming: A comparison of two methods. *Journal of Sport Sciences*, 17, 97–105. https://doi.org/10.1080/026404199366190.

6. Bixler, B., & Riewald, S. (2002). Analysis of a swimmer's hand and arm in steady flow conditions using computational fluid dynamics. *Journal of Biomechanics*, 35(5), 713–717. https://doi.org/10.1016/S0021-9290(01)00246-9.
7. Cohen, R. C. Z., Cleary, P. W., Mason, B. R., & Pease, D. L. (2018). Forces during front crawl swimming at different stroke rates. *Sports Engineering*, 21, 63–73. https://doi.org/10.1007/s12283-017-0246-x
8. Havriluk, R (2007). Variability in measurement of swimming forces: A meta-analysis of passive and active drag. *Research Quarterly for Exercise and Sport*, 78(2), 32–39. https://doi.org/10.1080/02701367.2007.10599401
9. Heinlein S. A., & Cosgarea, A. J. (2010). Biomechanical considerations in the competitive swimmer's shoulder. *Sports Health*, 2(6), 519–525. https://doi.org/10.1177/1941738110377611.
10. Kolmogorov, S. V., & Duplishcheva, O. A. (1992). Active drag, useful mechanical power output and hydrodynamic force coefficient in different swimming strokes at maximal velocity. *Journal of Biomechanics*, 25(3), 311–318. https://doi.org/10.1016/0021-9290(92)90028-Y.
11. Kolmogorov, S. V., Rumyantseva, O. A., Gordon, B.J., & Cappaert, J. M. (1997) Hydrodynamic characteristics of competitive swimmers of different genders and performance levels. *Journal of Applied Biomechanics*, 13(1), 88–97. https://doi.org/10.1123/jab.13.1.88.
12. Lecrivain, G., Slaouti, A., Payton, C., & Kennedy, I. (2008). Using reverse engineering and computational fluid dynamics to investigate a lower arm amputee swimmer's performance. *Journal of Biomechanics*, 41(13), 2855–2859. https://doi.org/10.1016/j.jbiomech.2008.06.036
13. MacIntosh, B. R., Gardiner, P. F., & McComas, A. J. (2006). *Skeletal muscle form and function.* Human Kinetics.
14. Marinho, D. A., Rouboa, A. I., Alves, F. B., Vilas-Boas, J. P., Machado, L., Reis, V. M., & Silva, A. J. (2009). Hydrodynamic analysis of different thumb positions in swimming. *Journal of Sports Science & Medicine, 8*(1), 58–66.
15. McCabe, C. B., & Sanders, R. H. (2012) Kinematic differences between front crawl sprint and distance swimmers at a distance pace. *Journal of Sports Sciences*, 30(6), 601–608. http://dx.doi.org/10.1080/02640414.2012.660186
16. McLeod, I. (2010). *Swimming anatomy.* Human Kinetics.
17. McMaster WC. (1999). Shoulder injuries in competitive swimmers. *Clinical Sports Medicine*, 18(2):349–5.
18. Minetti, A. E., Machtsiras, G., & Masters, J. C. (2009). The optimum finger spacing in human swimming. *Journal of Biomechanics*, 42(13), 2188–2190. https://doi.org/10.1016/j.jbiomech.2009.06.012
19. Newsome, P. S., & Young, A. (2012). *Swim smooth: The complete coaching programme for swimmers and triathletes.* Wiley.
20. Rouboa, A., Silva, A., Leal, L., Rocha, J., & Alves, F. (2006). The effect of swimmer's hand/forearm acceleration on propulsive forces generation using computational fluid dynamics. *Journal of Biomechanics, 39(7)*, 1239–1248. https://doi.org/10.1016/J.JBIOMECH.2005.03.012.
21. Silva, A. J., Rouboa, A., Moreira, A., Reis, V. M., Alves, F., Vilas-Boas, J. P., & Marinho, D. A. (2008). Analysis of drafting effects in swimming using computational fluid dynamics. *Journal of Sports Science & Medicine*, 7(1), 60–66.

22. Swan, J. W., Brady, J. F., Moore, R. S., Dooling, L., Hoh, N., Choi, J., & Zia, R. (2011) Modeling hydrodynamic self-propulsion with Stokesian dynamics or teaching Stokesian Dynamics to swim. *Physics of Fluids*, 23. https://doi.org/10.1063/1.3594790
23. Tanner, R. K., & Gore, C. J. (2013). *Physiological tests for elite athletes* (2nd ed.) Human Kinetics.
24. Toussaint, H. M. (1990). Differences in propelling efficiency between competitive and triathlon swimmers. *Medicine and Science in Sports and Exercise*, 22(3), 409–415.
25. Toussaint, H. M., Roos, P. E., & Kolmogorov, S. (2004). The determination of drag in front crawl swimming. *Journal of Biomechanics, 37(11)*, 1655–1663. https://doi.org/10.1016/j.jbiomech.2004.02.020
26. van Houwelingen, J., Willemsen, D. H. J., Kunnen, R. P. J., van Heijst, G. J. F., Grift, E. J., Breugem, W. P., Delfos, R., Westerweel, J., Clercx, H. J. H., & van de Water, W. (2017) The effect of finger spreading on drag of the hand in human swimming. *Journal of Biomechanics*, 63, 67–73. https://doi.org/10.1016/j.jbiomech.2017.08.002

Image Credits

Fig. 3.1a: Copyright © 2017 Depositphotos/watchara.tk@gmail.com.

Fig. 3.1b: Source: https://smartpaddle.trainesense.com. Copyright © 2019 by Trainesense.

Fig. 3.5: Source: https://smartpaddle.trainesense.com. Copyright © 2019 by Trainesense.

Fig. 3.7: Adapted from Source: https://coachsci.sdsu.edu/swim/bullets/forces3.htm.

Chapter 4

"On the DECK" Swimming Power Analysis

Power theory for swimming is an excellent tool for training and analysis. Learning your current baseline fitness and threshold pace and applying it to create your training zones is one of the most exciting ways that you can train more scientifically and maximize your limited training time. We all want to ensure that our training is effective, and we are improving. We do this through using the tools, techniques, and theories presented in the previous 3 chapters which allows you to train with personalized training intensities. Furthermore, power provides formidable analytics on performance and biomechanics. Some of these analytics include but are not limited to dead spot detection, force generation efficiency, arm patterns through the water, and so on. These are important because swimming is the one sport where fitness does not necessarily correlate to speed. To be fast in swimming, the athlete needs to be just as efficient as aerobically fit. Now, that you have done some of the background work, and understand the "why" and "how" of swimming, you need to learn how to analyze this data correctly in order to make critical training decisions. One of our "tests" of a new training tool or theory has always been to ask the question, "Will this help me make a training decision in order to help me improve?" If you apply that question to any and all of the latest tech devices, then you'll quickly learn which are just toys and which are true training tools. We love data analysis and squiggly lines on graphs, and have been accused of spending more time analyzing our training than training itself. However, we know that the analysis of our data is one of the most important aspects of training with data. Of course, if you have a fancy downloadable swimming tool, but never download it, then it just becomes an expensive watch. We encourage you to read carefully our examples of analysis below so that you may be able to apply these to your own personal data. Our jobs as coaches is not only to help inspire, motivate, and focus you on the correct training, but to also teach you, so that you can make these decisions for yourself and become an even more successful triathlete.

Case Study #1: 1500 m sFTP Test

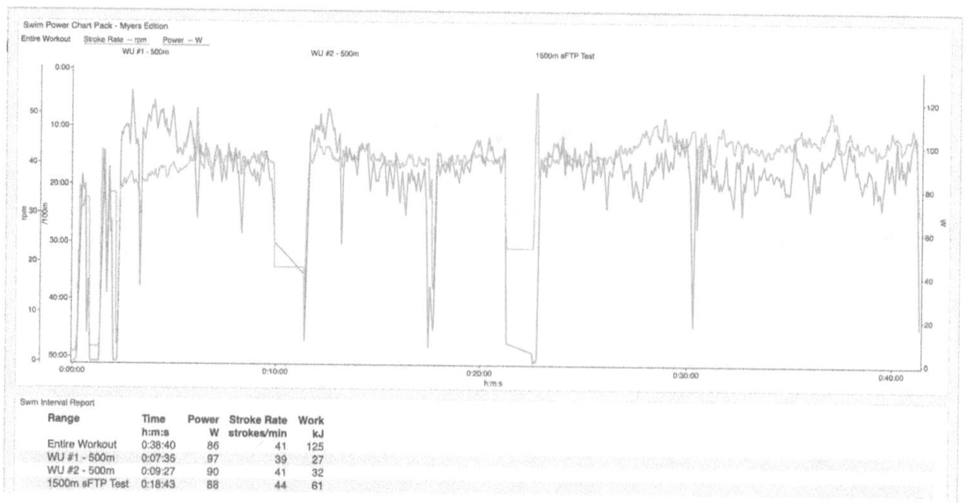

Range	Time h:m:s	Power W	Stroke Rate strokes/min	Work kJ
Entire Workout	0:38:40	86	41	125
WU #1 - 500m	0:07:35	97	39	27
WU #2 - 500m	0:09:27	90	41	32
1500m sFTP Test	0:18:43	88	44	61

FIGURE 4.1 1500 m sFTP power test results on Vasa Trainer.

In case study #1, a 39-year-old male experienced triathlete performed a 1500 m sFTP test on the Vasa Trainer. The intensity setting for the trainer was set at a 2. Before beginning the test, the triathlete performed 2 x 500 m warm-up intervals at a moderate intensity. Once he was confident he was warmed up, he performed the 1500 m swim test. The results of the test, as shown in Figure 4.1, were as follows:

NP = 89 W
SR = 44 SPM

Based on this result, the sFTP was calculated as follows:

$$\text{sFTP} = 89 \text{ W} \times .95 = 85 \text{ W}$$

Note: The coefficient of .95 or 95% was used since the triathlete is an experienced triathlete. Now that the triathlete has a sFTP metric, he was able to create power training zones. The triathlete used Dr. Coggan's power-based training zones. The result was as follows:

SFTP = 85 W: POWER TRAINING ZONES

LEVEL	DESCRIPTION	PERCENT	POWER RANGE	SUGGESTED DISTANCE
1	Active recovery	56% or less	< 46 W	Easy end/recovery
2	Endurance	56% to 76%	47–65 W	4000 m-plus

LEVEL	DESCRIPTION	PERCENT	POWER RANGE	SUGGESTED DISTANCE
3	Tempo	76% to 91%	66–77 W	1500–4000 m
4	Threshold	91% to 106%	77–90 W	400–1500 m
5	$VO_{2\,Max}$	106% to 121%	90–103 W	100–400 m
6	Anaerobic capacity	121% or more	> 103 W	< 100 m

This test provided personalized training zones for the triathlete to use on his Vasa Trainer. The next case studies highlight usage of these zones and how the workouts were analyzed.

Case Study #2: 200 and 400 m Intervals

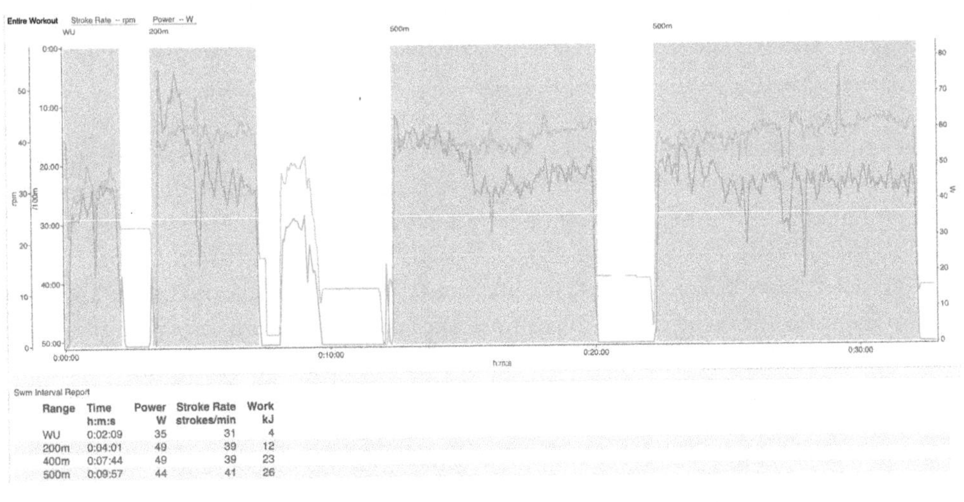

Range	Time h:m:s	Power W	Stroke Rate strokes/min	Work kJ
WU	0:02:09	35	31	4
200m	0:04:01	49	39	12
400m	0:07:44	49	39	23
500m	0:09:57	44	41	26

FIGURE 4.2 200 and 400 m intervals.

With case study #1, the triathlete performed the sFTP test. With his new power-based training zones, the triathlete performed his first workout, as shown in Figure 4.2. The prescribed workout was follows:

WU: Swim for 15 minutes at active recovery (power Z1, < 46 W, RPE 1) (data not shown)

MS: Perform 1×200 m, 1×400 m, 1×500 m at Endurance (power Z2, 47–65 W, RPE 2–3)

CD: Swim for 10 min at Active Recovery (power Z1, < 46 W, RPE 1) (data not shown)

The NP for the 200, 400, and 500 m intervals were 49, 48, and 44 W, respectively. The triathlete took a little time to settle into a good, consistent power output. Looking at the 200 m interval, the triathlete surged during the first 90 seconds of the interval. The NP for this half was 63 W. The power for the rest of the interval was 43 W. The triathlete pushed too hard and could not maintain the power output. Similarly, during the 400 m interval, the triathlete pushed too hard during the first half of the interval. The noticeable dip at the 16-minute mark demonstrates fatigue starting to affect performance. Similarly, the same effects are illustrated during the 500 m interval. From minute 22:31–24:42 of Figure 4.2 or the first 2:17 of the 500 m interval, NP = 49 W. The last 7:20 of the 500 m interval, NP = 43 W. These drops in power, especially during the 400 and 500 m intervals, demonstrates the difficulty the triathlete has keeping a consistent power output.

This type of characteristic, when translated to the pool, can indicate uneven pacing. During future training sessions, the triathlete took note and concentrated on pacing. He needs to focus on not surging during the initial minutes of his intervals. Besides gaining insight on his pacing, the triathlete was able to gain some valuable insight on his stroke rate and power balance between both arms, as shown in Figure 4.2.

From the sFTP test, as shown in Figure 4.1, the triathlete's sFTP SR = 44 SPM. During this interval session, two stroke characteristics are apparent. The first is the triathlete's stroke rate. The average stroke rate for the 39 strokes per minute is shown in Figure 4.2. This stroke rate is considered low for efficient swimming. According to Paul Newsome from Swim Smooth, this stroke rate is very characteristic of a "glider" (5). A low stroke rate entails inconsistency and reduces consistent power output. The triathlete tends to speed up and then slowing down due to a lack of consistent propulsion through the catch and pull phases. For example, imagine your arms are the propeller for a boat. For the boat to keep a consistent speed, the propeller needs to continuously spin. However, once the propeller slows down or stops, the boat meets resistance from the water and loses speed The same applies to a slow stroke rate. The left and right arms are not providing a consistent propulsion to overcome the resistance of the water to keep a consistent speed. To overcome this resistance at lower stroke rates, the triathlete needs to pull harder to keep consistent propulsion (2). However, at higher stroke rates, the arms increase their contribution to propulsion almost two-fold (2). No one consensus exists on the "sweet spot" for stroke rate; this metric varies from person to person. However, based on our discussion in the previous chapter on how SR and SL effect power production, field reports and certain computational fluid dynamic models suggest strokes over 50 strokes per minute is the minimum threshold to maintain a consistent propulsion in the pool (1, 2, 4, 5).

The second aspect gleaned from this workout is the power imbalance between the left and right arms. In Figure 4.3, the left arm power (purple line) has greater output than the right arm power (orange line). The scatterplots in Figures 4.4a–c further illustrate difference in power output. According to Table 4.1, the left arm produces about 6–8% more power than the right arm. This means the left arm does more work than the right.

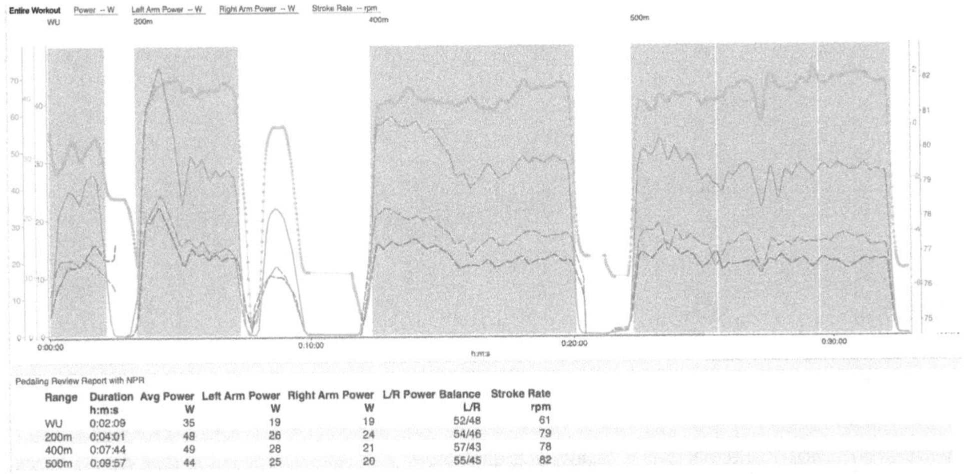

Pedaling Review Report with NPR

Range	Duration h:m:s	Avg Power W	Left Arm Power W	Right Arm Power W	L/R Power Balance L/R	Stroke Rate rpm
WU	0:02:09	35	19	19	52/48	61
200m	0:04:01	48	26	24	54/46	79
400m	0:07:44	49	28	21	57/43	78
500m	0:09:57	44	25	20	55/45	82

FIGURE 4.3 Left and right arm power balance.

TABLE 4.1 Left and Right Arm Power Balance Chart From Figure 4.2

RANGE	DURATION H:M:S	AVG POWER W	STROKE RATE STROKES/MIN	LEFT ARM POWER OUTPUT W	RIGHT ARM POWER OUTPUT W	POWER BALANCE L/R
WU	0:03:19	23	30	19	19	52/48
200 m	0:04:01	49	39	26	24	54/46
400 m	0:07:51	48	39	28	21	57/43
500 m	0:10:07	44	40	24	20	56/44

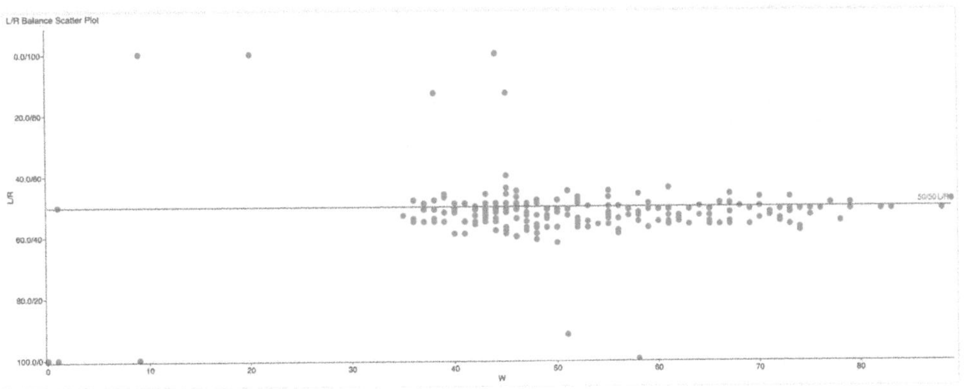

FIGURE 4.4A 200 m interval power balance scatter plot.

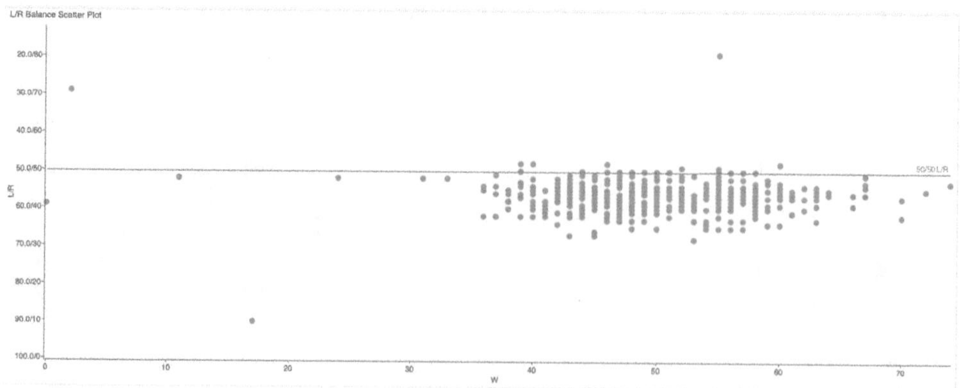

FIGURE 4.4B 400 m interval power balance scatter plot.

A power imbalance coupled with a low stroke rate signifies an inefficient stroke technique. The low stroke rate could be gleaned from testing in the pool; however, the power imbalance could not. This aspect shows a characteristic that needs to be improved. The triathlete needed to incorporate certain strength and swimming drills to correct this inefficiency and significantly improve swim speed.

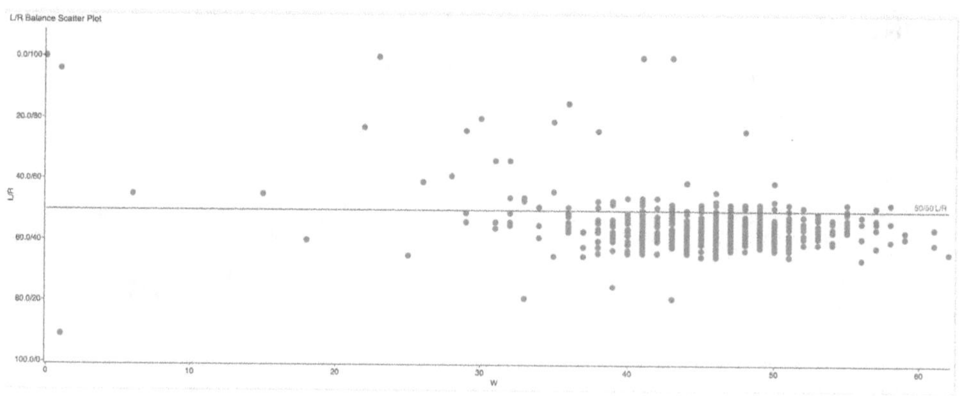

FIGURE 4.4C 500 m interval power balance scatter plot.

Case Study #3: 8–10 × 1-minute $VO_{2\,Max}$ Intervals

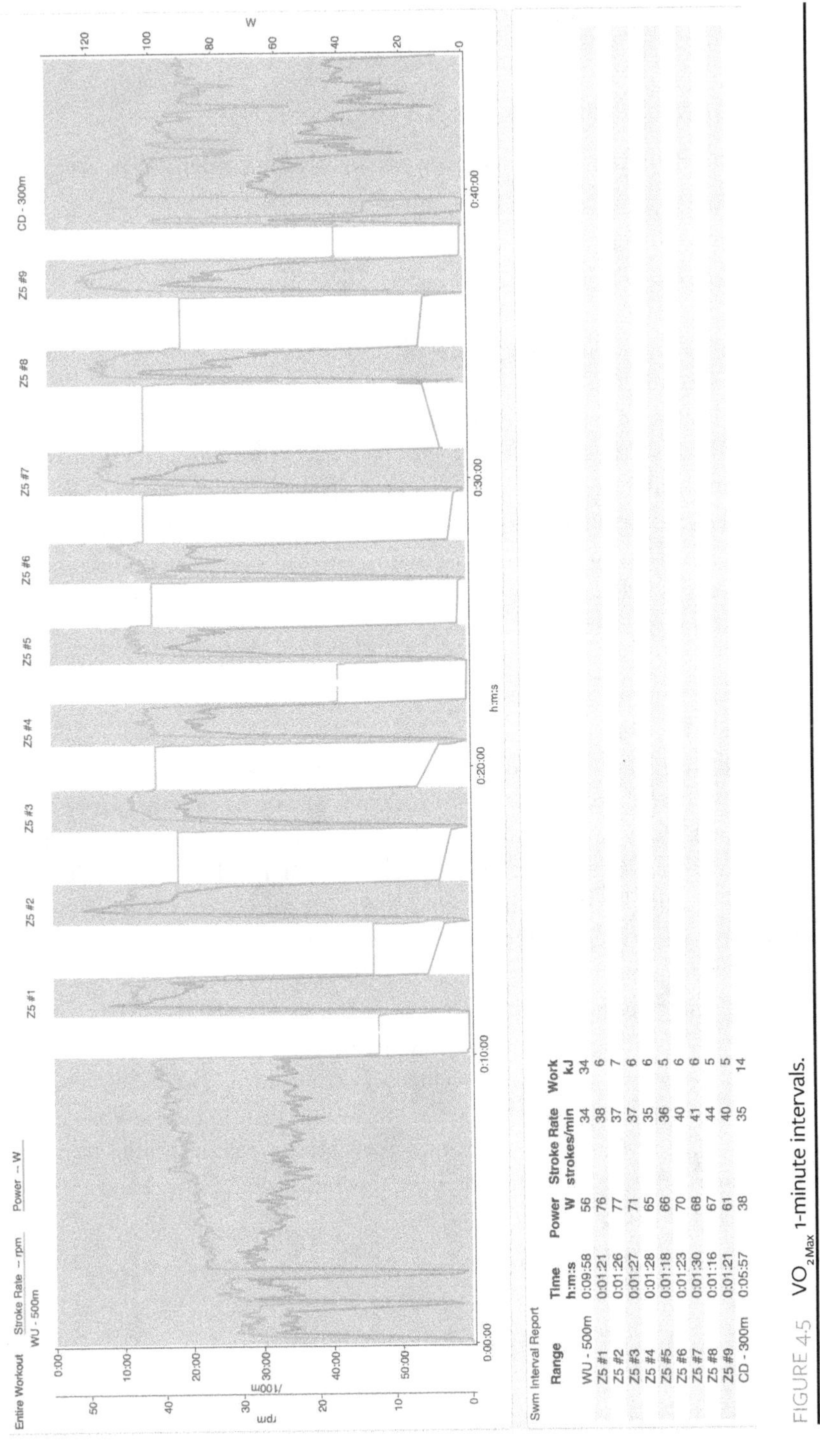

Range	Time h:m:s	Power W	Stroke Rate strokes/min	Work kJ
WU - 500m	0:09:58	56	34	34
Z5 #1	0:01:21	76	38	6
Z5 #2	0:01:26	77	37	7
Z5 #3	0:01:27	71	37	6
Z5 #4	0:01:28	65	35	6
Z5 #5	0:01:18	66	36	5
Z5 #6	0:01:23	70	40	6
Z5 #7	0:01:30	68	41	6
Z5 #8	0:01:16	67	44	5
Z5 #9	0:01:21	61	40	5
CD - 300m	0:05:57	38	35	14

FIGURE 4.5 $VO_{2\,Max}$ 1-minute intervals.

The purpose of this workout was to work on swimming speed. The workout description was as follows:

WU: Swim for 500 m at endurance (57–65 W)

MS: Perform 8–10 1-minute intervals at $VO_{2\,Max}$ (90–103W)

Note: The one-minute Z5 intervals were slightly longer than 50 m per interval.

CD: Swim 300 m at active recovery (< 46 W)

The first aspect shown with the Z5 intervals is the triathlete's ability to produce high power. For the nine intervals, he reached the prescribed power output of 90–103 W. However, the triathlete could not maintain the power throughout the 1-min interval. If we look at intervals 1,2, 7, and 8 in Figure 4.5, the triathlete is unable to maintain the power output during the entire interval. He appears to push too hard in the initial seconds of the interval, leaving himself unable to maintain the power output. Based on this information, the triathlete needs to be cognizant not to start the intervals too hard. This little detail could help him complete all 10 intervals and improve the overall quality of this type of training session.

Conclusion

Swim training has come a long way. Until recently, performance was based on a stopwatch and feedback from video analysis. Now, technology has advanced to being able to provide instant analysis in the pool. The application of sFTP allows the athlete to create and train within personalized training zones. These are steps 1 and 2 in swimming with power system and are critical to reducing your swimming times. Testing your current fitness using the testing protocols and then establishing your training zones allows you to easily quantify your current ability and then to train scientifically using accurate and well-defined zones. Training in your well defined training zones using discipline and consistency practically guarantees improvement. Furthermore, it provides near real-time data for analysis to better improve one's swim stroke and training. Post workout analysis truly turns your "tech toy" into a real training tool, giving you the ability to understand where improvements can be made for the next session, decide if you need a rest day, or if you should have trained even harder.

References

1. Barbosa, T. M., Bragada, J. A., Reis, V. M., Marinho, D. A., Carvalho, C., & Silva, A. J. (2010). Energetics and biomechanics as determining factors of swimming performance: Updating the state of the art. *Journal of Science and Medicine in Sport*, 13(2), 262–269.
2. Cohen, R. C. Z., Cleary, P. W., Mason, B. R., & Pease, D. L. (2018). Forces during front crawl swimming at different stroke rates. *Sports Engineering*, 21, 63–73. https://doi.org/10.1007/s12283-017-0246-x
3. Ginn, E. (1993). *Critical speed and training intensities for swimming*. National Sports Research Centre.
4. Knechtle, B., Baumann, B., Knechtle, P., & Rosemann, T. (2010). Speed during training and anthropometric measures in relation to race performance by male and female open-water ultra-endurance swimmers. *Perceptual Motor Skills*, 111(2), 463–474. https://doi.org/10.2466/05.25.pms.111.5.463-474
5. Newsome, P. S., & Young, A. (2012). *Swim smooth: The complete coaching programme for swimmers and triathletes*. Wiley.

Chapter 5

WATTAGE! Cycling Power Basics

Cycling Power Meters started it all and created the "data acquisition" revolution in endurance sports. They have been in use since the late 1990s, and while the first units were very finicky, the current power meters are incredibly reliable and long lasting. When Hunter first coauthored *Training and Racing with a Power Meter* with Dr. Andrew R. Coggan in 2006, we knew that power meter usage on bicycles would fundamentally change how all cyclists train, but we did not quite know the true scope of the "revolution." Fast forward to the current day and if you do not have a cycling power meter on your bike you are most likely in the minority as a serious triathlete. Of course, many recreational triathletes who are just competing and training for fun do not use them, but there comes a time when you decide to become more serious about your triathlon and you want to truly improve and that is the time you buy your first cycling power meter.

Which Power Meter Should You Buy?

Every power meter has pluses and minuses. The reasons are varied, but ultimately there are five questions you should ask yourself before purchasing a power meter. We do recommend that you buy a power meter that measures both sides of your power, as you need to understand exactly how both legs are contributing to the total load. A one-sided power meter only tells you half the story and can be misleading in your analysis, pacing, and training.

1. **What is your budget?** This is always a factor, and you have to look at the prices of the power meters in order to determine which one fits your budget. This is especially important if you will end up having to purchase more than one for multiple bikes. Ideally, you want the same kind of power meter on each bike.
2. **What pedals do you use?** There are different pedal platforms on the market from the "delta cleat" like the "Look" or "Shimano" pedals and there are also others

like the "Speedplay" platform. We believe it's important to maintain your pedal platform especially if you have been using one platform for a long time. Pedal choice is very personal and a power meter in your pedals could be a great option for you.

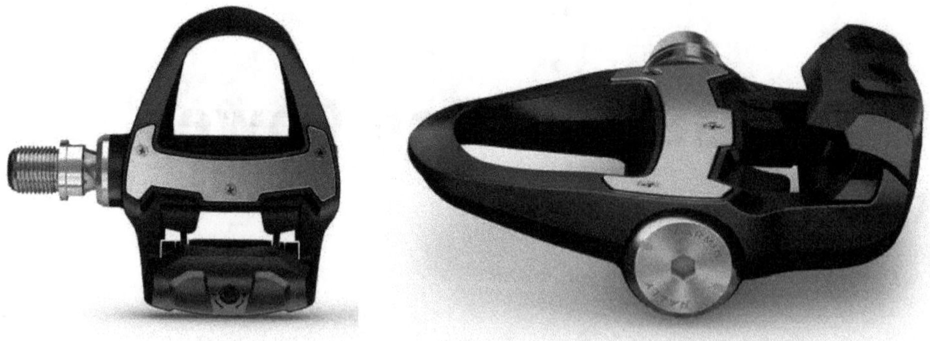

FIGURE 5.1 This figure depicts a pedal based power meter.

3. **Do you travel a lot?** If you travel, then a pedal-based platform is very convenient. You can take your pedals, shoes, and a couple of tools with you on your trip, rent any bike, or just use the hotel gym bike, and instantly you have a power meter on this bike and can train accurately.
4. **What bike frame do you have?** This is a factor because many bike frames have unique bottom bracket sizes and chain-stay widths and lengths that just do not accommodate some power meters. So, be sure to check if the power meter you are looking at will fit on your bike frame.
5. **Buying a new bike soon?** If you are considering a new bike, or if you buy new bikes every couple of years, then the power meter that you have on your current bike might not fit the new bike you are considering. So, take care in considering which power meter you might want to purchase; future proofing yourself might be a good idea.

How Do Power Meters Measure and What are the Different Types of Power Meters?

Power meters measure the torque or twisting of some part on a bicycle (1). This twisting occurs when you apply a load to the part; for example, the bottom bracket axle twists each time you push on the pedal and the distance that the part twists can be measured very precisely. This torque is then multiplied by your angular velocity or cadence. Very simply,

$$\text{power} = \text{torque} \times \text{cadence.}$$

(Equation 1)

So, you can produce 1000 watts by pedaling a hard gear (53:12) at a slow cadence (50 rpm, or you can produce 1000 watts by pedaling an easy gear (34:28) at a very fast cadence (130 rpm) (2). This is similar to what was discussed in Chapter 1 on how to increase your swim power through varying your stroke rate. A power meter measures the cadence by placing a small reed switch inside the power, and each revolution that reed switch is activated and then tells the internal computer chip that 1 revolution has occurred. Each power meter measures at different rates or hertz. Some power meters sample at 200x per second and then average those 200 measurements and send that average to the computer head unit every second. So, each reading that you see on the head unit, for example, 300 watts, could be an average of 200 measurements taken in the last second of your pedaling (2). Your torque is highly variable throughout the pedal stroke, and you could produce 100 lbs. of force at 3 o'clock and then 20 lbs. of force at 6 o'clock, and even 20 lbs. of negative forces at 10 o'clock. All of this torque is taken into account every second and then multiplied by the rpm in that second to give you a single wattage number. This number is then recorded in your computer head unit for later download and analysis.

There are many best practices for using your computer head unit with your power meter, but we only have space for the two most important. The first one applies to Garmin head units only, so ignore this is if you are not using a Garmin. With Garmin, you want to set your recording time to one second recording. Garmin head units come defaulted to "smart recording," which works well for recording GPS locations but eliminates thousands of data points per ride, so you could miss a tremendous amount important data. The second best practice is to make sure your head unit records zeroes for power but does *not* record zeroes for cadence. You want to have the time you spent *not* pedaling averaged into your average power and also to be able to see exactly when you did not pedal; but for cadence, if you the time you spent not pedaling it will erroneously lower your cadence average. For example, let's say I give you a workout in which you need to hold 90 rpm for 5 minutes. You hold 90 rpm for 3 minutes and then a dog runs out in front of you, and you have to stop pedaling for 30 seconds. The final minute and half you pedal at 90 rpm again. If you averaged zeroes for cadence in that 5 minute interval your average cadence would be 87 rpm; however, you know that while you were actually pedaling you averaged 90 rpm.

Where Do Power Meters Measure?

There are so many different kinds of power meters now on the market and the market is changing regularly, so it is beyond the scope of this chapter to review them. We suggest you do a Google search for "DC Rainmaker Power meter buyers guide" for an extensive power meter guide with excellent descriptions of each power meter that is updated on a regular basis. You can buy power meters that measure both legs, which we recommend, or just a one-sided power meter. For example, the Quarq power meter measures both left and right power and combines that into a single number, but as an option you can buy single-sided Garmin power meter pedals that only measure the left leg. Some power meters measure each side independently as well, and that can be an advantage to understand exactly how each leg contributes to the total power. For example, the Favero Assisimo pedals have a power meter in each pedal (you can buy just a single-sided one as well), and then you will have independent left and right power that would contribute to the total and also have the ability to separate each leg's contribution. What you should know is the philosophy of how power meters measure power, and this knowledge might help you in your purchase.

There are 6 locations that power meters measure power:

1. **Spider based.** This is the most popular location to measure power, and there are more than 5 companies that produce power meters in the spider of the cranks. SRM from Germany was the very first power meter produced and has been making spider-based power meters since the early 1990s.

FIGURE 5.2 The spider is the part of the bicycle crank between the crank arms and the chainrings. This is a very good place to measure power because it is close to where it is produced (your leg) and every bicycle has a spider, so it can be designed for different cranks. The inside of the spider has internal supports that twist very slightly when torque is applied to them.

2. **Crank based.** These power meters are the second most popular place to measure power, and companies will glue strain gauges to the inside of the crank arm itself and then place the electronics pod over top of them to read the torsion on the crank and send this data to the head unit. An example of this is the stages power meter. One manufacturer, Infocrank, actually places the strain gauges inside the crank arm itself, and this is a highly accurate way to measure power.
3. **Bottom bracket axle based.** By applying strain gauges to the bottom bracket axel or using optical sensors, the torsion of the bottom bracket can be determined. The downside to this is that only the left leg is measured. Therefore, companies like Shimano actually use two power meters in their product. They use a bottom bracket power meter to measure the left side, and then a crank-based power meter with strain gauges glued onto the crank arm for the right side power.
4. **Hub based.** We have included this power meter because the PowerTap hub for your rear wheel has been one of the most popular power meters in the United States for many years; however, this product was discontinued in 2021. There is also an Asian-based power meter in the hub as well. The advantage to this power meter was its simplicity and ease of use, along with its simple ability to move between bikes, as it's built into the rear wheel. The downside is that you

are then dedicated to that specific wheel (or you have to buy multiple rear wheels for different needs), and the power is measured downstream of the cranks, chain and cogs, so the power measured at the hub is consistently 7–10 watts lower than measured at the pedals, spider or cranks.

5. **Pedal based.** Pedals are an excellent place to measure power because the measurement occurs right where the power is transferred from the foot to the pedal, they are easy to charge or replace the batteries, you can switch them between bikes, and for the dual-sided power meter you have independent left and right power data. Pedals do take a fair bit of abuse though, so sometimes these power meters can be more problematic from a reliability standpoint.
6. **Opposing forces based.** There is only one company that uses this method, and that is the iBike powerpod. This method measures all of the forces that oppose you from moving forward on the bicycle and then back calculates the wattage from those opposite forces. This requires the user to do a calibration ride in which the power pod learns the rolling resistance of the tires, the aerodynamic resistance of your body and bike, along other important variables. This can be a very effective and great way to measure power, especially for triathletes that tend to stay in their tri-bars for most of their training and racing, thereby keeping the aerodynamic resistance a relative constant. The downside to this method is if you do your rolling resistance calibration on a smooth road, but then in training you ride on rough roads, the rolling resistance difference will make the wattage inaccurate. So, it's important to do the calibration correctly.

Conclusion

In this chapter, we discussed the different types of cycling power meters found on the market. Choosing the right power meter for your bike(s), is important. Ultimately, all cycling power meters measure power via the same equation. However, where the power meter measures power might be quite different and if you switch from one power meter to another one, especially if they measure in different locations, your data will be different. For example, if you use a pedal based power meter on your tri bike, but have a hub based power meter on your road bike, your road bike data will be 7–10 watts lower. This is always important to remember when analyzing your post workout data. There are many reasons why you should own a power meter and hopefully these reasons will help to motivate you as you understand the "why" behind using a power meter. Ultimately, no matter the type of cycling power meter you use, it is a tool to make you faster! In the next chapter, we will discuss how to use cycling power to improve your cycling performance.

References

1. Allen, H., & Cheung, S. (2012). *Cutting-edge cycling.* Human Kinetics.
2. Allen, H., Coggan, A., & McGregor, S. (2019). *Training and racing with a power meter* (3rd ed.). VeloPress.

Image Credits

Fig. 5.1: Source: https://buy.garmin.com/en-US/US/p/573589#overview. Copyright © by GARMIN.

Fig. 5.2a: Source: https://store.stagescycling.com/STAGES-POWER-L-ULTEGRA-R8000. Copyright © by STAGES Cycling.

Fig. 5.2b: Source: https://www.bike24.com/p2125073.html. Copyright © by Shimano.

Chapter 6

Pedal HARDER! and FASTER! Cycling Power Testing and Training Levels

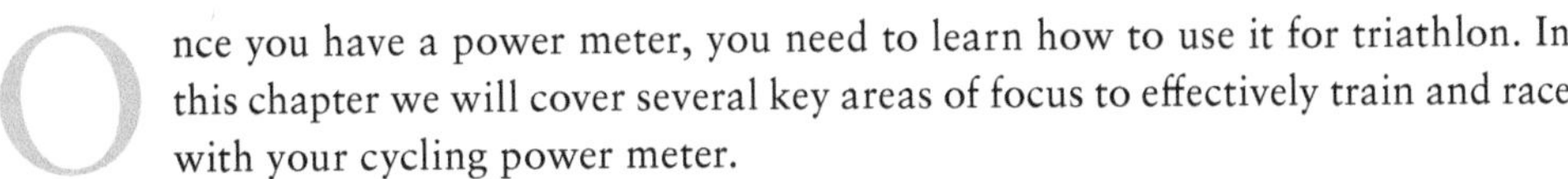

Once you have a power meter, you need to learn how to use it for triathlon. In this chapter we will cover several key areas of focus to effectively train and race with your cycling power meter.

Collect and Test Data

Your first job is to collect data, learn about yourself, and create a personal relationship with the data. What does 200 watts feel like to you? What is your heart rate when you ride at 200 watts and 90 rpm versus 200 watts and 60 rpm? How many watts do you need to produce to go up a hard and steep hill? How many watts can you maintain on a long 10 mile climb? All these questions and more need to be answered along your power training journey. Start with basic testing, and that means learning your functional threshold power or FTP. Dr. Andrew R. Coggan and I initially defined FTP back in 2006, and the definition remains the same today. FTP is the highest power a rider *can maintain in a quasi-steady state without fatiguing.* When power exceeds FTP, fatigue will occur much sooner, whereas power just below FTP can be maintained much longer. Or, in simpler terms, FTP is the highest average watts you can maintain for roughly an hour. Many people over the years have come up with different ways to measure FTP besides a pure one hour test, and many of those other tests are also valid. What we want to make sure that you know FTP can be determined a variety of ways, and you should always rely on at least three points of triangulation in order to determine your exact FTP if you do not do a 60 minute test. The most popular proxy for the 60 minute test is a testing protocol that Hunter developed and has used for over 15 years now. This is doing a 20 minute test, similar to the protocols discussed in previous chapters, and then subtracting 5% off of the results of this test to give you a close approximation of the power you could maintain for 60 minutes. There are some people who need to subtract 2%, and others might need to subtract 10%, but as a general rule, you'll be in the ballpark with a 5% reduction. The most important part of using this number is actually in doing a 5 minute test before your 20 minute test. This is critical to reduce your anaerobic work capacity, create some fatigue, and ensure that you are not too fresh for the 20 minute test. See Table 6.1 for the full testing protocol that you should do in order to determine your FTP.

TABLE 6.1 FTP Testing Protocol

	Time	Description	% of FTP
Warm Up	20 Min	Endurance	65%
	3 x 1 Min (1 min. Ri)	Fast Pedaling, RPM 100+	N/A
	5 Min Easy	Easy Riding	65%
Main Set	5 Min	All - Out	110-120%
	5 Min	Easy Riding	65%
	20 Min	Do your best effort!	100-105%
Cool Down	15 Min	Easy Riding	<65

Once you have completed your testing, you should subtract 5% off of your 20 minute average power number and use that as your initial FTP number to set your training zones. Some questions that are often asked are "Where should I do my testing? Can I do it indoors? On a climb? On my tri bike?" We recommend that you do your tests so that the terrain best mimics your upcoming events and/or where you do your most training. So, if you are riding a flat event, then do your best to test on a flat road. Or if you do the majority of your training indoors on a smart trainer, then do your testing indoors. However, if this is the case, you will need to retest at least two weeks in advance your event so that you can determine if your indoor and outdoor FTPs are different, and they are in most cases. We also suggest you do the tests while riding in your aero position in order to best mimic how you will ride in a race. Lastly, do your best to do your FTP testing at the end of a rest week and retest yourself every 6 to 8 weeks as fitness changes occur in generally 6 to 8 week cycles. Now, re-read that sentence again.

Determine Your Training Zones

Dr. Andrew R. Coggan came up with what are now called the Coggan classic levels (zones), and they have been widely used throughout the world to direct training and ensure that you are training in the correct physiological energy system. These are excellent to use, but not everyone needs customized zones, which are called iLevels for individualized levels. We will focus on classic zones for this chapter. The Coggan classic levels help you to define exactly what intensity you should train in and for how long in order to achieve the desired adaptation. Each level has a purpose: the energy system that you are training. The upper levels (5, 6, 7) are largely unused for triathlon training, but we argue are still important to train as they give you a better well-rounded fitness level, and some courses demand that you ride at those levels. In Table 6.2, you will notice that each level has a corresponding percentage of threshold power, threshold heart rate, rate of perceived exertion (on the 0–10 scale) and a time in which you can either maintain that intensity or in which you should design your intervals around (in parentheses for the first 3 levels).

TABLE 6.2 Coggan Classic Levels (Zones)

LEVEL	NAME/ PURPOSE	% OF THRESHOLD POWER	% OF THRESHOLD HR	RPE	TIME
1	Active recovery	< 55%	< 68%	< 2	70–80 years (1.5 hours or less)
2	Endurance	56–75%	69–83%	2–3	2.5 hours to 14 days (3–5 hours)
3	Tempo	76–90%	84–94%	3–4	30 min to 8 hours (30–90 minutes)
4	Lactate threshold	91–105%	95–105%	4–5	10–60 min
5	$VO_{2\ Max}$	106–120%	> 106%	6–7	3–8 min
6	Anaerobic capacity	121–150%	N/A	> 7	30 sec – 2 min
7	Neuromuscular power	N/A	N/A	(Maximal)	5–15 sec

It is important to reiterate that the relationship between the time of the intervals and the intensity is of utmost importance. For example, if you want to improve your FTP, you need to do a minimum of 10 minutes at 105% of your FTP in order to cause enough training stress for adaption to occur. Riding at 105% of your FTP for 4 minutes is just not long enough to cause the training stress to your body in order for it to adapt and improve. The same goes for a lower level like the level 1 active recovery. If you ride at less than 55% of your FTP for 4 hours, that *is not* an active recovery ride! An active recovery ride is less than 55% of FTP and less than 1.5 hours long, not longer.

Diagnose Your Strengths and Limitations

Once you have determined your FTP and training levels, you should also learn about your unique strengths and limitations, or what we call your power profile. Ultimately, this means more testing! As Dr. Coggan always says, "Testing is training and training is testing," so let's get in some more training. You now need to test your $VO_{2\ Max}$, anaerobic capacity, and neuromuscular power, which correspond to 5 minutes, 1 minute, and 5 seconds, respectively. While these upper intensities are often not needed for most triathlons, you should still do some training here, and especially if you are doing draft legal triathlons, you will really need to do training in these upper zones. I would suggest that you do these tests on a day after you have a minimum of two very easy days or at the end of a rest week to capture the best numbers possible. You will test your one minute first, and this is best done on a slight hill to give you additional resistance to push against. Go as hard as you can in the first 30 seconds, pretending you are racing for your life, and then in the second 30 seconds hang on for dear life and finish completely exhausted. For the 5 minute test, you will need to pace yourself and start strong (roughly 110% of your FTP) and then build from there so that you finish completely exhausted as well, but with a strong final 20 seconds. For the 15 second sprints, in which you are testing your neuromuscular power, you will want to sprint out of the saddle for at least 250 meters, starting from a speed of around 18 mph (30 kph). You will do 2 sprints, as it's possible the first one you will not have the best form or be "in the groove." Once you have finished the power profile tests, we suggest you use the TrainingPeaks software to review the power profile chart to see exactly how you compare to others. For a full in-depth discussion of the different types of power profiles, we recommend you pick up a copy of Hunter and Dr. Coggan's book *Training and Racing with a Power Meter.*

TABLE 6.3 Power Profile Testing protocols

	Time	Description	% of FTP
Warm Up	20 Min	Endurance Pace	65%
	3 x 1 Min (1 min. Ri)	Fast Pedaling, RPM 100	na
	5 Min Easy Riding	Easy Riding	65%
Main Set	1 Min	All - Out Effort	100%
	10 Min	Easy Riding	65%
	1 Min	All - Out Effort	Max
	5 Min	Easy Riding	65%
	5 Min	All - Out Effort	Max
	5 Min	Easy Riding	65%
	2 x 15 sec (2 min RI)	All - Out Effort	Max
Cool Down	15 Min	Easy Riding	<65%

Using the Training Levels

Next, we describe sample workouts that correspond to different cycling goals. Here, we use the fictitious Triathlete Flynn to give you some ideas about how to train at the specific Coggan classic training levels that you learned about earlier.

By reading the following workout descriptions and charting the best routes on your local terrain, you'll be better prepared to adhere to the intended philosophy of each workout. Be sure to always be safe and careful in your workouts and think about the big picture; don't just focus on the numbers.

Our hypothetical Flynn is an age group racer, aged 43, with some success at the local and regional level, and his functional threshold power wattage is 290. His heart rate at this level is 175 bpm, and his max heart rate is 200. Flynn weighs 160 pounds, and his ratio of watts per kilogram at threshold is about 4. He is a typical steady state rider and triathlete with his strengths at his FTP and longer endurance. His power profile in the TrainingPeaks software is upward sloping to the right (the typical time trialist/steady state rider).

In these workouts, we are assuming the best of conditions, from weather to road surface, to a strong and healthy Flynn. Flynn also pedals at his normal self-selected cadence unless the workout description says otherwise.

Level 1: Active Recovery

Flynn does his active recovery (level 1) workout when he needs to recover from a hard workout the day before or cool down at the end of a hard workout.

The classic active recovery ride is a total of 1 hour, warming up for 10 minutes, with his watts under 140 (a range of 45% to 48%), then keeps his cadence about 5 to 8 rpm higher than his normal, self-selected cadence for the next 40 minutes, maintaining his watts at 145 to 160 (50% to 55%). He cools down at his normal cadence, with watts under 140 (48%).

Because this is a very slow pace, many elite triathletes do not do enough riding at this level. When you are going out for a recovery ride, it should really be slow and all about recovery. If you go above the upper limit of the wattage range for this level, then you are riding too hard to recover properly, but not hard enough to train. It is very important physically to do active recovery rides because they help to flush built-up waste products out of your system, keep your body in a rhythm of riding, and maintain suppleness in your muscles.

Level 2: Endurance

When Flynn wants to build a base of endurance and enhance his aerobic fitness, he emphasizes endurance rides (level 2). Over time, training in this range will lead to the development of a stronger heart muscle, increased mitochondrial levels in the cells, development of more capillaries in his muscles, and an overall increase in stamina. This is an important level for triathletes to train in, especially if you are training for your first full Ironman-length event.

For this workout, Flynn really needs to ride for 4.5 hours total, warming up for 15 minutes while keeping his watts under 190 (65%). He then rides with his watts at 200 to 220 (69–75%) for 4 hours, but includes some bursts of faster riding once every 10 minutes (8 seconds, seated, taking rpm to 130 and watts to 300, or 103%). The rest of the ride is at a normal, self-selected cadence, and he cools down for 15 minutes, keeping his watts under 150.

It is very important that you do enough of these longer rides to prepare your body for harder levels of training and also to prepare for a full 112-mile distance event. The longer you can ride, the better.

Level 3: Tempo

The tempo level is the meat and potatoes of every triathlete, and it is probably the level that triathletes ride in more than any other. A tempo ride should be done at a level that feels fast and takes some work to maintain.

Do not underestimate the amount of work that training in this level requires. However, this level of training is also one of the most beneficial for most triathletes. Riding in level 3 causes some of the greatest physiological adaptations. It's the best bang for the buck, so to speak. There are a variety of ways to effectively train in level 3, and one great example follows. But remember to keep the big picture in mind: Do not worry, for example, if your watts go above 90% of your threshold (the upper limit of level 3) on a few hills or in a short headwind section. It's the average watts (or normalized watts, discussed in more detail later) that are important.

Many a coach has referred to this level as a cyclist's and triathlete's no-man's land, and it's true that training in this level will not make you either a better sprinter or a better hill climber. If you spend too much time here, you just get very good at riding at level 3 and not much else. It is wise not to get caught in the trap of constantly spending valuable training time in this level. If you want to improve your power at $VO_{2\,Max}$, then you will have to train at $VO_{2\,Max}$ power, and tempo power just won't be sufficient. However, that being said, in most triathlons, you will ride here for the majority of the bike leg.

If you have limited time, however, or if you are trying to increase your muscular endurance, then this level is just what the doctor called for. If all you have is 5 hours a week to ride, drill it in the upper range of level 3 and get in a great workout; or, if you are getting prepped for a full Ironman, then being able to ride in this zone for 3-plus hours will pay off with a possible podium finish.

For the tempo ride, he warms up for 15 minutes, keeping his watts under 200, or 68%, which is a good intensity to begin warming up the muscles. It's not as easy as recovery pace, but it's not so hard that it will undermine the entire workout. Flynn then rides at tempo pace, between 76% and 90% of his threshold (220 to 260 watts). He tries his best to hold this range over hills, on flats, and even on downhill runs. The emphasis is on spending as much time as possible in the 240 to 260 (82% to 90%) range. He keeps his cadence at his self-selected level, metering his efforts on hills. He may go over 260 watts, and that's fine, but he does not sprint up hills.

Lower Level 4: Sub-threshold, or the Sweet Spot

The lower part of level 4 is what we call the sub-threshold level, or the "sweet spot." This occurs at about 88% to 94% of your functional threshold power. That means that it is on the cusp of both the tempo level and the lactate threshold level. Although this is not exactly an official level of its own, it is an excellent place to begin building your FTP and pushing it higher. In our coaching, we encourage the athletes we work with to train heavily in this area at the beginning of the season, before moving into training right at their FTP (91% to 105%). This intensity level is also great to revisit right around the middle of June in order to achieve a second peak in the fall. Even if an athlete is not trying to achieve a second peak, we incorporate this sweet spot training into their schedule at least once or twice every 14 days. Figure 6.1 highlights this important training zone.

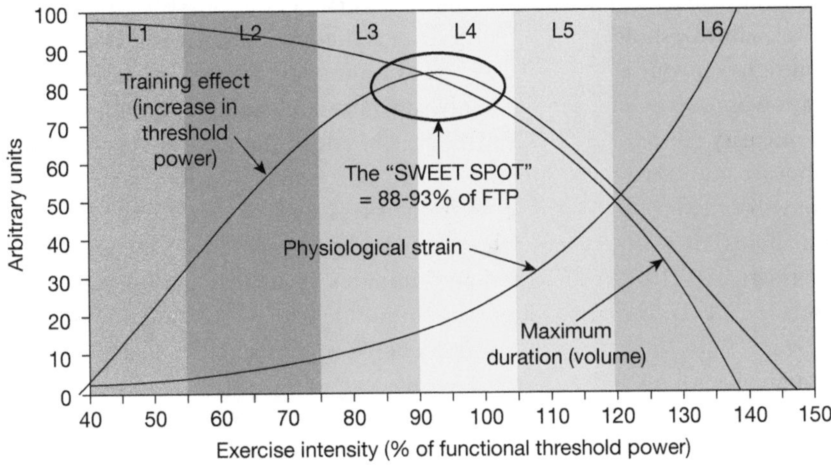

FIGURE 6.1 Sweet Spot zone

Riding in this range certainly does not help significantly with your sprint, your power at $VO_{2\,Max}$, or your anaerobic capacity. Nor will it make you the best draft legal racer. But at the same time, if all your training were in this area, at least you probably wouldn't get dropped. All in all, it's one of the most beneficial places to spend your training time. Just make sure that you are training the other systems as well.

To train at this level, Flynn rides for 2 to 2.5 hours, warming up well for 15 minutes at below 200 watts (68%), then does one 5 minute effort at 290 watts, or 100% of threshold power. This is to get his body ready for some solid work. He then does two efforts of 20 minutes each with his watts at a range of 255 to 272 (88% to 93% of threshold power). It is critical for him to stay in this range as best he can. He should rest for 15 minutes after each 20 minute effort. He uses a gear that allows him to keep his cadence in his self-selected range or challenges himself to pedal just a touch faster than he normally would. He finishes the workout with several (eight or ten) 1 minute intervals of fast pedaling with a high cadence (over 105 rpm), holding his watts under 280 (85% to 95% range), and resting for 2 minutes between efforts. The goal is not to go super hard, but to spin a high cadence at subthreshold power. Then, he goes into his cooldown.

Flynn should do at least six to eight of these workouts before moving to specific threshold work. This type of workout is a good base on which to build threshold work, so he should be sure to make it a base that is wide and strong. If he moves to upper level 4 work and above too soon, he could compromise the solidity of this foundation.

Remember: When you are working at this level, don't hammer over hills; instead, keep your pedaling pressure steady up to the crest of the hill.

Typical Level 4: Threshold

Threshold-level workouts are meant to focus directly on improving your FTP, and they are done right at FTP and just above. They are strenuous and require a solid recovery between efforts and also between workouts. Otherwise, they are very similar to the previous level, sub-threshold. The only difference is that the intensity is increased a notch to hold you right on your edge. These are painful intervals when done correctly. They are important workouts to perform, not only so you can increase your ability to handle the level of intensity needed to maintain this type of effort, but also so that you can continually improve your threshold power.

Flynn will ride for 2 to 2.5 hours to train at this level, with a 15-minute warm-up in which he holds his watts under 200 (68%). He then gets in one 5 minute all-out effort with watts at 290 (100%), followed by 5 minutes at an easy pace—that is, less than 200 watts (68%). After that, he does two 20-minute efforts at 288 to 305 watts (96% to 105%), with 10 to. 15 minutes of resting in between. After the second effort, he cruises for 15 minutes with his watts below 220 (76%).

Flynn could have used other options that parallel those described in the previous level for building up to the 20-minute efforts. If he chose to do so, he could have simply followed those same plans at FTP wattage instead of the sweet spot.

If your goal is to become a strong age grouper, we suggest building up to riding for at least 1 hour at this power level.

Level 5: $VO_{2\,Max}$

As mentioned previously in this chapter, most triathlons do not include this intensity in the actual event itself, except for draft legal events; however, training at $VO_{2\,Max}$ can make a significant contribution to improving your FTP and giving a better rounded level of fitness. Designed to elicit improvements in your $VO_{2\,Max}$, or your maximal volume of oxygen uptake, efforts for level 5 range from 3 to 8 minutes, with the majority of work typically done in the lower end of this range of time.

Flynn, for example, out on a 2-hour ride, may want to work at this level to boost his $VO_{2\,Max}$. If so, he would begin with a 15-minute warm-up, keeping his wattage at less than 200 (that is, less than 68% of FTP). Then he would do one 5-minute interval at 290 watts (100%), followed by 5 minutes at an easy pace. The main part of the workout would then begin. He would do six 3-minute efforts, trying for an average of 340 watts (117% of FTP or greater) in each effort. He would rest for 3 minutes between efforts. Following the sixth one, he would cruise easy for 10 minutes and then do four 2-minute efforts with 4 minutes of rest between them. In these four efforts, he would try to average between 330 and 350 watts (113% to 120%). Finally, he would cool down.

Be sure to apply the intervals-to-exhaustion concept to this workout.

Level 6: Anaerobic Capacity

Even more intense than $VO_{2\,Max}$, anaerobic capacity (AC) efforts are usually completed in time intervals of 2 minutes or less. These are very intense, short, hard efforts, and they are difficult to do correctly without the use of a power meter. The intensity of these efforts is far beyond what can be maintained aerobically. It is a supra-maximal intensity—that is, it requires more than 100% of your $VO_{2\,Max}$. These also are not used in triathlon events unless you are racing in a draft legal event, but you should still do some occasional work here (2 times a month) to make sure your fitness is well rounded and also prepares you for any group rides you might do.

Level 6 efforts are much higher in intensity than level 5 efforts, and they are carried out long enough to stress the anaerobic capacity system, which means they hurt! Training at this level includes the greatest variety of efforts, however. There is a huge difference between a 30 second effort and a 2 minute effort, although both train the AC system. This variety makes it exciting to create lots of different intervals and workouts. The key is to reach the required intensity; the duration of the effort can change somewhat. These level 6 exercises should be performed when you are fresh in your training week, so most likely at the beginning of the week.

To add some anaerobic capacity work to your training plan in a 2-hour ride, start with a standard warm-up, then set your power meter to show average watts in interval mode. Then do about eight 2-minute efforts pedaling as hard as you can, using average watts as a carrot to push all the way to the end. The goal? Average 135% of FTP (390 watts, for example, for Flynn Triathlete). Reach for that and stop when you can no longer reach 120% to 122% of FTP, which would be a 10% to 12% drop in power, in your average. Flynn Triathlete, for example, would stop when he could no longer reach an average of 348 to 355 watts. Recover for at least 2 to 3 minutes, more if needed, then finish with eight 1-minute efforts, trying to average at least 145% of FTP (420 watts, for John), with 3-minute rest periods between efforts. Do all of these efforts unless you are unable to reach 128% to 131%, which would represent a 10% to 12% drop in power (370 to 380 watts in our hypothetical example). This guideline follows the intervals to exhaustion idea which is covered in the next chapter.

Level 7: Neuromuscular Power

Level 7 exercises are very short, high-intensity efforts usually lasting less than 10 seconds each. They place a larger load on the musculoskeletal system than on the metabolic systems. In these short efforts, it would be difficult to use power as a guide for training, since the efforts themselves are so explosive and short that you would have to focus more on handling the bike than on reading your power meter. It would be exceedingly rare to have to do this kind of an effort in any triathlon, even a draft legal one. This level just isn't used in triathlons and it does not really make much sense to train in this level for any triathlete. Only if you also do some intense group rides or other rides in a peloton, would it make sense as a triathlete to train level 7. We still include it because it is part of the Coggan training levels and should be addressed for those triathletes that need it.

When you do these efforts, do not concern yourself with looking at your power meter. You can review the data later, while you are cooling down between sprints. The most important thing is to get all the sprints done and continue to add more repetitions as you get stronger.

The sprints done in the small chainring typically do not involve gear changes. The objective is to wind the gear out and increase cadence to 120 rpm by the end of the interval. The sprints in the big chainring include one or two gear changes, with an emphasis on a hard jump at the start of the interval and winding out the gear at a high cadence (110 to 120 rpm) before shifting.

One of the goals of this workout is to show that you do not need to dump the chain into the hardest gear for a sprint. Sprinting starts out with a hard jump in a gear that you can turn over. Then, as you wind out each gear, you shift down one. It's just like driving a car with a stick shift: You work down the gears when the rpm reaches the correct range.

Conclusion

In this chapter, we laid out how to perform a cycling FTP test and create your personalized power training zones. These personalized zones are important to tailor your training to your strengths and limiters and the characteristics of the race you are targeting. By following this methodology, you will set yourself up for success in achieving your athletic goals As you do these workouts, keep in mind that all the training levels are continuous: There is no definitive starting or stopping point for any of them. You do not just go from training your aerobic capacity while you are riding in level 3 (76% to 90% of FTP) to magically training your threshold at 91% of FTP in level 4. The physiological systems in the human body that you are training meld into one another; if you are training in level 3, you are using a larger percentage of that particular system than you are using for other systems at that intensity, but that does not mean the other systems are unaffected. It's important to remain aware of the big picture, or the philosophy of the workout, and not to get too caught up in becoming a slave to the numbers. Now, the other half of applying power training to your bike is analyzing the data. In the next chapter, we will examine on how to interpret all those squiggly lines and bars.

Image Credits

Fig. 6.1: Source: https://fascatcoaching.com/training-plans/gravel/. Copyright © by Frank Overton/Fascat Coaching.

Chapter 7

On the ROAD! Training, Racing, and Pacing!

Align Your Abilities with the Demands of the Event

The next area of focus is taking your abilities and making sure that your event demands are very similar. For example, if your event is a very hilly Ironman, like Ironman Wisconsin, which is very demanding of the anaerobic capacity energy system, but your level 6 is on the poor side, you might want to consider doing a different event. Alternatively, if you have an incredible FTP and are very good at long steady events but have signed up for a draft legal short course, you might have trouble riding with the pack unless you do some very specific training. As well, you must consider your ability to improve. In the example of Ironman Wisconsin, knowing that you might lack the anaerobic capacity, you could always just train it! Training your limiters is a strategy that can pay off with a great event, especially if you are willing to put in the hard, smart work. It's this work that allows you to improve both your strengths and your limiters so that you can successfully accomplish any key event on the calendar.

Training: How Many Intervals Should You Do?

Using your power meter in training is one of the most important parts of training with power. It defines your intensity on a second-by-second basis, gives you clear goals, helps you with your pacing and provides you with motivation. We have all done intervals in our training, and this is one of the many places that a power meter really shines. One concept that is very important to understand is the concept that Hunter wrote about in *Training and Racing with a Power Meter* book, which is called "intervals to exhaustion" or determining the correct number of intervals.

When should you stop doing repeats? Is there a point at which doing just one more interval is not helping you anymore? Can you do too many intervals? It depends on your goal for that particular workout, your current level of fitness, the big picture of how that session fits into the goals you have for your training, and your own ability to dig deep and put out a 110% effort. Since there are so many factors involved in making a decision about when to end an interval session, it is difficult to provide precise guidelines, and any guidelines put forth will likely not address all the issues. Nevertheless, we have presented a way to determine the optimum number of repeats in Table 7.1.

Before athletes could train with power, the problem was that there was no way to accurately quantify diminishing marginal returns when doing intervals. The question "How many intervals is enough?" just couldn't be answered. Now, with your power meter and the information in Table 7.1, an answer is possible: You can do intervals to exhaustion, or accurately determine the correct number of intervals to do in each session, without going too far over the hump in the diminishing marginal returns curve.

In the table, we have based the percentage drop-off on the third interval because typically the effort that a rider can put forth in the first two intervals will be much higher than what that rider could actually repeat multiple times. Since we assume you are fresh when you begin your interval session, we throw out those first two efforts for the purpose of determining when to stop a workout. Obviously, if you are doing longer intervals in which you might complete only two intervals total, then this rule does not apply.

Let's look at an example. Let's say that Flynn wants to work on his FTP power to prepare for a race with four solid 12 minute climbs. From our Coggan classic levels, we know that his FTP is stressed when he is riding at between 91–105% of his functional threshold power. The intensity must be in the correct training range in order to place enough stress on the FTPsystem and stimulate improvement. At the same time, the duration of the effort must be long enough to stress that energy system. If the athlete rode at 100% of FTP for only 4 minutes, he would not have ridden long enough for an adaptation to occur. For the FTP system to adapt to a training stimulus, a minimal effort of 10 minutes is necessary, with the maximum duration being as long as 60 minutes. After 60 minutes, by definition, you are no longer able to train at your FTP.

Understanding this relationship between time and intensity will allow our rider to set some guidelines about the optimal number of intervals to do in his workouts. For instance, since he is trying to improve his FTP system, and wants to prepare for an event with four 12 minute climbs, then he should do at least five 12 minute intervals at 91–105% of FTP (let's use an FTP of 250 watts in this example). The first interval could be at 260 watts, the second at 260, and the third at 255 This third interval is what we call the *repeatable* interval. The watts that Flynn does in that interval are the watts that he can repeat multiple times. The first two efforts are the fresh efforts, when he has plenty of glycogen in his muscles and enough anaerobic work capacity available to produce big wattage; once that anaerobic work capacity is used up, he is left with just the right amount of energy to produce an effort that can be repeated.

The reason this is so important is that we must take the wattage in the third effort and subtract 5% from it (in this case, 255 × 0.05 = 12, and 250 – 12 = 238 = watts) to determine when to stop the repeats. When the athlete cannot average at least this wattage (238) for his interval, he is going to stop, as he would now not be training intensely enough to elicit enough stress to cause a training improvement or adaptation. Let's say that in the fifth interval he produces 240 watts, and because he is an overachiever (like many serious triathletes) and he wants to make certain that he has done as much as possible, he does one more interval. But then let's suppose that by the time he is in the second minute of the interval he sees that he cannot even maintain 230 watts, much less 238 or more. This immediately lets him know that he is now working below the intensity needed to stimulate his FTP and therefore should stop doing the interval. Flynn has exhausted his FTP and it's time to either ride home or address a different training level.

We are all limited by the time we have to train, and we all want to train in the most efficient way possible. Using your power meter allows you to figure out the optimal number of training intervals for each workout. With a power meter, you can quantify your optimal training load in the grand scheme and truly optimize your training each day. As a result, you can improve at the highest rate that you are capable. And when you can train at an optimal level, you'll be assured of success.

TABLE 7.1 When to Stop Intervals

INTERVAL	AVERAGE DROP IN POWER
20 min	3–5%
10 min	4–6%
5 min	5–7%
3 min	8–9%
2 min	10–12%
1 min	10–12%
30 sec	12–15%
15 sec	**10–15% peak power drops by (15–20% peak power); average power for interval drops by**

Note: The drop in power is based on the number of watts achieved in the third effort. For example, when doing 5 minute intervals, a rider is ready for a rest when their average watts for an interval are 5% to 7% percent lower than they were for the third effort.

Pacing and Racing

After training and pushing yourself to the limit, you will be prepared to take all that hard-won fitness and do your best on race day. Pacing yourself correctly on the bike is critical. Most triathletes do not understand how easy it is to ride too fast on the bike leg; it's the number one cause of DNFs in triathlons. The difference between a well-paced bike leg and a poorly paced one can be as little as 15 watts (normalized) for an average in the event. Sure, you need to know how to swim efficiently, ride your bike solidly, and run fast, but once you have those skills down, the event itself is about metering out your energy for the entire event so that you finish strong on the run. If you go too fast on your bike leg, you are going to be in serious trouble on the run, but if you hold back too much on the bike, you will not always have a faster run. In many ways, a power meter is even better suited for use with triathlon than for use with bicycle racing. Most triathlons do not have complicated racing tactics—which increases the relative importance of pacing—and most are performed on the same course every year—which means that you can plan your pace in advance and test your pacing choices as you prepare for an event. Pacing, in short, is critical to triathlon success.

In pacing for a triathlon, no matter the distance, it is best to use normalized power (NP) because it accounts for the differences in terrain and allows you to focus on pedaling smoothly and steadily. What is normalized power? This is a mathematical formula applied to your average watts that takes into account the varying terrain, varying power output, and the time course of athlete's ability to recover from harder efforts. More simply, this is the power output you would have maintained had you pedaled smoothly throughout the entire ride or race and is what your body felt like it was producing. A power meter that displays NP on the head unit can be a real advantage. If this isn't possible with your unit, you will need to pace yourself based on average power as a percentage of FTP.

One other concept that you need to understand in order understand the pacing guidelines is a term called *intensity factor* (IF). The IF is the normalized power divided by your threshold power, and an IF of 1.0 is 100% of your FTP, whereas an IF of .65 is roughly 65% of your FTP. This is used in helping to determine the correct intensity for pacing for your length event.

See Table 7.2 for general pacing guidelines. But bear in mind that the levels provided in the table may not be exactly right for you. A newbie will need to be at the lower edge of the percentages and an experienced top age grouper might be able to handle the upper edges. It is important for you to do some rehearsal rides in which you try to hold particular levels of intensity for the entire length of the event you are planning to enter. If your event is longer than Olympic distance, try to hold a particular pace for half the race distance, followed by a half-distance run, for a solid brick workout. Pacing at this distance will provide you with a good indication of exactly how much energy you will have left at the beginning and end of the run.

TABLE 7.2 General Pacing Guidelines

TYPE OF TRIATHLON	DISTANCE	INTENSITY FACTOR (FRACTION OF NP)	AVERAGE POWER (% OF FTP)	TRAINING LEVEL
Sprint	10 km (6.2 mi.)	1.03–1.07	100–103	4
Olympic	40 km (24.8 mi.)	0.95–1.00	95–100	4
Half Ironman	90 km (56 mi.)	0.83–0.87	80–85	3
Ironman	180 km (112 mi.)	0.70–0.76	68–78	2–3
Double Ironman	361 km (224 mi.)	0.55–0.67	56–70	2

Smoother Is Better!

It's not just about average watts; it's about how you produce those watts, how many bursts you make, and whether you go harder in the beginning or save some for the finish. All these factors can dramatically impact your run time. How you will produce watts is the first consideration when developing a tri racing strategy—after all, not all watts are created equal. Recall the discussion of how power is created earlier in the chapter. You can create 1000 watts by pedaling in the 53:12 gear at a very high force but slow cadence, or you can produce 1000 watts by pedaling in the 34:28 gear at a low force but very fast cadence. The watts are the same in the end, but each effort called on very different muscle fiber types. We use a special tool called quadrant analysis in order to plot how the wattages are created in each training and racing ride. Quadrant I is fast cadence and high force, and more fast twitch muscle fibers are recruited here. More fast-twitch (type II) muscle fibers are also recruited when you are in quadrant II or pedaling in a high-force, low-cadence situation, whereas more slow-twitch (type I) fibers are recruited in a quadrant IV, or low-force, high-cadence, situation. Quadrant III is also slow twitch fibers, in a low force and lower cadence power creation scenario.

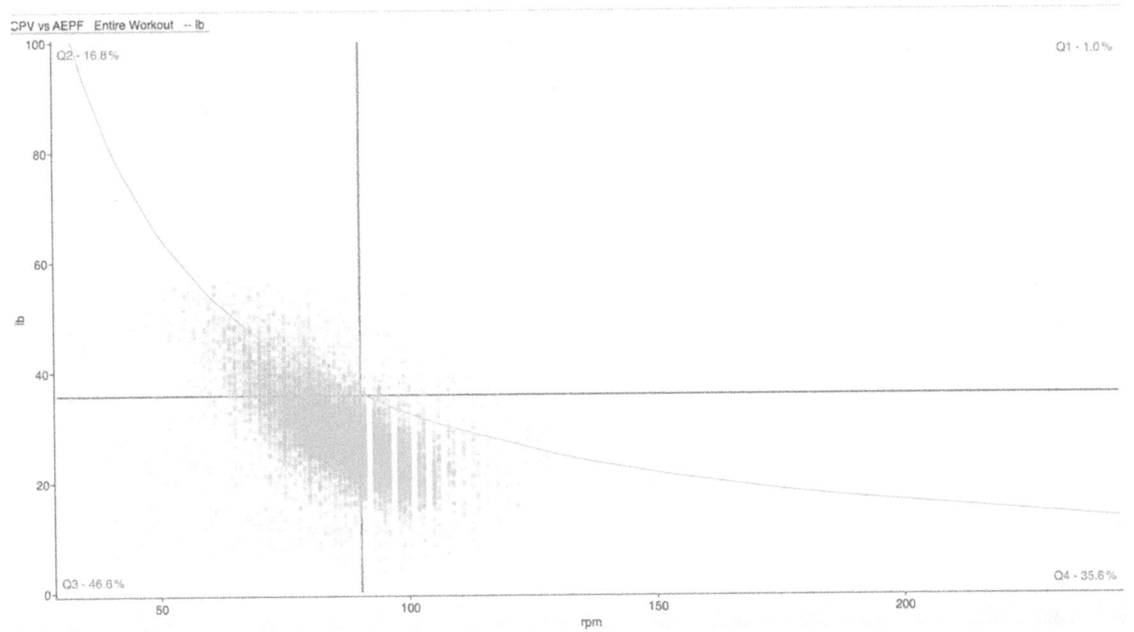

FIGURE 7.1 Quadrant analysis of a typical triathlon.

This matters in triathlon because your energy expenditure in each situation will be quite different. When fast-twitch muscle fibers are recruited, more muscle glycogen is used in the contractions than when slow-twitch fibers are recruited. Pedaling as smoothly and steadily as possible is key in triathlon. By keeping the normalized power and average power as close to the same as you can, you save valuable energy for the run. When normalized power is very high relative to average power, or when the variability index is high, this means that your power fluctuated too much. By smoothing your effort on hills and avoiding bursts of wattage, you can keep your variability index low and therefore reduce the amount of muscle glycogen used on the bike leg. *Variability index* (VI) is another important term you should understand when using a power meter in triathlon; it is the normalized power divided by the average power. When the normalized power is very high, for example 250 watts, in relation to the average power 150 watts, then the VI would be 1.66, which means the power was very "bursty" in nature and used more energy than needed for a triathlon. Triathletes should strive to have a VI between 1.00 and 1.07, so that it minimizes the amount of muscle glycogen usage on the bike and saving it for the run.

When considering quadrant analysis and smooth pedaling, even an effort that isn't fully in quadrants I or II will cost you more than you want to expend, and this is a critical waste of muscle glycogen and could impact you negatively on the run. Just as when you are driving a car your fuel consumption will be much higher if you are constantly flooring it and accelerating hard at every chance you get than if you just drive smoothly and consistently, your muscle glycogen expenditure will be greatest on the bike when you are fluctuating your power between low and high forces. We are not necessarily advocating high cadence in triathlon; we are, however, advising greater mindfulness about how you create your watts in a race. Stay light on the pedals, use your gearing to keep your cadence consistent, and if you are a gear masher spend plenty of time in training trying to achieve a more consistent, smooth pedaling stroke and we encourage you to do your best to increase your cadence so that is close to 90 rpm.

Let's examine two different race files from an Ironman event to better illustrate this point. In Figure 7.2, the athlete spent over 25.5% of his race in quadrant II, which

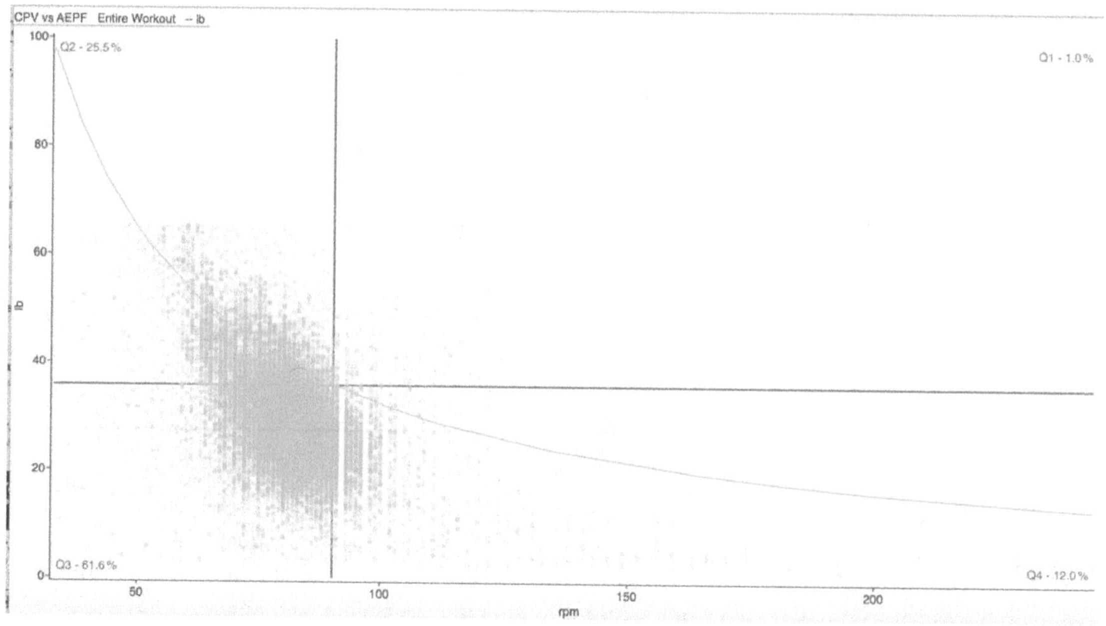

FIGURE 7.2 Too much time spent in quadrant II costs precious energy.

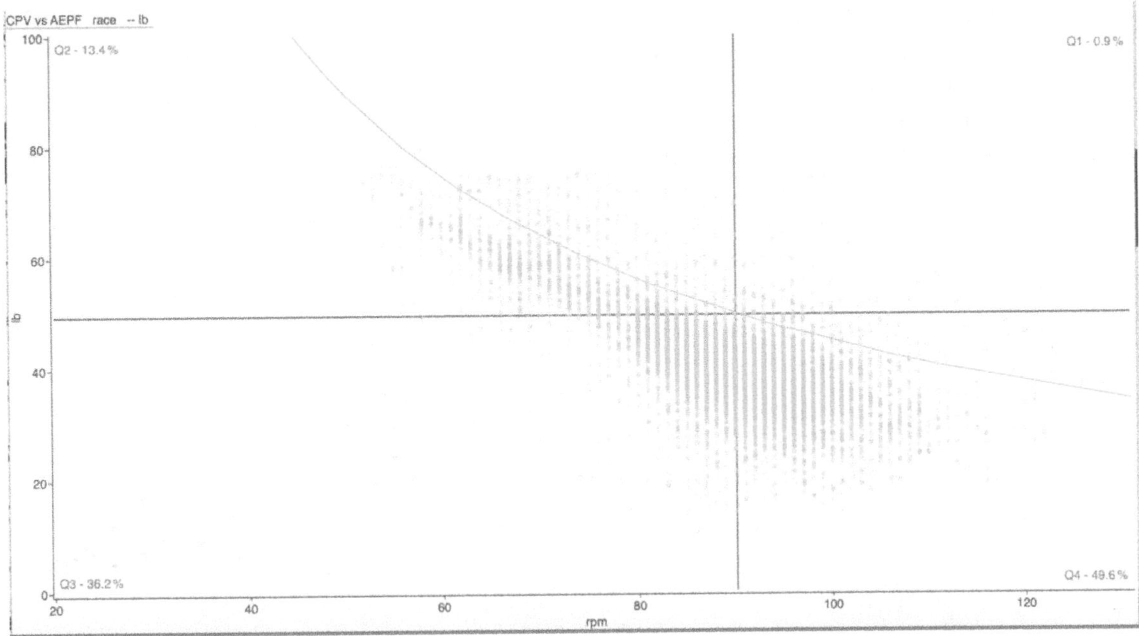

FIGURE 7.3 Good example of how an athlete creates watts in a triathlon.

represents high force and low cadence. From an energy conservation standpoint, this is the worst quadrant: Quadrant II requires a particularly large amount of muscle glycogen.

In the quadrant analysis shown in Figure 7.3, we see a much better example of how an athlete can create watts. This athlete shows nearly perfect wattage creation for over 86% of the race. He pedaled with low force and a slower cadence as you would in a recovery/endurance ride, staying in quadrant III. He avoided any hard power spikes and maintained a comfortable and steady pace throughout the ride, thus preserving his glycogen stores for the run. In fact, he was able to set a personal record on the run and easily won his age group as well, and in a tough event, Ironman Canada. Riding as smoothly as possible, avoiding hard surges of power throughout the ride, and being sure not to push a big gear can dramatically enhance your ability to conserve energy for the run. The best triathletes not only ride fast but also know exactly how to create watts in order to conserve energy—and the energy they conserve is energy that can be used on the run.

This quadrant analysis shows a well-paced Ironman distance race with proper selection of gears. Note that this athlete spent only 13% of his time in quadrant II and 86% in quadrant III and IV. He conserved a lot of glycogen in this way and consequently set a personal record on the run. He easily won in his age group.

Conclusion

A cycling power meter is an indispensable tool for training, and racing in triathlons and can be used in so many ways to help you improve. It's the perfect pacing tool for races, it helps you create wattage correctly, it ensures that you are training in the correct zone, and of course analysis after your workout or event can reveal areas of improvement needed or if you executed your strategy perfectly. There are so many ways that you can use your cycling power meter effectively for triathlon that it is hard to edit into one single chapter for this book. Following the areas of focus for power training will ensure that you are on the right track and training correctly with a power meter. Be sure that you test your FTP every six to eight weeks and reset your training levels(zones) as needed. This will ensure that you are applying a progressive overload to your body to continue to improve. Your FTP is the most important factor in your performance and a higher FTP; no matter what distance of triathlon or triathlon type you do; it will make you ride faster and finish sooner.

Chapter 8

Ready, Set, GO! Running and Power Meters

We all have the natural ability to run. However, we are not all great runners! Some of us can run long distances, some are better sprinters, and some of us trip over our own two feet. No matter our ability, running is a skill we can continue to improve throughout our lifetime. Running is essential to a good triathlete and many times is neglected in training, as it can feel so simple and natural that triathletes might not feel the need to train for it as seriously as swimming and cycling. With the advent of inexpensive running power meters, triathletes and runners alike have the ability to track data like power, flight time, vertical oscillation, and impact. These metrics have only been available to elite runners and researchers in the lab, but now are available to anyone with a device. Triathletes are traditionally quick to adopt and test out new technologies, and running devices are no exception. Like swimming devices and cycling power meters, running power meters have the ability to significantly enhance your running economy, pace, and endurance.

Many runners and multisport athletes focus on speed and steady-state endurance when it comes to running. To do this, the primary metrics used are heart rate and pace. However, these two metrics are highly susceptible to environmental factors such as heat, weather, terrain, and dehydration. Running power offers a different parameter to better measure speed and pacing. This metric is not reliant on some of the same factors as pace and heart rate. In this chapter, we will discuss how running power can assist with improving training, running economy, and post-training analysis. Before we dive into these elements of running power, we want to review the running power meters briefly.

The Running Power Meter

Running power meters have been on the market for the past few years. In theory, these devices provide a running metric that is independent of environmental factors that affect pace and heart rate. For example, your running power on flat terrain could be 200 W at an 8:00 minute/mile pace. However, later in the run, if you hit a hill with a 5% gradient, your power is still 200 W, but your pace drops to 9:00 minutes/mile. With a metric that is independent of environmental factors, you can create training zones to better dial in your training without the worry of outside elements interfering with the power metric.

Running and Cycling Power Meter Differences

The fundamentals of running and cycling power meters are quite different. Earlier, we discussed how cycling power meters calculate power through the following equation:

$$\text{Power} = \text{cadence} \times \text{torque} \qquad (1)$$

(Equation 1)

However, not all running power meters derive power this way. There are two classes of running power meters found on the market. For simplicity, we will differentiate these as direct and indirect power meters. Let us start with direct power meters.

Direct power meters measure running power in a similar fashion as cycling power meters. The base power equation is similar to Equation 1. However, we can change out the cycling metrics and utilize running metrics to get the following:

$$\text{Power} = \text{stride rate} \times \text{torque}$$

(Equation 2)

You might be wondering how a direct running power meter may be able to calculate your power. These power meters typically measure the force you produce while running at the sole of your foot. Direct running power meters are usually sole inserts that you put in your shoe. Prime examples of this type of power meter are RPM^2 and FeetMe. These products have several force meters imbedded in the insole you place in your shoe. These bilateral power meters measure the force vectors you create every time your foot hits the ground. These sensors can calculate your stride rate, stride length, and force production which gives you power.

As you learned earlier, running power is stride rate times torque (Equation 2). In cycling, this is how hard you are pedaling multiplied by how fast you are pedaling. So, if you pedal harder your wattage increases, or if you pedal faster your wattage increases (Equation 1). In running, it does not work that way. The power measured by direct power meters is susceptible to the types of shoes you are wearing or the terrain you are running on. For example, running on a treadmill is softer than running on dirt or on concrete. This material property is termed the elastic modulus. The elastic modulus of a treadmill is significantly lower than that of concrete. This stiffness property of materials effects the amount of force you produce. The same holds true if you run in different running shoes. So, your power output can change due to the change in running surface or shoe type even though your pace and incline did not.

The second class, indirect power meters, use sophisticated accelerometers to calculate the power (wattage) that is created during a running session. Force can be measured via the following equation:

$$F = MA$$

(Equation 3)

Where

F = force (N)

M = mass (kg)

A = acceleration (m/s^2)

This class of power meters utilize accelerometers, gyroscopes, and magnetometers to calculate force. With this metric, torque and power can be calculated via Equation 2. Indirect running power meters are found in foot pods, watches, and heart rate monitors. The main foot pod power meters are Stryd and RunScribe. Others are found in smartwatches such as the Garmin Running Power App and Polar Vantage V. One of the central running power meters in today's market, Stryd, describes itself as a 3D power meter (2). All running indirect power meters can measure, but are not limited to, the following metrics: power, ground impact, vertical oscillation, ground contact time, and stride length.

Differences in cycling and running threshold powers exist. Typically, an athlete's running power is higher than their cycling power. This is due to several factors, such as running economy and efficiency. Additionally, many athletes have a higher lactate threshold when running compared to cycling. Physiologically, this makes sense. Put simply, an athlete uses more muscles during running than during cycling and that demand is spread across more working muscles, thus allowing the athlete to work at a higher intensity.

Running economy is defined as "typically defined as the energy demand for a given velocity of submaximal running, and is determined by measuring the steady-state consumption of oxygen (VO_2) and the respiratory exchange ratio" (3). Running efficiency is not a true physiological term. In physics, efficiency is defined as the ratio of energy output to the energy input to a system (4). This definition cannot be applied to physiology and running. We must think in terms of running economy; how can we improve our running speed with the lowest cost of oxygen utilization. Running power meters can help you improve your running economy and speed. Over the next few chapters, we will dive into running power theory and show you how to apply it.

Conclusion

Running power meters are here to stay and will continue to improve. Choosing which option is right for you, has to do more with how much data do you want and how important is it to wear a specific brand of shoes. If you are very committed to a particular brand, an insole power meter might not work for you. Whereas an indirect power meter might be just the thing for your style and shoe choice. Even though each class of power meter measures power differently, they give you the same power metric. Power can be used to improve your speed and running economy. In the next chapter, we will discuss how to create and train with running power.

References

1. Allen, H., Coggan, A., & McGregor, S. (2019). *Training and racing with a power meter* (3rd ed.). VeloPress.
2. https://www.stryd.com/en/.
3. Saunders, P. U., Pyne, D. B., Telford, R. D., & Hawley, J. A. (2004). Factors affecting running economy in trained distance runners. *Sports Medicine (Auckland, N.Z.)*, *34*(7), 465–485. https://doi.org/10.2165/00007256-200434070-00005
4. Saw, V. L., & Chew, L. Y. (2020). No-boarding buses: Synchronization for efficiency. *PlOS One*, *15*(3), e0230377. https://doi.org/10.1371/journal.pone.0230377

Chapter 9

Dropping the HAMMER! Running and Training with Power

As discussed in the previous chapters, a threshold test needs to be performed to establish running power training zones and baseline metrics. This section will discuss the different types of methodologies utilized and their strengths and weaknesses. Lace up your shoes, and let's go on this journey together.

Critical Power

Using a running power meter is very similar to a cycling power meter. You will need to perform a running functional threshold power (rFTP) test. Previously, we discussed the usage of the 20 minute protocol to determine your FTP, and here we are presenting multiple options. The most essential aspect with any FTP test is it is designed to be the upper end of your aerobic capability (1, 2). A well-performed FTP test correlates well with laboratory mean lactate steady state tests (1, 2).

This is the issue with some of the popular methodologies. One commonly used run test is the critical power (CP) protocol. The CP test is another cycling power methodology adopted for running and is generally interchangeable with FTP. However, CP and FTP are not the same. Technically, CP is a two-parameter nonlinear mathematical model that describes the difference between steady-state and not steady-state metabolic work (mean metabolic steady-state, or MMSS) (7, 13). It does not represent the mean lactate steady-state (MLSS), which is highly correlated with the 20 minute FTP field test (1–3, 6). MLSS is accepted as the metabolic measurement denoting the line between aerobic and anaerobic work at a steady-state intensity for a given period of time (10, 11). Additionally, CP and FTP tests provide different power threshold estimates that can cause significant differences in individualized power training zones (7). In simple terms, your critical power is determined based on how quickly (or slowly) you fatigue from an all-out running effort. By looking at the reduction in your power over the test protocol, a modeled power is calculated that is your running threshold power for a longer time, say 45–60 minutes.

Several different CP protocols exist. The most common is the 3 minute, all-out running test. As with other power training protocols, it was adapted from cycling critical power testing theory. This protocol is useful in determining shorter distance anaerobic efforts. However, it has very little correlation with longer distances (i.e., 10 km and longer) (8). To mitigate this low correlation to long-distance running, a 6 and 9 minute all-out effort protocol is commonly used in conjunction with the 3 minute test.

When you perform these tests, you need to record your running power. This involves using a foot pod that measures running power. Additionally, you will need to plan 2 separate days to perform the 3 minute and 6 and 9 minute tests. This will ensure you are well rested and can give your maximum effort. The 9 minute test is more representative of a threshold effort than the 6 minute test. For this reason, only the 9 minute test will be used for the following example.

Three Minute CP Test Protocol

Perform 5 minutes of dynamic warm-up:

1. Leg swings: 10–20 per leg
2. Marches: 10–15 per leg
3. Leg side swings: 10–20 per leg

Build to warm-up pace from active recovery (power Z1, pace Z1, HR Z1, RPE 1–2) to endurance (power Z2, pace Z2, HR Z2, RPE 2–3) for 10 minutes. Then perform 4x10 s strides with 30 s rest in between.

MS: Immediately after the warm-up, increase your pace to tempo pace (power Z3, pace Z3, HR Z3, RPE 3–4). Once comfortable, quickly ramp up your pace/power to a maximal effort you think you can hold for 3 minutes. Your effort should range between upper $VO_{2\,Max}$ (power Z5, pace Z5, HR Z5, RPE 6–7) to anaerobic capacity (power Z6, pace Z6, HR Z6, RPE 7–8). Once you hit your desired pace, start recording your effort.

Once you finish the 3 minute test, ramp down you pace to low endurance (power Z2, pace Z2, HR Z2, RPE 2–3) for 3 to 5 minutes.

CD: Walk for 10 minutes until your heart rate reaches 100 BPM.

NINE MINUTE CP TEST PROTOCOL

Perform 5 minutes of dynamic warm-up:
1. Leg swings: 10–20 per leg
2. Marches: 10–15 per leg
3. Leg side swings: 10–20 per leg

Build to warm-up pace from active recovery (power Z1, pace Z1, HR Z1, RPE 1–2) to endurance (power Z2, pace Z2, HR Z2, RPE 2–3) for 10 min. Then perform 4×10 s strides with 30 s rest in between.

MS: Immediately after the warm-up, increase your pace to tempo pace (power Z3, pace Z3, HR Z3, RPE 3–4). Once comfortable, quickly ramp up your pace/power to a maximal effort you think you can hold for 9 minutes. Your effort should range between threshold (power Z4, pace Z4, HR Z4, RPE 5–6) to $VO_{2\,Max}$ (power Z5, pace Z5, HR Z5, RPE 7–8). Once you hit your desired pace, start recording your effort.

Once you finish the 9 minute test, ramp down you pace to low endurance (power Z2, pace Z2, HR Z2, RPE 2–3) for 3 to 5 minutes.

CD: Walk for 10 minutes until your heart rate reaches 100 BPM.

The CP equation is as follows (3, 5):

$$T_{lim} = W' / (P - CP)$$

(Equation 1)

where

W' = finite amount of work CP (J)

CP = critical power (W)

T_{lim} = time limit (s)

P = power output (W)

Sophisticated software is needed to perform the mathematical modeling to calculate CP. Research shows that CP modeling produces higher wattage compared to the 20 minute test (9). This overestimation could have you training in the wrong metabolic pathways (i.e., the wrong training zone). Remember, the CP protocols are very limited in their ability to accurately predict running threshold, as presented at the beginning of this chapter.

Look at it this way, the 3 minute test is very close to running an 800 m interval, and the 9 minute test is close to running 1.5 miles. These efforts are not generally considered threshold efforts. These efforts cover more of the anaerobic energy pathway than the aerobic pathway (10, 14). Due to these performance and metabolic aspects, using the 3 minute test metric alone would overestimate your training zones, as seen in the research presented by Karsten et al. (7). Remember, threshold testing mimics MLSS efforts. The CP tests produce blood lactate markers higher than 4 mmol, which is the standard as the lactate threshold (LT) (i.e., the theoretical physiological marker between aerobic and anaerobic work). To meet this standard, the testing efforts need to have lower intensities and longer lengths of time. As stated at the beginning of this chapter, to be considered an FTP test, the effort must cover the aerobic metabolic pathway, not anaerobic (10). The 5 km protocol meets this standard and is widely used in human performance research, whereas the CP test does and is not.

The 5 km test serves as the rFTP metric in order calculate your training zones (11). Endurance athletes can run 5 k between 19 and 25 minutes (6, 11). This timeframe matches the scientifically proven 20 minute FTP test protocol (2, 6, 11). However, if performed properly, it elicits the same cardiovascular and respiratory metrics characteristic of lactate threshold efforts (11). This is the reason many laboratory protocols utilize 5 km running tests, not CP, as part of their studies. The best part about this protocol is it can be performed anywhere, and you do not need expensive computer modeling to calculate your rFTP.

It is important to note that for a small number of individuals, primarily well-trained to elite triathletes and runners, the 5 km test may be too short. This is why we suggest using the 10 km protocol to verify your rFTP a few days after performing the 5 km rFTP test to ensure your zones are correct.

The 10 km test serves to measure the endurance component of your power. Typically, one's 10 km pace falls within the tempo (power Z3) range. This data point serves as a check to ensure the zones calculated from your 5 km test are accurate. In Chapters 1 and 2 we discussed similar strategies you should perform the first time you use a power meter. The 5 and 10 km protocols should be tested on different days, with a minimum of 24 hours of rest in between. However, the more experienced and trained you become, you can perform these two protocols together (as discussed in case study 1).

5 KM RUN TEST:

Perform 5 minutes of dynamic warm-up:

1. Leg swings: 10–20 per leg
2. Toe touches: 10 per leg
3. Leg side swings: 10–20 per leg

Build to warm-up pace from active recovery (power Z1, pace Z1, HR Z1, RPE 1–2) to endurance (power Z2, pace Z2, HR Z2, RPE 2–3) for 10 minutes. Then perform 4x10 s strides with 30 s rest in between.

MS: Immediately after the warm-up, increase your pace to tempo pace (power Z3, pace Z3, HR Z3, RPE 3–4). Once comfortable, quickly ramp up your pace/power to the maximal effort you think you can hold for 5 km (power Z4, pace Z4, HR Z4, RPE 6–7). Once you hit your desired pace, start recording your effort.

Once you finish the test, ramp down you pace to low endurance (power Z2, pace Z2, HR Z2, RPE 2–3) for 3 to 5 minutes.
CD: Walk for 10 minutes until your heart rate reaches 100 BPM.

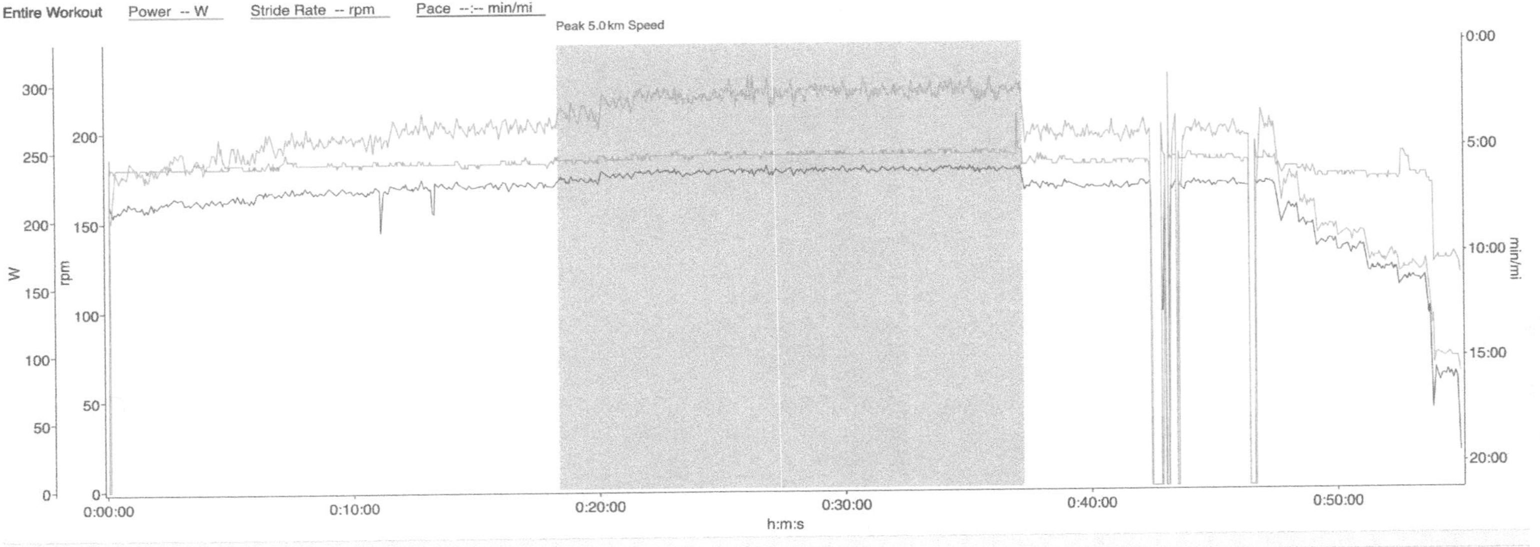

Range	Duration h:m:s	Avg Power W	NP W	Stride Rate steps/min	Avg Pace min/mi
Entire Workout	0:54:59	251	262	178	7:04
Peak 5.0 km Speed	0:18:53	290	290	186	6:05

FIGURE 9.1 This figure depicts the results of a well-executed 5 km rFTP test. The test yielded a 5 km test result of 290 W. This triathlete was a season triathlete, so the coefficient of .95 was used to calculate the rFTP. The triathlete's calculated rFTP = 275 W.

10 KM RUN TEST:

Perform 5 minutes of dynamic warm-up:

1. Leg swings: 10–20 per leg
2. Toe touches: 10 per leg
3. Leg side swings: 10–20 per leg

Build to warm-up pace from active recovery (power Z1, pace Z1, HR Z1, RPE 1–2) to endurance (power Z2, pace Z2, HR Z2, RPE 2–3) for 10 minutes. Then perform 4x10 s strides with 30 s rest in between.

MS: Immediately after the warm-up, increase your pace to upper endurance pace (power Z2, pace Z2, HR Z2, RPE 2–3). Once comfortable, quickly ramp up your pace/power to the maximal effort you think you can hold for 10 km. This effort should be tempo (power Z3, pace Z3, HR Z3, RPE 3–4) to low threshold (power Z4, pace Z4, HR Z4, RPE 5–6). Once you hit your desired pace, start recording your effort.

Once you finish the test, ramp down you pace to low endurance (Power Z2, Pace Z2, HR Z2, RPE 2–3) for 3 to 5 minutes.

CD: Walk for 10 minutes until your heart rate reaches 100 BPM.

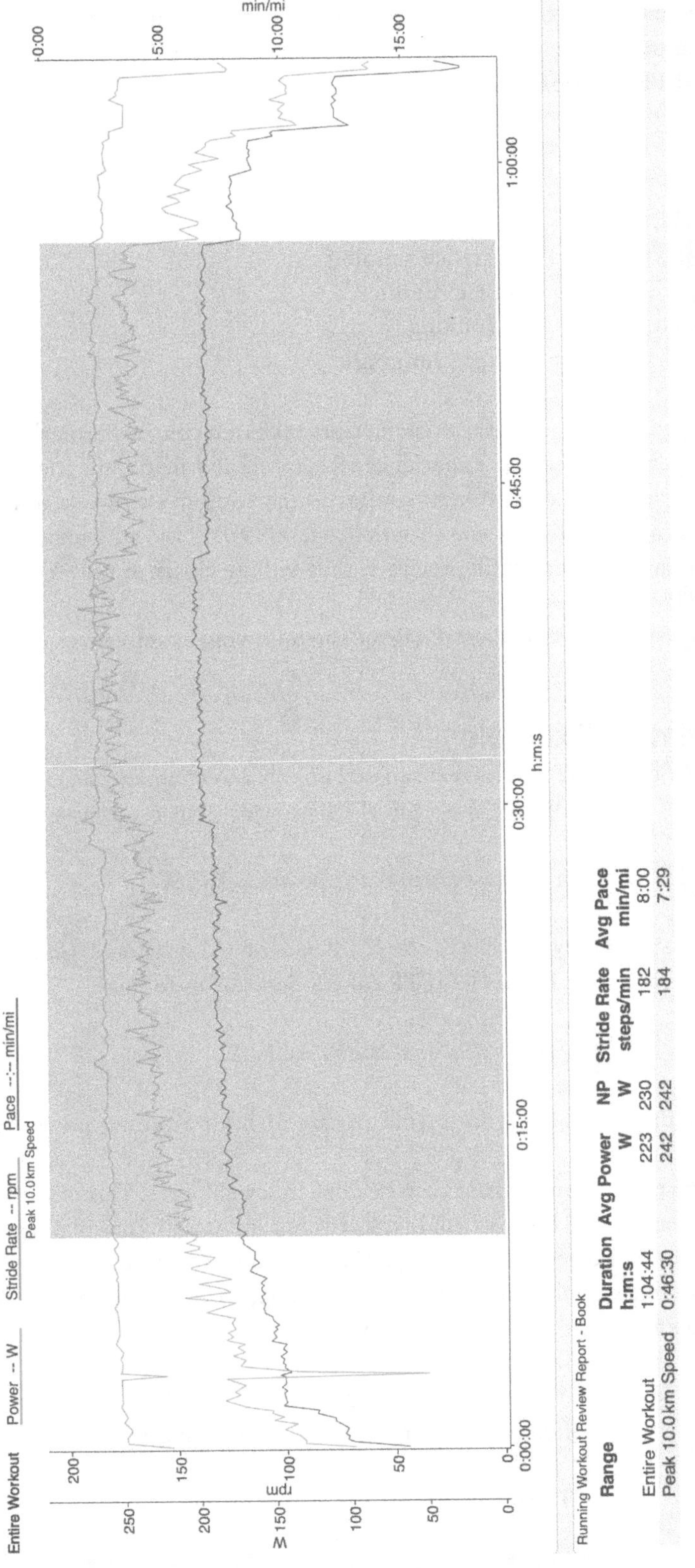

Running Workout Review Report - Book

Range	Duration h:m:s	Avg Power W	NP W	Stride Rate steps/min	Avg Pace min/mi
Entire Workout	1:04:44	223	230	182	8:00
Peak 10.0km Speed	0:46:30	242	242	184	7:29

FIGURE 9.2 This figure depicts a well-executed 10 km run test. The athlete's calculated rFTP was 275W. The tempo power range was 209–250 W. The 10 km test wattage was at 242 W after the 10 min warm-up period. This test validated the triathlete's rFTP.

Once an athlete completes the 5 km run test, the normalized power (NP) for the test needs to be determined. This can be found via your data collection device, Training Peaks, Strava, Final Surge, or other data collection platforms. The NP is necessary to calculate the rFTP. The rFTP equation is as follows:

$$\text{rFTP} = 5 \text{ km NP} \times \text{coefficient}$$

(Equation 2)

Experience Coefficients
92%: New or inexperienced to distance running
93%: Some experience with distance running
94%: Experienced with distance running
95%: Very experienced with distance running

Note: As presented in Chapter 2, these coefficients take into consideration this variation in steady-state performance and experience. Research and field data suggest performance can fade over the 5 km distance (similar to the 1500 m swim test) and is highly dependent on the athlete's fitness and experience level (9). As the athlete becomes more and more experienced at performing the test, they will be closer to the 95% coefficient to calculate rFTP.

To better discuss how to calculate rFTP, see the following example.

rFTP Calculation Example

Flynn, the same long-course triathlete discussed in previous chapters, decided to test his rFTP. During his test, he followed the 5 km rFTP protocol. His result was as follows:

5 km run test normalized power = 262 W

To calculate his rFTP, Flynn utilized the rFTP equation (Equation 2) and considered himself an experienced triathlete. His rFTP calculation was as follows:

$$\text{rFTP} = 95\% \text{ x } 262 \text{ W} = 250 \text{ W}$$

With his calculated rFTP, Flynn is able to establish his running power training/pacing zones.

Calculating the power training zones can be done in several ways. TrainingPeaks, Final Surge, Garmin Connect, and other scheduling software automatically calculate the training zones and apply them to scheduled workouts. The traditional way is to calculate the zones oneself. All power zones, similar to swimming and cycling, are based on a percentage of the athlete's FTP. Again, as with swimming power training zones, very little research exists on how to calculate running power training zones. The application of cycling power training zones, as discussed earlier, is the best course of action since it is well researched and verified. The following is the calculation of Flynn's running power training zones.

rFTP from the 5 km run test = 250 W

DR. COGGAN'S CLASSIC POWER LEVELS

LEVEL	DESCRIPTION	PERCENT	SUGGESTED DISTANCE
1	Active recovery	56% or less	N/A
2	Endurance	56% to 76%	Marathon, IRONMAN, IRONMAN 70.3
3	Tempo	76% to 91%	Half-marathon, IRONMAN 70.3, 10 km
4	Threshold	91% to 106%	5 km, 10 km
5	VO_{2max}	106% to 121%	800 m, 1 mile
6	Anaerobic capacity	121% or more	400 m, sprints

RFTP = 250 W POWER TRAINING ZONES

LEVEL	DESCRIPTION	PERCENT	POWER RANGE
1	Active recovery	56% or less	< 140 W
2	Endurance	56% to 76%	141–190 W
3	Tempo	76% to 91%	191–277 W
4	Threshold	91% to 106%	228–265 W
5	VO_{2max}	106% to 121%	266–302 W
6	Anaerobic capacity	121% or more	➤ 303 W

Please note the suggested distances are just suggestions. The power pacing over the distances is individualistic. For example, professional triathletes can perform IRONMAN 70.3 run at zone 4, whereas others can only run the IRONMAN 70.3 run at zone 1. You are encouraged to find out what zone works best for you through training.

Once established, the individualized running power zones allow the runner to create customized workouts. These types of workouts address the specific athlete's running strengths and limitations and allows for proper training of targeted metabolic pathways. Another interesting aspect with these zones is the athlete can utilize them both indoors and outdoors. It is critical for triathletes to train specifically to the demands of the event and also to your own strengths and limiters. One of the major benefits of training with a power meter in running is ensuring that you are indeed training the zone that you want to train and not just estimating based on an outdated zone system that might be dependent on many factors.

Continuing with the example of Flynn, he created his first running workout based on his newly established running power zones. The workout is as follows:

3x5 Race Pace Intervals

Warm-up: Jog at active recovery (< 140 W) for 10 minutes.

After the 10 minute jog, perform the following:
1. Marches: 15 per leg
2. Toe touches: 10 per leg
3. Leg side swings: 10–20 per leg

MS: Start main set at low endurance (141–155 W). Once comfortable, complete 3×5 minute 10 km race pace intervals at upper tempo (250–270 W) with 10 minutes rest in between each interval at middle endurance (150–170 W).

CD: Jog for 10 minutes at active recovery (< 140 W).

Conclusion

Two prevailing methodologies exist to determine running training zones, CP and rFTP. Each utilizes different methodologies to calculate the key power metric. No matter the methodology, the way to determine your running training zones is the same. With these zones, you can create tailored power zones to address your running strengths and limitations. The next step is to understand what this power data is telling you. In the next chapter, we will discuss how to perform analysis on your running power data.

References

1. Allen, H., & Cheung, S. (2012). *Cutting-edge cycling.* Human Kinetics.
2. Allen, H., Coggan, A., & McGregor, S. (2019). *Training and racing with a power meter* (3rd ed.). VeloPress.
3. Black, M. I., Jones, A. M., Kelly, J. A. Bailey, S. J., & Vanhatalo, A. (2016). The constant work rate critical power protocol overestimates ramp incremental exercise performance. *European Journal of Applied Physiology*, 116, 2415–2422. https://doi.org/10.1007/s00421-016-3491-y
4. Borszcz, F. K., Tramontin, A. F., Bossi, A. H., Carminatti, L. J., & Costa, V. P. (2018). Functional threshold power in cyclists: Validity of the concept and physiological responses. *International Journal of Sports Medicine*, *39*, 737–742. https://doi.org/10.1055/s-0044-101546

5. Chorley, A., & Lamb, K. L. (2020). The application of critical power, the work capacity above critical power (W'), and its reconstitution: A narrative review of current evidence and implications for cycling training prescription. *Sports*, *8*(9), 123. https://doi.org/10.3390/sports8090123
6. Haverty M., Kenney W., & Hodgson, J. (1988). Lactate and gas exchange responses to incremental and steady state running. *British Journal of Sports Medicine*, 22, 51–54. http://dx.doi.org/10.1136/bjsm.22.2.51
7. Karsten, B., Petrigna L., Klose A., Bianco A., Townsend N., & Triska C. (2021). Relationship between the critical power test and a 20-min functional threshold power test in cycling. *Frontiers in Physiology*, *11*, 1877. https://doi.org/10.3389/fphys.2020.613151
8. Kolbe, T., Dennis, S. C., Selley, E., Noakes, T. D., & Lambert, M. I. (1995). The relationship between critical power and running performance. *Journal of Sports Sciences, 13*(3), 265–269. https://doi.org/10.1080/02640419508732236.
9. Muniz-Pumares, D., Karsten, B., Triska, C., & Glaister, M. (2018). Methological approaches and related challenges associated with the determination of critical power and W'. *Journal of Strength and Conditioning Research.*
10. Powers, S. K., & Howley, E. T. (2011). *Exercise physiology: Theory and application to fitness and performance* (8th ed.). McGraw-Hill.
11. Ramsbottom, R., Williams, C., Kerwin D., & Nute N. (1992) Physiological and metabolic responses of men and women to a 5-km treadmill time trial. *Journal of Sports Sciences*, *10*(2), 119–129. https://doi.org/10.1080/02640419208729914.
12. Tanner, A. V., Nielsen, B. V., & Allgrove, J. (2014). Salivary and plasma cortisol and testosterone responses to interval and tempo runs and a bodyweight-only circuit session in endurance-trained men. *Journal of Sports Sciences, 32*(7), 680–689. https://doi.org/10.1080/02640414.2013.850594.
13. Vanhatalo, A., Jones, A. M., & Burnley, M. (2011). Application of critical power in sport. *International Journal of Sports Physiology and Performance*, 6(1), 128–136. https://doi.org/10.1123/ijspp.6.1.128
14. Vuorimaa, T., Ahotupa, M., Häkkinen, K., & Vasankari, T. (2008). Different hormonal response to continuous and intermittent exercise in middle-distance and marathon runners. *Scandinavian Journal of Medicine and Science in Sport,* 18(5), 565–572. https://doi.org/10.1111/j.1600-0838.2007.00733.x.

Chapter 10

PR

Analyzing Running Power

Running with power provides more than just a pacing measurement. This metric provides a formidable set of parameters to analyze your performance during training and racing. It's important that you clearly understand what all those squiggly lines and graphs mean in your downloaded running data. This is when the tech toy turns into a training tool. By learning how to quickly analyze your data, understand the key metrics, and then learn when you need to make a training decision, you will be training more effectively. In this section, we will look at several examples of how run power can be used for training and pacing and how to analyze performance. Before we get to the case studies, we want to explain, albeit quickly, the phases of the running gait. This will be very helpful when analyzing your running power metrics.

The Running Gait

Running performance is primarily based on two factors: endurance and biomechanics. No matter the type of runner you are (e.g., heel strike, mid-foot strike, or toe strike), the elements of the gait are the same. The critical difference between the running style is how the foot hits the ground; the ankle, knee, and hip angles; and how the impact forces are translated through the musculoskeletal system. Each leg goes through the same gait cycle, as shown in Figure 10.1. Due to the nature of how we evolved to run, the sequences for each leg are offset.

The running cycle begins with the initial contact of the foot (heel or other portion of the foot). This starts the stance phase. As your weight propels forward and the opposite leg swings through the initial swing phase, you roll along your foot. You begin to move from absorbing the forces of the impact to the midstance. As your body continues to move forward, your foot transitions into a position to start pushing off the ground. At the midstance, your body is directly over your foot. Simultaneously, the opposite leg begins to transition from the mid-swing to the terminal swing. Once you push off with your foot, the opposite leg swings into the terminal swing. This motion causes you to be propelled forward in the air with neither foot touching the ground. This portion of your gait is typically termed *floating* or the *float phase*. Both legs are extended in front and behind you during the float phase. The foot you just pushed off enters the initial swing phase at the end of the float phase. Simultaneously, the opposite foot hits the ground (initial contact). This process repeatedly occurs for each leg as you run.

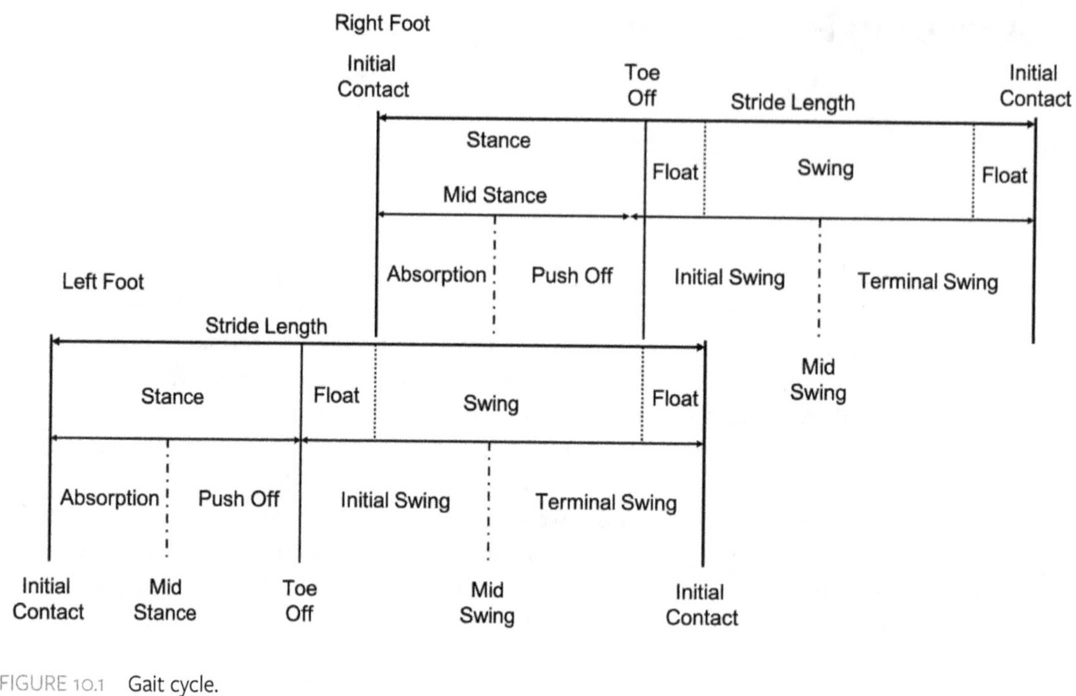

FIGURE 10.1 Gait cycle.

Having a basic understanding of your running gait will help with your power analysis. We will build on this foundational knowledge in the case studies in this chapter and the next.

Case Study 1: rFTP Field Test

The first case study we will dive into is a rFTP field test. We present this case to illustrate what a good rFTP test looks like and some test characteristics to analyze for the accuracy of the rFTP test. The triathlete in this case study followed the same 5 km and 10 km protocols described in the previous chapter and performed the protocol on the treadmill.

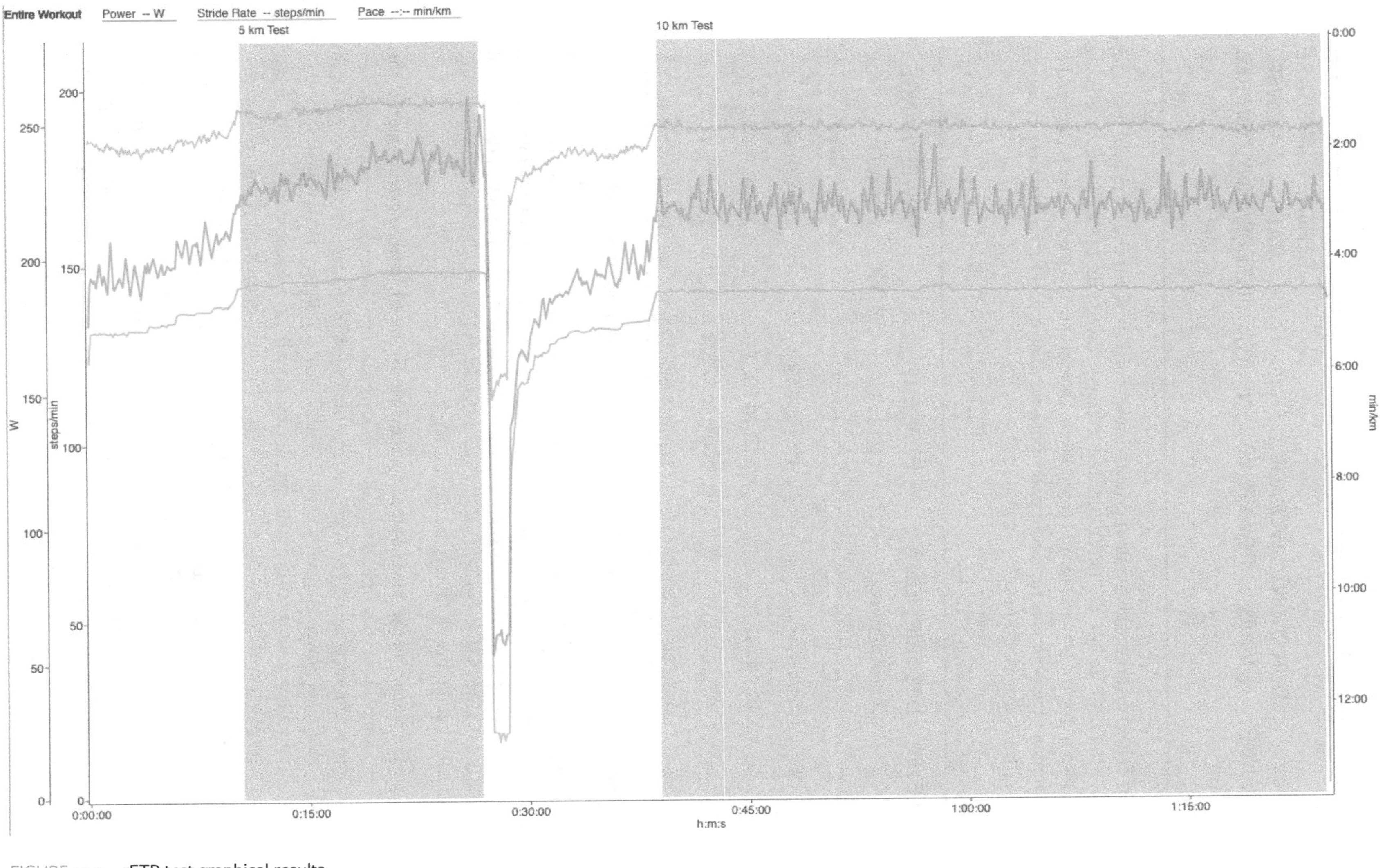

FIGURE 10.2 rFTP test graphical results.

TABLE 10.1 rFTP Results

RANGE	DURATION (H/M/S)	AVERAGE POWER (W)	NP (W)	STRIDE RATE (STEPS/MIN)	AVERAGE POWER (MIN/KM)
5 km test	0:16:19	233	233	195	4:17
10 km test	0:45:20	219	219	188	4:34

In Table 10.1, the athlete ran an average power of 233 W for the 5 km field test. This places the rFTP at 221 W. The 10 km test average power was 219W. These results are significant due the way the results corroborate each other. The 10 km test is designed to be an upper tempo/lower threshold pace. With the 219 W rFTP, the triathlete's running power zones are as follows:

rFTP = 219 W: Power Training Zones

LEVEL	DESCRIPTION	PERCENT	POWER RANGE
1	Active recovery	56% or less	< 124W
2	Endurance	56% to 76%	125–167 W
3	Tempo	76% to 91%	168–201 W
4	Threshold	91% to 106%	202–234 W
5	$VO_{2\,Max}$	106% to 121%	235–267 W
6	Anaerobic capacity	121% or more	> 268 W

The 10 km average power of 219 W falls in the middle of the threshold power range of 202–234 W. This is the result one should expect from a properly ran power test.

In this case study, this particular triathlete is a high-performing long-course age grouper. This triathlete had trained and raced at a high level for over 15 years before this test. Given this history, we should expect a consistent testing result. However, this type of result is not always so consistent. A few key areas to pay particular attention to ensure you have high quality rFTP test are as follows:

1. **Consistency of the power output.** As shown in Figure 10.3a, the power output for the 5 km field was 6% or a change of 15 W over the total distance. It is not uncommon to see an increase of 4–7% or less over the length of the test. It is best to get up to the target power as quickly as possible, as shown in Figure 10.3a. However, it can take a few minutes to get up to speed. Additionally, as evident in Figure 10.1, a last surge of effort is typically seen in the final 1 minute of the test. A general guideline is that a rate change of 7% or lower confirms a valid rFTP test result.
2. **Consistency of the 5 and 10 km test results.** The entire purpose of the 10 km field test is to confirm the rFTP result. The average power of the 10 km field test should fall between the upper tempo and the mid-threshold power ranges. If this does not occur, double-check the validity of the 5 km test. If the 5 km test appears to be valid, consider the athlete's endurance capacity or the constant (92–95%) used to calculate the rFTP.

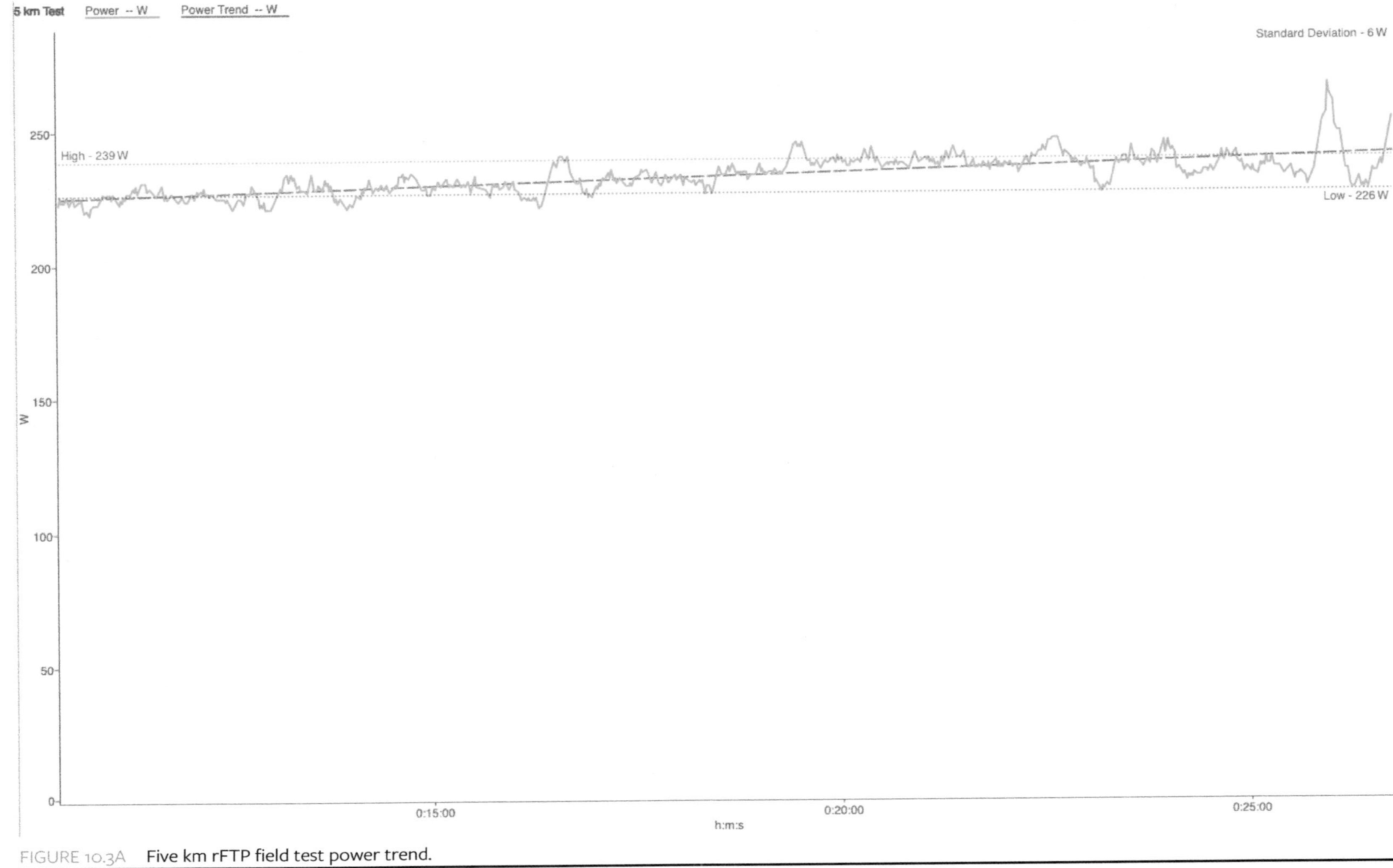

FIGURE 10.3A Five km rFTP field test power trend.

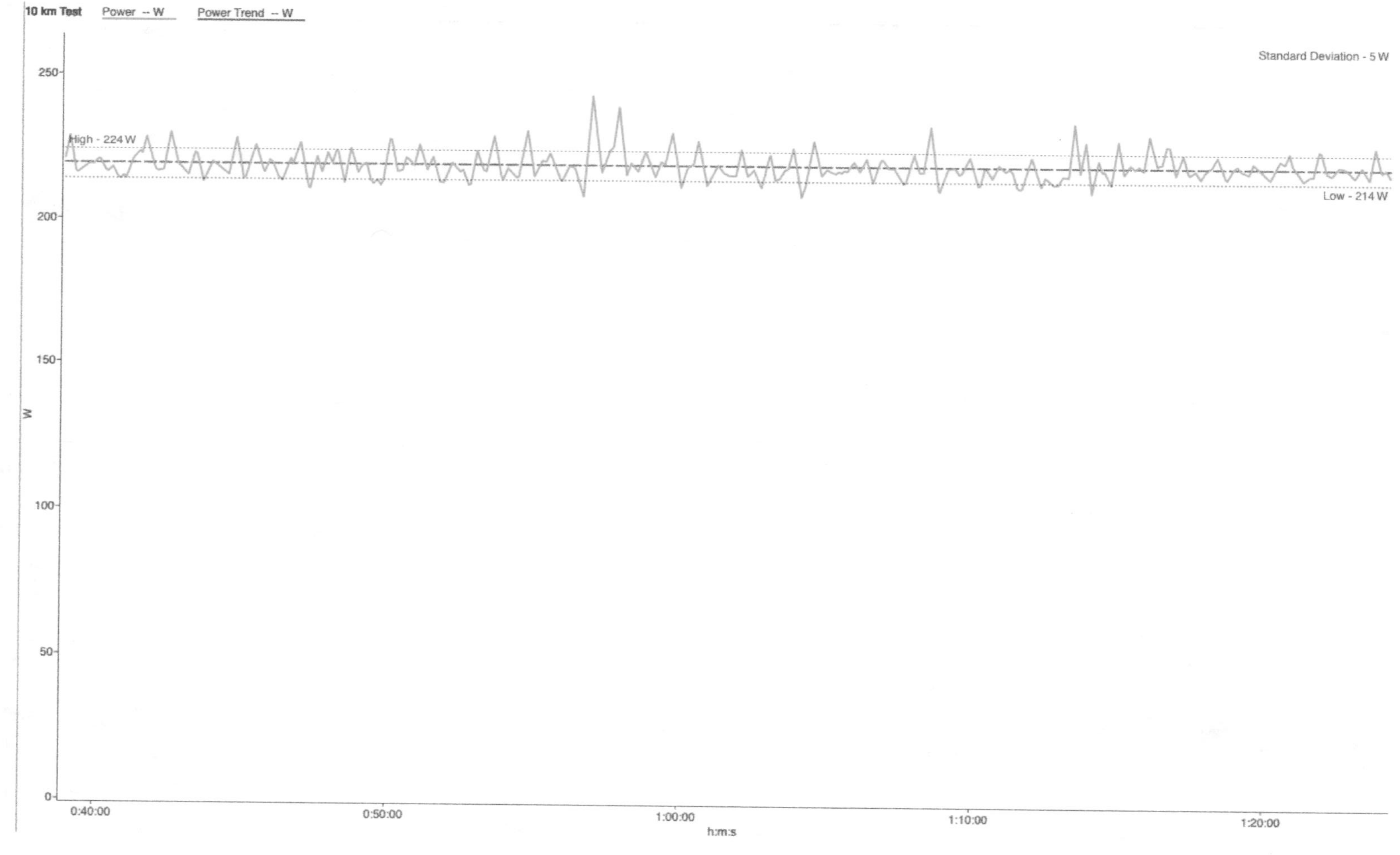

FIGURE 10.3B Ten km running field test power trend.

3. **Athlete endurance capacity.** New multisport athletes may not have extensive aerobic capabilities. This athletic limitation can confound the result of the 10 km field test. If this is the case, you may want to consider retesting the 10 km test after the athlete has built up enough aerobic endurance.

Case Study 2: Tempo Run

The staple of any run component of the multisport training program is the tempo run. Tempo pace is very similar to long-course race pace, as discussed in the previous chapter. Additionally, the physiological stress is moderate, but not to the point to require large amounts of recovery (3, 4). This training aspect is highly important to those multisport athletes who are limited on training time. Tempo run effects are similar to cycling sweet-spot intervals (1).

In this case study, the example triathlete is a seasoned age-group triathlete. This triathlete had a rFTP of 205 W. Following are the triathlete's power training zones based on his most recent field test.

rFTP = 205W: Power Training Zones

LEVEL	DESCRIPTION	PERCENT	POWER RANGE
1	Active recovery	56% or less	< 114 W
2	Endurance	56% to 76%	115–155 W
3	Tempo	76% to 91%	158–186 W
4	Threshold	91% to 106%	187–217 W
5	$VO_{2\,Max}$	106% to 121%	218–248 W
6	Anaerobic capacity	121% or more	> 249 W

The triathlete's first workout after the field test was to perform a 60 minute tempo run at 168–180 W. As shown in Figure 10.4 and Table 10.2, the triathlete ran for 1:05:08 at 170 W. Overall, the power output (yellow line) was very consistent over the hilly terrain, with no significant issues with heart rate. Looking closer at Figure 10.4, this tempo run was performed on terrain (gray line) with rolling hills. The pace (blue line) changes with the terrain. With each climb, the pace drops, and vice versa. However, the power stays consistent going up and down the hills. The aspect case study 2 highlights is how power can be used for pacing over rolling terrain.

This is the awesome aspect of running with power. The ability to pace consistently through undulating terrain is a major advance in running and pacing. As you know, you pace changes when going up and down hills, and it is hard to gauge a consistent effort. Running power changes this aspect of your training, and now you can maintain a consistent power pace over the changing terrain by using your power output. You can modulate your effort to maintain the proper wattage, ensuring you don't "blow up" or go too easy and leave something on the table. This will help you maintain consistent efforts and not push (or not push hard enough) on hilly terrain. How well does this strategy work for marathon distance runs and runs up a mountain?

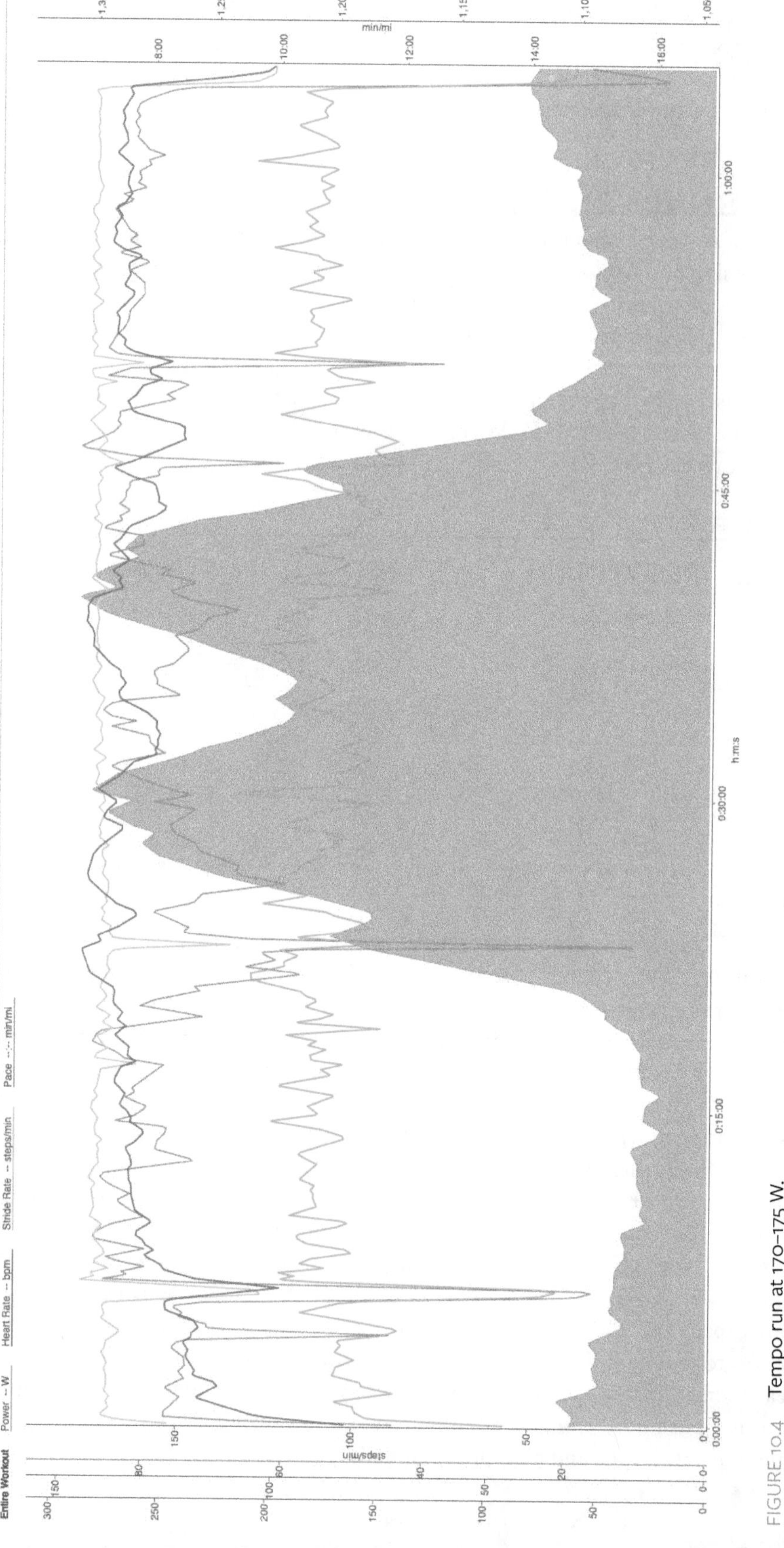

FIGURE 10.4 Tempo run at 170–175 W.

TABLE 10.2 Tempo Run Overall Metrics

RANGE	DURATION (H/M/S)	AVERAGE POWER (W)	NP (W)	STRIDE RATE (STEPS/MIN)
1:05:08	173	176	171	5:01

Case Study 3: Half-Marathon in the Mountains

For this case study, we will examine how to utilize and analyze power metrics for a half marathon performed in the mountains. This particular event was a 13.1 half-marathon ran by a master's age group long-course triathlete. The triathlete ran the course in the spring with mild temperatures and moderate wind. The course consisted of over 1,700 feet of climbing. Before the event, the triathlete completed the rFTP test. The results of the test put the triathlete's rFTP at 255 W. The training and pacing zones based on this rFTP were as follows:

RFTP = 255 W: POWER TRAINING ZONES

LEVEL	DESCRIPTION	PERCENT	POWER RANGE
1	Active recovery	56% or less	< 142 W
2	Endurance	56% to 76%	143–193 W
3	Tempo	76% to 91%	194–232 W
4	Threshold	91% to 106%	233–270 W
5	$VO_{2\ Max}$	106% to 121%	271–308 W
6	Anaerobic capacity	121% or more	> 309 W

With this extreme change in terrain, it is challenging to prescribe a consistent pace. This triathlete had trained with running power for a few months. Over this time period, we determined that his power zones were correct. During testing, the triathlete's 255W rFTP equated to 6:51 min/mi on flat terrain. Additionally, prior training sessions confirmed the triathlete's power was very consistent on rolling terrain. With this being the triathlete's "A race" for the first part of the year, an aggressive race plan was set to obtain two goals: (a) win the master's age group and (b) achieve a new personal record (PR). The end result was the triathlete placing first overall in the master's age group; however, a new PR was not set.

Figure 10.5a illustrates the extreme terrain change throughout the half-marathon. Based the triathlete's rFTP pacing zones and training performance, we set an overall pacing goal of 245 W. Figure 10.6 (red square) shows the triathlete's power output was 248 W for the entire race. Furthermore, Figure 10.5b demonstrates how even the triathlete's power output was throughout the event. The race plan was based on the aspect that he could consistently control his power-based pace over the mountain. The plan of running at 245 W for the entire race worked to the triathlete's advantage. The power metric gave the triathlete a consistent parameter to be used for proper pacing. Figure 10.5a shows how variable the pacing (blue line) was during the event. With the power metric, a stable pacing metric of 245 W was the goal for the entire course. The course was broken into three pacing sections that equated to the 245 W average power.

Based on past iterations of this half-marathon, the triathlete and coach knew the race participants tended to attack the first mountain. Previous data demonstrated the triathlete could maintain an upper threshold power pace for about 30 minutes without sacrificing further aerobic performance.

For the first third of the race (Figure 10.5c), the strategy was to pace up the first mountain at mid-threshold wattage (250–265 W), as shown in Figures 10.5c and 10.6. This strategy allowed for the triathlete to pace well with the lead runners over the first climb. However, the triathlete was able to gauge the efforts as to not push into the red. The power trend (red line) in Figure 10.5c has a slope of zero, which means the power output did not change through the initial portion of the race. Following this strategy and using power to ensure real-time pacing allowed the triathlete to be in the top third in the overall category when cresting the first mountain.

The second portion of the race strategy was to reduce the overall power output between 240–250 W. Based on previous training data analysis, we knew the triathlete could hold this low-threshold power output for about 55 minutes, even after a period of hard exertion. As shown in Figure 10.5d and Figure 10.6, the average power output for segments 3–7 were 244 W. Again, the triathlete power trend (red line in Figure 10.5d) has a minimal change in slope. This negative slope in the power output details how even the triathlete's power output was during this portion of the race. The threshold pace of the first one third of the race did not inhibit the triathlete's pace. With this strategy, the triathlete broke away from the other competitors in the master's category. By the end of segment 7, which was the top of the second mountain, as shown in Figure 10.5a, the triathlete was in first place for the master's category.

Over the last one third of the race (segments 8–10), the triathlete kept an average power output of 243 W (Figure 10.6, blue square). This result shows how the triathlete was able to keep the same power output as laid out in the initial race plan. By following the race plan and using power as a real-time, consistent measurement, the triathlete was able to properly pace and win the master's category without burning any matches or showing severe declines in performance due to fatigue.

Case Study 3 serves to show what running power can do for you. It shows how running power can provide you with a pacing metric that does not change over variable terrain. Additionally, we demonstrated how running power can help you control your efforts and save your matches for when you may need them.

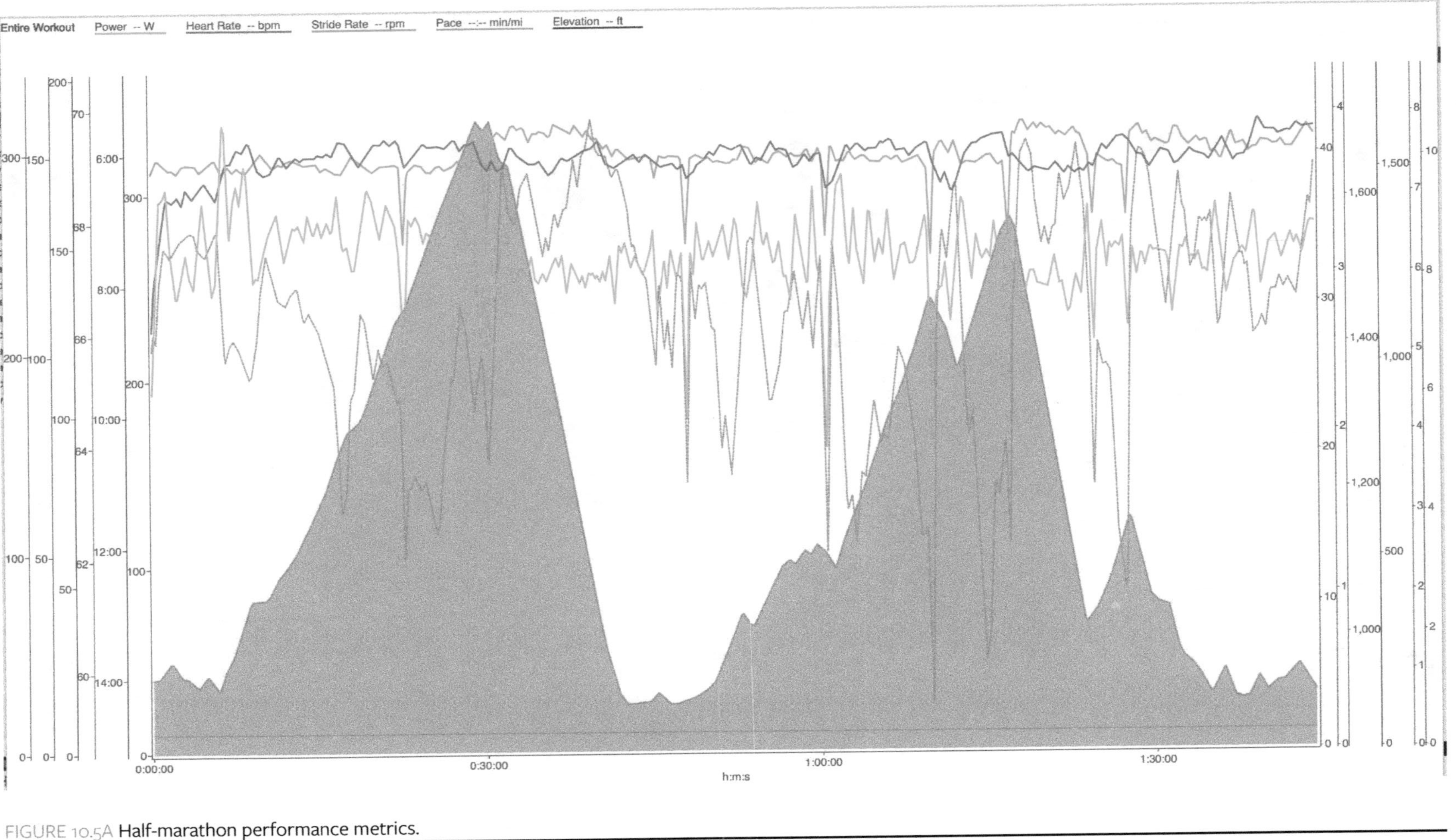

FIGURE 10.5A Half-marathon performance metrics.

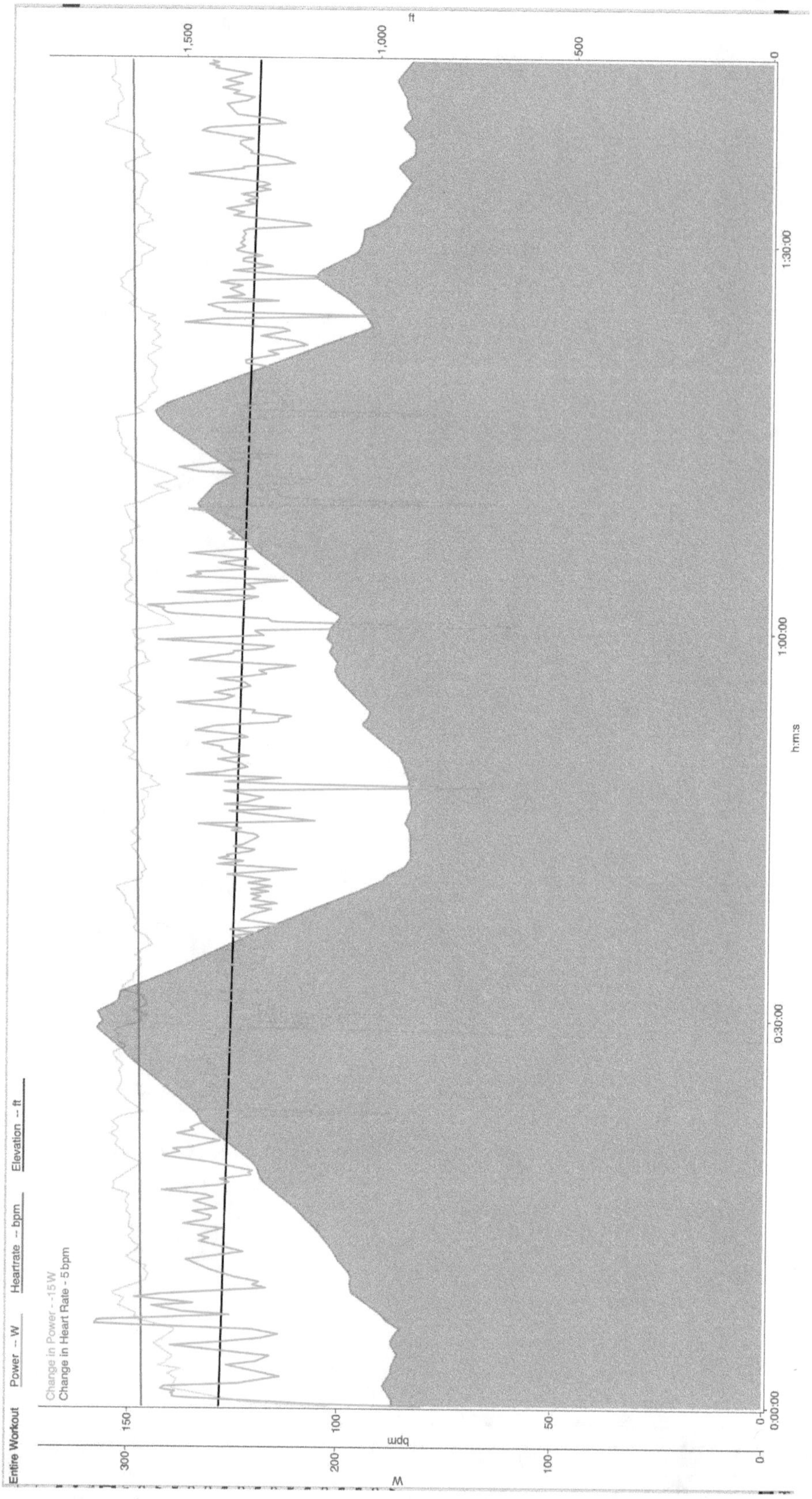

FIGURE 10.5B Trendline (black line) for power (orange line) output for half marathon. The trendline (red line) is for heart rate (red dotted line).

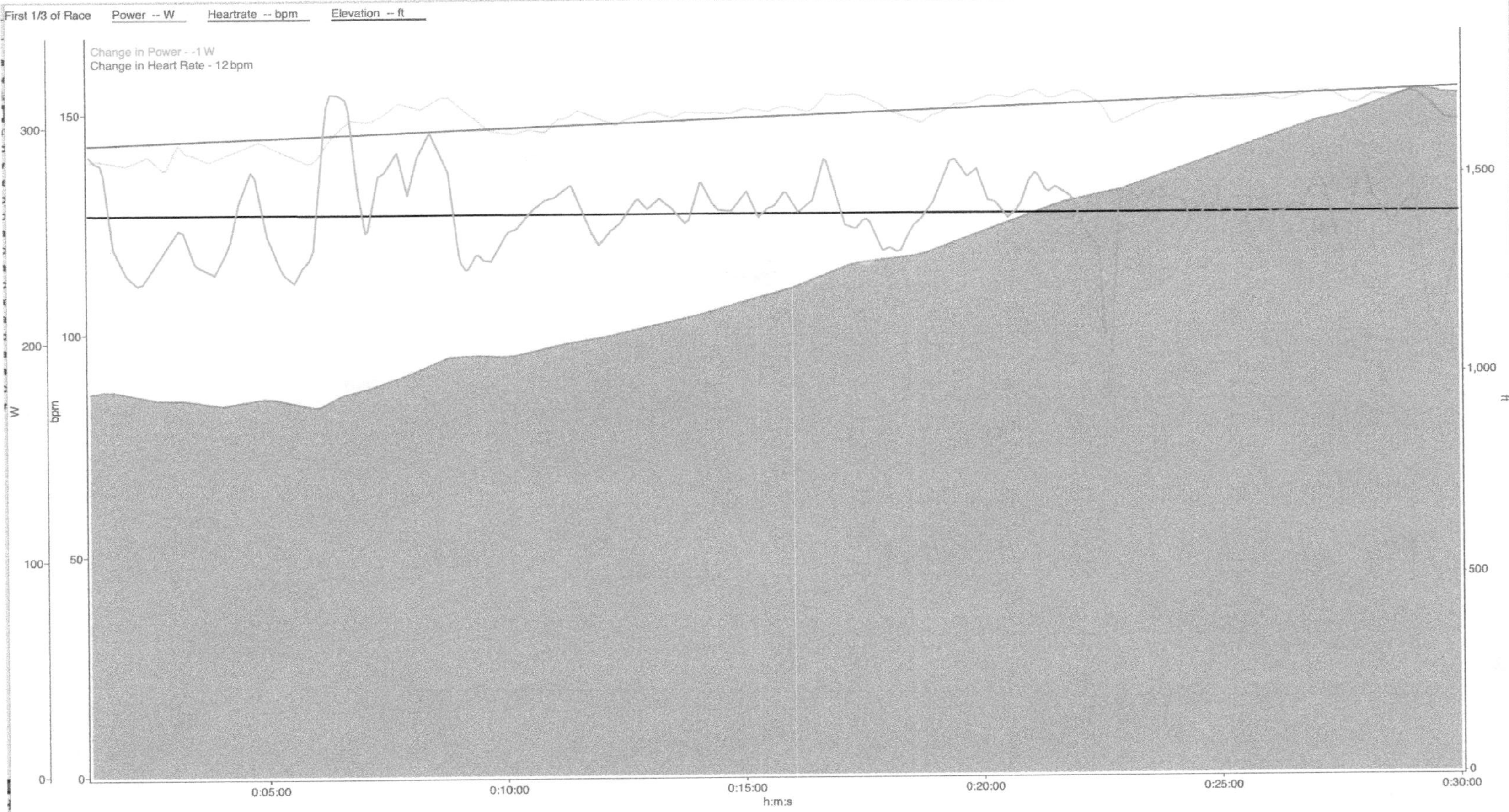

FIGURE 10.5C Trendline (black line) for power (orange line) output for segments 1-3 half marathon (first one third of the race). The average power for this portion of the race was 260W. The trendline (red line) is for heart rate (red dotted line).

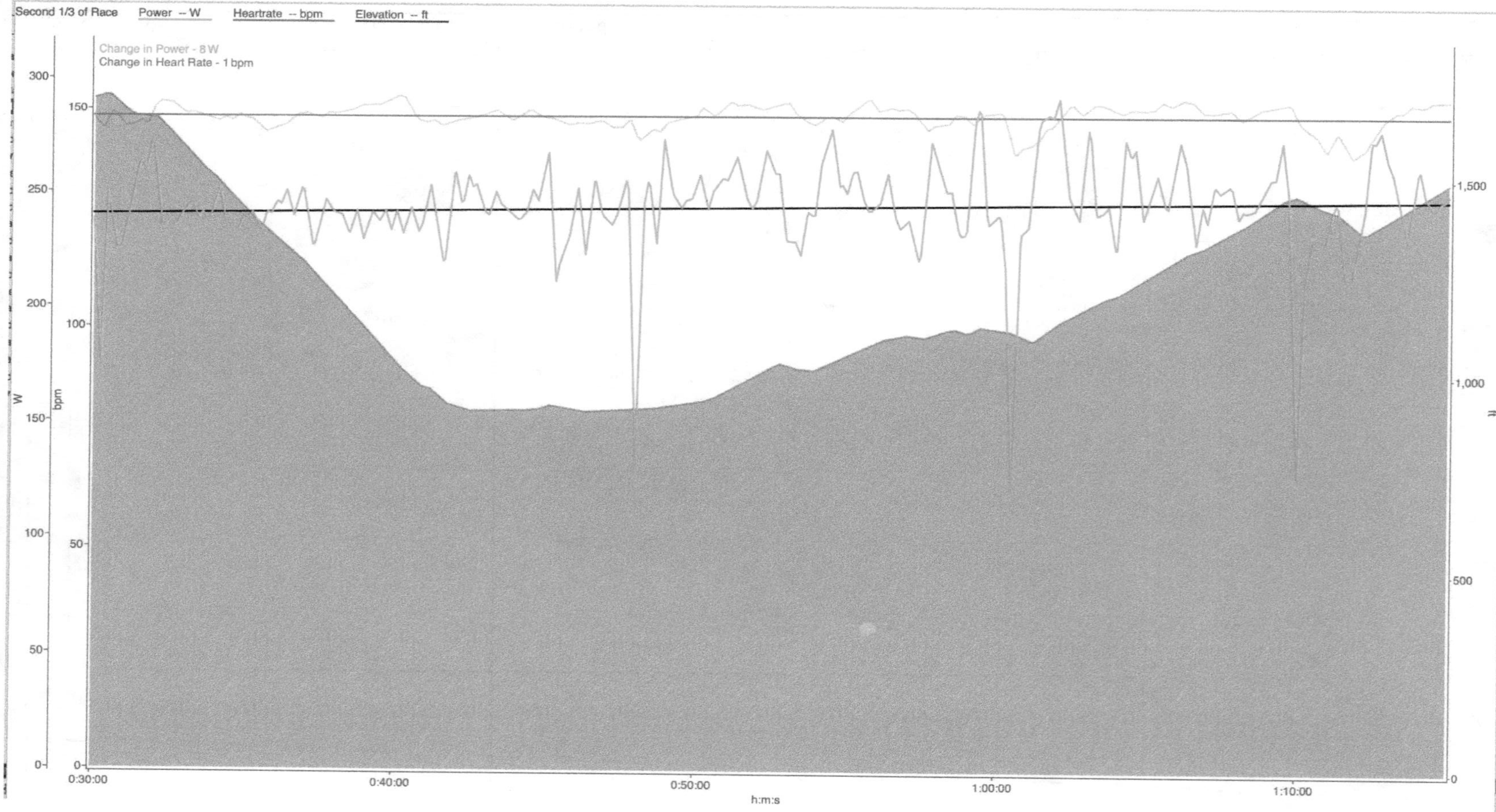

FIGURE 10.5D Trendline (black line) for power (orange line) output for segments 4-7 half marathon (middle third of the race). The average power for this portion of the race was 244W. The trendline (red line) is for heart rate (red dotted line).

Running Workout Review Report - Book Edition

Range	Duration h:m:s	Climbing ft	Descending ft	NGP min/mi	Avg Pace min/mi	Avg Hr bpm	Max HR bpm	EF	PaHR %	Avg Power W
Entire Workout	1:44:14	1,921	1,952	8:11	7:58	149	159	1.68	2.85	248
Seg 1	0:09:58	168	61	7:26	7:51	142	154	1.83	17.20	257
Seg 2	0:10:00	302	0	7:10	8:42	150	156	1.74	14.95	261
Seg 3	0:10:00	357	12	7:25	9:41	152	155	1.70	-4.94	256
Seg 4	0:10:00	8	673	11:13	6:23	149	153	1.62	-8.95	240
Seg 5	0:10:00	43	150	8:13	7:26	148	154	1.63	17.42	241
Seg 6	0:10:00	223	32	7:35	8:31	150	156	1.68	-2.94	251
Seg 7	0:10:00	369	28	7:39	10:12	150	154	1.68	7.50	248
Seg 8	0:10:00	204	333	8:59	8:15	148	155	1.62	-9.05	238
Seg 9	0:10:00	144	429	9:37	7:19	148	155	1.63	14.68	241
Seg 10	0:13:37	101	214	8:05	7:16	151	159	1.64	9.72	248

FIGURE 10.6 Half-marathon raw data. The data were broken down into 10-minute increments, except for segment 10, in order to provide a better resolution of what occurred during the event.

Conclusion

In this chapter, we discussed three different case studies and how to analyze power data. Running power zones can be an incredible tool for training and pacing in triathlons. Additionally, power is more consistent than pacing, especially over undulating terrain, and could make the difference between a great race and a DNF. However, the power data in these examples only gives a glimpse into the triathlete's overall performance. If we combine the power data with the advanced analytics provided by the power meter, we can gain a better sense of the triathlete's running performance. We will discuss these advanced metrics in the next chapter.

References

1. Allen, H., Coggan, A., & McGregor, S. (2019). *Training and racing with a power meter* (3rd ed.). VeloPress.
2. Tanner, A. V., Nielsen, B. V., & Allgrove, J. (2014). Salivary and plasma cortisol and testosterone responses to interval and tempo runs and a bodyweight-only circuit session in endurance-trained men. *Journal of Sports Sciences, 32*(7), 680–689. https://doi.org/10.1080/02640414.2013.850594
3. Vanhatalo, A., Jones, A. M., & Burnley, M. (2011). Application of critical power in sport. *International Journal of Sports Physiology and Performance*, *6*(1), 128–136. https://doi.org/10.1123/ijspp.6.1.128

Chapter 11

Runners High

Beyond Running With Power

Improving your running economy (the measure of oxygen utilization while running) is directly related to your running gait (10). Your running gait has many different elements that can be measured. The advantage of many of today's wearable technology, especially running power meters, is the secondary measurements given to you. This chapter will cover those metrics. Each metric looks at small pieces of your running gait, and when all the metrics are put together, they give you a complete picture of your gait. It's like having your running lab on your watch! The key gait metrics are as follows:

1. **Stride rate (i.e., cadence)**: The number of strides (or steps) you take in a minute.
2. **Stride length**: The distance taken between each step or the total distance covered in one complete stride cycle.
3. **Ground contact time** (GCT): The amount of time (milliseconds) your foot is in contact with the ground. The time begins when your heel touches the ground and ends when your toe leaves the ground.
4. **Flight time**: Ratio amount of time you are not in contact with the ground. In Chapter 10, we introduced the float phase of your running gait. This metric is measuring this phase.
5. **Leg spring stiffness**: A mathematical model assuming your leg is a spring, compressing when your foot hits the ground and lengthening when you toe lifts off the ground. When you are fatigued, a drop in this metric can indicate your run form is changing to a less economical state (7).
6. **Flight ratio/phase**: Ratio of flight time to step time. The higher this metric, the more time you are spending in the air. Having a high flight ratio does not necessarily mean you are going in the right direction. You can have a high vertical oscillation and still have a high flight ratio. You need to look at this metric in conjunction with your horizontal and vertical oscillation metrics to fully understand your flight ratio's meaning. Also, this metric is dependent on the type of terrain and the speed you are running. You should consider these elements as well.

7. **Pronation and supination angles:** The pronation angle is the foot's inward flexion when contacting the ground. The supination angle is the outward flexion of the foot when contacting with the ground. These metrics are good to know, as they can help you decide on the right type of shoes.
8. **Vertical and horizontal oscillation:** Vertical oscillation is how high (cm) you move upward during the flight phase, and horizontal oscillation is how far forward (cm) you move during the flight phase.
9. **Impact and braking Gs:** Typically, these two metrics are found separately. However, they describe two components of the force impulse of the foot strike. When the foot hits the ground, it creates a force impulse. Impact and braking Gs describe the strength of the impulse. The impulse G is the peak measurement of the horizontal component of the impulse, whereas the braking G is the peak measurement of the vertical component (Figure 11.1).

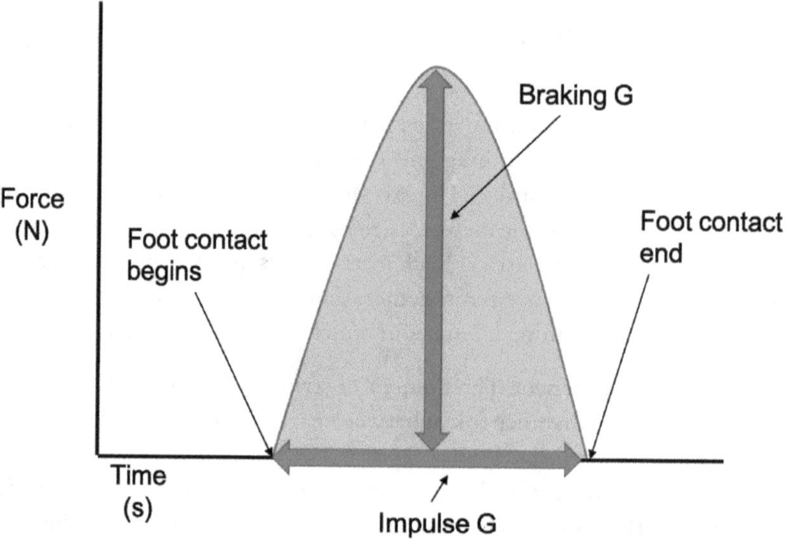

FIGURE 11.1 The components of a force impulse as the foot hits the ground while running.

Before you start using all these metrics, you should perform a video gait analysis. Having a certified professional conducting this analysis will give you foundational knowledge to know what kind of runner you are (e.g., heel strike versus midfoot strike versus toe strike). Also, the analysis can provide you with your ankle, knee, hip, and torso angles. Knowing this information will allow you to understand what you need to address to improve your running economy.

Why is this important? Let's go back to Chapter 8, where we defined the running economy: the oxygen cost at running a certain speed during submaximal efforts. Determining your running economy "is a complex, multifactorial concept that represents the sum of various metabolic, cardiorespiratory, biomechanical and neuromuscular characteristics during submaximal running" (2, p. 71). Your running gait feeds into this calculation.

The biomechanical traits of your gait determine how fast you go and at what cost. These advanced metrics can help you to identify the limitations in your running gait. By improving on your gait limitations, you will gain speed and improve your running economy.

However, not everyone can have a gait video analysis performed. Another excellent approach is to record as many of the metrics as possible (if not all of them) during your rFTP test. By collecting these metrics during the 5 and 10 km tests, you will have a strong baseline of your running efficiency at threshold and upper endurance efforts. As you work on your limiting areas, you will see how these metrics change when you retest your rFTP. With the right combination of resistance training and running form drills identified by the recorded parameters, you will improve running efficiency.

Before we get into a case study involving these metrics, let's look at some of the relationships between them and what they can tell you about your running gait.

1. **Stride rate and stride length**. Naturally, these tend to be inverses of each other. For example, as you increase your stride rate, your stride length will typically go down. This relationship has to do with your running gait. The idea is to get through the gait cycle faster. Most runners, age groupers, and elites have to shorten their stride length to increase their stride rate. It is rare to see an athlete have significant increases in the stride rate with little to no reduction in stride length.

   Looking at your stride rate is another way to increase your speed. Increasing your stride rate usually equates to free speed. This feeds back into the running power equation discussed in Chapter 8. We discussed the way to calculate power for running as follows:

   $$\text{Power} = \text{stride rate} \times \text{torque}$$

   If you keep torque constant while increasing your stride rate, you will improve your power. Increasing your power will increase your speed.

   You might be asking, "How is this so?" This is directly related to the running economy. Increasing your stride rate tends to lower the oxygen cost with muscle fiber recruitment (2). Research shows that longer stride lengths recruit more muscle fibers when compared to lower stride lengths (2), so less oxygen is used when fewer muscle fibers are recruited.

   An exciting aspect of the stride rate versus stride length relationship is the aspect of self-selection. As supported by research, we find that the more experienced you are, the closer you are to your optimal stride rate and length ratio (2). The reasoning for this is two-fold. First, you might be able to find this optimal ratio over time due to personal experience (2). Second, chronic training at a specific stride rate and length ratio at certain speeds helps you physiologically adapt to the optimal running economy for that particular speed (2).
2. **GCT**. This metric deals with the amount of time your foot is in contact with the ground. Furthermore, this metric gives us some insight into lower leg power (1, 2). The faster the GCT, the quicker the muscle contracts (13). A faster muscular contraction means more power with an improved running economy (14, 15). More power means a strong push-off phase of the running gait and more distance covered during the flight phase.

3. **Horizontal oscillation versus vertical oscillation.** When we run, we want to move forward. In other words, we want to move horizontally. As we run, we have to strike this balance between bounding up and down (vertical) versus forward momentum (horizontal). Ideally, you want to have the maximum amount of horizontal oscillation with the lowest vertical oscillation. Why do we say this? The more you push off vertically, the less your momentum is being translated horizontally (i.e., you cover less ground per step). You want the majority of the propulsion you create to push you forward, not upward. You can address vertical oscillation issues through proper upper body lean, increasing your stride rate, and lowering your GCT.
4. **Impact and braking Gs.** The force you produce when hitting the ground may have a significant effect on your musculoskeletal health. Triathletes and runners with chronic high-impact Gs tend to see increased rates of plantar fasciitis, stress fractures, and patellofemoral pain (3). In comparison, high braking forces appear to be somewhat associated with Achilles tendinopathy and other types of knee pain (1). For chronic injuries, research is unclear if high force impulses cause osteoarthritis (4). As a rule of thumb, we suggest trying to keep this number on the lower side. Runscribe suggests that the optimal range is 5–14 Gs for impulse and 5–13 Gs for braking.

   So, how do you do this? Controlling your force impulse is directly related to your stride rate, stride length relationship, and GCT (1). Having a high stride rate and low GCT tends to reduce these forces. This relationship between stride rate and GCT is one reason mid-foot and toe strikers tend to see more minor impact injuries during running (2, 3). Another reason is mid-foot and toe-strikers tend to have their knees bent when their foot hits the ground. This striking pattern allows the musculoskeletal system to absorb a significant amount of the force impulse, thus reducing any possible injuries.
5. **Braking Gs versus vertical oscillation, GCT, and stride rate.** We want to note one possible side effect if you increase your stride rate and decrease your GCT and vertical oscillation. Adams et al. found this combination in changes to a runner's stride cause increases in the brake Gs (1). However, the increase was statistically significant but not enough to cause injury. This slight increase means the speed benefits of having a high stride rate and low vertical oscillation and GCT outweigh the small but statistically significant increase in brake Gs.
6. **Leg spring stiffness.** This metric is highly individualistic. Your musculotendinous is structurally different, albeit slightly, from everyone else (9). This difference is due to genetics. Greater leg spring stiffness is typically associated with better running economy, whereas lower leg spring stiffness is not (5–7). With this metric, you will need to perform several short and long-distance runs to understand how fatigue affects this metric. However, one of the best ways to increase your leg spring stiffness is to decrease your GCT (11). This increase in the stiffness is due to maximizing the muscle stretch-shortening cycle associated with shortening your GCT.

The leg spring stiffness metric is an excellent metric for long-distance running and is highly susceptible to fatigue. As you get fatigued, your running form deteriorates, reducing your running economy. One aspect of your running form you will see change when your leg spring stiffness drops is an increase in your vertical oscillation and increases in your GCT. If you start to see increases in vertical oscillation and GCT, you are beginning to lose power and momentum.

You might be asking, "What can I do with these relationships?" Well, they give you some great insights into what type of foot striker you are. Here are a few rules of thumb to help you understand:

A. **Heel strike.** With heel-strike running mechanics, the running form is typically associated with low stride rates, longer stride lengths, longer GCT, and more significant impact Gs. The vertical oscillation can vary but tends to be high and have lower flight times.
B. **Midfoot strike.** The midfoot strike running mechanics differ significantly from the heel-strike method. Midfoot running is considered the most efficient running style. It is typically characterized by high stride rates (between 175-plus steps/minute), lower stride lengths, shorter GCT, and lower impact Gs. The vertical oscillation is typically low with longer flight times.
C. **Toe strike.** The toe-strike method is typically seen in sprinting and some elite marathoners. The mechanics are similar to that of the midfoot strike. It is generally characterized by high stride rates (between 190-plus steps/minute), lower stride lengths, very short GCT, and lower impact Gs. The vertical oscillation is typically low, with longer flight times than the midfoot strike.

Another practical approach with these metrics is to see how they change while you fatigue. During strenuous or long-distance efforts, the body becomes fatigued. It becomes more challenging for the body to maintain proper form. Thus, your running economy decreases. The target power you want to keep could become harder to maintain due to fatigue-induced changes in your running form. Tracking these metrics in real time or during post-analysis will allow you to identify changes in these metrics affected by your fatigue. By seeing how these metrics change, you can work on form. Case study 1 demonstrates how to apply these metrics in addition to analyzing running power.

Case Study 1: Biomechanical Analysis

Advanced analytics provide a wealth of information to dive deeper into performance. This case study focuses on many of the running biomechanical metrics discussed in this chapter so far. Figure 11.2 provides a complete listing of advanced analytics for the half-marathon discussed in case study 3 from the previous chapter.

Your analysis of these metrics should focus on the relationships between each parameter and how they affect each other. When examining stride mechanics, stride rate, stride length, GCT, vertical oscillation, impact Gs, and flight time, metrics give insight into the running style and how fatigue changes your running form, and we can begin to understand how training and fatigue may cause positive or negative changes to the running economy. In the continuation of case study 3 from Chapter 10, we will focus on how fatigue may or may not affect your running biomechanics metrics.

Data Series	Entire Workout	Seg 1	Seg 2	Seg 3	Seg 4	Seg 5	Seg 6	Seg 7	Seg 8	Seg 9	Seg 10
	h:m:s	h:m:s	h:m:s	h:m:s	h:m:s	h:m:s	h:m:s	h:m:s	h:m:s	h:m:s	h:m:s
Time	1:44:14	0:09:58	0:10:00	0:10:00	0:10:00	0:10:00	0:10:00	0:10:00	0:10:00	0:10:00	0:13:37

Data Series	Entire Workout	Seg 1	Seg 2	Seg 3	Seg 4	Seg 5	Seg 6	Seg 7	Seg 8	Seg 9	Seg 10
	mi	mi	mi	mi	mi	mi	mi	mi	mi	mi	mi
Distance	13.08	1.27	1.15	1.03	1.57	1.35	1.17	0.98	1.21	1.37	1.87

Data Series	Entire Workout	Seg 1	Seg 2	Seg 3	Seg 4	Seg 5	Seg 6	Seg 7	Seg 8	Seg 9	Seg 10
	min/mi	min/mi	min/mi	min/mi	min/mi	min/mi	min/mi	min/mi	min/mi	min/mi	min/mi
Pace	7:58	7:51	8:42	9:41	6:23	7:26	8:31	10:12	8:15	7:19	7:16

Data Series	Entire Workout	Seg 1	Seg 2	Seg 3	Seg 4	Seg 5	Seg 6	Seg 7	Seg 8	Seg 9	Seg 10
	m/s	m/s	m/s	m/s	m/s	m/s	m/s	m/s	m/s	m/s	m/s
Speed	3.27	3.36	3.06	2.70	3.95	3.56	3.06	2.67	3.20	3.55	3.50

Data Series	Entire Workout	Seg 1	Seg 2	Seg 3	Seg 4	Seg 5	Seg 6	Seg 7	Seg 8	Seg 9	Seg 10
	W	W	W	W	W	W	W	W	W	W	W
AP	248	257	261	256	240	241	251	248	238	241	248

Data Series	Entire Workout	Seg 1	Seg 2	Seg 3	Seg 4	Seg 5	Seg 6	Seg 7	Seg 8	Seg 9	Seg 10
	ms	ms	ms	ms	ms	ms	ms	ms	ms	ms	ms
GCT	215	213	221	232	192	203	218	241	225	214	198

Data Series	Entire Workout	Seg 1	Seg 2	Seg 3	Seg 4	Seg 5	Seg 6	Seg 7	Seg 8	Seg 9	Seg 10
	steps/min	steps/min	steps/min	steps/min	steps/min	steps/min	steps/min	steps/min	steps/min	steps/min	steps/min
Str Rate	176	174	174	173	182	175	176	174	177	178	179

Data Series	Entire Workout	Seg 1	Seg 2	Seg 3	Seg 4	Seg 5	Seg 6	Seg 7	Seg 8	Seg 9	Seg 10
	m	m	m	m	m	m	m	m	m	m	m
Stride length	1.11	1.16	1.05	0.94	1.30	1.22	1.04	0.92	1.08	1.19	1.17

Data Series	Entire Workout	Seg 1	Seg 2	Seg 3	Seg 4	Seg 5	Seg 6	Seg 7	Seg 8	Seg 9	Seg 10
	%	%	%	%	%	%	%	%	%	%	%
Flight phase	34	35	34	33	35	35	34	32	34	34	35

Data Series	Entire Workout	Seg 1	Seg 2	Seg 3	Seg 4	Seg 5	Seg 6	Seg 7	Seg 8	Seg 9	Seg 10
	cm	cm	cm	cm	cm	cm	cm	cm	cm	cm	cm
Vert Oscil	8.6	9.3	8.8	8.4	8.5	9.0	8.5	8.1	8.4	8.5	8.6

Data Series	Entire Workout	Seg 1	Seg 2	Seg 3	Seg 4	Seg 5	Seg 6	Seg 7	Seg 8	Seg 9	Seg 10
	g	g	g	g	g	g	g	g	g	g	g
Impact Gs	2.52	2.54	2.45	2.34	2.69	2.67	2.47	2.26	2.44	2.54	2.66

FIGURE 11.2 Half-marathon in-depth metrics part 1. The is broken into 10-minute increments.

The triathlete is classified as a midfoot strike runner. The running style was confirmed via video analysis and previous training sessions. His advanced metrics from the training data building up to the half-marathon event mirrored those listed as the general characteristics of a midfoot strike runner.

The first step in analyzing these metrics is investigating if the stride rate, stride length, and ground contact time (GCT) (red boxes) in Figure 11.2 changed throughout the race. During the half-marathon, the triathlete had an average stride rate of 176 steps/min. This stride rate is characteristic of an athlete with a midfoot strike and a high turnover rate. If we match segments 1–10 from Figure 11.2 with Figure 10.6, we can see how specific form characteristics change concerning the terrain. Segments 2–3 and 6–8 cover the two mountain passes during the event. The triathlete's GCT increases between 8–20 ms during these segments with lower stride lengths. However, his stride rate did not change and had little effect on his power output.

Why did this occur? This change in his running mechanics was due to the incline of the mountain's slope in segments 2–3 and 6–8. To keep consistent power output, the triathlete's running gait needed to change. The increase in the incline reduces the triathlete's ability to cover the same distance with each stride in relation to a flat surface. The uphill segments are the cause of the reduction in the stride length. Also, we generally see slight increases in GCT during significant increases in terrain inclination. If these changes in the running gait were due to fatigue, we would see a reduction in the stride rate and, most likely, an increase in the vertical oscillation. Since we do not see any changes in the stride rate and vertical oscillation (Figure 11.2), and the specified fluctuations only coincide with the terrain changes, we know the changes in GCT and stride length are due to the incline of the mountain.

The next aspect to investigate is the changes to the flight phase and vertical oscillation (blue boxes). During the entire race, the triathlete's flight phase percentage and vertical oscillation did not change. Even though we do not directly measure horizontal oscillation, we can infer it did not change since no change was seen in the flight phase and vertical oscillations. We can safely conclude this due to the relationship between these two metrics. As stated at the beginning of the chapter, flight ratio/phase is the ratio of your flight time to your step time. This metric measures how long you are in the air or the flight phase of your running gait (Figure 10.1). This metric cannot be analyzed alone. You need to look at either your vertical oscillation or horizontal oscillation as well. Having a high flight phase/ratio metric does not necessarily mean you are moving in the right direction! You get this information from the oscillation metrics. In this example, we only have vertical oscillation. The triathlete's vertical oscillation stays mostly consistent between 8.5–8.7 cm. This is a little high for a vertical oscillation, and we will discuss this in the next case study. However, the metric does not change except for segments 1 and 5, which were downhill. This lack of change in the flight phase and vertical oscillation now allows us to look at their relationship to each other. This relationship means he was able to transfer his forward momentum consistently throughout the entire half-marathon, especially on the two uphill sections of the race.

Another metric that will help us understand the meaning of the vertical oscillation and flight phase relationship is looking at the changes of GCT. On the uphill sections (segments 2–3 and 6–8), we can see his flight phase and vertical oscillation do not change even though we saw increases in his GCT and reductions in stride length. We can infer from these relationship that the terrain caused the GCT and stride length changes but had no effect on his running power production. Also, understanding how the landscape affected his stride rate and stride length (as discussed earlier) helped us understand these changes. This combination of metrics means he maintained his running form on the two uphill segments and could translate more of his consistent power output to forward movement.

Additionally, when we look at the race as a whole, we see little change in his metrics. There is no point where we see a drastic decoupling in the relationships of the variables. This relationship means the triathlete did not have any effect of fatigue on his running form or performance. We attribute his running performance to his fitness. This race was his "A" race for the first half of the season (we discuss what an "A" race is in the next chapter). His training plan focused on being able to maintain form and power output over this type of terrain. His performance, both by winning his age group and running metrics, demonstrated the plan worked!

Finally, let us revisit the impact Gs. Earlier, we discussed them in their relationship to running uphill. With a race route like this, a significant portion of the race is downhill. This change could cause increases in the impact Gs. As stated at the beginning of this chapter, high-impact Gs can cause injury. We do see moderate increases in the impact Gs on the downhill segments (4 and 9). However, the increase was controlled. This means the triathlete was able to control the descent and running form. We had practiced maintaining downhill running form as part of his training program. When he performed hills repeats, we would practice good running form on the downhill recovery segments. We focused on proper body position and controlling his descent. Additionally, we had him perform squats and deadlifts as part of his resistance training program. These compound lifts are great for building run power and muscular compliance to the demands of running downhill.

Overall, we can see the triathlete's run form did not change throughout the half-marathon. This aspect is a function of two things. The first is the triathlete focusing on his power output for pacing and running metrics in real time. The second aspect is a function of great coaching! We were able to identify the triathlete's strengths and limitations and build a training plan that addressed these items to put the triathlete in an excellent state of fitness in time for the race, so he maintained power and form that guaranteed a personal best and won.

Case Study 2: Speed and Stride Rate

This section will demonstrate how specific drills can improve your stride rate, vertical oscillation, speed, and power. The workouts are shown in Figures 11.3 and 11.4, performed by a 38-year-old male long-course triathlete. Both workouts were performed on a treadmill about 6 months apart. We want to point out the workouts were performed on different treadmills and different shoes, which did cause some differences in the power data. We will address this aspect later in the case study.

The triathlete wanted to improve his run speed. He had been training with a running power meter for a few months, so we reviewed his historical data. In Figure 11.3, you can see a 3.5-mile tempo run. The tempo segment occurred between segments 2–5. With this being a treadmill run, the pace was consistent throughout the workout. However, we can see the speed started to fall to the lower side of the tempo range.

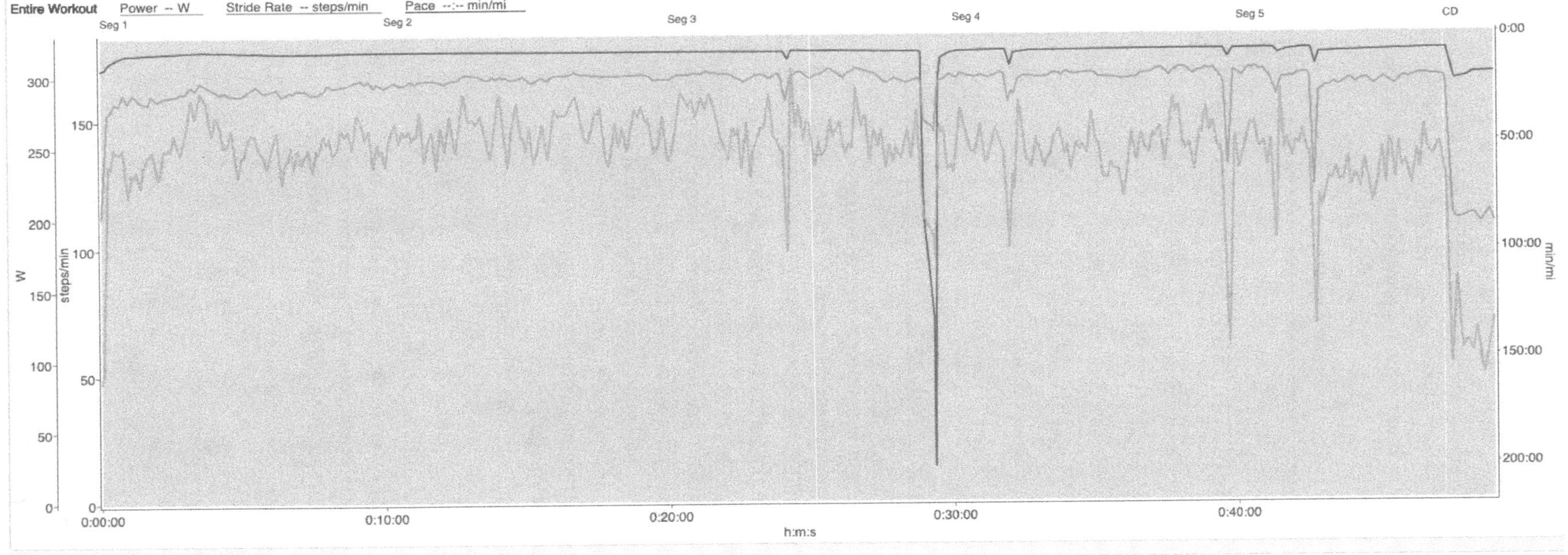

Range	Duration h:m:s	Avg Power W	NP W	Stride Rate steps/min	Avg Pace min/mi
Entire Workout	0:48:38	273	277	163	7:54
Seg 1	0:09:59	276	276	161	7:23
Seg 2	0:10:00	290	290	166	7:28
Seg 3	0:09:39	286	283	166	7:51
Seg 4	0:09:59	273	275	166	7:55
Seg 5	0:07:15	262	262	164	8:18
CD	0:01:44	136	184	115	18:05

FIGURE 11.3 This figure depicts the tempo run at the beginning of the 6-month training period.

In Table 11.1 we depict his running gait metrics measured by his running power meter. You will notice he has a high vertical oscillation. Even though no definitive research depicts an optimal vertical oscillation measurement, we suggest anything over 8 cm is too high. We have found that in working with runners when the vertical oscillation is less than 8 cm, the runner has lower impact Gs, a slightly higher power output, and a faster pace. The rule of thumb is shorter is better!

TABLE 11.1

DATA SERIES	ENTIRE WORKOUT	SEG 1	SEG 2	SEG 3	SEG 4	SEG 5	CD
NP (W)	264	276	270	263	260	252	184
Pace (min/mi)	7:47	7:23	7:28	7:51	7:55	8:18	18:05
GCT (ms)	218	211	211	220	220	229	354
Stride rate (steps/min)	164	161	166	166	166	164	115
Stride length (m)	1.16	1.24	1.21	1.13	1.13	1.09	0.73
Vertical osc. (cm)	8.84	9.8	8.7	8.5	8.6	8.6	6.3
Impact Gs	2.45	2.60	2.50	2.41	2.40	2.34	1.99

This table details the metrics of a 3-mile tempo run at the beginning of the 6-month training program. Segment 1 was the warm-up. Segments 2–4 were the tempo run, and segment 5 was an endurance segment. Each segment was a mile in length except for CD. The CD metrics were not included in the Entire Workout metrics column.

After finding this information, we knew how to address this issue. This triathlete has excellent running speed. However, his vertical oscillation was above 8 cm. This means he was not translating all his running momentum forward. He could increase his speed with a bit of work on his running form. We stated earlier a high vertical oscillation could be fixed through correct body position, increasing your stride rate, and lowering your GCT. These are resolved is through running drills. Over the next 6 months, we focused on two main workouts and one piece of equipment.

The first workout we performed at least once a week was turnovers. This workout is also known as strides and pickups. During this session, you focus on increasing your stride rate and lowering your stride length while maintaining a consistent endurance (usually zone 2 and 3). You do not want significant stride rate increases. You want to take it gradually. Usually, slow increments of two steps/minute will do the trick. Once you start to feel comfortable at the increased stride rate during the turnovers, increase the stride rate by another two steps/min. An example of one of the turnover workouts is as follows:

Perform 5 mins of dynamic warm-up:

1. Leg swings: 10–20 per leg
2. Marches: 10–15 per leg
3. Leg side swings: 10–20 per leg

Build warm-up pace from active recovery (Power Z1, Pace Z1, HR Z1, RPE 1) to endurance (Power Z2, Pace Z2, HR Z2, RPE 2–3) for 10 minutes.

MS1: 10 x 30-sec turnovers with a stride rate of 168 steps/min while maintaining endurance (Power Z2, Pace Z2, HR Z2, RPE 2–3) with 1 minute rest interval at active recovery (Power Z1, Pace Z1, HR Z1, RPE 1) between

MS2: Run 5 km at endurance (Power Z2, Pace Z2, HR Z2, RPE 2–3)

MS2: 5 x 60-sec turnovers with a stride rate of 168 steps/min while maintaining endurance (Power Z2, Pace Z2, HR Z2, RPE 2–3) with 2-minute rest interval at active recovery (Power Z1, Pace Z1, HR Z1, RPE 1) between.

CD: 15 mins active recovery (Power Z1, HR Z1, Pace Z1, RPE 1) and static stretching.

As the triathlete became more comfortable with the progression of the turnover workout, we started to add this workout to the end of his long runs. We made this change based on two data points. The first was the subjective feedback of the triathlete. Just communicating with the triathlete regularly let us know how he felt he was adapting to the increased stride rate. Once we felt comfortable, we knew he was adapting. The second piece was the data. If you do these drills, you will see increases in your HR during the drills. This increase in HR is due to the increase in muscle fiber recruitment and energy demand. As your body gets used to performing these drills, the HR will not rise as quickly. Once you see this type of HR response, it is a great indicator you are adapting well to the drills. So, armed with these two pieces of information, we knew we had to change the training stimulus and started to add the turnovers at the end of long runs to mimic a race-day scenario. He would have to maintain his stride rate when fatigued at the end of the race. At the end of a long run, the turnovers help with concentrating on his run form while fatigued and maintaining his run pace.

The second workout we utilized was hill repeats. This workout is excellent for developing your hip flexor and gluteal muscles. By strengthening these muscles, you can move your leg velocity through the swing phase of the gait, which can translate to a faster stride rate and decreased GCT. Additionally, running up a hill forces you to work on your knee drive, increasing your stride rate and body lean as well. This aspect is the incredible thing about hills. You have to take smaller steps to maintain a good pace up them! They force you to focus on increasing your stride rate, keep a forward upper body lean, and high knee drive. Over time, you will find you can translate this work to the flats. The improvements in your running form from hill repeats will translate to increased speed.

During this workout, he did not sprint or run anaerobically up the hill. We still kept the efforts aerobic. The idea is to work on run form and maintain a consistent endurance or tempo power output. We had him focus on his knee drive and increased stride rate during these workouts. We felt concentrating on these two aspects of his running form would produce the best outcome.

The triathlete began doing hill repeats on a treadmill almost once every week after performing the turnover workouts for several weeks. Doing these intervals on a treadmill was due to the triathlete's limited training time during the week. He had a treadmill available during his lunch hour to train. The great thing about this workout is it can be performed on a treadmill or outside. It all depends on where you want to do them! An example of one of his hill repeat sessions is as follows:

Perform 5 mins of dynamic warm-up:

1. Leg swings: 10–20 per leg
2. Marches: 10–15 per leg
3. Leg side swings: 10–20 per leg

Build warm-up pace from active recovery (Power Z1, HR Z1, Pace Z1, RPE 1) to endurance (Power Z2, HR Z2, Pace Z2, RPE 2–3) for 10 minutes. Then perform 4×10 s strides.

MS: Mid-endurance (Power Z2, HR Z2, Pace Z2, RPE 2–3): Keep the pace steady throughout the run. On a treadmill or long climb, perform 5 x 5 mins hill repeats at 3–5% with 3 minutes recovery at 0% grade. Try to keep the same endurance pace throughout the workout.

Focus on driving your knee through each stride and lean into the hill.

CD: 10 minutes at active recovery (Power Z1, HR Z1, Pace Z1, RPE 1) and static stretching.

The last aspect of his training progression was the introduction of the metronome. This piece of equipment allowed him to focus on a particular stride rate at a certain speed. He had downloaded an application on his phone that played the metronome through his wireless headphones. A metronome is a device that produces an audible click or sound at regular intervals and is excellent for keeping a consistent rhythm. A metronome can be used for swimming to maintain a constant stroke rate or, in this case, a consistent stride rate for running. We introduced this about 3 months into the training progression. As with the turnovers, we gradually increased the stride rate. The metronome was used on long runs. This helped train muscle memory when fresh and fatigued.

At this point, you might be asking, "What was the target stride rate?" This is a great question! It is suggested your stride rate should match your bike cadence. This suggestion has morphed into the optimal stride rate being 180 steps/minute. This stride metric comes from the thought that the optimal bike cadence is 90 rpm. These optimum rates are not necessarily accurate. There are merits to having high biking and running cadences. But what you find is every athlete is different; every athlete has their optimal cadence. We wanted to improve his stride rate by five to seven steps/minute over the 6 months for this triathlete.

Without getting into the cadence debate, we did feel the triathlete needed to increase his stride rate. The main question was, "By how much?" We did not want to go too high.

We took a conservative approach and settled on five to seven steps/minute over the 6 months. We would have increased the stride rate if he adapted quickly. However, it took him almost the entire 6-month period to increase his stride rate by 5 steps/min. You might be asking, "How do I figure this out?" You already have the tools at your disposal! You can look at your stride rate and gait metrics from your rFTP test. How fast is your stride rate? Is it 186 steps per minute, or is it 155 steps per minute? What are your GCT, stride length, vertical oscillation, and flight phase metrics telling you? Analyzing these metrics and relationships will help you answer this question.

We had seen improvements in his stride rate and vertical oscillation during his training, but we wanted to recreate the conditions from the data shown in Figure 11.3 and Table 11.1. For the data in Table 11.2, the triathlete ran another 3-mile tempo run. It is important to note that his power and pace zones were adjusted over the 6 months due to increased running performance. Additionally, he was wearing a new but different brand of running shoes and performed the workout on a different treadmill. These changes in the training conditions did cause some minor differences in the data. However, we were able to see significant improvements in his gait mechanics (Table 11.2).

As shown in Table 11.2, you can see his vertical oscillation dropped below 8 cm! Also, his stride rate increased by seven to eight steps/minute, with a significant decrease in his GCT. These gait improvements helped increase his pace by 8–10 s per mile in the 6 months. Furthermore, he was capable of holding the power pace consistently throughout the 3-mile tempo run (segments 2–3). If you compare these results with Table 11.1, you can see his power faded in segments 3 and 4. This was partially due to him starting too hard in segment 2, but we did see this issue with other runs that are not shown in this case study.

This table details a 3-mile tempo run at the end of the 6-month training program. Segment 1 is the warm-up period, and segments 2–4 are the tempo run. Each segment is a mile in length except for the CD. The CD metrics were not included in the Entire Workout metrics column.

With this information, we knew he was ready for his race. The main goal for this training plan was to reduce his vertical oscillation. We saw this as his limiting factor in increasing his speed. When we first looked at his vertical oscillation metric, it was well above 8 cm. We stated earlier that vertical oscillations above 8 cm tend to reduce forward momentum, so, we built a strategy to reduce this metric through increasing his stride rate and working on his running gait mechanics. Over the 6 months of training, he was able to reduce his vertical oscillation between 0.5–0.7 cm, as shown in Table 11.2. Additionally, he saw, on average, about a 15 s min/mile increase in his speed. We used the strategy of increasing the stride rate and working on gait mechanics to move more of his vertical momentum to horizontal (forward) momentum to increase his speed without spending extra time on speed work. By fixing his running gait, he was able to maintain his running form for longer periods of time, translated more of his momentum forward rather than vertically, and had greater confidence in his ability.

This training strategy to reduce his vertical oscillation and increase his speed was part of his build targeting a long-course duathlon. This race was his first duathlon of this distance. He knew he needed to increase his run speed in order to be competitive. Over the course of the 6 months, we performed regular communication sessions with the client. We reviewed the data and let the data guide training. We saw steady improvements

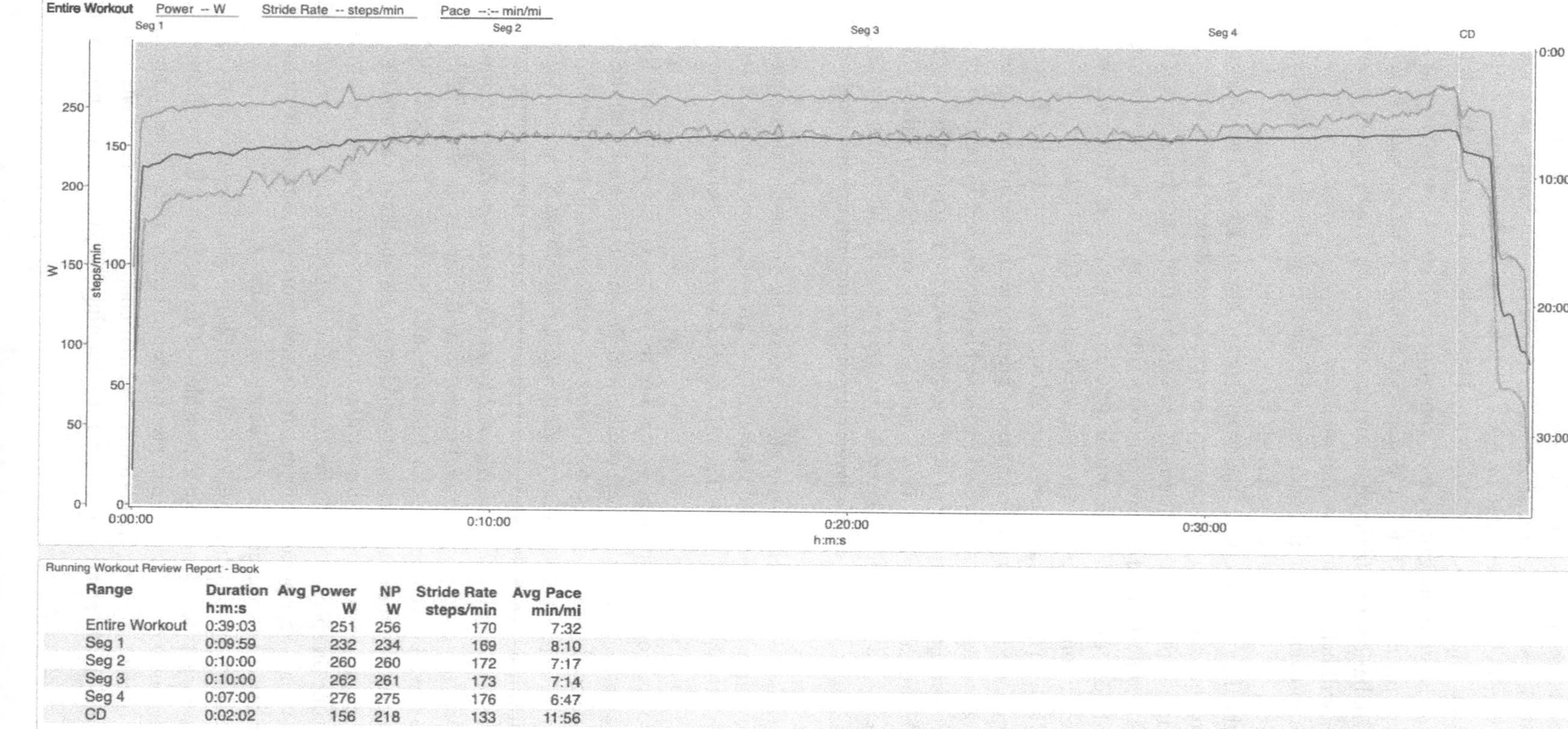

Running Workout Review Report - Book

Range	Duration h:m:s	Avg Power W	NP W	Stride Rate steps/min	Avg Pace min/mi
Entire Workout	0:39:03	251	256	170	7:32
Seg 1	0:09:59	232	234	169	8:10
Seg 2	0:10:00	260	260	172	7:17
Seg 3	0:10:00	262	261	173	7:14
Seg 4	0:07:00	276	275	176	6:47
CD	0:02:02	156	218	133	11:56

FIGURE 11.4 This figure depicts the tempo run at the end of the 6-month training period.

TABLE 11.2

DATA SERIES	ENTIRE WORKOUT	SEG 1	SEG 2	SEG 3	SEG 4	CD
NP (W)	263	234	271	272	277	218
Pace (min/mi)	7:28	8:10	7:17	7:17	7:10	11:56
GCT (ms)	206	210	207	207	203	301
Stride rate (steps/min)	172.5	169	172	173	176	133
Stride length (m)	1.17	1.22	1.17	1.16	1.14	0.74
Vertical osc. (cm)	7.78	8.1	7.7	7.7	7.6	6.3
Impact Gs	2.51	2.56	2.51	2.51	2.49	1.96

in his vertical oscillation and stride rate. Both we and the client had confidence that the plan was working. The final coup de grace was the changes he saw with the tempo run, detailed in Table 11.2. With this knowledge, the client knew he was ready for the race. The great news is he went on to win his first long-course duathlon!

Conclusion

This chapter defined several biomechanical metrics that running power meters can provide. Over two case studies, we discussed the relationships between these metrics, which need to be analyzed in conjunction with other metrics (i.e., stride rate and stride length or vertical oscillation and flight phase). Knowing the relationships between these variables will give you great insight into your running form. Also, you can monitor these metrics in real time to see how fatigue is changing your form. You do not need to monitor all these metrics in real time. You only need to pick a few that are important to you. For example, you may want to monitor your stride rate, GCT, and vertical oscillation. By making sure that you are keeping your GCT to a minimum, reducing your vertical oscillation below 8 cm, and keeping your stride rate between 170–180, you will be well on your way to an optimal running form.

Running form is very complicated, and using the data from your running power meter can make a significant difference in improving your running economy and increasing your speed. You do not need a lab to improve your running form, but understand that data you have at your fingertips is like having a lab! This is why data analysis is just as important at performing the work. The data will tell you if you are improving. Seeing how key metrics such as power, stride rate, GCT, and so on change over time gives powerful insight on how you are reacting to your training program. The data will help you to decide if you need to make adjustments to the program or continue with what you are doing.

At the same time, it's important that you also seek the help of a running coach, use video analysis, and employ different running drills to enhance your running form. We cannot be experts on everything. A well-educated, well-trained coach can provide you with the guidance and analysis you might be looking to obtain. Ultimately, whatever tool you utilize to improve your training program, you are that much closer to achieving your athletic goals!

References

1. Adams, D., Pozzi, F., Willy, R. W., Carrol, A., & Zeni, J. (2018). Altering cadence or vertical oscillation during running: effects on running-related injury factors. *International Journal of Sports Physical Therapy*, *13*(4), 633–642.
2. Barnes, K. R., & Kilding, A. E. (2015). Running economy: Measurement, norms, and determining factors. *Sports medicine - open*, *1*(1), 8. https://doi.org/10.1186/s40798-015-0007-y.
3. Bowser, B. J., Fellin, R., Milner, C. E., Pohl, M. B., & Davis, I. S. (2018). Reducing impact loading in runners: a one-year follow-up. *Medicine and Science in Sports and Exercise*, *50*(12), 2500–2506. https://doi.org/10.1249/MSS.0000000000001710.
4. Clatterbuck, J., Fridley J., & Myers, C. (2020) Endurance running and its effect on the development of osteoarthritis. *Archives of Rheumatology & Arthritis Research*, *1*(1). http://dx.doi.org/10.33552/ARAR.2020.01.000504
5. Dalleau G., Belli A., Bourdin M., & Lacour J. (1998) The spring-mass model and the energy cost of treadmill running. *European Journal of Applied Physiology*, *77*, 257–263.
6. Fourchet F., Girard O., Kelly L., Horobeanu, C., & Millet, G. (2014). Changes in leg spring behavior, plantar loading and foot mobility magnitude induced by an exhaustive treadmill run in adolescent middle-distance runners. *Journal of Science and Medicine in Sport*, *18*(2),199–203.
7. García-Pinillos, F., Cartón-Llorente, A., Jaén-Carrillo, D., Delgado-Floody, P., Carrasco-Alarcón, V., Martínez, C., & Roche-Seruendo, L. E. (2020). Does fatigue alter step characteristics and stiffness during running? *Gait & posture*, *76*, 259–263. https://doi.org/10.1016/j.gaitpost.2019.12.018
8. Hayes P., & Caplan N. (2014). Leg stiffness decreases during a run to exhaustion at the speed at VO2max. *European Journal of Sport Science*, *14*, 556–562.
9. Heise, G., & Martin, P. (1998). "Leg spring" characteristics and the aerobic demand of running. *Medicine & Science in Sports & Exercise*, *30*(5), 750–754.
10. Moore, I. (2016). Is there an economical running technique? A review of modifiable biomechanical factors affecting running economy. *Sports Medicine*, *46*, 793–807. https://doi.org/10.1007/s40279-016-0474-4.
11. Morin J., Samozino P., Zameziati K., & Belli A. (2007). Effects of altered stride frequency and contact time on leg-spring behavior in human running. *Journal of Biomechanics*, *40*(15), 3341–3348. https://doi.org/10.1016/j.jbiomech.2007.05.001.
12. Nishida, K., Hagio, S., Kibushi, B., Moritani, T., & Kouzaki, M. (2017). Comparison of muscle synergies for running between different foot strike patterns. *PLOS One*, 12(2). https://doi.org/10.1371/journal.pone.0171535
13. Paavolainen, L., Häkkinen, K., Hämäläinen, I., Nummela, A., & Rusko, H. (1999). Explosive-strength training improves 5-km running time by improving running economy and muscle power. *Journal of Applied Physiology*, *86*(5), 1527–1533. https://doi.org/10.1152/jappl.1999.86.5.1527.
14. Paavolainen, L. M., Nummela, A. T., & Rusko, H. K. (1999). Neuromuscular characteristics and muscle power as determinants of 5-km running performance. *Medicine and Science in Sports and Exercise*, *31*(1), 124–130. https://doi.org/10.1097/00005768-199901000-00020.
15. Paavolainen, L., Nummela, A., Rusko, H., & Häkkinen, K. (1999). Neuromuscular characteristics and fatigue during 10 km running. *International Journal of Sports Medicine*, *20*(8), 516–521. https://doi.org/10.1055/s-1999-8837

Chapter 12

Laying the Foundation

How to Create a Training Program

Knowing, understanding, and applying your data to training is only part of the process. In previous chapters, we focused on teaching you the mechanics and action steps you need to train for each of the three sports. These steps should allow you to easily train more scientifically, efficiently, and effectively and ultimately shortcut your learning curve. We often lose sight of the forest through the trees, and the trees do make up the forest, but it's also important to step back and take a look at the forest. This allows planning for a specific event, a certain period of time, or even a season to guide and direct your daily training. An overall training program allows the athlete to build to a higher level of fitness, better ensure a peak of fitness exactly when they want it, and also help maintain an overall better level of health and fitness throughout the season. As coaches, we believe that the holy grail of coaching is to deliver the peak of fitness exactly on the day the athletes wants to have their peak performance. Any structured training plan will help to improve your fitness, but when an athlete comes to us and says, "I want to have the triathlon of my life on June 10," then creating that peak on that day is really the most complicated and challenging thing to make happen. And this is what separates the real coaches from the pretenders. There are so many factors that go into developing a peaking plan, but each plan has critical components. This chapter lays out a systematic approach to create a personalized and individualized program that trains the correct metabolic pathways and addresses the athlete's strengths and limitations.

Needs Analysis—What Is It?

A needs analysis is deciding the physical and performance attributes necessary for an athlete to be successful in a particular sport. This process identifies an athlete's individual and sport-specific strengths and limitations. As part of the process, the person performing the needs analysis will complete an individual and sport-specific injury analysis. This part of the needs analysis helps tailor the training toward preventing such injures. Overall, the primary aim of a needs analysis is twofold: prevent and reduce injury, and enhance athletic performance (9).

A proper needs analysis process involves three steps. The first step includes conducting the sport-oriented needs analysis. The second step comprises the athlete-oriented needs analysis. The third and ultimate step is comparing the sport and athlete needs analyses. The process looks as follows:

Step 1: Sports-oriented needs analysis

a. Needs of the sport
b. Injury analysis of the sport

Step 2: Athlete needs analysis/athlete profile
Step 3: Comparative analysis of the sports-oriented and athlete needs analysis

The following section will cover these steps and utilize a real-world case study.

Step 1: The Sport-Oriented Needs Analysis

A sport-oriented needs analysis helps the coach or athlete fully understand the needs and demands of the sport. Defining the demands of your event is absolutely critical to your success. A proper sports-oriented needs analysis consists of two sections: (a) sport characteristics and (b) injury analysis.

This first part of the needs analysis looks at the various aspects and skill sets in which a particular athlete needs to be successful within the sport. Elements considered with this analysis are as follows:

1. What is the sport? Is it a single- or multiple-sport modality?
2. How long is the competition schedule? Is it a single event or a season-long schedule?
3. Is the sport individual or team focused? Is it a team sport based on individual athlete performances?
4. What are different sets of skills necessary to be successful in the sport? Are there general skills versus specialty skills for a particular position?
5. What is the competition level? Amateur versus professional?
6. What is the typical duration of the event? Is it continuous, or does it have stoppages? Is it a multiday event?
7. Does the sport occur on land or water?

This part of the analysis gives the coach a clear picture of the sport's demands. However, this list is not exhaustive (13). Showing the key aspects and the sport's needs further identifies the athlete's key strengths and limitations. By first understanding the demands of the sport, one can match the athlete's needs to be successful in that event. Many times the event's demands and the athlete's abilities do not match, and in that case one needs to decide on a different event (or sport altogether) or to push on through and do the best with the talents they have. The list of the sport's needs is compared to the athlete needs analysis in the third step of the process. The following section details how Dr. Myers conducted the needs analysis for his coaching client Geir Omarsson.

Sport-Oriented Needs Analysis: Case Study

Geir is a 45-year-old male long-course triathlete with several racing experience years as a high-performing age grouper. Geir wanted to win his age group in the IRONMAN Tallinn, and the first order of business was for Dr. Myers to perform the needs analysis of this particular event. Detailed in Table 12.1, the needs analysis investigated the general and critical aspects of an IRONMAN event.

TABLE 12.1 Sport-Oriented Needs Analysis for IRONMAN Tallinn

ACTIVITY	SPEED OF MOVEMENT	TOTAL DISTANCE COVERED	PERCENTAGE OF TIME IN ACTIVITY
Swim	1:40 min/100 m	3.86 km	11%
Bike	37.6 kph	180 km	51%
Run	4:54 min/km	44.2 km	36%
Walking	N/A	-	0%
Jogging	N/A	-	0%
Running	4:54 min/km	-	100%
Transition 1	3:23	-	1%
Transition 2	2:52	-	1%
PHYSIOLOGICAL ASPECT		**ESTIMATED DEMAND**	
Metabolic			
Anaerobic (phosphagen and glycolytic)		2% (5)	
Aerobic (oxidative phosphorylation)		98% (5)	
Range of motion (ROM)			
Shoulders and back		Necessary for swim propulsion (3, 4, 11, 12)	
Hips		Propulsion: All three events (10)	
Knees		Propulsion: Bike and run (10)	
Ankles		Propulsion: All three events (10)	

(Continued)

PHYSIOLOGICAL ASPECT	ESTIMATED DEMAND
Flexibility	
Shoulders and back	Reduces drag for swimming (3, 4, 11, 12). Aids within the best aerodynamic and powerful bike position (7).
Hips Knees Ankles	Running and cycling involve movement in a unilateral plane. The flexibility of these joints and associated muscle group will help with ROM and reduce injury (8).

Note: Dr. Myers performed this needs analysis with one of his athletes who was targeted to win the male 45–49 age group at the 2020 IRONMAN Tallinn. The swim, bike, and run metrics were taken from the 2019 race results, which can be found at www.ironman.com/im-tallinn-results as of 11/1/2020.

By performing the needs analysis early in the training program, the information gleaned from Table 12.1 supplied insight on how fast Geir would need to be in order to win his age group. Also, the analysis provided a pivotal foundation to identify some of his crucial performance strengths and limitations. This information alone does not supply much insight into his stance within the age group performance metrics. However, it guides the performance metrics he will need to win his age group based on historical race performance measures. For example, as shown in Table 12.1, the swim, bike, and run components of the race were the results of the 45–49 age group winner of the 2019 IRONMAN Tallinn. These times guided the athlete and Dr. Myers to the performance metrics he would need to meet to increase his chances of winning the race.

In this example, the IRONMAN Tallinn race was Geir's sole "A" event for the 2020 season. This choice meant Dr. Myers tailored his training program specifically to peak for the IRONMAN Tallinn. The training program's design focused heavily on the course profile and how Geir's actual abilities (his performance strengths and limitations) fit the course profile. So, as part of this section of the needs analysis, an in-depth look at the course was performed. The following is a summary of the analysis.

Sport-Oriented Needs Analysis: IRONMAN Tallin—Swim

The swim course was a lake swim that used several left and right turns, as shown in Figure 12.1. The swim course layout was unusual for an IRONMAN event. Most swim courses require a triathlete to make only left or right turns; however, this course meant the athlete needed to turn left and right around buoys. Geir was required to be proficient in open-water sighting and bilateral breathing to properly perform this athletic skill. Dr. Myers added these skills to the general makeup of his swimming workouts. By working on these unique skills, Geir focused on positioning and pace during the swim.

Another attribute of the swim leg is the average water temperature. The average reported temperature was between 18–20 degrees Celsius. This temperature meant the race would be wetsuit legal. Furthermore, the average water temperature was warmer than what Geir was accustomed to during open-water swims in Iceland. This information was important due to the wetsuit equipment necessary to take part in the race. Also, this showed the water temperature was closer to that seen in a swimming pool. Consequently, it was determined that only a small adjustment period would be necessary to be comfortable in the lake water upon arrival at the race venue.

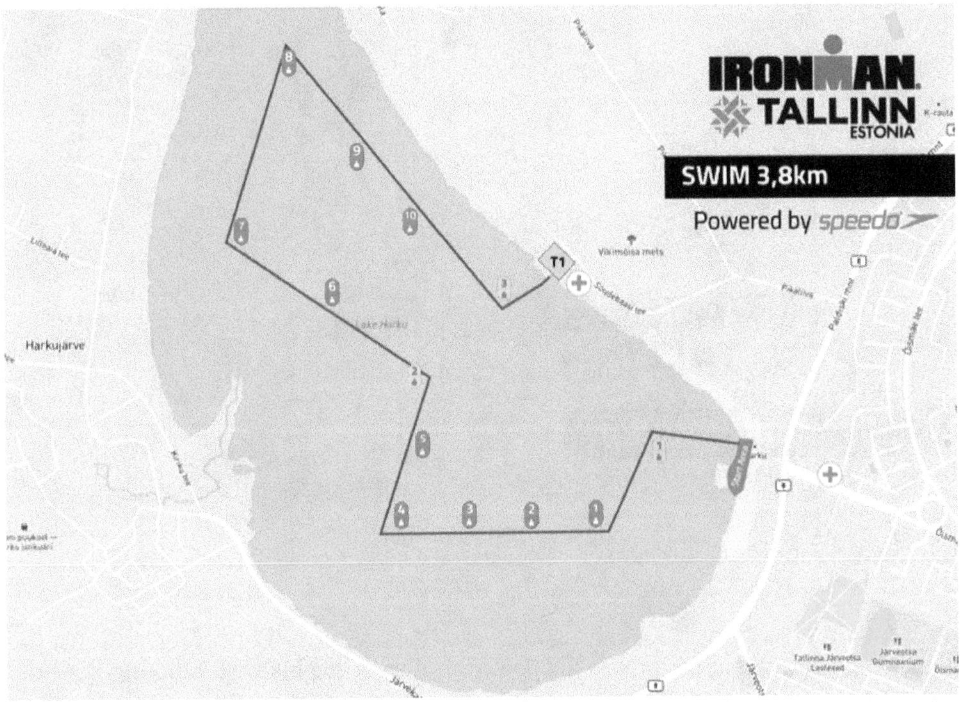

FIGURE 12.1 Swim course for IRONMAN Tallinn.

Finally, the lake swim meant the athlete did not contend with waves as seen in ocean water swims. The water conditions were closer to those observed in a pool. The minimization of outside variables meant that pace calculations would be similar to those seen in the pool. This aspect aided in predicting Geir's overall swim time and meant he could utilize his rate of perceived exertion to gauge his swimming pace during this leg of the event.

Sport-Oriented Needs Analysis: IRONMAN Tallin—Bike

The focus of bike needs analysis was multifold and looked at some of the following: terrain changes, wind directions and speed, feeding stations, and other factors that may affect the athlete's performance. Figure 12.2 shows the entirety of the bike course. Initially, the route looks very hilly. However, this was not the case. Further investigation revealed the course was very flat. The average elevation change was only around 2%, as shown in Figure 12.3. This information was one of the foundational factors in determining Geir's overall power pacing and power range.

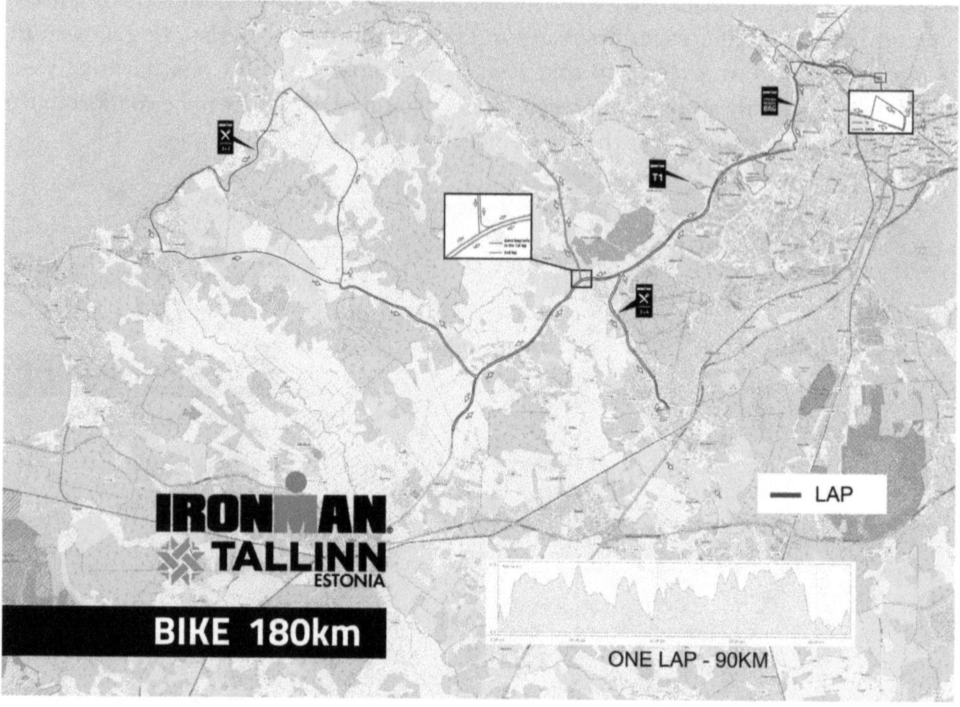

FIGURE 12.2 Bike course for IRONMAN Tallinn.

The next important factor was his power output for the bike leg. Looking at historical data from professional and high-performing age-group long-distance triathletes, we knew he would have to target an FTP in mid to upper endurance/power Z2 range. If you look at Table 6.2, you will see zone is an effort one can hold for 2–5 hours. Computer modeling of some of the historical data from the previous IRONMAN Tallin race and experience from coaching other long-course triathletes strongly suggested this was the correct zone he would need to target.

Next, the historical weather forecast showed the temperature at 15–16 degrees C. Even though the ambient temperature was not too hot or humid, this information helps to figure out a few key hydration aspects of Geir's nutrition plan for the race. Knowing that his sweat rate would be close to average, he could use his specific nutritional products. The temperature knowledge also helped to calculate hydration timing and an overall mixture of food and liquid nutrition to obtain the targeted glucose ingestion rate. Knowing this, we planned for half of his liquid intake to be split evenly through Maurten 320 drink mix and pure water. He would finish half a bottle of drink mix about every 62 minutes and half a bottle of water every 25–27 minutes. Also, Geir was scheduled to have a gel shot or chew about every 20 miles. He could substitute two of the gels for bananas depending on how he felt. This nutrition strategy on the bike was imperative in hitting the 60 g/hr glucose ingestion rate we were targeting.

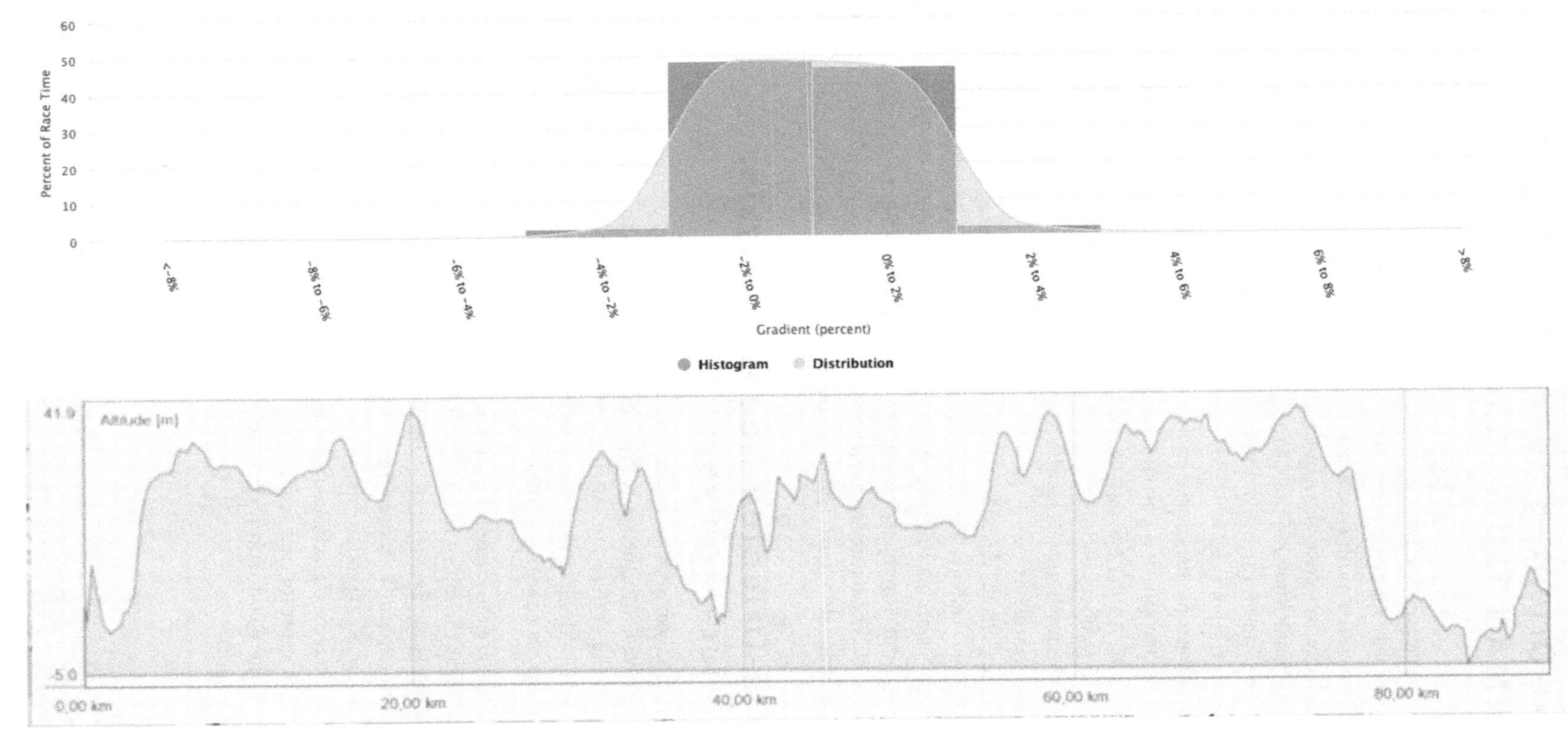

FIGURE 12.3 Bike course terrain profile for IRONMAN Tallinn.

Sport-Oriented Needs Analysis: IRONMAN Tallin—Run

Like the bike course, the run leg was flat, and since it was in the middle of the city, the wind was not a factor. However, with this part of the race happening later in the day, the temperature was slightly warmer with little shade. This meant hydration was even more crucial. The course profile detailed where each feed station was located on the course. The knowledge was critical when developing Geir's nutritional plan for this part of the race. Even though knowing the location of each feeding station did not change what Geir brought with him to eat, we did have to use several of the stations for water to ensure a consistent hydration rate.

The course profile meant the pacing strategy would be a consistent pace. Little to no change in the terrain profile would not cause issues with his pace. This knowledge made calculating the correct pacing and overall completion predictions possible. We decided to target mid to upper endurance/zone 2. This targeted pace was based on the historical data from the previous IRONMAN Tallin race and experience from coaching other long-course triathletes.

The course elements described (along with those not described) are essential to developing the race day strategy. Yet these elements are more critical in developing the specificity of the athlete's training toward a single event. In this example, the first analysis occurred 20 weeks (about 5 months) before the event. One of the critical skills found was the open-water skills necessary to navigate the swim section's unique layout successfully. The process does not stop here. The next step is to perform the injury analysis of the sport.

Sports-Oriented Needs Analysis: The Injury Analysis

The injury analysis section of the sports-oriented needs analysis looks at the common injuries involved with the sport (9). This part of the analysis does not consider injuries common to the athlete himself; the athlete-specific injury analysis occurs during the building and analysis of the athlete profile. Some frequent questions investigated in this section of the process are as follows:

1. What are the current injuries associated with the sport?
2. What is the injury frequency rate?
3. What is the average time loss with these injuries? What is the expected amount of time to fully recover from the injury?
4. Is there a particular time in the year when specific injuries occur?
5. Are there specific chronic injuries that occur with an athlete who has been involved in the sport for an exceptionally long time?
6. Are there common predisposing factors for specific injuries that occur within the sport?

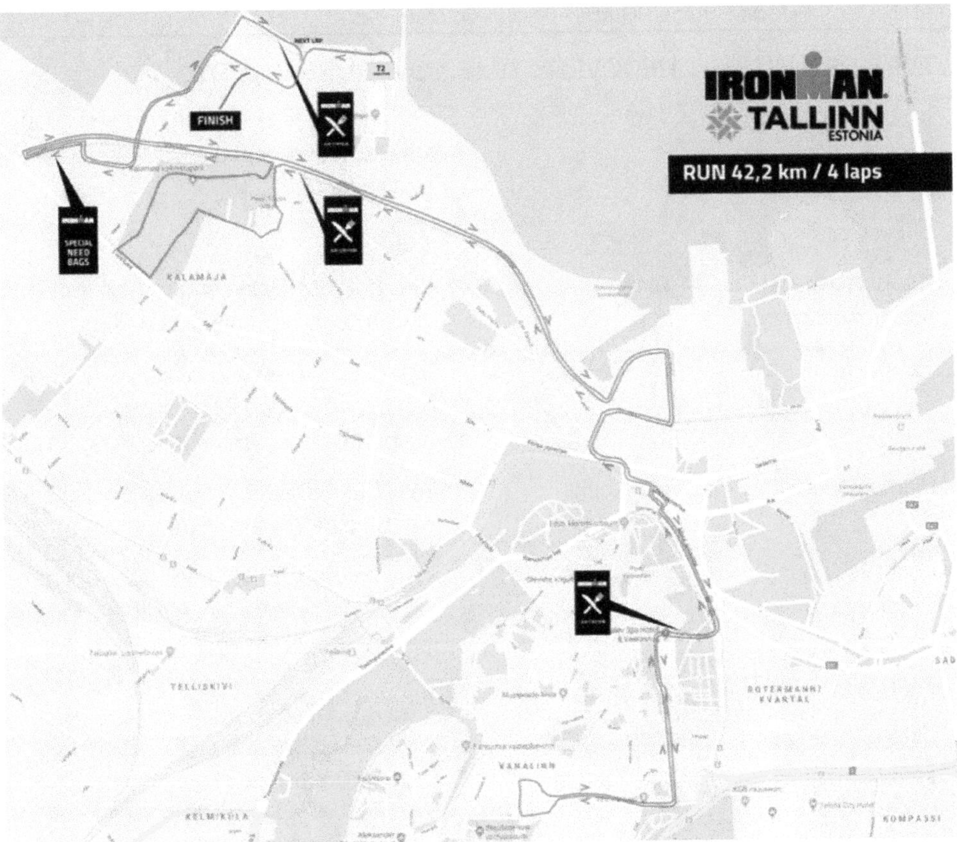

FIGURE 12.4 Run course for IRONMAN Tallinn.

The list of injuries shown in Table 12.2 details the most common that occur in triathlons. Even though this is not an exhaustive list, Table 12.2 sheds light on many of the injuries caused by overuse or overtraining. The coach and athlete cannot discount the fact that some of these injuries can be caused by normal, everyday accidents. This table shows that proper recovery needs to occur and be part of the training program for the athlete and the coach. It also shows the expected recovery time if one of the injuries occurs. This knowledge can help with planning and strategies to continue training around the injury.

Overall, the sports-oriented needs analysis gives a picture of the demands to succeed in the sport and strong insight on common injuries. With this picture, the coach and the athlete have a better conceptual understanding of the sport's demands. This information helps create the pillars for a complete and robust macro cycle. This part of the analysis provides insights where time is better used if the athlete has a limited time to train. However, this information supplies little insight without the athlete's profile.

TABLE 12.2 The Most Common Injuries Appearing in Triathletes

TYPE OF INJURY	RECOVERY TIME	OVERUSE INJURY
Shoulder injury	3 weeks (15)	Yes. However, poor swimming mechanics and muscle imbalance is a predisposing factor (2, 15).
Shin splints	6 weeks	Yes.
Chondromalacia patella (runner's knee)	Various	Yes, but foot issues and muscle imbalance in legs can cause as well.
Patellar knee pain	1–2 weeks	Mostly due to an improper bike fit. Can be caused by running in shoes that are beyond their recommended life span (6).
Plantar fasciitis	4–8 weeks	Yes (17). However, previous foot issues can be a predisposing factor.
Iliotibial (IT) band syndrome	4–8 weeks	Yes. However, predisposing factors of the hips or an imbalance with the glutes (16) contribute.
Achilles tendonitis	4–8 weeks	Yes.
Muscle strains and sprains	6–10 weeks (about 2.5 months)	Yes and no. Inadequate recovery can cause this; however, improper mechanics or accidents contribute to this injury (6).

Step 2: The Athlete's Needs Analysis/Athlete Profile

The previous section looked at the sport's demands, and the next step is to look at the athlete themself. The athlete profile can have the following:

1. Goal setting
2. Athlete body composition/body type
3. Experience and competition level
4. Medical history
5. Training availability
6. Available equipment
7. Identification of the athlete's strengths and limitations

Goal setting is arguably the most essential part of the athlete profile; goals set the stage for the upcoming season's expectations. Goals are set by the athlete and what intrinsically motivates them during hard training sessions, in bad weather, at the end of a hard training block, and during emotionally turbulent times. Setting goals can be a daunting and challenging process. One way to make it easier is to create goals that are achievable, realistic, and tangible. The last thing an athlete or coach should do is to create an unattainable goal. A challenging goal is one that can be achieved with hard work. Setting the right goal(s) can set the stage for a strong season and supply guidance on how the training program should be structured.

Geir's goal was to take the overall victory for his age group (men's 45–49) and qualify for the IRONMAN world championships in Kona. We knew this was a realistic and achievable goal because he had won other long-course triathlon events such as Iceland Extreme Triathlon in 2019 where he set the course record.

Gathering the athlete's anthropometrics provides insight into the athlete's body composition. These metrics include height, weight, and body fat percentage. Geir could be classified between an ectomorph and mesomorph. What we mean by this is he had a low body fat percentage and body build for endurance sports. However, he could build muscle mass if he wanted through the proper resistance training program. This information gives an excellent indication of the athlete's physical fitness level and relative power for performance metrics.

The next component in building the athlete profile is understanding the athlete's experience and competition level. With this information, one can begin to answer some of the following questions:

1. How long has the athlete been participating in the sport?
    a. Geir had participated in triathlon for well over 10 years at this point. He had an extensive background in endurance sports during his young adulthood. Running was his strongest sport and swimming was his limitation.
2. Does the athlete have the necessary skills and experience to reach the current goals?
    a. At this point, he did. Geir had won a few long-course events prior to setting this goal.
3. What level of competition does the athlete take part?
    a. Geir participated in age-group level events. However, many of the events included retired professional triathletes and cyclists. The quality of the competition would be considered very high.

With this information, one can begin to build a picture of the athlete. Understanding the athlete's experiences and competition level within the sport starts to lay the foundation for the skills and intensity that the training program should incorporate.

The next step is gathering the athlete's medical history. This history provides the athlete or coach with valuable information that might supply insights into limitations to training and provides insight into possible predisposing factors for injury. The medical history should be compared to the injury analysis performed in step 3. This part of step 2 provides the information necessary to see if the athlete is prone to or overly prone to common injuries that occur in the sport. Geir did not have a significant medical history or issues that would impair his training or athletic performance.

Training and equipment availability are usually taken for granted. Attempting to create a training plan where the athlete needs to train for 20 hours per week but only has 10 hours to spare is not possible. Also, ensuring the athlete has the correct equipment to train properly sets the athlete up for success. Knowing the available training time and equipment available helps provide information on the type of training strategies that could aid the athlete in achieving their goals.

Geir was able to dedicate up to 20 hours per week to train toward this goal. We were able to maximize this time through a periodized approach to address his strengths and limitations. He was able to train due to the flexibility of his work schedule and did not have to sacrifice his professional career to train properly. Furthermore, he had the support from his family, which was the most important aspect of his training.

The second crucial aspect of the athlete-oriented needs analysis is understanding the athlete's key limitations and strengths. This section is just as important as goal setting, but it must be performed last. Identifying an athlete's key strengths and limitations can come from two different avenues: objective or subjective means. This process means an athlete can perform a self-analysis and identify their strengths and limitations. Another way to do this is by analyzing the athlete's historical data. Some data that can be examined are past workouts, past field tests, and past competition performances. However, the optimal way to identify these aspects of the athlete profile is through testing.

For Geir, we had some work to do in order to ensure he was ready for IRONMAN Tallinn. Geir's weight was 70 kilograms at the beginning of the training and did not change throughout the program. His run was his strength. His run rFTP was 322 W, which equated to a 3:51 min/km threshold pace. He had a threshold stride rate of 176 steps per minute, stride length of 1.13, and vertical oscillation of 7.2 cm. These metrics denoted he was a mid-foot striker. The swim and bike were his limitations. Geir had a strong bike, but we still need to close the gap based on historical numbers. His FTP at the beginning of the build was 300 W (4.28 W/kg) with a cadence of 87 rpm. We knew, based on the sport-oriented needs analysis, he would need to increase his FTP by 30–50 W. His swim was his most significant limitation. His swim threshold was 1:44 min/100 m with as stroke rate of 39 strokes per minute. We would need to increase his threshold swim pace by 10–15 s in order to ensure his endurance/zone 2–tempo/zone 3 swim pace would increase. In Table 12.3, we discuss his progression throughout the training program. Finally, his threshold heart rates for the bike and run were 175 BPM and 178 BPM, respectively.

The earlier sections of this book provide several types of field tests. This section of the needs analysis is where these types of tests become crucial. They provide objective insights into the athlete's capabilities and limitations. When building a new training program, this is the point in the process to perform the proper field tests specific to the sport, which creates a baseline for comparing improvements and deciding if the training program is working. Furthermore, the field test results provide the essential metrics to develop personalized training zones.

The information gleaned from steps 1 and 2 provides the framework for creating a personalized training program. However, the needs analysis process is incomplete until these two steps are compared. This process occurs in step 3 of the needs analysis process, the comparative analysis.

Step 3: Comparative Analysis

The comparative analysis allows the athlete or the coach to compare the information gleaned from the sports- and athlete-oriented needs analyses. This comparison provides insights into how the athlete performs in the sport. Step 3 provides further and specific insight into the athlete's strengths and limitations. This information is then incorporated into the athlete's training plan. By addressing and integrating the information gleaned through steps 1–3, the training plan is tailored specifically to the athlete and reduces chances for injury.

Step 3 occurs several times in the build-up toward the "A" event or competition season. As the athlete improves, the analysis of the variables changes. An example of this is shown with Geir's build-up toward IRONMAN Tallinn. As stated earlier, the original needs analysis was conducted 20 weeks before the event. A second analysis was performed 2 weeks before the event, as shown in Table 12.3. As part of the race preparation, Geir's predictive performance outcomes were recalculated. The performance predictions were based on his training data.

1. Table 12.3 denotes how Geir's training program closed the performance gaps to increase his chances of winning the race. We focused on increasing his swim speed and bike power. To increase his swim pace, we worked on speed and endurance. Geir had a very good swim stroke. However, we were faced with a problem. The COVID-19 pandemic started, and all local pools were closed. To address this obstacle, a robust dryland strength training program was created and used to keep up his swimming performance.

   The dryland program consisted of bands and weights. Until the pools opened, he was doing bands three times per week. We focused on his stroke rate and mechanics through the catch, pull, and push phases. Early on, we noticed his threshold stroke rate ranged between 39–41 strokes/minute. We wanted to increase this to

TABLE 12.3 Winner of the 2019 IRONMAN Tallinn and the Estimated Performance of the Athlete Training for the Event

ACTIVITY	2019 WINNER'S TIME PER EVENT	GEIR'S PREDICTED TIME 20 WEEKS (ABOUT 4.5 MONTHS) BEFORE EVENT	GEIR'S PREDICTED TIMES 3 WEEKS BEFORE EVENT	GEIR'S IRONMAN TALLINN RACE WINNING PERFORMANCE
Swim	1:05.21	1:07.36	1:06.30	1:07.46
Transition 1	3.23	3.00	3.00	3.03
Bike	4:47.40	5:22.00	4:47.22	4:42.42
Transition 2	2.52	3.00	3.00	2.15
Run	3:26.51	3:32.43 (~290W)	3:26.17 (~295W)	3:13.19
Total time	9:26.07	10:08.19	9:20.09	9:09.05

47–50 strokes/minute while maintaining his stroke power and mechanics. The bands were very effective. By the time he was able to get back into the pool, he had increased his stroke rate to 46 strokes per minute. On race day, he was able to hold the 47–50 strokes per minute target. An example of one of the many band workouts is as follows:

Warm-up:

1. Jog for 10 min at active recovery (power Z1, pace Z1, HR Z1, RPE 1) building to endurance (power Z2, pace Z2, HR Z2, RPE 2–3)
2. Perform static stretch routine 2

MS1: With resistance cords, mimic the freestyle swim catch, pull, and push at a resistance that is easy to medium effort. Perform the following pyramid:

a. 1 minute on, 1 minute off
b. 2 minutes on, 1 minute off
c. 3 minutes on, 1 minute off
d. 2 minutes on, 1 minute off
e. 1 minute on, 1 minute off

MS2: Core: Do this set three times. Rest 30–45 s between each exercise.

a. 30 s flutter kicks
b. 10x pushups
c. 10x each side bird dog
d. 30 s high-to-low planks

CD: Perform foam roller routine 1

After a few months, the pools began to open. We knew we had to translate his band training to swim speed. We had Geir perform four swim sessions per week. One of the sessions was a 10x100 m threshold swim session. The swim workout was as follows:

Warm-up:

1. Shoulder mobility routine 1: 10 minutes
2. 400 free building from active recovery (pace Z1, power Z1, HR Z1, RPE 1) to endurance (pace Z2, power Z2, HR Z2, RPE 2–3).
3. 200 kicks: Free with fins

Set 1:
10x100 s swim with 15 s rest at threshold (pace Z4, power Z4, HR Z4, RPE 5–6).
I want you to try to keep a consistent endurance pace for each 100 m (within 1 sec).

If your pace drops, stop the workout and finish the balance of the swim at endurance (pace Z2, power Z2, HR Z2, RPE 2–3).

CD: 200 free at active recovery (pace Z1, power Z1, HR Z1, RPE 1)

The second session was a finisher sprint session. The idea was to work on anaerobic capacity toward the end of the swim session when he was fatigued. An example of this type of session is as follows:

Warm-up:

1. Shoulder mobility routine 2: 10 minutes
2. 200 kicks with fins: 100 free/100 back
3. 200 pull with fins building from active recovery (pace Z1, power Z1, HR Z1, RPE 1) to endurance (pace Z2, power Z2, HR Z2, RPE 2–3).

Preset: 5x75 s build (slow, fast, sprint)

Main set: 10x200s

1. One to four your best time plus 25 seconds
2. Five fast with last 50 m sprint
3. Six to nine your best time plus 20 seconds
4. Ten fast with last 50 m sprint

CD: 400 free at active recovery (pace Z1, power Z1, HR Z1, RPE 1).

The second aspect addressed was his bike power. We needed to increase his endurance capacity and increase his FTP. We did not do anything fancy; we kept the approach simple. The plan focused on steady state SST (sweet-spot training) and FTP intervals. The choice of SST versus FTP intervals was dependent on the goal of the second workout of the day. An example of the one of the SST bike workouts is as follows:

> WU: 10–15 minutes working into endurance (power Z2, HR Z2, pace Z2, RPE 2–3) with 3 x 1 minute fast pedals to wake up legs.
>
> -------
>
> MS1: Complete 3 x 12 s max sprint with 24 s recovery between VO2 max (power Z5, HR Z5, pace Z5, RPE 6–7). Immediately following last sprint (do not rest) complete a 15 minute interval in the SST zone (power Z3.5, HR Z3.5, RPE 5.5–6). Cadence should be 85–95; rest and pedal easy for 5 minutes at active recovery (power Z1, Pace Z1, HR Z1, RPE 1) between each interval.
>
> -------
>
> CD: 10 minutes of easy spinning in your active recovery (power Z1, Pace Z1, HR Z1, RPE 1).

To increase his endurance capacity, we need to increase his time in the saddle. Going back to the sports-oriented needs analysis in Table 12.1, we had calculated half the race was spent on the bike. We knew at a minimum over half of his training time per week needed to be on the bike. Additionally, the training times need to be longer volume and lower intensity. As part of the training mix, we did one tempo session and at least one 4–5 hour endurance session. This mix helped increase his volume but not cause exponential increases in his weekly TSS.

For his runs, we kept a similar approach. He did one to two tempo sessions per week, one track session, and one to two long slow-distance (LSD) runs. We chose to do the tempo and LSD runs because Geir responded well to those types of runs. Additionally, he was accumulating a large amount of training stress per week. We did not want to add more from high-intensity running work as that may cause an injury. When it came to the track sessions, we primarily focused on 400 s, 800 s, and mile repeats.

Toward the end of the training build, we performed field testing about 3 weeks prior to the event. We used the new metrics to tailor his peak period and race day strategy. The predicted times shown in Table 12.3 came from the results of the field testing. Geir's performance during these field tests showed he had closed the performance gaps to do well, if not win, IRONMAN Tallinn.

This information supplied guidance for the race day strategy. During the needs analysis process, the items showed increased specificity of the program to meet Geir's needs and the conditions he would encounter at the 2020 IRONMAN Tallinn event.

The needs analysis process may sound like a magic bullet. However, this is not the case. The needs analysis is merely the first step in creating a proper, individualized, periodized macrocycle. The results shown in Table 12.3 are the results of that type of training plan. The next section in this chapter will explain how to plan an individualized, periodized macrocycle carefully.

Testing: The Keys to Identifying Strengths and Limitations

Testing can be performed in a laboratory or the field. Since many athletes do not have access to laboratory testing, this section will focus on field testing. When testing, the athlete's coach should look at the following areas: aerobic endurance, muscular power, muscular strength, muscular endurance, range of motion, and flexibility. With multisports, all these areas apply. A standard error typically encountered in multisport athletes is ignoring the testing of muscular power, muscular strength, and muscular endurance. Ignoring these areas typically sets up areas of muscular imbalance and limitations to increasing performance. This section of the chapter will discuss the essential characteristics of how to perform a proper field test.

How to Perform Field Testing: The Warm-Up

Whether performing endurance or strength testing, a proper warm-up must be completed. The warm-up should be geared toward the exercise modality being performed in the main set of the workout. For example, as shown with the 5 km rFTP test, at least 20 minutes of dynamic and static exercises are prescribed to ensure the athlete is adequately prepared for the test. As part of the warm-up, the athlete is to jog or run, starting in zone 1 active recovery and slowly building up to zone 2 endurance for 10 to 15 minutes. The suggested dynamic exercises are geared toward warming up the primary ancillary muscle groups associated with running. These exercises prepare the body, especially the targeted muscle groups, for the rigors of the testing. The goal is to increase blood flow to the working muscles and increase body temperature. A proper warm-up helps prevent injuries that can be sustained while performing higher than usual intensity exercises.

The same is true when performing muscular strength, muscular endurance, and muscular power testing protocols. The leading national body for strength and conditioning governance and certification, the National Strength and Conditioning Association (NCSA), suggests 5–10 minutes of dynamic movements, including jogging or skipping, followed by a set of stretches to the targeted exercise modality (14). The NSCA builds on this basic warm-up protocol by adding a series of warm-up exercises geared toward the target exercise modality shown in Figure 12.4 as part of the 1 RM testing protocol. For example, if performing a one-repetition maximum (1 RM) test on the bench press, the added warm-up is performed on the bench press. With each succession of the warm-up, the weight lifted is increased.

No matter the field test's target (i.e., endurance testing versus muscular strength), a proper warm-up should be part of the testing protocol.

Best Practices: Ensuring Quality Testing

A critical aspect of performing an excellent field test is making the results valid and reliable. Reliable field test results allow the athlete or the coach to compare results with previous tests. This analysis helps determine if progress is being made, if the training plan is working, or if changes need to be made. Some key considerations to increase the validity and reliability of a field test as suggested by the NSCA are as follows:

- The testing equipment
- The method of calculation
- Method of instruction to the athlete
- Time of day
- The athlete's fatigue status and familiarity with the testing protocol
- The athlete's experience or training status
- The temperature of the testing environment
- The warm-up protocol before testing
- Order of testing (if other tests are also being performed)
- Modality of exercise to the specificity to the sport (9)

The bottom line to a reliable field test protocol is to keep the testing conditions as consistent as possible. This protocol eliminates the possibility of any peripheral variables that may confound the results.

1 RM Testing Protocol

1. Instruct the athlete to warm up with a light resistance that easily allows 5 to 10 repetitions.
2. Provide a 1-minute rest period.
3. Estimate a warm-up load that will allow the athlete to complete three to five repetitions by adding
   - 10 to 20 pounds (4–9 kg) or 5% to 10% for upper body exercise or
   - 30 to 40 pounds (14–18 kg) or 10% to 20% for lower body exercise.
4. Provide a 2-minute rest period.
5. Estimate a conservative, near-maximal load that will allow the athlete to complete two or three repetitions by adding
   - 10 to 20 pounds (4–9 kg) or 5% to 10% for upper body exercise or
   - 30 to 40 pounds (14–18 kg) or 10% to 20% for lower body exercise.
6. Provide a 2- to 4-minute rest period.
7. Make a load increase:
   - 10 to 20 pounds (4–9 kg) or 5% to 10% for upper body exercise or
   - 30 to 40 pounds (14–18 kg) or 10% to 20% for lower body exercise.
8. Instruct the athlete to attempt a 1RM.
9. If the athlete was successful, provide a 2- to 4-minute rest period and go back to step 7. If the athlete failed, provide a 2- to 4-minute rest period; then decrease the load by subtracting
   - 5 to 10 pounds (2–4 kg) or 2.5% to 5% for upper body exercise or
   - 15 to 20 pounds (7–9 kg) or 5% to 10% for lower body exercise.

   AND then go back to step 8.

Continue increasing or decreasing the load until the athlete can complete one repetition with proper exercise technique. Ideally, the athlete's 1 RM will be measured within three to five testing sets.

FIGURE 12.5 NSCA's guidelines for performing 1 RM testing (9).

Take Action: Data Analysis

The analysis of the data is the most critical aspect of field testing. Looking at the data and comparing it to other athletic normative data allows the athlete and coach to identify strengths and limitations. An in-depth analysis of the testing data is usually overlooked. One of the aspects that can be gleaned from testing is how the athlete compares to other athletes in the same category. Another way to look at the data is through the lens of the goal-oriented performance of an "A" event.

As part of the sport-oriented needs-analysis for Geir Omarsson (Table 12.3), his event time to win his age group was identified. However, the needs analysis results do not translate directly to the metrics he needed to use for his training. This is where a little ingenuity on applying the information gleaned from the historical data and his field testing came into play.

As shown in Table 12.3, at 20 weeks from the event Geir needed to significantly increase his bike power and run speed to win the event. His tested IRONMAN marathon pace was at 5:03 min/km. Comparing this result to the 2019 IRONMAN Tallinn winner's result, Geir needed to cut 4 to 5 minutes off his marathon time. He would have to increase his run speed to 4:54 minute per kilometer. Also, looking at his 20-week projected bike performance time, Geir needed to cut 40 minutes of his total projected bike time. At this point of his training cycle, his bike FTP was at 305 watts. From modeling predictions, his FTP needed to be increased by 25–30 watts to close the time gap. We used this information to determine where we should focus his training and the balance between intensity versus duration.

Putting It All Together: The Application to the Annual Training Plan (ATP)/Macro Cycle

The penultimate step in the process is applying what is gleaned from the needs and field test analysis. One involves the aspects identified through the needs analysis and field testing processes to build the training program. The following is a systematic approach on how to create an ATP:

1. Identify and schedule dates for key athletic events. Prioritize events in the following categories:
   a. "A" event—Most crucial race. The race(s) the athlete wants to be at peak performance and achieve their best results. Typically, only one or two "A" events occur in a macro cycle.
   b. "B" events—Good races to practice racing strategy. Not as important as "A" events but provide a good challenge and motivation to train toward. These events should feed into the overarching goals outlined for the "A" event. Typically, only two to four "B" events occur in a macro cycle.
   c. "C" events—Races and events that work well for training. They provide an opportunity to work on skills and strategies that cannot be recreated under normal training conditions. These events are treated as a typical training session.
2. Begin backward planning and outlining the mesocycles.
   a. Determine the large chunks of time the athlete cannot train, for example, priority races versus training races, family vacations, work conferences, holidays, and so on.
   b. Utilizing mesocycles, create a progressive build (preparatory phase, base phase, build phase, peak phase, taper phase, and transition phase) to the "A" event (1, 5).
   c. Identify the type of work-to-rest ratio cycles. An example of this is a work-to-rest cycle of 3:1. This ratio means that every fourth week is a recovery week.
   d. Identify the critical training goals for each mesocycle. This method helps guide training for that training block and allows the athlete to know the training's focus. These goals should address the strengths and limitations of the athlete's performance.
3. Begin building the micro cycles.
   a. Outline the goals for each micro cycle. These are two to three goals that address vital components identified as part of the athlete's strengths and limitations. This approach provides each micro cycle's purpose and shows the athlete and coach how the individual workouts feed into the overall build of the training program.
   b. Start building workouts that feed into the micro cycle goals in the following order:
      i. Program in weekly rest/recovery days.
      ii. Program specialization works to address athlete's limitations.
      iii. Program resistance training workouts.
      iv. Program workouts to address the athlete's strengths.

4. Identify the types of field tests and when the tests should occur within the training build. These metrics should be performance based. Looking back at Geir's training build, he performed an FTP test after his first build meso cycle. The performance benchmark was for a 3–4% increase in his FTP. The result from the test was 318 watts. This performance was a 4.2% increase in his FTP. Since he succeeded in increasing his FTP, he knew the training plan was addressing his cycling limitations.

Let's see how these four steps were applied to Geir's training program.

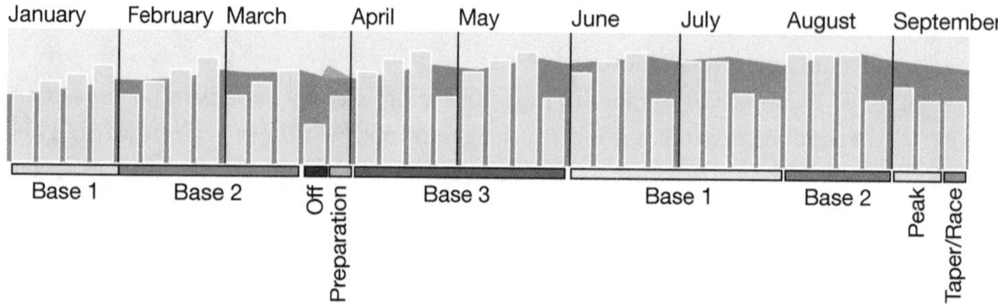

FIGURE 12.6 Initial ATP template for Geir's training program targeting IRONMAN Tallinn.

In step 1, Geir wanted to participate in several events. The "A" event was IRONMAN Tallinn in September 2020. Additionally, he wanted to participate in a few local area races, which included a 70.3 distance triathlon, local 10 km run race, and a few local individual cycling time trials. In our discussions, we had to categorize the priorities of these races. This is important when creating a training plan. This determines if you are creating a single or double event peak or a plan with a competition season. In Geir's case, we wanted to go for a single event peak, so we saw the 70.3 distance triathlon as a great event to test our racing and nutrition strategy. We categorized the 70.3 triathlon as a "B" event and the other events as "C" events.

Before we started the backward planning, we identified a time period where training would be minimal. At the end of March, Geir planned on taking a local family vacation. We were able to identify this early on in the planning to work his training schedule around the family event. Also, we would have tried to identify any work-related activities (such as seminars, business trips, etc.) that might need to be planned around. Due to the nature of his job, this was not an issue. The identification of the races and the family vacation laid the pillars ATP.

In step 2, we began the backward planning. We knew the week of the race he would have to travel. We estimated he would travel 3 days prior to the race. This would allow him enough time to preview the course and adjust from any possible jet lag. From here we planned the peak and the taper. We had the luxury of working with Geir for a significant period of time prior to this build. We knew a 7–10-day exponential fast decay taper strategy was the best solution, so, we planned for 7 days for the taper and about

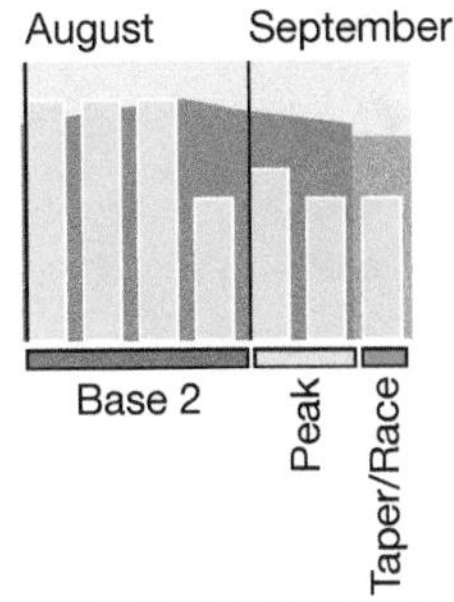

Event	Microcycle	Planned TSS	Focus - Swim	Focus - Bike	Focus - Run	Strength
	Peak 1	1200	Endurance, Speed Skill, Anaerobic Capacity	Muscular Endurance, Power	Endurance, Speed Skill	N/A
	Peak 2	700	Endurance	Endurance	Endurance	N/A
IRONMAN© Tallinn	Taper/Race	500	None	None	None	N/A

FIGURE 12.7 Key goals and intensity planned Geir's peak phase and taper for IRONMAN Tallinn.

10 days for the peak. As shown in Figure 12.7, we laid out the goals of these two meso cycles, which are listed under the Limitations columns.

The next step was to determine the optimal work-to-rest ratio for his meso cycles. Due to his experience and current aerobic conditioning, we chose to utilize the 3:1 approach for each meso cycle. Identifying this early allowed us to plan regular recovery periods to regulate overtraining. Additionally, this allowed for us to plan field tests at regular intervals.

Field tests are best performed after about 96 hours of recovery at the end of a meso cycle. The body needs a chance to recovery from the training stress accumulated during the meso cycle. This is called functional overreaching. The body recovers and adapts to the training stress. This change usually results in you becoming stronger and faster. In order to keep moving forward, a field test should be conducted about every 8 weeks in order to see if changes are needed to the training zones, as shown in Figure 12.8.

With each field test, we set a performance goal. During the base periods we set a goal of a 1–2% increase in power and pace based on the goals and intensity of the meso cycle. Base meso cycles are more aerobic in nature. When you increase the aerobic foundation, you will see increases in your power and pace. However, those changes will not occur as quickly as they would during a build or peak meso cycle. During the build meso cycles, we want to target 3–5% increases in power and pace. We did not set a performance goal for the peak meso cycle because the results would not be seen until race day. Step 2 is arguably the longest step in the entire process. Once you complete this process, you are ready to start planning your micro cycles.

Step 3 is where you start putting your ATP into action. Each micro cycle should have a goal that feeds into each meso cycle goal, and each mesocycle goal feeds into the overarching. In Geir's case, the main goal was to win IRONMAN Tallinn. Once you lay out the goal of the micro cycle, you can begin planning the key workouts for the week. Goal setting helps to pick and create workouts that address your strengths and limitations. As shown in Figure 12.9, Monday was set as active recovery, with Friday as a lighter day. The recovery was planned like this to help Geir be more fresh for key workouts on Tuesday,

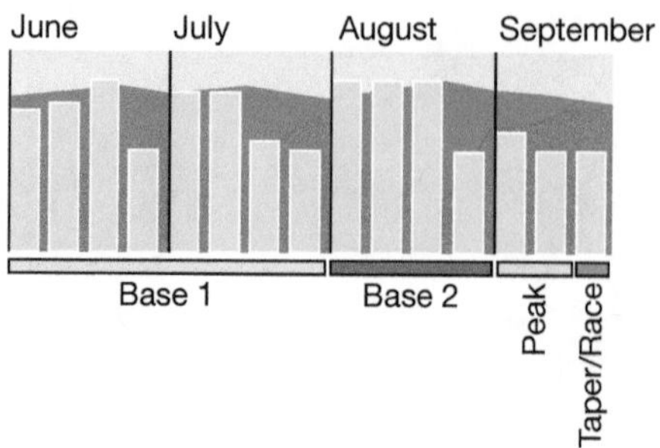

Event	Microcycle	Planned TSS	Focus - Swim	Focus - Bike	Focus - Run	Strength
	Build 1	1000	Endurance, Speed Skill	Muscular Endurance, Force	Endurance, Speed Skill	Maintenance
	Build 2	1090	Endurance, Speed Skill	Muscular Endurance, Force	Endurance, Speed Skill	Maintenance
Local HIM Distance Race	Build 3	1100	Open Water Drills, Race Pace	Race Pace	Race Pace	Maintenance
	Recovery and Test Week	500	Test	Test	None	N/A

FIGURE 12.8 Key goals and planned field test at the end of the build 1 meso cycle.

Wednesday, and Saturday. These days addressed Geir's limitations of swim speed and endurance and bike power and endurance.

Moving to step 4, you need to go back and address your planned field tests. In the sport of triathlon, you can test many, many different aspects. Field testing could be an entire mesocycle in itself! You need to be choosy on what you test. You may need to test every sport during every planned testing period. However, be cautious of this. The tests you plan should follow what the data is telling you and what training goal you trained. For example, you may not need to a run threshold test if you performed a swim-specific training block. In Figure 12.8, we only tested bike and swim: the two modalities that received specific attention during the meso cycle. We did not see any indication that the training intensity needed to be changed.

Finally, remember, the ATP is a living document. It may change several times during your training progression. You may have a life event that takes priority, or you may need to reevaluate your goals based on how you are progressing in your training. The ATP is a guide; it is not set in stone. Let the data guide you. It will provide you insights on how your training is progressing and where you need to focus your training. And, most of all, have fun!

MONDAY	TUESDAY	WEDNESDAY	THURSDAY	FRIDAY	SATURDAY	SUNDAY
Recovery - Swim **0:45:00** **1640 yds** **35 TSS** WU: 200m Free easy, 100m drill (2/3 catch up) MS1: 2x250m at low ENDURANCE (1:20-1:27 min/mi) ...	**Pre-swim Warm up - Shoulder Mobility Routine #1** **5x400 Middle Distance Mix** **0:50:00** **3062 yds** **40 TSS** Warm Up: 1. 200 free at Active Recovery (>1:35 min/100) 2. 200 kick with board and fins - focu...	**Pre-swim Warm up - Shoulder Mobility Routine #2** **10 x 100s - Pace Focus** **0:49:35** **2017 yds** **39 TSS** Warm Up: 400 free, 200 kick Set 1: 10 x 100s Swim with 40 sec. rest @ 1:10 min/100yd pace ... P: I want you to try to keep a consistent endurance pace for each 100m (within 1 sec). If you pac...	**Track Day!!!** **SST 2 x 12** **1:30:00** **97 TSS** WU: 10 minutes with effort at Endurance (180-220W). ------- MS: Sweet Spot Training. Perform 2...	**Pre-swim Warm up - Shoulder Mobility Routine #1** **Endurance 3000 (4 x 250 pulls, 4x500)** **0:55:00** **4156 yds** **50 TSS** WU: 200 free, 200 kick with fins, 100 drill (Shark fin) ------------- MS: 1.4 x 250 pulls at...	**ENDURANCE Day (3:00) WU 10' CD 15'** **3:00:00** **162 TSS** WU: 10 minutes working at Endurance (180-230W) with 2 x 1-minute Fast Pedals to wake up your legs ...	**11 Mile Endurance Run - LSD** **2:42:30** **12.5 mi** **138 TSS** WU: Perform 5 mins of dynamic warm up: 1. Leg swings - 10-20 per leg 2. Marches - 10-15 per leg ...
Recovery - Jog 40 Min **0:40:00** **15 TSS** WU: Jog for 15 min at ACTIVE RECOVERY (>7:15 min/mi), then Perform the following dynamic stretches ...	**12 KM Run at LSD** **1:46:33** **8.91 mi** **107 TSS** WU: Perform 5 mins of dynamic warm up: 1. Leg swings - 10-20 per leg 2. Marches - 10-15 per leg ...	**Recovery spin - 30 min** **1:00:00** **20 TSS** WU: 10 minutes working into ACTIVE RECOVERY (<190W) with 2 x 1 minute Fast Pedals to wake up legs ...	**4 x 50s - Float Drills, 6x75s Low Pulls, & 6-Switch** **0:50:00** **1550 yds** **50 TSS** Warm Up: 5x25s free, 3x50 kick with kick board Set 1: Floats with kicks. 4 x 50s with 15s re... P: When swimming, do not forget to slow down your swim stroke and stretch your arm out during the ex...	**20 Minute run with 4x10s Pickups** **0:30:00** **25 TSS** WU: Perform 5 mins of dynamic warm up: 1. Leg swings - 10-20 per leg 2. Marches - 10-15 per leg ...	**Power Cycle Workout 2** WARM-UP • 5 Minute cardio exercise (treadmill, stationary bike, trainer, fast walking ...) ----- ...	**ENDURANCE Day (1:00) WU 15' CD 10'** **1:00:00** **36 TSS** WU: 15 minutes working at Endurance (190-220W) with 2 x 1-minute Fast Pedals to wake up your legs ... P: Coach note. Stay low Z2. The objective is to spin out the legs.
Foam Rolling **0:15:00** Perform foam rolling on hamstrings, it band, quads, hips, adductors, and abductors.	**VO2 Max/Z5 4x3min/4 min** **1:40:00** **101 TSS** WU: 15 minutes with effort working into Endurance (<180W). 2-3 accelerations to open up the legs ...	**Recovery - Jog 40 min** **0:40:00** **15 TSS** WU: Jog for 15 min at ACTIVE RECOVERY (>7:15 pace), then Perform the following dynamic stretches ...	**Speed - 400/200** **1:03:59** **5.79 mi** **74 TSS** WU: 15 min warm-up with 6 strides MS: Perform 6 times 400m at 5K pace (5:30 min/mi) with 2 ...	**Core and Hip Routine - Pilates Style** **0:25:00** **10 TSS** WU: Jog for 10 min building from Active Recovery (<7:15 min/mi) building to Endurance (7-7:15 min ...		
		Power Cycle Workout 1 WARM-UP • 5 Minute cardio exercise (treadmill, stationary bike, trainer, fast walking ...) -----				

FIGURE 12.9 Micro cycle 2 of build 1 meso cycle.

Conclusion

There are many ways to create a training plan to aid an athlete in achieving their athletic goals. However, using fundamental tenets of a periodized approach and individualization requires the athletes and coach to create realistic, achievable, and tangible goals. The training program must have periodic field testing to ensure the proper physiological adaptations are occurring. A peak of fitness is the ultimate goal of every periodization plan and ensures that the athlete will peak on time, and with the highest level of fitness they can achieve in the given training time. A peak is fleeting as well, and sometimes only lasts for 2–3 weeks, so timing of the peak is crucial to plan out and depends largely on the athlete doing the needed hard training. Plans are critical, but only when you do the hard work and push yourself farther than you have pushed before will you achieve great things. Following the essential elements in this chapter will help you utilize the power information in the earlier chapters of this book to create a power training program dialed explicitly to your athletic needs.

References

1. Allen, H., Coggan, A., & McGregor S. (2019). *Training and racing with a power meter* (3rd ed.). VeloPress.
2. Batalha, N. M., Raimundo, A. M., Tomas-Carus, P., Barbosa, T. M., & Silva, A. J. (2013). Shoulder rotator cuff balance, strength, and endurance in young swimmers during a competitive season. *Journal of Strength and Conditioning Research*, *27*, 2562–2568. https://doi.org/10.1519/JSC.0b013e31827fd849
3. Bixler, B., Pease, D., & Fairhurst, F. (2007). The accuracy of computational fluid dynamics analysis of the passive drag of a male swimmer. *Sport Biomechanics*, *6*, 81–98. https://doi.org/10.1080/14763140601058581
4. Bixler, B., & Riewald, S. (2002). Analysis of a swimmer's hand and arm in steady flow conditions using computational fluid dynamics. *Journal of Biomechanics*, *35*, 713–717. https://doi.org/10.1016/S0021-9290(01)00246-9
5. Bompa, T., & Buzzichelli, C. (2018). *Periodization: Theory and methodology of training* (6th ed.). Human Kinetics.
6. Egermann, M., Brocai, D., Lill, C. A., & Schmitt, H. (2003). Analysis of injuries in long-distance triathletes. *International Journal of Sports Medicine*, *24*, 271–276, 2003. https://doi.org/10.1055/s-2003-39498.
7. Fonda, B. (2015). Redefining the definition of bike fitting.
8. Fredericson, M., & Moore, T. (2005). Muscular balance, core stability, and injury prevention for middle- and long-distance runners. *Phys. Med. Rehabil. Clin. N. Am.*
9. Haff, G., & Triplett, N. T. (2014). *Essentials of strength training and conditioning.*
10. Jobson, S. A., Hopker, J., Arkesteijn, M., & Passfield, L. (2013). Inter- and intra-session reliability of muscle activity patterns during cycling. *Journal of Electromyography and Kinesiology*, *23*, 230–237. https://doi.org/10.1016/j.jelekin.2012.08.013

11. Myers, C., Maken, K., Peaks, C. G., Alford, K., & Colvin, L. (2013). *The calculation of torque generated by a swimmer's arm during the free-style swim stroke*. University of Louisiana at Monroe.
12. Newsome, P. S., & Young, A. (2012). *Swim smooth: The complete coaching programme for swimmers and triathletes*. Wiley.
13. Pandelo, D. R., & Myers, C. M. (2020). Decision making in triathlon races with analytical hierarchy process assistance. *Arch Rheum Arthritis Res*, *1*, 1–5.
14. Sands, W. A., Wurth, J. J., & Hewit, J. K. B*asics of strength and conditioning manual*. National Strength and Conditioning Asscociation.
15. Schorn, D., Vogler, T., Gosheger, G., Schneider, K., Klingebiel, S., Rickert, C., Andreou, D., & Liem, D. (2018). Risk factors for acute injuries and overuse syndromes of the shoulder in amateur triathletes: A retrospective analysis. *PLOS One*, *13*, 1–10. https://doi.org/10.1371/journal.pone.0198168
16. Spiker, A. M., Dixit, S., & Cosgarea, A. J. (2012). *Triathlon: Running Injuries*, *20*, 206–213.
17. Wilk, B. R., Fisher, K. L., & Gutierrez, W. (2000). Defective running shoes as a contributing factor in plantar fasciitis in a triathlete. *Journal of Orthopedic Sports and Physical Therapy*, *30*, 21–31. https://doi.org/10.2519/jospt.2000.30.1.21

Image Credits

Fig. 12.1: Source: https://www.ironman.com/im-tallinn-course. Copyright © by World Triathlon Corporation.

Fig. 12.2: Source: https://www.ironman.com/im-tallinn-course. Copyright © by World Triathlon Corporation.

Fig. 12.3: Source: https://www.ironman.com/im-tallinn-course. Copyright © by World Triathlon Corporation.

Fig. 12.4: Source: https://www.ironman.com/im-tallinn-course. Copyright © by World Triathlon Corporation.

Fig. 12.5: Source: https://www.slideshare.net/coach_sanders/chap15-copy.

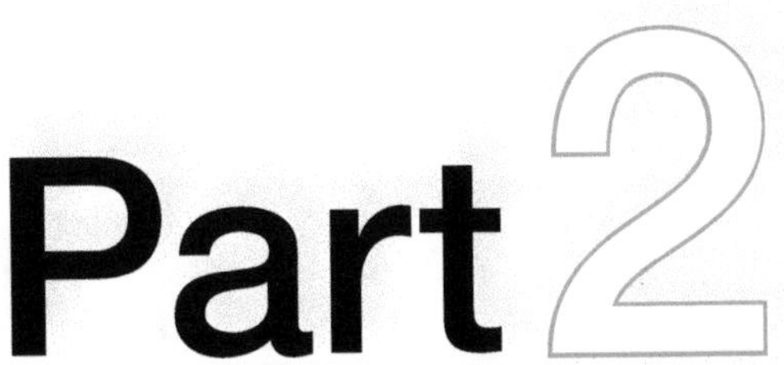

Part 2

Training Plans

Plan 1

Power Based Short Course Triathlon Training Plan

For this plan, please reference the following Test Interpretation Notes on p. 493 of this book:

- CSS Interpretation Notes (p. 493)
- Critical Run Speed/rFTP Test Calculations (p. 493)

WEEK #1

Training Focus: Base #1 - Week #1 - Test Week

MONDAY

PLANNED METRICS	
DURATION	01:00:00
DISTANCE	Various
TSS	38

PRE-TEST

WU: 15 Minutes in the Endurance zone (Power Z2, HR Z2, RPE 2–3). Get in 2 or 3 fast pedals of about 1 minute each.

MS: Your Pre-Test workout is about opening up the legs and keeping the lactate-processing plant sharp. As part of the Main Set do 3 × 90 seconds "Hard Efforts" at Zone 5/ VO2MAX (Power Z5, HR Z5 RPE 6–7), rest for 5 minutes at Active Recovery (Power Z1, HR Z1, RPE <2) between efforts. Focus on tomorrow's FTP test during the efforts, breath deep and pedal smooth.

CD: 15 minutes easy pedaling in Active Recovery (Power Z1, HR Z1, RPE <2)

TUESDAY

PLANNED METRICS		
DURATION	01:30:00	**WU**: 10–20 minutes working into Endurance Zone (Power Z2, HR Z2, RPE 2–3) with 3 × 1-minute fast pedals to wake up legs. ------- **MS1**: 5-Minute Hard Effort. This 5-minute effort should be done at maximum. Start the effort at a high pace, but not so hard that you cannot finish strong. Really hammer out the last 45 seconds. The goal is to generate a max 5-minute VO2 Max test while really opening up the legs for the test and really dispense the initial freshness to help produce more accurate power in the 20-minute test. Once complete, spin easily for 15 minutes of recovery, working back into Endurance Zone (Power Z2, HR Z2, RPE 2–3), and then go on to MS2. ------- **MS2**: 20-Minute Time Trial. Try to do this on a road that is fairly flat and allows you to put out strong, steady power for the entire 20-minute effort. Don't start too hard! You can do this on a steady climb or into a headwind to help produce steady power throughout the 20-minute effort. Once complete, spin easy for 10 minutes in Endurance Zone (Power Z2, HR Z2, RPE 2–3). Your FTP is the power average for the 20-minute effort minus 3–5%. ------- **CD**: 10–15 minutes of easy spinning.
DISTANCE	Various	
TSS	80	
THRESHOLD PLAN – FTP 20 MINUTE/ VO2 MAX TEST		

WEDNESDAY

PLANNED METRICS		
DURATION	00:30:00	**WU**: 200 swim, 100 kick, 100 drill (3/4 catch up drill) **MS**: 2 × 250 easy pace. Do not focus on speed or time. Work on form. Focus on full extension and follow through with your stroke. **CD**: 100 easy
DISTANCE	1000 m	
TSS	20	
RECOVERY - SWIM		

THURSDAY

PLANNED METRICS		
DURATION	00:45:00	
DISTANCE	1300 m	
TSS	40	
CRITICAL SWIM SPEED SWIM TEST #1		**WU**: 200 m at an easy pace **Pull**: 200 m pull (100 m follow through drill/ 100 m finger tip drill) **Kick**: 100 m with fins **MS1**: 1 × 400 m timed. This is a 400 m time-trial. Swim as hard as you can but do not start so hard as you fade in the last meters. You want your pace to be as even as possible during the entire 400 m. If possible, have someone count your strokes during a length near the 200 m point of the test (you can also find this information if you are using a smart watch such as the Garmin Swim or 920XT). Once finished, recover for 5–10 min. You can get out of the pool or slowly swim. The point is to recover but stay loose. **MS2**: 1 × 200 m time trial. Swim as hard as you can. Ensure your 200 m time is faster than 1/2 of your 400 m time. **CD**: 200 m easy

FRIDAY

PLANNED METRICS		
DURATION		
DISTANCE		
TSS		
REST DAY		Actively focus on recovery today: 1) avoid unneccessary physical exertion, 2) watch nutrition closely (healthy carbs, lean protein, and good fats), 3) stretch, and 4) drink when thirsty. Other common recovery aids include massage, napping, elevating legs, floating in water, and listening to music.

SATURDAY

PLANNED METRICS		
DURATION	00:35:00	
DISTANCE	4 mi	
TSS	35	
CRITICAL RUN SPEED TEST - 5 KM RFTP TEST		**WU**: Perform 5 mins of dynamic warm up: 1. Leg swings - 10–20 per leg 2. Marches - 10–15 per leg 3. Leg side swings - 10–20 per leg Build WU pace from ACTIVE RECOVERY (Power Z1, HR Z1, RPE 1) to ENDURANCE (Power Z2, HR Z2, RPE 2–3) for 10 min. Then perform 4 × 10s strides. **MS1**: Run 5 km at maximal pace. Do not go out too fast as to slow down over the course of the interval. **CD**: Jog for 10 at ACTIVE RECOVERY (Power Z1, HR Z1, RPE 1)

SUNDAY

PLANNED METRICS		
DURATION	00:30:00	**WU**: 200 m at an easy pace **Pull**: 200 m pull (100 m follow through drill/ 100 m finger tip drill) **Kick**: 100 m with fins **MS1**: Perform 1 × 1000 m time trial. Just like you performed with the 400 m time trial, do not start so hard that you fade in the final meters. Ensure you swim as hard and even as possible during the entire time trial. At about the 500 m point, if possible, have someone count your stroke rate (you can use a smartwatch to capture this information such as a Garmin Swim or Garmin 920XT). **CD**: 200 m easy
DISTANCE	1700 m	
TSS	30	
CRITICAL SWIM SPEED TEST #2		

WEEK #2

Training Focus: Base #1 - Week #2

MONDAY (AM)

PLANNED METRICS		
DURATION		Actively focus on recovery today: 1) avoid unneccessary physical exertion, 2) watch nutrition closely (healthy carbs, lean protein, and good fats), 3) stretch, and 4) drink when thirsty. Other common recovery aids include massage, napping, elevating legs, floating in water, and listening to music.
DISTANCE		
TSS		
REST DAY		

TUESDAY (AM)

PLANNED METRICS		
DURATION	01:15:00	**WU**: 15 minutes working into Endurance (Power Z2, HR Z2, RPE 2–3) with 3 × 1-minute fast pedals to wake up legs. ------- **MS**: Start out with a 15-minute effort with watts at Endurance (Power Z2, HR Z2, RPE 2–3), smooth and steady. Then pick up the intensity and complete 1 × 30-minute Tempo (Power Z3, HR Z3, RPE 3–4). Do 10 bursts within this half hour to watts at FTP (Power Z4, HR Z4, RPE 4–5) for 20 seconds each. Space the bursts at least 2 minutes apart. ------- **CD**: 10–15 minutes with watts at Active Recovery (Power Z1, HR Z1, RPE <2)
DISTANCE	Various	
TSS	65	
ENDURANCE 1 × 15 & TEMPO 1 × 30 W/ BURSTS 10 × :20 (1:15)		

WEDNESDAY (AM)

PLANNED METRICS		
DURATION	00:40:00	**WU**: 1. 200 swim at Active Recovery (Power Z1, HR Z1, Pace Z1, RPE 1) 2. 200 kick with fins and board - focus on kicking with the ankles and hips 3. 200 drill (Tarzan Drill)
DISTANCE	1850 m	
TSS	45	
		MS1: 5 × 50 Free with 15 sec. rest Odds are fast (not sprint), evens are moderate **MS2**: 2 × 400 Swim at Endurance (Power Z2, HR Z2, Pace Z2, RPE 2–3) with 20 sec. rest
10 × 50 × & 4 × 400 BUILDS		**CD**: 200 at Active Recovery (Power Z1, HR Z1, Pace Z1, RPE 1)

WEDNESDAY (PM)

PLANNED METRICS		Strength Protocol - Week 2
DURATION	00:45:00	**Goal**: Endurance / Adaptation
DISTANCE	N/A	**Intensity**: 60% of 1 RM
TSS	25	**Exercises**:
STRENGTH WORK - WEEK 2		**Strength**: 1. Bench Press (3 × 20) 2. Lateral Pull Down (3 × 20) 3. Seated Row (3 × 20) 4. Tricep Pulldown (3 × 20) 5. Bicep Curl (3 × 20) 6. Leg Press (3 × 30) 7. Leg Extension (3 × 20) 8. Leg Curl (3 × 20) 9. Calf Raises (3 × 20) 10. Back Extension (3 × 20) 11. Ab Curl (3 × 20) 12. Leg Tucked Rotation (3 × 20)

THURSDAY (AM)

PLANNED METRICS		
DURATION	00:30:00	**WU**: Perform 5 mins of dynamic warm up: 1. Leg swings - 10–20 per leg 2. Marches - 10–15 per leg 3. Leg side swings - 10–20 per leg
DISTANCE	3.6 mi	
TSS	35	Build WU pace from ACTIVE RECOVERY (Power Z1, HR Z1, Pace Z1, RPE 1) to ENDURANCE (Power Z2, HR Z2, Pace Z2, RPE 2–3) for 10 min. Then perform 4 × 10s strides. **MS**: Run 5 km at your ENDURANCE (Power Z2, HR Z2, Pace Z2, RPE 2–3) pace.
5 KM RUN		**CD**: Jog 10 min

FRIDAY (AM)

PLANNED METRICS		
DURATION	00:51:00	**WU**: 1. 300 free at Active Recovery (Power Z1, HR Z1, Pace Z1, RPE 1)
DISTANCE	2100	2. 200 kick with fins (100 back, 50 breast, 50 dolphin)
TSS	45	3. 100 free at Endurance (Power Z2, HR Z2, Pace Z2, RPE 2–3)
		MS1: 2 × 250 Pull with paddles with 30 sec. rest **MS2**: 4 × 200 Free with 20 sec. rest #1: 150 at Endurance (Power Z2, HR Z2, Pace Z2, RPE 2–3), 50 at Tempo (Power Z3, HR Z3, Pace Z3, RPE 3–4) #2: 100 at Endurance (Power Z2, HR Z2, Pace Z2, RPE 2–3), 100 at Tempo (Power Z3, HR Z3, Pace Z3, RPE 3–4) #3: 50 at Endurance (Power Z2, HR Z2, Pace Z2, RPE 2–3), 150 at Tempo (Power Z3, HR Z3, Pace Z3, RPE 3–4) #4: 200 at Tempo (Power Z3, HR Z3, Pace Z3, RPE 3–4)
2 × 250 & 4 × 200S		**CD**: 200 at Active Recovery (Power Z1, HR Z1, Pace Z1, RPE 1)

SATURDAY (AM)

PLANNED METRICS		
DURATION	02:30:00	
DISTANCE	Various	
TSS	133	
ENDURANCE DAY (2:30)		**WU**: 10 minutes working at Endurance (Power Z2, HR Z2, RPE 2–3) with 2 × 1-minute Fast Pedals to wake up your legs. ------- **MS**: Today is simple, ride the prescribed time your Endurance Zone (Power Z2, HR Z2, RPE 2–3). Vary your cadence throughout ride and work on pedaling form. Practice "coming over the top" and "pulling through the bottom" of the pedal (pretend there is glass in shoes). Enjoy the day!! Terrain: Flat to Rolling; Cadence: 85–105. -------- **CD**: 10 minutes of easy pedaling.

SATURDAY (PM)

PLANNED METRICS		
DURATION	00:45:00	
DISTANCE	N/A	
TSS	25	
STRENGTH WORK - WEEK 2		Strength Protocol - Week 2 **Goal**: Endurance / Adaptation **Intensity**: 60% of 1 RM **Exercises**: **Strength**: 1. Bench Press (3 × 20) 2. Lateral Pull Down (3 × 20) 3. Seated Row (3 × 20) 4. Tricep Pulldown (3 × 20) 5. Bicep Curl (3 × 20) 6. Leg Press (3 × 30) 7. Leg Extension (3 × 20) 8. Leg Curl (3 × 20) 9. Calf Raises (3 × 20) 10. Back Extension (3 × 20) 11. Ab Curl (3 × 20) 12. Leg Tucked Rotation (3 × 20)

SUNDAY (AM)

PLANNED METRICS		
DURATION	00:40:00	**WU**: 1. 200 m free at Active Recovery (Power Z1, HR Z1, Pace Z1, RPE 1) 2. 200 m kick with fins and board - focus on kicking with the ankles and hips 3. 100 m drill (Shark fin) -------------- **MS**: 1. 1 × 1000 m at ENDURANCE (Pace Z2, HR Z2, RPE 2–3) with 20s rest. 2. 2 × 250 m at ENDURANCE (Pace Z2, HR Z2, RPE 2–3) with 10s rest ---------------- **CD**: 200 m at Active Recovery (Power Z1, HR Z1, Pace Z1, RPE 1)
DISTANCE	2200 m	
TSS	40	
ENDURANCE 1500 - 1 × 1000, 2 × 250		

SUNDAY (PM)

PLANNED METRICS		
DURATION	00:45:00	**WU**: Perform 5 mins of dynamic warm up: 1. Leg swings - 10–20 per leg 2. Marches - 10–15 per leg 3. Leg side swings - 10–20 per leg Build WU pace from ACTIVE RECOVERY (Power Z1, HR Z1, Pace Z1, RPE 1) to ENDURANCE (Power Z2, HR Z2, Pace Z2, RPE 2–3) for 10 min. Then perform 4 × 10s strides. **MS**: Run 4 mi at your low ENDURANCE (Power Z2, HR Z2, Pace Z2, RPE 2–3) or better pace. **CD**: Jog 10 min
DISTANCE	4.5 mi	
TSS	45	
4 MILE LSD RUN		

WEEK #3

Training Focus: Base #1 - Week #3

MONDAY (AM)

PLANNED METRICS		Actively focus on recovery today: 1) avoid unneccessary physical exertion, 2) watch nutrition closely (healthy carbs, lean protein, and good fats), 3) stretch, and 4) drink when thirsty. Other common recovery aids include massage, napping, elevating legs, floating in water, and listening to music.
DURATION		
DISTANCE		
TSS		
REST DAY		

TUESDAY (AM)

PLANNED METRICS		
DURATION	01:00:00	
DISTANCE	Various	
TSS	60	
TRAINER: FORCE		

WU: 10 minutes working into your Endurance (Power Z2, HR Z2, RPE 2–3). Then complete 3 sets of 1 minute fast pedals with 1 minute rest in between to open up your legs.

MS1: Once warmed up, chose a big gear / high resistance (this will depend on your trainer) combination. Use the big chain ring and a gear that allows only about 50–60 rpm. While in the saddle, drive the pedals down as hard as possible for 15 to 20 revolutions of the cranks. Do 6 to 10 sets of these, with about 4 minutes rest in between at Z1 (Power Z1, HR Z1, RPE 1–2). Recover for 10 minutes before starting MS2.

MS2: Using a similar big chain ring / trainer resistance combo as above, complete 5 force intervals in at low FTP Zone (Power Z4, HR Z4, RPE 24–5) at a cadence of 50–60 rpm, with 5 minutes of rest in between. During the 5 minute rest, complete one fast pedal effort between minutes 3 and 4 of the recovery period. This fast pedal effort should be low power with little resistance, just focus on spin speed.

CD: 10 minutes of easy spinning in Active Recovery (Power Z1, HR Z1, RPE <2)

WEDNESDAY (AM)

PLANNED METRICS		
DURATION	00:40:00	**WU**: 1. 200 free at Active Recovery (Power Z1, HR Z1, Pace Z1, RPE 1) 2. 200 kick with fins and board - focus on kicking with the ankles and hips
DISTANCE	2200	
TSS	40	
10 × 50, 3 × 300 PULL		**MS1**: 10 × 50 Swim with 15 sec. rest a. Sets #1–4 at Endurance (Power Z2, HR Z2, Pace Z2, RPE 2–3) b. Set #5 at VO2 Max (Power Z5, HR Z5, Pace Z5, RPE 6–7) c. Sets #6–9 at Endurance (Power Z2, HR Z2, Pace Z2, RPE 2–3) d. Set #10 at VO2 Max (Power Z5, HR Z5, Pace Z5, RPE 6–7) **MS2**: 3 × 300 Pull with paddles at Endurance (Power Z2, HR Z2, Pace Z2, RPE 2–3) with 15 sec. rest **CD**: 200 at Active Recovery (Power Z1, HR Z1, Pace Z1, RPE 1)

WEDNESDAY (PM)

PLANNED METRICS		
DURATION	00:45:00	Strength Protocol - Week 3 **Goal**: Hypertrophy **Intensity**: 70% of 1 RM **Note**: 3d set should be performed until exhaustion.
DISTANCE	N/A	
TSS	25	
STRENGTH WORK - WEEK 3		**Exercises**: **Strength**: 1. Bench Press (3 × 8–12) 2. Lateral Pull Down (3 × 8–12) 3. Seated Row (3 × 8–12) 4. Tricep Pulldown (3 × 8–12) 5. Bicep Curl (3 × 8–12) 6. Leg Press (3 × 8–12) 7. Leg Extension (3 × 8–12) 8. Leg Curl (3 × 8–12) 9. Calf Raises (3 × 8–12) 10. Back Extension (3 × 8–12) 11. Ab Curl (3 × 8–12) 12. Leg Tucked Rotation (3 × 8–12)

THURSDAY (AM)

PLANNED METRICS		
DURATION	00:50:00	**WU**: Perform 5 mins of dynamic warm up: 1. Leg swings - 10–20 per leg 2. Marches - 10–15 per leg 3. Leg side swings - 10–20 per leg
DISTANCE	Various	
TSS	40	Build WU pace from ACTIVE RECOVERY (Power Z1, HR Z1, Pace Z1, RPE 1) to ENDURANCE (Power Z2, HR Z2, Pace Z2, RPE 2–3) for 10 min. Then perform 4 × 10s strides. **MS**: Start main set run at mid ENDURANCE (Power Z2, HR Z2, Pace Z2, RPE 2–3). Once comfortable, complete 3 × 5 min intervals at upper TEMPO (Power Z3, HR Z3, Pace Z3, RPE 3–4). Recover for 5 min ENDURANCE (Power Z2, HR Z2, Pace Z2, RPE 2–3) in between each interval.
3 × 5 TEMPO PACE INTERVALS		**CD**: Jog at ACTIVE RECOVERY (Power Z1, HR Z1, Pace Z1, RPE 1) for 10 min or until HR comes below 100 BPM

FRIDAY (AM)

PLANNED METRICS		
DURATION	00:40:00	**WU**: 1. 300 Free at Active Recovery (Power Z1, HR Z1, Pace Z1, RPE 1) 2. 200 pull with paddles at Endurance (Power Z2, HR Z2, Pace Z2, RPE 2–3) 3. 100 drill (3/4 catch up)
DISTANCE	2200 m	
TSS	40	**MS1**: 4 × 100 Kick with board and fins with 15 sec. rest - focus on kicking with the ankles and hips **MS2**: 4 × 200 Swim with 15 sec. rest a. 1 & 3 are at Tempo (Power Z3, HR Z3, Pace Z3, RPE 3–4) 2 & 4 are at Endurance (Power Z2, HR Z2, Pace Z2, RPE 2–3)
4 × 100 KICK, 4 × 200		**CD**: 200 at Active Recovery (Power Z1, HR Z1, Pace Z1, RPE 1)

SATURDAY (AM)

PLANNED METRICS		
DURATION	01:20:00	**WU**: 10–15 minutes working into Endurance (Power Z2, HR Z2, RPE 2–3), with 3 × 1-minute fast pedals to wake up legs.
DISTANCE	Various	-------
TSS	80	**MS**: Complete 3 × 10-minute intervals at Tempo (Power Z3, HR Z3, RPE 3–4), with 5 minutes of rest and easy spinning between intervals. 10 minutes at Endurance (Power Z2, HR Z2, RPE 2–3). -------
TEMPO 3 × 10/5 (1:25)		**CD**: 15 minutes of easy spinning in Active Recovery (Power Z1, HR Z1, RPE <2).

SATURDAY (PM)

PLANNED METRICS		Core, Balance, and Plyometrics Protocol - Week 3
DURATION	00:45:00	**Goal**: Endurance / Adaptation
DISTANCE	N/A	**Intensity**: 70% of 1 RM
TSS	25	**Exercises**:
CORE, BALANCE, AND PLYOMETRICS - WEEK 3		**CBP 1**: 1. Slow Side Kick (4 × 8–12) 2. Bulgarian Sidekick (4 × 8–12) 3. Knee Balance (4 × 8–12) 4. Ball Row (4 × 8–12) 5. Two Point Pushup (4 × 8–12) 6. Turkish Get Up (4 × 8–12) 7. Split Squat Jumps (4 × 8–12) 8. Lateral Box Push Of (4 × 8–12) 9. Lateral Jumps (4 × 8–12)

SUNDAY (AM)

PLANNED METRICS		
DURATION	00:40:00	**WU**: 1. 200 m free at Active Recovery (Power Z1, HR Z1, Pace Z1, RPE 1) 2. 200 m kick with fins and board - focus on kicking with the ankles and hips 3. 100 m drill (Shark fin) -------------- **MS**: 1. 1 × 1000 m at ENDURANCE (Pace Z2, HR Z2, RPE 2–3) with 20s rest. 2. 2 × 250 m at ENDURANCE (Pace Z2, HR Z2, RPE 2–3) with 10s rest ---------------- **CD**: 200 m at Active Recovery (Power Z1, HR Z1, Pace Z1, RPE 1)
DISTANCE	2200 m	
TSS	40	
ENDURANCE 1500 - 1 × 1000, 2 × 250		

SUNDAY (PM)

PLANNED METRICS		
DURATION	00:45:00	**WU**: Perform 5 mins of dynamic warm up: 1. Leg swings - 10–20 per leg 2. Marches - 10–15 per leg 3. Leg side swings - 10–20 per leg Build WU pace from ACTIVE RECOVERY (Power Z1, HR Z1, Pace Z1, RPE 1) to ENDURANCE (Power Z2, HR Z2, Pace Z2, RPE 2–3) for 10 min. Then perform 4 × 10s strides. **MS**: Run 4 mi at your low ENDURANCE (Power Z2, HR Z2, Pace Z2, RPE 2–3) or better pace. **CD**: Jog 10 min
DISTANCE	4.5 mi	
TSS	45	
4 MILE LSD RUN		

WEEK #4

Training Focus: Recovery Week

MONDAY (AM)

PLANNED METRICS		
DURATION		Actively focus on recovery today: 1) avoid unneccessary physical exertion, 2) watch nutrition closely (healthy carbs, lean protein, and good fats), 3) stretch, and 4) drink when thirsty. Other common recovery aids include massage, napping, elevating legs, floating in water, and listening to music.
DISTANCE		
TSS		
REST DAY		

TUESDAY (AM)

PLANNED METRICS		
DURATION	00:30:00	**WU**: 200 easy, 100 drill (2/3 catch up) **MS**: 2 × 250 moderate. Focus on form **CD**: 200 pull, easy
DISTANCE	1100 m	
TSS	20	
RECOVERY - SWIM		

WEDNESDAY (AM)

PLANNED METRICS		
DURATION	00:45:00	Strength Protocol - Week 4 **Goal**: Hypertrophy **Intensity**: 90% of 1 RM **Note**: Last rep should performed until exhaustion. **Exercises**: **Strength**: 1. Bench Press (6 × 4–6) 2. Lateral Pull Down (6 × 4–6) 3. Seated Row (6 × 4–6) 4. Tricep Pulldown (6 × 4–6) 5. Bicep Curl (6 × 4–6) 6. Leg Press (6 × 4–6) 7. Leg Extension (6 × 4–6) 8. Leg Curl (6 × 4–6) 9. Calf Raises (6 × 4–6) 10. Back Extension (6 × 4–6) 11. Ab Curl (6 × 4–6) 12. Leg Tucked Rotation (6 × 4–6)
DISTANCE	N/A	
TSS	25	
STRENGTH WORK - WEEK 4		

THURSDAY (AM)

PLANNED METRICS		Very easy recovery spin on a mostly flat course in small chain ring. Active Recovery Power Zone (Power Z1, HR Z1, RPE 1–2). Light on the pedals. Comfortably high rpm focusing on pedaling skills.
DURATION	00:45:00	
DISTANCE	Various	
TSS	25	
RECOVERY SPIN - 45		

FRIDAY (AM)

PLANNED METRICS		Actively focus on recovery today: 1) avoid unneccessary physical exertion, 2) watch nutrition closely (healthy carbs, lean protein, and good fats), 3) stretch, and 4) drink when thirsty. Other common recovery aids include massage, napping, elevating legs, floating in water, and listening to music.
DURATION		
DISTANCE		
TSS		
REST DAY		

SATURDAY (AM)

PLANNED METRICS		**WU**: 15 minutes at Z1 (Power Z1, HR Z1, RPE 1–2).
DURATION	02:00:00	**MS**: 90 minutes of riding with watts at Z2 (Power Z2, HR Z2, RPE 2–3), just nice and steady. If you have to go over hills and your watts go higher, that's OK, but generally average between Endurance watts today.
DISTANCE	Various	
TSS	100	
MEDIUM, ENDURANCE RIDE		**CD**: 15 minutes just easy pedaling.

SUNDAY (AM)

PLANNED METRICS		**WU**: Perform 5 mins of dynamic warm up: 1. Leg swings - 10–20 per leg 2. Marches - 10–15 per leg 3. Leg side swings - 10–20 per leg
DURATION	00:45:00	
DISTANCE	4.5 mi	
TSS	40	
		Build WU pace from ACTIVE RECOVERY (Power Z1, HR Z1, Pace Z1, RPE 1) to ENDURANCE (Power Z2, HR Z2, Pace Z2, RPE 2–3) for 10 min. Then perform 4 × 10s strides. **MS**: Run 4 mi at your low ENDURANCE (Power Z2, HR Z2, Pace Z2, RPE 2–3) or better pace.
4 MILE LSD RUN		**CD**: Jog 10 min

WEEK #5

Training Focus: Base #2 - Week #1

MONDAY (AM)

PLANNED METRICS		
DURATION		Actively focus on recovery today: 1) avoid unneccessary physical exertion, 2) watch nutrition closely (healthy carbs, lean protein, and good fats), 3) stretch, and 4) drink when thirsty. Other common recovery aids include massage, napping, elevating legs, floating in water, and listening to music.
DISTANCE		
TSS		
REST DAY		

TUESDAY (BRICK)

PLANNED METRICS		
DURATION	01:17:00	**WU**: To Endurance (Power Z2, HR Z2, Pace Z2, RPE 2–3) for 3 minutes, then do 4 reps of 30 seconds at FTP (Power Z4, HR Z4, Pace Z4, RPE 5–6), 30 seconds easy. Then ride another 3 minutes at Endurance (Power Z2, HR Z2, Pace Z2, RPE 2–3). ---------- **MS1**: First, start in your 53 on the front and your 21 on the rear. Ride 16 minutes at Tempo (Power Z3, HR Z3, Pace Z3, RPE 3–4), shifting down one cog in the back every 2 minutes. Your cadence will decrease - keep the power in the Tempo. You can stand up as needed. Spin at an easy pace for 5 minutes to recover. Next, start in your 53 on the front and your 12 on the rear. Ride 16 minutes at Tempo (Power Z3, HR Z3, Pace Z3, RPE 3–4), shifting up one cog in the back every 2 minutes. Increase your cadence and keep the power in the Tempo. You can stand up as needed. Spin at an easy pace for 5 minutes to recover. **MS2**: Finally, ride for 30 seconds at 100% of FTP (Power Z4, HR Z4, Pace Z4, RPE 5–6) followed by 30 seconds at 60% of FTP (Endurance (Power Z2, HR Z2, Pace Z2, RPE 2–3)). Repeat this combination 10 times, for a total of 10 minutes. You're done! ---------- **CD**: For 5–10 minutes, then go get the mop!
DISTANCE	Various	
TSS	65	
TRAINER: TEMPO GEARAMIDS - 1 HOUR (WITH WO BUILDER)		

TUESDAY (BRICK)

PLANNED METRICS		
DURATION	00:20:00	**WU**:
DISTANCE	4 km	**MS**: Run 3 km at your ENDURANCE (Power Z2, HR Z2, Pace Z2, RPE 2–3) pace. Focus on getting up to pace as quickly as possible.
TSS	20	**CD**: Jog 10 min
3 KM RUN		

WEDNESDAY (AM)

PLANNED METRICS		
DURATION	00:35:00	**WU**: 1. 200 free at Active Recovery (Power Z1, HR Z1, Pace Z1, RPE 1)
DISTANCE	2600	2. 200 kick (100 on back) - focus on kicking with the ankles and hips
TSS	40	3. 200 drill (3/4 catch up)
		MS1: 2 × 300 Pull with paddles at Endurance (Power Z2, HR Z2, Pace Z2, RPE 2–3)with 20 sec. rest
		MS2: Do this four times through: 200 Free with at Tempo (Power Z3, HR Z3, Pace Z3, RPE 3–4) with 25 sec. rest 4 × 25 Alternating Build & Fast by 25 with 10 sec. rest
2 × 300 PULL & 4 × 25S		**CD**: 200 at Active Recovery (Power Z1, HR Z1, Pace Z1, RPE 1)

WEDNESDAY (PM)

PLANNED METRICS		Strength Protocol - Week 5
DURATION	00:45:00	**Goal**: Hypertrophy
DISTANCE	N/A	**Intensity**: 75% of 1 RM
TSS	25	**Note**: 1. 3d set should be performed until exhaustion. 2. Only 3 upper body sets. **Exercises**: **Strength**: 1. Bench Press (3 × 8–12) 2. Lateral Pull Down (3 × 8–12) 3. Seated Row (3 × 8–12) 4. Tricep Pulldown (3 × 8–12) 5. Bicep Curl (3 × 8–12) 6. Leg Press (3 × 8–12) 7. Leg Extension (3 × 8–12) 8. Leg Curl (3 × 8–12) 9. Calf Raises (3 × 8–12) 10. Back Extension (3 × 8–12) 11. Ab Curl (4 × 8–12) 12. Leg Tucked Rotation (4 × 8–12)
STRENGTH WORK - WEEK 5		

THURSDAY (AM)

PLANNED METRICS		**WU**: Perform 5 mins of dynamic warm up: 1. Leg swings - 10–20 per leg 2. Marches - 10–15 per leg 3. Leg side swings - 10–20 per leg
DURATION	01:00:00	
DISTANCE	4 mi	
TSS	45	Build WU pace from ACTIVE RECOVERY (Power Z1, HR Z1, Pace Z1, RPE 1) to ENDURANCE (Power Z2, HR Z2, Pace Z2, RPE 2–3) for 10 min. Then perform 4 × 10s strides. **MS**: 0.5 mile at low Endurance (Power Z2, HR Z2, Pace Z2, RPE 2–3). Then crank it to Tempo (Power Z3, HR Z3, Pace Z3, RPE 3–4) for 2 mi. Then back down to Endurance (Power Z2, HR Z2, Pace Z2, RPE 2–3) for 0.5 mi
ENDURANCE-TEMPO SANDWICH		**CD**: Jog for 10 min at Active Recovery (Power Z1, HR Z1, Pace Z1, RPE 1)

FRIDAY (AM)

PLANNED METRICS		
DURATION	00:50:00	**WU**: 400 free, 200 kick **MS1**: 10 × 100s Swim with 40 sec. rest @ Threshold (Power Z4, Pace Z4, RPE 5–6) min/100 m pace **CD**: 200 Easy
DISTANCE	1800 m	
TSS	45	
10 × 100S - PACE FOCUS		

SATURDAY (AM)

PLANNED METRICS		
DURATION	01:25:00	**WU**: 15 Minutes working into ENDURANCE (Power Z2, HR Z2, RPE 2–3) with 2 × 1 minute Fast Pedals to wake up legs ------ **MS**: SST Intervals. On trainer, out on road or in a group, SST intervals are part of our continued effort to build and maintain base. Complete 2 × 15 Minute Intervals at SST (Sweet Spot) (Power Z3.5, Heart Rate Z3.5, RPE 4) with 5 minutes recovery in-between. Ride all other time at ENDURANCE (Power Z2, HR Z2, RPE 2–3). **Terrain**: Flat to Rolling; Cadence: 85–105. ------ **CD**: 10 Minutes at ACTIVE RECOVERY (Power Z1, HR Z1, RPE <2)
DISTANCE	Various	
TSS	90	
ENDURANCE & SST 2 × 15		

SUNDAY (AM)

PLANNED METRICS		
DURATION	00:45:00	**WU**: Perform 5 mins of dynamic warm up: 1. Leg swings - 10–20 per leg 2. Marches - 10–15 per leg 3. Leg side swings - 10–20 per leg Build WU pace from ACTIVE RECOVERY (Power Z1, HR Z1, Pace Z1, RPE 1) to ENDURANCE (Power Z2, HR Z2, Pace Z2, RPE 2–3) for 10 min. Then perform 4 × 10s strides. **MS**: Run 6 km at your low ENDURANCE (Power Z2, HR Z2, Pace Z2, RPE 2–3) pace. **CD**: Jog 10 min
DISTANCE	7 km	
TSS	45	
6 KM LSD RUN		

SUNDAY (PM)

PLANNED METRICS		
DURATION	00:40:00	**WU**: 1. 200 m free at Active Recovery (Power Z1, HR Z1, Pace Z1, RPE 1) 2. 200 m kick with fins and board - focus on kicking with the ankles and hips 3. 100 m drill (Shark fin) -------------- **MS**: 1. 1 × 1000 m at ENDURANCE (Pace Z2, HR Z2, RPE 2–3) with 20s rest. 2. 2 × 250 m at ENDURANCE (Pace Z2, HR Z2, RPE 2–3) with 10s rest ----------------
DISTANCE	2200	
TSS	40	
ENDURANCE 1500 - 1 × 1000, 2 × 250		**CD**: 200 m at Active Recovery (Power Z1, HR Z1, Pace Z1, RPE 1)

WEEK #6

Training Focus: Base #2 - Week #2

MONDAY (AM)

PLANNED METRICS		
DURATION		Actively focus on recovery today: 1) avoid unneccessary physical exertion, 2) watch nutrition closely (healthy carbs, lean protein, and good fats), 3) stretch, and 4) drink when thirsty. Other common recovery aids include massage, napping, elevating legs, floating in water, and listening to music.
DISTANCE		
TSS		
REST DAY		

TUESDAY (AM)

PLANNED METRICS		
DURATION	01:05:00	**WU**: 20 minutes working into ENDURANCE (Power Z2, HR Z2, RPE 2–3). ---------- **MS**: Then 5 minutes with FAST pedaling – Cadence over 105!!! SPIN those legs. Then 3 minutes easy.
DISTANCE	Various	
TSS	40	
PM TRAINER FAST PEDALS 1 × 5/3, ONE LEG PEDALING 20 × :60 (1:02) WU 20'		Then, do (10) 1 legged pedaling efforts. ONE minute each leg. FOCUS on smoothing out the stroke. NO dead spots. So, 10× on each leg … ---------- **CD**: Ride for at least 15 minutes spinning 90–100 rpm after that to cool down. OK, the legs should feel balanced now.

TUESDAY (PM)

PLANNED METRICS		
DURATION	00:30:00	**WU**: Perform 5 mins of dynamic warm up: 1. Leg swings - 10–20 per leg 2. Marches - 10–15 per leg 3. Leg side swings - 10–20 per leg Build WU pace from ACTIVE RECOVERY (Power Z1, HR Z1, Pace Z1, RPE 1) to ENDURANCE (Power Z2, HR Z2, Pace Z2, RPE 2–3) for 10 min. Then perform 4 × 10s strides. **MS**: Run 3–4 km at your ENDURANCE (Power Z2, HR Z2, Pace Z2, RPE 2–3) pace. **CD**: Jog 10 min
DISTANCE	4.5 km	
TSS	35	
3–4 KM RUN		

WEDNESDAY (AM)

PLANNED METRICS		
DURATION	01:00:00	**WU**: 1. 200 swim at Active Recovery (Power Z1, HR Z1, Pace Z1, RPE 1) 2. 100 kick with fins and board - focus on kicking with the ankles and hips 3. 300 swim at Active Recovery (Power Z1, HR Z1, Pace Z1, RPE 1) **MS**: 1. 4 × 25 w/ :30 rest w/band only - focus on keeping your hips up 2. 4 × 50 swim w/ :20 rest at Tempo (Power Z3, HR Z3, Pace Z3, RPE 3–4) 3. 100 free at Active Recovery (Power Z1, HR Z1, Pace Z1, RPE 1) 4. (do the following sets continuous, no extra rest, all swim freestyle) and at Tempo (Power Z3, HR Z3, Pace Z3, RPE 3–4) 4 × 25 w/ :10 rest 4 × 50 w/ :15 rest 4 × 75 w/ :20 rest 4 × 100 w/ :25 rest 4 × 125 w/ :30 rest **CD**: 200 at Active Recovery (Power Z1, HR Z1, Pace Z1, RPE 1)
DISTANCE	2900	
TSS	55	
CLIMB THE LADDER 4×		

WEDNESDAY (PM)

PLANNED METRICS		Strength Protocol - Week 6
DURATION	00:45:00	**Goal**: Hypertrophy
DISTANCE	N/A	**Intensity**: 75% of 1 RM
TSS	25	**Note**: 1. 3d set should be performed until exhaustion. 2. Only 3 upper body sets.
STRENGTH WORK - WEEK 6		**Exercises**: **Strength**: 1. Bench Press (3 × 8–12) 2. Lateral Pull Down (3 × 8–12) 3. Seated Row (3 × 8–12) 4. Tricep Pulldown (3 × 8–12) 5. Bicep Curl (3 × 8–12) 6. Leg Press (5 × 8–12) 7. Leg Extension (5 × 8–12) 8. Leg Curl (5 × 8–12) 9. Calf Raises (5 × 8–12) 10. Back Extension (3 × 8–12) 11. Ab Curl (5 × 8–12) 12. Leg Tucked Rotation (5 × 8–12)

THURSDAY (AM)

PLANNED METRICS		**WU**:
DURATION	00:45:00	Perform 5 mins of dynamic warm up: 1. Leg swings - 10–20 per leg 2. Marches - 10–15 per leg 3. Leg side swings - 10–20 per leg
DISTANCE	Various	
TSS	35	
20 MIN LOW TEMPO RUN		Build WU pace from ACTIVE RECOVERY (Power Z1, HR Z1, Pace Z1, RPE 1) to ENDURANCE (Power Z2, HR Z2, Pace Z2, RPE 2–3) for 10 min. Then perform 4 × 10s strides. **MS**: Tempo run: 20' Low TEMPO (Power Z3, HR Z3, Pace Z3, RPE 3–4). **CD**: Jog for 10 min ACTIVE RECOVERY (Power Z1, HR Z1, Pace Z1, RPE 1)

FRIDAY (AM)

<table>
<tr><td colspan="2">PLANNED METRICS</td><td rowspan="5">WU:
1. 200 free at Active Recovery (Power Z1, HR Z1, Pace Z1, RPE 1)
2. 200 kick with board and fins
- focus on kicking with the ankles and hips
3. 200 drill (50 × 3/4 catch up, 50 free, repeat)

MS:
3 × 400 Swim with 15 sec. rest
#1–3: Free descending 1 to 3 within Endurance (Power Z2, HR Z2, Pace Z2, RPE 2–3)

CD: 200 free at Active Recovery (Power Z1, HR Z1, Pace Z1, RPE 1)</td></tr>
<tr><td>DURATION</td><td>00:50:00</td></tr>
<tr><td>DISTANCE</td><td>2000</td></tr>
<tr><td>TSS</td><td>40</td></tr>
<tr><td colspan="2">3 × 400 MIDDLE DISTANCE MIX</td></tr>
</table>

SATURDAY (AM)

<table>
<tr><td colspan="2">PLANNED METRICS</td><td rowspan="5">WU: 10 Minutes working into ENDURANCE (Power Z2, HR Z2, RPE 2–3) with 2 × 1 minute Fast Pedals to wake up legs
------
MS: Today is simple, ride prescribed time at ENDURANCE (Power Z2, HR Z2, RPE 2–3). Vary cadence throughout ride and work on pedaling form. Practice “coming over the top” and “pulling through the bottom” of the pedal (pretend there is glass in shoes). Enjoy the day!!

Terrain: Flat to Rolling;

Cadence: 85–105. During the ENDURANCE effort add 20 second BURSTS at FTP (Functional Threshold Power)/ LT (Lactate Threshold) (Power Z4, HR Z4, RPE 4–5) every 5 minutes.

CD: 15 minutes of easy pedaling at ACTIVE RECOVERY (Power Z1, HR Z1, RPE <2)</td></tr>
<tr><td>DURATION</td><td>02:20:00</td></tr>
<tr><td>DISTANCE</td><td>Various</td></tr>
<tr><td>TSS</td><td>130</td></tr>
<tr><td colspan="2">ENDURANCE DAY WITH FTP BURSTS 21 × :20/5</td></tr>
</table>

SATURDAY (PM)

PLANNED METRICS		Core, Balance, and Plyometrics Protocol - Week 6
DURATION	00:45:00	**Goal**: Endurance / Adaptation
DISTANCE	N/A	**Intensity**: 75% of 1 RM
TSS	25	**Note**: 1. Last Rep performed until exhaustion. 2. Only 3 upper body sets.
CORE, BALANCE, AND PLYOMETRICS - WEEK 6		**Exercises**: **CBP 1**: 1. Slow Side Kick (5 × 8–12) 2. Bulgarian Sidekick (5 × 8–12) 3. Knee Balance (5 × 8–12) 4. Ball Row (5 × 8–12) 5. Two Point Pushup (3 × 8–12) 6. Turkish Get Up (5 × 8–12) 7. Split Squat Jumps (5 × 8–12) 8. Lateral Box Push Of (5 × 8–12) 9. Lateral Jumps (5 × 8–12)

SUNDAY (AM)

PLANNED METRICS		**WU**:
DURATION	00:40:00	Perform 5 mins of dynamic warm up: 1. Leg swings - 10–20 per leg
DISTANCE	6.5 km	2. Marches - 10–15 per leg
TSS	45	3. Leg side swings - 10–20 per leg
6 KM RUN WITH TURN OVERS		Build WU pace from ACTIVE RECOVERY (Power Z1, HR Z1, Pace Z1, RPE 1) to ENDURANCE (Power Z2, HR Z2, Pace Z2, RPE 2–3) for 10 min. Then perform 4 × 10s strides. **MS**: Run 6 km at your ENDURANCE (Power Z2, HR Z2, Pace Z2, RPE 2–3) pace. Starting at mile 2, perform 2 × 20s Turn Overs at Threshold (Power Z4, HR Z4, Pace Z4, RPE 5–6) pace with 2 min rest in between. Focus on a quick cadence. Your stride rate should increase by at least 10 steps per minute during these turnovers. **CD**: Jog 10 min

SUNDAY (PM)

PLANNED METRICS		
DURATION	00:40:00	**WU**: 1. 200 m free at Active Recovery (Power Z1, HR Z1, Pace Z1, RPE 1) 2. 200 m kick with fins and board - focus on kicking with the ankles and hips 3. 100 m drill (Shark fin) -------------- **MS**: 1. 2 × 500 m at ENDURANCE (Pace Z2, HR Z2, RPE 2–3) with 20s rest. 2. 2 × 250 m at ENDURANCE (Pace Z2, HR Z2, RPE 2–3) with 10s rest ---------------- **CD**: 200 m at Active Recovery (Power Z1, HR Z1, Pace Z1, RPE 1)
DISTANCE	2200	
TSS	40	
ENDURANCE 1500 - 2 × 500, 2 × 250		

WEEK #7

Training Focus: Base #2 - Week #3

MONDAY (AM)

PLANNED METRICS		
DURATION		Actively focus on recovery today: 1) avoid unneccessary physical exertion, 2) watch nutrition closely (healthy carbs, lean protein, and good fats), 3) stretch, and 4) drink when thirsty. Other common recovery aids include massage, napping, elevating legs, floating in water, and listening to music.
DISTANCE		
TSS		
REST DAY		

TUESDAY (AM)

PLANNED METRICS		
DURATION	01:10:00	**WU**: 10–15 minutes working into Endurance (Power Z2, HR Z2, RPE 2–3), with 3 × 1-minute fast pedals to wake up legs.
DISTANCE	Various	-------
TSS	65	**MS**: Sweet Spot Crisscross 2 × 15-minute intervals. A crisscross interval is an interval in which you vary your efforts to really teach your body to clear lactate. Complete 2 × 15-minute intervals at low Z3 (Power Z3, HR Z3, RPE 3–5), then every 2 minutes pop it up to 100% of FTP (Power Z4, HR Z4, RPE 4–5) for 30 seconds and recover back to 89–92% (nothing below 85%). Rest 5 minutes between intervals. Ride all other times at Endurance (Power Z2, HR Z2, RPE 2–3) pace. Cadence: Self-selected. Terrain: Flat to low grade climbing.

TEMPO CRISS-CROSS 2 × 15		**CD**: 10–15 minutes of easy spinning in Active Recovery (Power Z1, HR Z1, RPE <2).

TUESDAY (PM)

PLANNED METRICS		
DURATION	00:30:00	**WU**: Perform 5 mins of dynamic warm up: 1. Leg swings - 10–20 per leg
DISTANCE	4 km	2. Marches - 10–15 per leg
TSS	40	3. Leg side swings - 10–20 per leg
		Build WU pace from ACTIVE RECOVERY (Power Z1, HR Z1, Pace Z1, RPE 1) to ENDURANCE (Power Z2, HR Z2, Pace Z2, RPE 2–3) for 10 min. Then perform 4 × 10s strides.
		MS: Run 4–5 km at your ENDURANCE (Power Z2, HR Z2, Pace Z2, RPE 2–3) pace.
4–5 KM RUN		**CD**: Jog 10 min

WEDNESDAY (AM)

PLANNED METRICS	
DURATION	01:15:00
DISTANCE	2600
TSS	60

MAYAN PYRAMID (FLAT TOP)

WU:
1. 200 free at Active Recovery (Power Z1, HR Z1, Pace Z1, RPE 1)
2. 200 Kick with fins and board
   - focus on kicking with the ankles and hips

MS: All 10–15s between each set.

All sets at Endurance (Power Z2, HR Z2, Pace Z2, RPE 2–3)

8 × 50
4 × 100
1 × 200
1 × 400
1 × 200
4 × 100
8 × 50

CD: 100 free at Active Recovery (Power Z1, HR Z1, Pace Z1, RPE 1)

WEDNESDAY (PM)

PLANNED METRICS	
DURATION	00:45:00
DISTANCE	N/A
TSS	25

STRENGTH WORK - WEEK 7

Strength Protocol - Week 7

Goal: Hypertrophy

Intensity: 90% of 1 RM

Note:
1. 3d set should be performed until exhaustion.
2. Only 3 upper body sets.

Exercises:

Strength:
1. Bench Press (3 × 4–6)
2. Lateral Pull Down (3 × 4–6)
3. Seated Row (3 × 4–6)
4. Tricep Pulldown (3 × 4–6)
5. Bicep Curl (3 × 4–6)
6. Leg Press (6 × 4–6)
7. Leg Extension (6 × 4–6)
8. Leg Curl (6 × 4–6)
9. Calf Raises (6 × 4–6)
10. Back Extension (3 × 4–6)
11. Ab Curl (3 × 4–6)
12. Leg Tucked Rotation (6 × 4–6)

THURSDAY (AM)

<table>
<tr><th colspan="2">PLANNED METRICS</th><td rowspan="5">**WU**: Jog at Z1 (Pace Z1, Power Z1, HR Z1, RPE 1–2) for 15 min.

MS: Start main set run at Z2 (Pace Z2, Power Z2, HR Z2, RPE 2–3). Once comfortable, complete 3 × 3 min intervals at Z3 (Pace 3, Power Z3, HR Z3, RPE 3–5) with 5 min rest in between each interval at RPE of 3 (slow jog).

CD: Walk for 10 min or until HR comes below 100 BPM</td></tr>
<tr><td>**DURATION**</td><td>00:50:00</td></tr>
<tr><td>**DISTANCE**</td><td>Various</td></tr>
<tr><td>**TSS**</td><td>40</td></tr>
<tr><td colspan="2">**3 × 3 TEMPO PACE INTERVALS**</td></tr>
</table>

FRIDAY (AM)

<table>
<tr><th colspan="2">PLANNED METRICS</th><td rowspan="5">**WU**: 300 at Active Recovery (Power Z1, HR Z1, Pace Z1, RPE 1) building to Endurance (Power Z2, HR Z2, Pace Z2, RPE 2–3)

MS: 2000 at Endurance (Power Z2, HR Z2, Pace Z2, RPE 2–3)

CD: 200 at Active Recovery (Power Z1, HR Z1, Pace Z1, RPE 1)</td></tr>
<tr><td>**DURATION**</td><td>00:45:00</td></tr>
<tr><td>**DISTANCE**</td><td>2500 m</td></tr>
<tr><td>**TSS**</td><td>60</td></tr>
<tr><td colspan="2">**ENDURANCE SWIM 2000 METER**</td></tr>
</table>

SATURDAY (AM)

<table>
<tr><th colspan="2">PLANNED METRICS</th><td rowspan="5">**WU**: 5 minutes working from Active Recovery (Power Z1, HR Z1, RPE <2) training zone into Endurance (Power Z2, HR Z2, RPE 2–3).

MS:
1 × 10 min at 65% of FTP (Power Z2, HR Z2, Pace Z2, RPE 2–3)
1 × 10 min at 72% of FTP (Power Z2, HR Z2, Pace Z2, RPE 2–3)
1 × 10 min at 82% of FTP (Power Z3, HR Z3, Pace Z3, RPE 3–4)
1 × 10 min at 88% of FTP (Power Z3, HR Z3, Pace Z3, RPE 3–4)
1 × 10 min at 82% of FTP (Power Z3, HR Z3, Pace Z3, RPE 3–4)
1 × 10 min at 72% of FTP (Power Z2, HR Z2, Pace Z2, RPE 2–3)
1 × 10 min at 65% of FTP (Power Z2, HR Z2, Pace Z2, RPE 2–3)

CD: 5 minutes of easy pedaling in Active Recovery (Power Z1, HR Z1, RPE <2)</td></tr>
<tr><td>**DURATION**</td><td>01:25:00</td></tr>
<tr><td>**DISTANCE**</td><td>Various</td></tr>
<tr><td>**TSS**</td><td>80</td></tr>
<tr><td colspan="2">**ENDURANCE/TEMPO/ SST PYRAMID**</td></tr>
</table>

SATURDAY (PM)

PLANNED METRICS		Core, Balance, and Plyometrics Protocol - Week 7
DURATION	00:45:00	**Goal**: Endurance / Adaptation
DISTANCE	N/A	**Intensity**: 90% of 1 RM
TSS	25	**Note**: 1. Last Rep performed until exhaustion. 2. Only 3 upper body sets.
CORE, BALANCE, AND PLYOMETRICS - WEEK 7		**Exercises**: **CBP 1**: 1. Slow Side Kick (6 × 4–6) 2. Bulgarian Sidekick (6 × 4–6) 3. Knee Balance (6 × 4–6) 4. Ball Row (6 × 4–6) 5. Two Point Pushup (3 × 4–6) 6. Turkish Get Up (6 × 4–6) 7. Split Squat Jumps (6 × 4–6) 8. Lateral Box Push Of (6 × 4–6) 9. Lateral Jumps (6 × 4–6)

SUNDAY (AM)

PLANNED METRICS		**WU**:
DURATION	00:50:00	Perform 5 mins of dynamic warm up: 1. Leg swings - 10–20 per leg
DISTANCE	7.5 km	2. Marches - 10–15 per leg
TSS	50	3. Leg side swings - 10–20 per leg
7 KM LSD RUN		Build WU pace from ACTIVE RECOVERY (Power Z1, HR Z1, Pace Z1, RPE 1) to ENDURANCE (Power Z2, HR Z2, Pace Z2, RPE 2–3) for 10 min. Then perform 4 × 10s strides. **MS**: Run 7 km at your low ENDURANCE (Power Z2, HR Z2, Pace Z2, RPE 2–3) pace. **CD**: Jog 10 min

SUNDAY (PM)

PLANNED METRICS		
DURATION	00:55:00	**WU**: 1. 200 m free at Active Recovery (Power Z1, HR Z1, Pace Z1, RPE 1) 2. 200 m kick with fins and board - focus on kicking with the ankles and hips 3. 100 m drill (Shark fin) -------------- **MS**: 1. 4 × 500 m at ENDURANCE (Pace Z2, HR Z2, RPE 2–3) with 20s rest. 2. 2 × 250 m at ENDURANCE (Pace Z2, HR Z2, RPE 2–3) with 10s rest ---------------- **CD**: 200 m at Active Recovery (Power Z1, HR Z1, Pace Z1, RPE 1)
DISTANCE	3200	
TSS	55	
ENDURANCE 2500 - 4 × 500, 2 × 250		

WEEK #8

Training Focus: Recovery Week

MONDAY (AM)

PLANNED METRICS		
DURATION		Actively focus on recovery today: 1) avoid unneccessary physical exertion, 2) watch nutrition closely (healthy carbs, lean protein, and good fats), 3) stretch, and 4) drink when thirsty. Other common recovery aids include massage, napping, elevating legs, floating in water, and listening to music.
DISTANCE		
TSS		
REST DAY		

TUESDAY (AM)

PLANNED METRICS		
DURATION	00:30:00	**WU**: 200 easy, 100 drill (2/3 catch up) **MS**: 2 × 250 moderate. Focus on form **CD**: 200 pull, easy
DISTANCE	1100 m	
TSS	20	
RECOVERY - SWIM		

WEDNESDAY (AM)

PLANNED METRICS		Strength Protocol - Week 8
DURATION	00:45:00	**Goal**: Hypertrophy
DISTANCE	N/A	**Intensity**: 95% of 1 RM
TSS	25	**Note**: 1. 3d set should be performed until exhaustion. 2. Only 3 upper body sets. **Exercises**: **Strength**: 1. Bench Press (3 × 4–6) 2. Lateral Pull Down (3 × 4–6) 3. Seated Row (3 × 4–6) 4. Tricep Pulldown (3 × 4–6) 5. Bicep Curl (3 × 4–6) 6. Leg Press (7 × 4–6) 7. Leg Extension (7 × 4–6) 8. Leg Curl (7 × 4–6) 9. Calf Raises (7 × 4–6) 10. Back Extension (3 × 4–6) 11. Ab Curl (3 × 4–6) 12. Leg Tucked Rotation (7 × 4–6)
STRENGTH WORK - WEEK 8		

THURSDAY (AM)

PLANNED METRICS		Very easy recovery spin on a mostly flat course in small chain ring. Active Recovery Power Zone (Power Z1, HR Z1, RPE 1–2). Light on the pedals. Comfortably high rpm focusing on pedaling skills.
DURATION	00:45:00	
DISTANCE	Various	
TSS	25	
RECOVERY SPIN - 45		

FRIDAY (AM)

PLANNED METRICS		Actively focus on recovery today: 1) avoid unneccessary physical exertion, 2) watch nutrition closely (healthy carbs, lean protein, and good fats), 3) stretch, and 4) drink when thirsty. Other common recovery aids include massage, napping, elevating legs, floating in water, and listening to music.
DURATION		
DISTANCE		
TSS		
REST DAY		

SATURDAY (AM)

PLANNED METRICS		WU: 15 minutes at Z1 (Power Z1, HR Z1, RPE 1–2).
DURATION	02:00:00	**MS**: 90 minutes of riding with watts at Z2 (Power Z2, HR Z2, RPE 2–3), just nice and steady. If you have to go over hills and your watts go higher, that's OK, but generally average between Endurance watts today.
DISTANCE	Various	
TSS	100	
MEDIUM, ENDURANCE RIDE		**CD**: 15 minutes just easy pedaling.

SUNDAY (AM)

PLANNED METRICS		**WU**:
DURATION	00:50:00	Perform 5 mins of dynamic warm up: 1. Leg swings - 10–20 per leg 2. Marches - 10–15 per leg 3. Leg side swings - 10–20 per leg
DISTANCE	7.5 km	
TSS	55	
		Build WU pace from ACTIVE RECOVERY (Power Z1, HR Z1, Pace Z1, RPE 1) to ENDURANCE (Power Z2, HR Z2, Pace Z2, RPE 2–3) for 10 min. Then perform 4 × 10s strides.
		MS: Run 7 km at your low-ENDURANCE (Power Z2, HR Z2, Pace Z2, RPE 2–3) pace.
7 KM RUN AT LSD		**CD**: Jog 10 min

WEEK #9

Training Focus: Base #3 - Week #1

MONDAY (AM)

PLANNED METRICS		Actively focus on recovery today: 1) avoid unneccessary physical exertion, 2) watch nutrition closely (healthy carbs, lean protein, and good fats), 3) stretch, and 4) drink when thirsty. Other common recovery aids include massage, napping, elevating legs, floating in water, and listening to music.
DURATION		
DISTANCE		
TSS		
REST DAY		

TUESDAY (BRICK)

PLANNED METRICS	
DURATION	01:15:00
DISTANCE	Various
TSS	65

TRAINER: TEMPO GEARAMIDS

WU: To Endurance (Power Z2, HR Z2, Pace Z2, RPE 2–3) for 3 minutes, then do 4 reps of 30 seconds at FTP (Power Z4, HR Z4, Pace Z4, RPE 5–6), 30 seconds easy. Then ride another 3 minutes at Endurance (Power Z2, HR Z2, Pace Z2, RPE 2–3).

MS1: First, start in your 53 on the front and your 21 on the rear. Ride 16 minutes at Tempo (Power Z3, HR Z3, Pace Z3, RPE 3–4), shifting down one cog in the back every 2 minutes. Your cadence will decrease - keep the power in the Tempo. You can stand up as needed.
Spin at an easy pace for 5 minutes to recover.

Next, start in your 53 on the front and your 12 on the rear. Ride 16 minutes at Tempo (Power Z3, HR Z3, Pace Z3, RPE 3–4), shifting up one cog in the back every 2 minutes. Increase your cadence and keep the power in the Tempo. You can stand up as needed. Spin at an easy pace for 5 minutes to recover.

MS2: Finally, ride for 30 seconds at 100% of FTP (Power Z4, HR Z4, Pace Z4, RPE 5–6) followed by 30 seconds at 60% of FTP (Endurance (Power Z2, HR Z2, Pace Z2, RPE 2–3)). Repeat this combination 10 times, for a total of 10 minutes.

You're done!

CD: For 5–10 minutes, then go get the mop!

TUESDAY (BRICK)

PLANNED METRICS	
DURATION	00:30:00
DISTANCE	5 km
TSS	35

5 KM RUN

WU: Long ride

MS: Run 5 km at your ENDURANCE (Power Z2, HR Z2, Pace Z2, RPE 2–3) pace.

CD: Jog 10 min

WEDNESDAY (AM)

PLANNED METRICS		WU:
DURATION	00:45:00	1. 300 free at Active Recovery (Power Z1, HR Z1, Pace Z1, RPE 1) building to Endurance (Power Z2, HR Z2, Pace Z2, RPE 2–3) 2. 200 kick (100 back, 50 breast, 50 dolphin) with fins 3. 100 free at Endurance (Power Z2, HR Z2, Pace Z2, RPE 2–3) with fins
DISTANCE	2400	
TSS	40	
4 × 400 PYRAMIDS		**MS1**: 4 × 400 Free with 20 sec. rest #1: 300 at Endurance (Power Z2, HR Z2, Pace Z2, RPE 2–3), 100 at Tempo (Power Z3, HR Z3, Pace Z3, RPE 3–4) #2: 200 at Endurance (Power Z2, HR Z2, Pace Z2, RPE 2–3), 200 at Tempo (Power Z3, HR Z3, Pace Z3, RPE 3–4) #3: 100 at Endurance (Power Z2, HR Z2, Pace Z2, RPE 2–3), 300 at Tempo (Power Z3, HR Z3, Pace Z3, RPE 3–4) #4: 400 at Tempo (Power Z3, HR Z3, Pace Z3, RPE 3–4) **CD**: 200 at Active Recovery (Power Z1, HR Z1, Pace Z1, RPE 1)

WEDNESDAY (PM)

PLANNED METRICS		Strength Protocol - Week 9
DURATION	00:45:00	**Goal**: Hypertrophy
DISTANCE	N/A	**Intensity**: 75% of 1 RM
TSS	25	**Note**: 1. 3d set should be performed until exhaustion. 2. Only 3 upper body sets.
STRENGTH WORK - WEEK 9		**Exercises**: **Strength**: 1. Bench Press (3 × 8–12) 2. Lateral Pull Down (3 × 8–12) 3. Seated Row (3 × 8–12) 4. Tricep Pulldown (3 × 8–12) 5. Bicep Curl (3 × 8–12) 6. Leg Press (5 × 8–12) 7. Leg Extension (5 × 8–12) 8. Leg Curl (5 × 8–12) 9. Calf Raises (5 × 8–12) 10. Back Extension (3 × 8–12) 11. Ab Curl (3 × 8–12) 12. Leg Tucked Rotation (5 × 8–12)

THURSDAY (AM)

PLANNED METRICS		
DURATION	01:10:00	**WU**: Perform 5 mins of dynamic warm up: 1. Leg swings - 10–20 per leg 2. Marches - 10–15 per leg 3. Leg side swings - 10–20 per leg Build WU pace from ACTIVE RECOVERY (Power Z1, HR Z1, Pace Z1, RPE 1) to ENDURANCE (Power Z2, HR Z2, Pace Z2, RPE 2–3) for 10 min. Then perform 4 × 10s strides. ---------- **MS**: Run 10–5–3–2–1 minutes at 5 K pace (THRESH-OLD (Power Z4, HR Z4, Pace Z4, RPE 4–5) and jog equal amounts between each segment. ---------- **CD**: 10 minute cool down at (ACTIVE RECOVERY (Power Z1, HR Z1, Pace Z1, RPE 1)
DISTANCE	Various	
TSS	65	
FARTLEK RUN		

FRIDAY (AM)

PLANNED METRICS		
DURATION	00:50:00	**WU**: 400 free, 200 kick **MS**: 10 × 100s Swim with 40 sec. rest @ Threshold (Power Z4, Pace Z4, RPE 5–6) min/100 m pace **CD**: 200 Easy
DISTANCE	1800 m	
TSS	45	
10 × 100S - PACE FOCUS		

SATURDAY (AM)

PLANNED METRICS		
DURATION	01:45:00	**WU**: 10–15 minutes working into Endurance (Power Z2, HR Z2, RPE 2–3), with 3 × 1-minute fast pedals to wake up legs. ------- **MS**: Complete 3 × 10-minute intervals at Tempo (Power Z3, HR Z3, RPE 3–4), with 5 minutes of rest and easy spinning between intervals. 10 minutes at Endurance (Power Z2, HR Z2, RPE 2–3). ------- **CD**: 15 minutes of easy spinning in Active Recovery (Power Z1, HR Z1, RPE <2).
DISTANCE	Various	
TSS	100	
TEMPO 3 × 10/15		

SATURDAY (PM)

PLANNED METRICS		Core, Balance, and Plyometrics Protocol - Week 8
DURATION	00:45:00	**Goal**: Endurance/Adaptation
DISTANCE	N/A	**Intensity**: 95% of 1 RM
TSS	25	**Note**: 1. Last Rep performed until exhaustion. 2. Only 3 upper body sets.
CORE, BALANCE, AND PLYOMETRICS - WEEK 8		**Exercises**: **CBP 1**: 1. Slow Side Kick (7 × 4–6) 2. Bulgarian Sidekick (7 × 4–6) 3. Knee Balance (7 × 4–6) 4. Ball Row (7 × 4–6) 5. Two Point Pushup (3 × 4–6) 6. Turkish Get Up (3 × 4–6) 7. Split Squat Jumps (7 × 4–6) 8. Lateral Box Push Of (7 × 4–6) 9. Lateral Jumps (7 × 4–6)

SUNDAY (AM)

PLANNED METRICS		**WU**:
DURATION	00:50:00	Perform 5 mins of dynamic warm up: 1. Leg swings - 10–20 per leg
DISTANCE	7.5 km	2. Marches - 10–15 per leg
TSS	55	3. Leg side swings - 10–20 per leg
7 KM RUN AT LSD		Build WU pace from ACTIVE RECOVERY (Power Z1, HR Z1, Pace Z1, RPE 1) to ENDURANCE (Power Z2, HR Z2, Pace Z2, RPE 2–3) for 10 min. Then perform 4 × 10s strides. **MS**: Run 7 km at your low-ENDURANCE (Power Z2, HR Z2, Pace Z2, RPE 2–3) pace. **CD**: Jog 10 min

SUNDAY (PM)

PLANNED METRICS		
DURATION	01:00:00	**WU**: 300 at Active Recovery (Power Z1, HR Z1, Pace Z1, RPE 1) building to Endurance (Power Z2, HR Z2, Pace Z2, RPE 2–3) ------------- **MS**: 1500 at Endurance (Power Z2, HR Z2, Pace Z2, RPE 2–3) ------------- **CD**: 200 at Active Recovery (Power Z1, HR Z1, Pace Z1, RPE 1)
DISTANCE	2000 m	
TSS	60	
ENDURANCE SWIM 1500 METER		

WEEK #10

Training Focus: Base #3 - Week #2

MONDAY (AM)

PLANNED METRICS		
DURATION		Actively focus on recovery today: 1) avoid unneccessary physical exertion, 2) watch nutrition closely (healthy carbs, lean protein, and good fats), 3) stretch, and 4) drink when thirsty. Other common recovery aids include massage, napping, elevating legs, floating in water, and listening to music.
DISTANCE		
TSS		
REST DAY		

TUESDAY (BRICK)

PLANNED METRICS		
DURATION	01:15:00	**WU**: 10 minutes with effort at Endurance (Power Z2, HR Z2, RPE 2–3). ------- **MS**: Sweet Spot Training. Perform 2 × 12-minute efforts in your Sweet Spot (Power Z3.5, HR Z3.5, RPE 3–5) with 10 minutes of easy pedaling between efforts. ------- **CD**: 5–10 minutes with effort at Active Recovery (Power Z1, HR Z1, RPE <2)
DISTANCE	Various	
TSS	75	
SST 2 × 12		

TUESDAY (BRICK)

PLANNED METRICS		
DURATION	00:30:00	**WU**: Long ride **MS**: Run 5 km at your ENDURANCE (Power Z2, HR Z2, Pace Z2, RPE 2–3) pace. **CD**: Jog 10 min
DISTANCE	5 km	
TSS	35	
5 KM RUN		

WEDNESDAY (AM)

PLANNED METRICS		
DURATION	00:45:00	**WU**: 200 free, 200 kick (back), 200 pull with paddles **MS1**: 8 × 125 Free with 15 sec. rest **MS2**: 3 × 300 Swim with 15 sec. rest Build each 300 **CD**: 200 Easy **Total Workout**: 2,700
DISTANCE	2700	
TSS	40	
8 × 125 & 3 × 300 BUILD		

WEDNESDAY (PM)

PLANNED METRICS		
DURATION	00:45:00	Strength Protocol - Week 10 **Goal**: Hypertrophy **Intensity**: 90% of 1 RM **Note**: 1. 3d set should be performed until exhaustion. 2. Only 3 upper body sets. **Exercises**: **Strength**: 1. Bench Press (3 × 4–6) 2. Lateral Pull Down (3 × 4–6) 3. Seated Row (3 × 4–6) 4. Tricep Pulldown (3 × 4–6) 5. Bicep Curl (3 × 4–6) 6. Leg Press (7 × 4–6) 7. Leg Extension (7 × 4–6) 8. Leg Curl (7 × 4–6) 9. Calf Raises (7 × 4–6) 10. Back Extension (3 × 4–6) 11. Ab Curl (3 × 4–6) 12. Leg Tucked Rotation (7 × 4–6)
DISTANCE	N/A	
TSS	25	
STRENGTH WORK - WEEK 10		

THURSDAY (AM)

PLANNED METRICS		
DURATION	00:55:00	**WU**: Jog at Active Recovery (Pace Z1, Power Z1, HR Z1, RPE 1–2) for 10 min. **MS**: Start main set run at Endurance pace (Pace Z2, Power Z2, HR Z2, RPE 2–4). Once comfortable, complete 4 × 5 min intervals at low-mid Tempo (Pace Z3, Power Z3, HR Z3, RPE 4–5) with 10 min rest in between each interval at RPE of 3 (slow jog). **CD**: Walk for 10 min or until HR comes below 100 BPM
DISTANCE	Various	
TSS	50	
4 × 5 RACE PACE INTERVALS		

FRIDAY (AM)

PLANNED METRICS		
DURATION	00:50:00	**WU**: 200 pull with paddles **MS1**: 2 × 100 Kick with 15 sec. rest **MS2**: 3 × 600 Swim with 20 sec. rest #1: Do as 2 × 300 with 15 sec. rest between 300s #2: Pull with paddles #3: Do as 3 × 200 with 15 sec. rest between 200s - last 200 is choice drill **CD**: 200 Easy **Total Workout**: 3,000
DISTANCE	2400 m	
TSS	45	
2 × 100 KICK, 3 × 600		

SATURDAY (AM)

PLANNED METRICS		
DURATION	01:50:00	**WU**: 10 minutes working at Endurance (Power Z2, HR Z2, RPE 2–3) with 2 × 1-minute Fast Pedals to wake up your legs. ------- **MS**: For today's ride find a course with 3 longer hill climbs. Start out in Endurance Zone (Power Z2, HR Z2, RPE 2–3) and with each climb put in a 3 × 5 minute effort in your SST (Power Z3.5, HR Z3.5, RPE 4.5–5). After each effort, ride at low Endurance for at least 5 minutes to recover, then back up to the prescribed endurance zone. **Terrain**: Rolling to Hill Climbs **Cadence**: 85–105 for Endurance / 75–85 during ------- **CD**: 10 minutes of easy spinning.
DISTANCE	Various	
TSS	105	
ENDURANCE & SST 3 × 5		

SATURDAY (PM)

PLANNED METRICS		Core, Balance, and Plyometrics Protocol - Week 9
DURATION	00:45:00	**Goal**: Endurance / Adaptation
DISTANCE	N/A	**Intensity**: 75% of 1 RM
TSS	25	**Note**: 1. Last Rep performed until exhaustion. 2. Only 3 upper body sets.
CORE, BALANCE, AND PLYOMETRICS - WEEK 9		**Exercises**: **CBP 1**: 1. Slow Side Kick (5 × 8–12) 2. Bulgarian Sidekick (5 × 8–12) 3. Knee Balance (5 × 8–12) 4. Ball Row (5 × 8–12) 5. Two Point Pushup (3 × 8–12) 6. Turkish Get Up (3 × 8–12) 7. Split Squat Jumps (5 × 8–12) 8. Lateral Box Push Of (5 × 8–12) 9. Lateral Jumps (5 × 8–12)

SUNDAY (AM)

PLANNED METRICS		**WU**:
DURATION	00:55:00	Perform 5 mins of dynamic warm up: 1. Leg swings - 10–20 per leg
DISTANCE	8.5 km	2. Marches - 10–15 per leg
TSS	55	3. Leg side swings - 10–20 per leg
8 KM RUN AT LSD		Build WU pace from ACTIVE RECOVERY (Power Z1, HR Z1, Pace Z1, RPE 1) to ENDURANCE (Power Z2, HR Z2, Pace Z2, RPE 2–3) for 10 min. Then perform 4 × 10s strides. **MS**: Run 8 km at your low-ENDURANCE (Power Z2, HR Z2, Pace Z2, RPE 2–3) pace. **CD**: Jog 10 min

SUNDAY (PM)

PLANNED METRICS		
DURATION	00:50:00	
DISTANCE	1400 m	
TSS	30	
10 × 50S - FLOAT DRILLS & 6–8 × 75S LOW PULLS		

WU: 5 × 25s free, 3 × 50 kick with kick board

MS1:
Floats with kicks.
10 × 50s with 15s rest in b/w. Start each from the streamline floating position. Focus on keeping the hips and legs up. As your hips start to sink, start kick. As you hips come to the surface and you start to move forward, add in your swim stroke. Complete the rest of the 50 swimming.

MS2: Low buoy pulls.
6–8 × 75s with 20s rest in b/w. Perform low buoy pulls. Do not forget to slow down your swim stroke and stretch your arm out during the extension phase.

CD: 4 × 50s Easy

WEEK #11

Training Focus: Base #3 - Week #3

MONDAY (AM)

PLANNED METRICS	
DURATION	
DISTANCE	
TSS	
REST DAY	

Actively focus on recovery today: 1) avoid unneccessary physical exertion, 2) watch nutrition closely (healthy carbs, lean protein, and good fats), 3) stretch, and 4) drink when thirsty. Other common recovery aids include massage, napping, elevating legs, floating in water, and listening to music.

TUESDAY (BRICK)

PLANNED METRICS		
DURATION	01:00:00	**WU**: 10 minutes working from Active Recovery (Power Z1, HR Z1, RPE <2) training zone into Endurance (Power Z2, HR Z2, RPE 2–3). ---------- **MS1**: High Pedaling Cadence Efforts. Complete 10 one minute ON, one minute OFF intervals. During the ON section, cadence should be 105 rpm. During the OFF section, cadence should be 85 rpm. Do not worry about wattage or heart rate during these efforts. Once complete, ride for 5 minutes easy and then onto MS2: ---------- **MS2**: Complete 2 × 5 minutes at FTP (Power Z4, HR Z4, RPE 4–5). Keep cadence at 100 rpm. These efforts are about improving your cadence at FTP. Rest for 3 minutes between each effort. ---------- Go into the run.
DISTANCE	Various	
TSS	60	
TRAINER: FAST PEDALING EFFORTS		

TUESDAY (BRICK)

PLANNED METRICS		
DURATION	00:40:00	**WU**: Long ride. **MS**: Run 8 km at your ENDURANCE (Power Z2, HR Z2, Pace Z2, RPE 2–3) pace. **CD**: Jog 10 min
DISTANCE	8 km	
TSS	45	
8 KM RUN		

WEDNESDAY (AM)

PLANNED METRICS	
DURATION	00:55:00
DISTANCE	2900
TSS	45

10 × 50 & 4 × 400 Builds
0:55:00
2900
01:44
45
0.79

WU:

1. 200 swim at Active Recovery (Power Z1, HR Z1, Pace Z1, RPE 1)
2. 200 kick with fins and board
   - focus on kicking with the ankles and hips
3. 200 drill (Tarzan Drill)

MS1:
10 × 50 Free with 15 sec. rest
Odds are fast (not sprint), evens are moderate

MS2:
4 × 400 Swim at Endurance (Power Z2, HR Z2, Pace Z2, RPE 2–3) with 20 sec. rest

10 × 50 & 4 × 400 BUILDS

CD: 200 at Active Recovery (Power Z1, HR Z1, Pace Z1, RPE 1)

WEDNESDAY (PM)

PLANNED METRICS		Strength Protocol - Week 11
DURATION	00:45:00	**Goal**: Hypertrophy
DISTANCE	N/A	**Intensity**: 95+% of 1 RM
TSS	25	**Note**: 1. 3d set should be performed until exhaustion. 2. Only 3 upper body sets.
STRENGTH WORK - WEEK 11		**Exercises**: **Strength**: 1. Bench Press (3 × 4–6) 2. Lateral Pull Down (3 × 4–6) 3. Seated Row (3 × 4–6) 4. Tricep Pulldown (3 × 4–6) 5. Bicep Curl (3 × 4–6) 6. Leg Press (8 × 4–6) 7. Leg Extension (8 × 4–6) 8. Leg Curl (8 × 4–6) 9. Calf Raises (7 × 4–6) 10. Back Extension (3 × 4–6) 11. Ab Curl (3 × 4–6) 12. Leg Tucked Rotation (8 × 4–6)

THURSDAY (AM)

PLANNED METRICS		**WU**:
DURATION	01:05:00	Perform 5 mins of dynamic warm up: 1. Leg swings - 10–20 per leg
DISTANCE	Various	2. Marches - 10–15 per leg
TSS	60	3. Leg side swings - 10–20 per leg
40 MIN LOW TEMPO RUN		Build WU pace from ACTIVE RECOVERY (Power Z1, HR Z1, Pace Z1, RPE 1) to ENDURANCE (Power Z2, HR Z2, Pace Z2, RPE 2–3) for 10 min. Then perform 4 × 10s strides. **MS**: Tempo run: 40' Low TEMPO (Power Z3, HR Z3, Pace Z3, RPE 3–4). **CD**: Jog for 10 min ACTIVE RECOVERY (Power Z1, HR Z1, Pace Z1, RPE 1)

FRIDAY (AM)

PLANNED METRICS		
DURATION	00:50:00	**WU**: 400 free, 200 kick **MS**: 10 × 100s Swim with 40 sec. rest @ Threshold (Power Z4, Pace Z4, RPE 5–6) min/100 m pace **CD**: 200 Easy
DISTANCE	1800 m	
TSS	45	
10 × 100S - PACE FOCUS		

SATURDAY (AM)

PLANNED METRICS		
DURATION	02:30:00	**WU**: 15 minutes working from Active Recovery (Power Z1, HR Z1, RPE <2) training zone into Endurance (Power Z2, HR Z2, RPE 2–3) with 2–3 × 1-minute Fast Pedals to wake up your legs. ---------- **MS**: Endurance ride. Set a pace at Endurance (Power Z2, HR Z2, RPE 2–3) and hold this pace for the rest of the ride. Throughout the ride, do 10 × 15-second FTP/Threshold (Power Z4, HR Z4, Pace Z4, RPE 5–6). Make sure cadence stays high. Vary terrain. --------- **CD**: 15 minutes of easy pedaling in Active Recovery (Power Z1, HR Z1, RPE <2)
DISTANCE	Various	
TSS	150	
ENDURANCE WITH FTP BURSTS 7 × :10 & SST 1 × 20		

SATURDAY (PM)

PLANNED METRICS		
DURATION	00:45:00	Core, Balance, and Plyometrics Protocol - Week 10 **Goal**: Endurance/Adaptation **Intensity**: 90% of 1 RM **Note**: 1. Last Rep performed until exhaustion. 2. Only 3 upper body sets. **Exercises**: **CBP 1**: 1. Slow Side Kick (7 × 4–6) 2. Bulgarian Sidekick (7 × 4–6) 3. Knee Balance (7 × 4–6) 4. Ball Row (7 × 4–6) 5. Two Point Pushup (3 × 4–6) 6. Turkish Get Up (3 × 4–6) 7. Split Squat Jumps (7 × 4–6) 8. Lateral Box Push Of (7 × 4–6) 9. Lateral Jumps (7 × 4–6)
DISTANCE	N/A	
TSS	25	
CORE, BALANCE, AND PLYOMETRICS - WEEK 11		

SUNDAY (AM)

PLANNED METRICS		
DURATION	00:55:00	**WU**: Perform 5 mins of dynamic warm up: 1. Leg swings - 10–20 per leg 2. Marches - 10–15 per leg 3. Leg side swings - 10–20 per leg
DISTANCE	8.5 km	
TSS	55	
8 KM RUN AT LSD WITH TURN OVERS		Build WU pace from ACTIVE RECOVERY (Power Z1, HR Z1, Pace Z1, RPE 1) to ENDURANCE (Power Z2, HR Z2, Pace Z2, RPE 2–3) for 10 min. Then perform 4 × 10s strides. **MS**: Run 8 km at your low-ENDURANCE (Power Z2, HR Z2, Pace Z2, RPE 2–3) pace. Starting at km 5, perform 2 × 20s Turn Overs at Threshold (Power Z4, HR Z4, Pace Z4, RPE 5–6) pace with 2 min rest in between. Focus on a quick cadence. Your stride rate should increase by at least 10 steps per minute during these turnovers. **CD**: Jog 10 min

WEEK #12

Training Focus: Recovery Week

MONDAY (AM)

PLANNED METRICS		
DURATION		Actively focus on recovery today: 1) avoid unneccessary physical exertion, 2) watch nutrition closely (healthy carbs, lean protein, and good fats), 3) stretch, and 4) drink when thirsty. Other common recovery aids include massage, napping, elevating legs, floating in water, and listening to music.
DISTANCE		
TSS		
REST DAY		

TUESDAY (AM)

PLANNED METRICS		
DURATION	00:30:00	**WU**: 200 easy, 100 drill (2/3 catch up)
DISTANCE	1100 m	**MS**: 2 × 250 moderate. Focus on form
TSS	20	**CD**: 200 pull, easy
RECOVERY - SWIM		

WEDNESDAY (AM)

PLANNED METRICS		
DURATION	00:45:00	Strength Protocol - Week 8
DISTANCE	N/A	**Goal**: Hypertrophy
TSS	25	**Intensity**: 95% of 1 RM
STRENGTH WORK - WEEK 8		**Note**: 1. 3d set should be performed until exhaustion. 2. Only 3 upper body sets. **Exercises**: **Strength**: 1. Bench Press (3 × 4–6) 2. Lateral Pull Down (3 × 4–6) 3. Seated Row (3 × 4–6) 4. Tricep Pulldown (3 × 4–6) 5. Bicep Curl (3 × 4–6) 6. Leg Press (7 × 4–6) 7. Leg Extension (7 × 4–6) 8. Leg Curl (7 × 4–6) 9. Calf Raises (7 × 4–6) 10. Back Extension (3 × 4–6) 11. Ab Curl (3 × 4–6) 12. Leg Tucked Rotation (7 × 4–6)

THURSDAY (AM)

PLANNED METRICS		
DURATION	00:45:00	Very easy recovery spin on a mostly flat course in small chain ring. Active Recovery Power Zone (Power Z1, HR Z1, RPE 1–2). Light on the pedals. Comfortably high rpm focusing on pedaling skills.
DISTANCE	Various	
TSS	25	
RECOVERY SPIN - 45		

FRIDAY (AM)

PLANNED METRICS		
DURATION		Actively focus on recovery today: 1) avoid unneccessary physical exertion, 2) watch nutrition closely (healthy carbs, lean protein, and good fats), 3) stretch, and 4) drink when thirsty. Other common recovery aids include massage, napping, elevating legs, floating in water, and listening to music.
DISTANCE		
TSS		
REST DAY		

SATURDAY (AM)

PLANNED METRICS		**WU**: 15 minutes at Z1 (Power Z1, HR Z1, RPE 1–2).
DURATION	02:00:00	**MS**: 90 minutes of riding with watts at Z2 (Power Z2, HR Z2, RPE 2–3), just nice and steady. If you have to go over hills and your watts go higher, that's OK, but generally average between Endurance watts today.
DISTANCE	Various	
TSS	100	
MEDIUM, ENDURANCE RIDE		**CD**: 15 minutes just easy pedaling.

SUNDAY (AM)

PLANNED METRICS		**WU**:
DURATION	00:50:00	Perform 5 mins of dynamic warm up: 1. Leg swings - 10–20 per leg 2. Marches - 10–15 per leg 3. Leg side swings - 10–20 per leg
DISTANCE	7.5 km	
TSS	55	
		Build WU pace from ACTIVE RECOVERY (Power Z1, HR Z1, Pace Z1, RPE 1) to ENDURANCE (Power Z2, HR Z2, Pace Z2, RPE 2–3) for 10 min. Then perform 4 × 10s strides. **MS**: Run 7 km at your low-ENDURANCE (Power Z2, HR Z2, Pace Z2, RPE 2–3) pace.
7 KM RUN AT LSD		**CD**: Jog 10 min

WEEK #13

Training Focus: Test Week

MONDAY

PLANNED METRICS		
DURATION	01:00:00	**WU**: 15 Minutes in the Endurance zone (Power Z2, HR Z2, RPE 2–3). Get in 2 or 3 fast pedals of about 1 minute each. ------- **MS**: Your Pre-Test workout is about opening up the legs and keeping the lactate-processing plant sharp. As part of the Main Set do 3 × 90 seconds "Hard Efforts" at Zone 5/ VO2MAX (Power Z5, HR Z5 RPE 6–7), rest for 5 minutes at Active Recovery (Power Z1, HR Z1, RPE <2) between efforts. Focus on tomorrow's FTP test during the efforts, breath deep and pedal smooth. ------- **CD**: 15 minutes easy pedaling in Active Recovery (Power Z1, HR Z1, RPE <2)
DISTANCE	Various	
TSS	38	
PRE-TEST		

TUESDAY

PLANNED METRICS		
DURATION	01:30:00	**WU**: 10–20 minutes working into Endurance Zone (Power Z2, HR Z2, RPE 2–3) with 3 × 1-minute fast pedals to wake up legs. ------- **MS1**: 5-Minute Hard Effort. This 5-minute effort should be done at maximum. Start the effort at a high pace, but not so hard that you cannot finish strong. Really hammer out the last 45 seconds. The goal is to generate a max 5-minute VO2 Max test while really opening up the legs for the test and really dispense the initial freshness to help produce more accurate power in the 20-minute test. Once complete, spin easily for 15 minutes of recovery, working back into Endurance Zone (Power Z2, HR Z2, RPE 2–3), and then go on to MS2. ------- **MS2**: 20-Minute Time Trial. Try to do this on a road that is fairly flat and allows you to put out strong, steady power for the entire 20-minute effort. Don't start too hard! You can do this on a steady climb or into a headwind to help produce steady power throughout the 20-minute effort. Once complete, spin easy for 10 minutes in Endurance Zone (Power Z2, HR Z2, RPE 2–3). Your FTP is the power average for the 20-minute effort minus 3–5%. ------- **CD**: 10–15 minutes of easy spinning.
DISTANCE	Various	
TSS	80	
THRESHOLD PLAN – FTP 20 MINUTE/ VO2 MAX TEST		

WEDNESDAY

PLANNED METRICS		
DURATION	00:30:00	**WU**: 200 swim, 100 kick, 100 drill (3/4 catch up drill)
DISTANCE	1000 m	**MS**: 2 × 250 easy pace. Do not focus on speed or time. Work on form. Focus on full extension and follow through with your stroke.
TSS	20	**CD**: 100 easy
RECOVERY - SWIM		

THURSDAY

PLANNED METRICS		
DURATION	00:45:00	**WU**: 200 m at an easy pace
DISTANCE	1300 m	**Pull**: 200 m pull (100 m follow through drill/ 100 m finger tip drill)
TSS	40	**Kick**: 100 m with fins
		MS1: 1 × 400 m timed. This is a 400 m time-trial. Swim as hard as you can but do not start so hard as you fade in the last meters. You want your pace to be as even as possible during the entire 400 m. If possible, have someone count your strokes during a length near the 200 m point of the test (you can also find this information if you are using a smart watch such as the Garmin Swim or 920XT). Once finished, recover for 5–10 min. You can get out of the pool or slowly swim. The point is to recover but stay loose.
		MS2: 1 × 200 m time trial. Swim as hard as you can. Ensure your 200 m time is faster than 1/2 of your 400 m time.
CRITICAL SWIM SPEED SWIM TEST #1		**CD**: 200 m easy

FRIDAY

PLANNED METRICS		
DURATION		Actively focus on recovery today: 1) avoid unneccessary physical exertion, 2) watch nutrition closely (healthy carbs, lean protein, and good fats), 3) stretch, and 4) drink when thirsty. Other common recovery aids include massage, napping, elevating legs, floating in water, and listening to music.
DISTANCE		
TSS		
REST DAY		

SATURDAY

PLANNED METRICS		
DURATION	00:35:00	**WU**: Perform 5 mins of dynamic warm up: 1. Leg swings - 10–20 per leg 2. Marches - 10–15 per leg 3. Leg side swings - 10–20 per leg
DISTANCE	4 mi	
TSS	35	
CRITICAL RUN SPEED TEST - 5 KM RFTP TEST		Build WU pace from ACTIVE RECOVERY (Power Z1, HR Z1, RPE 1) to ENDURANCE (Power Z2, HR Z2, RPE 2–3) for 10 min. Then perform 4 × 10s strides. **MS**: Run 5 km at maximal pace. Do not go out too fast as to slow down over the course of the interval. **CD**: Jog for 10 at ACTIVE RECOVERY (Power Z1, HR Z1, RPE 1)

SUNDAY

PLANNED METRICS		
DURATION	00:30:00	**WU**: 200 m at an easy pace **Pull**: 200 m pull (100 m follow through drill/ 100 m finger tip drill)
DISTANCE	1700 m	
TSS	30	**Kick**: 100 m with fins
CRITICAL SWIM SPEED TEST #2		**MS**: Perform 1 × 1000 m time trial. Just like you performed with the 400 m time trial, do not start so hard that you fade in the final meters. Ensure you swim as hard and even as possible during the entire time trial. At about the 500 m point, if possible, have someone count your stroke rate (you can use a smartwatch to capture this information such as a Garmin Swim or Garmin 920XT). **CD**: 200 m easy

Plan 2

Power Based Long Course Triathlon Training Plan

For this plan, please reference the following Test Interpretation Notes on p. 493 of this book:

- CSS Interpretation Notes (p. 493)
- Critical Run Speed/rFTP Test Calculations (p. 493)

WEEK #1

Training Focus: Base #1 - Week #1 - Test Week

MONDAY

PLANNED METRICS		
DURATION	01:00:00	**WU**: 15 Minutes in the Endurance zone (Power Z2, HR Z2, RPE 2–3). Get in 2 or 3 fast pedals of about 1 minute each. ------- **MS**: Your Pre-Test workout is about opening up the legs and keeping the lactate-processing plant sharp. As part of the Main Set do 3 × 90 seconds "Hard Efforts" at Zone 5/VO2MAX (Power Z5, HR Z5 RPE 6–7), rest for 5 minutes at Active Recovery (Power Z1, HR Z1, RPE <2) between efforts. Focus on tomorrow's FTP test during the efforts, breath deep and pedal smooth. ------- **CD**: 15 minutes easy pedaling in Active Recovery (Power Z1, HR Z1, RPE <2)
DISTANCE	Various	
TSS	38	
PRE-TEST		

TUESDAY

PLANNED METRICS		
DURATION	01:30:00	**WU**: 10–20 minutes working into Endurance Zone (Power Z2, HR Z2, RPE 2–3) with 3 × 1-minute fast pedals to wake up legs. ------- **MS1**: 5-Minute Hard Effort. This 5-minute effort should be done at maximum. Start the effort at a high pace, but not so hard that you cannot finish strong. Really hammer out the last 45 seconds. The goal is to generate a max 5-minute VO2 Max test while really opening up the legs for the test and really dispense the initial freshness to help produce more accurate power in the 20-minute test. Once complete, spin easily for 15 minutes of recovery, working back into Endurance Zone (Power Z2, HR Z2, RPE 2–3), and then go on to MS2. ------- **MS2**: 20-Minute Time Trial. Try to do this on a road that is fairly flat and allows you to put out strong, steady power for the entire 20-minute effort. Don't start too hard! You can do this on a steady climb or into a headwind to help produce steady power throughout the 20-minute effort. Once complete, spin easy for 10 minutes in Endurance Zone (Power Z2, HR Z2, RPE 2–3). Your FTP is the power average for the 20-minute effort minus 3–5%. ------- **CD**: 10–15 minutes of easy spinning.
DISTANCE	Various	
TSS	75	
FTP 20 MINUTE & VO2 MAX TEST		

WEDNESDAY

PLANNED METRICS		
DURATION	00:30:00	**WU**: 200 swim, 100 kick, 100 drill (3/4 catch up drill) **MS**: 2 × 250 easy pace. Do not focus on speed or time. Work on form. Focus on full extension and follow through with your stroke. **CD**: 100 easy
DISTANCE	1000 m	
TSS	20	
RECOVERY - SWIM		

THURSDAY

PLANNED METRICS		
DURATION	00:45:00	**WU**: 200 m at an easy pace **Pull**: 200 m pull (100 m follow through drill/ 100 m finger tip drill) **Kick**: 100 m with fins
DISTANCE	1300 m	
TSS	40	
CRITICAL SWIM SPEED SWIM TEST #1		**MS1**: 1 × 400 m timed. This is a 400 m time-trial. Swim as hard as you can but do not start so hard as you fade in the last meters. You want your pace to be as even as possible during the entire 400 m. If possible, have someone count your strokes during a length near the 200 m point of the test (you can also find this information if you are using a smart watch such as the Garmin Swim or 920XT). Once finished, recover for 5–10 min. You can get out of the pool or slowly swim. The point is to recover but stay loose. **MS2**: 1 × 200 m time trial. Swim as hard as you can. Ensure your 200 m time is faster than 1/2 of your 400 m time. **CD**: 200 m easy

FRIDAY

PLANNED METRICS		
DURATION		Actively focus on recovery today: 1) avoid unneccessary physical exertion, 2) watch nutrition closely (healthy carbs, lean protein, and good fats), 3) stretch, and 4) drink when thirsty. Other common recovery aids include massage, napping, elevating legs, floating in water, and listening to music.
DISTANCE		
TSS		
DAY OFF		

SATURDAY

PLANNED METRICS		
DURATION	00:45:00	**WU**: Perform 5 mins of dynamic warm up: 1. Leg swings - 10–20 per leg 2. Marches - 10–15 per leg 3. Leg side swings - 10–20 per leg
DISTANCE	5.5 km	
TSS	45	
CRITICAL RUN SPEED TEST #1–5 KM RFTP TEST		Build WU pace from ACTIVE RECOVERY (Power Z1, HR Z1, RPE 1) to ENDURANCE (Power Z2, HR Z2, RPE 2–3) for 10 min. Then perform 4 × 10s strides. **MS**: Run 5 km at maximal pace. Do not go out too fast as to slow down over the course of the interval. **CD**: Jog for 10 at ACTIVE RECOVERY (Power Z1, HR Z1, RPE 1)

SUNDAY

PLANNED METRICS		
DURATION	00:30:00	**WU**: 200 m at an easy pace **Pull**: 200 m pull (100 m follow through drill/ 100 m finger tip drill) **Kick**: 100 m with fins
DISTANCE	1700 m	
TSS	30	
CRITICAL SWIM SPEED TEST #2		**MS**: Perform 1 × 1000 m time trial. Just like you performed with the 400 m time trial, do not start so hard that you fade in the final meters. Ensure you swim as hard and even as possible during the entire time trial. At about the 500 m point, if possible, have someone count your stroke rate (you can use a smartwatch to capture this information such as a Garmin Swim or Garmin 920XT). **CD**: 200 m easy

WEEK #2

Training Focus: Base #1 - Week #2

MONDAY (AM)

PLANNED METRICS		
DURATION		Actively focus on recovery today: 1) avoid unneccessary physical exertion, 2) watch nutrition closely (healthy carbs, lean protein, and good fats), 3) stretch, and 4) drink when thirsty. Other common recovery aids include massage, napping, elevating legs, floating in water, and listening to music.
DISTANCE		
TSS		
REST DAY		

TUESDAY (AM)

PLANNED METRICS		
DURATION	01:00:00	**WU**: Perform 5 mins of dynamic warm up: 1. Leg swings - 10–20 per leg 2. Toe Touches - 10–15 per leg 3. Leg tucks - 10–20 per leg
DISTANCE	10.5 km	
TSS	60	
CRITICAL RUN SPEED TEST #2–10 KM TEST		Build WU pace from ACTIVE RECOVERY (Power Z1, HR Z1, RPE 1) to ENDURANCE (Power Z2, HR Z2, RPE 2–3) for 10 min. Then perform 4 × 10s strides. **MS**: Run 10 km at a maximal pace. Do not go out too fast as to slow down over the course of the interval. **CD**: Jog for 10 at ACTIVE RECOVERY (Power Z1, HR Z1, RPE 1)

TUESDAY (PM)

PLANNED METRICS		
DURATION	01:15:00	**WU**: 10 minutes working from Active Recovery (0–99 Watts) training zone into Endurance (100–135 Watts). ---------- **MS1**: Begin in the small ring for 15 minutes. Focus on keeping your cadence in the 100+ rpm range. The continue onto MS2: ---------- **MS2**: Complete 30 minutes in the same gear you were previously riding in but ride in a more normal cadence. During this 30 minutes, add in a burst every 2 minutes and hold it for 8 seconds. During the bursts, go two gears harder. Return back to your previous gear and cadence in between bursts. ---------- **CD**: 10 minutes of easy pedaling in Active Recovery (0–99 Watts)
DISTANCE	Various	
TSS	75	
TRAINER: CADENCE DRILLS		

WEDNESDAY (AM)

PLANNED METRICS		Strength Protocol - Week 2
DURATION	00:45:00	**Goal**: Endurance / Adaptation
DISTANCE	N/A	**Intensity**: 60% of 1 RM
TSS	25	**Exercises**:
STRENGTH WORK - WEEK 2		**Strength**: 1. Bench Press (3 × 20) 2. Lateral Pull Down (3 × 20) 3. Seated Row (3 × 20) 4. Tricep Pulldown (3 × 20) 5. Bicep Curl (3 × 20) 6. Leg Press (3 × 30) 7. Leg Extension (3 × 20) 8. Leg Curl (3 × 20) 9. Calf Raises (3 × 20) 10. Back Extension (3 × 20) 11. Ab Curl (3 × 20) 12. Leg Tucked Rotation (3 × 20)

WEDNESDAY (PM)

PLANNED METRICS		
DURATION	00:40:00	**WU**: 1. 200 swim at Active Recovery (Power Z1, HR Z1, Pace Z1, RPE 1) 2. 200 kick with fins and board - focus on kicking with the ankles and hips 3. 200 drill (Tarzan Drill)
DISTANCE	2900 m	
TSS	40	
		MS1: 10 × 50 Free with 15 sec. rest Odds are fast (not sprint), evens are moderate
		MS2: 4 × 400 Swim at Endurance (Power Z2, HR Z2, Pace Z2, RPE 2–3) with 20 sec. rest
10 × 50 × & 4 × 400 BUILDS		**CD**: 200 at Active Recovery (Power Z1, HR Z1, Pace Z1, RPE 1)

THURSDAY (AM)

PLANNED METRICS		
DURATION	00:35:00	**WU**: Perform 5 mins of dynamic warm up: 1. Leg swings - 10–20 per leg 2. Marches - 10–15 per leg 3. Leg side swings - 10–20 per leg
DISTANCE	5.5 km	
TSS	35	
		Build WU pace from ACTIVE RECOVERY (Power Z1, HR Z1, Pace Z1, RPE 1) to ENDURANCE (Power Z2, HR Z2, Pace Z2, RPE 2–3) for 10 min. Then perform 4 × 10s strides.
		MS: Run 5 km at your ENDURANCE (Power Z2, HR Z2, Pace Z2, RPE 2–3) pace.
5 KM RUN		**CD**: Jog 10 min

THURSDAY (PM)

PLANNED METRICS		
DURATION	01:15:00	**WU**: 15 minutes working into Endurance (Power Z2, HR Z2, RPE 2–3) with 3 × 1-minute fast pedals to wake up legs. ------- **MS**: Start out with a 15-minute effort with watts at Endurance (Power Z2, HR Z2, RPE 2–3), smooth and steady. Then pick up the intensity and complete 1 × 30-minute Tempo (Power Z3, HR Z3, RPE 3–4). Do 10 bursts within this half hour to watts at FTP (Power Z4, HR Z4, RPE 4–5) for 20 seconds each. Space the bursts at least 2 minutes apart. ------- **CD**: 10–15 minutes with watts at Active Recovery (Power Z1, HR Z1, RPE <2)
DISTANCE	Various	
TSS	65	
ENDURANCE 1 × 15 & TEMPO 1 × 30 W/ BURSTS 10 × :20 (1:15)		

FRIDAY (AM)

PLANNED METRICS		
DURATION	01:00:00	**WU**: 1. 300 free at Active Recovery (Power Z1, HR Z1, Pace Z1, RPE 1) 2. 200 kick with fins (100 back, 50 breast, 50 dolphin) 3. 100 free at Endurance (Power Z2, HR Z2, Pace Z2, RPE 2–3) **MS1**: 2 × 250 Pull with paddles with 30 sec. rest **MS2**: 4 × 400 Free with 20 sec. rest #1: 300 at Endurance (Power Z2, HR Z2, Pace Z2, RPE 2–3), 100 at Tempo (Power Z3, HR Z3, Pace Z3, RPE 3–4) #2: 200 at Endurance (Power Z2, HR Z2, Pace Z2, RPE 2–3), 200 at Tempo (Power Z3, HR Z3, Pace Z3, RPE 3–4) #3: 100 at Endurance (Power Z2, HR Z2, Pace Z2, RPE 2–3), 300 at Tempo (Power Z3, HR Z3, Pace Z3, RPE 3–4) #4: 400 at Tempo (Power Z3, HR Z3, Pace Z3, RPE 3–4) **CD**: 200 at Active Recovery (Power Z1, HR Z1, Pace Z1, RPE 1)
DISTANCE	3000	
TSS	65	
2 × 400, 8 × 100, 2 × 400		

SATURDAY (AM)

PLANNED METRICS		
DURATION	02:30:00	**WU**: 10 minutes working at Endurance (Power Z2, HR Z2, RPE 2–3) with 2 × 1-minute Fast Pedals to wake up your legs. ------- **MS**: Today is simple, ride the prescribed time your Endurance Zone (Power Z2, HR Z2, RPE 2–3). Vary your cadence throughout ride and work on pedaling form. Practice "coming over the top" and "pulling through the bottom" of the pedal (pretend there is glass in shoes). Enjoy the day!! Terrain: Flat to Rolling; Cadence: 85–105. -------- **CD**: 10 minutes of easy pedaling.
DISTANCE	Various	
TSS	130	
ENDURANCE DAY		

SATURDAY (PM)

PLANNED METRICS		
DURATION	00:45:00	Strength Protocol - Week 2 **Goal**: Endurance / Adaptation **Intensity**: 60% of 1 RM **Exercises**: **Strength**: 1. Bench Press (3 × 20) 2. Lateral Pull Down (3 × 20) 3. Seated Row (3 × 20) 4. Tricep Pulldown (3 × 20) 5. Bicep Curl (3 × 20) 6. Leg Press (3 × 30) 7. Leg Extension (3 × 20) 8. Leg Curl (3 × 20) 9. Calf Raises (3 × 20) 10. Back Extension (3 × 20) 11. Ab Curl (3 × 20) 12. Leg Tucked Rotation (3 × 20)
DISTANCE	N/A	
TSS	25	
STRENGTH WORK - WEEK 2		

SUNDAY (AM)

PLANNED METRICS		
DURATION	00:40:00	
DISTANCE	2200 m	
TSS	40	
ENDURANCE 1500 - 1 × 1000, 2 × 250		

WU:
1. 200 m free at Active Recovery (Power Z1, HR Z1, Pace Z1, RPE 1)
2. 200 m kick with fins and board
   - focus on kicking with the ankles and hips
3. 100 m drill (Shark fin)

MS:
1. 1 × 1000 m at ENDURANCE (Pace Z2, HR Z2, RPE 2–3) with 20s rest.
2. 2 × 250 m at ENDURANCE (Pace Z2, HR Z2, RPE 2–3) with 10s rest

----

CD: 200 m at Active Recovery (Power Z1, HR Z1, Pace Z1, RPE 1)

SUNDAY (PM)

PLANNED METRICS	
DURATION	00:50:00
DISTANCE	5.5 mi
TSS	60
5 MILE ENDURANCE RUN	

WU:
Perform 5 mins of dynamic warm up:
1. Leg swings - 10–20 per leg
2. Marches - 10–15 per leg
3. Leg side swings - 10–20 per leg

Build WU pace from ACTIVE RECOVERY (Power Z1, HR Z1, Pace Z1, RPE 1) to ENDURANCE (Power Z2, HR Z2, Pace Z2, RPE 2–3) for 10 min. Then perform 4 × 10s strides.

MS: Run 5 mi at your low ENDURANCE (Power Z2, HR Z2, Pace Z2, RPE 2–3) or better pace.

CD: Jog 10 min

WEEK #3

Training Focus: Base #1 - Week #3

MONDAY (AM)

PLANNED METRICS	
DURATION	
DISTANCE	
TSS	
DAY OFF	

Actively focus on recovery today: 1) avoid unneccessary physical exertion, 2) watch nutrition closely (healthy carbs, lean protein, and good fats), 3) stretch, and 4) drink when thirsty. Other common recovery aids include massage, napping, elevating legs, floating in water, and listening to music.

TUESDAY (AM)

PLANNED METRICS		
DURATION	01:00:00	**WU**: 10 minutes working into your Endurance (Power Z2, HR Z2, RPE 2–3). Then complete 3 sets of 1 minute fast pedals with 1 minute rest in between to open up your legs. ------ **MS1**: Once warmed up, chose a big gear / high resistance (this will depend on your trainer) combination. Use the big chain ring and a gear that allows only about 50- 60 rpm. While in the saddle, drive the pedals down as hard as possible for 15 to 20 revolutions of the cranks. Do 6 to 10 sets of these, with about 4 minutes rest in between at Z1 (Power Z1, HR Z1, RPE 1–2). Recover for 10 minutes before starting MS2. ------ **MS2**: Using a similar big chain ring / trainer resistance combo as above, complete 5 force intervals in at low FTP Zone (Power Z4, HR Z4, RPE 24–5) at a cadence of 50–60 rpm, with 5 minutes of rest in between. During the 5 minute rest, complete one fast pedal effort between minutes 3 and 4 of the recovery period. This fast pedal effort should be low power with little resistance, just focus on spin speed. ------- **CD**: 10 minutes of easy spinning in Active Recovery (Power Z1, HR Z1, RPE <2)
DISTANCE	Various	
TSS	60	
TRAINER: FORCE		

TUESDAY (PM)

PLANNED METRICS		
DURATION	00:50:00	**WU**: Perform 5 mins of dynamic warm up: 1. Leg swings - 10–20 per leg 2. Marches - 10–15 per leg 3. Leg side swings - 10–20 per leg Build WU pace from ACTIVE RECOVERY (Power Z1, HR Z1, Pace Z1, RPE 1) to ENDURANCE (Power Z2, HR Z2, Pace Z2, RPE 2–3) for 10 min. Then perform 4 × 10s strides. **MS**: Start main set run at mid ENDURANCE (Power Z2, HR Z2, Pace Z2, RPE 2–3). Once comfortable, complete 3 × 5 min intervals at upper TEMPO (Power Z3, HR Z3, Pace Z3, RPE 3–4). Recover for 5 min ENDURANCE (Power Z2, HR Z2, Pace Z2, RPE 2–3) in between each interval. **CD**: Jog at ACTIVE RECOVERY (Power Z1, HR Z1, Pace Z1, RPE 1) for 10 min or until HR comes below 100 BPM.
DISTANCE	Various	
TSS	40	
3 × 5 TEMPO PACE INTERVALS		

WEDNESDAY (AM)

PLANNED METRICS	
DURATION	00:40:00
DISTANCE	2200 m
TSS	45
10 × 50, 3 × 300 PULL	

WU:
1. 200 free at Active Recovery (Power Z1, HR Z1, Pace Z1, RPE 1)
2. 200 kick with fins and board
   - focus on kicking with the ankles and hips

MS1:
10 × 50 Swim with 15 sec. rest
a. Sets #1–4 at Endurance (Power Z2, HR Z2, Pace Z2, RPE 2–3)
b. Set #5 at VO2 Max (Power Z5, HR Z5, Pace Z5, RPE 6–7)
c. Sets #6–9 at Endurance (Power Z2, HR Z2, Pace Z2, RPE 2–3)
d. Set #10 at VO2 Max (Power Z5, HR Z5, Pace Z5, RPE 6–7)

MS2:
3 × 300 Pull with paddles at Endurance (Power Z2, HR Z2, Pace Z2, RPE 2–3) with 15 sec. rest

CD: 200 at Active Recovery (Power Z1, HR Z1, Pace Z1, RPE 1)

WEDNESDAY (PM)

PLANNED METRICS	
DURATION	00:45:00
DISTANCE	N/A
TSS	25
STRENGTH WORK - WEEK 3	

Strength Protocol - Week 3

Goal: Hypertrophy

Intensity: 70% of 1 RM

Note: 3d set should be performed until exhaustion.

Exercises:

Strength:
1. Bench Press (3 × 8–12)
2. Lateral Pull Down (3 × 8–12)
3. Seated Row (3 × 8–12)
4. Tricep Pulldown (3 × 8–12)
5. Bicep Curl (3 × 8–12)
6. Leg Press (3 × 8–12)
7. Leg Extension (3 × 8–12)
8. Leg Curl (3 × 8–12)
9. Calf Raises (3 × 8–12)
10. Back Extension (3 × 8–12)
11. Ab Curl (3 × 8–12)
12. Leg Tucked Rotation (3 × 8–12)

THURSDAY (AM)

PLANNED METRICS		
DURATION	01:15:00	**WU**: 15 minutes working Endurance (Power Z2, HR Z2, RPE 2–3) with 2 × 1-minute Fast Pedals to wake up your legs.
DISTANCE	Various	-------
TSS	65	**MS**: Ride to a hill of 5–8% grade then do 3 × 90-second Hill Climb Intervals at Z3 (Pace Z3, Power Z3, HR Z3, RPE 4–5). Complete the first 75 seconds of each interval seated, then stand and power the last 15 seconds. Recover for 3 minutes between intervals.

ENDURANCE & Z3 3 × :90 (1:15)		**CD**: 15 minutes of easy spinning.

THURSDAY (PM)

PLANNED METRICS		
		WU:
DURATION	00:30:00	Perform 5 mins of dynamic warm up: 1. Leg swings - 10–20 per leg 2. Marches - 10–15 per leg 3. Leg side swings - 10–20 per leg
DISTANCE	5.5 km	
TSS	40	
		Build WU pace from ACTIVE RECOVERY (Power Z1, HR Z1, Pace Z1, RPE 1) to ENDURANCE (Power Z2, HR Z2, Pace Z2, RPE 2–3) for 10 min. Then perform 4 × 10s strides.
		MS: Run 5 km at your ENDURANCE (Power Z2, HR Z2, Pace Z2, RPE 2–3) pace.
5 KM RUN		**CD**: Jog 10 min

FRIDAY (AM)

PLANNED METRICS		
DURATION	00:40:00	
DISTANCE	2200 m	
TSS	40	
4 × 100 KICK, 4 × 200		

WU:
1. 300 Free at Active Recovery (Power Z1, HR Z1, Pace Z1, RPE 1)
2. 200 pull with paddles at Endurance (Power Z2, HR Z2, Pace Z2, RPE 2–3)
3. 100 drill (3/4 catch up)

MS1:
4 × 100 Kick with board and fins with 15 sec. rest
- focus on kicking with the ankles and hips

MS2:
4 × 200 Swim with 15 sec. rest
a. 1 & 3 are at Tempo (Power Z3, HR Z3, Pace Z3, RPE 3–4)
2 & 4 are at Endurance (Power Z2, HR Z2, Pace Z2, RPE 2–3)

CD: 200 at Active Recovery (Power Z1, HR Z1, Pace Z1, RPE 1)

SATURDAY (AM)

PLANNED METRICS	
DURATION	02:00:00
DISTANCE	Various
TSS	100
MEDIUM, ENDURANCE RIDE	

WU: 10 minutes working at Endurance (Power Z2, HR Z2, RPE 2–3) with 2 × 1-minute Fast Pedals to wake up your legs.

MS: Today is simple, ride the prescribed time your Endurance Zone (Power Z2, HR Z2, RPE 2–3). Vary your cadence throughout ride and work on pedaling form. Practice “coming over the top” and “pulling through the bottom” of the pedal (pretend there is glass in shoes). Enjoy the day!! Terrain: Flat to Rolling; Cadence: 85–105.

CD: 10 minutes of easy pedaling.

SATURDAY (PM)

PLANNED METRICS		Core, Balance, and Plyometrics Protocol - Week 3
DURATION	00:45:00	**Goal**: Endurance / Adaptation
DISTANCE	N/A	**Intensity**: 70% of 1 RM
TSS	25	**Exercises**:
CORE, BALANCE, AND PLYOMETRICS - WEEK 3		**CBP 1**: 1. Slow Side Kick (4 × 8–12) 2. Bulgarian Sidekick (4 × 8–12) 3. Knee Balance (4 × 8–12) 4. Ball Row (4 × 8–12) 5. Two Point Pushup (4 × 8–12) 6. Turkish Get Up (4 × 8–12) 7. Split Squat Jumps (4 × 8–12) 8. Lateral Box Push Of (4 × 8–12) 9. Lateral Jumps (4 × 8–12)

SUNDAY (AM)

PLANNED METRICS		**WU**:
DURATION	00:50:00	Perform 5 mins of dynamic warm up: 1. Leg swings - 10–20 per leg
DISTANCE	5.5 mi	2. Marches - 10–15 per leg
TSS	60	3. Leg side swings - 10–20 per leg
5 MILE ENDURANCE RUN		Build WU pace from ACTIVE RECOVERY (Power Z1, HR Z1, Pace Z1, RPE 1) to ENDURANCE (Power Z2, HR Z2, Pace Z2, RPE 2–3) for 10 min. Then perform 4 × 10s strides. **MS**: Run 5 mi at your low ENDURANCE (Power Z2, HR Z2, Pace Z2, RPE 2–3) or better pace. **CD**: Jog 10 min

SUNDAY (PM)

PLANNED METRICS		
DURATION	00:40:00	**WU**: 1. 200 free at Active Recovery (Power Z1, HR Z1, Pace Z1, RPE 1) 2. 200 kick with fins - focus on kicking with the ankles and hips 3. 100 drill (Shark fin) -------------- **MS**: 1. 4 × 250 pulls at ENDURANCE (Pace Z2, HR Z2, RPE 2–3) with 20s rest. 2. 1 × 500 at ENDURANCE (Pace Z2, HR Z2, RPE 2–3) ---------------- **CD**: 200 at ACTIVE RECOVERY (Pace Z1, HR Z1, RPE 1)
DISTANCE	2300 m	
TSS	45	
ENDURANCE 1500 (4 × 250 PULLS, 1 × 500)		

WEEK #4

Training Focus: Recovery Week

MONDAY

PLANNED METRICS		
DURATION		Actively focus on recovery today: 1) avoid unneccessary physical exertion, 2) watch nutrition closely (healthy carbs, lean protein, and good fats), 3) stretch, and 4) drink when thirsty. Other common recovery aids include massage, napping, elevating legs, floating in water, and listening to music.
DISTANCE		
TSS		
REST DAY		

TUESDAY (AM)

PLANNED METRICS		
DURATION	00:30:00	**WU**: 200 easy, 100 drill (2/3 catch up) **MS**: 2 × 250 moderate. Focus on form **CD**: 200 pull, easy
DISTANCE	1100 m	
TSS	20	
RECOVERY - SWIM		

WEDNESDAY (AM)

PLANNED METRICS	
DURATION	00:45:00
DISTANCE	N/A
TSS	25
STRENGTH WORK - WEEK 4	

Strength Protocol - Week 4

Goal: Hypertrophy

Intensity: 90% of 1 RM

Note: Last rep should performed until exhaustion.

Exercises:

Strength:

1. Bench Press (6 × 4–6)
2. Lateral Pull Down (6 × 4–6)
3. Seated Row (6 × 4–6)
4. Tricep Pulldown (6 × 4–6)
5. Bicep Curl (6 × 4–6)
6. Leg Press (6 × 4–6)
7. Leg Extension (6 × 4–6)
8. Leg Curl (6 × 4–6)
9. Calf Raises (6 × 4–6)
10. Back Extension (6 × 4–6)
11. Ab Curl (6 × 4–6)
12. Leg Tucked Rotation (6 × 4–6)

THURSDAY (AM)

PLANNED METRICS	
DURATION	00:45:00
DISTANCE	Various
TSS	25
RECOVERY SPIN - 45	

Very easy recovery spin on a mostly flat course in small chain ring. Active Recovery Power Zone (Power Z1, HR Z1, RPE 1–2). Light on the pedals. Comfortably high rpm focusing on pedaling skills.

FRIDAY (AM)

PLANNED METRICS	
DURATION	
DISTANCE	
TSS	
REST DAY	

Actively focus on recovery today: 1) avoid unneccessary physical exertion, 2) watch nutrition closely (healthy carbs, lean protein, and good fats), 3) stretch, and 4) drink when thirsty. Other common recovery aids include massage, napping, elevating legs, floating in water, and listening to music.

SATURDAY (AM)

PLANNED METRICS		
DURATION	02:00:00	**WU**: 15 minutes at Z1 (Power Z1, HR Z1, RPE 1–2).
DISTANCE	Various	**MS**: 90 minutes of riding with watts at Z2 (Power Z2, HR Z2, RPE 2–3), just nice and steady. If you have to go over hills and your watts go higher, that's OK, but generally average between Endurance watts today.
TSS	100	
MEDIUM, ENDURANCE RIDE		**CD**: 15 minutes just easy pedaling.

SUNDAY (AM)

PLANNED METRICS		
DURATION	00:50:00	**WU**: Perform 5 mins of dynamic warm up: 1. Leg swings - 10–20 per leg 2. Marches - 10–15 per leg 3. Leg side swings - 10–20 per leg
DISTANCE	10.5 km	Build WU pace from ACTIVE RECOVERY (Power Z1, HR Z1, Pace Z1, RPE 1) to ENDURANCE (Power Z2, HR Z2, Pace Z2, RPE 2–3) for 10 min. Then perform 4 × 10s strides.
TSS	55	**MS**: Run 10 km at your low-ENDURANCE (Power Z2, HR Z2, Pace Z2, RPE 2–3) pace.
10 KM RUN AT LSD		**CD**: Jog 10 min

WEEK #5

Training Focus: Base #2 - Week #1

MONDAY (AM)

PLANNED METRICS		
DURATION		Actively focus on recovery today: 1) avoid unneccessary physical exertion, 2) watch nutrition closely (healthy carbs, lean protein, and good fats), 3) stretch, and 4) drink when thirsty. Other common recovery aids include massage, napping, elevating legs, floating in water, and listening to music.
DISTANCE		
TSS		
DAY OFF		

TUESDAY (AM)

<table>
<tr><td colspan="2">PLANNED METRICS</td><td rowspan="5">WU: To Endurance (Power Z2, HR Z2, Pace Z2, RPE 2–3) for 3 minutes, then do 4 reps of 30 seconds at FTP (Power Z4, HR Z4, Pace Z4, RPE 5–6), 30 seconds easy. Then ride another 3 minutes at Endurance (Power Z2, HR Z2, Pace Z2, RPE 2–3).

MS1: First, start in your 53 on the front and your 21 on the rear. Ride 16 minutes at Tempo (Power Z3, HR Z3, Pace Z3, RPE 3–4), shifting down one cog in the back every 2 minutes. Your cadence will decrease - keep the power in the Tempo. You can stand up as needed.
Spin at an easy pace for 5 minutes to recover.

Next, start in your 53 on the front and your 12 on the rear. Ride 16 minutes at Tempo (Power Z3, HR Z3, Pace Z3, RPE 3–4), shifting up one cog in the back every 2 minutes. Increase your cadence and keep the power in the Tempo. You can stand up as needed. Spin at an easy pace for 5 minutes to recover.

MS2: Finally, ride for 30 seconds at 100% of FTP (Power Z4, HR Z4, Pace Z4, RPE 5–6) followed by 30 seconds at 60% of FTP (Endurance (Power Z2, HR Z2, Pace Z2, RPE 2–3)). Repeat this combination 10 times, for a total of 10 minutes.
You're done!

CD: For 5–10 minutes, then go get the mop!</td></tr>
<tr><td>DURATION</td><td>01:17:00</td></tr>
<tr><td>DISTANCE</td><td>Various</td></tr>
<tr><td>TSS</td><td>65</td></tr>
<tr><td colspan="2">TRAINER: TEMPO GEARAMIDS</td></tr>
</table>

TUESDAY (PM)

PLANNED METRICS		WU:
DURATION	00:45:00	Perform 5 mins of dynamic warm up: 1. Leg swings - 10–20 per leg 2. Marches - 10–15 per leg 3. Leg side swings - 10–20 per leg
DISTANCE	4.5 mi	
TSS	55	
		Build WU pace from ACTIVE RECOVERY (Power Z1, HR Z1, Pace Z1, RPE 1) to ENDURANCE (Power Z2, HR Z2, Pace Z2, RPE 2–3) for 10 min. Then perform 4 × 10s strides. **MS**: 1 mile at low Endurance (Power Z2, HR Z2, Pace Z2, RPE 2–3). Then crank it to Tempo (Power Z3, HR Z3, Pace Z3, RPE 3–4) for 3 mi. Then back down to Endurance (Power Z2, HR Z2, Pace Z2, RPE 2–3) for 1 mi
ENDURANCE-TEMPO SANDWICH		**CD**: Jog for 10 min at Active Recovery (Power Z1, HR Z1, Pace Z1, RPE 1)

WEDNESDAY (AM)

PLANNED METRICS		WU:
DURATION	00:35:00	1. 200 free at Active Recovery (Power Z1, HR Z1, Pace Z1, RPE 1) 2. 200 kick (100 on back) - focus on kicking with the ankles and hips 3. 200 drill (3/4 catch up)
DISTANCE	2600 m	
TSS	40	
		MS1: 2 × 300 Pull with paddles at Endurance (Power Z2, HR Z2, Pace Z2, RPE 2–3)with 20 sec. rest **MS2**: Do this four times through: 200 Free with at Tempo (Power Z3, HR Z3, Pace Z3, RPE 3–4) with 25 sec. rest 4 × 25 Alternating Build & Fast by 25 with 10 sec. rest
2 × 300 PULL & 4 × 25S		**CD**: 200 at Active Recovery (Power Z1, HR Z1, Pace Z1, RPE 1)

WEDNESDAY (PM)

PLANNED METRICS	
DURATION	00:45:00
DISTANCE	N/A
TSS	25

STRENGTH WORK - WEEK 5

Strength Protocol - Week 5

Goal: Hypertrophy

Intensity: 75% of 1 RM

Note:

1. 3d set should be performed until exhaustion.
2. Only 3 upper body sets.

Exercises:

Strength:

1. Bench Press (3 × 8–12)
2. Lateral Pull Down (3 × 8–12)
3. Seated Row (3 × 8–12)
4. Tricep Pulldown (3 × 8–12)
5. Bicep Curl (3 × 8–12)
6. Leg Press (3 × 8–12)
7. Leg Extension (3 × 8–12)
8. Leg Curl (3 × 8–12)
9. Calf Raises (3 × 8–12)
10. Back Extension (3 × 8–12)
11. Ab Curl (4 × 8–12)
12. Leg Tucked Rotation (4 × 8–12)

THURSDAY (AM)

PLANNED METRICS	
DURATION	01:25:00
DISTANCE	Various
TSS	90

ENDURANCE & SST 2 × 15 MIN

WU: 15 Minutes working into ENDURANCE (Power Z2, HR Z2, RPE 2–3) with 2 × 1 minute Fast Pedals to wake up legs

------

MS: SST Intervals. On trainer, out on road or in a group, SST intervals are part of our continued effort to build and maintain base. Complete 2 × 15 Minute Intervals at SST (Sweet Spot) (Power Z3.5, Heart Rate Z3.5, RPE 4) with 5 minutes recovery in-between.
Ride all other time at ENDURANCE (Power Z2, HR Z2, RPE 2–3).
Terrain: Flat to Rolling;
Cadence: 85–105.

CD: 10 Minutes at ACTIVE RECOVERY (Power Z1, HR Z1, RPE <2)

THURSDAY (PM)

PLANNED METRICS		
DURATION	00:40:00	**WU**: Perform 5 mins of dynamic warm up: 1. Leg swings - 10–20 per leg 2. Marches - 10–15 per leg 3. Leg side swings - 10–20 per leg Build WU pace from ACTIVE RECOVERY (Power Z1, HR Z1, Pace Z1, RPE 1) to ENDURANCE (Power Z2, HR Z2, Pace Z2, RPE 2–3) for 10 min. Then perform 4 × 10s strides. **MS**: Run 6 km at your ENDURANCE (Power Z2, HR Z2, Pace Z2, RPE 2–3) pace. **CD**: Jog 10 min
DISTANCE	6.5 km	
TSS	40	
6 KM RUN		

FRIDAY (AM)

PLANNED METRICS		
DURATION	00:50:00	**WU**: 1. 300 free at Active Recovery (Power Z1, HR Z1, Pace Z1, RPE 1) building to Endurance (Power Z2, HR Z2, Pace Z2, RPE 2–3) 2. 300 pull with paddles at Endurance (Power Z2, HR Z2, Pace Z2, RPE 2–3) **MS1**: 8 × 75 Kick with fins and board with 10 sec. rest - focus on kicking with the ankles and hips 8 × 75 Pull with at Endurance (Power Z2, HR Z2, Pace Z2, RPE 2–3) 10 sec. rest **MS2**: 500 Swim at Endurance (Power Z2, HR Z2, Pace Z2, RPE 2–3) with 60 sec. rest **MS3**: 5 × 100 free at Tempo (Power Z3, HR Z3, Pace Z3, RPE 3–4) with 15 sec. rest **CD**: 200 free at Active Recovery (Power Z1, HR Z1, Pace Z1, RPE 1)
DISTANCE	3000	
TSS	65	
16 × 75 KICK AND PULLS & 500		

SATURDAY (AM)

PLANNED METRICS		
DURATION	02:15:00	**WU**: 15 minutes working into Endurance (Power Z2, HR Z2, RPE 2–3), with 3 × 1-minute fast pedals to wake up legs. ------- **MS1**: Race Winning Sweet Spot Intervals are intervals that are the exact replica of how most road races are won from a breakaway. The power profile produced is very specific and is a great interval to work on. Complete 3 × 15-minute intervals at 89–92% of FTP (Power Z3.5, HR Z3.5, RPE 3–5), with 5 minutes of rest and easy spinning between intervals. Start each interval with a sprint out of the saddle, go hard for 30 seconds, and then nail your wattage on your SST Goal. In the last 30 seconds get back out of the saddle and sprint for the finish line! Ride all other times at Endurance (Power Z2, HR Z2, RPE 2–3) pace. Cadence: Self-selected. Terrain: Flat to low grade climbing. ------ **MS2**: Ride at TEMPO (Power Z3, HR Z3, RPE 3–4) for 45 minutes. ------- **CD**: 15 minutes of easy spinning in Active Recovery (Power Z1, HR Z1, RPE <2).
DISTANCE	Various	
TSS	160	
SST 3 × 15 & TEMPO 1 × 45 MIN		

SATURDAY (PM)

PLANNED METRICS		
DURATION	00:45:00	Core, Balance, and Plyometrics Protocol - Week 5 **Goal**: Endurance / Adaptation **Intensity**: 75% of 1 RM **Note**: 1. Last Rep performed until exhaustion. 2. Only 3 upper body sets. **Exercises**: **CBP 1**: 1. Slow Side Kick (4 × 8–12) 2. Bulgarian Sidekick (4 × 8–12) 3. Knee Balance (4 × 8–12) 4. Ball Row (4 × 8–12) 5. Two Point Pushup (3 × 8–12) 6. Turkish Get Up (4 × 8–12) 7. Split Squat Jumps (4 × 8–12) 8. Lateral Box Push Of (4 × 8–12) 9. Lateral Jumps (4 × 8–12)
DISTANCE	N/A	
TSS	25	
CORE, BALANCE, AND PLYOMETRICS - WEEK 5		

SUNDAY (AM)

PLANNED METRICS		WU:
DURATION	00:50:00	Perform 5 mins of dynamic warm up: 1. Leg swings - 10–20 per leg 2. Marches - 10–15 per leg 3. Leg side swings - 10–20 per leg
DISTANCE	10.5 km	
TSS	55	
		Build WU pace from ACTIVE RECOVERY (Power Z1, HR Z1, Pace Z1, RPE 1) to ENDURANCE (Power Z2, HR Z2, Pace Z2, RPE 2–3) for 10 min. Then perform 4 × 10s strides.
		MS: Run 10 km at your low-ENDURANCE (Power Z2, HR Z2, Pace Z2, RPE 2–3) pace.
10 KM RUN AT LSD		**CD**: Jog 10 min

SUNDAY (PM)

PLANNED METRICS		WU:
DURATION	00:40:00	1. 200 m free at Active Recovery (Power Z1, HR Z1, Pace Z1, RPE 1) 2. 200 m kick with fins and board - focus on kicking with the ankles and hips 3. 100 m drill (Shark fin)
DISTANCE	2200 m	
TSS	40	

		MS: 1. 1 × 1000 m at ENDURANCE (Pace Z2, HR Z2, RPE 2–3) with 20s rest. 2. 2 × 250 m at ENDURANCE (Pace Z2, HR Z2, RPE 2–3) with 10s rest ----------------
ENDURANCE 1500 - 1 × 1000, 2 × 250		**CD**: 200 m at Active Recovery (Power Z1, HR Z1, Pace Z1, RPE 1)

WEEK #6

Training Focus: Base #2 - Week #2

MONDAY (AM)

PLANNED METRICS		Actively focus on recovery today: 1) avoid unneccessary physical exertion, 2) watch nutrition closely (healthy carbs, lean protein, and good fats), 3) stretch, and 4) drink when thirsty. Other common recovery aids include massage, napping, elevating legs, floating in water, and listening to music.
DURATION		
DISTANCE		
TSS		
REST DAY		

TUESDAY (AM)

PLANNED METRICS		**WU**: 20 minutes working into ENDURANCE (Power Z2, HR Z2, RPE 2–3). ---------- **MS**: Then 5 minutes with FAST pedaling – Cadence over 105!!! SPIN those legs. Then 3 minutes easy. Then, do (10) 1 legged pedaling efforts. ONE minute each leg. FOCUS on smoothing out the stroke. NO dead spots. So, 10× on each leg … ---------- **CD**: Ride for at least 15 minutes spinning 90–100 rpm after that to cool down. OK, the legs should feel balanced now.
DURATION	01:05:00	
DISTANCE	Various	
TSS	40	
PM TRAINER FAST PEDALS 1 × 5/3, ONE LEG PEDALING 20 × :60		

TUESDAY (PM)

PLANNED METRICS		**WU**: Perform 5 mins of dynamic warm up: 1. Leg swings - 10–20 per leg 2. Marches - 10–15 per leg 3. Leg side swings - 10–20 per leg Build WU pace from ACTIVE RECOVERY (Power Z1, HR Z1, Pace Z1, RPE 1) to ENDURANCE (Power Z2, HR Z2, Pace Z2, RPE 2–3) for 10 min. Then perform 4 × 10s strides. **MS**: Tempo run: 40' Low TEMPO (Power Z3, HR Z3, Pace Z3, RPE 3–4). **CD**: Jog for 10 min ACTIVE RECOVERY (Power Z1, HR Z1, Pace Z1, RPE 1)
DURATION	01:05:00	
DISTANCE	Various	
TSS	60	
40 MIN LOW TEMPO RUN		

WEDNESDAY (AM)

PLANNED METRICS	
DURATION	00:50:00
DISTANCE	2900,
TSS	50

WU:
1. 200 swim at Active Recovery (Power Z1, HR Z1, Pace Z1, RPE 1)
2. 100 kick with fins and board
   - focus on kicking with the ankles and hips
3. 300 swim at Active Recovery (Power Z1, HR Z1, Pace Z1, RPE 1)

MS:
1. 4 × 25 w/ :30 rest w/band only
   - focus on keeping your hips up
2. 4 × 50 swim w/ :20 rest at Tempo (Power Z3, HR Z3, Pace Z3, RPE 3–4)
3. 100 free at Active Recovery (Power Z1, HR Z1, Pace Z1, RPE 1)
4. (do the following sets continuous, no extra rest, all swim freestyle) and at Tempo (Power Z3, HR Z3, Pace Z3, RPE 3–4)

   4 × 25 w/ :10 rest
   4 × 50 w/ :15 rest
   4 × 75 w/ :20 rest
   4 × 100 w/ :25 rest
   4 × 125 w/ :30 rest

CLIMB THE LADDER 4×

CD: 200 at Active Recovery (Power Z1, HR Z1, Pace Z1, RPE 1)

WEDNESDAY (PM)

PLANNED METRICS		Strength Protocol - Week 6
DURATION	00:45:00	**Goal**: Hypertrophy
DISTANCE	N/A	**Intensity**: 75% of 1 RM
TSS	25	**Note**: 1. 3d set should be performed until exhaustion. 2. Only 3 upper body sets.
STRENGTH WORK - WEEK 6		**Exercises**: **Strength**: 1. Bench Press (3 × 8–12) 2. Lateral Pull Down (3 × 8–12) 3. Seated Row (3 × 8–12) 4. Tricep Pulldown (3 × 8–12) 5. Bicep Curl (3 × 8–12) 6. Leg Press (5 × 8–12) 7. Leg Extension (5 × 8–12) 8. Leg Curl (5 × 8–12) 9. Calf Raises (5 × 8–12) 10. Back Extension (3 × 8–12) 11. Ab Curl (5 × 8–12) 12. Leg Tucked Rotation (5 × 8–12)

THURSDAY (AM)

PLANNED METRICS		**WU**: 15 Minutes working into ENDURANCE (Power Z2, HR Z2, RPE 2–3) with 2 × 1 minute Fast Pedals to wake up legs
DURATION	01:25:00	------
DISTANCE	Various	
TSS	90	**MS**: SST Intervals. On trainer, out on road or in a group, SST intervals are part of our continued effort to build and maintain base. Complete 2 × 15 Minute Intervals at SST (Sweet Spot) (Power Z3.5, Heart Rate Z3.5, RPE 4) with 5 minutes recovery in-between. Ride all other time at ENDURANCE (Power Z2, HR Z2, RPE 2–3). **Terrain**: Flat to Rolling; **Cadence**: 85–105. ------
ENDURANCE & SST 2 × 15		**CD**: 10 Minutes at ACTIVE RECOVERY (Power Z1, HR Z1, RPE <2)

THURSDAY (PM)

PLANNED METRICS		WU:
DURATION	00:40:00	Perform 5 mins of dynamic warm up: 1. Leg swings - 10–20 per leg
DISTANCE	6.5 km	2. Marches - 10–15 per leg
TSS	40	3. Leg side swings - 10–20 per leg
		Build WU pace from ACTIVE RECOVERY (Power Z1, HR Z1, Pace Z1, RPE 1) to ENDURANCE (Power Z2, HR Z2, Pace Z2, RPE 2–3) for 10 min. Then perform 4 × 10s strides.
		MS: Run 6 km at your ENDURANCE (Power Z2, HR Z2, Pace Z2, RPE 2–3) pace.
6 KM RUN		**CD**: Jog 10 min

FRIDAY (AM)

PLANNED METRICS		WU:
DURATION	00:50:00	1. 200 free at Active Recovery (Power Z1, HR Z1, Pace Z1, RPE 1)
DISTANCE	2800 m	2. 200 kick with board and fins - focus on kicking with the ankles and hips
TSS	45	3. 200 drill (50 × 3/4 catch up, 50 free, repeat)
		MS: 5 × 400 Swim with 15 sec. rest #1–3: Free descending 1 to 3 within Endurance (Power Z2, HR Z2, Pace Z2, RPE 2–3) #4: 4 × 100 Free on 2 minutes descending 1 to 4 within Endurance (Power Z2, HR Z2, Pace Z2, RPE 2–3) #5: 8 × 50 on one minute
5 × 400 MIDDLE DISTANCE MIX		**CD**: 200 free at Active Recovery (Power Z1, HR Z1, Pace Z1, RPE 1)

SATURDAY (AM)

PLANNED METRICS		
DURATION	02:20:00	**WU**: 10 Minutes working into ENDURANCE (Power Z2, HR Z2, RPE 2–3) with 2 × 1 minute Fast Pedals to wake up legs ------
DISTANCE	Various	
TSS	130	**MS**: Today is simple, ride prescribed time at ENDURANCE (Power Z2, HR Z2, RPE 2–3). Vary cadence throughout ride and work on pedaling form. Practice "coming over the top" and "pulling through the bottom" of the pedal (pretend there is glass in shoes). Enjoy the day!! **Terrain**: Flat to Rolling; **Cadence**: 85–105. During the ENDURANCE effort add 20 second BURSTS at FTP (Functional Threshold Power)/ LT (Lactate Threshold) (Power Z4, HR Z4, RPE 4–5) every 5 minutes. ------
ENDURANCE DAY WITH FTP BURSTS 21 × :20/5		**CD**: 15 minutes of easy pedaling at ACTIVE RECOVERY (Power Z1, HR Z1, RPE <2)

SATURDAY (PM)

PLANNED METRICS		Core, Balance, and Plyometrics Protocol - Week 6
DURATION	00:45:00	**Goal**: Endurance / Adaptation
DISTANCE	N/A	**Intensity**: 75% of 1 RM
TSS	25	**Note**: 1. Last Rep performed until exhaustion. 2. Only 3 upper body sets. **Exercises**: **CBP 1**: 1. Slow Side Kick (5 × 8–12) 2. Bulgarian Sidekick (5 × 8–12) 3. Knee Balance (5 × 8–12) 4. Ball Row (5 × 8–12) 5. Two Point Pushup (3 × 8–12) 6. Turkish Get Up (5 × 8–12)
CORE, BALANCE, AND PLYOMETRICS - WEEK 6		7. Split Squat Jumps (5 × 8–12) 8. Lateral Box Push Of (5 × 8–12) 9. Lateral Jumps (5 × 8–12)

SUNDAY (AM)

PLANNED METRICS		
DURATION	01:00:00	
DISTANCE	6.5 km	
TSS	45	
10 KM RUN WITH TURN OVERS		**WU**: Perform 5 mins of dynamic warm up: 1. Leg swings - 10–20 per leg 2. Marches - 10–15 per leg 3. Leg side swings - 10–20 per leg Build WU pace from ACTIVE RECOVERY (Power Z1, HR Z1, Pace Z1, RPE 1) to ENDURANCE (Power Z2, HR Z2, Pace Z2, RPE 2–3) for 10 min. Then perform 4 × 10s strides. **MS**: Run 10 km at your ENDURANCE (Power Z2, HR Z2, Pace Z2, RPE 2–3) pace. Starting at mile 4, perform 2 × 20s Turn Overs at Threshold (Power Z4, HR Z4, Pace Z4, RPE 5–6) pace with 2 min rest in between. Focus on a quick cadence. Your stride rate should increase by at least 10 steps per minute during these turnovers. **CD**: Jog 10 min

SUNDAY (PM)

PLANNED METRICS		
DURATION	00:40:00	
DISTANCE	2200 m	
TSS	40	
ENDURANCE 1500 - 2 × 500, 2 × 250		**WU**: 1. 200 m free at Active Recovery (Power Z1, HR Z1, Pace Z1, RPE 1) 2. 200 m kick with fins and board - focus on kicking with the ankles and hips 3. 100 m drill (Shark fin) -------------- **MS**: 1. 2 × 500 m at ENDURANCE (Pace Z2, HR Z2, RPE 2–3) with 20s rest. 2. 2 × 250 m at ENDURANCE (Pace Z2, HR Z2, RPE 2–3) with 10s rest ---------------- **CD**: 200 m at Active Recovery (Power Z1, HR Z1, Pace Z1, RPE 1)

WEEK #7

Training Focus: Base #2 - Week #3

MONDAY (AM)

PLANNED METRICS		
DURATION		Actively focus on recovery today: 1) avoid unneccessary physical exertion, 2) watch nutrition closely (healthy carbs, lean protein, and good fats), 3) stretch, and 4) drink when thirsty. Other common recovery aids include massage, napping, elevating legs, floating in water, and listening to music.
DISTANCE		
TSS		
DAY OFF		

TUESDAY (AM)

PLANNED METRICS		
DURATION	01:00:00	**WU**: 10 minutes working from Active Recovery (Power Z1, HR Z1, RPE <2) training zone into Endurance (Power Z2, HR Z2, RPE 2–3). ---------- **MS1**: High Pedaling Cadence Efforts. Complete 10 one minute ON, one minute OFF intervals. During the ON section, cadence should be 105 rpm. During the OFF section, cadence should be 85 rpm. Do not worry about wattage or heart rate during these efforts. Once complete, ride for 5 minutes easy and then onto MS2: ---------- **MS2**: Complete 2 × 5 minutes SST efforts (Power Z3.55, HR Z3.55, RPE 5). Cadence at 100 rpm. Rest for 3 minutes between each effort. ----------
DISTANCE	Various	
TSS	60	
TRAINER: CADENCE DRILLS, SST		**CD**: 15 minutes of easy pedaling in Active Recovery (Power Z1, HR Z1, RPE <2)

TUESDAY (PM)

PLANNED METRICS		
DURATION	00:50:00	**WU**: Jog at Z1 (Pace Z1, Power Z1, HR Z1, RPE 1–2) for 15 min.
DISTANCE	Various	**MS**: Start main set run at Z2 (Pace Z2, Power Z2, HR Z2, RPE 2–3). Once comfortable, complete 3 × 3 min intervals at Z3 (Pace 3, Power Z3, HR Z3, RPE 3–5) with 5 min rest in between each interval at RPE of 3 (slow jog).
TSS	40	
3 × 3 TEMPO PACE INTERVALS		**CD**: Walk for 10 min or until HR comes below 100 BPM.

WEDNESDAY (AM)

PLANNED METRICS	
DURATION	01:15:00
DISTANCE	3400 m
TSS	80

MAYAN PYRAMID (FLAT TOP)

WU:

1. 200 free at Active Recovery (Power Z1, HR Z1, Pace Z1, RPE 1)
2. 200 Kick with fins and board
   - focus on kicking with the ankles and hips

MS: All 10–15s between each set.

All 50s to 200s at Tempo (Power Z3, HR Z3, Pace Z3, RPE 3–4) & 400s at Endurance (Power Z2, HR Z2, Pace Z2, RPE 2–3)

8 × 50
4 × 100
2 × 200
1 × 400
1 × 400
2 × 200
4 × 100
8 × 50

CD: 100 free at Active Recovery (Power Z1, HR Z1, Pace Z1, RPE 1)

WEDNESDAY (PM)

PLANNED METRICS	
DURATION	00:45:00
DISTANCE	N/A
TSS	25

STRENGTH WORK - WEEK 7

Strength Protocol - Week 7

Goal: Hypertrophy

Intensity: 90% of 1 RM

Note:

1. 3d set should be performed until exhaustion.
2. Only 3 upper body sets.

Exercises:

Strength:

1. Bench Press (3 × 4–6)
2. Lateral Pull Down (3 × 4–6)
3. Seated Row (3 × 4–6)
4. Tricep Pulldown (3 × 4–6)
5. Bicep Curl (3 × 4–6)
6. Leg Press (6 × 4–6)
7. Leg Extension (6 × 4–6)
8. Leg Curl (6 × 4–6)
9. Calf Raises (6 × 4–6)
10. Back Extension (3 × 4–6)
11. Ab Curl (3 × 4–6)
12. Leg Tucked Rotation (6 × 4–6)

THURSDAY (AM)

PLANNED METRICS		
DURATION	01:10:00	**WU**: 10–15 minutes working into Endurance (Power Z2, HR Z2, RPE 2–3), with 3 × 1-minute fast pedals to wake up legs. ------- **MS**: Sweet Spot Crisscross 2 × 15-minute intervals. A crisscross interval is an interval in which you vary your efforts to really teach your body to clear lactate. Complete 2 × 15-minute intervals at low Z3 (Power Z3, HR Z3, RPE 3–5), then every 2 minutes pop it up to 100% of FTP (Power Z4, HR Z4, RPE 4–5) for 30 seconds and recover back to 89–92% (nothing below 85%). Rest 5 minutes between intervals. Ride all other times at Endurance (Power Z2, HR Z2, RPE 2–3) pace. Cadence: Self-selected. Terrain: Flat to low grade climbing. ------- **CD**: 10–15 minutes of easy spinning in Active Recovery (Power Z1, HR Z1, RPE <2).
DISTANCE	Various	
TSS	70	
TEMPO CRISS-CROSS 2 × 15		

THURSDAY (PM)

PLANNED METRICS		
DURATION	00:45:00	**WU**: Perform 5 mins of dynamic warm up: 1. Leg swings - 10–20 per leg 2. Marches - 10–15 per leg 3. Leg side swings - 10–20 per leg Build WU pace from ACTIVE RECOVERY (Power Z1, HR Z1, Pace Z1, RPE 1) to ENDURANCE (Power Z2, HR Z2, Pace Z2, RPE 2–3) for 10 min. Then perform 4 × 10s strides. **MS**: Run 7 km at your ENDURANCE (Power Z2, HR Z2, Pace Z2, RPE 2–3) pace. **CD**: Jog 10 min
DISTANCE	7.5 km	
TSS	45	
7 KM RUN		

FRIDAY (AM)

PLANNED METRICS		
DURATION	01:00:00	**WU**: 300 at Active Recovery (Power Z1, HR Z1, Pace Z1, RPE 1) building to Endurance (Power Z2, HR Z2, Pace Z2, RPE 2–3) ------------- **MS**: 2000 at Endurance (Power Z2, HR Z2, Pace Z2, RPE 2–3) ------------- **CD**: 200 at Active Recovery (Power Z1, HR Z1, Pace Z1, RPE 1)
DISTANCE	2500 m	
TSS	60	
ENDURANCE SWIM 2000 METER		

SATURDAY (AM)

PLANNED METRICS	
DURATION	02:30:00
DISTANCE	Various
TSS	170

TRAINER: 24 MINUTE SETS

WU: 20 minutes in Endurance (Power Z2, HR Z2, RPE 2–3). Include a few fast pedaling efforts to get the blood pumping.

MS: 24 minute sets of increasing watts:
1 × 24 minutes at upper Tempo (Power Z3, HR Z3, RPE 3–4).
5 minutes at Endurance (Power Z2, HR Z2, RPE 2–3).
2 × 10 minutes at sub-FTP, lower zone 4 (Power Z4, HR Z4, RPE 4–5), with 2 minutes at Active Recovery (Power Z1, HR Z1, RPE <2) in between each set.
5 minutes at Endurance (Power Z2, HR Z2, RPE 2–3).
3 × 6 minutes at upper FTP, zone 4 (Power Z4, HR Z4, RPE 4–5), with 2 minutes at Active Recovery (Power Z1, HR Z1, RPE <2) in between each set.
5 minutes at Endurance (Power Z2, HR Z2, RPE 2–3).
4 × 3 minutes at lower VO2 (Power Z5, HR Z5, RPE 6–7) with 3 minutes at Active Recovery (Power Z1, HR Z1, RPE <2) in between each set.
5 minutes at Endurance (Power Z2, HR Z2, RPE 2–3).

CD: 14 minutes at Endurance (Power Z2, HR Z2, RPE 2–3)

SATURDAY (PM)

PLANNED METRICS	
DURATION	00:45:00
DISTANCE	N/A
TSS	25

CORE, BALANCE, AND PLYOMETRICS - WEEK 7

Core, Balance, and Plyometrics Protocol - Week 7

Goal: Endurance / Adaptation

Intensity: 90% of 1 RM

Note:
1. Last Rep performed until exhaustion.
2. Only 3 upper body sets.

Exercises:

CBP 1:
1. Slow Side Kick (6 × 4–6)
2. Bulgarian Sidekick (6 × 4–6)
3. Knee Balance (6 × 4–6)
4. Ball Row (6 × 4–6)
5. Two Point Pushup (3 × 4–6)
6. Turkish Get Up (6 × 4–6)
7. Split Squat Jumps (6 × 4–6)
8. Lateral Box Push Of (6 × 4–6)
9. Lateral Jumps (6 × 4–6)

SUNDAY (AM)

PLANNED METRICS		**WU**:
DURATION	01:00:00	Perform 5 mins of dynamic warm up: 1. Leg swings - 10–20 per leg 2. Marches - 10–15 per leg 3. Leg side swings - 10–20 per leg
DISTANCE	12.5 km	
TSS	65	
		Build WU pace from ACTIVE RECOVERY (Power Z1, HR Z1, Pace Z1, RPE 1) to ENDURANCE (Power Z2, HR Z2, Pace Z2, RPE 2–3) for 10 min. Then perform 4 × 10s strides.
		MS: Run 12 km at your low-ENDURANCE (Power Z2, HR Z2, Pace Z2, RPE 2–3) pace.
12 KM RUN AT LSD		**CD**: Jog 10 min

SUNDAY (PM)

PLANNED METRICS		**WU**:
DURATION	01:05:00	1. 200 m free at Active Recovery (Power Z1, HR Z1, Pace Z1, RPE 1)
DISTANCE	3200 m	2. 200 m kick with fins and board - focus on kicking with the ankles and hips
TSS		3. 100 m drill (Shark fin)

		MS: 1. 4 × 500 m at ENDURANCE (Pace Z2, HR Z2, RPE 2–3) with 20s rest. 2. 2 × 250 m at ENDURANCE (Pace Z2, HR Z2, RPE 2–3) with 10s rest
		----------------
ENDURANCE 2500 - 4 × 500, 2 × 250		**CD**: 200 m at Active Recovery (Power Z1, HR Z1, Pace Z1, RPE 1)

WEEK #8

Training Focus: Recovery Week

MONDAY

PLANNED METRICS		Actively focus on recovery today: 1) avoid unneccessary physical exertion, 2) watch nutrition closely (healthy carbs, lean protein, and good fats), 3) stretch, and 4) drink when thirsty. Other common recovery aids include massage, napping, elevating legs, floating in water, and listening to music.
DURATION		
DISTANCE		
TSS		
REST DAY		

TUESDAY (AM)

PLANNED METRICS		**WU**: 200 easy, 100 drill (2/3 catch up) **MS**: 2 × 250 moderate. Focus on form **CD**: 200 pull, easy
DURATION	00:30:00	
DISTANCE	1100 m	
TSS	20	
RECOVERY - SWIM		

WEDNESDAY (AM)

PLANNED METRICS		Strength Protocol - Week 8 **Goal**: Hypertrophy **Intensity**: 95% of 1 RM **Note**: 1. 3d set should be performed until exhaustion. 2. Only 3 upper body sets. **Exercises**: **Strength**: 1. Bench Press (3 × 4–6) 2. Lateral Pull Down (3 × 4–6) 3. Seated Row (3 × 4–6) 4. Tricep Pulldown (3 × 4–6) 5. Bicep Curl (3 × 4–6) 6. Leg Press (7 × 4–6) 7. Leg Extension (7 × 4–6) 8. Leg Curl (7 × 4–6) 9. Calf Raises (7 × 4–6) 10. Back Extension (3 × 4–6) 11. Ab Curl (3 × 4–6) 12. Leg Tucked Rotation (7 × 4–6)
DURATION	00:45:00	
DISTANCE	N/A	
TSS	25	
STRENGTH WORK - WEEK 8		

THURSDAY (AM)

PLANNED METRICS		Very easy recovery spin on a mostly flat course in small chain ring. Active Recovery Power Zone (Power Z1, HR Z1, RPE 1–2). Light on the pedals. Comfortably high rpm focusing on pedaling skills.
DURATION	00:45:00	
DISTANCE	Various	
TSS	25	
RECOVERY SPIN - 45		

FRIDAY (AM)

PLANNED METRICS		Actively focus on recovery today: 1) avoid unneccessary physical exertion, 2) watch nutrition closely (healthy carbs, lean protein, and good fats), 3) stretch, and 4) drink when thirsty. Other common recovery aids include massage, napping, elevating legs, floating in water, and listening to music.
DURATION		
DISTANCE		
TSS		
REST DAY		

SATURDAY (AM)

PLANNED METRICS		**WU**: 15 minutes at Z1 (Power Z1, HR Z1, RPE 1–2). **MS**: 90 minutes of riding with watts at Z2 (Power Z2, HR Z2, RPE 2–3), just nice and steady. If you have to go over hills and your watts go higher, that's OK, but generally average between Endurance watts today. **CD**: 15 minutes just easy pedaling.
DURATION	02:00:00	
DISTANCE	Various	
TSS	100	
MEDIUM, ENDURANCE RIDE		

SUNDAY (AM)

PLANNED METRICS		**WU**: Perform 5 mins of dynamic warm up: 1. Leg swings - 10–20 per leg 2. Marches - 10–15 per leg 3. Leg side swings - 10–20 per leg Build WU pace from ACTIVE RECOVERY (Power Z1, HR Z1, Pace Z1, RPE 1) to ENDURANCE (Power Z2, HR Z2, Pace Z2, RPE 2–3) for 10 min. Then perform 4 × 10s strides. **MS**: Run 14 km at your low-ENDURANCE (Power Z2, HR Z2, Pace Z2, RPE 2–3) pace. **CD**: Jog 10 min
DURATION	01:10:00	
DISTANCE	14.5 km	
TSS	75	
14 KM RUN AT LSD		

WEEK #9

Training Focus: Base #3 - Week #1

MONDAY (AM)

PLANNED METRICS		
DURATION		Actively focus on recovery today: 1) avoid unneccessary physical exertion, 2) watch nutrition closely (healthy carbs, lean protein, and good fats), 3) stretch, and 4) drink when thirsty. Other common recovery aids include massage, napping, elevating legs, floating in water, and listening to music.
DISTANCE		
TSS		
REST DAY		

TUESDAY (AM)

PLANNED METRICS		
DURATION	01:20:00	**WU**: To endurance (150–200 W) for 3 minutes, then do 4 reps of 30 seconds at threshold (260 W), 30 seconds easy. Then ride another 3 minutes at endurance pace (150–200 W). ---------- **MS**: First, start in your 53 on the front and your 21 on the rear. Ride 16 minutes at Sweet Spot (235–245W), shifting down one cog in the back every 2 minutes. Your cadence will decrease—keep the power in the sweet spot. You can stand up as needed. Spin at an easy pace for 5 minutes to recover. Next, start in your 53 on the front and your 12 on the rear. Ride 16 minutes at Sweet Spot (235–245W), shifting up one cog in the back every 2 minutes. Increase your cadence and keep the power in the sweet spot. You can stand up as needed. Spin at an easy pace for 5 minutes to recover. Finally, ride for 30 seconds at 100% of FTP (260 W) followed by 30 seconds at 60% of FTP (160 W). Repeat this combination 10 times, for a total of 10 minutes. You're done! ---------- **CD**: For 5–10 minutes, then go get the mop!
DISTANCE	Various	
TSS	80	
TRAINER: SST GEAR-AMIDS		

TUESDAY (PM)

PLANNED METRICS		
DURATION	01:10:00	**WU**: Perform 5 mins of dynamic warm up: 1. Leg swings - 10–20 per leg 2. Marches - 10–15 per leg 3. Leg side swings - 10–20 per leg Build WU pace from ACTIVE RECOVERY (Power Z1, HR Z1, Pace Z1, RPE 1) to ENDURANCE (Power Z2, HR Z2, Pace Z2, RPE 2–3) for 10 min. Then perform 4 × 10s strides. ---------- **MS**: Run 10–5–3–2–1 minutes at 5 K pace (THRESHOLD (Power Z4, HR Z4, Pace Z4, RPE 4–5) and jog equal amounts between each segment. ---------- **CD**: 10 minute cool down at (ACTIVE RECOVERY (Power Z1, HR Z1, Pace Z1, RPE 1)
DISTANCE	Various	
TSS	65	
FARTLEK RUN		

WEDNESDAY (AM)

PLANNED METRICS		
DURATION	00:45:00	**WU**: 1. 300 free at Active Recovery (Power Z1, HR Z1, Pace Z1, RPE 1) building to Endurance (Power Z2, HR Z2, Pace Z2, RPE 2–3) 2. 200 kick (100 back, 50 breast, 50 dolphin) with fins 3. 100 free at Endurance (Power Z2, HR Z2, Pace Z2, RPE 2–3) with fins **MS**: 4 × 400 Free with 20 sec. rest #1: 300 at Endurance (Power Z2, HR Z2, Pace Z2, RPE 2–3), 100 at Tempo (Power Z3, HR Z3, Pace Z3, RPE 3–4) #2: 200 at Endurance (Power Z2, HR Z2, Pace Z2, RPE 2–3), 200 at Tempo (Power Z3, HR Z3, Pace Z3, RPE 3–4) #3: 100 at Endurance (Power Z2, HR Z2, Pace Z2, RPE 2–3), 300 at Tempo (Power Z3, HR Z3, Pace Z3, RPE 3–4) #4: 400 at Tempo (Power Z3, HR Z3, Pace Z3, RPE 3–4) **CD**: 200 at Active Recovery (Power Z1, HR Z1, Pace Z1, RPE 1)
DISTANCE	2400 m	
TSS	50	
4 × 400 PYRAMIDS		

WEDNESDAY (PM)

PLANNED METRICS		Strength Protocol - Week 9
DURATION	00:45:00	**Goal**: Hypertrophy
DISTANCE	N/A	**Intensity**: 75% of 1 RM
TSS	25	**Note**: 1. 3d set should be performed until exhaustion. 2. Only 3 upper body sets. **Exercises**: **Strength**: 1. Bench Press (3 × 8–12) 2. Lateral Pull Down (3 × 8–12) 3. Seated Row (3 × 8–12) 4. Tricep Pulldown (3 × 8–12) 5. Bicep Curl (3 × 8–12) 6. Leg Press (5 × 8–12) 7. Leg Extension (5 × 8–12) 8. Leg Curl (5 × 8–12) 9. Calf Raises (5 × 8–12) 10. Back Extension (3 × 8–12) 11. Ab Curl (3 × 8–12) 12. Leg Tucked Rotation (5 × 8–12)
STRENGTH WORK - WEEK 9		

THURSDAY (AM)

PLANNED METRICS		**WU**: 10–15 minutes working into Endurance (Power Z2, HR Z2, RPE 2–3), with 3 × 1-minute fast pedals to wake up legs.
DURATION	01:15:00	-------
DISTANCE	Various	**MS**: Complete 3 × 10-minute intervals at Tempo (Power Z3, HR Z3, RPE 3–4), with 5 minutes of rest and easy spinning between intervals. 10 minutes at Endurance (Power Z2, HR Z2, RPE 2–3).
TSS	70	-------
TEMPO 3 × 10/5		**CD**: 15 minutes of easy spinning in Active Recovery (Power Z1, HR Z1, RPE <2).

THURSDAY (PM)

PLANNED METRICS		WU:
DURATION	00:55:00	Perform 5 mins of dynamic warm up: 1. Leg swings - 10–20 per leg 2. Marches - 10–15 per leg 3. Leg side swings - 10–20 per leg
DISTANCE	7.5 km	
TSS	65	
		Build WU pace from ACTIVE RECOVERY (Power Z1, HR Z1, Pace Z1, RPE 1) to ENDURANCE (Power Z2, HR Z2, Pace Z2, RPE 2–3) for 10 min. Then perform 4 × 10s strides.
		MS: Run 7 km at your ENDURANCE (Power Z2, HR Z2, Pace Z2, RPE 2–3) pace.
7 KM RUN		**CD**: Jog 10 min

FRIDAY (AM)

PLANNED METRICS		**WU**: 400 free at Active Recovery (Power Z1, HR Z1, Pace Z1, RPE 1) building to Endurance (Power Z2, HR Z2, Pace Z2, RPE 2–3)
DURATION	00:50:00	
DISTANCE	1800 m	2. 200 kick with fins and board - focus on kicking with the ankles and hips
TSS	50	
10 × 100S - PACE FOCUS		**MS**: 10 × 100s Swim with 40 sec. rest @ Tempo (Power Z3, HR Z3, Pace Z3, RPE 3–4) pace
		CD: 200 Easy

SATURDAY (AM)

PLANNED METRICS		
DURATION	02:00:00	
DISTANCE	Various	
TSS	115	

WU: 10 minutes working at Endurance (Power Z2, HR Z2, RPE 2–3) with 2 × 1-minute Fast Pedals to wake up your legs.

MS: For today's ride find a course with 3 longer hill climbs. Start out in Endurance Zone (Power Z2, HR Z2, RPE 2–3) and with each climb put in a 3–5 minute effort in your VO2 Max Zone (Power Z5, HR Z5, RPE 6–7). After each effort, ride at low Endurance for at least 5 minutes to recover, then back up to the prescribed endurance zone. Take each effort to the MAX!

Terrain: Rolling to Hill Climbs

Cadence: 85–105 for Endurance / 75–85 during VO2Max Efforts!

CD: 10 minutes of easy spinning.

ENDURANCE & SST 3 × 5

SATURDAY (PM)

PLANNED METRICS	
DURATION	00:45:00
DISTANCE	N/A
TSS	25

Core, Balance, and Plyometrics Protocol - Week 9

Goal: Endurance / Adaptation

Intensity: 75% of 1 RM

Note:
1. Last Rep performed until exhaustion.
2. Only 3 upper body sets.

Exercises:

CBP 1:
1. Slow Side Kick (5 × 8–12)
2. Bulgarian Sidekick (5 × 8–12)
3. Knee Balance (5 × 8–12)
4. Ball Row (5 × 8–12)
5. Two Point Pushup (3 × 8–12)
6. Turkish Get Up (3 × 8–12)
7. Split Squat Jumps (5 × 8–12)
8. Lateral Box Push Of (5 × 8–12)
9. Lateral Jumps (5 × 8–12)

CORE, BALANCE, AND PLYOMETRICS - WEEK 9

SUNDAY (AM)

PLANNED METRICS		
DURATION	01:10:00	**WU**: Perform 5 mins of dynamic warm up: 1. Leg swings - 10–20 per leg 2. Marches - 10–15 per leg 3. Leg side swings - 10–20 per leg
DISTANCE	14.5 km	
TSS	75	
14 KM RUN AT LSD		Build WU pace from ACTIVE RECOVERY (Power Z1, HR Z1, Pace Z1, RPE 1) to ENDURANCE (Power Z2, HR Z2, Pace Z2, RPE 2–3) for 10 min. Then perform 4 × 10s strides. **MS**: Run 14 km at your low-ENDURANCE (Power Z2, HR Z2, Pace Z2, RPE 2–3) pace. **CD**: Jog 10 min

SUNDAY (PM)

PLANNED METRICS		
DURATION	01:00:00	**WU**: 300 at Active Recovery (Power Z1, HR Z1, Pace Z1, RPE 1) building to Endurance (Power Z2, HR Z2, Pace Z2, RPE 2–3) -------------
DISTANCE	3500 m	**MS**: 2500 at Endurance (Power Z2, HR Z2, Pace Z2, RPE 2–3) -------------
TSS	60	
ENDURANCE SWIM 2500 METER		**CD**: 200 at Active Recovery (Power Z1, HR Z1, Pace Z1, RPE 1)

WEEK #10

Training Focus: Base #3 - Week #2

MONDAY (AM)

PLANNED METRICS		
DURATION		Actively focus on recovery today: 1) avoid unneccessary physical exertion, 2) watch nutrition closely (healthy carbs, lean protein, and good fats), 3) stretch, and 4) drink when thirsty. Other common recovery aids include massage, napping, elevating legs, floating in water, and listening to music.
DISTANCE		
TSS		
DAY OFF		

TUESDAY (AM)

PLANNED METRICS		
DURATION	01:00:00	**WU**: Build from Active Recovery (Power Z1, HR Z1, RPE 1) to Endurance (Power Z2, HR Z2, RPE 2–3) for 12 minutes, then recovery for 3 min at (Power Z1, HR Z1, RPE 1) ---------- **MS**: Perform 3x Perform 30s at VO2 (Power Z5, HR Z5, RPE 6–7), then go straight into the 8 min OU set. Ride for 1 min at SST (Power Z3.5, HR 3.5, RPE 3–4) then down to 1 min at Tempo (Power Z3, HR Z3, RPE 3–4). Perform this OU 4 times per set. Recover for 5 min at low Endurance (Power Z2, HR Z2, RPE 2–3). After the recovery, go into the next set ---------- **CD**: 10 minutes of easy spinning.
DISTANCE	Various	
TSS	60	
EDP OVER UNDER SST: 3 × 8 MIN		

TUESDAY (PM)

PLANNED METRICS		
DURATION	00:45:00	**WU**: Perform 5 mins of dynamic warm up: 1. Leg swings - 10–20 per leg 2. Marches - 10–15 per leg 3. Leg side swings - 10–20 per leg Build WU pace from ACTIVE RECOVERY (Power Z1, HR Z1, Pace Z1, RPE 1) to ENDURANCE (Power Z2, HR Z2, Pace Z2, RPE 2–3) for 10 min. Then perform 4 × 10s strides. **MS**: Run 7 km at your ENDURANCE (Power Z2, HR Z2, Pace Z2, RPE 2–3) pace. **CD**: Jog 10 min
DISTANCE	7.5 km	
TSS	45	
7 KM RUN		

WEDNESDAY (AM)

PLANNED METRICS		
DURATION	00:55:00	**WU**: 200 free, 200 kick (back), 200 pull with paddles **MS1**: 8 × 125 Free with 15 sec. rest **MS2**: 3 × 300 Swim with 15 sec. rest Build each 300 **CD**: 200 Easy **Total Workout**: 2,700
DISTANCE	2700 m	
TSS	50	
8 × 125 & 3 × 300 BUILD		

WEDNESDAY (PM)

PLANNED METRICS	
DURATION	00:45:00
DISTANCE	N/A
TSS	25

STRENGTH WORK - WEEK 10

Strength Protocol - Week 10

Goal: Hypertrophy

Intensity: 90% of 1 RM

Note:
1. 3d set should be performed until exhaustion.
2. Only 3 upper body sets.

Exercises:

Strength:
1. Bench Press (3 × 4–6)
2. Lateral Pull Down (3 × 4–6)
3. Seated Row (3 × 4–6)
4. Tricep Pulldown (3 × 4–6)
5. Bicep Curl (3 × 4–6)
6. Leg Press (7 × 4–6)
7. Leg Extension (7 × 4–6)
8. Leg Curl (7 × 4–6)
9. Calf Raises (7 × 4–6)
10. Back Extension (3 × 4–6)
11. Ab Curl (3 × 4–6)
12. Leg Tucked Rotation (7 × 4–6)

THURSDAY (AM)

PLANNED METRICS	
DURATION	01:15:00
DISTANCE	Various
TSS	65

ENDURANCE 1 × 15 & TEMPO 1 × 30 W/ BURSTS 10 × :20

WU: 15 minutes working into Endurance (Power Z2, HR Z2, RPE 2–3) with 3 × 1-minute fast pedals to wake up legs.

MS: Start out with a 15-minute effort with watts at Endurance (Power Z2, HR Z2, RPE 2–3), smooth and steady. Then pick up the intensity and complete 1 × 30-minute Tempo (Power Z3, HR Z3, RPE 3–4). Do 10 bursts within this half hour to watts at FTP (Power Z4, HR Z4, RPE 4–5) for 20 seconds each. Space the bursts at least 2 minutes apart.

CD: 10–15 minutes with watts at Active Recovery (Power Z1, HR Z1, RPE <2).

THURSDAY (PM)

PLANNED METRICS		
DURATION	00:55:00	**WU**: Jog at Active Recovery (Pace Z1, Power Z1, HR Z1, RPE 1–2) for 10 min.
DISTANCE	Various	**MS**: Start main set run at Endurance pace (Pace Z2, Power Z2, HR Z2, RPE 2–4). Once comfortable, complete 4 × 5 min intervals at low-mid Tempo (Pace Z3, Power Z3, HR Z3, RPE 4–5) with 10 min rest in between each interval at RPE of 3 (slow jog).
TSS	50	
4 × 5 TEMPO PACE INTERVALS		**CD**: Walk for 10 min or until HR comes below 100 BPM.

FRIDAY (AM)

PLANNED METRICS		
DURATION	00:50:00	**WU**: 200 pull with paddles
DISTANCE	2400 m	**MS1**: 2 × 100 Kick with 15 sec. rest
TSS	50	**MS2**: 3 × 600 Swim with 20 sec. rest #1: Do as 2 × 300 with 15 sec. rest between 300s #2: Pull with paddles #3: Do as 3 × 200 with 15 sec. rest between 200s - last 200 is choice drill **CD**: 200 Easy
2 × 100 KICK, 3 × 600		**Total Workout**: 3,000

SATURDAY (AM)

PLANNED METRICS		
DURATION	02:30:00	**WU**: 10 minutes working at Endurance (Power Z2, HR Z2, RPE 2–3) with 2 × 1-minute Fast Pedals to wake up your legs. -------
DISTANCE	Various	**MS**: For today's ride find a course with 3 longer hill climbs. Start out in Endurance Zone (Power Z2, HR Z2, RPE 2–3) and with each climb put in a 3 × 5 minute effort in your SST (Power Z3.5, HR Z3.5, RPE 4.5–5). After each effort, ride at low Endurance for at least 5 minutes to recover, then back up to the prescribed endurance zone. Terrain: Rolling to Hill Climbs Cadence: 85–105 for Endurance / 75–85 during -------
TSS	145	
ENDURANCE & SST 3 × 5		**CD**: 10 minutes of easy spinning.

SATURDAY (PM)

PLANNED METRICS		Core, Balance, and Plyometrics Protocol - Week 10
DURATION	00:45:00	**Goal**: Endurance / Adaptation
DISTANCE	N/A	**Intensity**: 90% of 1 RM
TSS	25	**Note**: 1. Last Rep performed until exhaustion. 2. Only 3 upper body sets.
CORE, BALANCE, AND PLYOMETRICS - WEEK 10		**Exercises**: **CBP 1**: 1. Slow Side Kick (7 × 4–6) 2. Bulgarian Sidekick (7 × 4–6) 3. Knee Balance (7 × 4–6) 4. Ball Row (7 × 4–6) 5. Two Point Pushup (3 × 4–6) 6. Turkish Get Up (3 × 4–6) 7. Split Squat Jumps (7 × 4–6) 8. Lateral Box Push Of (7 × 4–6) 9. Lateral Jumps (7 × 4–6)

SUNDAY (AM)

PLANNED METRICS		**WU**:
DURATION	01:15:00	Perform 5 mins of dynamic warm up: 1. Leg swings - 10–20 per leg
DISTANCE	15.5 km	2. Marches - 10–15 per leg
TSS	80	3. Leg side swings - 10–20 per leg
15 KM RUN AT LSD		Build WU pace from ACTIVE RECOVERY (Power Z1, HR Z1, Pace Z1, RPE 1) to ENDURANCE (Power Z2, HR Z2, Pace Z2, RPE 2–3) for 10 min. Then perform 4 × 10s strides. **MS**: Run 15 km at your low-ENDURANCE (Power Z2, HR Z2, Pace Z2, RPE 2–3) pace. **CD**: Jog 10 min

SUNDAY (PM)

PLANNED METRICS		**WU**: 5 × 25s free, 3 × 50 kick with kick board **MS1**: Floats with kicks. 10 × 50s with 15s rest in b/w. Start each from the streamline floating position. Focus on keeping the hips and legs up. As your hips start to sink, start kick. As you hips come to the surface and you start to move forward, add in your swim stroke. Complete the rest of the 50 swimming. **MS2**: Low buoy pulls. 6–8 × 75s with 20s rest in b/w. Perform low buoy pulls. Do not forget to slow down your swim stroke and stretch your arm out during the extension phase. **CD**: 4 × 50s Easy
DURATION	00:50:00	
DISTANCE	1400 m	
TSS	50	
10 × 50S - FLOAT DRILLS & 6–8 × 75S LOW PULLS		

WEEK #11

Training Focus: Base #3 - Week #3

MONDAY (AM)

PLANNED METRICS		Actively focus on recovery today: 1) avoid unneccessary physical exertion, 2) watch nutrition closely (healthy carbs, lean protein, and good fats), 3) stretch, and 4) drink when thirsty. Other common recovery aids include massage, napping, elevating legs, floating in water, and listening to music.
DURATION		
DISTANCE		
TSS		
DAY OFF		

TUESDAY (AM)

PLANNED METRICS	
DURATION	01:00:00
DISTANCE	Various
TSS	60

TRAINER: FAST PEDALING EFFORTS

WU: 10 minutes working from Active Recovery (Power Z1, HR Z1, RPE <2) training zone into Endurance (Power Z2, HR Z2, RPE 2–3).

MS1: High Pedaling Cadence Efforts. Complete 10 one minute ON, one minute OFF intervals. During the ON section, cadence should be 105 rpm. During the OFF section, cadence should be 85 rpm. Do not worry about wattage or heart rate during these efforts. Once complete, ride for 5 minutes easy and then onto MS2:

MS2: Complete 2 × 5 minutes at FTP (Power Z4, HR Z4, RPE 4–5). Keep cadence at 100 rpm. These efforts are about improving your cadence at FTP. Rest for 3 minutes between each effort.

CD: 10 minutes of easy pedaling in Active Recovery (Power Z1, HR Z1, RPE <2).

TUESDAY (PM)

PLANNED METRICS	
DURATION	01:05:00
DISTANCE	Various
TSS	60

40 MIN LOW TEMPO RUN

WU:

Perform 5 mins of dynamic warm up:

1. Leg swings - 10–20 per leg
2. Marches - 10–15 per leg
3. Leg side swings - 10–20 per leg

Build WU pace from ACTIVE RECOVERY (Power Z1, HR Z1, Pace Z1, RPE 1) to ENDURANCE (Power Z2, HR Z2, Pace Z2, RPE 2–3) for 10 min. Then perform 4 × 10s strides.

MS: Tempo run: 40' Low TEMPO (Power Z3, HR Z3, Pace Z3, RPE 3–4).

CD: Jog for 10 min ACTIVE RECOVERY (Power Z1, HR Z1, Pace Z1, RPE 1)

WEDNESDAY (AM)

PLANNED METRICS	
DURATION	00:50:00
DISTANCE	2900 m
TSS	45

10 × 50 & 4 × 400 BUILDS

WU:
1. 200 swim at Active Recovery (Power Z1, HR Z1, Pace Z1, RPE 1)
2. 200 kick with fins and board
   - focus on kicking with the ankles and hips
3. 200 drill (Tarzan Drill)

MS1:
10 × 50 Free with 15 sec. rest
Odds are fast (not sprint), evens are moderate

MS2:
4 × 400 Swim at Endurance (Power Z2, HR Z2, Pace Z2, RPE 2–3) with 20 sec. rest

CD: 200 at Active Recovery (Power Z1, HR Z1, Pace Z1, RPE 1)

WEDNESDAY (PM)

PLANNED METRICS	
DURATION	00:45:00
DISTANCE	N/A
TSS	25

STRENGTH WORK - WEEK 11

Strength Protocol - Week 11

Goal: Hypertrophy

Intensity: 95+% of 1 RM

Note:
1. 3d set should be performed until exhaustion.
2. Only 3 upper body sets.

Exercises:

Strength:
1. Bench Press (3 × 4–6)
2. Lateral Pull Down (3 × 4–6)
3. Seated Row (3 × 4–6)
4. Tricep Pulldown (3 × 4–6)
5. Bicep Curl (3 × 4–6)
6. Leg Press (8 × 4–6)
7. Leg Extension (8 × 4–6)
8. Leg Curl (8 × 4–6)
9. Calf Raises (7 × 4–6)
10. Back Extension (3 × 4–6)
11. Ab Curl (3 × 4–6)
12. Leg Tucked Rotation (8 × 4–6)

THURSDAY (AM)

PLANNED METRICS		
DURATION	01:15:00	**WU**: 10–15 minutes working into Endurance (Power Z2, HR Z2, RPE 2–3), with 3 × 1-minute fast pedals to wake up legs.
DISTANCE	Various	-------
TSS	70	**MS**: Complete 3 × 10-minute intervals at Tempo (Power Z3, HR Z3, RPE 3–4), with 5 minutes of rest and easy spinning between intervals. 10 minutes at Endurance (Power Z2, HR Z2, RPE 2–3).

TEMPO 3 × 10/5		**CD**: 15 minutes of easy spinning in Active Recovery (Power Z1, HR Z1, RPE <2).

THURSDAY (PM)

PLANNED METRICS		
DURATION	00:50:00	**WU**: Perform 5 mins of dynamic warm up: 1. Leg swings - 10–20 per leg 2. Marches - 10–15 per leg 3. Leg side swings - 10–20 per leg
DISTANCE	8.5 km	Build WU pace from ACTIVE RECOVERY (Power Z1, HR Z1, Pace Z1, RPE 1) to ENDURANCE (Power Z2, HR Z2, Pace Z2, RPE 2–3) for 10 min. Then perform 4 × 10s strides.
TSS	60	**MS**: Run 8 km at your ENDURANCE (Power Z2, HR Z2, Pace Z2, RPE 2–3) pace.
8 KM RUN		**CD**: Jog 10 min

FRIDAY (AM)

PLANNED METRICS		
DURATION	01:00:00	**WU**: 200 free, 200 pull with paddles, 200 free
DISTANCE	3000 m	**MS1**: 4 × 50 Kick with 15 sec. rest
TSS	65	**MS2**: 4 × 500 with 30 sec. rest Build within each 500
		CD: 200 Easy
4 × 50 KICK, 4 × 500 BUILD		**Total Workout**: 3,000

SATURDAY (AM)

PLANNED METRICS		
DURATION	02:30:00	**WU**: 15 minutes working from Active Recovery (Power Z1, HR Z1, RPE <2) training zone into Endurance (Power Z2, HR Z2, RPE 2–3) with 2–3 × 1-minute Fast Pedals to wake up your legs. ---------- **MS**: Endurance ride. Set a pace at Endurance (Power Z2, HR Z2, RPE 2–3) and hold this pace for the rest of the ride. Throughout the ride, do 10 × 15-second FTP/Threshold (Power Z4, HR Z4, Pace Z4, RPE 5–6). Make sure cadence stays high. Vary terrain. --------- **CD**: 15 minutes of easy pedaling in Active Recovery (Power Z1, HR Z1, RPE <2).
DISTANCE	Various	
TSS	150	
ENDURANCE WITH FTP BURSTS 7 × :10 & SST 1 × 20		

SATURDAY (PM)

PLANNED METRICS		
DURATION	00:45:00	Core, Balance, and Plyometrics Protocol - Week 11 **Goal**: Endurance / Adaptation **Intensity**: 95+% of 1 RM **Note**: 1. Last Rep performed until exhaustion. 2. Only 3 upper body sets. **Exercises**: **CBP 1**: 1. Slow Side Kick (8 × 4–6) 2. Bulgarian Sidekick (8 × 4–6) 3. Knee Balance (8 × 4–6) 4. Ball Row (8 × 4–6) 5. Two Point Pushup (3 × 4–6) 6. Turkish Get Up (3 × 4–6) 7. Split Squat Jumps (8 × 4–6) 8. Lateral Box Push Of (8 × 4–6) 9. Lateral Jumps (8 × 4–6)
DISTANCE	N/A	
TSS	25	
CORE, BALANCE, AND PLYOMETRICS - WEEK 11		

SUNDAY (AM)

PLANNED METRICS		
DURATION	01:15:00	**WU**: Perform 5 mins of dynamic warm up: 1. Leg swings - 10–20 per leg 2. Marches - 10–15 per leg 3. Leg side swings - 10–20 per leg
DISTANCE	15.5 km	
TSS	80	
15 KM RUN AT LSD WITH TURN OVERS		Build WU pace from ACTIVE RECOVERY (Power Z1, HR Z1, Pace Z1, RPE 1) to ENDURANCE (Power Z2, HR Z2, Pace Z2, RPE 2–3) for 10 min. Then perform 4 × 10s strides. **MS**: Run 15 km at your low-ENDURANCE (Power Z2, HR Z2, Pace Z2, RPE 2–3) pace. Starting at km 9, perform 2 × 20s Turn Overs at Threshold (Power Z4, HR Z4, Pace Z4, RPE 5–6) pace with 2 min rest in between. Focus on a quick cadence. Your stride rate should increase by at least 10 steps per minute during these turnovers. **CD**: Jog 10 min

SUNDAY (PM)

PLANNED METRICS		
DURATION	01:00:00	**WU**: 300 at Active Recovery (Power Z1, HR Z1, Pace Z1, RPE 1) building to Endurance (Power Z2, HR Z2, Pace Z2, RPE 2–3) -------------
DISTANCE	3500 m	
TSS	60	**MS**: 2500 at Endurance (Power Z2, HR Z2, Pace Z2, RPE 2–3) -------------
ENDURANCE SWIM 2500 METER		**CD**: 200 at Active Recovery (Power Z1, HR Z1, Pace Z1, RPE 1)

WEEK #12

Training Focus: Recovery Week

MONDAY (AM)

PLANNED METRICS		
DURATION		Actively focus on recovery today: 1) avoid unneccessary physical exertion, 2) watch nutrition closely (healthy carbs, lean protein, and good fats), 3) stretch, and 4) drink when thirsty. Other common recovery aids include massage, napping, elevating legs, floating in water, and listening to music.
DISTANCE		
TSS		
REST DAY		

TUESDAY (AM)

PLANNED METRICS		
DURATION	00:30:00	**WU**: 200 easy, 100 drill (2/3 catch up)
DISTANCE	1100 m	**MS**: 2 × 250 moderate. Focus on form
TSS	20	**CD**: 200 pull, easy
RECOVERY - SWIM		

WEDNESDAY (AM)

PLANNED METRICS		Strength Protocol - Week 8
DURATION	00:45:00	**Goal**: Hypertrophy
DISTANCE	N/A	**Intensity**: 95% of 1 RM
TSS	25	**Note**: 1. 3d set should be performed until exhaustion. 2. Only 3 upper body sets.
STRENGTH WORK - WEEK 8		**Exercises**: **Strength**: 1. Bench Press (3 × 4–6) 2. Lateral Pull Down (3 × 4–6) 3. Seated Row (3 × 4–6) 4. Tricep Pulldown (3 × 4–6) 5. Bicep Curl (3 × 4–6) 6. Leg Press (7 × 4–6) 7. Leg Extension (7 × 4–6) 8. Leg Curl (7 × 4–6) 9. Calf Raises (7 × 4–6) 10. Back Extension (3 × 4–6) 11. Ab Curl (3 × 4–6) 12. Leg Tucked Rotation (7 × 4–6)

THURSDAY (AM)

PLANNED METRICS		Very easy recovery spin on a mostly flat course in small chain ring. Active Recovery Power Zone (Power Z1, HR Z1, RPE 1–2). Light on the pedals. Comfortably high rpm focusing on pedaling skills.
DURATION	00:45:00	
DISTANCE	Various	
TSS	25	
RECOVERY SPIN - 45		

FRIDAY (AM)

PLANNED METRICS		Actively focus on recovery today: 1) avoid unneccessary physical exertion, 2) watch nutrition closely (healthy carbs, lean protein, and good fats), 3) stretch, and 4) drink when thirsty. Other common recovery aids include massage, napping, elevating legs, floating in water, and listening to music.
DURATION		
DISTANCE		
TSS		
REST DAY		

SATURDAY (AM)

PLANNED METRICS		
DURATION	02:00:00	**WU**: 15 minutes at Z1 (Power Z1, HR Z1, RPE 1–2).
DISTANCE	Various	**MS**: 90 minutes of riding with watts at Z2 (Power Z2, HR Z2, RPE 2–3), just nice and steady. If you have to go over hills and your watts go higher, that's OK, but generally average between Endurance watts today.
TSS	100	
MEDIUM, ENDURANCE RIDE		**CD**: 15 minutes just easy pedaling.

SUNDAY (AM)

PLANNED METRICS		
DURATION	00:50:00	**WU**: Perform 5 mins of dynamic warm up: 1. Leg swings - 10–20 per leg 2. Marches - 10–15 per leg 3. Leg side swings - 10–20 per leg
DISTANCE	5.5 mi	Build WU pace from ACTIVE RECOVERY (Power Z1, HR Z1, Pace Z1, RPE 1) to ENDURANCE (Power Z2, HR Z2, Pace Z2, RPE 2–3) for 10 min. Then perform 4 × 10s strides.
TSS	60	**MS**: Run 5 mi at your low ENDURANCE (Power Z2, HR Z2, Pace Z2, RPE 2–3) or better pace.
5 MILE ENDURANCE RUN		**CD**: Jog 10 min

WEEK #13

Training Focus: Test Week

MONDAY

PLANNED METRICS		
DURATION	01:00:00	**WU**: 15 Minutes in the Endurance zone (Power Z2, HR Z2, RPE 2–3). Get in 2 or 3 fast pedals of about 1 minute each. ------- **MS**: Your Pre-Test workout is about opening up the legs and keeping the lactate-processing plant sharp. As part of the Main Set do 3 × 90 seconds "Hard Efforts" at Zone 5/ VO2MAX (Power Z5, HR Z5 RPE 6–7), rest for 5 minutes at Active Recovery (Power Z1, HR Z1, RPE <2) between efforts. Focus on tomorrow's FTP test during the efforts, breath deep and pedal smooth. ------- **CD**: 15 minutes easy pedaling in Active Recovery (Power Z1, HR Z1, RPE <2)
DISTANCE	Various	
TSS	38	
PRE-TEST		

TUESDAY

PLANNED METRICS		
DURATION	01:30:00	**WU**: 10–20 minutes working into Endurance Zone (Power Z2, HR Z2, RPE 2–3) with 3 × 1-minute fast pedals to wake up legs. ------- **MS1**: 5-Minute Hard Effort. This 5-minute effort should be done at maximum. Start the effort at a high pace, but not so hard that you cannot finish strong. Really hammer out the last 45 seconds. The goal is to generate a max 5-minute VO2 Max test while really opening up the legs for the test and really dispense the initial freshness to help produce more accurate power in the 20-minute test. Once complete, spin easily for 15 minutes of recovery, working back into Endurance Zone (Power Z2, HR Z2, RPE 2–3), and then go on to MS2. ------- **MS2**: 20-Minute Time Trial. Try to do this on a road that is fairly flat and allows you to put out strong, steady power for the entire 20-minute effort. Don't start too hard! You can do this on a steady climb or into a headwind to help produce steady power throughout the 20-minute effort. Once complete, spin easy for 10 minutes in Endurance Zone (Power Z2, HR Z2, RPE 2–3). Your FTP is the power average for the 20-minute effort minus 3–5%. ------- **CD**: 10–15 minutes of easy spinning.
DISTANCE	Various	
TSS	75	
FTP 20 MINUTE & VO2 MAX TEST		

WEDNESDAY

PLANNED METRICS		
DURATION	00:30:00	**WU**: 200 swim, 100 kick, 100 drill (3/4 catch up drill) **MS**: 2 × 250 easy pace. Do not focus on speed or time. Work on form. Focus on full extension and follow through with your stroke. **CD**: 100 easy
DISTANCE	1000 m	
TSS	20	
RECOVERY - SWIM		

THURSDAY

PLANNED METRICS		
DURATION	00:45:00	**WU**: 200 m at an easy pace **Pull**: 200 m pull (100 m follow through drill/ 100 m finger tip drill) **Kick**: 100 m with fins **MS1**: 1 × 400 m timed. This is a 400 m time-trial. Swim as hard as you can but do not start so hard as you fade in the last meters. You want your pace to be as even as possible during the entire 400 m. If possible, have someone count your strokes during a length near the 200 m point of the test (you can also find this information if you are using a smart watch such as the Garmin Swim or 920XT). Once finished, recover for 5–10 min. You can get out of the pool or slowly swim. The point is to recover but stay loose. **MS2**: 1 × 200 m time trial. Swim as hard as you can. Ensure your 200 m time is faster than 1/2 of your 400 m time. **CD**: 200 m easy
DISTANCE	1300 m	
TSS	40	
CRITICAL SWIM SPEED SWIM TEST #1		

FRIDAY

PLANNED METRICS		
DURATION		Actively focus on recovery today: 1) avoid unneccessary physical exertion, 2) watch nutrition closely (healthy carbs, lean protein, and good fats), 3) stretch, and 4) drink when thirsty. Other common recovery aids include massage, napping, elevating legs, floating in water, and listening to music.
DISTANCE		
TSS		
REST DAY		

SATURDAY

PLANNED METRICS		
DURATION	00:45:00	**WU**: Perform 5 mins of dynamic warm up: 1. Leg swings - 10–20 per leg 2. Marches - 10–15 per leg 3. Leg side swings - 10–20 per leg
DISTANCE	5.5 km	
TSS	45	
CRITICAL RUN SPEED TEST #1–5 KM RFTP TEST		Build WU pace from ACTIVE RECOVERY (Power Z1, HR Z1, RPE 1) to ENDURANCE (Power Z2, HR Z2, RPE 2–3) for 10 min. Then perform 4 × 10s strides. **MS**: Run 5 km at maximal pace. Do not go out too fast as to slow down over the course of the interval. **CD**: Jog for 10 at ACTIVE RECOVERY (Power Z1, HR Z1, RPE 1)

SUNDAY

PLANNED METRICS		CRITICAL SWIM SPEED TEST #2
DURATION	00:30:00	
DISTANCE	1700 m	
TSS	30	

Plan 3

Power Based Short Course SwimRun Training Plan

For this plan, please reference the following Test Interpretation Notes on p. 493 of this book:

- CSS Interpretation Notes (p. 493)
- Critical Run Speed/rFTP Test Calculations (p. 493)

WEEK #1

Training Focus: Test Week - The focus of this week is to set your personalized power and pace zones for swimming and runing.

MONDAY

PLANNED METRICS		
DURATION	0:45:00	**WU**: 200m at an easy pace **Pull**: 200m pull (100m follow through drill/ 100m finger tip drill) **Kick**: 100 m with fins **MS1**: 1 x 400m timed. This is a 400 m time-trial. Swim as hard as you can but do not start so hard as you fade in the last meters. You want your pace to be as even as possible during the entire 400m. If possible, have someone count your strokes during a length near the 200m point of the test (you can also find this information if you are using a smart watch such as the Garmin Swim or 920XT). Once finished, recover for 5–10 min. You can get out of the pool or slowly swim. The point is to recover but stay loose. **MS2**: 1 x 200m time trial. Swim as hard as you can. Ensure your 200m time is faster than 1/2 of your 400m time. **CD**: 200m easy
DISTANCE	1300	
TSS	40	
CRITICAL SWIM SPEED SWIM TEST #1		

TUESDAY

PLANNED METRICS		
DURATION	0:45:00	**WU**: Perform 5 mins of dynamic warm up: 1. Leg swings - 10–20 per leg 2. Marches - 10–15 per leg 3. Leg side swings - 10–20 per leg Build WU pace from ACTIVE RECOVERY (Power Z1, HR Z1, RPE 1) to ENDURANCE (Power Z2, HR Z2, RPE 2–3) for 10 min. Then perform 4 × 10s strides. **MS**: Run 5 km at maximal pace. Do not go out too fast as to slow down over the course of the interva. **CD**: Jog for 10 at ACTIVE RECOVERY (Power Z1, HR Z1, RPE 1)
DISTANCE	5 mi	
TSS	35	
CRITICAL RUN SPEED TEST #1–5 KM RFTP TEST		

WEDNESDAY

PLANNED METRICS		
DURATION	0:45:00	**WU**: 200m at an easy pace **Pull**: 200m pull (100m follow through drill/ 100m finger tip drill) **Kick**: 100 m with fins **MS**: Perform 1 × 1000m time trial. Just like you performed with the 400 m time trial, do not start so hard that you fade in the final meters. Ensure you swim as hard and even as possible during the entire time trial. At about the 500m point, if possible, have someone count your stroke rate (you can use a smartwatch to capture this information such as a Garmin Swim or Garmin 920XT). **CD**: 200m easy
DISTANCE	1700	
TSS	30	
CRITICAL SWIM SPEED TEST #2		

THURSDAY

PLANNED METRICS		DAY OFF
DURATION		
DISTANCE		
TSS		

FRIDAY

PLANNED METRICS		
DURATION	0:50:00	**WU**: Perform 5 mins of dynamic warm up: 1. Leg swings - 10–20 per leg 2. Toe Touches - 10–15 per leg 3. Leg tucks - 10–20 per leg
DISTANCE	7 mi	
TSS	60	Build WU pace from ACTIVE RECOVERY (Power Z1, HR Z1, RPE 1) to ENDURANCE (Power Z2, HR Z2, RPE 2–3) for 10 min. Then perform 4 × 10s strides.
		MS: Run 10 km at a maximal pace. Do not go out too fast as to slow down over the course of the interval.
CRITICAL RUN SPEED TEST #2–10 KM TEST		**CD**: Jog for 10 at ACTIVE RECOVERY (Power Z1, HR Z1, RPE 1)

SATURDAY

PLANNED METRICS		
DURATION	1:10:00	**WU**: 300m free/200m kick with fins/200m drill (6–3-6 switch kick)
DISTANCE	3400	**MS1**: 1 × 1000m at ENDURANCE (Pace Z2, HR Z2, RPE 2–3) with 20s rest
TSS	71	**MS2**: 3 × 500m meters at ENDURANCE (Pace Z2, HR Z2, RPE 2–3) with 10s rest
ENDURANCE SWIM 2000 METE		**CD**: 200 m easy swimming (stroke of choice) at ACTIVE RECOVERY (Pace Z1, HR Z1, RPE 1)

SUNDAY

PLANNED METRICS		
DURATION	1:05:00	**WU**: Perform 5 mins of dynamic warm up: 1. Leg swings - 10–20 per leg 2. Marches - 10–15 per leg 3. Leg side swings - 10–20 per leg
DISTANCE	7 mi	
TSS	65	Build WU pace from ACTIVE RECOVERY (Power Z1, HR Z1, RPE 1) to ENDURANCE (Power Z2, HR Z2, RPE 2–3) for 10 min. Then perform 4 × 10s strides.
		MS: Run 10 km at ENDURANCE (Power Z2, HR Z2, RPE 2–3).
10 KM ENDURANCE RUN		**CD**: Jog 10 min

WEEK #2

Training Focus: Build #1 - Week #1

MONDAY (AM)

PLANNED METRICS		
DURATION		Actively focus on recovery today: 1) avoid unneccessary physical exertion, 2) watch nutrition closely (healthy carbs, lean protein, and good fats), 3) stretch, and 4) drink when thirsty. Other common recovery aids include massage, napping, elevating legs, floating in water, and listening to music.
DISTANCE		
TSS		
REST DAY		

TUESDAY (AM)

PLANNED METRICS		
DURATION	0:50:00	**WU**: 1. 400 free at Active Recovery (Power Z1, HR Z1, Pace Z1, RPE 1) building to Endurance (Power Z2, HR Z2, Pace Z2, RPE 2–3) 2. 200 kick with board and fins – focus on kicking with the ankles and hips
DISTANCE	1800	**MS**: 10 × 100s Swim with 40 sec. rest @ Tempo (Power Z3, HR Z3, Pace Z3, RPE 3–4)
TSS	50	**CD**: 200 Easy
		****Note**: Try to keep a consistent endurance pace for each 100m (within 1 sec).
10 × 100S - PACE FOCUS		If you pace drops, give yourself a few more seconds of recovery in between each 100.

TUESDAY (PM)

PLANNED METRICS		
DURATION	0:40:00	**WU**: Perform 5 mins of dynamic warm up: 1. Leg swings - 10–20 per leg 2. Marches - 10–15 per leg 3. Leg side swings - 10–20 per leg
DISTANCE	4 mi	
TSS	40	Build WU pace from ACTIVE RECOVERY (Power Z1, HR Z1, Pace Z1, RPE 1) to ENDURANCE (Power Z2, HR Z2, Pace Z2, RPE 2–3) for 10 min. Then perform 4 × 10s strides.
		MS: Run 5 km at your ENDURANCE (Power Z2, HR Z2, Pace Z2, RPE 2–3) pace.
5 KM RUN		**CD**: Jog 10 min

WEDNESDAY (AM)

PLANNED METRICS		Strength Protocol - Week 2
DURATION	0:45:00	**Goal**: Endurance / Adaptation
DISTANCE		**Intensity**: 60% of 1 RM
TSS	20	**Exercises**:
STRENGTH WORK - WEEK 2		**Strength**: 1. Bench Press (3 × 20) 2. Lateral Pull Down (3 × 20) 3. Seated Row (3 × 20) 4. Tricep Pulldown (3 × 20) 5. Bicep Curl (3 × 20) 6. Leg Press (3 × 30) 7. Leg Extension (3 × 20) 8. Leg Curl (3 × 20) 9. Calf Raises (3 × 20) 10. Back Extension (3 × 20) 11. Ab Curl (3 × 20) 12. Leg Tucked Rotation (3 × 20)

WEDNESDAY (PM)

PLANNED METRICS		
DURATION	1:05:00	**WU**: Perform 5 mins of dynamic warm up: 1. Leg swings - 10–20 per leg 2. Marches - 10–15 per leg 3. Leg side swings - 10–20 per leg
DISTANCE	Various	
TSS	65	Build WU pace from ACTIVE RECOVERY (Power Z1, HR Z1, Pace Z1, RPE 1) to ENDURANCE (Power Z2, HR Z2, Pace Z2, RPE 2–3) for 10 min. Then perform 4 × 10s strides. ---------- **MS**: Run 10-5-3-2-1 minutes at 5 K pace (THRESHOLD (Power Z4, HR Z4, Pace Z4, RPE 4–5) and jog equal amounts between each segment. ---------- **CD**: 10 minute cool down at (ACTIVE RECOVERY (Power Z1, HR Z1, Pace Z1, RPE 1)
FARTLEK RUN		

THURSDAY (AM)

PLANNED METRICS		
DURATION	1:10:00	**WU**: 1. 300 free at Active Recovery (Power Z1, HR Z1, Pace Z1, RPE 1) 2. 300 drill (100 tarzan/100 Fist/ 2/3 catch up)
DISTANCE	3300	
TSS	40	**MS**: 1. 8 x 75 Kick with fins with 10s rest – focus on kicking with the ankles and hips 2. 8 x 75 Pull with **DAY OFF**
12 × 75 STROKE MIX & 4 × 400		

FRIDAY (AM)

PLANNED METRICS	
DURATION	1:05:00
DISTANCE	7 mi
TSS	65
10 KM ENDURANCE RUN	

WU: Perform 5 mins of dynamic warm up:
1. Leg swings - 10–20 per leg
2. Marches - 10–15 per leg
3. Leg side swings - 10–20 per leg

Build WU pace from Z1 to Z2 for 10 min. Then perform 4 × 10s strides.

MS: Run 10 km at your marathon pace or better pace.

CD: Jog 10 min

FRIDAY (PM)

PLANNED METRICS	
DURATION	0:30:00
DISTANCE	1000
TSS	15
RECOVERY SWIM	

WU: Perform 5 mins of dynamic warm up:
1. 200m Free at ACTIVE RECOVERY (Power Z1, HR Z1, Pace Z1, RPE 1)
2. 100m drill (2/3 catch up)

MS: 2 × 250m at low ENDURANCE (Pace Z2, HR Z2, RPE 2). Focus on form

CD: 200 pull at ACTIVE RECOVERY (Power Z1, HR Z1, Pace Z1, RPE 1)

SATURDAY (AM)

PLANNED METRICS	
DURATION	1:30:00
DISTANCE	Various
TSS	125
SWIMRUN BRICK #2	

WU:
1. 200m Free at ACTIVE RECOVERY (Power Z1, HR Z1, Pace Z1, RPE 1)
2. 100m drill (2/3 catch up)

MS: 2 × 250m at low ENDURANCE (Pace Z2, HR Z2, RPE 2). Focus on form

CD: 200 pull at ACTIVE RECOVERY (Power Z1, HR Z1, Pace Z1, RPE 1)

SUNDAY (AM)

PLANNED METRICS		
DURATION	1:17:00	**WU**: Perform 5 mins of dynamic warm up: 1. Leg swings - 10–20 per leg 2. Marches - 10–15 per leg 3. Leg side swings - 10–20 per leg
DISTANCE	8	
TSS	75	Build WU pace from ACTIVE RECOVERY (Power Z1, HR Z1, Pace Z1, RPE 1) to ENDURANCE (Power Z2, HR Z2, Pace Z2, RPE 2–3) for 10 min. Then perform 4 × 10s strides.
		MS: Run 7 mi at upper ENDURANCE (Power Z2, HR Z2, Pace Z2, RPE 2–3). During this 6 mile main set, run 2 mi at TEMPO (Power Z3, HR Z3, Pace Z3, RPE 3–4). You can do the 2 mi TEMPO segment at any point during the run.
7 MI RUN WITH TEMPO		**CD**: Walk for 10 min to bring HR down to 100 BPM.

SUNDAY (PM)

PLANNED METRICS		
DURATION	0:40:00	
DISTANCE		
TSS	33	
RESISTANCE BANDS - SWIMMING #1		Total workout duration should be 20–25 min. Try to do 3–4 rounds of 2 minutes of each exercise. **Butterfly (double-arm pull-back)**: Holding the cords in front of you, stand far enough away to create some tension in them. Bend over at the waist and lower your head. With arms straight and outstretched in front of you, pull your arms down to your sides as if doing an actual butterfly stroke. Remember to start the pull phase with your palms and forearms. Make sure to keep your elbows pointed out and at your shoulder line. Finish with your hands past your hips. **Single arm (freestyle pull-back)**: Same as the butterfly, but alternate one arm at a time. **Tricep pull-back**: Use the same starting position as the butterfly but keep your elbows tucked into your sides and press your arms behind you. Make sure to squeeze the muscles at the back of your arms at the end of each stroke. **Breaststroke pull**: Use the same bent-over starting position as above. Make breaststroke motions with your arms. Maintain a high elbow position and execute the motion with your palms and forearms. Be careful not to let your elbows drop below a line parallel to your shoulders. **Chest fly**: Stand upright holding the cords in front of you with a little bit of tension. Start with arms outstretched in front of you. While keeping arms at chest height, pull each arm to the side and back until your hands are in line with your shoulders. **Reverse fly**: Standing upright and facing away from the cords, position your hands next to your shoulders and your elbows at shoulder level. Keeping your arms parallel to your shoulders, push out until you can press your hands together in front of your chest.

WEEK #3

Training Focus: Build #1 - Week #2

MONDAY (AM)

PLANNED METRICS		
DURATION		Actively focus on recovery today: 1) avoid unneccessary physical exertion, 2) watch nutrition closely (healthy carbs, lean protein, and good fats), 3) stretch, and 4) drink when thirsty. Other common recovery aids include massage, napping, elevating legs, floating in water, and listening to music.
DISTANCE		
TSS		
REST DAY		

TUESDAY (AM)

PLANNED METRICS		
DURATION	1:00:00	**WU**: 1. 200 free at Active Recovery (Power Z1, HR Z1, Pace Z1, RPE 1) 2. 200 pull at Active Recovery (Power Z1, HR Z1, Pace Z1, RPE 1) with paddles - Focus on the catch phase of your stroke 3. 200 drill (100 - Tarzan and 100 - 3/4 catch up)
DISTANCE	3500	
TSS	45	
		MS1: 8 x 75 Kick with 10 sec. rest (Odds with fins, evens without fins) **MS2**: 6 x 150 at Endurance (Power Z2, HR Z2, Pace Z2, RPE 2–3) Swim with 15 sec. rest-Middle 50 change stroke to breast or back **MS3**: 16 x 25 Swim at VO2 Max (Pace Z5, HR Z5, RPE 5–6) with 10 sec. rest-All are fast, but not sprint. Try to keep times within 2s of each, **MS4**: 2 × 400 at ENDURANCE (Pace Z2, HR Z2, RPE 2–3)
8 × 75,16 × 25 FAST, & 2 × 400S		**CD**: 200 at Active Recovery (Power Z1, HR Z1, Pace Z1, RPE 1)

TUESDAY (PM)

PLANNED METRICS		
DURATION	0:40:00	**WU**: Perform 5 mins of dynamic warm up: 1. Leg swings - 10–20 per leg 2. Marches - 10–15 per leg 3. Leg side swings - 10–20 per leg Build WU pace from ACTIVE RECOVERY (Power Z1, HR Z1, Pace Z1, RPE 1) to ENDURANCE (Power Z2, HR Z2, Pace Z2, RPE 2–3) for 10 min. **MS**: Run 4 mi at ENDURANCE (Power Z2, HR Z2, Pace Z2, RPE 2–3) with 10 x 60 sec pick-ups with 2 mins easy between interval. **CD**: Jog 15 mins at ACTIVE RECOVERY (Power Z1, HR Z1, Pace Z1, RPE 1)
DISTANCE	4.5 mi	
TSS	40	
4 MI ENDURANCE RUN WITH PICK UPS		

WEDNESDAY (AM)

PLANNED METRICS		
DURATION	1:10:00	**WU**: Perform 5 mins of dynamic warm up: 1. Leg swings - 10–20 per leg 2. Marches - 10–15 per leg 3. Leg side swings - 10–20 per leg Build WU pace from ACTIVE RECOVERY (Power Z1, HR Z1, Pace Z1, RPE 1) to ENDURANCE (Power Z2, HR Z2, Pace Z2, RPE 2–3) for 10 min. Then perform 4 × 10s strides. **MS**: 4 × 1 mile at target 5K race pace or THRESHOLD (Power Z4, HR Z4, Pace Z4, RPE 4–5) with 4–5' low ENDURANCE (Power Z2, HR Z2, Pace Z2, RPE 2–3) between each interval. **CD**: Jog for 10 min at ACTIVE RECOVERY (Power Z1, HR Z1, Pace Z1, RPE 1)
DISTANCE	Various	
TSS	55	
4 × 1 MILE RUN AT TARGET 5K RACE PACE		

WEDNESDAY (PM)

PLANNED METRICS	
DURATION	0:45:00
DISTANCE	
TSS	20

STRENGTH WORK - WEEK 3

Strength Protocol - Week 3
Goal: Hypertrophy
Intensity: 70% of 1 RM
Note: 3d set should be performed until exhaustion.

Exercises:
Strength:

1. Bench Press (3 × 8–12)
2. Lateral Pull Down (3 × 8–12)
3. Seated Row (3 × 8–12)
4. Tricep Pulldown (3 × 8–12)
5. Bicep Curl (3 × 8–12)
6. Leg Press (3 × 8–12)
7. Leg Extension (3 × 8–12)
8. Leg Curl (3 × 8–12)
9. Calf Raises (3 × 8–12)
10. Back Extension (3 × 8–12)
11. Ab Curl (3 × 8–12)
12. Leg Tucked Rotation (3 × 8–12)

THURSDAY (AM)

PLANNED METRICS	
DURATION	1:05:00
DISTANCE	2700
TSS	50

20 × 50, 3 × 300 PULL

WU:

1. 400 free at Active Recovery (Power Z1, HR Z1, Pace Z1, RPE 1) building to Endurance (Power Z2, HR Z2, Pace Z2, RPE 2–3)
2. 200 kick with fins at Endurance (Power Z2, HR Z2, Pace Z2, RPE 2–3)

MS1:
20 x 50 Swim with 15 sec. rest
Do as 4 sets of 5 building 1 to 4 with the 5th being all out. Start at ENDURANCE (Pace Z2, HR Z2, RPE 2–3). Increase intensity with each 50 with the 5th iteration at VO2 Max (Power Z5, HR Z5, Pace Z5, RPE 6–7)
MS2: 5 x 300 Pull at ENDURANCE (Pace Z2, HR Z2, RPE 2–3) with 15 sec. rest

1. With paddles
2. Focus on form
3. Odds are breathing 3/5/7 by 25
4. With paddles
5. Odds are breathing 3/5/7 by 25

CD: 200 at Active Recovery (Power Z1, HR Z1, Pace Z1, RPE 1)

FRIDAY (AM)

PLANNED METRICS		
DURATION	1:05	**WU**: Perform 5 mins of dynamic warm up: 1. Leg swings - 10–20 per leg 2. Marches - 10–15 per leg 3. Leg side swings - 10–20 per leg Build WU pace from ACTIVE RECOVERY (Power Z1, HR Z1, Pace Z1, RPE 1) to ENDURANCE (Power Z2, HR Z2, Pace Z2, RPE 2–3) for 10 min. Then perform 4 × 10 s strides. **MS**: Run 10 km ranging between your Endurance (Power Z2, HR Z2, Pace Z2, RPE 2–3) and Tempo (Power Z3, HR Z3, Pace Z3, RPE 3–4) pacing. **CD**: Jog 10 min at ACTIVE RECOVERY (Power Z1, HR Z1, Pace Z1, RPE 1)
DISTANCE	7 mi	
TSS	65	
10 KM ENDURANCE RUN		

FRIDAY (PM)

PLANNED METRICS		
DURATION	0:30:00	**WU**: 200m Free at at ACTIVE RECOVERY (Power Z1, HR Z1, Pace Z1, RPE 1), 100m drill (2/3 catch up) **MS**: 2 × 250m at low ENDURANCE (Pace Z2, HR Z2, RPE 2). Focus on form **CD**: 200 pull at ACTIVE RECOVERY (Power Z1, HR Z1, Pace Z1, RPE 1)
DISTANCE	1000	
TSS	20	
RECOVERY - SWIM		

SATURDAY (AM)

<table>
<tr><td>PLANNED METRICS</td><td></td><td rowspan="5">WU: Perform 5 mins of dynamic warm up:
1. Leg swings - 10–20 per leg
2. Leg Tucks - 10–15 per leg
3. Toe touches - 10–20 per leg

Build WU pace from ACTIVE RECOVERY (Power Z1, HR Z1, Pace Z1, RPE 1) to ENDURANCE (Power Z2, HR Z2, Pace Z2, RPE 2–3) for 10 min. Then perform 4 × 10s strides.

MS:
1. Run 1 mi at THRESHOLD (Power Z4, HR Z4, Pace Z4, RPE 4–5)
2. Swim 500m at ENDURANCE (Power Z2, HR Z2, Pace Z2, RPE 2–3)
3. Run 1 mi at ENDURANCE (Power Z2, HR Z2, Pace Z2, RPE 3–4)
4. Swim 500m at TEMPO (Pace Z3, HR Z3, RPE 3–4)
5. Run 1 mi at TEMPO (Power Z3, HR Z3, Pace Z3, RPE 3–4)
6. Swim 500m at ENDURANCE (Power Z2, HR Z2, Pace Z2, RPE 2–3).
7. Run 1 mi at ENDURANCE (Power Z2, HR Z2, Pace Z2, RPE 3–4)</td></tr>
<tr><td>DURATION</td><td>1:28</td></tr>
<tr><td>DISTANCE</td><td>Various</td></tr>
<tr><td>TSS</td><td>106</td></tr>
<tr><td></td><td></td></tr>
<tr><td colspan="2">SWIMRUN BRICK #3</td><td>CD: Walk for 15 min until HR comes down to 100 BPM.</td></tr>
</table>

SUNDAY (AM)

<table>
<tr><td>PLANNED METRICS</td><td></td><td rowspan="5">WU: Perform 5 mins of dynamic warm up:
1. Leg swings - 10–20 per leg
2. Marches - 10–15 per leg
3. Leg side swings - 10–20 per leg

Build WU pace from ACTIVE RECOVERY (Power Z1, HR Z1, Pace Z1, RPE 1) to ENDURANCE (Power Z2, HR Z2, Pace Z2, RPE 2–3) for 10 min. Then perform 4 × 10s strides.

MS: Start main set run at mid ENDURANCE (Power Z2, HR Z2, Pace Z2, RPE 2–3). Once comfortable, complete 4 × 7 min intervals at upper TEMPO (Power Z3, HR Z3, Pace Z3, RPE 3–4). Recover for 5 min ENDURANCE (Power Z2, HR Z2, Pace Z2, RPE 2–3) in between each interval.</td></tr>
<tr><td>DURATION</td><td>1:08:00</td></tr>
<tr><td>DISTANCE</td><td>Various</td></tr>
<tr><td>TSS</td><td>71</td></tr>
<tr><td></td><td></td></tr>
<tr><td colspan="2">4 × 7 RACE PACE RUN INTERVALS</td><td>CD: Jog at ACTIVE RECOVERY (Power Z1, HR Z1, Pace Z1, RPE 1) for 10 min or until HR comes below 100 BPM.</td></tr>
</table>

SUNDAY (PM)

PLANNED METRICS	
DURATION	0:25:00
DISTANCE	
TSS	20

Curls for Biceps – 2 × 20 repetitions per arm

1. Hook the band underneath your foot and stand up straight.
2. Make sure the band is fairly tight.
3. Grip the other end of the band with your right hand, and rest it near your side. If you're gripping the band correctly, your palms will be facing outward.
4. Bend your right elbow, and pull the band toward your shoulder.
5. Slowly bring your arm back to your side and repeat. Practice the curls with each arm.

Pulls for Internal Rotation – 2 × 15 repetitions per arm

1. Loop the band at shoulder height around a fence or sturdy object.
2. Stand away from the fence or object so that the band is taut, but not strained.
3. Turn your right side toward the object, and grip the band with your right hand.
4. Straighten your right arm out from your shoulder.
5. Raise your arm so that it is shoulder-height.
6. Bend your right elbow, and pull the band in toward your shoulder.
7. Slowly straighten your arm and repeat. Switch hands and repeat with your left arm.

Pulls for External Rotation – 2 × 15 repetitions per arm

1. Loop the band at shoulder-height around a fence or sturdy object.
2. Stand away from the fence or object so that the band is taut, but not strained.
3. Turn your left side toward the fence and grip the band with your right hand.
4. Straighten your right arm out from your shoulder.
5. Raise your arm so that it is shoulder-height.
6. Bend your right elbow and pull the band in toward your shoulder.
7. Slowly straighten your arm and repeat. Switch hands and repeat this rotation with your left arm.

Flaps for Lateral & Deltoid Muscles – 2 × 20 repetitions per arm

1. Grip the ends of the band with both of your hands.
2. Hold the band straight above your head with your elbows locked.
3. While keeping your arms straight, pull downward from your shoulders. If you're performing this correctly, you should feel like a bird flapping its wings.

Outward Pulls for Lateral & Trapezius Muscles

1. Stand on the band with both of your feet.
2. Rest your right arm near your side.
3. Lift your right arm straight out from your side. Keep your elbow locked.
4. When you reach the height of your shoulder, lower your arm back to your side and repeat.

RESISTANCE BANDS - SWIMMING #2

WEEK #4

Training Focus: Build #1 - Week 3

MONDAY (AM)

PLANNED METRICS		Actively focus on recovery today: 1) avoid unneccessary physical exertion, 2) watch nutrition closely (healthy carbs, lean protein, and good fats), 3) stretch, and 4) drink when thirsty. Other common recovery aids include massage, napping, elevating legs, floating in water, and listening to music.
DURATION		
DISTANCE		
TSS		
REST DAY		

TUESDAY (AM)

PLANNED METRICS		**WU**: 1. 200m Free at Active Recovery (Power Z1, HR Z1, Pace Z1, RPE 1) 2. 200m Pull with paddles at Endurance (Power Z2, HR Z2, Pace Z2, RPE 2–3) - Focus on hand entry and extension
DURATION	1:00:00	
DISTANCE	3100	
TSS	55	
		MS1: 8 × 75 m Kick with fins with 10 sec. rest **MS2**: 4 × 250m Swim with 30 sec. rest at TEMPO (Pace Z3, HR Z3, RPE 3–4) **MS3**: 4 × 50m at VO2 max (Pace Z5, HR Z5, RPE 5–6) with 20 sec. rest **MS4**: 8 × 25 m Sprint!! with 15 sec. rest **MS5**: 1 × 500m with paddles at ENDURANCE (Pace Z2, HR Z2, RPE 2–3)
8 × 75 KICK, 4 × 250, 8 × 25 SPEED WORK		**CD**: 200m at Active Recovery (Power Z1, HR Z1, Pace Z1, RPE 1)

TUESDAY (PM)

PLANNED METRICS		
DURATION	0:34:00	**WU**: Perform 5 mins of dynamic warm up: 1. Leg swings - 10–20 per leg 2. Leg Tucks - 10–15 per leg 3. Toe touches - 10–20 per leg
DISTANCE	Various	
TSS	50	Build WU pace from ACTIVE RECOVERY (Power Z1, HR Z1, Pace Z1, RPE 1) to ENDURANCE (Power Z2, HR Z2, Pace Z2, RPE 2–3) for 10 min. Then perform 4 × 10s strides. -------- **3 × Progressive Ramps**: 1 minute at ENDURANCE (Power Z2, HR Z2, Pace Z2, RPE 2–3) 2 minutes at upper TEMPO (Power Z3, HR Z3, Pace Z3, RPE 3–4) 3 minutes at low THRESHOLD (Power Z4, HR Z4, Pace Z4, RPE 4–5) 2 minutes at upper THRESHOLD (Power Z4, HR Z4, Pace Z4, RPE 4–5) 1 minute at VO2 (Power Z5, HR Z5, Pace Z5, RPE 5–6) -------- Rest 2 minutes then repeat ------
PROGRESSIVE 34 MINUTE RUN		**CD**: Easy Jog for 10 minutes at ACTIVE RECOVERY (Power Z1, HR Z1, Pace Z1, RPE 1. Stretch and drink wen you are finished.

WEDNESDAY (AM)

PLANNED METRICS		
DURATION	1:05:00	**WU**: Perform 5 mins of dynamic warm up: 1. Leg swings - 10–20 per leg 2. Marches - 10–15 per leg 3. Leg side swings - 10–20 per leg
DISTANCE	Various	
TSS	60	Build WU pace from ACTIVE RECOVERY (Power Z1, HR Z1, Pace Z1, RPE 1) to ENDURANCE (Power Z2, HR Z2, Pace Z2, RPE 2–3) for 10 min. Then perform 4 × 10s strides. **MS**: Tempo run: 40' Low TEMPO (Power Z3, HR Z3, Pace Z3, RPE 3–4).
LOW TEMPO RUN - 40 MIN		**CD**: Jog for 10 min ACTIVE RECOVERY (Power Z1, HR Z1, Pace Z1, RPE 1)

WEDNESDAY (PM)

PLANNED METRICS		
DURATION	0:45:00	Strength Protocol - Week 4 **Goal**: Hypertrophy **Intensity**: 90% of 1 RM **Note**: Last rep should performed until exhaustion.
DISTANCE		
TSS	20	**Exercises**: **Strength**: 1. Bench Press (6 × 4–6) 2. Lateral Pull Down (6 × 4–6) 3. Seated Row (6 × 4–6) 4. Tricep Pulldown (6 × 4–6) 5. Bicep Curl (6 × 4–6) 6. Leg Press (6 × 4–6) 7. Leg Extension (6 × 4–6) 8. Leg Curl (6 × 4–6) 9. Calf Raises (6 × 4–6) 10. Back Extension (6 × 4–6) 11. Ab Curl (6 × 4–6) 12. Leg Tucked Rotation (6 × 4–6)
STRENGTH WORK - WEEK 4		

THURSDAY (AM)

PLANNED METRICS		
DURATION	1:10:00	**WU**: 200 free at Active Recovery (Power Z1, HR Z1, Pace Z1, RPE 1)
DISTANCE	3100	**MS**: Take 10 sec rest with 100 and longer; 5 sec rest between 50s. All pacing at (Pace Z2, HR Z2, RPE 2–3). 8 × 50 - use the first 4 50's to finish warming up 4 × 100 2 × 200 1 × 400 2 × 200 4 × 100 8 50
TSS	50	
EGYPTIAN PYRAMID SWIM - (POINTY TOP)		**CD**: 100 free at Active Recovery (Power Z1, HR Z1, Pace Z1, RPE 1)

FRIDAY (AM)

PLANNED METRICS		
DURATION	1:05	**WU**: Perform 5 mins of dynamic warm up: 1. Leg swings - 10–20 per leg 2. Marches - 10–15 per leg 3. Leg side swings - 10–20 per leg Build WU pace from ACTIVE RECOVERY (Power Z1, HR Z1, Pace Z1, RPE 1) to ENDURANCE (Power Z2, HR Z2, Pace Z2, RPE 2–3) for 10 min. Then perform 4 × 10s strides. **MS**: Run 10 km ranging between your Endurance (Power Z2, HR Z2, Pace Z2, RPE 2–3) and Tempo (Power Z3, HR Z3, Pace Z3, RPE 3–4) pacing. **CD**: Jog 10 min at ACTIVE RECOVERY (Power Z1, HR Z1, Pace Z1, RPE 1)
DISTANCE	7 mi	
TSS	65	
10 KM ENDURANCE RUN		

FRIDAY (PM)

PLANNED METRICS		
DURATION	0:30:00	**WU**: 200m Free at at ACTIVE RECOVERY (Power Z1, HR Z1, Pace Z1, RPE 1), 100m drill (2/3 catch up) **MS**: 2 × 250m at low ENDURANCE (Pace Z2, HR Z2, RPE 2). Focus on form **CD**: 200 pull at ACTIVE RECOVERY (Power Z1, HR Z1, Pace Z1, RPE 1)
DISTANCE	1000	
TSS	20	
RECOVERY - SWIM		

SATURDAY (AM)

PLANNED METRICS	
DURATION	1:45:00
DISTANCE	Various
TSS	102

SWIMRUN BRICK #1

SWIM

WU: 100m free, 100m kick without fins, 100m pull

Pre-set: 4 × 50 free with paddles

MS:

1. 10 × 100m at TEMPO (Pace Z3, HR Z3, RPE 3–4) with 0:10s rest
2. 200m pull at low ENDURANCE (Pace Z2, HR Z3, RPE 2–3)
3. 500m build. Each length should be faster than the previous.
4. 3 × 200m free. 1 & 3 at ENDURANCE (Pace Z2, HR Z3, RPE 2–3). 2nd at TEMPO (Pace Z3, HR Z3, RPE 3–4) with 0:15s rest between each interval.

CD: 100m easy swimming

Throw on shoes and head to treadmill as quickly as possible.

RUN

WU: 10 min at low ENDURANCE (Power Z2, HR Z2, Pace Z2, RPE 2–3) building to middle ENDURANCE.

MS: Start main set run at ENDURANCE (Power Z2, HR Z2, Pace Z2, RPE 2–3). Once comfortable, complete 4 × 5 min intervals at upper TEMPO (Power Z3, HR Z3, Pace Z3, PRE 304) with 10 min rest in between each interval at ENDURANCE (Power Z2, HR Z2, Pace Z2, RPE 2–3).

CD: Walk for 10 min or until HR comes below 100 BPM.

SUNDAY (AM)

PLANNED METRICS		
DURATION	1:15:00	**WU**: Perform 5 mins of dynamic warm up: 1. Leg swings - 10–20 per leg 2. Leg Tucks - 10–15 per leg 3. Toe touches - 10–20 per leg
DISTANCE	8 mi	
TSS	80	Build WU pace from ACTIVE RECOVERY (Power Z1, HR Z1, Pace Z1, RPE 1) to ENDURANCE (Power Z2, HR Z2, Pace Z2, RPE 2–3) for 10 min. Then perform 4 × 10s strides.
		MS: Keep upper ENDURANCE (Power Z2, HR Z2, Pace Z2, RPE 2–3) throughout the MS. The effort will increase with hills.
		Perform 10×: 90 sec at 3%, then 90s back at 0%
		Run balance of time at ENDURANCE (Power Z2, HR Z2, Pace Z2, RPE 2–3). Your total distance should be 8 mi.
RUN THE HILLS, HILLS, HILLS!!!!!		**CD**: Jog at ACTIVE RECOVERY (Power Z1, HR Z1, Pace Z1, RPE 1) for 10 min.

SUNDAY (PM)

PLANNED METRICS	
DURATION	0:30:00
DISTANCE	
TSS	20

RESISTANCE BANDS - SWIMMING #1

Total workout duration should be 20–25 min. Try to do 3–4 rounds of 2 minutes of each exercise. Butterfly (double-arm pull-back): Holding the cords in front of you, stand far enough away to create some tension in them. Bend over at the waist and lower your head. With arms straight and outstretched in front of you, pull your arms down to your sides as if doing an actual butterfly stroke. Remember to start the pull phase with your palms and forearms. Make sure to keep your elbows pointed out and at your shoulder line. Finish with your hands past your hips.

Single arm (freestyle pull-back): Same as the butterfly, but alternate one arm at a time.

Tricep pull-back: Use the same starting position as the butterfly but keep your elbows tucked into your sides and press your arms behind you. Make sure to squeeze the muscles at the back of your arms at the end of each stroke.

Breaststroke pull: Use the same bent-over starting position as above. Make breaststroke motions with your arms. Maintain a high elbow position and execute the motion with your palms and forearms. Be careful not to let your elbows drop below a line parallel to your shoulders.

Chest fly: Stand upright holding the cords in front of you with a little bit of tension. Start with arms outstretched in front of you. While keeping arms at chest height, pull each arm to the side and back until your hands are in line with your shoulders.

Reverse fly: Standing upright and facing away from the cords, position your hands next to your shoulders and your elbows at shoulder level. Keeping your arms parallel to your shoulders, push out until you can press your hands together in front of your chest.

WEEK #5

Training Focus: Recovery Week

MONDAY (AM)

PLANNED METRICS		Actively focus on recovery today: 1) avoid unneccessary physical exertion, 2) watch nutrition closely (healthy carbs, lean protein, and good fats), 3) stretch, and 4) drink when thirsty. Other common recovery aids include massage, napping, elevating legs, floating in water, and listening to music.
DURATION		
DISTANCE		
TSS		
REST DAY		

TUESDAY (AM)

PLANNED METRICS		**WU**: 200m Free at at ACTIVE RECOVERY (Power Z1, HR Z1, Pace Z1, RPE 1), 100m drill (2/3 catch up) **MS**: 2 × 250m at low ENDURANCE (Pace Z2, HR Z2, RPE 2). Focus on form **CD**: 200 pull at ACTIVE RECOVERY (Power Z1, HR Z1, Pace Z1, RPE 1)
DURATION	0:30:00	
DISTANCE	1000	
TSS	20	
RECOVERY - SWIM		

WEDNESDAY (AM)

PLANNED METRICS		
DURATION	0:45:00	Strength Protocol - Week 5 **Goal**: Hypertrophy **Intensity**: 75% of 1 RM **Note**: 1. 3d set should be performed until exhaustion. 2. Only 3 upper body sets. **Exercises**: **Strength**: 1. Bench Press (3 × 8–12) 2. Lateral Pull Down (3 × 8–12) 3. Seated Row (3 × 8–12) 4. Tricep Pulldown (3 × 8–12) 5. Bicep Curl (3 × 8–12) 6. Leg Press (3 × 8–12) 7. Leg Extension (3 × 8–12) 8. Leg Curl (3 × 8–12) 9. Calf Raises (3 × 8–12) 10. Back Extension (3 × 8–12) 11. Ab Curl (4 × 8–12) 12. Leg Tucked Rotation (4 × 8–12)
DISTANCE		
TSS	20	
STRENGTH WORK - WEEK 5		

WEDNESDAY (PM)

PLANNED METRICS		
DURATION	0:40:00	**WU**: Jog for 15 min at ACTIVE RECOVERY (Power Z1, HR Z1, Pace Z1, RPE 1), then **Perform the following dynamic stretches**: 1. Toe Touches - 2 × 15 per leg 2. Leg Tucks - 2 × 15 per leg **MS**: Jog at ACTIVE RECOVERY (Power Z1, HR Z1, Pace Z1, RPE 1) **CD**: Walk for 10 min or until your HR drops below 100 BPM.
DISTANCE	Various	
TSS	19	
RECOVERY - JOG 40 MIN		

THURSDAY (AM)

PLANNED METRICS	DAY OFF
DURATION	
DISTANCE	
TSS	

FRIDAY (AM)

PLANNED METRICS	WU:
DURATION	1. 200m free at Active Recovery (Power Z1, HR Z1, Pace Z1, RPE 1)
DISTANCE	2. 200m pull with paddles at Endurance (Power Z2, HR Z2, Pace Z2, RPE 2–3) – Focus on the catch phase of swim stroke.
TSS	3. 200m kick with fins at Endurance (Power Z2, HR Z2, Pace Z2, RPE 2–3)
300S & PULLS SWIM	**MS**: 1. 6 × 50m w/ 10s rest (descend stroke count 1–6) 2. 2 × 300m w/ 20s rest (50 kick/100 swim at Endurance (Power Z2, HR Z2, Pace Z2, RPE 2–3), repeat) 3. 2 × 50m pull at Active Recovery (Power Z1, HR Z1, Pace Z1, RPE 1) with paddles with 10s rest 4. 100m pull w/ 10s rest at ENDURANCE (Pace Z2, HR Z2, RPE 2–3) 5. 150m pull w/ 15s rest at ENDURANCE (Pace Z2, HR Z2, RPE 2–3) 6. 2 × 150m at ENDURANCE (Pace Z2, HR Z2, RPE 2–3) (50 free/50 non-free/50 free) **CD**: 200m at Active Recovery (Power Z1, HR Z1, Pace Z1, RPE 1)

SATURDAY (AM)

PLANNED METRICS		
DURATION	1:00:00	**WU**: 1. 300m free at Active Recovery (Power Z1, HR Z1, Pace Z1, RPE 1) 2. 200m kick with board and fins - focus on kicking with the ankles and hips 3. 200m drill (6–3-6 switch kick)
DISTANCE	2900	**MS1**: 1 × 1000m at ENDURANCE (Pace Z2, HR Z2, RPE 2–3) with 20s rest
TSS	72	**MS2**: 2 × 500m meters at ENDURANCE (Pace Z2, HR Z2, RPE 2–3) with 10s rest
ENDURANCE SWIM 2000 METER		**CD**: 200 m easy swimming (stroke of choice) at ACTIVE RECOVERY (Pace Z1, HR Z1, RPE 1)

SATURDAY (PM)

PLANNED METRICS		
DURATION	1:05	**WU**: Perform 5 mins of dynamic warm up: 1. Leg swings - 10–20 per leg 2. Marches - 10–15 per leg 3. Leg side swings - 10–20 per leg
DISTANCE	7 mi	Build WU pace from ACTIVE RECOVERY (Power Z1, HR Z1, Pace Z1, RPE 1) to ENDURANCE (Power Z2, HR Z2, Pace Z2, RPE 2–3) for 10 min. Then perform 4 × 10s strides.
TSS	65	**MS**: Run 10 km ranging between your Endurance (Power Z2, HR Z2, Pace Z2, RPE 2–3) and Tempo (Power Z3, HR Z3, Pace Z3, RPE 3–4) pacing.
10 KM ENDURANCE RUN		**CD**: Jog 10 min at ACTIVE RECOVERY (Power Z1, HR Z1, Pace Z1, RPE 1)

SUNDAY (AM)

PLANNED METRICS		
DURATION	1:20:00	**WU**: Perform 5 mins of dynamic warm up: 1. Leg swings - 10–20 per leg 2. Marches - 10–15 per leg 3. Leg side swings - 10–20 per leg
DISTANCE	8 mi	Build WU pace from ACTIVE RECOVERY (Power Z1, HR Z1, Pace Z1, RPE 1) to ENDURANCE (Power Z2, HR Z2, Pace Z2, RPE 2–3) for 10 min. Then perform 4 × 10s strides.
TSS	75	**MS**: Run 7 mi at your ENDURANCE (Power Z2, HR Z2, Pace Z2, RPE 2–3) pace.
7 MILE ENDURANCE RUN		**CD**: Jog 10 min

SUNDAY (PM)

PLANNED METRICS	
DURATION	0:25:00
DISTANCE	
TSS	15

Curls for Biceps – 2 × 20 repetitions per arm

1. Hook the band underneath your foot and stand up straight.
2. Make sure the band is fairly tight.
3. Grip the other end of the band with your right hand, and rest it near your side. If you're gripping the band correctly, your palms will be facing outward.
4. Bend your right elbow, and pull the band toward your shoulder.
5. Slowly bring your arm back to your side and repeat. Practice the curls with each arm.

Pulls for Internal Rotation – 2 × 15 repetitions per arm

1. Loop the band at shoulder height around a fence or sturdy object.
2. Stand away from the fence or object so that the band is taut, but not strained.
3. Turn your right side toward the object, and grip the band with your right hand.
4. Straighten your right arm out from your shoulder.
5. Raise your arm so that it is shoulder-height.
6. Bend your right elbow, and pull the band in toward your shoulder.
7. Slowly straighten your arm and repeat. Switch hands and repeat with your left arm.

Pulls for External Rotation – 2 × 15 repetitions per arm

1. Loop the band at shoulder-height around a fence or sturdy object.
2. Stand away from the fence or object so that the band is taut, but not strained.
3. Turn your left side toward the fence and grip the band with your right hand.
4. Straighten your right arm out from your shoulder.
5. Raise your arm so that it is shoulder-height.
6. Bend your right elbow and pull the band in toward your shoulder.
7. Slowly straighten your arm and repeat. Switch hands and repeat this rotation with your left arm.

	Flaps for Lateral & Deltoid Muscles – 2 × 20 repetitions per arm 1. Grip the ends of the band with both of your hands. 2. Hold the band straight above your head with your elbows locked. 3. While keeping your arms straight, pull downward from your shoulders. If you're performing this correctly, you should feel like a bird flapping its wings. Outward Pulls for Lateral & Trapezius Muscles 1. Stand on the band with both of your feet. 2. Rest your right arm near your side. 3. Lift your right arm straight out from your side. Keep your elbow locked. 4. When you reach the height of your shoulder, lower your arm back to your side and repeat.
RESISTANCE BANDS - SWIMMING #2	

WEEK #6

Training Focus: Peak Week #1

MONDAY (AM)

PLANNED METRICS		Actively focus on recovery today: 1) avoid unneccessary physical exertion, 2) watch nutrition closely (healthy carbs, lean protein, and good fats), 3) stretch, and 4) drink when thirsty. Other common recovery aids include massage, napping, elevating legs, floating in water, and listening to music.
DURATION		
DISTANCE		
TSS		
REST DAY		

TUESDAY (AM)

PLANNED METRICS		**WU**: 1. 400 free at Active Recovery (Power Z1, HR Z1, Pace Z1, RPE 1) building to Endurance (Power Z2, HR Z2, Pace Z2, RPE 2–3) 2. 200 kick with board and fins – focus on kicking with the ankles and hips
DURATION	0:50:00	
DISTANCE	1800	
TSS	50	
10 × 100S - PACE FOCUS		**MS**: 10 × 100s Swim with 40 sec. rest @ Tempo (Power Z3, HR Z3, Pace Z3, RPE 3–4) **CD**: 200 Easy **Note: Try to keep a consistent endurance pace for each 100m (within 1 sec). If you pace drops, give yourself a few more seconds of recovery in between each 100.

TUESDAY (PM)

PLANNED METRICS		
DURATION	1:01:15	**WU**: 15 minutes working into ENDURANCE (Power Z2, HR Z2, Pace Z2, RPE 2–3). Perform 4 × 30 s strides during this time. ------- **MS**: 1. 10 min @ ENDURANCE (Power Z2, HR Z2, Pace Z2, RPE 2–3) 2. 10 min @ mid TEMPO (Power Z3, HR Z3, Pace Z3, RPE 3–4) 3. 10 min @ upper TEMPO (Power Z3, HR Z3, Pace Z3, RPE 3–4) 4. 15 min @ low THRESHOLD (Power Z4, HR Z4 ,Pace Z4, RPE 4–5) -------- **CD**: 10 minutes at ACTIVE ENDURANCE (Power Z1, HR Z1, Pace Z1, RPE Z1)
DISTANCE	Various	
TSS	70	
TEMPO/SST RAMP RUN 1 × 45		

WEDNESDAY (AM)

PLANNED METRICS		
DURATION	0:50:00	**WU**: Perform 5 mins of dynamic warm up: 1. Toe Touches - 10–20 per leg 2. Marches - 10–15 per leg 3. Leg side swings - 10–20 per leg Build WU pace from ACTIVE RECOVERY (Power Z1, HR Z1, Pace Z1, RPE 1) to ENDURANCE (Power Z2, HR Z2, Pace Z2, RPE 2–3) for 10 min. Then perform 4 × 10s strides. **MS**: Perform twice (2×) at THRESHOLD (Power Z4, HR Z4, Pace Z4, RPE 4–5) 1 × 4 minutes fast 3 × 2 minutes fast 2 × 3 minutes fast 4 × 1 minute fast All with 1 minute easy recovery at low ENDURANCE (Power Z2, HR Z2, Pace Z2, RPE 2–3) **CD**: 1 mile at own pace
DISTANCE	Various	
TSS	50	
ENDURANCE RUN - SPEED LADDERS (DECLINE TIMED)		

WEDNESDAY (PM)

PLANNED METRICS		
DURATION	0:45:00	
DISTANCE		
TSS	20	
STRENGTH WORK - WEEK 6		

Strength Protocol - Week 6
Goal: Hypertrophy
Intensity: 75% of 1 RM
Note:
1. 3d set should be performed until exhaustion.
2. Only 3 upper body sets.

Exercises:
Strength:
1. Bench Press (3 × 8–12)
2. Lateral Pull Down (3 × 8–12)
3. Seated Row (3 × 8–12)
4. Tricep Pulldown (3 × 8–12)
5. Bicep Curl (3 × 8–12)
6. Leg Press (5 × 8–12)
7. Leg Extension (5 × 8–12)
8. Leg Curl (5 × 8–12)
9. Calf Raises (5 × 8–12)
10. Back Extension (3 × 8–12)
11. Ab Curl (5 × 8–12)
12. Leg Tucked Rotation (5 × 8–12)

THURSDAY (AM)

PLANNED METRICS	
DURATION	1:15:00
DISTANCE	3900
TSS	76
ENDURANCE SWIM 3000 METER	

WU:
1. 300m free at Active Recovery (Power Z1, HR Z1, Pace Z1, RPE 1)
2. 200m kick with board and fins at Endurance (Power Z2, HR Z2, Pace Z2, RPE 2–3)
3. 200m drill (6–3-6 switch kick)

MS1: 2 × 1000m at ENDURANCE (Pace Z2, HR Z2, RPE 2–3) with 20s rest

MS2: 2 × 500m meters at ENDURANCE (Pace Z2, HR Z2, RPE 2–3) with 10s rest

CD: 200 m at ACTIVE RECOVERY (Pace Z1, HR Z1, RPE 1)

THURSDAY (PM)

PLANNED METRICS		
DURATION	0:40:00	**WU**: Perform 5 mins of dynamic warm up: 1. Leg swings - 10–20 per leg 2. Marches - 10–15 per leg 3. Leg side swings - 10–20 per leg
DISTANCE	4 mi	
TSS	40	
		Build WU pace from ACTIVE RECOVERY (Power Z1, HR Z1, Pace Z1, RPE 1) to ENDURANCE (Power Z2, HR Z2, Pace Z2, RPE 2–3) for 10 min. Then perform 4 × 10s strides.
		MS: Run 5 km at your ENDURANCE (Power Z2, HR Z2, Pace Z2, RPE 2–3) pace.
5 KM RUN		**CD**: Jog 10 min

FRIDAY (AM)

PLANNED METRICS		
DURATION	0:40:00	**WU**: Jog for 15 min at ACTIVE RECOVERY (Power Z1, HR Z1, Pace Z1, RPE 1), then
DISTANCE	Various	Perform the following dynamic stretches: 1. Toe Touches - 2 × 15 per leg 2. Leg Tucks - 2 × 15 per leg
TSS	19	
		MS: Jog at ACTIVE RECOVERY (Power Z1, HR Z1, Pace Z1, RPE 1)
RECOVERY - JOG 40 MIN		**CD**: Walk for 10 min or until your HR drops below 100 BPM.

SATURDAY (AM)

PLANNED METRICS	
DURATION	1:45:00
DISTANCE	Various
TSS	102

SWIMRUN BRICK #1

SWIM

WU: 100m free, 100m kick without fins, 100m pull

Pre-set: 4 × 50 free with paddles

MS:

1. 10 × 100m at TEMPO (Pace Z3, HR Z3, RPE 3–4) with 0:10s rest
2. 200m pull at low ENDURANCE (Pace Z2, HR Z3, RPE 2–3)
3. 500m build. Each length should be faster than the previous.
4. 3 × 200m free. 1 & 3 at ENDURANCE (Pace Z2, HR Z3, RPE 2–3). 2nd at TEMPO (Pace Z3, HR Z3, RPE 3–4) with 0:15s rest between each interval.

CD: 100m easy swimming

Throw on shoes and head to treadmill as quickly as possible.

RUN

WU: 10 min at low ENDURANCE (Power Z2, HR Z2, Pace Z2, RPE 2–3) building to middle ENDURANCE.

MS: Start main set run at ENDURANCE (Power Z2, HR Z2, Pace Z2, RPE 2–3). Once comfortable, complete 4 × 5 min intervals at upper TEMPO (Power Z3, HR Z3, Pace Z3, PRE 304) with 10 min rest in between each interval at ENDURANCE (Power Z2, HR Z2, Pace Z2, RPE 2–3).

CD: Walk for 10 min or until HR comes below 100 BPM.

SUNDAY (AM)

PLANNED METRICS	
DURATION	1:25:00
DISTANCE	9 mi
TSS	75

8 MILE ENDURANCE RUN

WU: Perform 5 mins of dynamic warm up:

1. Leg swings - 10–20 per leg
2. Marches - 10–15 per leg
3. Leg side swings - 10–20 per leg

Build WU pace from ACTIVE RECOVERY (Power Z1, HR Z1, Pace Z1, RPE 1) to ENDURANCE (Power Z2, HR Z2, Pace Z2, RPE 2–3) for 10 min. Then perform 4 × 10s strides.

MS: Run 8 mi at your ENDURANCE (Power Z2, HR Z2, Pace Z2, RPE 2–3) pace.

CD: Jog 10 min

SUNDAY (PM)

PLANNED METRICS		
DURATION	0:30:00	Total workout duration should be 20–25 min. Try to do 3–4 rounds of 2 minutes of each exercise. Butterfly (double-arm pull-back): Holding the cords in front of you, stand far enough away to create some tension in them. Bend over at the waist and lower your head. With arms straight and outstretched in front of you, pull your arms down to your sides as if doing an actual butterfly stroke. Remember to start the pull phase with your palms and forearms. Make sure to keep your elbows pointed out and at your shoulder line. Finish with your hands past your hips. **Single arm (freestyle pull-back)**: Same as the butterfly, but alternate one arm at a time. **Tricep pull-back**: Use the same starting position as the butterfly but keep your elbows tucked into your sides and press your arms behind you. Make sure to squeeze the muscles at the back of your arms at the end of each stroke. **Breaststroke pull**: Use the same bent-over starting position as above. Make breaststroke motions with your arms. Maintain a high elbow position and execute the motion with your palms and forearms. Be careful not to let your elbows drop below a line parallel to your shoulders. **Chest fly**: Stand upright holding the cords in front of you with a little bit of tension. Start with arms outstretched in front of you. While keeping arms at chest height, pull each arm to the side and back until your hands are in line with your shoulders. **Reverse fly**: Standing upright and facing away from the cords, position your hands next to your shoulders and your elbows at shoulder level. Keeping your arms parallel to your shoulders, push out until you can press your hands together in front of your chest.
DISTANCE		
TSS	20	
RESISTANCE BANDS - SWIMMING #1		

WEEK #7

Training Focus: Peak Week #2

MONDAY (AM)

PLANNED METRICS	
DURATION	
DISTANCE	
TSS	
REST DAY	

Actively focus on recovery today: 1) avoid unneccessary physical exertion, 2) watch nutrition closely (healthy carbs, lean protein, and good fats), 3) stretch, and 4) drink when thirsty. Other common recovery aids include massage, napping, elevating legs, floating in water, and listening to music.

TUESDAY (AM)

PLANNED METRICS	
DURATION	1:00:00
DISTANCE	3300
TSS	65
SWIM BUILD SETS WITH RECOVERY KICKS (3300M)	

WU: 500m (200 free at Endurance (Power Z2, HR Z2, Pace Z2, RPE 2–3)/50 kick, repeat)

Pre-Set:

1. 300m pull at Endurance (Power Z2, HR Z2, Pace Z2, RPE 2–3)(3/5/3 breathing pattern by 100)
2. 100m kick with board and fins (50 easy/50 FAST)

MS:

1. 2 × 300m swim at Endurance (Power Z2, HR Z2, Pace Z2, RPE 2–3) building to Threshold (Power Z4, HR Z4, Pace Z4, RPE 5–6) by last 50.
2. 50m at Active Recovery (Power Z1, HR Z1, Pace Z1, RPE 1)/recovery kick w/ :30 rest
3. 3 × 200m pull at Endurance (Power Z2, HR Z2, Pace Z2, RPE 2–3) building to Threshold (Power Z4, HR Z4, Pace Z4, RPE 5–6) by last 50.
4. 50m at Active Recovery (Power Z1, HR Z1, Pace Z1, RPE 1)/recovery kick w/ :30 rest
5. 4 × 100m swim at Endurance (Power Z2, HR Z2, Pace Z2, RPE 2–3) building to Threshold (Power Z4, HR Z4, Pace Z4, RPE 5–6) by last 25.
6. 50m at Active Recovery (Power Z1, HR Z1, Pace Z1, RPE 1)/recovery kick w/ :30 rest
7. 6 × 50m pull at Tempo (Power Z3, HR Z3, Pace Z3, RPE 3–4)
8. 50m at Active Recovery (Power Z1, HR Z1, Pace Z1, RPE 1)/recovery kick w/ :30 rest

CD: 300m free at Active Recovery (Power Z1, HR Z1, Pace Z1, RPE 1)

TUESDAY (PM)

PLANNED METRICS		
DURATION	0:48:00	**WU**: Perform 5 mins of dynamic warm up: 1. Leg swings - 10–20 per leg 2. Marches - 10–15 per leg 3. Leg side swings - 10–20 per leg
DISTANCE	5 mi	
TSS	45	Build WU pace from ACTIVE RECOVERY (Power Z1, HR Z1, Pace Z1, RPE 1) to ENDURANCE (Power Z2, HR Z2, Pace Z2, RPE 2–3) for 10 min. Then perform 4 × 10s strides.
		MS: Run 6 km at your ENDURANCE (Power Z2, HR Z2, Pace Z2, RPE 2–3) pace.
6 KM ENDURANCE RUN		**CD**: Jog 10 min

WEDNESDAY (AM)

PLANNED METRICS		
DURATION	1:05:00	**WU**: Jog at ACTIVE RECOVERY (Power Z1, HR Z1, Pace Z1, RPE 1) to ENDURANCE (Power Z2, HR Z2, Pace Z2, RPE 2–3) for 10 min. Perform 4 × 30s strides during the WU.
DISTANCE	Various	
TSS	66	**MS**: Run: 3 × 12' at Upper TEMPO (Power Z3, HR Z3, Pace Z3, RPE 3–4) pace with 3' at ENDURANCE (Power Z2, HR Z2, Pace Z2, RPE 2–3) between each interval.
TEMPO RUN - 3 × 12'		**CD**: Jog for 10 min at ACTIVE RECOVERY (Power Z1, HR Z1, Pace Z1, RPE 1)

WEDNESDAY (PM)

PLANNED METRICS		
DURATION	0:45:00	Strength Protocol - Week 7 **Goal**: Hypertrophy **Intensity**: 90% of 1 RM **Note**: 1. 3d set should be performed until exhaustion. 2. Only 3 upper body sets.
DISTANCE		
TSS	20	
STRENGTH WORK - WEEK 7		**Exercises**: **Strength**: 1. Bench Press (3 × 4–6) 2. Lateral Pull Down (3 × 4–6) 3. Seated Row (3 × 4–6) 4. Tricep Pulldown (3 × 4–6) 5. Bicep Curl (3 × 4–6) 6. Leg Press (6 × 4–6) 7. Leg Extension (6 × 4–6) 8. Leg Curl (6 × 4–6) 9. Calf Raises (6 × 4–6) 10. Back Extension (3 × 4–6) 11. Ab Curl (3 × 4–6) 12. Leg Tucked Rotation (6 × 4–6)

THURSDAY (AM)

PLANNED METRICS		
DURATION	1:15:00	**WU**: 1. 300m free at Active Recovery (Power Z1, HR Z1, Pace Z1, RPE 1) 2. 200m kick with board and fins at Endurance (Power Z2, HR Z2, Pace Z2, RPE 2–3) 3. 200m drill (6–3-6 switch kick)
DISTANCE	3900	
TSS	76	
ENDURANCE SWIM 3000 METER		**MS1**: 2 × 1000m at ENDURANCE (Pace Z2, HR Z2, RPE 2–3) with 20s rest **MS2**: 2 × 500m meters at ENDURANCE (Pace Z2, HR Z2, RPE 2–3) with 10s rest **CD**: 200 m at ACTIVE RECOVERY (Pace Z1, HR Z1, RPE 1)

THURSDAY (PM)

PLANNED METRICS		
DURATION	1:00:00	**WU**: Perform 5 mins of dynamic warm up: 1. Leg swings - 10–20 per leg 2. Marches - 10–15 per leg 3. Leg side swings - 10–20 per leg Build WU pace from ACTIVE RECOVERY (Power Z1, HR Z1, Pace Z1, RPE 1) to ENDURANCE (Power Z2, HR Z2, Pace Z2, RPE 2–3) for 10 min. Then perform 4 × 10s strides. **MS**: Run 10 km at your ENDURANCE (Power Z2, HR Z2, Pace Z2, RPE 2–3) pace. **CD**: Jog 10 min
DISTANCE	8 mi	
TSS	70	
10 KM ENDURANCE RUN		

FRIDAY (AM)

PLANNED METRICS		
DURATION	0:30:00	**WU**: 1. 200m Free at at ACTIVE RECOVERY (Power Z1, HR Z1, Pace Z1, RPE 1) 2. 100m drill (2/3 catch up) **MS**: 2 × 250m at low ENDURANCE (Pace Z2, HR Z2, RPE 2). Focus on form **CD**: 200 pull at ACTIVE RECOVERY (Power Z1, HR Z1, Pace Z1, RPE 1)
DISTANCE	1000	
TSS	25	
RECOVERY - SWIM		

SATURDAY (AM)

PLANNED METRICS	
DURATION	1:48:00
DISTANCE	Various
TSS	130

SWIMRUN BRICK #4

WU: Perform 5 mins of dynamic warm up:
1. Leg swings - 10–20 per leg
2. Leg Tucks - 10–15 per leg
3. Toe touches - 10–20 per leg

Build WU pace from ACTIVE RECOVERY (Power Z1, HR Z1, Pace Z1, RPE 1) to ENDURANCE (Power Z2, HR Z2, Pace Z2, RPE 2–3) for 10 min. Then perform 4 × 10s strides.

MS:
1. Run 1 mi at THRESHOLD (Power Z4, HR Z4, Pace Z4, RPE 4–5)
2. Swim 500m at ENDURANCE (Power Z2, HR Z2, Pace Z2, RPE 2–3)
3. Run 1 mi at ENDURANCE (Power Z2, HR Z2, Pace Z2, RPE 3–4)
4. Swim 500m at TEMPO (Pace Z3, HR Z3, RPE 3–4)
5. Run 1 mi at TEMPO (Power Z3, HR Z3, Pace Z3, RPE 3–4)
6. Swim 500m at ENDURANCE (Power Z2, HR Z2, Pace Z2, RPE 2–3).
7. Run 3 mi at ENDURANCE (Power Z2, HR Z2, Pace Z2, RPE 3–4).

CD: Walk for 15 min until HR comes down to 100 BPM.

SUNDAY (AM)

PLANNED METRICS	
DURATION	1:25:00
DISTANCE	9 mi
TSS	75

8 MILE ENDURANCE RUN

WU: Perform 5 mins of dynamic warm up:
1. Leg swings - 10–20 per leg
2. Marches - 10–15 per leg
3. Leg side swings - 10–20 per leg

Build WU pace from ACTIVE RECOVERY (Power Z1, HR Z1, Pace Z1, RPE 1) to ENDURANCE (Power Z2, HR Z2, Pace Z2, RPE 2–3) for 10 min. Then perform 4 × 10s strides.

MS: Run 8 mi at your ENDURANCE (Power Z2, HR Z2, Pace Z2, RPE 2–3) pace.

CD: Jog 10 min

SUNDAY (PM)

PLANNED METRICS	
DURATION	0:30:00
DISTANCE	
TSS	25

Curls for Biceps – 2 × 20 repetitions per arm

1. Hook the band underneath your foot and stand up straight.
2. Make sure the band is fairly tight.
3. Grip the other end of the band with your right hand, and rest it near your side. If you're gripping the band correctly, your palms will be facing outward.
4. Bend your right elbow, and pull the band toward your shoulder.
5. Slowly bring your arm back to your side and repeat. Practice the curls with each arm.

Pulls for Internal Rotation – 2 × 15 repetitions per arm

1. Loop the band at shoulder height around a fence or sturdy object.
2. Stand away from the fence or object so that the band is taut, but not strained.
3. Turn your right side toward the object, and grip the band with your right hand.
4. Straighten your right arm out from your shoulder.
5. Raise your arm so that it is shoulder-height.
6. Bend your right elbow, and pull the band in toward your shoulder.
7. Slowly straighten your arm and repeat. Switch hands and repeat with your left arm.

Pulls for External Rotation – 2 × 15 repetitions per arm

1. Loop the band at shoulder-height around a fence or sturdy object.
2. Stand away from the fence or object so that the band is taut, but not strained.
3. Turn your left side toward the fence and grip the band with your right hand.
4. Straighten your right arm out from your shoulder.
5. Raise your arm so that it is shoulder-height.
6. Bend your right elbow and pull the band in toward your shoulder.
7. Slowly straighten your arm and repeat. Switch hands and repeat this rotation with your left arm.

RESISTANCE BANDS - SWIMMING #2	Flaps for Lateral & Deltoid Muscles – 2 × 20 repetitions per arm 1. Grip the ends of the band with both of your hands. 2. Hold the band straight above your head with your elbows locked. 3. While keeping your arms straight, pull downward from your shoulders. If you're performing this correctly, you should feel like a bird flapping its wings. Outward Pulls for Lateral & Trapezius Muscles 1. Stand on the band with both of your feet. 2. Rest your right arm near your side. 3. Lift your right arm straight out from your side. Keep your elbow locked. 4. When you reach the height of your shoulder, lower your arm back to your side and repeat.

WEEK #8

Training Focus: Taper Week

MONDAY

PLANNED METRICS		
DURATION		Actively focus on recovery today: 1) avoid unneccessary physical exertion, 2) watch nutrition closely (healthy carbs, lean protein, and good fats), 3) stretch, and 4) drink when thirsty. Other common recovery aids include massage, napping, elevating legs, floating in water, and listening to music.
DISTANCE		
TSS		
REST DAY		

TUESDAY

PLANNED METRICS		
DURATION	0:31:00	**WU**: Perform 5 mins of dynamic warm up: 1. Leg swings - 10–20 per leg 2. Marches - 10–15 per leg 3. Leg side swings - 10–20 per leg Build WU pace from ACTIVE RECOVERY (Power Z1, HR Z1, Pace Z1, RPE 1) to ENDURANCE (Power Z2, HR Z2, Pace Z2, RPE 2–3) for 10 min. Then perform 4 × 10s strides. **MS**: 4 × 3 min progression run - increase pace/effort with each 3 minute interval on 1 min walking recovery. 1: Low-TEMPO (Power Z3, HR Z3, Pace Z3, RPE 3–4) 2: Mid TEMPO (Power Z3, HR Z3, Pace Z3, RPE 3–4) 3: Upper TEMPO (Power Z3, HR Z3, Pace Z3, RPE 3–4) 4: Low THRESHOLD (Power Z4, HR Z4, RPE 4–5) **CD**: 10 min jog at ACTIVE RECOVERY (Power Z1, HR Z1, Pace Z1, RPE 1)
DISTANCE	Various	
TSS	36	
RUN TAPER RACE EFFORTS: 4 × 3 PROGRESSION ON 1 MIN WALKING RECOVERY		

WEDNESDAY

PLANNED METRICS		
DURATION	0:30:00	**WU**: 1. 200m Free at at ACTIVE RECOVERY (Power Z1, HR Z1, Pace Z1, RPE 1) 2. 100m drill (2/3 catch up)
DISTANCE	1000	
TSS	25	**MS**: 2 × 250m at low ENDURANCE (Pace Z2, HR Z2, RPE 2). Focus on form
RECOVERY - SWIM		**CD**: 200 pull at ACTIVE RECOVERY (Power Z1, HR Z1, Pace Z1, RPE 1)

THURSDAY

PLANNED METRICS		
DURATION	0:40:00	**WU**: Jog for 15 min at ACTIVE RECOVERY (Power Z1, HR Z1, Pace Z1, RPE 1), then
DISTANCE	Various	Perform the following dynamic stretches: 1. Toe Touches - 2 × 15 per leg 2. Leg Tucks - 2 × 15 per leg
TSS	19	**MS**: Jog at ACTIVE RECOVERY (Power Z1, HR Z1, Pace Z1, RPE 1)
RECOVERY - JOG 40 MIN		**CD**: Walk for 10 min or until your HR drops below 100 BPM.

FRIDAY

PLANNED METRICS		
DURATION	0:38:00	**WU**: Perform 5 mins of dynamic warm up: 1. Leg swings - 10–20 per leg 2. Marches - 10–15 per leg 3. Leg side swings - 10–20 per leg
DISTANCE	Various	Build WU pace from ACTIVE RECOVERY (Power Z1, HR Z1, Pace Z1, RPE 1) to ENDURANCE (Power Z2, HR Z2, Pace Z2, RPE 2–3) for 10 min. Then perform 4 × 10s strides.
TSS	26	**MS**: Start main set run at mid ENDURANCE (Power Z2, HR Z2, Pace Z2, RPE 2–3). Once comfortable, complete 3 × 3 min intervals at low TEMPO (Power Z3, HR Z3, Pace Z3, RPE 3–4). Recover for 3 min low ENDURANCE (Power Z2, HR Z2, Pace Z2, RPE 2–3) in between each interval.
EVENT PRIMER - RUN		**CD**: Jog at ACTIVE RECOVERY (Power Z1, HR Z1, Pace Z1, RPE 1) for 10 min or until HR comes below 100 BPM.

SATURDAY

PLANNED METRICS	Today is the big day! Make sure you do the prescribed warm up you are on early. Stay relaxed and ready to race. You will crush it!
DURATION	
DISTANCE	
TSS	
THE BIG EVENT!!!	

SUNDAY

PLANNED METRICS	DAY OFF
DURATION	
DISTANCE	
TSS	

Plan 4

Power Based Long Course SwimRun Training Plan

For this plan, please reference the following Test Interpretation Notes on p. 493 of this book:

- CSS Interpretation Notes (p. 493)
- Critical Run Speed/rFTP Test Calculations (p. 493)

WEEK #1

Training Focus: Test Week - The focus of this week is to set your personalized power and pace zones for swimming and runing.

MONDAY

PLANNED METRICS		
DURATION	0:45:00	**WU**: 200m at an easy pace
DISTANCE	1300	**Pull**: 200m pull (100m follow through drill/ 100m finger tip drill)
TSS	40	**Kick**: 100 m with fins
		MS1: 1 × 400m timed. This is a 400 m time-trial. Swim as hard as you can but do not start so hard as you fade in the last meters. You want your pace to be as even as possible during the entire 400m. If possible, have someone count your strokes during a length near the 200m point of the test (you can also find this information if you are using a smart watch such as the Garmin Swim or 920XT). Once finished, recover for 5–10 min. You can get out of the pool or slowly swim. The point is to recover but stay loose.
		MS2: 1 × 200m time trial. Swim as hard as you can. Ensure your 200m time is faster than 1/2 of your 400m time.
CRITICAL SWIM SPEED SWIM TEST #1		**CD**: 200m easy

TUESDAY

PLANNED METRICS		
DURATION	0:45:00	**WU**: Perform 5 mins of dynamic warm up: 1. Leg swings - 10–20 per leg 2. Marches - 10–15 per leg 3. Leg side swings - 10–20 per leg
DISTANCE	5 mi	
TSS	35	Build WU pace from ACTIVE RECOVERY (Power Z1, HR Z1, RPE 1) to ENDURANCE (Power Z2, HR Z2, RPE 2–3) for 10 min. Then perform 4 × 10s strides.
CRITICAL RUN SPEED TEST #1–5 KM RFTP TEST		**MS**: Run 5 km at maximal pace. Do not go out too fast as to slow down over the course of the interval. **CD**: Jog for 10 at ACTIVE RECOVERY (Power Z1, HR Z1, RPE 1)

WEDNESDAY

PLANNED METRICS		
DURATION	0:45:00	**WU**: 200m at an easy pace **Pull**: 200m pull (100m follow through drill/ 100m finger tip drill)
DISTANCE	1700	
TSS	30	**Kick**: 100 m with fins
CRITICAL SWIM SPEED TEST #2		**MS**: Perform 1 × 1000m time trial. Just like you performed with the 400 m time trial, do not start so hard that you fade in the final meters. Ensure you swim as hard and even as possible during the entire time trial. At about the 500m point, if possible, have someone count your stroke rate (you can use a smartwatch to capture this information such as a Garmin Swim or Garmin 920XT). **CD**: 200m easy.

THURSDAY

PLANNED METRICS		
DURATION		Actively focus on recovery today: 1) avoid unneccessary physical exertion, 2) watch nutrition closely (healthy carbs, lean protein, and good fats), 3) stretch, and 4) drink when thirsty. Other common recovery aids include massage, napping, elevating legs, floating in water, and listening to music.
DISTANCE		
TSS		
REST DAY		

FRIDAY

PLANNED METRICS		
DURATION	0:50:00	**WU**: Perform 5 mins of dynamic warm up: 1. Leg swings - 10–20 per leg 2. Toe Touches - 10–15 per leg 3. Leg tucks - 10–20 per leg
DISTANCE	7 mi	
TSS	60	Build WU pace from ACTIVE RECOVERY (Power Z1, HR Z1, RPE 1) to ENDURANCE (Power Z2, HR Z2, RPE 2–3) for 10 min. Then perform 4 × 10s strides.
		MS: Run 10 km at a maximal pace. Do not go out too fast as to slow down over the course of the interval.
CRITICAL RUN SPEED TEST #2–10 KM TEST		**CD**: Jog for 10 at ACTIVE RECOVERY (Power Z1, HR Z1, RPE 1)

SATURDAY

PLANNED METRICS		
DURATION	1:10:00	**WU**: 300m free/200m kick with fins/200m drill (6-3-6 switch kick) -------------
DISTANCE	3400	**MS1**: 1 × 1000m at ENDURANCE (Pace Z2, HR Z2, RPE 2–3) with 20s rest
TSS	71	
		MS2: 4 × 500m meters at ENDURANCE (Pace Z2, HR Z2, RPE 2–3) with 10s rest -------------
ENDURANCE SWIM 3000 METER		**CD**: 200 m easy swimming (stroke of choice) at ACTIVE RECOVERY (Pace Z1, HR Z1, RPE 1)

SUNDAY

PLANNED METRICS		
DURATION	1:05:00	**WU**: Perform 5 mins of dynamic warm up: 1. Leg swings - 10–20 per leg 2. Marches - 10–15 per leg 3. Leg side swings - 10–20 per leg
DISTANCE	7 mi	
TSS	65	Build WU pace from ACTIVE RECOVERY (Power Z1, HR Z1, RPE 1) to ENDURANCE (Power Z2, HR Z2, RPE 2–3) for 10 min. Then perform 4 × 10s strides.
		MS: Run 10 km at ENDURANCE (Power Z2, HR Z2, RPE 2–3).
10 KM ENDURANCE RUN		**CD**: Jog 10 min

WEEK #2

Training Focus: Build #1 - Week #1

MONDAY (AM)

PLANNED METRICS		Actively focus on recovery today: 1) avoid unneccessary physical exertion, 2) watch nutrition closely (healthy carbs, lean protein, and good fats), 3) stretch, and 4) drink when thirsty. Other common recovery aids include massage, napping, elevating legs, floating in water, and listening to music.
DURATION		
DISTANCE		
TSS		
REST DAY		

TUESDAY (AM)

PLANNED METRICS		Strength Protocol - Week 2 **Goal**: Endurance / Adaptation **Intensity**: 60% of 1 RM
DURATION	0:45:00	
DISTANCE		**Exercises**:
TSS	20	**Strength**:
STRENGTH WORK - WEEK 2		1. Bench Press (3 × 20) 2. Lateral Pull Down (3 × 20) 3. Seated Row (3 × 20) 4. Tricep Pulldown (3 × 20) 5. Bicep Curl (3 × 20) 6. Leg Press (3 × 30) 7. Leg Extension (3 × 20) 8. Leg Curl (3 × 20) 9. Calf Raises (3 × 20) 10. Back Extension (3 × 20) 11. Ab Curl (3 × 20) 12. Leg Tucked Rotation (3 × 20)

TUESDAY (PM)

PLANNED METRICS		
DURATION	1:04:55	**WU**: Perform 5 mins of dynamic warm up: 1. Leg swings - 10–20 per leg 2. Marches - 10–15 per leg 3. Leg side swings - 10–20 per leg Build WU pace from ACTIVE RECOVERY (Power Z1, HR Z1, Pace Z1, RPE 1) to ENDURANCE (Power Z2, HR Z2, Pace Z2, RPE 2–3) for 10 min. Then perform 4 × 10s strides. **MS**: Run 6 mi at upper ENDURANCE (Power Z2, HR Z2, Pace Z2, RPE 2–3). During this 6 mile main set, run 2 mi at TEMPO (Power Z3, HR Z3, Pace Z3, RPE 3–4). You can do the 2 mi TEMPO segment at any point during the run. **CD**: Walk for 10 min to bring HR down to 100 BPM.
DISTANCE	7.5 mi	
TSS	70	
6 MILE RUN WITH TEMPO		

WEDNESDAY (AM)

PLANNED METRICS		
DURATION	1:05:00	**WU**: 400m free at Active Recovery (Power Z1, HR Z1, Pace Z1, RPE 1) 200m pull with paddles at Endurance (Power Z2, HR Z2, Pace Z2, RPE 2–3) **MS1**: 4 × 100m Kick without fins 15 sec. rest **MS2**: 4 × 600m free at Endurance (Power Z2, HR Z2, Pace Z2, RPE 2–3) with 20 sec. rest #1: Do as 2 × 300 with 15 sec. rest between 300s #2: Pull with paddles #3: Do as 3 × 200 with 15 sec. rest between #4 Pull with paddles **CD**: 200 free at Active Recovery (Power Z1, HR Z1, Pace Z1, RPE 1)
DISTANCE	3600m	
TSS	55	
4 × 100 KICK, 3 × 600		

WEDNESDAY (PM)

PLANNED METRICS		
DURATION	1:06:00	**WU**: Perform 5 mins of dynamic warm up: 1. Leg swings - 10–20 per leg 2. Marches - 10–15 per leg 3. Leg side swings - 10–20 per leg Build WU pace from ACTIVE RECOVERY (Power Z1, HR Z1, Pace Z1, RPE 1) to ENDURANCE (Power Z2, HR Z2, Pace Z2, RPE 2–3) for 10 min. Then perform 4 × 10s strides. ---------- **MS**: Run 10–5-3–2-1 minutes at 5 K pace (THRESHOLD (Power Z4, HR Z4, Pace Z4, RPE 4–5) and jog equal amounts between each segment. ---------- **CD**: 10 minute cool down at (ACTIVE RECOVERY (Power Z1, HR Z1, Pace Z1, RPE 1)
DISTANCE	Various	
TSS	65	
FARTLEK RUN		

THURSDAY (AM)

PLANNED METRICS		
DURATION	1:05:00	**WU**: 400m free at Active Recovery (Power Z1, HR Z1, Pace Z1, RPE 1) 200m pull with paddles at Endurance (Power Z2, HR Z2, Pace Z2, RPE 2–3) **MS1**: 4 × 100m Kick without fins 15 sec. rest **MS2**: 4 × 600m free at Endurance (Power Z2, HR Z2, Pace Z2, RPE 2–3) with 20 sec. rest #1: Do as 2 × 300 with 15 sec. rest between 300s #2: Pull with paddles #3: Do as 3 × 200 with 15 sec. rest between #4 Pull with paddles **CD**: 200 free at Active Recovery (Power Z1, HR Z1, Pace Z1, RPE 1)
DISTANCE	3600m	
TSS	55	
4 × 100 KICK, 3 × 600		

THURSDAY (PM)

PLANNED METRICS		
DURATION	1:05:00	**WU**: Perform 5 mins of dynamic warm up: 1. Leg swings - 10–20 per leg 2. Marches - 10–15 per leg 3. Leg side swings - 10–20 per leg
DISTANCE	6.2 mi	
TSS	70	Build WU pace from ACTIVE RECOVERY (Power Z1, HR Z1, Pace Z1, RPE 1) to ENDURANCE (Power Z2, HR Z2, Pace Z2, RPE 2–3) for 10 min. Then perform 4 × 10s strides.
		MS: Run 10 km at your marathon pace / ENDURANCE (Power Z2, HR Z2, Pace Z2, RPE 2–3) or better pace.
10 KM RUN		**CD**: Jog 10 min

FRIDAY (AM)

PLANNED METRICS		
DURATION	0:40:00	**WU**: Jog for 15 min at ACTIVE RECOVERY (Power Z1, HR Z1, Pace Z1, RPE 1), then
DISTANCE	Various	**Perform the following dynamic stretches**: 1. Toe Touches - 2 × 15 per leg 2. Leg Tucks - 2 × 15 per leg
TSS	19	
		MS: Jog at ACTIVE RECOVERY (Power Z1, HR Z1, Pace Z1, RPE 1)
40 MIN RECOVERY JOG		**CD**: Walk for 10 min or until your HR drops below 100 BPM.

SATURDAY (AM)

PLANNED METRICS		
DURATION	1:45:00	
DISTANCE	Various	
TSS	102	
SWIMRUN BRICK #1		

SWIM

WU: 100m free, 100m kick without fins, 100m pull
Pre-set: 4 × 50 free with paddles

MS:

1. 10 × 100m at TEMPO (Pace Z3, HR Z3, RPE 3–4) with 0:10s rest
2. 200m pull at low ENDURANCE (Pace Z2, HR Z3, RPE 2–3)
3. 500m build. Each length should be faster than the previous.
4. 3 × 200m free. 1 & 3 at ENDURANCE (Pace Z2, HR Z3, RPE 2–3). 2nd at TEMPO (Pace Z3, HR Z3, RPE 3–4) with 0:15s rest between each interval.

CD: 100m easy swimming
Throw on shoes and head to treadmill as quickly as possible.

RUN

WU: 10 min at low ENDURANCE (Power Z2, HR Z2, Pace Z2, RPE 2–3) building to middle ENDURANCE.

MS: Start main set run at ENDURANCE (Power Z2, HR Z2, Pace Z2, RPE 2–3). Once comfortable, complete 4 × 5 min intervals at upper TEMPO (Power Z3, HR Z3, Pace Z3, PRE 304) with 10 min rest in between each interval at ENDURANCE (Power Z2, HR Z2, Pace Z2, RPE 2–3).

CD: Walk for 10 min or until HR comes below 100 BPM.

SUNDAY (AM)

PLANNED METRICS		
DURATION	0:25:00	Total workout duration should be 20–25 min. Try to do 3–4 rounds of 2 minutes of each exercise. **Butterfly (double-arm pull-back)**: Holding the cords in front of you, stand far enough away to create some tension in them. Bend over at the waist and lower your head. With arms straight and outstretched in front of you, pull your arms down to your sides as if doing an actual butterfly stroke. Remember to start the pull phase with your palms and forearms. Make sure to keep your elbows pointed out and at your shoulder line. Finish with your hands past your hips. **Single arm (freestyle pull-back)**: Same as the butterfly, but alternate one arm at a time. **Tricep pull-back**: Use the same starting position as the butterfly but keep your elbows tucked into your sides and press your arms behind you. Make sure to squeeze the muscles at the back of your arms at the end of each stroke. **Breaststroke pull**: Use the same bent-over starting position as above. Make breaststroke motions with your arms. Maintain a high elbow position and execute the motion with your palms and forearms. Be careful not to let your elbows drop below a line parallel to your shoulders. **Chest fly**: Stand upright holding the cords in front of you with a little bit of tension. Start with arms outstretched in front of you. While keeping arms at chest height, pull each arm to the side and back until your hands are in line with your shoulders. **Reverse fly**: Standing upright and facing away from the cords, position your hands next to your shoulders and your elbows at shoulder level. Keeping your arms parallel to your shoulders, push out until you can press your hands together in front of your chest.
DISTANCE		
TSS	21	
RESISTANCE BANDS #1		

SUNDAY (PM)

PLANNED METRICS		
DURATION	1:30:00	**WU**: Perform 5 mins of dynamic warm up: 1. Leg swings - 10–20 per leg 2. Marches - 10–15 per leg 3. Leg side swings - 10–20 per leg Build WU pace from Active Recovery (Power Z1, HR Z1, Pace Z1, RPE 1) to Endurance (Power Z2, HR Z2, Pace Z2, RPE 2–3) for 10 min. Then perform 4 × 10s strides. **MS**: Run 10 mi at Endurance (Power Z2, HR Z2, Pace Z2, RPE 2–3) **CD**: Jog 10 min at Active Recovery (Power Z1, HR Z1, Pace Z1, RPE 1)
DISTANCE	10 mi	
TSS	100	
LONG RUN - 10 MILES		

WEEK #3

Training Focus: Build #1 - Week #2

MONDAY (AM)

PLANNED METRICS		Actively focus on recovery today: 1) avoid unneccessary physical exertion, 2) watch nutrition closely (healthy carbs, lean protein, and good fats), 3) stretch, and 4) drink when thirsty. Other common recovery aids include massage, napping, elevating legs, floating in water, and listening to music.
DURATION		
DISTANCE		
TSS		
REST DAY		

TUESDAY (AM)

PLANNED METRICS		
DURATION	1:20:00	
DISTANCE	3700	
TSS	60	
SWIM - 8 × 75 &16 × 25 FAST, 2 × 500		**WU**: 1. 200 free Active Recovery (Power Z1, HR Z1, Pace Z1, RPE 1) 2. 200 pull with paddles Endurance (Power Z2, HR Z2, Pace Z2, RPE 2–3) 3. 200 drill (100 Tarzan and 100 3/4 catch up) **MS1**: 8 × 75 Kick with 10 sec. rest (Odds with fins, evens without fins) **MS2**: 6 × 150 at Swim at Endurance (Power Z2, HR Z2, Pace Z2, RPE 2–3) with 15 sec. rest -Middle 50 change stroke to breast or back **MS3**: 16 × 25 Swim with 5 sec. rest -All are fast, but not sprint. Try to keep times within 2s of each, VO2 Max (Pace Z5, HR Z5, RPE 5–6) **MS4**: 2 × 500 moderate ENDURANCE (Pace Z2, HR Z2, RPE 2–3). Focus on form. Do one set with paddles. **CD**: 200 at Active Recovery (Power Z1, HR Z1, Pace Z1, RPE 1)

TUESDAY (PM)

PLANNED METRICS		
DURATION	1:05:00	**WU**: Perform 5 mins of dynamic warm up: 1. Leg swings - 10–20 per leg 2. Marches - 10–15 per leg 3. Leg side swings - 10–20 per leg Build WU pace from ACTIVE RECOVERY (Power Z1, HR Z1, Pace Z1, RPE 1) to ENDURANCE (Power Z2, HR Z2, Pace Z2, RPE 2–3) for 10 min. Then perform 4 × 10s strides. **MS**: Run 10 km at your marathon pace/ENDURANCE (Power Z2, HR Z2, Pace Z2, RPE 2–3) or better pace. **CD**: Jog 10 min
DISTANCE	6.2 mi	
TSS	70	
10 KM RUN		

WEDNESDAY (AM)

PLANNED METRICS		
DURATION	0:45:00	Strength Protocol - Week 3 **Goal**: Hypertrophy **Intensity**: 70% of 1 RM **Note**: 3d set should be performed until exhaustion. **Exercises**: **Strength**: 1. Bench Press (3 × 8–12) 2. Lateral Pull Down (3 × 8–12) 3. Seated Row (3 × 8–12) 4. Tricep Pulldown (3 × 8–12) 5. Bicep Curl (3 × 8–12) 6. Leg Press (3 × 8–12) 7. Leg Extension (3 × 8–12) 8. Leg Curl (3 × 8–12) 9. Calf Raises (3 × 8–12) 10. Back Extension (3 × 8–12) 11. Ab Curl (3 × 8–12) 12. Leg Tucked Rotation (3 × 8–12)
DISTANCE		
TSS	25	
STRENGTH WORK - WEEK 3		

WEDNESDAY (PM)

PLANNED METRICS		
DURATION	1:00:00	**WU**: Perform 5 mins of dynamic warm up: 1. Leg swings - 10–20 per leg 2. Marches - 10–15 per leg 3. Leg side swings - 10–20 per leg Build WU pace from ACTIVE RECOVERY (Power Z1, HR Z1, Pace Z1, RPE 1) to ENDURANCE (Power Z2, HR Z2, Pace Z2, RPE 2–3) for 10 min. Then perform 4 × 10s strides. **MS**: Mid ENDURANCE (Power Z2, HR Z2, Pace Z2, RPE 2–3) - keep pace steady throughout. On a treadmill or long climb, perform 5 × 5 mins hill repeats at 3% to 5% with 3 min recovery at 0% grade. Try to keep the same ENDURANCE pace throughout the workout. **CD**: 10 min at ACTIVE RECOVERY (Power Z1, HR Z1, Pace Z1, RPE 1)
DISTANCE	6.5 mi	
TSS	80	
RUN - LONG HILLS		

THURSDAY (AM)

PLANNED METRICS		
DURATION	1:10:00	Active Recovery (Power Z1, HR Z1, Pace Z1, RPE 1)
DISTANCE	3100	
TSS	47	
SWIM - 20 × 50, 4 × 300 PULL		

THURSDAY (PM)

PLANNED METRICS		
DURATION	0:56:00	**WU**: Perform 5 mins of dynamic warm up: 1. Leg swings - 10–20 per leg 2. Marches - 10–15 per leg 3. Leg side swings - 10–20 per leg
DISTANCE	Various	Build WU pace from ACTIVE RECOVERY (Power Z1, HR Z1, Pace Z1, RPE 1) to ENDURANCE (Power Z2, HR Z2, Pace Z2, RPE 2–3) for 10 min. Then perform 4 × 10s strides.
TSS	57	**MS**: Start main set run at mid ENDURANCE (Power Z2, HR Z2, Pace Z2, RPE 2–3). Once comfortable, complete 3 × 7 min intervals at upper TEMPO (Power Z3, HR Z3, Pace Z3, RPE 3–4). Recover for 5 min ENDURANCE (Power Z2, HR Z2, Pace Z2, RPE 2–3) in between each interval.
RUN - 3 × 7 RACE PACE INTERVALS		**CD**: Jog at ACTIVE RECOVERY (Power Z1, HR Z1, Pace Z1, RPE 1) for 10 min or until HR comes below 100 BPM.

FRIDAY (AM)

PLANNED METRICS		
DURATION	0:30:00	**WU**: 200m Free easy, 100m drill (2/3 catch up)
DISTANCE	1000	**MS**: 2 × 250m at low ENDURANCE (Pace Z2, HR Z2, RPE 2). Focus on form
TSS	20	**CD**: 200 pull at ACTIVE RECOVERY (Power Z1, HR Z1, Pace Z1, RPE 1)
RECOVERY - SWIM		

SATURDAY (AM)

PLANNED METRICS		
DURATION	1:35:00	**Warm-up** **WU**: Perform 5 mins of dynamic warm up: 1. Leg Tucks - 10–20 per leg 2. Marches - 10–15 per leg 3. Toe Touches - 10–20 per leg
DISTANCE	Various	Build WU pace from ACTIVE RECOVERY (Power Z1, HR Z1, Pace Z1, RPE 1) to ENDURANCE (Power Z2, HR Z2, Pace Z2, RPE 2–3) for 10 min. Then perform 4 × 10s strides.
TSS	125	**MS**: Repeat 3–5× 1. 400m swim at TEMPO (Pace Z3, HR Z3, RPE 3–4). The put on your run shoes and immediately go into 2. 1 mile run at TEMPO (Power Z3, HR Z3, Pace Z3, RPE 3–4) 3. 1 minute walk, then 50 swim easy recovery
SWIMRUN BRICK #2		**CD**: 200 m of easy pulls or 10–15 min of walking.

SUNDAY (AM)

PLANNED METRICS	
DURATION	0:25:00
DISTANCE	
TSS	20

Curls for Biceps – 2 × 20 repetitions per arm

1. Hook the band underneath your foot and stand up straight.
2. Make sure the band is fairly tight.
3. Grip the other end of the band with your right hand, and rest it near your side. If you're gripping the band correctly, your palms will be facing outward.
4. Bend your right elbow, and pull the band toward your shoulder.
5. Slowly bring your arm back to your side and repeat. Practice the curls with each arm.

Pulls for Internal Rotation – 2 × 15 repetitions per arm

1. Loop the band at shoulder height around a fence or sturdy object.
2. Stand away from the fence or object so that the band is taut, but not strained.
3. Turn your right side toward the object, and grip the band with your right hand.
4. Straighten your right arm out from your shoulder.
5. Raise your arm so that it is shoulder-height.
6. Bend your right elbow, and pull the band in toward your shoulder.
7. Slowly straighten your arm and repeat. Switch hands and repeat with your left arm.

Pulls for External Rotation – 2 × 15 repetitions per arm

1. Loop the band at shoulder-height around a fence or sturdy object.
2. Stand away from the fence or object so that the band is taut, but not strained.
3. Turn your left side toward the fence and grip the band with your right hand.
4. Straighten your right arm out from your shoulder.
5. Raise your arm so that it is shoulder-height.
6. Bend your right elbow and pull the band in toward your shoulder.
7. Slowly straighten your arm and repeat. Switch hands and repeat this rotation with your left arm.

RESISTANCE BANDS - SWIMMING #2	Flaps for Lateral & Deltoid Muscles – 2 × 20 repetitions per arm 1. Grip the ends of the band with both of your hands. 2. Hold the band straight above your head with your elbows locked. 3. While keeping your arms straight, pull downward from your shoulders. If you're performing this correctly, you should feel like a bird flapping its wings. Outward Pulls for Lateral & Trapezius Muscles 1. Stand on the band with both of your feet. 2. Rest your right arm near your side. 3. Lift your right arm straight out from your side. Keep your elbow locked. 4. When you reach the height of your shoulder, lower your arm back to your side and repeat.

SUNDAY (PM)

PLANNED METRICS		
DURATION	1:30:00	**WU**: Perform 5 mins of dynamic warm up: 1. Leg swings - 10–20 per leg 2. Marches - 10–15 per leg 3. Leg side swings - 10–20 per leg Build WU pace from Active Recovery (Power Z1, HR Z1, Pace Z1, RPE 1) to Endurance (Power Z2, HR Z2, Pace Z2, RPE 2–3) for 10 min. Then perform 4 × 10s strides. **MS**: Run 10 mi at Endurance (Power Z2, HR Z2, Pace Z2, RPE 2–3) **CD**: Jog 10 min at Active Recovery (Power Z1, HR Z1, Pace Z1, RPE 1)
DISTANCE	10 mi	
TSS	100	
LONG RUN - 10 MILES		

WEEK #4

Training Focus: Build #1 - Week 3

MONDAY (AM)

PLANNED METRICS		Actively focus on recovery today: 1) avoid unneccessary physical exertion, 2) watch nutrition closely (healthy carbs, lean protein, and good fats), 3) stretch, and 4) drink when thirsty. Other common recovery aids include massage, napping, elevating legs, floating in water, and listening to music.
DURATION		
DISTANCE		
TSS		
REST DAY		

TUESDAY (AM)

PLANNED METRICS		**WU**: 1. 200 Free at Active Recovery (Power Z1, HR Z1, Pace Z1, RPE 1) 2. 200 Pull with paddles at Endurance (Power Z2, HR Z2, Pace Z2, RPE 2–3)
DURATION	1:15:00	
DISTANCE	3600	
TSS	56	
SWIM - 8 × 75 KICK, 4 × 250, 8 × 25 SPEED WORK		**MS1**: 8 × 75 Kick with 10 sec. rest. - focus on kicking with the ankles and hips **MS2**: 4 × 250 Swim with 30 sec. rest at TEMPO (Pace Z3, HR Z3, RPE 3–4) **MS3**: 4 × 50 at VO2 max (Pace Z5, HR Z5, RPE 5–6) with 20 sec. rest 8 × 25 Sprint!! with 15 sec. rest **MS4**: 2 × 500 pulls with paddles **CD**: 200 at Active Recovery (Power Z1, HR Z1, Pace Z1, RPE 1)

TUESDAY (PM)

PLANNED METRICS		
DURATION	1:05:00	**WU**: Perform 5 mins of dynamic warm up: 1. Leg swings - 10–20 per leg 2. Marches - 10–15 per leg 3. Leg side swings - 10–20 per leg Build WU pace from ACTIVE RECOVERY (Power Z1, HR Z1, Pace Z1, RPE 1) to ENDURANCE (Power Z2, HR Z2, Pace Z2, RPE 2–3) for 10 min. Then perform 4 × 10s strides. **MS**: Run 10 km at your marathon pace/ENDURANCE (Power Z2, HR Z2, Pace Z2, RPE 2–3) or better pace. **CD**: Jog 10 min
DISTANCE	6.2 mi	
TSS	70	
10 KM RUN		

WEDNESDAY (AM)

PLANNED METRICS		
DURATION	0:45:00	Strength Protocol - Week 4 **Goal**: Hypertrophy **Intensity**: 90% of 1 RM **Note**: Last rep should performed until exhaustion. **Exercises**: **Strength**: 1. Bench Press (6 × 4–6) 2. Lateral Pull Down (6 × 4–6) 3. Seated Row (6 × 4–6) 4. Tricep Pulldown (6 × 4–6) 5. Bicep Curl (6 × 4–6) 6. Leg Press (6 × 4–6) 7. Leg Extension (6 × 4–6) 8. Leg Curl (6 × 4–6) 9. Calf Raises (6 × 4–6) 10. Back Extension (6 × 4–6) 11. Ab Curl (6 × 4–6) 12. Leg Tucked Rotation (6 × 4–6)
DISTANCE		
TSS	25	
STRENGTH WORK - WEEK 4		

WEDNESDAY (PM)

PLANNED METRICS		
DURATION	1:00:00	**WU**: Perform 5 mins of dynamic warm up: 1. Leg swings - 10–20 per leg 2. Leg Tucks - 10–15 per leg 3. Toe touches - 10–20 per leg Build WU pace from ACTIVE RECOVERY (Power Z1, HR Z1, Pace Z1, RPE 1) to ENDURANCE (Power Z2, HR Z2, Pace Z2, RPE 2–3) for 10 min. Then perform 4 × 10s strides. **MS**: Keep upper ENDURANCE (Power Z2, HR Z2, Pace Z2, RPE 2–3) throughout the MS. The effort will increase with hills. **Perform 10×**: 90 sec at 3%, then 90s back at 0% Run balance of time at ENDURANCE (Power Z2, HR Z2, Pace Z2, RPE 2–3). **CD**: Jog at ACTIVE RECOVERY (Power Z1, HR Z1, Pace Z1, RPE 1) for 10 min.
DISTANCE	6.0 mi	
TSS	65	
RUN - HILLS, HILLS, HILLS!!!!!		

THURSDAY (AM)

PLANNED METRICS		
DURATION	1:10:00	**WU**: 200m free nice and easy **MS1**: Take 10 sec rest with 100 and longer; 5 sec rest between 50s. All pacing at (Pace Z2, HR Z2, RPE 2–3). 8 × 50m - use the first 4 50's to finish warming up 4 × 100m 2 × 200m 1 × 400m 2 × 200m 4 × 100m 8 × 50m **MS2**: 2 × 500m at ENDURANCE (Pace Z2, HR Z2, RPE 2–3) **CD**: 100m choice
DISTANCE	3835	
TSS	50	
SWIM - EGYPTIAN PYRAMID (POINTY TOP)		

THURSDAY (PM)

PLANNED METRICS		
DURATION	1:05:00	**WU**: Perform 5 mins of dynamic warm up: 1. Leg swings - 10–20 per leg 2. Marches - 10–15 per leg 3. Leg side swings - 10–20 per leg Build WU pace from ACTIVE RECOVERY (Power Z1, HR Z1, Pace Z1, RPE 1) to ENDURANCE (Power Z2, HR Z2, Pace Z2, RPE 2–3) for 10 min. Then perform 4 × 10s strides. **MS**: Tempo run: 40' Low TEMPO (Power Z3, HR Z3, Pace Z3, RPE 3–4).
DISTANCE	Various	
TSS	59	
LOW TEMPO RUN - 40 MIN		**CD**: Jog for 10 min ACTIVE RECOVERY (Power Z1, HR Z1, Pace Z1, RPE 1)

FRIDAY (AM)

PLANNED METRICS		
DURATION	1:00:00	**WU**: 300m free/200m kick with fins/200m drill (6–3-6 switch kick) -------------
DISTANCE	2900	**MS1**: 1 × 1000m at ENDURANCE (Pace Z2, HR Z2, RPE 2–3) with 20s rest
TSS	52	
		MS2: 2 × 500m meters at ENDURANCE (Pace Z2, HR Z2, RPE 2–3) with 10s rest -------------
ENDURANCE SWIM 2000 METER		**CD**: 200 m easy swimming (stroke of choice) at ACTIVE RECOVERY (Pace Z1, HR Z1, RPE 1)

SATURDAY (AM)

PLANNED METRICS	
DURATION	1:28:00
DISTANCE	Various
TSS	106

SWIMRUN BRICK #3

WU: Perform 5 mins of dynamic warm up:
1. Leg swings - 10–20 per leg
2. Leg Tucks - 10–15 per leg
3. Toe touches - 10–20 per leg

Build WU pace from ACTIVE RECOVERY (Power Z1, HR Z1, Pace Z1, RPE 1) to ENDURANCE (Power Z2, HR Z2, Pace Z2, RPE 2–3) for 10 min. Then perform 4 × 10s strides.

MS:
1. Run 1 mi at THRESHOLD (Power Z4, HR Z4, Pace Z4, RPE 4–5)
2. Swim 500m at ENDURANCE (Power Z2, HR Z2, Pace Z2, RPE 2–3)
3. Run 1 mi at ENDURANCE (Power Z2, HR Z2, Pace Z2, RPE 3–4)
4. Swim 500m at TEMPO (Pace Z3, HR Z3, RPE 3–4)
5. Run 1 mi at TEMPO (Power Z3, HR Z3, Pace Z3, RPE 3–4)
6. Swim 500m at ENDURANCE (Power Z2, HR Z2, Pace Z2, RPE 2–3).
7. Run 1 mi at ENDURANCE (Power Z2, HR Z2, Pace Z2, RPE 3–4)

CD: Walk for 15 min until HR comes down to 100 BPM.

SUNDAY (AM)

PLANNED METRICS	
DURATION	0:25:00
DISTANCE	
TSS	21

RESISTANCE BANDS #1

Total workout duration should be 20–25 min. Try to do 3–4 rounds of 2 minutes of each exercise.

Butterfly (double-arm pull-back): Holding the cords in front of you, stand far enough away to create some tension in them. Bend over at the waist and lower your head. With arms straight and outstretched in front of you, pull your arms down to your sides as if doing an actual butterfly stroke. Remember to start the pull phase with your palms and forearms. Make sure to keep your elbows pointed out and at your shoulder line. Finish with your hands past your hips.

Single arm (freestyle pull-back): Same as the butterfly, but alternate one arm at a time.

Tricep pull-back: Use the same starting position as the butterfly but keep your elbows tucked into your sides and press your arms behind you. Make sure to squeeze the muscles at the back of your arms at the end of each stroke.

Breaststroke pull: Use the same bent-over starting position as above. Make breaststroke motions with your arms. Maintain a high elbow position and execute the motion with your palms and forearms. Be careful not to let your elbows drop below a line parallel to your shoulders.

Chest fly: Stand upright holding the cords in front of you with a little bit of tension. Start with arms outstretched in front of you. While keeping arms at chest height, pull each arm to the side and back until your hands are in line with your shoulders.

Reverse fly: Standing upright and facing away from the cords, position your hands next to your shoulders and your elbows at shoulder level. Keeping your arms parallel to your shoulders, push out until you can press your hands together in front of your chest.

SUNDAY (PM)

PLANNED METRICS		
DURATION	1:30:00	**WU**: Perform 5 mins of dynamic warm up: 1. Leg swings - 10–20 per leg 2. Marches - 10–15 per leg 3. Leg side swings - 10–20 per leg
DISTANCE	11 mi	
TSS	110	Build WU pace from Active Recovery (Power Z1, HR Z1, Pace Z1, RPE 1) to Endurance (Power Z2, HR Z2, Pace Z2, RPE 2–3) for 10 min. Then perform 4 × 10s strides.
		MS: Run 11 mi at Endurance (Power Z2, HR Z2, Pace Z2, RPE 2–3)
LONG RUN - 11 MILES		**CD**: Jog 10 min at Active Recovery (Power Z1, HR Z1, Pace Z1, RPE 1)

WEEK #5

Training Focus: Recovery Week

MONDAY (AM)

PLANNED METRICS		Actively focus on recovery today: 1) avoid unneccessary physical exertion, 2) watch nutrition closely (healthy carbs, lean protein, and good fats), 3) stretch, and 4) drink when thirsty. Other common recovery aids include massage, napping, elevating legs, floating in water, and listening to music.
DURATION		
DISTANCE		
TSS		
REST DAY		

TUESDAY (AM)

PLANNED METRICS		**WU**: 200m Free easy, 100m drill (2/3 catch up)
DURATION	0:30:00	**MS**: 2 × 250m at low ENDURANCE (Pace Z2, HR Z2, RPE 2). Focus on form
DISTANCE	1000	
TSS	20	**CD**: 200 pull at ACTIVE RECOVERY (Power Z1, HR Z1, Pace Z1, RPE 1)
RECOVERY - SWIM		

WEDNESDAY (AM)

PLANNED METRICS		
DURATION	0:45:00	Strength Protocol - Week 5 **Goal**: Hypertrophy **Intensity**: 75% of 1 RM **Note**: 1. 3d set should be performed until exhaustion. 2. Only 3 upper body sets.
DISTANCE		
TSS	25	
STRENGTH WORK - WEEK 5		**Exercises**: **Strength**: 1. Bench Press (3 × 8–12) 2. Lateral Pull Down (3 × 8–12) 3. Seated Row (3 × 8–12) 4. Tricep Pulldown (3 × 8–12) 5. Bicep Curl (3 × 8–12) 6. Leg Press (3 × 8–12) 7. Leg Extension (3 × 8–12) 8. Leg Curl (3 × 8–12) 9. Calf Raises (3 × 8–12) 10. Back Extension (3 × 8–12) 11. Ab Curl (4 × 8–12) 12. Leg Tucked Rotation (4 × 8–12)

WEDNESDAY (PM)

PLANNED METRICS		
DURATION	0:40:00	**WU**: Jog for 15 min at ACTIVE RECOVERY (Power Z1, HR Z1, Pace Z1, RPE 1), then
DISTANCE	Various	Perform the following dynamic stretches: 1. Toe Touches - 2 × 15 per leg 2. Leg Tucks - 2 × 15 per leg
TSS	19	
40 MIN RECOVERY JOG		**MS**: Jog at ACTIVE RECOVERY (Power Z1, HR Z1, Pace Z1, RPE 1) **CD**: Walk for 10 min or until your HR drops below 100 BPM.

THURSDAY (AM)

PLANNED METRICS		
DURATION	0:45:00	Active Recovery (Power Z1, HR Z1, Pace Z1, RPE 1)
DISTANCE	2600	
TSS	45	
SWIM - 300S & PULLS		

FRIDAY (AM)

PLANNED METRICS		
DURATION	1:05:00	**WU**: Perform 5 mins of dynamic warm up: 1. Leg swings - 10–20 per leg 2. Marches - 10–15 per leg 3. Leg side swings - 10–20 per leg
DISTANCE	6.2 mi	
TSS	70	Build WU pace from ACTIVE RECOVERY (Power Z1, HR Z1, Pace Z1, RPE 1) to ENDURANCE (Power Z2, HR Z2, Pace Z2, RPE 2–3) for 10 min. Then perform 4 × 10s strides. **MS**: Run 10 km at your marathon pace/ENDURANCE (Power Z2, HR Z2, Pace Z2, RPE 2–3) or better pace.
10 KM RUN		**CD**: Jog 10 min

SATURDAY (AM)

PLANNED METRICS		
DURATION	1:00:00	**WU**: 300m free/200m kick with fins/200m drill (6-3-6 switch kick) -------------
DISTANCE	2900	**MS1**: 1 × 1000m at ENDURANCE (Pace Z2, HR Z2, RPE 2–3) with 20s rest
TSS	72	**MS2**: 2 × 500m meters at ENDURANCE (Pace Z2, HR Z2, RPE 2–3) with 10s rest -------------
ENDURANCE SWIM 2000 METER		**CD**: 200 m easy swimming (stroke of choice) at ACTIVE RECOVERY (Pace Z1, HR Z1, RPE 1)

SUNDAY (AM)

PLANNED METRICS	
DURATION	0:25:00
DISTANCE	
TSS	20

Curls for Biceps – 2 × 20 repetitions per arm

1. Hook the band underneath your foot and stand up straight.
2. Make sure the band is fairly tight.
3. Grip the other end of the band with your right hand, and rest it near your side. If you're gripping the band correctly, your palms will be facing outward.
4. Bend your right elbow, and pull the band toward your shoulder.
5. Slowly bring your arm back to your side and repeat. Practice the curls with each arm.

Pulls for Internal Rotation – 2 × 15 repetitions per arm

1. Loop the band at shoulder height around a fence or sturdy object.
2. Stand away from the fence or object so that the band is taut, but not strained.
3. Turn your right side toward the object, and grip the band with your right hand.
4. Straighten your right arm out from your shoulder.
5. Raise your arm so that it is shoulder-height.
6. Bend your right elbow, and pull the band in toward your shoulder.
7. Slowly straighten your arm and repeat. Switch hands and repeat with your left arm.

Pulls for External Rotation – 2 × 15 repetitions per arm

1. Loop the band at shoulder-height around a fence or sturdy object.
2. Stand away from the fence or object so that the band is taut, but not strained.
3. Turn your left side toward the fence and grip the band with your right hand.
4. Straighten your right arm out from your shoulder.
5. Raise your arm so that it is shoulder-height.
6. Bend your right elbow and pull the band in toward your shoulder.
7. Slowly straighten your arm and repeat. Switch hands and repeat this rotation with your left arm.

RESISTANCE BANDS - SWIMMING #2	Flaps for Lateral & Deltoid Muscles – 2 × 20 repetitions per arm 1. Grip the ends of the band with both of your hands. 2. Hold the band straight above your head with your elbows locked. 3. While keeping your arms straight, pull downward from your shoulders. If you're performing this correctly, you should feel like a bird flapping its wings. Outward Pulls for Lateral & Trapezius Muscles 1. Stand on the band with both of your feet. 2. Rest your right arm near your side. 3. Lift your right arm straight out from your side. Keep your elbow locked. 4. When you reach the height of your shoulder, lower your arm back to your side and repeat

SUNDAY (PM)

PLANNED METRICS		
DURATION	1:30:00	**WU**: Perform 5 mins of dynamic warm up: 1. Leg swings - 10–20 per leg 2. Marches - 10–15 per leg 3. Leg side swings - 10–20 per leg Build WU pace from Active Recovery (Power Z1, HR Z1, Pace Z1, RPE 1) to Endurance (Power Z2, HR Z2, Pace Z2, RPE 2–3) for 10 min. Then perform 4 × 10s strides. **MS**: Run 10 mi at Endurance (Power Z2, HR Z2, Pace Z2, RPE 2–3) **CD**: Jog 10 min at Active Recovery (Power Z1, HR Z1, Pace Z1, RPE 1)
DISTANCE	10 mi	
TSS	100	
LONG RUN - 10 MILES		

WEEK #6

Training Focus: Peak Week #1

MONDAY (AM)

PLANNED METRICS	
DURATION	
DISTANCE	
TSS	
REST DAY	

Actively focus on recovery today: 1) avoid unneccessary physical exertion, 2) watch nutrition closely (healthy carbs, lean protein, and good fats), 3) stretch, and 4) drink when thirsty. Other common recovery aids include massage, napping, elevating legs, floating in water, and listening to music.

TUESDAY (AM)

PLANNED METRICS	
DURATION	1:30:00
DISTANCE	4600
TSS	100
SWIM - SHORT SPRINTS AND PULLS	

WU:

1. 300 free at Active Recovery (Power Z1, HR Z1, Pace Z1, RPE 1)
2. Kick with fins - focus on kicking with the ankles and hips

MS:

1. 400 pull with paddles (3/5 breathing pattern by 100) at Endurance (Power Z2, HR Z2, Pace Z2, RPE 2–3)
2. 16 × 25 @ :30 (free/back/breast/free by 25)
3. 8 × 125 @ 1:50 (25 sprint/100 smooth)
4. 8 × 75 pull @ :55 (all strong)
5. 8 × 25 @ :45 (sprint for half of the pool, swim easy to the wall)
6. 600 swim (100 IM/100 free, repeat) at at Endurance (Power Z2, HR Z2, Pace Z2, RPE 2–3)
7. 8 × 25 kick with fins
8. 4 × 150 pull at Endurance (Power Z2, HR Z2, Pace Z2, RPE 2–3)

CD: 200 easy Active Recovery (Power Z1, HR Z1, Pace Z1, RPE 1)

TUESDAY (PM)

PLANNED METRICS		
DURATION	1:05:00	**WU**: Perform 5 mins of dynamic warm up: 1. Leg swings - 10–20 per leg 2. Marches - 10–15 per leg 3. Leg side swings - 10–20 per leg Build WU pace from ACTIVE RECOVERY (Power Z1, HR Z1, Pace Z1, RPE 1) to ENDURANCE (Power Z2, HR Z2, Pace Z2, RPE 2–3) for 10 min. Then perform 4 × 10s strides. **MS**: Tempo run: 40' Low TEMPO (Power Z3, HR Z3, Pace Z3, RPE 3–4). **CD**: Jog for 10 min ACTIVE RECOVERY (Power Z1, HR Z1, Pace Z1, RPE 1)
DISTANCE	Various	
TSS	59	
LOW TEMPO RUN - 40 MIN		

WEDNESDAY (AM)

PLANNED METRICS		
DURATION	0:45:00	Strength Protocol - Week 6 **Goal**: Hypertrophy **Intensity**: 75% of 1 RM **Note**: 1. 3d set should be performed until exhaustion. 2. Only 3 upper body sets. **Exercises**: **Strength**: 1. Bench Press (3 × 8–12) 2. Lateral Pull Down (3 × 8–12) 3. Seated Row (3 × 8–12) 4. Tricep Pulldown (3 × 8–12) 5. Bicep Curl (3 × 8–12) 6. Leg Press (5 × 8–12) 7. Leg Extension (5 × 8–12) 8. Leg Curl (5 × 8–12) 9. Calf Raises (5 × 8–12) 10. Back Extension (3 × 8–12) 11. Ab Curl (5 × 8–12) 12. Leg Tucked Rotation (5 × 8–12)
DISTANCE		
TSS	25	
STRENGTH WORK - WEEK 6		

WEDNESDAY (PM)

PLANNED METRICS		
DURATION	0:50:00	**WU**: Perform 5 mins of dynamic warm up: 1. Toe Touches - 10–20 per leg 2. Marches - 10–15 per leg 3. Leg side swings - 10–20 per leg Build WU pace from ACTIVE RECOVERY (Power Z1, HR Z1, Pace Z1, RPE 1) to ENDURANCE (Power Z2, HR Z2, Pace Z2, RPE 2–3) for 10 min. Then perform 4 × 10s strides. **MS**: Perform twice (2×) at THRESHOLD (Power Z4, HR Z4, Pace Z4, RPE 4–5) 1 × 4 minutes fast 3 × 2 minutes fast 2 × 3 minutes fast 4 × 1 minute fast All with 1 minute easy recovery at low ENDURANCE (Power Z2, HR Z2, Pace Z2, RPE 2–3) **CD**: 1 mile at own pace
DISTANCE	Various	
TSS	46	
RUN - ENDURANCE SPEED LADDERS (DECLINE TIMED)		

THURSDAY (AM)

PLANNED METRICS		
DURATION	1:20:00	**WU**: 300m free/200m kick with fins/200m drill (6-3-6 switch kick) ------------- **MS1**: 2 × 1000m at ENDURANCE (Pace Z2, HR Z2, RPE 2–3) with 20s rest **MS2**: 3 × 500m meters at ENDURANCE (Pace Z2, HR Z2, RPE 2–3) with 10s rest ------------- **CD**: 200 m easy swimming (stroke of choice) at ACTIVE RECOVERY (Pace Z1, HR Z1, RPE 1)
DISTANCE	4400	
TSS	82	
ENDURANCE SWIM 3500 METER		

THURSDAY (PM)

PLANNED METRICS		
DURATION	1:05:00	**WU**: Perform 5 mins of dynamic warm up: 1. Leg swings - 10–20 per leg 2. Marches - 10–15 per leg 3. Leg side swings - 10–20 per leg Build WU pace from ACTIVE RECOVERY (Power Z1, HR Z1, Pace Z1, RPE 1) to ENDURANCE (Power Z2, HR Z2, Pace Z2, RPE 2–3) for 10 min. Then perform 4 × 10s strides. **MS**: Run 10 km at your marathon pace/ENDURANCE (Power Z2, HR Z2, Pace Z2, RPE 2–3) or better pace. **CD**: Jog 10 min
DISTANCE	6.2 mi	
TSS	70	
10 KM RUN		

FRIDAY (AM)

PLANNED METRICS		
DURATION	0:40:00	**WU**: Jog for 15 min at ACTIVE RECOVERY (Power Z1, HR Z1, Pace Z1, RPE 1), then Perform the following dynamic stretches: 1. Toe Touches - 2 × 15 per leg 2. Leg Tucks - 2 × 15 per leg **MS**: Jog at ACTIVE RECOVERY (Power Z1, HR Z1, Pace Z1, RPE 1) **CD**: Walk for 10 min or until your HR drops below 100 BPM.
DISTANCE	Various	
TSS	19	
40 MIN RECOVERY JOG		

SATURDAY (AM)

PLANNED METRICS	
DURATION	1:45:00
DISTANCE	Various
TSS	102
SWIMRUN BRICK #1	

SWIM

WU: 100m free, 100m kick without fins, 100m pull
Pre-set: 4 × 50 free with paddles

MS:

1. 10 × 100m at TEMPO (Pace Z3, HR Z3, RPE 3–4) with 0:10s rest
2. 200m pull at low ENDURANCE (Pace Z2, HR Z3, RPE 2–3)
3. 500m build. Each length should be faster than the previous.
4. 3 × 200m free. 1 & 3 at ENDURANCE (Pace Z2, HR Z3, RPE 2–3). 2nd at TEMPO (Pace Z3, HR Z3, RPE 3–4) with 0:15s rest between each interval.

CD: 100m easy swimming
Throw on shoes and head to treadmill as quickly as possible.

RUN

WU: 10 min at low ENDURANCE (Power Z2, HR Z2, Pace Z2, RPE 2–3) building to middle ENDURANCE.

MS: Start main set run at ENDURANCE (Power Z2, HR Z2, Pace Z2, RPE 2–3). Once comfortable, complete 4 × 5 min intervals at upper TEMPO (Power Z3, HR Z3, Pace Z3, PRE 304) with 10 min rest in between each interval at ENDURANCE (Power Z2, HR Z2, Pace Z2, RPE 2–3).

CD: Walk for 10 min or until HR comes below 100 BPM.

SUNDAY (AM)

PLANNED METRICS	
DURATION	0:25:00
DISTANCE	
TSS	21

RESISTANCE BANDS #1

Total workout duration should be 20–25 min. Try to do 3–4 rounds of 2 minutes of each exercise.

Butterfly (double-arm pull-back): Holding the cords in front of you, stand far enough away to create some tension in them. Bend over at the waist and lower your head. With arms straight and outstretched in front of you, pull your arms down to your sides as if doing an actual butterfly stroke. Remember to start the pull phase with your palms and forearms. Make sure to keep your elbows pointed out and at your shoulder line. Finish with your hands past your hips.

Single arm (freestyle pull-back): Same as the butterfly, but alternate one arm at a time.

Tricep pull-back: Use the same starting position as the butterfly but keep your elbows tucked into your sides and press your arms behind you. Make sure to squeeze the muscles at the back of your arms at the end of each stroke.

Breaststroke pull: Use the same bent-over starting position as above. Make breaststroke motions with your arms. Maintain a high elbow position and execute the motion with your palms and forearms. Be careful not to let your elbows drop below a line parallel to your shoulders.

Chest fly: Stand upright holding the cords in front of you with a little bit of tension. Start with arms outstretched in front of you. While keeping arms at chest height, pull each arm to the side and back until your hands are in line with your shoulders.

Reverse fly: Standing upright and facing away from the cords, position your hands next to your shoulders and your elbows at shoulder level. Keeping your arms parallel to your shoulders, push out until you can press your hands together in front of your chest.

SUNDAY (PM)

PLANNED METRICS		
DURATION	1:40:00	**WU**: Perform 5 mins of dynamic warm up: 1. Leg swings - 10–20 per leg 2. Marches - 10–15 per leg 3. Leg side swings - 10–20 per leg
DISTANCE	12 mi	
TSS	110	
		Build WU pace from Active Recovery (Power Z1, HR Z1, Pace Z1, RPE 1) to Endurance (Power Z2, HR Z2, Pace Z2, RPE 2–3) for 10 min. Then perform 4 × 10s strides.
		MS: Run 12 mi at Endurance (Power Z2, HR Z2, Pace Z2, RPE 2–3)
LONG RUN - 12 MILES		**CD**: Jog 10 min at Active Recovery (Power Z1, HR Z1, Pace Z1, RPE 1)

WEEK #7

Training Focus: Peak Week #2

MONDAY (AM)

PLANNED METRICS		
DURATION		Actively focus on recovery today: 1) avoid unneccessary physical exertion, 2) watch nutrition closely (healthy carbs, lean protein, and good fats), 3) stretch, and 4) drink when thirsty. Other common recovery aids include massage, napping, elevating legs, floating in water, and listening to music.
DISTANCE		
TSS		
REST DAY		

TUESDAY (AM)

PLANNED METRICS		
DURATION	1:20:00	**WU**: 500m (200 free at Active Recovery (Power Z1, HR Z1, Pace Z1, RPE 1) /50 kick, repeat)
DISTANCE	3900	**Pre-Set**: 1. 3 × 300m pulls with paddles at Endurance (Power Z2, HR Z2, Pace Z2, RPE 2–3) 2. 100m kick (50 easy/50 FAST)
TSS	65	**MS**: 1. 2 × 300m swim at Tempo (Power Z3, HR Z3, Pace Z3, RPE 3–4) 2. 50m easy/recovery kick w/ :30 rest 3. 3 × 200m pull @ Tempo (Power Z3, HR Z3, Pace Z3, RPE 3–4) 4. 50m easy/recovery kick w/ :30 rest 5. 4 × 100m swim @ Threshold (Power Z4, HR Z4, Pace Z4, RPE 5–6) 6. 50m easy/recovery kick w/ :30 rest 7. 6 × 50m pull @ :55 (all strong effort) 8. 50m at Active Recovery (Power Z1, HR Z1, Pace Z1, RPE 1)
SWIM - BUILD SETS WITH RECOVERY KICKS		**CD**: 300 at Active Recovery (Power Z1, HR Z1, Pace Z1, RPE 1)

TUESDAY (PM)

PLANNED METRICS		
DURATION	1:05:00	**WU**: Perform 5 mins of dynamic warm up: 1. Leg swings - 10–20 per leg 2. Marches - 10–15 per leg 3. Leg side swings - 10–20 per leg Build WU pace from ACTIVE RECOVERY (Power Z1, HR Z1, Pace Z1, RPE 1) to ENDURANCE (Power Z2, HR Z2, Pace Z2, RPE 2–3) for 10 min. Then perform 4 × 10s strides. **MS**: Run 10 km at your marathon pace/ENDURANCE (Power Z2, HR Z2, Pace Z2, RPE 2–3) or better pace. **CD**: Jog 10 min
DISTANCE	6.2 mi	
TSS	70	
10 KM RUN		

WEDNESDAY (AM)

PLANNED METRICS		
DURATION	0:45:00	Strength Protocol - Week 7 **Goal**: Hypertrophy **Intensity**: 90% of 1 RM **Note**: 1. 3d set should be performed until exhaustion. 2. Only 3 upper body sets. **Exercises**: **Strength**: 1. Bench Press (3 × 4–6) 2. Lateral Pull Down (3 × 4–6) 3. Seated Row (3 × 4–6) 4. Tricep Pulldown (3 × 4–6) 5. Bicep Curl (3 × 4–6) 6. Leg Press (6 × 4–6) 7. Leg Extension (6 × 4–6) 8. Leg Curl (6 × 4–6) 9. Calf Raises (6 × 4–6) 10. Back Extension (3 × 4–6) 11. Ab Curl (3 × 4–6) 12. Leg Tucked Rotation (6 × 4–6)
DISTANCE		
TSS	25	
STRENGTH WORK - WEEK 7		

WEDNESDAY (PM)

PLANNED METRICS		
DURATION	1:00:00	**WU**: Perform 5 mins of dynamic warm up: 1. Leg swings - 10–20 per leg 2. Marches - 10–15 per leg 3. Leg side swings - 10–20 per leg Build WU pace from ACTIVE RECOVERY (Power Z1, HR Z1, Pace Z1, RPE 1) to ENDURANCE (Power Z2, HR Z2, Pace Z2, RPE 2–3) for 10 min. Then perform 4 × 10s strides. **MS**: Mid ENDURANCE (Power Z2, HR Z2, Pace Z2, RPE 2–3) - keep pace steady throughout. On a treadmill or long climb, perform 5 × 5 mins hill repeats at 3% to 5% with 3 min recovery at 0% grade. Try to keep the same ENDURANCE pace throughout the workout. **CD**: 10 min at ACTIVE RECOVERY (Power Z1, HR Z1, Pace Z1, RPE 1)
DISTANCE	6.5	
TSS	80	
RUN - LONG HILLS		

THURSDAY (AM)

PLANNED METRICS		
DURATION	1:45:00	**WU**: 300m free/200m kick with fins/200m drill (6-3-6 switch kick) ------------- **MS1**: 3 × 1000m at ENDURANCE (Pace Z2, HR Z2, RPE 2–3) with 20s rest **MS2**: 2 × 500m meters at ENDURANCE (Pace Z2, HR Z2, RPE 2–3) with 10s rest ------------- **CD**: 200 m easy swimming (stroke of choice) at ACTIVE RECOVERY (Pace Z1, HR Z1, RPE 1)
DISTANCE	4900	
TSS	85	
ENDURANCE SWIM 4000 METER		

THURSDAY (PM)

PLANNED METRICS		
DURATION	1:15:00	**WU**: Perform 5 mins of dynamic warm up: 1. Leg swings - 10–20 per leg 2. Marches - 10–15 per leg 3. Leg side swings - 10–20 per leg Build WU pace from Active Recovery (Power Z1, HR Z1, Pace Z1, RPE 1) to Endurance (Power Z2, HR Z2, Pace Z2, RPE 2–3) for 10 min. Then perform 4 × 10s strides. **MS**: 5 × 1 mile at Threshold (Power Z4, HR Z4, Pace Z4, RPE 5–6) pace with 4–5' at Endurance (Power Z2, HR Z2, Pace Z2, RPE 2–3) between each interval. **CD**: Jog for 10 min
DISTANCE	Various	
TSS	95	
5 × 1 MILE AT TARGET 5K RACE PACE		

FRIDAY (AM)

PLANNED METRICS		
DURATION	1:00:00	**WU**: 300m free/200m kick with fins/200m drill (6–3-6 switch kick) ------------- **MS1**: 1 × 1000m at ENDURANCE (Pace Z2, HR Z2, RPE 2–3) with 20s rest **MS2**: 2 × 500m meters at ENDURANCE (Pace Z2, HR Z2, RPE 2–3) with 10s rest ------------- **CD**: 200 m easy swimming (stroke of choice) at ACTIVE RECOVERY (Pace Z1, HR Z1, RPE 1)
DISTANCE	2900	
TSS	52	
ENDURANCE SWIM 2000 METER		

SATURDAY (AM)

PLANNED METRICS		
DURATION	1:28:00	**WU**: Perform 5 mins of dynamic warm up: 1. Leg swings - 10–20 per leg 2. Leg Tucks - 10–15 per leg 3. Toe touches - 10–20 per leg
DISTANCE	Various	
TSS	106	
		Build WU pace from ACTIVE RECOVERY (Power Z1, HR Z1, Pace Z1, RPE 1) to ENDURANCE (Power Z2, HR Z2, Pace Z2, RPE 2–3) for 10 min. Then perform 4 × 10s strides. **MS**: 1. Run 1 mi at THRESHOLD (Power Z4, HR Z4, Pace Z4, RPE 4–5) 2. Swim 500m at ENDURANCE (Power Z2, HR Z2, Pace Z2, RPE 2–3) 3. Run 1 mi at ENDURANCE (Power Z2, HR Z2, Pace Z2, RPE 3–4) 4. Swim 500m at TEMPO (Pace Z3, HR Z3, RPE 3–4) 5. Run 1 mi at TEMPO (Power Z3, HR Z3, Pace Z3, RPE 3–4) 6. Swim 500m at ENDURANCE (Power Z2, HR Z2, Pace Z2, RPE 2–3). 7. Run 1 mi at ENDURANCE (Power Z2, HR Z2, Pace Z2, RPE 3–4)
SWIMRUN BRICK #3		**CD**: Walk for 15 min until HR comes down to 100 BPM.

SUNDAY (AM)

PLANNED METRICS		
DURATION	0:40:00	**WU**: 200m free, 200m kick with fins, 100m drill (Shark fin) ---------------
DISTANCE	2200	**MS**: 1. 1 × 1000m at ENDURANCE (Pace Z2, HR Z2, RPE 2–3) with 20s rest. 2. 2 × 250m at ENDURANCE (Pace Z2, HR Z2, RPE 2–3) with 10s rest ----------------
TSS	40	
ENDURANCE SWIM - 1×1000, 2×250		**CD**: 200m easy

SUNDAY (PM)

PLANNED METRICS		
DURATION	1:10:00	**WU**: Perform 5 mins of dynamic warm up: 1. Leg swings - 10–20 per leg 2. Marches - 10–15 per leg 3. Leg side swings - 10–20 per leg
DISTANCE	8–10 mi	Build WU pace from Active Recovery (Power Z1, HR Z1, Pace Z1, RPE 1) to Endurance (Power Z2, HR Z2, Pace Z2, RPE 2–3) for 10 min. Then perform 4 × 10s strides.
TSS	110	**MS**: Run 8–10 mi at Endurance (Power Z2, HR Z2, Pace Z2, RPE 2–3)
LONG RUN - 8–10 MILES		**CD**: Jog 10 min at Active Recovery (Power Z1, HR Z1, Pace Z1, RPE 1)

WEEK #8

Training Focus: Taper Week

MONDAY

PLANNED METRICS		Actively focus on recovery today: 1) avoid unneccessary physical exertion, 2) watch nutrition closely (healthy carbs, lean protein, and good fats), 3) stretch, and 4) drink when thirsty. Other common recovery aids include massage, napping, elevating legs, floating in water, and listening to music.
DURATION		
DISTANCE		
TSS		
REST DAY		

TUESDAY

PLANNED METRICS		**WU**: Perform 5 mins of dynamic warm up: 1. Leg swings - 10–20 per leg 2. Marches - 10–15 per leg 3. Leg side swings - 10–20 per leg Build WU pace from ACTIVE RECOVERY (Power Z1, HR Z1, Pace Z1, RPE 1) to ENDURANCE (Power Z2, HR Z2, Pace Z2, RPE 2–3) for 10 min. Then perform 4 × 10s strides. **MS**: 4 × 3 min progression run - increase pace/effort with each 3 minute interval on 1 min walking recovery. 1: Low-TEMPO (Power Z3, HR Z3, Pace Z3, RPE 3–4) 2: Mid TEMPO (Power Z3, HR Z3, Pace Z3, RPE 3–4) 3: Upper TEMPO (Power Z3, HR Z3, Pace Z3, RPE 3–4) 4: Low THRESHOLD (Power Z4, HR Z4, RPE 4–5) **CD**: 10 min jog at ACTIVE RECOVERY (Power Z1, HR Z1, Pace Z1, RPE 1)
DURATION	0:31:00	
DISTANCE	Various	
TSS	36	
TAPER RACE EFFORTS: 4 × 3 PROGRESSION ON 1 MIN WALKING RECOVERY		

WEDNESDAY

PLANNED METRICS	
DURATION	0:30:00
DISTANCE	1000
TSS	20
RECOVERY - SWIM	

WU: 200m Free easy, 100m drill (2/3 catch up)

MS: 2 × 250m at low ENDURANCE (Pace Z2, HR Z2, RPE 2). Focus on form

CD: 200 pull at ACTIVE RECOVERY (Power Z1, HR Z1, Pace Z1, RPE 1)

THURSDAY

PLANNED METRICS	
DURATION	0:40:00
DISTANCE	Various
TSS	19
40 MIN RECOVERY JOG	

WU: Jog for 15 min at ACTIVE RECOVERY (Power Z1, HR Z1, Pace Z1, RPE 1), then

Perform the following dynamic stretches:
1. Toe Touches - 2 × 15 per leg
2. Leg Tucks - 2 × 15 per leg

MS: Jog at ACTIVE RECOVERY (Power Z1, HR Z1, Pace Z1, RPE 1)

CD: Walk for 10 min or until your HR drops below 100 BPM.

FRIDAY

PLANNED METRICS	
DURATION	0:40:00
DISTANCE	
TSS	26
EVENT PRIMER - RUN	

WU: Perform 5 mins of dynamic warm up:
1. Leg swings - 10–20 per leg
2. Marches - 10–15 per leg
3. Leg side swings - 10–20 per leg

Build WU pace from ACTIVE RECOVERY (Power Z1, HR Z1, Pace Z1, RPE 1) to ENDURANCE (Power Z2, HR Z2, Pace Z2, RPE 2–3) for 10 min. Then perform 4 × 10s strides.

MS: Start main set run at mid ENDURANCE (Power Z2, HR Z2, Pace Z2, RPE 2–3). Once comfortable, complete 3 × 3 min intervals at low TEMPO (Power Z3, HR Z3, Pace Z3, RPE 3–4). Recover for 3 min low ENDURANCE (Power Z2, HR Z2, Pace Z2, RPE 2–3) in between each interval.

CD: Jog at ACTIVE RECOVERY (Power Z1, HR Z1, Pace Z1, RPE 1) for 10 min or until HR comes below 100 BPM.

SATURDAY

PLANNED METRICS	Today is the big day! Make sure you do the prescribed warm up you are on early. Stay relaxed and ready to race. Work hard to stay in the front of the pack!
DURATION	
DISTANCE	
TSS	
RACE DAY	

SUNDAY

PLANNED METRICS	Actively focus on recovery today: 1) avoid unneccessary physical exertion, 2) watch nutrition closely (healthy carbs, lean protein, and good fats), 3) stretch, and 4) drink when thirsty. Other common recovery aids include massage, napping, elevating legs, floating in water, and listening to music.
DURATION	
DISTANCE	
TSS	
REST DAY	

Plan 5

Power Based Swim Training Plan for Long Course Distance Triathlon

For this plan, please reference the following Test Interpretation Notes on p. 493 of this book:

- CSS Interpretation Notes (p. 493)
- Swimming Key Terms (p. 495)

WEEK #1

Training Focus: Test Week

MONDAY

PLANNED METRICS		
DURATION	00:40:00	**WU**: 200 free, 200 kick with fins, 200 drill (100 3/4 catch up/100 shark fin) ---------- **MS**: 3 × 250 at steady pace ---------- **CD**: 200 easy
DISTANCE	1550	
TSS	25	
PRE-TEST WARM UP		

TUESDAY

PLANNED METRICS		
DURATION	00:45:00	**WU**: 200 m at an easy pace **Pull**: 200 m pull (100 m follow through drill/ 100 m finger tip drill) **Kick**: 100 m with fins **MS1**: 1 × 400 m timed. This is a 400 m time-trial. Swim as hard as you can but do not start so hard as you fade in the last meters. You want your pace to be as even as possible during the entire 400 m. If possible, have someone count your strokes during a length near the 200 m point of the test (you can also find this information if you are using a smart watch such as the Garmin Swim or 920XT). Once finished, recover for 5–10 min. You can get out of the pool or slowly swim. The point is to recover but stay loose. **MS2**: 1 × 200 m time trial. Swim as hard as you can. Ensure your 200 m time is faster than 1/2 of your 400 m time. **CD**: 200 m easy
DISTANCE	1300	
TSS	30	
CRITICAL SWIM SPEED SWIM TEST #1		

WEDNESDAY

PLANNED METRICS		DAY OFF
DURATION		
DISTANCE		
TSS		

THURSDAY

PLANNED METRICS		DAY OFF
DURATION		
DISTANCE		
TSS		

FRIDAY

PLANNED METRICS		
DURATION	00:40:00	**WU**: 200 free, 200 kick with fins, 200 drill (100 3/4 catch up/100 shark fin) ---------- **MS**: 3 × 250 at steady pace ---------- **CD**: 200 easy
DISTANCE	1550	
TSS	20	
PRE-TEST WARM UP		

SATURDAY

PLANNED METRICS		
DURATION	00:30:00	**WU**: 200 m at an easy pace **Pull**: 200 m pull (100 m follow through drill/ 100 m finger tip drill) **Kick**: 100 m with fins **MS1**: Perform 1 × 1000 m time trial. Just like you performed with the 400 m time trial, do not start so hard that you fade in the final meters. Ensure you swim as hard and even as possible during the entire time trial. At about the 500 m point, if possible, have someone count your stroke rate (you can use a smartwatch to capture this information such as a Garmin Swim or Garmin 920XT). **CD**: 200 m easy.
DISTANCE	1700	
TSS	30	
CRITICAL SWIM SPEED TEST #2		

SUNDAY

PLANNED METRICS		
DURATION		DAY OFF
DISTANCE		
TSS		

WEEK #2

Training Focus: Base Training - This first microcycle will focus on building volume. You will have one day of drills, one day of strength/speed work, and two days of endurance volume.

On the volume days, the primary focus will be on short course intervals (distances under 400 m). I want you to get comfortable with doing the total volume first before moving onto longer intervals with the same amount of volume.

MONDAY

PLANNED METRICS		
DURATION	00:40:00	**WU**: 200 Free in Active Recovery Zone (Power Z1, HR Z1, Pace Z1, RPE 1) 200 kick (100 dolphin/100 back) with fins 200 pull with paddles Active Recovery Zone (Power Z1, HR Z1, Pace Z1, RPE 1) ----------- Drills 8 × 50 on 10 sec rest -Drill down/swim back Do this sequence twice: 1. Fist drill 2. Right arm only 3. Left arm only 4. 2/3 Catch-up drill ---------------- **MS**: 2 × (3 × 200) in low Endurance Zone (Power Z2, HR Z2, Pace Z2, RPE 1–2) -Descend - increase by 5W with 200 or increase pace by 1–2s with each 200. - start over on the second set of three 200s 3 × 100 in Endurance Zone (Power Z2, HR Z2, Pace Z2, RPE 1–2) on 10 sec rest -Breathe every 5 strokes ----------------- **CD**: 200 in Active Recovery Zone (Power Z1, HR Z1, Pace Z1, RPE 1)
DISTANCE	2770	
TSS	35	
ENDURANCE AND DRILL SWIM		

TUESDAY

PLANNED METRICS	
DURATION	00:45:00
DISTANCE	2900
TSS	50

12 × 50 KICK/SWIM MIX & MIDDLE DISTANCE PYRAMIDS

WU:
200 free, 200 Kick, 100 Pull, 100 Drill (Tarzan)

MS1:
12 × 50 with 15 sec. rest
Odds = kick
Evens = Free at Endurance (Power Z2, HR Z2, Pace Z2, RPE 2–3)

MS2:
Take 15 sec. rest between distances:
4 × 200 Swim at Tempo (Power Z3, HR Z3, Pace Z3, RPE 3–4)
2 × 50 Kick
4 × 100 Swim at Tempo (Power Z3, HR Z3, Pace Z3, RPE 3–4)
2 × 50 Kick
8 × 50 Swim at Tempo (Power Z3, HR Z3, Pace Z3, RPE 3–4)
2 × 50 Kick

CD: 200 at Active Recovery (Power Z1, HR Z1, Pace Z1, RPE 1)

WEDNESDAY

PLANNED METRICS	
DURATION	
DISTANCE	
TSS	

DAY OFF

THURSDAY

PLANNED METRICS	
DURATION	
DISTANCE	
TSS	

DAY OFF

FRIDAY

PLANNED METRICS		
DURATION	01:00:00	**WU**: 200 free, 200 kick, 200 pull with paddles
DISTANCE	3100	**MS1**: 16 × 25 with 10 sec. rest. Do four times 100 IM broken (free/back/breast/free).
TSS	50	**MS2**: 6 × 150 with 10 sec. rest 125 Free and 25 Back at Endurance (Power Z2, HR Z2, Pace Z2, RPE 2–3) **MS3**: 4 × 250 Swim with 15 sec. rest at Tempo (Power Z3, HR Z3, Pace Z3, RPE 3–4) -middle 50 back stroke
16 × 25 BROKEN IM, 4 × 250		**CD**: 200 at Active Recovery (Power Z1, HR Z1, Pace Z1, RPE 1)

SATURDAY

PLANNED METRICS		
DURATION	00:40:00	**WU**: 1. 200 free at Active Recovery (Power Z1, HR Z1, Pace Z1, RPE 1)
DISTANCE	2200	2. 200 kick with fins - focus on kicking with the ankles and hips
TSS	35	3. 100 drill (Shark fin) **MS**: 6 × 250 with 20s rest at Endurance (Power Z2, HR Z2, Pace Z2, RPE 2–3).
ENDURANCE 1500		**CD**: 200 at Active Recovery (Power Z1, HR Z1, Pace Z1, RPE 1)

SUNDAY

PLANNED METRICS	DAY OFF
DURATION	
DISTANCE	
TSS	

WEEK #3

Training Focus: Base Training - This first microcycle will focus on building volume. You will have one day of drills, one day of strength/speed work, and two days of endurance volume.

On the volume days, the primary focus will be on short course intervals (distances under 400 m). I want you to get comfortable with doing the total volume first before moving onto longer intervals with the same amount of volume.

MONDAY

PLANNED METRICS	DAY OFF
DURATION	
DISTANCE	
TSS	

TUESDAY

<table>
<tr><td colspan="2">PLANNED METRICS</td><td rowspan="5">WU: 300 Easy
----
Drill: 4 × 100: 50 Fists / 25 Scull / 25 Count strokes, take 1 stroke off each time through, 15-second rest
4 × 75: 25 Count strokes, take 1 stroke off each time through/50 Build, 10-second rest
4 × 25: Easy, focus on excellent technique, 5-second rest

MS:
1. 9 × 50: Descend 1–3, 4–6, 7–9 @ low Endurance (Power Z2, HR Z2, Pace Z2, RPE 2–3). Increase wattage by 2–4W/-5s with each lap and reset on every 3rd lap.

2. 3 × 300 at Tempo (Power Z3, HR Z3, Pace Z3, RPE 3–4) with 20s rest in between each 300. Make second 300 pull with paddles focusing on the catch portion of the stroke.

3. 9 × 50:
1,2 -- All at Threshold (Power Z4, HR Z4, Pace Z4, RPE 5–6) @ cruise +3W/-5 seconds per 50
3 -- All Active Recovery (Power Z1, HR Z1, Pace Z1, RPE 1)
4–6 -- Repeat 1–3
7–9 -- Repeat 1–3

Swim and Kick (No fins):
6 × 50: 25 Kick / 25 swim

CD: 200 m at Active Recovery (Power Z1, HR Z1, Pace Z1, RPE 1)</td></tr>
<tr><td>DURATION</td><td>00:50:00</td></tr>
<tr><td>DISTANCE</td><td>3200</td></tr>
<tr><td>TSS</td><td>40</td></tr>
<tr><td colspan="2">ENDURANCE/DRILL (3200)</td></tr>
</table>

WEDNESDAY

PLANNED METRICS		
DURATION	00:50:00	
DISTANCE	2700	
TSS	40	
20 × 50, 3 × 300 PULL		**WU**: 1. 400 free at Active Recovery (Power Z1, HR Z1, Pace Z1, RPE 1) building to Endurance (Power Z2, HR Z2, Pace Z2, RPE 2–3) 2. 200 kick with kick board. - focus on proper breathing technique and kicking from the ankles and hips. **MS1**: 5 × (4 × 50) with 15 sec rest. Perform the intervals as follows: 1. 50 at Active Recovery (Power Z1, HR Z1, Pace Z1, RPE 1) 2. 50 at Endurance (Power Z2, HR Z2, Pace Z2, RPE 2–3) 3. 50 at Tempo (Power Z3, HR Z3, Pace Z3, RPE 3–4) 4. 50 at Threshold (Power Z4, HR Z4, Pace Z4, RPE 5–6) 5. 50 at Anaerobic Capacity (Power Z6, HR Z6, Pace Z5, RPE 8–9). ALL OUT!!!! **MS2**: 3 × 300 Pull at Endurance (Power Z2, HR Z2, Pace Z2, RPE 2–3) with 15 sec. rest 1. With paddles 2. Focus on proper catch 3. Odds are breathing 3/5/7 by 25 **CD**: 200 at Active Recovery (Power Z1, HR Z1, Pace Z1, RPE 1)

THURSDAY

PLANNED METRICS		DAY OFF
DURATION		
DISTANCE		
TSS		

FRIDAY

<table>
<tr><th colspan="2">PLANNED METRICS</th><th rowspan="5">**WU**: 5 × 25s free, 3 × 50 kick with kick board

MS1:
Floats with kicks.
10 × 50s with 15s rest in b/w. Start each from the streamline floating position. Focus on keeping the hips and legs up. As your hips start to sink, start kick. As you hips come to the surface and you start to move forward, add in your swim stroke. Complete the rest of the 50 swimming.

MS2: Low buoy pulls.
6–8 × 75s with 20s rest in b/w. Perform low buoy pulls. Do not forget to slow down your swim stroke and stretch your arm out during the extension phase.

CD: 4 × 50s Easy</th></tr>
<tr><td>DURATION</td><td>00:50:00</td></tr>
<tr><td>DISTANCE</td><td>1550</td></tr>
<tr><td>TSS</td><td>50</td></tr>
<tr><td colspan="2">10 × 50S - FLOAT DRILLS & 6–8 × 75S LOW PULLS</td></tr>
</table>

SATURDAY

<table>
<tr><th colspan="2">PLANNED METRICS</th><th rowspan="5">**WU**:
1. 200 free at Active Recovery (Power Z1, HR Z1, Pace Z1, RPE 1) building to Endurance (Power Z2, HR Z2, Pace Z2, RPE 2–3)
2. 200 kick with fins
3. 100 drill (Shark fin)

MS:
1. 4 × 250 with 20s rest.
a. 250 at Endurance (Power Z2, HR Z2, Pace Z2, RPE 2–3).
b. 250 at Tempo (Power Z3, HR Z3, Pace Z3, RPE 3–4)
c. 250 at Endurance (Power Z2, HR Z2, Pace Z2, RPE 2–3).
d. 250 at Tempo (Power Z3, HR Z3, Pace Z3, RPE 3–4)
2. 1 × 500 at Endurance (Power Z2, HR Z2, Pace Z2, RPE 2–3)

CD: 200 at Active Recovery (Power Z1, HR Z1, Pace Z1, RPE 1)</th></tr>
<tr><td>DURATION</td><td>00:40:00</td></tr>
<tr><td>DISTANCE</td><td>2200</td></tr>
<tr><td>TSS</td><td>35</td></tr>
<tr><td colspan="2">4 × 250, 1 × 500</td></tr>
</table>

SUNDAY

PLANNED METRICS	DAY OFF
DURATION	
DISTANCE	
TSS	

WEEK #4

Training Focus: Base Training - This first microcycle will focus on building volume. You will have one day of drills, one day of strength/speed work, and two days of endurance volume.

On the volume days, the primary focus will be on short course intervals (distances under 400 m). I want you to get comfortable with doing the total volume first before moving onto longer intervals with the same amount of volume.

MONDAY

PLANNED METRICS	DAY OFF
DURATION	
DISTANCE	
TSS	

TUESDAY

PLANNED METRICS	
DURATION	00:50:00
DISTANCE	1550
TSS	40

10 × 50S - FLOAT DRILLS & 6–8 × 75S LOW PULLS

WU: 5 × 25s free, 3 × 50 kick with kick board

MS1:
Floats with kicks.
10 × 50s with 15s rest in b/w. Start each from the streamline floating position. Focus on keeping the hips and legs up. As your hips start to sink, start kick. As you hips come to the surface and you start to move forward, add in your swim stroke. Complete the rest of the 50 swimming.

MS2: Low buoy pulls.
6–8 × 75s with 20s rest in b/w. Perform low buoy pulls. Do not forget to slow down your swim stroke and stretch your arm out during the extension phase.

CD: 4 × 50s Easy

WEDNESDAY

PLANNED METRICS	
DURATION	00:45:00
DISTANCE	2900
TSS	50

12 × 50 KICK/ SWIM MIX & SHORT DISTANCE PYRAMIDS

WU:
1. 200 free Active Recovery (Power Z1, HR Z1, Pace Z1, RPE 1) building to Endurance (Power Z2, HR Z2, Pace Z2, RPE 2–3)
2. 200 Kick
3. 100 Pull with paddles focusing on hand entry and extension
4. 100 Drill (Tarzan)

MS1:
12 × 50 with 15 sec. rest
Odds = kick / Evens = Non free swim

MS2:
Take 15 sec. rest between distances:
a. 4 × 200 Swim at Endurance (Power Z2, HR Z2, Pace Z2, RPE 2–3)
b. 2 × 50 Kick
c. 4 × 100 Swim at Tempo (Power Z3, HR Z3, Pace Z3, RPE 3–4)
d. 2 × 50 Kick
e. 8 × 50 Swim at Threshold (Power Z4, HR Z4, Pace Z4, RPE 5–6)
f. 2 × 50 Kick

CD: 200 at Active Recovery (Power Z1, HR Z1, Pace Z1, RPE 1)

THURSDAY

PLANNED METRICS		DAY OFF
DURATION		
DISTANCE		
TSS		

FRIDAY

PLANNED METRICS		
DURATION	00:50:00	
DISTANCE	2500	
TSS	50	
FAST 25S TO FINISH		

WU:
1. 200 free at Active Recovery (Power Z1, HR Z1, Pace Z1, RPE 1) building to Endurance (Power Z2, HR Z2, Pace Z2, RPE 2–3)
2. 100 kick with board and fins.
   - focus on kicking with the hips and ankles
3. 200 swim (free/back per 100)

Pre-set:
4 × 50 w/ 10 sec rest (easy swim, kick hard on wall for :10)

MS:
1. 3 × 200 pull w/ 20 sec rest (descend 1–3)
2. 3 × 150 w/ 20 sec rest (50 free/50 non-free/50 free)
3. 3 × 100 w/ fins w/ 15 sec rest (50 dolphin kick on back/50 swim free)
4. 3 × 50 w/ fins @ 60 sec rest (kick as FAST! as possible!)

CD: 300 at Active Recovery (Power Z1, HR Z1, Pace Z1, RPE 1)

SATURDAY

PLANNED METRICS	
DURATION	01:00:00
DISTANCE	3800
TSS	55

WU:
1. 200 swim at Active Recovery (Power Z1, HR Z1, Pace Z1, RPE 1) building to Endurance (Power Z2, HR Z2, Pace Z2, RPE 2–3)
2. 100 kick with board and fins
   - focus on kicking with the ankles and hips

Pre-set:
1. 8 × 25 @ Endurance (Power Z2, HR Z2, Pace Z2, RPE 2–3) with 5 sec rest
   - w/band only on your ankles. Focus on keeping your hips up near the surface of the water.
2. 4 × 50 swim @ Endurance (Power Z2, HR Z2, Pace Z2, RPE 2–3) with 10 sec rest.
   - increase each 50 by +3W/-2s
3. 100 stroke of choice at Active Recovery (Power Z1, HR Z1, Pace Z1, RPE 1)

MS: (do the following sets continuous, no extra rest, all swim freestyle) all at Endurance (Power Z2, HR Z2, Pace Z2, RPE 2–3)
4 × 25 with 5s rest
4 × 50 with 5s rest
4 × 75 with 5s rest
4 × 100 with 10s rest
4 × 125 with 12s rest
4 × 150 with 15s rest
4 × 175 with 15s rest

CLIMB THE LADDER 4×

CD: 200 at Active Recovery (Power Z1, HR Z1, Pace Z1, RPE 1)

SUNDAY

PLANNED METRICS	
DURATION	
DISTANCE	
TSS	

DAY OFF

WEEK #5

Training Focus: Rest and Test Week - 1. The focus of the rest week is to allow your body to recover. This is the time period you start to reap the gains from the work you have performed over the previous weeks. Remember, less is more this week.

2. After the recovery portion of this week, you will retest your swim pace. You will be following the same testing and interpretation you did during the first week of this plan.

MONDAY

PLANNED METRICS		DAY OFF
DURATION		
DISTANCE		
TSS		

TUESDAY

PLANNED METRICS		
DURATION	00:30:00	**WU**: 200 easy, 100 drill (2/3 catch up)
DISTANCE	1100	**MS**: 2 × 250 at Active Recovery (Power Z1, HR Z1, Pace Z1, RPE 1) to low Endurance (Power Z2, HR Z2, Pace Z2, RPE 2–3). - Focus on an 1 aspect of your swim stroke that you feel is a weak point in you technique.
TSS	20	**CD**: 200 pull at Active Recovery (Power Z1, HR Z1, Pace Z1, RPE 1)
RECOVERY - SWIM		

WEDNESDAY

PLANNED METRICS		DAY OFF
DURATION		
DISTANCE		
TSS		

THURSDAY

PLANNED METRICS		
DURATION	00:30:00	**WU**: 200 easy, 100 drill (2/3 catch up) **MS**: 2 × 250 at Active Recovery (Power Z1, HR Z1, Pace Z1, RPE 1) to low Endurance (Power Z2, HR Z2, Pace Z2, RPE 2–3). - Focus on an 1 aspect of your swim stroke that you feel is a weak point in you technique. **CD**: 200 pull at Active Recovery (Power Z1, HR Z1, Pace Z1, RPE 1)
DISTANCE	1100	
TSS	20	
RECOVERY - SWIM		

FRIDAY

PLANNED METRICS		
DURATION	00:45:00	**WU**: 200 m at an easy pace **Pull**: 200 m pull (100 m follow through drill/100 m finger tip drill) **Kick**: 100 m with fins **MS1**: 1 × 400 m timed. This is a 400 m time-trial. Swim as hard as you can but do not start so hard as you fade in the last meters. You want your pace to be as even as possible during the entire 400 m. If possible, have someone count your strokes during a length near the 200 m point of the test (you can also find this information if you are using a smart watch such as the Garmin Swim or 920XT). Once finished, recover for 5–10 min. You can get out of the pool or slowly swim. The point is to recover but stay loose. **MS2**: 1 × 200 m time trial. Swim as hard as you can. Ensure your 200 m time is faster than 1/2 of your 400 m time. **CD**: 200 m easy
DISTANCE	1300	
TSS	30	
CRITICAL SWIM SPEED SWIM TEST #1		

SATURDAY

PLANNED METRICS		DAY OFF
DURATION		
DISTANCE		
TSS		

SUNDAY

PLANNED METRICS		
DURATION	00:30:00	**WU**: 200 m at an easy pace **Pull**: 200 m pull (100 m follow through drill/ 100 m finger tip drill) **Kick**: 100 m with fins **MS**: Perform 1 × 1000 m time trial. Just like you performed with the 400 m time trial, do not start so hard that you fade in the final meters. Ensure you swim as hard and even as possible during the entire time trial. At about the 500 m point, if possible, have someone count your stroke rate (you can use a smartwatch to capture this information such as a Garmin Swim or Garmin 920XT). **CD**: 200 m easy.
DISTANCE	1700	
TSS	30	
CRITICAL SWIM SPEED TEST #2		

WEEK #6

Training Focus: Base Training - This microcycle will have two goals:

1. You will start performing middle distance intervals (distance between 400–800 m) on the second endurance day.
2. You will perform individual medley (IM) strokes throughout the speed/interval day. This will help build other muscle groups that are not primarily used during the freestyle.

MONDAY

PLANNED METRICS		DAY OFF
DURATION		
DISTANCE		
TSS		

TUESDAY

PLANNED METRICS		
DURATION	00:50:00	**WU**: 1. 300 free at Active Recovery (Power Z1, HR Z1, Pace Z1, RPE 1) building to Endurance (Power Z2, HR Z2, Pace Z2, RPE 2–3) 2. 200 kick with board - focus on kicking with the ankles and hips 3. 100 drill (3/4 catch up)
DISTANCE	3300	
TSS	40	
		MS1: 12 × 75 with at Endurance (Power Z2, HR Z2, Pace Z2, RPE 2–3) with15 sec. rest - Odds are free and evens back/breast/free by 25 **MS2**: 4 × 400 Swim with 15 sec. rest 1 & 3 at Tempo (Power Z3, HR Z3, Pace Z3, RPE 3–4) 2 & 4 at Endurance (Power Z2, HR Z2, Pace Z2, RPE 2–3)
12 × 75 STROKE MIX & 4 × 400		**CD**: 200 at Active Recovery (Power Z1, HR Z1, Pace Z1, RPE 1)

WEDNESDAY

PLANNED METRICS		
DURATION	00:55:00	**WU**: 5 × 200 with fins - 50 drill (shark fin), 100 swim, 50 drill (3/4 catch up).
DISTANCE	2700	
TSS	45	**MS**: 3 × 400 1. First 400: a. 100 build within Endurance (Power Z2, HR Z2, Pace Z2, RPE 2–3) b. 200 at Threshold (Power Z4, HR Z4, Pace Z4, RPE 5–6) c. 100 at Tempo (Power Z3, HR Z3, Pace Z3, RPE 3–4) 2. Second 400: a. 100 at Active Recovery (Power Z1, HR Z1, Pace Z1, RPE 1) b. 50 at Threshold (Power Z4, HR Z4, Pace Z4, RPE 5–6) c. 50 at Active Recovery (Power Z1, HR Z1, Pace Z1, RPE 1) d. 50 at Threshold (Power Z4, HR Z4, Pace Z4, RPE 5–6) e. 100 at Active Recovery (Power Z1, HR Z1, Pace Z1, RPE 1) 3. Third 400: 200 build, 100 fast, 100 slow a. 2 × 200 i. First 200: Pull with paddles at Endurance (Power Z2, HR Z2, Pace Z2, RPE 2–3) **Second 200**: Kick with board and fins
MIDDLE DISTANCE INTERVALS		**CD**: 400 at Active Recovery (Power Z1, HR Z1, Pace Z1, RPE 1)

THURSDAY

PLANNED METRICS		DAY OFF
DURATION		
DISTANCE		
TSS		

FRIDAY

PLANNED METRICS		
DURATION	01:00:00	**WU**: 1. 300 Free at Active Recovery (Power Z1, HR Z1, Pace Z1, RPE 1) building to Endurance (Power Z2, HR Z2, Pace Z2, RPE 2–3) 2. 200 Kick with board and fins - focus on kicking with the ankles and hips 3. 100 Free at Endurance (Power Z2, HR Z2, Pace Z2, RPE 2–3) **MS1**: 2 × 200 (50 drill/50 free) with 20 sec. rest - drill = 3/4 catch up. **MS2**: 4 × 150 Swim (middle 50 Breast stroke) with 20 sec. rest at Endurance (Power Z2, HR Z2, Pace Z2, RPE 2–3) **MS3**: 12 × 100 with up to 30 sec. rest at Endurance (Power Z2, HR Z2, Pace Z2, RPE 2–3) a. Evens 100 free b. 100 IM (free/back/breast/free) **CD**: 200 at Active Recovery (Power Z1, HR Z1, Pace Z1, RPE 1)
DISTANCE	3000	
TSS	50	
2 × 200 MIX, 4 × 150, 12 × 100 IM MIX		

SATURDAY

PLANNED METRICS		
DURATION	01:00:00	**WU**: 1. 300 free at Active Recovery (Power Z1, HR Z1, Pace Z1, RPE 1) building to Endurance (Power Z2, HR Z2, Pace Z2, RPE 2–3) 2. 6 × 50 drills (Odds - Tarzan, Evens - 3/4 catch up) 3. 100 at Active Recovery (Power Z1, HR Z1, Pace Z1, RPE 1), form-focused **MS**: 1. 5 × 200 at Endurance (Power Z2, HR Z2, Pace Z2, RPE 2–3) (sprint the last 50 of each 200, moderate efforts in between) with 20 sec rest 2. 1000 at Endurance (Power Z2, HR Z2, Pace Z2, RPE 2–3) at sprint the last 25 of each 100. **CD**: 300 at Active Recovery (Power Z1, HR Z1, Pace Z1, RPE 1)
DISTANCE	3000	
TSS	55	
MIDDLE DISTANCE - HALF IM DISTANCE AND SPEED		

SUNDAY

PLANNED METRICS	DAY OFF
DURATION	
DISTANCE	
TSS	

WEEK #7

Training Focus: Base Training - This microcycle will have two goals:

1. You will start performing middle distance intervals (distance between 400–800 m) on the second endurance day.
2. You will perform individual medley (IM) strokes throughout the speed/interval day. This will help build other muscle groups that are not primarily used during the freestyle.

MONDAY

PLANNED METRICS	DAY OFF
DURATION	
DISTANCE	
TSS	

TUESDAY

PLANNED METRICS		
DURATION	00:50:00	**WU**: 5 × 25s free, 3 × 50 kick with kick board **MS1**: Floats with kicks. 10 × 50s with 15s rest in b/w. Start each from the streamline floating position. Focus on keeping the hips and legs up. As your hips start to sink, start kick. As you hips come to the surface and you start to move forward, add in your swim stroke. Complete the rest of the 50 swimming. **MS2**: Low buoy pulls. 6–8 × 75s with 20s rest in b/w. Perform low buoy pulls. Do not forget to slow down your swim stroke and stretch your arm out during the extension phase. **CD**: 4 × 50s Easy
DISTANCE	1550	
TSS	50	
10 × 50S - FLOAT DRILLS & 6–8 × 75S LOW PULLS		

WEDNESDAY

PLANNED METRICS		
DURATION	00:40:00	**WU**: 300 free, 300 drill (100 tarzan/100 Fist/2/3 catch up) **MS1**: 1. 8 × 75 Kick with fins with 10s rest 2. 8 × 75 Pull with paddles with 10s rest **MS2**: 1. 500 Swim with 60 sec. rest 2. 5 × 100 Swim with 15 sec. rest **CD**: 200 Easy
DISTANCE	3000	
TSS	55	
16 × 75 KICK AND PULLS & 500		

THURSDAY

PLANNED METRICS		
DURATION		DAY OFF
DISTANCE		
TSS		

FRIDAY

PLANNED METRICS		WU: 200 swim/200 pull with paddles/100 kick with fins
DURATION	00:40:00	MS:
DISTANCE	2500	4 × 150 w/ 20s rest (50 free/50 breast/50 free)
TSS	45	4 × 150 pull w/ :20 (with buoy and band) 6 × 50 w/ :5s rest (25 FAST/25 easy drill) 4 × 100 swim w/ :20 rest (descend 1–4)
150S WITH BUOY & BANDS, 50S		CD: 100 cool-down (50 kick/50 swim)

SATURDAY

PLANNED METRICS		WU: 300 free, 200 kick (100 back, 50 breast, 50 dolphin), 100 free
DURATION	00:50:00	
DISTANCE	2900	MS1:
TSS	40	2 × 250 Pull with paddles with 30 sec. rest
2 × 250 PULL, 4 × 400 PYRAMIDS		MS2: 4 × 400 Free with 20 sec. rest #1: 300 steady, 100 hard #2: 200 steady, 200 hard #3: 100 steady, 300 hard #4: 400 hard CD: 200 Easy

SUNDAY

PLANNED METRICS		DAY OFF
DURATION		
DISTANCE		
TSS		

WEEK #8

Training Focus: Base Training - This microcycle will have two goals:

1. You will start performing middle distance intervals (distance between 400–800 m) on the second endurance day.
2. You will perform individual medley (IM) strokes throughout the speed/interval day. This will help build other muscle groups that are not primarily used during the freestyle.

MONDAY

PLANNED METRICS		DAY OFF
DURATION		
DISTANCE		
TSS		

TUESDAY

PLANNED METRICS		
DURATION	00:30:00	**WU**: 400 swim with fins at Active Recovery (Power Z1, HR Z1, Pace Z1, RPE 1) building to Endurance (Power Z2, HR Z2, Pace Z2, RPE 2–3). **MS**: All with fins 1. 200 kick w/ fins at Tempo (Power Z3, HR Z3, Pace Z3, RPE 3–4) 2. 6 × 50 w/ :15 rest (2/3 catch-up drill) 3. 6 × 50 w/ :15 rest (25 Fist/Golf Drill/25 swim) 4. 6 × 50 w/ :20 rest (25 kick/25 swim) 5. 200 kick - focus on kicking with the ankles and hips 6. 6 × 50 w/fins w/ :30 rest - Odds - (25 kick on your back/25 swim) - Evens - (25 dolphin kick/25 swim)
DISTANCE	2300	
TSS	45	
DRILLS, DRILLS, DRILLS		**CD**: 300 at Active Recovery (Power Z1, HR Z1, Pace Z1, RPE 1)

WEDNESDAY

PLANNED METRICS	
DURATION	01:00:00
DISTANCE	3200
TSS	50

WU:
1. 200 at Active Recovery (Power Z1, HR Z1, Pace Z1, RPE 1)
2. 200 kick with fins
   - focus on kicking with the ankles and hips
3. 200 pull with paddles at Endurance (Power Z2, HR Z2, Pace Z2, RPE 2–3)

MS1:
4 × 100 Kick with 15 sec. rest
- 1 & 3 with fins
- 2 & 4 with no fins
- focus on kicking with the ankles and hips

MS2:
8 × 125 with 15 sec. rest at Tempo (Power Z3, HR Z3, Pace Z3, RPE 3–4)

MS3:
4 × 250 with 20 sec. rest at Endurance (Power Z2, HR Z2, Pace Z2, RPE 2–3)

a. Odds are pull
b. evens are free

8 × 125 & 4 × 250 PULL/SWIM MIX

CD: 200 at Active Recovery (Power Z1, HR Z1, Pace Z1, RPE 1)

THURSDAY

PLANNED METRICS	
DURATION	
DISTANCE	
TSS	

DAY OFF

FRIDAY

PLANNED METRICS		
DURATION	00:55:00	**WU**: 1. 200 free at Active Recovery (Power Z1, HR Z1, Pace Z1, RPE 1) building to Endurance (Power Z2, HR Z2, Pace Z2, RPE 2–3) 2. 200 kick with fins (100 dolphin/100 back) 3. 200 pull with paddles at Endurance (Power Z2, HR Z2, Pace Z2, RPE 2–3) - Focus on proper form of the catch of the stroke. **MS1**: 2 × (4 × 100) broken IM's with 25s rest **MS2**: 8 × 200 with 20 sec. rest a. Evens at Tempo (Power Z3, HR Z3, Pace Z3, RPE 3–4) b. Endurance (Power Z2, HR Z2, Pace Z2, RPE 2–3) **CD**: 200 at Active Recovery (Power Z1, HR Z1, Pace Z1, RPE 1)
DISTANCE	2800	
TSS	45	
2 × (4 × 100) BROKEN IM, 8 × 200 MIX		

SATURDAY

PLANNED METRICS		
DURATION	00:50:00	**WU**: 1. 400 free at Active Recovery (Power Z1, HR Z1, Pace Z1, RPE 1) building to Endurance (Power Z2, HR Z2, Pace Z2, RPE 2–3) 2. 200 pull with paddles at Endurance (Power Z2, HR Z2, Pace Z2, RPE 2–3) - focus on the entry and extension phase of stroke **MS1**: 4 × 100 Kick with fins with 15s rest - focus on kicking with the ankles and hips **MS2**: 3 × 600 Swim with 20s rest a. Set #1: Do as 2 × 300 at Tempo (Power Z3, HR Z3, Pace Z3, RPE 3–4) with 15s rest between 300s b. Set #2: Pull with paddles at Endurance (Power Z2, HR Z2, Pace Z2, RPE 2–3) c. Set #3: Do as 3 × 200 with 15s. rest between 200s - last 200 is choice drill **CD**: 200 at Active Recovery (Power Z1, HR Z1, Pace Z1, RPE 1)
DISTANCE	3000	
TSS	45	
4 × 100 KICK, 3 × 600		

SUNDAY

PLANNED METRICS	DAY OFF
DURATION	
DISTANCE	
TSS	

WEEK #9

Training Focus: Rest and Test Week - 1. The focus of the rest week is to allow your body to recover. This is the time period you start to reap the gains from the work you have performed over the previous weeks. Remember, less is more this week.

2. After the recovery portion of this week, you will retest your swim pace. You will be following the same testing and interpretation you did during the first week of this plan.

MONDAY

PLANNED METRICS	DAY OFF
DURATION	
DISTANCE	
TSS	

TUESDAY

PLANNED METRICS	
DURATION	00:30:00
DISTANCE	1100
TSS	20

RECOVERY - SWIM

WU: 200 easy, 100 drill (2/3 catch up)

MS: 2 × 250 at Active Recovery (Power Z1, HR Z1, Pace Z1, RPE 1) to low Endurance (Power Z2, HR Z2, Pace Z2, RPE 2–3).

- Focus on an 1 aspect of your swim stroke that you feel is a weak point in you technique.

CD: 200 pull at Active Recovery (Power Z1, HR Z1, Pace Z1, RPE 1)

WEDNESDAY

PLANNED METRICS		DAY OFF
DURATION		
DISTANCE		
TSS		

THURSDAY

PLANNED METRICS		
DURATION	00:30:00	
DISTANCE	1100	
TSS	20	
RECOVERY - SWIM		

WU: 200 easy, 100 drill (2/3 catch up)

MS: 2 × 250 at Active Recovery (Power Z1, HR Z1, Pace Z1, RPE 1) to low Endurance (Power Z2, HR Z2, Pace Z2, RPE 2–3).

- Focus on an 1 aspect of your swim stroke that you feel is a weak point in you technique.

CD: 200 pull at Active Recovery (Power Z1, HR Z1, Pace Z1, RPE 1)

FRIDAY

PLANNED METRICS		
DURATION	00:45:00	**WU**: 200 m at an easy pace **Pull**: 200 m pull (100 m follow through drill/ 100 m finger tip drill)
DISTANCE	1300	**Kick**: 100 m with fins
TSS	30	**MS1**: 1 × 400 m timed. This is a 400 m time-trial. Swim as hard as you can but do not start so hard as you fade in the last meters. You want your pace to be as even as possible during the entire 400 m. If possible, have someone count your strokes during a length near the 200 m point of the test (you can also find this information if you are using a smart watch such as the Garmin Swim or 920XT). Once finished, recover for 5–10 min. You can get out of the pool or slowly swim. The point is to recover but stay loose. **MS2**: 1 × 200 m time trial. Swim as hard as you can. Ensure your 200 m time is faster than 1/2 of your 400 m time.
CRITICAL SWIM SPEED SWIM TEST #1		**CD**: 200 m easy

SATURDAY

PLANNED METRICS		
DURATION		DAY OFF
DISTANCE		
TSS		

SUNDAY

PLANNED METRICS		
DURATION	00:30:00	**WU**: 200 m at an easy pace **Pull**: 200 m pull (100 m follow through drill/ 100 m finger tip drill)
DISTANCE	1700	Kick: 100 m with fins
TSS	30	**MS**: Perform 1 × 1000 m time trial. Just like you performed with the 400 m time trial, do not start so hard that you fade in the final meters. Ensure you swim as hard and even as possible during the entire time trial. At about the 500 m point, if possible, have someone count your stroke rate (you can use a smartwatch to capture this information such as a Garmin Swim or Garmin 920XT).
CRITICAL SWIM SPEED TEST #2		**CD**: 200 m easy

WEEK #10

Training Focus: Base Training - The goal is to still increase interval length and volume. By weeks 11 and 12, you will perform long distance intervals (distances 800 m+). These should be a challenge, but not out of your reach!

MONDAY

PLANNED METRICS		DAY OFF
DURATION		
DISTANCE		
TSS		

TUESDAY

PLANNED METRICS		
DURATION	00:40:00	
DISTANCE	2700	
TSS	35	
ENDURANCE AND DRILL SWIM		**WU**: 1. 200 free at Active Recovery (Power Z1, HR Z1, Pace Z1, RPE 1) 2. 200 kick (100 dolphin/100 back) with fins 3. 200 pull with paddles at Endurance (Power Z2, HR Z2, Pace Z2, RPE 2–3) - focus on the catch portion of the stroke. ----------- Drills 8 × 50 on 10 sec rest -Drill down/swim back Do this sequence twice: 1. Fist drill 2. Right arm only 3. Left arm only 4. 2/3 Catch-up drill **MS**: 2 × (3 × 200 on 20 sec rest) at Endurance (Power Z2, HR Z2, Pace Z2, RPE 2–3) a. Set #1. Increase effort by +4W/-2s with each 200. Start with each 300. b. Set #2 3 × 100 on 10 sec rest at Endurance (Power Z2, HR Z2, Pace Z2, RPE 2–3) while breathing every 5 strokes **CD**: 200 at Active Recovery (Power Z1, HR Z1, Pace Z1, RPE 1)

WEDNESDAY

PLANNED METRICS		
DURATION	00:50:00	**WU**: 1. 300 free at Active Recovery (Power Z1, HR Z1, Pace Z1, RPE 1) building to Endurance (Power Z2, HR Z2, Pace Z2, RPE 2–3) 2. 200 kick with fins (100 back, 50 breast, 50 dolphin) 3. 100 free at Endurance (Power Z2, HR Z2, Pace Z2, RPE 2–3) **MS1**: 2 × 250 Pull with paddles with 30 sec. rest **MS2**: 4 × 400 Free with 20 sec. rest #1: 300 at Endurance (Power Z2, HR Z2, Pace Z2, RPE 2–3), 100 at Tempo (Power Z3, HR Z3, Pace Z3, RPE 3–4) #2: 200 at Endurance (Power Z2, HR Z2, Pace Z2, RPE 2–3), 200 at Tempo (Power Z3, HR Z3, Pace Z3, RPE 3–4) #3: 300 at Endurance (Power Z2, HR Z2, Pace Z2, RPE 2–3), 300 at Tempo (Power Z3, HR Z3, Pace Z3, RPE 3–4) #4: 400 at Tempo (Power Z3, HR Z3, Pace Z3, RPE 3–4) **MS3**: Swim 1 × 300 at Tempo (Power Z3, HR Z3, Pace Z3, RPE 3–4)
DISTANCE	3100	
TSS	50	
2 × 250 PULL, 4 × 400 PYRAMIDS		**CD**: 200 at Active Recovery (Power Z1, HR Z1, Pace Z1, RPE 1)

THURSDAY

PLANNED METRICS		DAY OFF
DURATION		
DISTANCE		
TSS		

FRIDAY

PLANNED METRICS		
DURATION	00:45:00	**WU**: 200 free, 200 pull with paddles, 200 drill (Tarzan and Fist)
DISTANCE	2700	**MS1**: 8 × 75 Kick with board and fins with 10 sec. rest - focus on kicking with the ankles and hips
TSS	45	**MS2**: 6 × 150 Swim with 15 sec. rest at Endurance (Power Z2, HR Z2, Pace Z2, RPE 2–3) -Middle 50 change stroke to breast or back
		MS3: 16 × 25 Swim with 5 sec. rest a. Evens at Threshold (Power Z4, HR Z4, Pace Z4, RPE 5–6) b. Tempo (Power Z3, HR Z3, Pace Z3, RPE 3–4)
8 × 75 &16 × 25 FAST		**CD**: 200 atActive Recovery (Power Z1, HR Z1, Pace Z1, RPE 1)

SATURDAY

PLANNED METRICS		
DURATION	01:20:00	**WU**: 1. 200 free at Active Recovery (Power Z1, HR Z1, Pace Z1, RPE 1) 2. 200 kick board with fins - focus on kicking with the ankles and hips 3. 100 drill (Shark fin)
DISTANCE	4200	
TSS	70	**MS**: 1. 1 × 1000 at Endurance (Power Z2, HR Z2, Pace Z2, RPE 2–3) with 20s rest. The pace should be at or just below your predicted race pace. 2. 2 × 250 at Endurance (Power Z2, HR Z2, Pace Z2, RPE 2–3) with 10s rest
ENDURANCE 3500 - 3 × 1000, 2 × 250		**CD**: 200 at Active Recovery (Power Z1, HR Z1, Pace Z1, RPE 1)

SUNDAY

PLANNED METRICS	DAY OFF
DURATION	
DISTANCE	
TSS	

WEEK #11

Training Focus: Base Training - The goal is to still increase interval length and volume. By weeks 11 and 12, you will perform long distance intervals (distances 800 m+). These should be a challenge, but not out of your reach!

MONDAY

PLANNED METRICS	DAY OFF
DURATION	
DISTANCE	
TSS	

TUESDAY

PLANNED METRICS	
DURATION	00:40:00
DISTANCE	2400
TSS	40

WU:
1. 200 free at Active Recovery (Power Z1, HR Z1, Pace Z1, RPE 1)
2. 200 drill (2/3 catch up)
3. 200 free at Endurance (Power Z2, HR Z2, Pace Z2, RPE 2–3)

MS:
1. 6 × 50 w/ fins w/ 10s rest (25 kick/25 swim)
2. 6 × 150 pull w/ paddles w/ 20s rest
   a. (descend 1–3, 4–6)
3. 6 × 50 w/ fins w/ 10s rest (25 kick/25 swim)
4. 6 × 50 pull w/ 10s rest
   a. #1 & 2 at VO2 Max (Power Z5, HR Z5, Pace Z5, RPE 6–7)
   b. #3 at Active Recovery (Power Z1, HR Z1, Pace Z1, RPE 1)
   c. #4 & 5 at VO2 Max (Power Z5, HR Z5, Pace Z5, RPE 6–7)
   d. #6 at Active Recovery (Power Z1, HR Z1, Pace Z1, RPE 1)

KICK BETWEEN INTERVALS

CD: 200 at Active Recovery (Power Z1, HR Z1, Pace Z1, RPE 1)

WEDNESDAY

PLANNED METRICS	
DURATION	00:50:00
DISTANCE	2800
TSS	40

WU:
1. 200 free at Active Recovery (Power Z1, HR Z1, Pace Z1, RPE 1)
2. 200 kick with board and fins
   - focus on kicking with the ankles and hips
3. 200 drill
   a. First 100 is 3/4 catch up drill
   b. Second 200 is shark fin drill

MS:
5 × 400 Swim with 15s rest
   a. #1–3: Free at Endurance (Power Z2, HR Z2, Pace Z2, RPE 2–3). Increase pace by +4W/-2s per 400
   b. 4 × 100 Free with 5s rest b/w each 100 descending 1 to 4 at Endurance (Power Z2, HR Z2, Pace Z2, RPE 2–3). Increase pace by +6W/-3s per 400
   c. #5: 8 × 50 at Threshold (Power Z4, HR Z4, Pace Z4, RPE 5–6) with 15s rest

5 × 400 MIDDLE DISTANCE MIX

CD: 200 at Active Recovery (Power Z1, HR Z1, Pace Z1, RPE 1)

THURSDAY

PLANNED METRICS	DAY OFF
DURATION	
DISTANCE	
TSS	

FRIDAY

PLANNED METRICS	DAY OFF
DURATION	
DISTANCE	
TSS	

SATURDAY

PLANNED METRICS	DAY OFF
DURATION	
DISTANCE	
TSS	

SUNDAY

PLANNED METRICS	DAY OFF
DURATION	
DISTANCE	
TSS	

WEEK #12

Training Focus: Base Training - The goal is to still increase interval length and volume. By weeks 11 and 12, you will perform long distance intervals (distances 800 m+). These should be a challenge, but not out of your reach!

MONDAY

PLANNED METRICS		DAY OFF
DURATION		
DISTANCE		
TSS		

TUESDAY

PLANNED METRICS		
DURATION	00:40:00	
DISTANCE	2500	
TSS	40	
DRILLS, DRILLS, DRILLS		

WU:
1. 400 swim with fins at Active Recovery (Power Z1, HR Z1, Pace Z1, RPE 1) building to Endurance (Power Z2, HR Z2, Pace Z2, RPE 2–3)
2. 200 kick with board and fins
   - focus on kicking with the ankles and hips

MS:
1. 200 free at Tempo (Power Z3, HR Z3, Pace Z3, RPE 3–4)
2. 6 × 50 w/ :15 rest (2/3 catch-up drill
3. 6 × 50 w/ :15 rest (25 Fist/Golf Drill/25 swim)
4. 6 × 50 w/ :20 rest (25 kick/25 swim)
5. 200 w/buoy (25 scull/75 pull, repeat)
6. 6 × 50 w/fins w/ :30 rest
   - Odds - (25 kick on your back/25 swim)
   - Evens - (25 dolphin kick/25 swim)

CD: 300 at Active Recovery (Power Z1, HR Z1, Pace Z1, RPE 1)

WEDNESDAY

PLANNED METRICS	
DURATION	00:55:00
DISTANCE	3300
TSS	40

BUILD TO FAST

WU:
1. 200 at Active Recovery (Power Z1, HR Z1, Pace Z1, RPE 1)
2. 100 kick board with fins
   - focus on kicking with the ankles and hips
3. 300 pull with paddles at Endurance (Power Z2, HR Z2, Pace Z2, RPE 2–3)
   - (3/5/3 breathing pattern by 100)
4. 100 kick (50 easy/50 FAST) with fins

MS:
1. 2 × 300 swim with 15s rest building from Endurance (Power Z2, HR Z2, Pace Z2, RPE 2–3) to Tempo (Power Z3, HR Z3, Pace Z3, RPE 3–4)
2. 50 at Active Recovery (Power Z1, HR Z1, Pace Z1, RPE 1) w/:30 rest
3. 3 × 200 pull with 12s rest building from Endurance (Power Z2, HR Z2, Pace Z2, RPE 2–3) to Tempo (Power Z3, HR Z3, Pace Z3, RPE 3–4)
4. 50 50 at Active Recovery (Power Z1, HR Z1, Pace Z1, RPE 1) w/:30 rest
5. 4 × 100 swim at Tempo (Power Z3, HR Z3, Pace Z3, RPE 3–4) building to Threshold (Power Z4, HR Z4, Pace Z4, RPE 5–6) with 20s rest
6. 50 at Active Recovery (Power Z1, HR Z1, Pace Z1, RPE 1) w/:30 rest
7. 6 × 50 pull at Threshold (Power Z4, HR Z4, Pace Z4, RPE 5–6) with 7s rest
8. 50 at Active Recovery (Power Z1, HR Z1, Pace Z1, RPE 1) w/:30 rest

CD: 300 at Active Recovery (Power Z1, HR Z1, Pace Z1, RPE 1)

THURSDAY

PLANNED METRICS	
DURATION	
DISTANCE	
TSS	

DAY OFF

FRIDAY

PLANNED METRICS		
DURATION	00:50:00	**WU**: 1. 200 free at Active Recovery (Power Z1, HR Z1, Pace Z1, RPE 1) 2. 200 pull with paddles - Focus on the catch portion of your stroke 3. 200 drill (Shark fin)
DISTANCE	3000	
TSS	40	
		MS1: 8 × 75 Kick with 10s rest - with fins 1. 1 & 5 - free kick 2. 2 & 6 - breast kick (no fins) 3. 3 & 7 - dolphin kick 4. 4 & 8 - free kick **MS2**: 1. 400 Tempo (Power Z3, HR Z3, Pace Z3, RPE 3–4) Swim at with 30s rest 2. 4 × 200 Swim with 20 sec. rest a. 1 & 3 at Endurance (Power Z2, HR Z2, Pace Z2, RPE 2–3) b. 2 & 4 at Tempo (Power Z3, HR Z3, Pace Z3, RPE 3–4) 3. 4 × 100 Swim with 10 sec. rest. a. 1 & 3 at Endurance (Power Z2, HR Z2, Pace Z2, RPE 2–3) b. 2 & 4 at Threshold (Power Z4, HR Z4, Pace Z4, RPE 5–6)
8 × 75 IM KICK & MIDDLE DIST. INTERVALS		**CD**: 200 at Active Recovery (Power Z1, HR Z1, Pace Z1, RPE 1)

SATURDAY

PLANNED METRICS	
DURATION	01:00:00
DISTANCE	3200
TSS	55
4 × 600 TIME TRIAL	

WU:
1. 200 free at Active Recovery (Power Z1, HR Z1, Pace Z1, RPE 1)
2. 200 kick with fins
   - focus on kicking with the ankles and hips
3. 200 drill (100 3/4 catch up / 100 shark fin)

MS:
4 × 600 Time trial swim with up to 30 sec. rest
- This is a time trial swim at RACE PACE (pace should fall between upper Endurance (Power Z2, HR Z2, Pace Z2, RPE 2–3) to Tempo (Power Z3, HR Z3, Pace Z3, RPE 3–4). Each 600 should have same time. If your time drops more than 15s, stop the set.

CD: 200 at Active Recovery (Power Z1, HR Z1, Pace Z1, RPE 1)

SUNDAY

PLANNED METRICS	
DURATION	
DISTANCE	
TSS	

DAY OFF

WEEK #13

Training Focus: Rest and Test Week - 1. The focus of the rest week is to allow your body to recover. This is the time period you start to reap the gains from the work you have performed over the previous weeks. Remember, less is more this week.

2. After the recovery portion of this week, you will retest your swim pace. You will be following the same testing and interpretation you did during the first week of this plan.

MONDAY

PLANNED METRICS		DAY OFF
DURATION		
DISTANCE		
TSS		

TUESDAY

PLANNED METRICS		**WU**: 200 easy, 100 drill (2/3 catch up) **MS**: 2 × 250 at Active Recovery (Power Z1, HR Z1, Pace Z1, RPE 1) to low Endurance (Power Z2, HR Z2, Pace Z2, RPE 2–3). - Focus on an 1 aspect of your swim stroke that you feel is a weak point in you technique. **CD**: 200 pull at Active Recovery (Power Z1, HR Z1, Pace Z1, RPE 1)
DURATION	00:30:00	
DISTANCE	1100	
TSS	20	
RECOVERY - SWIM		

WEDNESDAY

PLANNED METRICS		DAY OFF
DURATION		
DISTANCE		
TSS		

THURSDAY

PLANNED METRICS	
DURATION	00:30:00
DISTANCE	1100
TSS	20

RECOVERY - SWIM

WU: 200 easy, 100 drill (2/3 catch up)

MS: 2 × 250 at Active Recovery (Power Z1, HR Z1, Pace Z1, RPE 1) to low Endurance (Power Z2, HR Z2, Pace Z2, RPE 2–3).

- Focus on an 1 aspect of your swim stroke that you feel is a weak point in you technique.

CD: 200 pull at Active Recovery (Power Z1, HR Z1, Pace Z1, RPE 1)

FRIDAY

PLANNED METRICS	
DURATION	00:45:00
DISTANCE	1300
TSS	30

CRITICAL SWIM SPEED SWIM TEST #1

WU: 200 m at an easy pace

Pull: 200 m pull (100 m follow through drill/ 100 m finger tip drill)

Kick: 100 m with fins

MS1: 1 × 400 m timed. This is a 400 m time-trial. Swim as hard as you can but do not start so hard as you fade in the last meters. You want your pace to be as even as possible during the entire 400 m. If possible, have someone count your strokes during a length near the 200 m point of the test (you can also find this information if you are using a smart watch such as the Garmin Swim or 920XT). Once finished, recover for 5–10 min. You can get out of the pool or slowly swim. The point is to recover but stay loose.

MS2: 1 × 200 m time trial. Swim as hard as you can. Ensure your 200 m time is faster than 1/2 of your 400 m time.

CD: 200 m easy

SATURDAY

PLANNED METRICS	
DURATION	
DISTANCE	
TSS	

DAY OFF

SUNDAY

PLANNED METRICS		
DURATION	00:30:00	**WU**: 200 m at an easy pace
DISTANCE	1700	**Pull**: 200 m pull (100 m follow through drill/ 100 m finger tip drill)
TSS	30	**Kick**: 100 m with fins
CRITICAL SWIM SPEED TEST #2		**MS**: Perform 1 × 1000 m time trial. Just like you performed with the 400 m time trial, do not start so hard that you fade in the final meters. Ensure you swim as hard and even as possible during the entire time trial. At about the 500 m point, if possible, have someone count your stroke rate (you can use a smartwatch to capture this information such as a Garmin Swim or Garmin 920XT). **CD**: 200 m easy

Plan 6

Power Based 10 km Base Training Plan

For this plan, please reference the following Test Interpretation Notes on p. 493 of this book:

- CSS Interpretation Notes (p. 493)

WEEK #1

Training Focus: Week 1 - Test Week

MONDAY

PLANNED METRICS		
DURATION	01:01:00	**WU**: Jog for 15 min progressing from ACTIVE RECOVERY (Pace Z1, HR Z1, Power Z1, RPE 1–2) to ENDURANCE (Pace Z2, HR Z2, Power Z2, PRE 2–3). Towards the end of the WU, perform 4 × 60s of strides to fully open up your muscles.
DISTANCE	Various	
TSS	40	
PRIMER (PRE-TEST)		**MS**: 1. 3 × 3 minutes @ 90% of your Threshold pace (Pace Z3, HR Z3, Power Z3, RPE 4–5) with 6 minutes of recovery at ENDURANCE Pace (Pace Z2, HR Z2, Power Z2, PRE 2–3). 2. 3 × 10s pick-ups with 3 min recovery at ENDURANCE Pace (Pace Z2, HR Z2, Power Z2, PRE 2–3) in between **CD**: 10 min at ACTIVE RECOVERY (Pace Z1, HR Z1, Power Z1, RPE 1–2

TUESDAY

PLANNED METRICS		
DURATION	00:45:00	
DISTANCE	Various	
TSS	35	
5 KM - RFTP TEST		

WU:
Perform 5 mins of dynamic warm up:
1. Leg swings - 10–20 per leg
2. Marches - 10–15 per leg
3. Leg side swings - 10–20 per leg

Build WU pace from Z1 to Z2 for 20 min. Then perform 4 × 10s strides.

MS: Run 5 km (3.1) as fast as you can. You can do this on a bike trail, track, or sidewalk. Try to find the most flat surface (no hills) as possible. However, do not do the test on a treadmill. Track you HR. The four metrics you are concerned with tracking is your running power, pace, and HR, and the time it took you to complete the 5 km.

CD: Jog in for 10 min until your HR comes down to about 100 BPM

WEDNESDAY

PLANNED METRICS	
DURATION	
DISTANCE	
TSS	
DAY OFF	

Actively focus on recovery today: 1) avoid unneccessary physical exertion, 2) watch nutrition closely (healthy carbs, lean protein, and good fats), 3) stretch, and 4) drink when thirsty. Other common recovery aids include massage, napping, elevating legs, floating in water, and listening to music.

THURSDAY

PLANNED METRICS	
DURATION	00:30:00
DISTANCE	Various
TSS	25

20 MINUTE RUN WITH 4 × 10S PICKUPS

WU:
Perform 5 mins of dynamic warm up:
1. Leg swings - 10–20 per leg
2. Marches - 10–15 per leg
3. Leg side swings - 10–20 per leg

Build WU pace from ACTIVE RECOVERY (Power Z1, HR Z1, Pace Z1, RPE 1–2) to ENDURANCE (Power Z2, HR Z2, Pace Z2, RPE 2–3) for 10 min.

MS: Complete this 20 minute run. Build into the run VERY easy. Walk for the first 5 minutes, start a steady, Low ENDURANCE Z2 (Power Z2, HR Z2, Pace Z2, RPE 2–3) jog and at the 10 minute mark, complete 4 × 10 second "pick ups" gradually building into your 10 km/THRESHOLD (Power Z4, HR Z4, Pace Z4, RPE 5–6). by the end of the 20s. 40s EASY Low ENDURANCE Z2 (Power Z2, HR Z2, Pace Z2, RPE 2–3) jog between.

Run the final 6 minutes at low ENDURANCE Z2 (Power Z2, HR Z2, Pace Z2, RPE 2–3) jog.

CD: Walk for 5–10 min. Perform static stretching as necessary.

FRIDAY

PLANNED METRICS	
DURATION	01:00:00
DISTANCE	11 km
TSS	55

CRITICAL RUN SPEED TEST/RFTP #2–10 KM RUN

WU:
Perform 5 mins of dynamic warm up:
1. Leg swings - 10–20 per leg
2. Marches - 10–15 per leg
3. Leg side swings - 10–20 per leg

Build WU pace from ACTIVE RECOVERY (Power Z1, HR Z1, RPE 1) to ENDURANCE (Power Z2, HR Z2, RPE 2–3) for 10 min. Then perform 4 × 10s strides.

MS: Run 10 km at a maximal pace. Do not go out too fast as to slow down over the course of the interval.

Try to find the most flat surface (no hills) as possible. However, do not do the test on a treadmill. Track you HR. The four metrics you are concerned with tracking is your running power, pace, and HR, and the time it took you to complete the 5 km.

CD: Jog for 10 at ACTIVE RECOVERY (Power Z1, HR Z1, RPE 1)

SATURDAY

PLANNED METRICS		
DURATION	00:40:00	**WU**: Jog for 15 min at ACTIVE RECOVERY (Power Z1, HR Z1, Pace Z1, RPE 1), then Perform the following dynamic stretches: 1. Toe Touches - 2 × 15 per leg 2. Leg Tucks - 2 × 15 per leg **MS**: Jog at ACTIVE RECOVERY (Power Z1, HR Z1, Pace Z1, RPE 1) **CD**: Walk for 10 min or until your HR drops below 100 BPM.
DISTANCE	Various	
TSS	15	
RECOVERY - JOG 40 MIN		

SUNDAY

PLANNED METRICS		
DURATION	00:35:00	**WU**: Perform 5 mins of dynamic warm up: 1. Leg swings - 10–20 per leg 2. Marches - 10–15 per leg 3. Leg side swings - 10–20 per leg Build WU pace from ACTIVE RECOVERY (Power Z1, HR Z1, Pace Z1, RPE 1) to ENDURANCE (Power Z2, HR Z2, Pace Z2, RPE 2–3) for 10 min. Then perform 4 × 10s strides. **MS**: Run 4 mi at your Low ENDURANCE (Power Z2, HR Z2, Pace Z2, RPE 2–3) pace. **CD**: Jog 10 min
DISTANCE	4 mi	
TSS	30	
4 MILE LSD ENDURANCE RUN		

WEEK #2

Training Focus: Week 2

MONDAY

PLANNED METRICS		Actively focus on recovery today: 1) avoid unneccessary physical exertion, 2) watch nutrition closely (healthy carbs, lean protein, and good fats), 3) stretch, and 4) drink when thirsty. Other common recovery aids include massage, napping, elevating legs, floating in water, and listening to music.
DURATION		
DISTANCE		
TSS		
DAY OFF		

TUESDAY

PLANNED METRICS		**WU**: Perform 5 mins of dynamic warm up: 1. Leg swings - 10–20 per leg 2. Marches - 10–15 per leg 3. Leg side swings - 10–20 per leg Build WU pace from ACTIVE RECOVERY (Power Z1, HR Z1, Pace Z1, RPE 1) to ENDURANCE (Power Z2, HR Z2, Pace Z2, RPE 2–3) for 10 min. Then perform 4 × 10s strides. **MS**: Run 3 mi at ENDURANCE (Pace Z2, Power Z2, HR Z2, RPE 2–3). **CD**: Walk for 10 min to bring HR down to 100 BPM.
DURATION	00:30:00	
DISTANCE	3 mi	
TSS	30	
ENDURANCE RUN - 3 MILES		

WEDNESDAY

PLANNED METRICS		
DURATION	00:40:00	**WU**: Perform 5 mins of dynamic warm up: 1. Leg swings - 10–20 per leg 2. Marches - 10–15 per leg 3. Leg side swings - 10–20 per leg Build WU pace from ACTIVE RECOVERY (Power Z1, HR Z1, Pace Z1, RPE 1) to ENDURANCE (Power Z2, HR Z2, Pace Z2, RPE 2–3) for 10 min. Then perform 4 × 10s strides. **MS**: 1 mile at low Endurance (Power Z2, HR Z2, Pace Z2, RPE 2–3). Then crank it to Tempo (Power Z3, HR Z3, Pace Z3, RPE 3–4) for 1 mi. Then back down to Endurance (Power Z2, HR Z2, Pace Z2, RPE 2–3) for 1 mi **CD**: Jog for 10 min at Active Recovery (Power Z1, HR Z1, Pace Z1, RPE 1).
DISTANCE	4 mi	
TSS	40	
ENDURANCE-TEMPO SANDWICH		

THURSDAY

PLANNED METRICS		
DURATION	00:35:00	**WU**: Perform 5 mins of dynamic warm up: 1. Leg swings - 10–20 per leg 2. Marches - 10–15 per leg 3. Leg side swings - 10–20 per leg Build WU pace from ACTIVE RECOVERY (Power Z1, HR Z1, Pace Z1, RPE 1) to ENDURANCE (Power Z2, HR Z2, Pace Z2, RPE 2–3) for 10 min. Then perform 4 × 10s strides. **MS**: Run 4 mi at your Low ENDURANCE (Power Z2, HR Z2, Pace Z2, RPE 2–3) pace. **CD**: Jog 10 min
DISTANCE	4 mi	
TSS	30	
4 MILE LSD ENDURANCE RUN		

FRIDAY

PLANNED METRICS		
DURATION		Actively focus on recovery today: 1) avoid unneccessary physical exertion, 2) watch nutrition closely (healthy carbs, lean protein, and good fats), 3) stretch, and 4) drink when thirsty. Other common recovery aids include massage, napping, elevating legs, floating in water, and listening to music.
DISTANCE		
TSS		
DAY OFF		

SATURDAY

PLANNED METRICS		
DURATION	00:55:00	**WU**: Perform 5 mins of dynamic warm up: 1. Leg swings - 10–20 per leg 2. Marches - 10–15 per leg 3. Leg side swings - 10–20 per leg
DISTANCE	Various	
TSS	55	
TEMPO - 2 × 2 MI		15 min at ACTIVE RECOVERY (Pace Z1, HR Z1, Power Z1, RPE 1–2). Perform 3 × 45s strides during the WU. **MS**: Perform 2 × 2 mi intervals at upper TEMPO (Pace Z3, HR Z3, Power Z3, RPE 4–5) … close to your goal 10K pace with 4 min rest in between at ENDURANCE (Pace Z2, Hr Z2, Power Z2, RPE 2–3) **CD**: Jog for 10 min at ACTIVE RECOVERY (Pace Z1, HR Z1, Power Z1, RPE 1–2)

SUNDAY

PLANNED METRICS		
DURATION	00:35:00	**WU**: Perform 5 mins of dynamic warm up: 1. Leg swings - 10–20 per leg 2. Marches - 10–15 per leg 3. Leg side swings - 10–20 per leg
DISTANCE	4 mi	
TSS	30	
4 MILE LSD ENDURANCE RUN		Build WU pace from ACTIVE RECOVERY (Power Z1, HR Z1, Pace Z1, RPE 1) to ENDURANCE (Power Z2, HR Z2, Pace Z2, RPE 2–3) for 10 min. Then perform 4 × 10s strides. **MS**: Run 4 mi at your Low ENDURANCE (Power Z2, HR Z2, Pace Z2, RPE 2–3) pace. **CD**: Jog 10 min

WEEK #3

Training Focus: Week 3

MONDAY

PLANNED METRICS		Actively focus on recovery today: 1) avoid unneccessary physical exertion, 2) watch nutrition closely (healthy carbs, lean protein, and good fats), 3) stretch, and 4) drink when thirsty. Other common recovery aids include massage, napping, elevating legs, floating in water, and listening to music.
DURATION		
DISTANCE		
TSS		
DAY OFF		

TUESDAY

PLANNED METRICS		
DURATION	00:30:00	**WU**: Perform 5 mins of dynamic warm up: 1. Leg swings - 10–20 per leg 2. Marches - 10–15 per leg 3. Leg side swings - 10–20 per leg Build WU pace from ACTIVE RECOVERY (Power Z1, HR Z1, Pace Z1, RPE 1) to ENDURANCE (Power Z2, HR Z2, Pace Z2, RPE 2–3) for 10 min. Then perform 4 × 10s strides. **MS**: Run 3 mi at ENDURANCE (Pace Z2, Power Z2, HR Z2, RPE 2–3). **CD**: Walk for 10 min to bring HR down to 100 BPM.
DISTANCE	3 mi	
TSS	30	
ENDURANCE RUN - 3 MILES		

WEDNESDAY

PLANNED METRICS		WU:
DURATION	01:07:30	Perform 5 mins of dynamic warm up: 1. Leg swings - 10–20 per leg 2. Marches - 10–15 per leg 3. Leg side swings - 10–20 per leg
DISTANCE	Various	
TSS	55	
FARTLEK: STEP DOWN INTERVALS (TEMPO)		Build WU pace from ACTIVE RECOVERY (Power Z1, HR Z1, Pace Z1, RPE 1) to ENDURANCE (Power Z2, HR Z2, Pace Z2, RPE 2–3) for 10 min. Then perform 4 × 10s strides. ---------- **MS**: Run 10–5-3–2-1 minutes at Tempo (Power Z3, HR Z3, Pace Z3, RPE 3–4) and jog equal amounts between each segment at Endurance (Power Z2, HR Z2, Pace Z2, RPE 2–3) ---------- **CD**: 10 minute cool down at (ACTIVE RECOVERY (Power Z1, HR Z1, Pace Z1, RPE 1)

THURSDAY

PLANNED METRICS		WU:
DURATION	00:35:00	Perform 5 mins of dynamic warm up: 1. Leg swings - 10–20 per leg 2. Marches - 10–15 per leg 3. Leg side swings - 10–20 per leg
DISTANCE	4 mi	
TSS	30	
4 MILE LSD ENDURANCE RUN		Build WU pace from ACTIVE RECOVERY (Power Z1, HR Z1, Pace Z1, RPE 1) to ENDURANCE (Power Z2, HR Z2, Pace Z2, RPE 2–3) for 10 min. Then perform 4 × 10s strides. **MS**: Run 4 mi at your Low ENDURANCE (Power Z2, HR Z2, Pace Z2, RPE 2–3) pace. **CD**: Jog 10 min

FRIDAY

PLANNED METRICS		Actively focus on recovery today: 1) avoid unneccessary physical exertion, 2) watch nutrition closely (healthy carbs, lean protein, and good fats), 3) stretch, and 4) drink when thirsty. Other common recovery aids include massage, napping, elevating legs, floating in water, and listening to music.
DURATION		
DISTANCE		
TSS		
DAY OFF		

SATURDAY

PLANNED METRICS		**WU**: Perform 5 mins of dynamic warm up: 1. Leg swings - 10–20 per leg 2. Marches - 10–15 per leg 3. Leg side swings - 10–20 per leg
DURATION	00:50:00	Build WU pace from ACTIVE RECOVERY (Power Z1, HR Z1, Pace Z1, RPE 1) to ENDURANCE (Power Z2, HR Z2, Pace Z2, RPE 2–3) for 10 min. Then perform 4 × 10s strides.
DISTANCE	Various	**MS**: Run: 2 × 12' at TEMPO (Pace Z3, HR Z3, Power, Z3, RPE 3–4) with 3–5 min easy ENDURANCE (Pace Z2, Power Z2, HR Z2, RPE 2–3) between.
TSS	45	
TEMPO RUN - 2 × 12 MIN		**CD**: Jog for 10 min at ACTIVE RECOVERY (Pace Z1, HR Z1, Power Z1, RPE 1–2).

SUNDAY

PLANNED METRICS		**WU**: Perform 5 mins of dynamic warm up: 1. Leg swings - 10–20 per leg 2. Marches - 10–15 per leg 3. Leg side swings - 10–20 per leg
DURATION	00:45:00	Build WU pace from ACTIVE RECOVERY (Power Z1, HR Z1, Pace Z1, RPE 1) to ENDURANCE (Power Z2, HR Z2, Pace Z2, RPE 2–3) for 10 min. Then perform 4 × 10s strides.
DISTANCE	5 mi	**MS**: Run 5 mi at your Low ENDURANCE (Power Z2, HR Z2, Pace Z2, RPE 2–3) pace.
TSS	40	
5 MILE LSD ENDURANCE RUN		**CD**: Jog 10 min

WEEK #4

Training Focus: Week 4

MONDAY

PLANNED METRICS		Actively focus on recovery today: 1) avoid unneccessary physical exertion, 2) watch nutrition closely (healthy carbs, lean protein, and good fats), 3) stretch, and 4) drink when thirsty. Other common recovery aids include massage, napping, elevating legs, floating in water, and listening to music.
DURATION		
DISTANCE		
TSS		
DAY OFF		

TUESDAY

PLANNED METRICS		**WU**: Perform 5 mins of dynamic warm up: 1. Leg swings - 10–20 per leg 2. Marches - 10–15 per leg 3. Leg side swings - 10–20 per leg Build WU pace from ACTIVE RECOVERY (Power Z1, HR Z1, Pace Z1, RPE 1) to ENDURANCE (Power Z2, HR Z2, Pace Z2, RPE 2–3) for 10 min. Then perform 4 × 10s strides. **MS**: Run 4 mi at ENDURANCE (Pace Z2, Power Z2, HR Z2, RPE 2–3). **CD**: Walk for 10 min to bring HR down to 100 BPM.
DURATION	00:40:00	
DISTANCE	4 mi	
TSS	40	
ENDURANCE RUN - 4 MILES		

WEDNESDAY

PLANNED METRICS		
DURATION	00:26:00	
DISTANCE	Various	
TSS	30	
HILLS, HILLS, HILLS!!!!!		**WU**: Perform 5 mins of dynamic warm up: 1. Leg swings - 10–20 per leg 2. Marches - 10–15 per leg 3. Leg side swings - 10–20 per leg Build WU pace from ACTIVE RECOVERY (Power Z1, HR Z1, Pace Z1, RPE 1) to ENDURANCE (Power Z2, HR Z2, Pace Z2, RPE 2–3) for 10 min. Then perform 4 × 10s strides. **MS**: Start at mid-ENDURANCE (Pace Z2, HR Z2, Power Z2, RPE 2–3) and hold through entire set. Perform 10 × 90 sec at 3% with 1–2 min at 0% between. **CD**: Jog for 10 min at ACTIVE RECOVERY (Pace Z1, HR Z1, Power Z1, RPE 1–2)

THURSDAY

PLANNED METRICS		
DURATION	00:40:00	
DISTANCE	4 mi	
TSS	40	
ENDURANCE RUN - 4 MILES		**WU**: Perform 5 mins of dynamic warm up: 1. Leg swings - 10–20 per leg 2. Marches - 10–15 per leg 3. Leg side swings - 10–20 per leg Build WU pace from ACTIVE RECOVERY (Power Z1, HR Z1, Pace Z1, RPE 1) to ENDURANCE (Power Z2, HR Z2, Pace Z2, RPE 2–3) for 10 min. Then perform 4 × 10s strides. **MS**: Run 4 mi at ENDURANCE (Pace Z2, Power Z2, HR Z2, RPE 2–3). **CD**: Walk for 10 min to bring HR down to 100 BPM.

FRIDAY

PLANNED METRICS		
DURATION		
DISTANCE		
TSS		
DAY OFF		Actively focus on recovery today: 1) avoid unneccessary physical exertion, 2) watch nutrition closely (healthy carbs, lean protein, and good fats), 3) stretch, and 4) drink when thirsty. Other common recovery aids include massage, napping, elevating legs, floating in water, and listening to music.

SATURDAY

PLANNED METRICS		
DURATION	00:55:00	**WU**: Perform 5 mins of dynamic warm up: 1. Leg swings - 10–20 per leg 2. Marches - 10–15 per leg 3. Leg side swings - 10–20 per leg Build WU pace from ACTIVE RECOVERY (Power Z1, HR Z1, Pace Z1, RPE 1) to ENDURANCE (Power Z2, HR Z2, Pace Z2, RPE 2–3) for 10 min. Then perform 4 × 10s strides. **MS**: Tempo run: 30' Low TEMPO (Power Z3, HR Z3, Pace Z3, RPE 3–4). **CD**: Jog for 10 min ACTIVE RECOVERY (Power Z1, HR Z1, Pace Z1, RPE 1)
DISTANCE	Various	
TSS	50	
30 MIN LOW TEMPO RUN		

SUNDAY

PLANNED METRICS		
DURATION	00:55:00	**WU**: Perform 5 mins of dynamic warm up: 1. Leg swings - 10–20 per leg 2. Marches - 10–15 per leg 3. Leg side swings - 10–20 per leg Build WU pace from ACTIVE RECOVERY (Power Z1, HR Z1, Pace Z1, RPE 1) to ENDURANCE (Power Z2, HR Z2, Pace Z2, RPE 2–3) for 10 min. Then perform 4 × 10s strides. **MS**: Run 5 mi at your Low ENDURANCE (Power Z2, HR Z2, Pace Z2, RPE 2–3) pace. **CD**: Jog 10 min
DISTANCE	5 mi	
TSS	55	
5 MILE LSD ENDURANCE RUN		

WEEK #5

Training Focus: Week 5

MONDAY

PLANNED METRICS		
DURATION		Actively focus on recovery today: 1) avoid unneccessary physical exertion, 2) watch nutrition closely (healthy carbs, lean protein, and good fats), 3) stretch, and 4) drink when thirsty. Other common recovery aids include massage, napping, elevating legs, floating in water, and listening to music.
DISTANCE		
TSS		
DAY OFF		

TUESDAY

PLANNED METRICS		
DURATION	00:40:00	**WU**: Perform 5 mins of dynamic warm up: 1. Leg swings - 10–20 per leg 2. Marches - 10–15 per leg 3. Leg side swings - 10–20 per leg Build WU pace from ACTIVE RECOVERY (Power Z1, HR Z1, Pace Z1, RPE 1) to ENDURANCE (Power Z2, HR Z2, Pace Z2, RPE 2–3) for 10 min. Then perform 4 × 10s strides. **MS**: Run 4 mi at ENDURANCE (Pace Z2, Power Z2, HR Z2, RPE 2–3). **CD**: Walk for 10 min to bring HR down to 100 BPM.
DISTANCE	4 mi	
TSS	40	
ENDURANCE RUN - 4 MILES		

WEDNESDAY

PLANNED METRICS		
DURATION	01:05:00	**WU**: Perform 5 mins of dynamic warm up: 1. Leg swings - 10–20 per leg 2. Marches - 10–15 per leg 3. Leg side swings - 10–20 per leg
DISTANCE	Various	
TSS	60	
40 MIN LOW TEMPO RUN		Build WU pace from ACTIVE RECOVERY (Power Z1, HR Z1, Pace Z1, RPE 1) to ENDURANCE (Power Z2, HR Z2, Pace Z2, RPE 2–3) for 10 min. Then perform 4 × 10s strides. **MS**: Tempo run: 40’ at TEMPO (Power Z3, HR Z3, Pace Z3, RPE 3–4). **CD**: Jog for 10 min ACTIVE RECOVERY (Power Z1, HR Z1, Pace Z1, RPE 1)

THURSDAY

PLANNED METRICS		
DURATION	00:40:00	**WU**: Perform 5 mins of dynamic warm up: 1. Leg swings - 10–20 per leg 2. Marches - 10–15 per leg 3. Leg side swings - 10–20 per leg
DISTANCE	4 mi	
TSS	40	
ENDURANCE RUN - 4 MILES		Build WU pace from ACTIVE RECOVERY (Power Z1, HR Z1, Pace Z1, RPE 1) to ENDURANCE (Power Z2, HR Z2, Pace Z2, RPE 2–3) for 10 min. Then perform 4 × 10s strides. **MS**: Run 4 mi at ENDURANCE (Pace Z2, Power Z2, HR Z2, RPE 2–3). **CD**: Walk for 10 min to bring HR down to 100 BPM.

FRIDAY

PLANNED METRICS		Actively focus on recovery today: 1) avoid unneccessary physical exertion, 2) watch nutrition closely (healthy carbs, lean protein, and good fats), 3) stretch, and 4) drink when thirsty. Other common recovery aids include massage, napping, elevating legs, floating in water, and listening to music.
DURATION		
DISTANCE		
TSS		
DAY OFF		

SATURDAY

PLANNED METRICS		**WU**: Perform 5 mins of dynamic warm up: 1. Leg swings - 10–20 per leg 2. Marches - 10–15 per leg 3. Leg side swings - 10–20 per leg
DURATION	00:40:00	
DISTANCE	4 mi	
TSS	40	
ENDURANCE-TEMPO SANDWICH		Build WU pace from ACTIVE RECOVERY (Power Z1, HR Z1, Pace Z1, RPE 1) to ENDURANCE (Power Z2, HR Z2, Pace Z2, RPE 2–3) for 10 min. Then perform 4 × 10s strides. **MS**: 1 mile at low Endurance (Power Z2, HR Z2, Pace Z2, RPE 2–3). Then crank it to Tempo (Power Z3, HR Z3, Pace Z3, RPE 3–4) for 1 mi. Then back down to Endurance (Power Z2, HR Z2, Pace Z2, RPE 2–3) for 1 mi **CD**: Jog for 10 min at Active Recovery (Power Z1, HR Z1, Pace Z1, RPE 1).

SUNDAY

PLANNED METRICS		**WU**: Perform 5 mins of dynamic warm up: 1. Leg swings - 10–20 per leg 2. Marches - 10–15 per leg 3. Leg side swings - 10–20 per leg
DURATION	01:05:00	
DISTANCE	7 mi	
TSS	60	
7 MILE LSD ENDURANCE RUN		Build WU pace from ACTIVE RECOVERY (Power Z1, HR Z1, Pace Z1, RPE 1) to ENDURANCE (Power Z2, HR Z2, Pace Z2, RPE 2–3) for 10 min. Then perform 4 × 10s strides. **MS**: Run 7 mi at your Low ENDURANCE (Power Z2, HR Z2, Pace Z2, RPE 2–3) pace. **CD**: Jog 10 min

WEEK #6

Training Focus: Week 6

MONDAY

PLANNED METRICS		
DURATION		Actively focus on recovery today: 1) avoid unneccessary physical exertion, 2) watch nutrition closely (healthy carbs, lean protein, and good fats), 3) stretch, and 4) drink when thirsty. Other common recovery aids include massage, napping, elevating legs, floating in water, and listening to music.
DISTANCE		
TSS		
DAY OFF		

TUESDAY

PLANNED METRICS		
DURATION	00:55:00	**WU**: Perform 5 mins of dynamic warm up: 1. Leg swings - 10–20 per leg 2. Marches - 10–15 per leg 3. Leg side swings - 10–20 per leg Build WU pace from ACTIVE RECOVERY (Power Z1, HR Z1, Pace Z1, RPE 1) to ENDURANCE (Power Z2, HR Z2, Pace Z2, RPE 2–3) for 10 min. Then perform 4x10s strides. **MS**: Start main set run at mid ENDURANCE (Power Z2, HR Z2, Pace Z2, RPE 2–3). Once comfortable, complete 3x7 min intervals at upper TEMPO (Power Z3, HR Z3, Pace Z3, RPE 3–4). Recover for 5 min ENDURANCE (Power Z2, HR Z2, Pace Z2, RPE 2–3) in between each interval. **CD**: Jog at ACTIVE RECOVERY (Power Z1, HR Z1, Pace Z1, RPE 1) for 10 min or until HR comes below 100 BPM.
DISTANCE	Various	
TSS	55	
3 × 7 TEMPO PACE INTERVALS		

WEDNESDAY

PLANNED METRICS		
DURATION	00:35:00	**WU**: Perform 5 mins of dynamic warm up: 1. Leg swings - 10–20 per leg 2. Marches - 10–15 per leg 3. Leg side swings - 10–20 per leg Build WU pace from ACTIVE RECOVERY for 10 min. Then perform 4x10s strides. **MS**: Jog a ACTIVE RECOVERY (Pace Z1, HR Z1, Power Z1, RPE 1–2) pace for 15–20 min. Enjoy yourself. **CD**: Walk home.
DISTANCE	Various	
TSS	10	
RECOVERY - JOG		

THURSDAY

PLANNED METRICS		
DURATION		Actively focus on recovery today: 1) avoid unneccessary physical exertion, 2) watch nutrition closely (healthy carbs, lean protein, and good fats), 3) stretch, and 4) drink when thirsty. Other common recovery aids include massage, napping, elevating legs, floating in water, and listening to music.
DISTANCE		
TSS		
DAY OFF		

FRIDAY

PLANNED METRICS		
DURATION	00:35:00	**WU**: Perform 5 mins of dynamic warm up: 1. Leg swings - 10–20 per leg 2. Marches - 10–15 per leg 3. Leg side swings - 10–20 per leg Build WU pace from ACTIVE RECOVERY for 10 min. Then perform 4x10s strides. **MS**: Jog a ACTIVE RECOVERY (Pace Z1, HR Z1, Power Z1, RPE 1–2) pace for 15–20 min. Enjoy yourself. **CD**: Walk home.
DISTANCE	Various	
TSS	10	
RECOVERY - JOG		

SATURDAY

PLANNED METRICS	
DURATION	00:30:00
DISTANCE	Various
TSS	25

PRE-TEST PRIMER - 20 MINUTE RUN WITH 4 × 10S PICKUPS

WU:
Perform 5 mins of dynamic warm up:
1. Leg swings - 10–20 per leg
2. Marches - 10–15 per leg
3. Leg side swings - 10–20 per leg

Build WU pace from ACTIVE RECOVERY (Power Z1, HR Z1, Pace Z1, RPE 1–2) to ENDURANCE (Power Z2, HR Z2, Pace Z2, RPE 2–3) for 10 min.

MS: Complete this 20 minute run. Build into the run VERY easy. Walk for the first 5 minutes, start a steady, Low ENDURANCE Z2 (Power Z2, HR Z2, Pace Z2, RPE 2–3) jog and at the 10 minute mark, complete 4x10 second "pick ups" gradually building into your 10k/THRESHOLD (Power Z4, HR Z4, Pace Z4, RPE 5–6). by the end of the 20s. 40s EASY Low ENDURANCE Z2 (Power Z2, HR Z2, Pace Z2, RPE 2–3) jog between.

Run the final 6 minutes at low ENDURANCE Z2 (Power Z2, HR Z2, Pace Z2, RPE 2–3) jog.

CD: Walk for 5–10 min. Perform static stretching as necessary.

SUNDAY

PLANNED METRICS	
DURATION	00:45:00
DISTANCE	Various
TSS	35

5 KM - RFTP TEST

WU:
Perform 5 mins of dynamic warm up:
1. Leg swings - 10–20 per leg
2. Marches - 10–15 per leg
3. Leg side swings - 10–20 per leg

Build WU pace from Z1 to Z2 for 20 min. Then perform 4 × 10s strides.

MS: Run 5 km (3.1) as fast as you can. You can do this on a bike trail, track, or sidewalk. Try to find the most flat surface (no hills) as possible. However, do not do the test on a treadmill. Track you HR. The four metrics you are concerned with tracking is your running power, pace, and HR, and the time it took you to complete the 5 km.

CD: Jog in for 10 min until your HR comes down to about 100 BPM

Plan 7

Power Based 10 km Peak Training Plan

For this plan, please reference the following Test Interpretation Notes on p. 493 of this book:

- Week 1: CSS Interpretation Notes (p. 493)

WEEK #1

Training Focus: Week 1 - Test Week

MONDAY

PLANNED METRICS		
DURATION	01:01:00	**WU**: Jog for 15 min progressing from ACTIVE RECOVERY (Pace Z1, HR Z1, Power Z1, RPE 1–2) to ENDURANCE (Pace Z2, HR Z2, Power Z2, PRE 2–3). Towards the end of the WU, perform 4 × 60s of strides to fully open up your muscles.
DISTANCE	Various	
TSS	40	
PRIMER (PRE-TEST)		**MS**: 1. 3 × 3 minutes @ 90% of your Threshold pace (Pace Z3, HR Z3, Power Z3, RPE 4–5) with 6 minutes of recovery at ENDURANCE Pace (Pace Z2, HR Z2, Power Z2, PRE 2–3). 2. 3 × 10s pick-ups with 3 min recovery at ENDURANCE Pace (Pace Z2, HR Z2, Power Z2, PRE 2–3) in between **CD**: 10 min at ACTIVE RECOVERY (Pace Z1, HR Z1, Power Z1, RPE 1–2)

TUESDAY

PLANNED METRICS		
DURATION	00:45:00	**WU**: Perform 5 mins of dynamic warm up: 1. Leg swings - 10–20 per leg 2. Marches - 10–15 per leg 3. Leg side swings - 10–20 per leg Build WU pace from Z1 to Z2 for 20 min. Then perform 4 × 10s strides. ------- **MS**: Run 5 km (3.1) as fast as you can. You can do this on a bike trail, track, or sidewalk. Try to find the most flat surface (no hills) as possible. However, do not do the test on a treadmill. Track you HR. The four metrics you are concerned with tracking is your running power, pace, and HR, and the time it took you to complete the 5 km. ------- **CD**: Jog in for 10 min until your HR comes down to about 100 BPM
DISTANCE	Various	
TSS	35	
5 KM - RFTP TEST		

WEDNESDAY

PLANNED METRICS		
DURATION		Actively focus on recovery today: 1) avoid unneccessary physical exertion, 2) watch nutrition closely (healthy carbs, lean protein, and good fats), 3) stretch, and 4) drink when thirsty. Other common recovery aids include massage, napping, elevating legs, floating in water, and listening to music.
DISTANCE		
TSS		
DAY OFF		

THURSDAY

PLANNED METRICS		
DURATION	00:30:00	**WU**: Perform 5 mins of dynamic warm up: 1. Leg swings - 10–20 per leg 2. Marches - 10–15 per leg 3. Leg side swings - 10–20 per leg
DISTANCE	Various	
TSS	25	Build WU pace from ACTIVE RECOVERY (Power Z1, HR Z1, Pace Z1, RPE 1–2) to ENDURANCE (Power Z2, HR Z2, Pace Z2, RPE 2–3) for 10 min. **MS**: Complete this 20 minute run. Build into the run VERY easy. Walk for the first 5 minutes, start a steady, Low ENDURANCE Z2 (Power Z2, HR Z2, Pace Z2, RPE 2–3) jog and at the 10 minute mark, complete 4 × 10 second "pick ups" gradually building into your 10k/THRESHOLD (Power Z4, HR Z4, Pace Z4, RPE 5–6). by the end of the 20s. 40s EASY Low ENDURANCE Z2 (Power Z2, HR Z2, Pace Z2, RPE 2–3) jog between. Run the final 6 minutes at low ENDURANCE Z2 (Power Z2, HR Z2, Pace Z2, RPE 2–3) jog.
20 MINUTE RUN WITH 4 × 10S PICKUPS		**CD**: Walk for 5–10 min. Perform static stretching as necessary.

FRIDAY

PLANNED METRICS		
DURATION	01:00:00	**WU**: Perform 5 mins of dynamic warm up: 1. Leg swings - 10–20 per leg 2. Marches - 10–15 per leg 3. Leg side swings - 10–20 per leg
DISTANCE	11 km	
TSS	55	Build WU pace from ACTIVE RECOVERY (Power Z1, HR Z1, RPE 1) to ENDURANCE (Power Z2, HR Z2, RPE 2–3) for 10 min. Then perform 4 × 10s strides. **MS**: Run 10 km at a maximal pace. Do not go out too fast as to slow down over the course of the interval. Try to find the most flat surface (no hills) as possible. However, do not do the test on a treadmill. Track you HR. The four metrics you are concerned with tracking is your running power, pace, and HR, and the time it took you to complete the 5 km.
CRITICAL RUN SPEED TEST/RFTP #2–10 KM RUN		**CD**: Jog for 10 at ACTIVE RECOVERY (Power Z1, HR Z1, RPE 1)

SATURDAY

PLANNED METRICS		
DURATION	00:40:00	**WU**: Jog for 15 min at ACTIVE RECOVERY (Power Z1, HR Z1, Pace Z1, RPE 1), then
DISTANCE	Various	Perform the following dynamic stretches: 1. Toe Touches - 2 × 15 per leg 2. Leg Tucks - 2 × 15 per leg
TSS	15	**MS**: Jog at ACTIVE RECOVERY (Power Z1, HR Z1, Pace Z1, RPE 1)
RECOVERY - JOG 40 MIN		**CD**: Walk for 10 min or until your HR drops below 100 BPM.

SUNDAY

PLANNED METRICS		
DURATION	01:05:00	**WU**: Perform 5 mins of dynamic warm up: 1. Leg swings - 10–20 per leg 2. Marches - 10–15 per leg 3. Leg side swings - 10–20 per leg
DISTANCE	7 mi	Build WU pace from ACTIVE RECOVERY (Power Z1, HR Z1, Pace Z1, RPE 1) to ENDURANCE (Power Z2, HR Z2, Pace Z2, RPE 2–3) for 10 min. Then perform 4 × 10s strides.
TSS	60	**MS**: Run 7 mi at your Low ENDURANCE (Power Z2, HR Z2, Pace Z2, RPE 2–3) pace.
7 MILE LSD ENDURANCE RUN		**CD**: Jog 10 min

WEEK #2

Training Focus: Week 2

MONDAY

PLANNED METRICS		
DURATION		Actively focus on recovery today: 1) avoid unneccessary physical exertion, 2) watch nutrition closely (healthy carbs, lean protein, and good fats), 3) stretch, and 4) drink when thirsty. Other common recovery aids include massage, napping, elevating legs, floating in water, and listening to music.
DISTANCE		
TSS		
DAY OFF		

TUESDAY

PLANNED METRICS		
DURATION	00:45:00	**WU**: Perform 5 mins of dynamic warm up: 1. Leg swings - 10–20 per leg 2. Marches - 10–15 per leg 3. Leg side swings - 10–20 per leg
DISTANCE	Various	
TSS	55	Build WU pace from ACTIVE RECOVERY (Power Z1, HR Z1, Pace Z1, RPE 1) to ENDURANCE (Power Z2, HR Z2, Pace Z2, RPE 2–3) for 10 min. Then perform 4 × 10s strides. **MS1**: 5 × 400 at 5K pace Threshold (Power Z4, HR Z4, Pace Z4, RPE 5–6) with 2 min at low ENDURANCE (Power Z2, HR Z2, Pace Z2, RPE 2–3) for recovery. **MS2**: Run 1.5 mi at ENDURANCE (Power Z2, HR Z2, Pace Z2, RPE 2–3). **CD**: Jog for 800 m at ACTIVE RECOVERY (Power Z1, HR Z1, Pace Z1, RPE 1)
5 × 400 AT 5K PACE		

WEDNESDAY

PLANNED METRICS		
DURATION	00:40:00	**WU**: Perform 5 mins of dynamic warm up: 1. Leg swings - 10–20 per leg 2. Marches - 10–15 per leg 3. Leg side swings - 10–20 per leg
DISTANCE	4	
TSS	55	Build WU pace from ACTIVE RECOVERY (Power Z1, HR Z1, Pace Z1, RPE 1) to ENDURANCE (Power Z2, HR Z2, Pace Z2, RPE 2–3) for 10 min. Then perform 4 × 10s strides. **MS**: 1/2 mile at low ENDURANCE (Pace Z2, Power Z2, HR Z2, RPE 3–4). Then crank it to TEMPO (Pace Z3, Power Z3, HR Z3, RPE 4–5) for 3 mi then bring it back down to ENDURANCE (Pace Z2, Power Z2, HR Z2, RPE 3–4) for 1/2 mi. **CD**: 10 min cool down ACTIVE RECOVERY (Pace Z1, Power Z1, HR Z1, RPE 1–2)
3 MI TEMPO RUN		

THURSDAY

PLANNED METRICS		
DURATION	00:30:00	**WU**: Perform 5 mins of dynamic warm up: 1. Leg swings - 10–20 per leg 2. Marches - 10–15 per leg 3. Leg side swings - 10–20 per leg Build WU pace from ACTIVE RECOVERY (Power Z1, HR Z1, Pace Z1, RPE 1) to ENDURANCE (Power Z2, HR Z2, Pace Z2, RPE 2–3) for 10 min. Then perform 4 × 10s strides. **MS**: Run 3 mi at ENDURANCE (Pace Z2, Power Z2, HR Z2, RPE 2–3). **CD**: Walk for 10 min to bring HR down to 100 BPM.
DISTANCE	3 mi	
TSS	30	
ENDURANCE RUN - 3 MILES		

FRIDAY

PLANNED METRICS		
DURATION		Actively focus on recovery today: 1) avoid unneccessary physical exertion, 2) watch nutrition closely (healthy carbs, lean protein, and good fats), 3) stretch, and 4) drink when thirsty. Other common recovery aids include massage, napping, elevating legs, floating in water, and listening to music.
DISTANCE		
TSS		
DAY OFF		

SATURDAY

PLANNED METRICS		
DURATION	00:50:00	**WU**: Perform 5 mins of dynamic warm up: 1. Leg swings - 10–20 per leg 2. Marches - 10–15 per leg 3. Leg side swings - 10–20 per leg 15 min at ACTIVE RECOVERY (Pace Z1, HR Z1, Power Z1, RPE 1–2). Perform 3 × 45s strides during the WU. **MS**: Perform 2 × 2 mi intervals at upper TEMPO (Pace Z3, HR Z3, Power Z3, RPE 4–5) … close to your goal 10K pace with 4 min rest in between at ENDURANCE (Pace Z2, Hr Z2, Power Z2, RPE 2–3) **CD**: Jog for 10 min at ACTIVE RECOVERY (Pace Z1, HR Z1, Power Z1, RPE 1–2)
DISTANCE	Various	
TSS	55	
TEMPO - 2 × 2 MI AT 10K		

SUNDAY

PLANNED METRICS		
DURATION	01:05:00	
DISTANCE	7 mi	
TSS	60	
7 MILE LSD ENDURANCE RUN		**WU**: Perform 5 mins of dynamic warm up: 1. Leg swings - 10–20 per leg 2. Marches - 10–15 per leg 3. Leg side swings - 10–20 per leg Build WU pace from ACTIVE RECOVERY (Power Z1, HR Z1, Pace Z1, RPE 1) to ENDURANCE (Power Z2, HR Z2, Pace Z2, RPE 2–3) for 10 min. Then perform 4 × 10s strides. **MS**: Run 7 mi at your Low ENDURANCE (Power Z2, HR Z2, Pace Z2, RPE 2–3) pace. **CD**: Jog 10 min

WEEK #3

Training Focus: Week 3

MONDAY

PLANNED METRICS		
DURATION		
DISTANCE		
TSS		
DAY OFF		Actively focus on recovery today: 1) avoid unneccessary physical exertion, 2) watch nutrition closely (healthy carbs, lean protein, and good fats), 3) stretch, and 4) drink when thirsty. Other common recovery aids include massage, napping, elevating legs, floating in water, and listening to music.

TUESDAY

PLANNED METRICS		
DURATION	00:40:00	
DISTANCE	Various	
TSS	55	
2 × 2 MILE AT THRESHOLD PACE		**WU**: Perform 5 mins of dynamic warm up: 1. Leg swings - 10–20 per leg 2. Marches - 10–15 per leg 3. Leg side swings - 10–20 per leg Build WU pace from ACTIVE RECOVERY (Power Z1, HR Z1, Pace Z1, RPE 1) to ENDURANCE (Power Z2, HR Z2, Pace Z2, RPE 2–3) for 10 min. Then perform 4 × 10s strides. **MS**: Run 2 × 2 mile intervals your THRESHOLD (Pace Z4, HR Z4, Power Z4, RPE 4–5) with 0.5 mile recovery at ENDURANCE (Z2, HR Z2, Power Z2, RPE 2–3) **CD**: Jog for 10 min at ACTIVE RECOVERY (Pace Z1, HR Z1, Power Z1, RPE 1–2)

WEDNESDAY

PLANNED METRICS		
DURATION	00:30:00	**WU**: Perform 5 mins of dynamic warm up: 1. Leg swings - 10–20 per leg 2. Marches - 10–15 per leg 3. Leg side swings - 10–20 per leg
DISTANCE	3 mi	
TSS	30	Build WU pace from ACTIVE RECOVERY (Power Z1, HR Z1, Pace Z1, RPE 1) to ENDURANCE (Power Z2, HR Z2, Pace Z2, RPE 2–3) for 10 min. Then perform 4 × 10s strides. **MS**: Run 3 mi at ENDURANCE (Pace Z2, Power Z2, HR Z2, RPE 2–3).
ENDURANCE RUN - 3 MILES		**CD**: Walk for 10 min to bring HR down to 100 BPM.

THURSDAY

PLANNED METRICS		
DURATION	01:07:00	**WU**: Perform 5 mins of dynamic warm up: 1. Leg swings - 10–20 per leg 2. Marches - 10–15 per leg 3. Leg side swings - 10–20 per leg
DISTANCE	Various	
TSS	65	Build WU pace from ACTIVE RECOVERY (Power Z1, HR Z1, Pace Z1, RPE 1) to ENDURANCE (Power Z2, HR Z2, Pace Z2, RPE 2–3) for 10 min. Then perform 4 × 10s strides. ------- **MS**: Run 10–5-3–2-1 minutes at 5 K pace (THRESHOLD (Power Z4, HR Z4, Pace Z4, RPE 4–5) and jog equal amounts between each segment. -------
FARTLEK: STEP DOWN INTERVALS		**CD**: 10 minute cool down at (ACTIVE RECOVERY (Power Z1, HR Z1, Pace Z1, RPE 1)

FRIDAY

PLANNED METRICS		
DURATION		Actively focus on recovery today: 1) avoid unneccessary physical exertion, 2) watch nutrition closely (healthy carbs, lean protein, and good fats), 3) stretch, and 4) drink when thirsty. Other common recovery aids include massage, napping, elevating legs, floating in water, and listening to music.
DISTANCE		
TSS		
DAY OFF		

SATURDAY

PLANNED METRICS		
DURATION	00:50:00	**WU**: Perform 5 mins of dynamic warm up: 1. Leg swings - 10–20 per leg 2. Marches - 10–15 per leg 3. Leg side swings - 10–20 per leg
DISTANCE	Various	
TSS	45	Build WU pace from ACTIVE RECOVERY (Power Z1, HR Z1, Pace Z1, RPE 1) to ENDURANCE (Power Z2, HR Z2, Pace Z2, RPE 2–3) for 10 min. Then perform 4 × 10s strides. **MS**: Run: 2 × 12' at TEMPO (Pace Z3, HR Z3, Power, Z3, RPE 3–4) with 3–5 min easy ENDURANCE (Pace Z2, Power Z2, HR Z2, RPE 2–3) between.
TEMPO RUN - 2 × 12 MIN		**CD**: Jog for 10 min at ACTIVE RECOVERY (Pace Z1, HR Z1, Power Z1, RPE 1–2).

SUNDAY

PLANNED METRICS		
DURATION	01:12:00	**WU**: Perform 5 mins of dynamic warm up: 1. Leg swings - 10–20 per leg 2. Marches - 10–15 per leg 3. Leg side swings - 10–20 per leg
DISTANCE	8 mi	
TSS	70	Build WU pace from ACTIVE RECOVERY (Power Z1, HR Z1, Pace Z1, RPE 1) to ENDURANCE (Power Z2, HR Z2, Pace Z2, RPE 2–3) for 10 min. Then perform 4 × 10s strides. **MS**: Run 8 mi at your Low ENDURANCE (Power Z2, HR Z2, Pace Z2, RPE 2–3) pace.
8 MILE LSD ENDURANCE RUN		**CD**: Jog 10 min

WEEK #4

Training Focus: Week 4

MONDAY

PLANNED METRICS		
DURATION		Actively focus on recovery today: 1) avoid unneccessary physical exertion, 2) watch nutrition closely (healthy carbs, lean protein, and good fats), 3) stretch, and 4) drink when thirsty. Other common recovery aids include massage, napping, elevating legs, floating in water, and listening to music.
DISTANCE		
TSS		
DAY OFF		

TUESDAY

PLANNED METRICS		
DURATION	00:40:00	**WU**: Perform 5 mins of dynamic warm up: 1. Leg swings - 10–20 per leg 2. Marches - 10–15 per leg 3. Leg side swings - 10–20 per leg Build WU pace from ACTIVE RECOVERY (Power Z1, HR Z1, Pace Z1, RPE 1) to ENDURANCE (Power Z2, HR Z2, Pace Z2, RPE 2–3) for 1.5 miles. **MS1**: 6 × 400 at 5K pace/Threshold (Power Z4, HR Z4, Pace Z4, RPE 5–6) with 2 min at low Endurance (Power Z2, HR Z2, Pace Z2, RPE 2–3) for recovery. **MS2**: Run 1.5 mi at Endurance (Power Z2, HR Z2, Pace Z2, RPE 2–3). **CD**: Jog for 10 min at ACTIVE RECOVERY (Power Z1, HR Z1, Pace Z1, RPE 1)
DISTANCE	Various	
TSS	40	
6 × 400 AT 5K PACE		

WEDNESDAY

PLANNED METRICS		
DURATION	00:40:00	**WU**: Perform 5 mins of dynamic warm up: 1. Leg swings - 10–20 per leg 2. Marches - 10–15 per leg 3. Leg side swings - 10–20 per leg Build WU pace from ACTIVE RECOVERY (Power Z1, HR Z1, Pace Z1, RPE 1) to ENDURANCE (Power Z2, HR Z2, Pace Z2, RPE 2–3) for 10 min. Then perform 4 × 10s strides. **MS**: Run 4 mi at ENDURANCE (Pace Z2, Power Z2, HR Z2, RPE 2–3). **CD**: Walk for 10 min to bring HR down to 100 BPM.
DISTANCE	4 mi	
TSS	40	
ENDURANCE RUN - 4 MILES		

THURSDAY

PLANNED METRICS		
DURATION	00:35:00	**WU**: Perform 5 mins of dynamic warm up: 1. Leg swings - 10–20 per leg 2. Marches - 10–15 per leg 3. Leg side swings - 10–20 per leg
DISTANCE	Various	
TSS	30	Build WU pace from ACTIVE RECOVERY (Power Z1, HR Z1, Pace Z1, RPE 1) to ENDURANCE (Power Z2, HR Z2, Pace Z2, RPE 2–3) for 10 min. Then perform 4 × 10s strides. **MS**: Start at mid-ENDURANCE (Pace Z2, HR Z2, Power Z2, RPE 2–3) and hold through entire set. Perform 10 × 90 sec at 3% with 1–2 min at 0% between.
HILLS, HILLS, HILLS!!!!!		**CD**: Jog for 10 min at ACTIVE RECOVERY (Pace Z1, HR Z1, Power Z1, RPE 1–2)

FRIDAY

PLANNED METRICS		
DURATION		Actively focus on recovery today: 1) avoid unneccessary physical exertion, 2) watch nutrition closely (healthy carbs, lean protein, and good fats), 3) stretch, and 4) drink when thirsty. Other common recovery aids include massage, napping, elevating legs, floating in water, and listening to music.
DISTANCE		
TSS		
DAY OFF		

SATURDAY

PLANNED METRICS		
DURATION	00:45:00	**WU**: Perform 5 mins of dynamic warm up: 1. Leg swings - 10–20 per leg 2. Marches - 10–15 per leg 3. Leg side swings - 10–20 per leg
DISTANCE	Various	
TSS	45	Build WU pace from ACTIVE RECOVERY (Power Z1, HR Z1, Pace Z1, RPE 1) to ENDURANCE (Power Z2, HR Z2, Pace Z2, RPE 2–3) for 10 min. Then perform 4 × 10s strides. ------- **MS**: 1. 5 min @ upper ENDURANCE (Pace Z2, HR Z2, Power Z2, RPE 2–3) 2. 5 min @ low TEMPO (Pace Z3, HR Z3, Power Z3, RPE 3–4) 3. 5 min at upper TEMPO (Pace Z3, HR Z3, Power Z3, RPE 3–4) min @ 7:35–7:40 min/mi 4. 5 min @ THRESHOLD (Pace Z4, HR Z4, Power Z4, RPE 5–6) --------
TEMPO RAMP RUN 1 × 45		**CD**: 10 minutes at ACTIVE RECOVERY (Pace Z1, HR Z1, Power Z1, RPE 1–2)

SUNDAY

PLANNED METRICS		
DURATION	01:12:00	WU: Perform 5 mins of dynamic warm up: 1. Leg swings - 10–20 per leg 2. Marches - 10–15 per leg 3. Leg side swings - 10–20 per leg
DISTANCE	8 mi	Build WU pace from ACTIVE RECOVERY (Power Z1, HR Z1, Pace Z1, RPE 1) to ENDURANCE (Power Z2, HR Z2, Pace Z2, RPE 2–3) for 10 min. Then perform 4 × 10s strides.
TSS	70	**MS**: Run 5 mi at your Low ENDURANCE (Power Z2, HR Z2, Pace Z2, RPE 2–3) pace.
5 MILE LSD ENDURANCE RUN		**CD**: Jog 10 min

WEEK #5

Training Focus: Week 5

MONDAY

PLANNED METRICS		
DURATION		Actively focus on recovery today: 1) avoid unneccessary physical exertion, 2) watch nutrition closely (healthy carbs, lean protein, and good fats), 3) stretch, and 4) drink when thirsty. Other common recovery aids include massage, napping, elevating legs, floating in water, and listening to music.
DISTANCE		
TSS		
DAY OFF		

TUESDAY

PLANNED METRICS		
DURATION	00:40:00	**WU**: Perform 5 mins of dynamic warm up: 1. Leg swings - 10–20 per leg 2. Marches - 10–15 per leg 3. Leg side swings - 10–20 per leg
DISTANCE	4 mi	Build WU pace from ACTIVE RECOVERY (Power Z1, HR Z1, Pace Z1, RPE 1) to ENDURANCE (Power Z2, HR Z2, Pace Z2, RPE 2–3) for 10 min. Then perform 4 × 10s strides.
TSS	40	**MS**: Run 4 mi at ENDURANCE (Pace Z2, Power Z2, HR Z2, RPE 2–3).
ENDURANCE RUN - 4 MILES		**CD**: Walk for 10 min to bring HR down to 100 BPM.

WEDNESDAY

PLANNED METRICS		
DURATION	01:05:00	**WU**: Perform 5 mins of dynamic warm up: 1. Leg swings - 10–20 per leg 2. Marches - 10–15 per leg 3. Leg side swings - 10–20 per leg
DISTANCE	Varous	Build WU pace from ACTIVE RECOVERY (Power Z1, HR Z1, Pace Z1, RPE 1) to ENDURANCE (Power Z2, HR Z2, Pace Z2, RPE 2–3) for 10 min. Then perform 4 × 10s strides.
TSS	60	**MS**: Tempo run: 40' at TEMPO (Power Z3, HR Z3, Pace Z3, RPE 3–4).
40 MIN LOW TEMPO RUN		**CD**: Jog for 10 min ACTIVE RECOVERY (Power Z1, HR Z1, Pace Z1, RPE 1)

THURSDAY

PLANNED METRICS		
DURATION	00:40:00	**WU**: Perform 5 mins of dynamic warm up: 1. Leg swings - 10–20 per leg 2. Marches - 10–15 per leg 3. Leg side swings - 10–20 per leg
DISTANCE	4 mi	Build WU pace from ACTIVE RECOVERY (Power Z1, HR Z1, Pace Z1, RPE 1) to ENDURANCE (Power Z2, HR Z2, Pace Z2, RPE 2–3) for 10 min. Then perform 4 × 10s strides.
TSS	40	**MS**: Run 4 mi at ENDURANCE (Pace Z2, Power Z2, HR Z2, RPE 2–3).
ENDURANCE RUN - 4 MILES		**CD**: Walk for 10 min to bring HR down to 100 BPM.

FRIDAY

PLANNED METRICS		
DURATION		Actively focus on recovery today: 1) avoid unneccessary physical exertion, 2) watch nutrition closely (healthy carbs, lean protein, and good fats), 3) stretch, and 4) drink when thirsty. Other common recovery aids include massage, napping, elevating legs, floating in water, and listening to music.
DISTANCE		
TSS		
DAY OFF		

SATURDAY

PLANNED METRICS		
DURATION	01:05:00	**WU**: Perform 5 mins of dynamic warm up: 1. Leg swings - 10–20 per leg 2. Marches - 10–15 per leg 3. Leg side swings - 10–20 per leg
DISTANCE	5 mi	Build WU pace from ACTIVE RECOVERY (Power Z1, HR Z1, Pace Z1, RPE 1) to ENDURANCE (Power Z2, HR Z2, Pace Z2, RPE 2–3) for 10 min. Then perform 4 × 10s strides.
TSS	70	**MS**: 1 mile at low Endurance (Power Z2, HR Z2, Pace Z2, RPE 2–3). Then crank it to Tempo (Power Z3, HR Z3, Pace Z3, RPE 3–4) for 3 mi. Then back down to Endurance (Power Z2, HR Z2, Pace Z2, RPE 2–3) for 1 mi
ENDURANCE-TEMPO SANDWICH		**CD**: Jog for 10 min at Active Recovery (Power Z1, HR Z1, Pace Z1, RPE 1).

SUNDAY

PLANNED METRICS		
DURATION	00:55:00	**WU**: Perform 5 mins of dynamic warm up: 1. Leg swings - 10–20 per leg 2. Marches - 10–15 per leg 3. Leg side swings - 10–20 per leg
DISTANCE	5 mi	Build WU pace from ACTIVE RECOVERY (Power Z1, HR Z1, Pace Z1, RPE 1) to ENDURANCE (Power Z2, HR Z2, Pace Z2, RPE 2–3) for 10 min. Then perform 4 × 10s strides.
TSS	55	**MS**: Run 5 mi at your Low ENDURANCE (Power Z2, HR Z2, Pace Z2, RPE 2–3) pace.
5 MILE LSD ENDURANCE RUN		**CD**: Jog 10 min

WEEK #6

Training Focus: Week 6

MONDAY

PLANNED METRICS		
DURATION		Actively focus on recovery today: 1) avoid unneccessary physical exertion, 2) watch nutrition closely (healthy carbs, lean protein, and good fats), 3) stretch, and 4) drink when thirsty. Other common recovery aids include massage, napping, elevating legs, floating in water, and listening to music.
DISTANCE		
TSS		
DAY OFF		

TUESDAY

PLANNED METRICS		
DURATION	00:40:00	**WU**: Perform 5 mins of dynamic warm up: 1. Leg swings - 10–20 per leg 2. Marches - 10–15 per leg 3. Leg side swings - 10–20 per leg
DISTANCE	4 mi	
TSS	40	Build WU pace from ACTIVE RECOVERY (Power Z1, HR Z1, Pace Z1, RPE 1) to ENDURANCE (Power Z2, HR Z2, Pace Z2, RPE 2–3) for 10 min. Then perform 4x10s strides. **MS**: Run 4 mi at ENDURANCE (Pace Z2, Power Z2, HR Z2, RPE 2–3). **CD**: Walk for 10 min to bring HR down to 100 BPM.
ENDURANCE RUN - 4 MILES		

WEDNESDAY

PLANNED METRICS		
DURATION	00:35:00	**WU**: Perform 5 mins of dynamic warm up: 1. Leg swings - 10–20 per leg 2. Marches - 10–15 per leg 3. Leg side swings - 10–20 per leg
DISTANCE	Various	
TSS	10	Build WU pace from ACTIVE RECOVERY for 10 min. Then perform 4x10s strides. **MS**: Jog a ACTIVE RECOVERY (Pace Z1, HR Z1, Power Z1, RPE 1–2) pace for 15–20 min. Enjoy yourself. **CD**: Walk home.
RECOVERY - JOG		

THURSDAY

PLANNED METRICS		
DURATION		Actively focus on recovery today: 1) avoid unneccessary physical exertion, 2) watch nutrition closely (healthy carbs, lean protein, and good fats), 3) stretch, and 4) drink when thirsty. Other common recovery aids include massage, napping, elevating legs, floating in water, and listening to music.
DISTANCE		
TSS		
DAY OFF		

FRIDAY

PLANNED METRICS		
DURATION	00:35:00	
DISTANCE	Various	
TSS	10	
RECOVERY - JOG		**WU**: Perform 5 mins of dynamic warm up: 1. Leg swings - 10–20 per leg 2. Marches - 10–15 per leg 3. Leg side swings - 10–20 per leg Build WU pace from ACTIVE RECOVERY for 10 min. Then perform 4x10s strides. **MS**: Jog a ACTIVE RECOVERY (Pace Z1, HR Z1, Power Z1, RPE 1–2) pace for 15–20 min. Enjoy yourself. **CD**: Walk home.

SATURDAY

PLANNED METRICS		
DURATION	00:30:00	
DISTANCE	Various	
TSS	25	
PRE-RACE PRIMER - 20 MINUTE RUN WITH 4 × 10S PICKUPS		**WU**: Perform 5 mins of dynamic warm up: 1. Leg swings - 10–20 per leg 2. Marches - 10–15 per leg 3. Leg side swings - 10–20 per leg Build WU pace from ACTIVE RECOVERY (Power Z1, HR Z1, Pace Z1, RPE 1–2) to ENDURANCE (Power Z2, HR Z2, Pace Z2, RPE 2–3) for 10 min. **MS**: Complete this 20 minute run. Build into the run VERY easy. Walk for the first 5 minutes, start a steady, Low ENDURANCE Z2 (Power Z2, HR Z2, Pace Z2, RPE 2–3) jog and at the 10 minute mark, complete 4x10 second "pick ups" gradually building into your 10k/THRESHOLD (Power Z4, HR Z4, Pace Z4, RPE 5–6). by the end of the 20s. 40s EASY Low ENDURANCE Z2 (Power Z2, HR Z2, Pace Z2, RPE 2–3) jog between. Run the final 6 minutes at low ENDURANCE Z2 (Power Z2, HR Z2, Pace Z2, RPE 2–3) jog. **CD**: Walk for 5–10 min. Perform static stretching as necessary.

SUNDAY

PLANNED METRICS		
DURATION	Various	
DISTANCE	10 km	
TSS	75	
RACE DAY!!!		You are ready to set your new PR. Remember your pacing and nutrition.

Plan 8

Power Based Marathon Based and Build Training Plan

For this plan, please reference the following Test Interpretation Notes on p. 493 of this book:

- CSS Interpretation Notes (p. 493)
- Critical Run Speed/rFTP Test Interpretation and Zone/Pacing Calculation #2 (p. 495)

WEEK #1

Training Focus: Test Week - The focus of this week is to set your personalized power and pace zones.

MONDAY

PLANNED METRICS		
DURATION	01:01:00	**WU**: Jog for 15 min progressing from ACTIVE RECOVERY (Pace Z1, HR Z1, Power Z1, RPE 1–2) to ENDURANCE (Pace Z2, HR Z2, Power Z2, PRE 2–3). Towards the end of the WU, perform 4 × 60s of strides to fully open up your muscles.
DISTANCE	Various	
TSS	40	
PRIMER (PRE-TEST)		**MS**: 1. 3 × 3 minutes @ 90% of your Threshold pace (Pace Z3, HR Z3, Power Z3, RPE 4–5) with 6 minutes of recovery at ENDURANCE Pace (Pace Z2, HR Z2, Power Z2, PRE 2–3). 2. 3 × 10s pick-ups with 3 min recovery at ENDURANCE Pace (Pace Z2, HR Z2, Power Z2, PRE 2–3) in between **CD**: 10 min at ACTIVE RECOVERY (Pace Z1, HR Z1, Power Z1, RPE 1–2

TUESDAY

PLANNED METRICS		WU: Perform 5 mins of dynamic warm up: 1. Leg swings - 10–20 per leg 2. Marches - 10–15 per leg 3. Leg side swings - 10–20 per leg Build WU pace from Z1 to Z2 for 20 min. Then perform 4 × 10s strides. ------- **MS**: Run 5 km (3.1) as fast as you can. You can do this on a bike trail, track, or sidewalk. Try to find the most flat surface (no hills) as possible. However, do not do the test on a treadmill. Track you HR. The four metrics you are concerned with tracking is your running power, pace, and HR, and the time it took you to complete the 5 km. ------- **CD**: Jog in for 10 min until your HR comes down to about 100 BPM.
DURATION	00:45:00	
DISTANCE	5 km	
TSS	35	
CRITICAL RUN SPEED/RFTP TEST - 5 KM		

WEDNESDAY

PLANNED METRICS		DAY OFF
DURATION		
DISTANCE		
TSS		

THURSDAY

PLANNED METRICS		
DURATION	00:30:00	**WU**: Perform 5 mins of dynamic warm up: 1. Leg swings - 10–20 per leg 2. Marches - 10–15 per leg 3. Leg side swings - 10–20 per leg
DISTANCE	Various	
TSS	25	Build WU pace from ACTIVE RECOVERY (Power Z1, HR Z1, Pace Z1, RPE 1–2) to ENDURANCE (Power Z2, HR Z2, Pace Z2, RPE 2–3) for 10 min. **MS**: Complete this 20 minute run. Build into the run VERY easy. Walk for the first 5 minutes, start a steady, Low ENDURANCE Z2 (Power Z2, HR Z2, Pace Z2, RPE 2–3) jog and at the 10 minute mark, complete 4 × 10 second "pick ups" gradually building into your 10k/THRESHOLD (Power Z4, HR Z4, Pace Z4, RPE 5–6). by the end of the 20s. 40s EASY Low ENDURANCE Z2 (Power Z2, HR Z2, Pace Z2, RPE 2–3) jog between. Run the final 6 minutes at low ENDURANCE Z2 (Power Z2, HR Z2, Pace Z2, RPE 2–3) jog.
20 MINUTE RUN WITH 4 × 10S PICKUPS		**CD**: Walk for 5–10 min. Perform static stretching as necessary.

FRIDAY

PLANNED METRICS		
DURATION	01:00:00	**WU**: Perform 5 mins of dynamic warm up: 1. Leg swings - 10–20 per leg 2. Marches - 10–15 per leg 3. Leg side swings - 10–20 per leg
DISTANCE	10 K	
TSS	70	Build WU pace from ACTIVE RECOVERY (Power Z1, HR Z1, RPE 1) to ENDURANCE (Power Z2, HR Z2, RPE 2–3) for 10 min. Then perform 4 × 10s strides. **MS**: Run 10 km at a maximal pace. Do not go out too fast as to slow down over the course of the interval. Try to find the most flat surface (no hills) as possible. However, do not do the test on a treadmill. Track you HR. The four metrics you are concerned with tracking is your running power, pace, and HR, and the time it took you to complete the 5 km.
CRITICAL RUN SPEED TEST #2–10 KM		**CD**: Jog for 10 at ACTIVE RECOVERY (Power Z1, HR Z1, RPE 1)

SATURDAY

PLANNED METRICS		
DURATION	00:40:00	**WU**: Jog for 15 min at ACTIVE RECOVERY (Power Z1, HR Z1, Pace Z1, RPE 1), then Perform the following dynamic stretches: 1. Toe Touches - 2 × 15 per leg 2. Leg Tucks - 2 × 15 per leg
DISTANCE	Various	
TSS	15	
RECOVERY - JOG 40 MIN		**MS**: Jog at ACTIVE RECOVERY (Power Z1, HR Z1, Pace Z1, RPE 1) **CD**: Walk for 10 min or until your HR drops below 100 BPM.

SUNDAY

PLANNED METRICS		
DURATION	01:30:00	**WU**: Perform 5 mins of dynamic warm up: 1. Leg swings - 10–20 per leg 2. Marches - 10–15 per leg 3. Leg side swings - 10–20 per leg
DISTANCE	10 mi	
TSS	90	
10 MILE LSD ENDURANCE RUN		Build WU pace from ACTIVE RECOVERY (Power Z1, HR Z1, Pace Z1, RPE 1) to ENDURANCE (Power Z2, HR Z2, Pace Z2, RPE 2–3) for 10 min. Then perform 4 × 10s strides. **MS**: Run 10 mi at your Low ENDURANCE (Power Z2, HR Z2, Pace Z2, RPE 2–3) pace. **CD**: Jog 10 min

WEEK #2

Training Focus: Base 1 - Week 2

MONDAY (AM)

PLANNED METRICS		
DURATION		Actively focus on recovery today: 1) avoid unneccessary physical exertion, 2) watch nutrition closely (healthy carbs, lean protein, and good fats), 3) stretch, and 4) drink when thirsty. Other common recovery aids include massage, napping, elevating legs, floating in water, and listening to music.
DISTANCE		
TSS		
DAY OFF		

TUESDAY (AM)

PLANNED METRICS		
DURATION	00:35:00	**WU**: Perform 5 mins of dynamic warm up: 1. Leg swings - 10–20 per leg 2. Marches - 10–15 per leg 3. Leg side swings - 10–20 per leg
DISTANCE	3.5 mi	Build WU pace from ACTIVE RECOVERY (Power Z1, HR Z1, Pace Z1, RPE 1) to ENDURANCE (Power Z2, HR Z2, Pace Z2, RPE 2–3) for 10 min. Then perform 4 × 10s strides.
TSS	35	**MS**: Run 3 mi at your Low ENDURANCE (Power Z2, HR Z2, Pace Z2, RPE 2–3) pace.
3 MILE LSD ENDURANCE RUN		**CD**: Jog 10 min

TUESDAY (PM)

PLANNED METRICS		
DURATION	00:25:00	**WU**: 1. Jog for 10 min building from Active Recovery (Power Z1, HR Z1, Pace Z1, RPE 1) building to Endurance (Power Z2, HR Z2, Pace Z2, RPE 2–3).
DISTANCE	N/A	2. Perform 15 reps per leg: a. knee hugs b. straight leg military march c. walking pigeon
TSS	8	**MS**: Lower Body & Core Strength: 12–15 reps of each 1. stability ball hamstring pull ins 2. ball transfer from hands to feet 3. top of the ball foot march 4. reverse crunch 5. low back/ glute & ham raise 6. single leg dead lift moderate weight dumb bell 7. side step up to box w/ moderate wt dumb bell pilates hip series 10 each without resting leg to floor until completion: 8. front circles with tow pointed quad firm 9. back circles with tow pointed quad firm 10. leg raise (controlled and slow) hold at the top after 10 for 10 sec then 10 fast pulses
LOWER BODY STRENGTH + HIP ROUTINE #1		**CD**: Static stretch for 10 min.

WEDNESDAY

PLANNED METRICS		
DURATION	00:56:00	**WU**: Perform 5 mins of dynamic warm up: 1. Leg swings - 10–20 per leg 2. Marches - 10–15 per leg 3. Leg side swings - 10–20 per leg Build WU pace from ACTIVE RECOVERY (Power Z1, HR Z1, Pace Z1, RPE 1) to ENDURANCE (Power Z2, HR Z2, Pace Z2, RPE 2–3) for 10 min. Then perform 4 × 10s strides. **MS**: Start main set run at mid ENDURANCE (Power Z2, HR Z2, Pace Z2, RPE 2–3). Once comfortable, complete 3 × 7 min intervals at upper TEMPO (Power Z3, HR Z3, Pace Z3, RPE 3–4). Recover for 5 min ENDURANCE (Power Z2, HR Z2, Pace Z2, RPE 2–3) in between each interval. **CD**: Jog at ACTIVE RECOVERY (Power Z1, HR Z1, Pace Z1, RPE 1) for 10 min or until HR comes below 100 BPM.
DISTANCE	Various	
TSS	57	
3 × 7 TEMPO PACE INTERVALS		

THURSDAY

PLANNED METRICS		
DURATION	00:45:00	**WU**: Perform 5 mins of dynamic warm up: 1. Leg swings - 10–20 per leg 2. Marches - 10–15 per leg 3. Leg side swings - 10–20 per leg Build WU pace from ACTIVE RECOVERY (Power Z1, HR Z1, Pace Z1, RPE 1) to ENDURANCE (Power Z2, HR Z2, Pace Z2, RPE 2–3) for 10 min. Then perform 4 × 10s strides. **MS**: Run 3 mi at your Low ENDURANCE (Power Z2, HR Z2, Pace Z2, RPE 2–3) pace. **CD**: Jog 10 min
DISTANCE	3.5	
TSS	35	
3 MILE LSD ENDURANCE RUN		

FRIDAY

PLANNED METRICS		
DURATION	00:20:00	
DISTANCE	N/A	
TSS	10	

HIP GIRDLE LOOP BAND WO#1

Equipment: 1 Loop resistance band.

WU: 1. Jog for 10 min building from Active Recovery (Power Z1, HR Z1, Pace Z1, RPE 1) building to Endurance (Power Z2, HR Z2, Pace Z2, RPE 2–3).

2. Perform 15 reps per leg:
   a. knee hugs
   b. straight leg military march
   c. walking pigeon

MS: Perform 3 rounds with 20s RI:
1. Abductor extensions (20–25/leg)
2. Adductor (20–25/leg)
3. Lateral Monster Walks (20 steps in each direction)
4. Good Mornings (20 per leg)
5. Hip Flexion (20 per leg)

CD: 5 min of static stretching focusing on flexibility.

SATURDAY

PLANNED METRICS		
DURATION	00:52:00	
DISTANCE	4.5	
TSS	42	

4 MILE LSD ENDURANCE RUN

WU: Perform 5 mins of dynamic warm up:
1. Leg swings - 10–20 per leg
2. Marches - 10–15 per leg
3. Leg side swings - 10–20 per leg

Build WU pace from ACTIVE RECOVERY (Power Z1, HR Z1, Pace Z1, RPE 1) to ENDURANCE (Power Z2, HR Z2, Pace Z2, RPE 2–3) for 10 min. Then perform 4 × 10s strides.

MS: Run 4 mi at your Low ENDURANCE (Power Z2, HR Z2, Pace Z2, RPE 2–3) pace.

CD: Jog 10 min

SUNDAY

PLANNED METRICS		
DURATION	02:00:00	
DISTANCE	12.5 mi	
TSS	88	

12 MILE LSD ENDURANCE RUN

WU: Perform 5 mins of dynamic warm up:
1. Leg swings - 10–20 per leg
2. Marches - 10–15 per leg
3. Leg side swings - 10–20 per leg

Build WU pace from ACTIVE RECOVERY (Power Z1, HR Z1, Pace Z1, RPE 1) to ENDURANCE (Power Z2, HR Z2, Pace Z2, RPE 2–3) for 10 min. Then perform 4 × 10s strides.

MS: Run 12 mi at your Low ENDURANCE (Power Z2, HR Z2, Pace Z2, RPE 2–3) pace.

CD: Jog 10 min

WEEK #3

Training Focus: Base 1 - Week 3

MONDAY (AM)

PLANNED METRICS		Actively focus on recovery today: 1) avoid unneccessary physical exertion, 2) watch nutrition closely (healthy carbs, lean protein, and good fats), 3) stretch, and 4) drink when thirsty. Other common recovery aids include massage, napping, elevating legs, floating in water, and listening to music.
DURATION		
DISTANCE		
TSS		
DAY OFF		

TUESDAY (AM)

PLANNED METRICS		**WU**: Perform 5 mins of dynamic warm up: 1. Leg swings - 10–20 per leg 2. Marches - 10–15 per leg 3. Leg side swings - 10–20 per leg
DURATION	00:35:00	
DISTANCE	3.5 mi	
TSS	35	Build WU pace from ACTIVE RECOVERY (Power Z1, HR Z1, Pace Z1, RPE 1) to ENDURANCE (Power Z2, HR Z2, Pace Z2, RPE 2–3) for 10 min. Then perform 4 × 10s strides. **MS**: Run 3 mi at your Low ENDURANCE (Power Z2, HR Z2, Pace Z2, RPE 2–3) pace. **CD**: Jog 10 min
3 MILE LSD ENDURANCE RUN		

TUESDAY (PM)

PLANNED METRICS	
DURATION	00:25:00
DISTANCE	N/A
TSS	8

LOWER BODY STRENGTH + HIP ROUTINE #2

WU: 1. Jog for 10 min building from Active Recovery (Power Z1, HR Z1, Pace Z1, RPE 1) building to Endurance (Power Z2, HR Z2, Pace Z2, RPE 2–3).

2. Perform 15 reps per leg:
   a. knee hugs
   b. straight leg military march
   c. walking pigeon

MS: Lower Body & Core Strength:
12–15 reps of each
1. stability ball hamstring pull ins
2. ball transfer from hands to feet
3. top of the ball foot march
4. reverse crunch
5. low back/ glute & ham raise
6. single leg dead lift moderate weight dumb bell
7. single leg wall squat.
8. 1 legged bosu ball balance - 15–20s / leg
9. 1 legged bosu ball squats

CD: Static stretch for 10 min.

WEDNESDAY

PLANNED METRICS	
DURATION	01:00:00
DISTANCE	Various
TSS	55

4 × 1 MILE AT NEGATIVE SPLIT TEMPO RUN

WU: Perform 5 mins of dynamic warm up:
1. Leg swings - 10–20 per leg
2. Marches - 10–15 per leg
3. Leg side swings - 10–20 per leg

Build WU pace from ACTIVE RECOVERY (Power Z1, HR Z1, Pace Z1, RPE 1) to ENDURANCE (Power Z2, HR Z2, Pace Z2, RPE 2–3) for 10 min. Then perform 4 × 10s strides.

MS: 4 × 1 mile at Tempo (Power Z3, HR Z3, Pace Z3, RPE 3–4) with 0.5 mi low ENDURANCE (Power Z2, HR Z2, Pace Z2, RPE 2–3) between each interval. With the first interval, start in low Z3. From there, make each interval consecutively faster.

CD: Jog for 10 min at ACTIVE RECOVERY (Power Z1, HR Z1, Pace Z1, RPE 1)

THURSDAY

PLANNED METRICS		
DURATION	00:35:00	**WU**: Perform 5 mins of dynamic warm up: 1. Leg swings - 10–20 per leg 2. Marches - 10–15 per leg 3. Leg side swings - 10–20 per leg
DISTANCE	3.5 mi	
TSS	35	Build WU pace from ACTIVE RECOVERY (Power Z1, HR Z1, Pace Z1, RPE 1) to ENDURANCE (Power Z2, HR Z2, Pace Z2, RPE 2–3) for 10 min. Then perform 4 × 10s strides. **MS**: Run 3 mi at your Low ENDURANCE (Power Z2, HR Z2, Pace Z2, RPE 2–3) pace.
3 MILE LSD ENDURANCE RUN		**CD**: Jog 10 min

FRIDAY

PLANNED METRICS		
DURATION	00:25:00	**WU**: Jog for 10 min building from Active Recovery (Power Z1, HR Z1, Pace Z1, RPE 1) building to Endurance (Power Z2, HR Z2, Pace Z2, RPE 2–3).
DISTANCE	N/A	
TSS	10	**MS1**: Perform 2 sets of the following with 1–2 min rest between each set: 1. Front plank x 1 min. During this one minute, perform 30 reps of isometric squeezes of all core muscles. Immediately after … 2. Press into a child's pose for 30 seconds. Then.. 3. Perform 15 reps of the bird dog on each side from all fours. Then … 4. Perform 30 reps of pilates roll ups from flat back **MS2**: Perform 2 sets x 10 reps on each side of the following Pilates hip routine with 1–2 min rest between each set: 1. Point your toes & kick powerfully up & flex to slow down pulse with shorter ROM as above 2. Circle clockwise stopping at 12 o'clock circle counter clockwise stopping at 12 o'clock 3. Kick pointed toe forward & flex slow kick back to the start position 4. Kick forward flexed & slow point toe back to the start position
CORE AND HIP ROUTINE - PILATES STYLE		**CD**: Perform 5–10 min of static stretching

SATURDAY

PLANNED METRICS		
DURATION	00:52:00	**WU**: Perform 5 mins of dynamic warm up: 1. Leg swings - 10–20 per leg 2. Marches - 10–15 per leg 3. Leg side swings - 10–20 per leg
DISTANCE	4.5	
TSS	42	Build WU pace from ACTIVE RECOVERY (Power Z1, HR Z1, Pace Z1, RPE 1) to ENDURANCE (Power Z2, HR Z2, Pace Z2, RPE 2–3) for 10 min. Then perform 4 × 10s strides.
4 MILE LSD ENDURANCE RUN		**MS**: Run 4 mi at your Low ENDURANCE (Power Z2, HR Z2, Pace Z2, RPE 2–3) pace. **CD**: Jog 10 min

SUNDAY

PLANNED METRICS		
DURATION	02:00:00	**WU**: Perform 5 mins of dynamic warm up: 1. Leg swings - 10–20 per leg 2. Marches - 10–15 per leg 3. Leg side swings - 10–20 per leg
DISTANCE	12.5 mi	
TSS	88	Build WU pace from ACTIVE RECOVERY (Power Z1, HR Z1, Pace Z1, RPE 1) to ENDURANCE (Power Z2, HR Z2, Pace Z2, RPE 2–3) for 10 min. Then perform 4 × 10s strides.
12 MILE LSD ENDURANCE RUN		**MS**: Run 12 mi at your Low ENDURANCE (Power Z2, HR Z2, Pace Z2, RPE 2–3) pace. **CD**: Jog 10 min

WEEK #4

Training Focus: Recovery Week

MONDAY (AM)

PLANNED METRICS		
DURATION		Actively focus on recovery today: 1) avoid unneccessary physical exertion, 2) watch nutrition closely (healthy carbs, lean protein, and good fats), 3) stretch, and 4) drink when thirsty. Other common recovery aids include massage, napping, elevating legs, floating in water, and listening to music.
DISTANCE		
TSS		
DAY OFF		

TUESDAY (AM)

PLANNED METRICS		
DURATION	00:45:00	**WU**: Jog for 15 min at ACTIVE RECOVERY (Power Z1, HR Z1, Pace Z1, RPE 1), then Perform the following dynamic stretches: 1. Toe Touches - 2 × 15 per leg 2. Leg Tucks - 2 × 15 per leg
DISTANCE	Various	
TSS	19	
RECOVERY - JOG 40 MIN		**MS**: Jog at ACTIVE RECOVERY (Power Z1, HR Z1, Pace Z1, RPE 1) **CD**: Walk for 10 min or until your HR drops below 100 BPM.

WEDNESDAY

PLANNED METRICS		
DURATION	00:52:00	**WU**: Perform 5 mins of dynamic warm up: 1. Leg swings - 10–20 per leg 2. Marches - 10–15 per leg 3. Leg side swings - 10–20 per leg
DISTANCE	4.5	
TSS	42	Build WU pace from ACTIVE RECOVERY (Power Z1, HR Z1, Pace Z1, RPE 1) to ENDURANCE (Power Z2, HR Z2, Pace Z2, RPE 2–3) for 10 min. Then perform 4 × 10s strides.
4 MILE LSD ENDURANCE RUN		**MS**: Run 4 mi at your Low ENDURANCE (Power Z2, HR Z2, Pace Z2, RPE 2–3) pace. **CD**: Jog 10 min

THURSDAY

PLANNED METRICS		
DURATION	00:30:00	**WU**: Perform 5 mins of dynamic warm up: 1. Leg swings - 10–20 per leg 2. Marches - 10–15 per leg 3. Leg side swings - 10–20 per leg
DISTANCE	Various	
TSS	25	Build WU pace from ACTIVE RECOVERY (Power Z1, HR Z1, Pace Z1, RPE 1–2) to ENDURANCE (Power Z2, HR Z2, Pace Z2, RPE 2–3) for 10 min.
		MS: Complete this 20 minute run. Build into the run VERY easy. Walk for the first 5 minutes, start a steady, Low ENDURANCE Z2 (Power Z2, HR Z2, Pace Z2, RPE 2–3) jog and at the 10 minute mark, complete 4 × 10 second "pick ups" gradually building into your 10k/THRESHOLD (Power Z4, HR Z4, Pace Z4, RPE 5–6). by the end of the 20s. 40s EASY Low ENDURANCE Z2 (Power Z2, HR Z2, Pace Z2, RPE 2–3) jog between. Run the final 6 minutes at low ENDURANCE Z2 (Power Z2, HR Z2, Pace Z2, RPE 2–3) jog.
20 MINUTE RUN WITH 4 × 10S PICKUPS		**CD**: Walk for 5–10 min. Perform static stretching as necessary.

FRIDAY

PLANNED METRICS		
DURATION	00:25:00	**WU**: 1. Jog for 10 min building from Active Recovery (Power Z1, HR Z1, Pace Z1, RPE 1) building to Endurance (Power Z2, HR Z2, Pace Z2, RPE 2–3). 2. Perform 15 reps per leg: a. knee hugs b. straight leg military march c. walking pigeon **MS**: Lower Body & Core Strength: 12–15 reps of each 1. stability ball hamstring pull ins 2. ball transfer from hands to feet 3. top of the ball foot march 4. reverse crunch 5. low back/ glute & ham raise 6. single leg dead lift moderate weight dumb bell 7. side step up to box w/ moderate wt dumb bell pilates hip series 10 each without resting leg to floor until completion: 8. leg raise (controlled and slow) hold at the top after 10 for 10 sec then 10 fast pulses 9. kicks - front/ front back long 10. kicks - back/ back/ front long 11. Bench Press - 2 × 15 - 18 repetitions at 65% of your 1 rep max 12. Dumbbell Pullovers - 2 × 15 - 18 repetitions 13. Dumbell Lateral Raises - 2 × 15 - 18 repetitions **CD**: Static stretch for 10 min.
DISTANCE	N/A	
TSS	10	
LOWER BODY STRENGTH + HIP ROUTINE + UPPER BODY #3		

SATURDAY

PLANNED METRICS		
DURATION	00:50:00	**WU**: Perform 5 mins of dynamic warm up: 1. Leg swings - 10–20 per leg 2. Marches - 10–15 per leg 3. Leg side swings - 10–20 per leg
DISTANCE	4.5	
TSS	50	Build WU pace from ACTIVE RECOVERY (Power Z1, HR Z1, Pace Z1, RPE 1) to ENDURANCE (Power Z2, HR Z2, Pace Z2, RPE 2–3) for 10 min. Then perform 4 × 10s strides.
4 MILE ENDURANCE RUN		**MS**: Run 4 mi at your ENDURANCE (Power Z2, HR Z2, Pace Z2, RPE 2–3) pace. **CD**: Jog 10 min

SUNDAY

PLANNED METRICS		
DURATION	01:25:00	**WU**: Perform 5 mins of dynamic warm up: 1. Leg swings - 10–20 per leg 2. Marches - 10–15 per leg 3. Leg side swings - 10–20 per leg
DISTANCE	10.5	
TSS	60	Build WU pace from ACTIVE RECOVERY (Power Z1, HR Z1, Pace Z1, RPE 1) to ENDURANCE (Power Z2, HR Z2, Pace Z2, RPE 2–3) for 10 min. Then perform 4 × 10s strides.
10 MILE LSD ENDURANCE RUN		**MS**: Run 10 mi at your Low ENDURANCE (Power Z2, HR Z2, Pace Z2, RPE 2–3) pace. **CD**: Jog 10 min

WEEK #5

Training Focus: Base 2 - Week 1

MONDAY (AM)

PLANNED METRICS		
DURATION		Actively focus on recovery today: 1) avoid unneccessary physical exertion, 2) watch nutrition closely (healthy carbs, lean protein, and good fats), 3) stretch, and 4) drink when thirsty. Other common recovery aids include massage, napping, elevating legs, floating in water, and listening to music.
DISTANCE		
TSS		
DAY OFF		

TUESDAY (AM)

PLANNED METRICS		
DURATION	00:52:00	**WU**: Perform 5 mins of dynamic warm up: 1. Leg swings - 10–20 per leg 2. Marches - 10–15 per leg 3. Leg side swings - 10–20 per leg
DISTANCE	4.5	
TSS	42	Build WU pace from ACTIVE RECOVERY (Power Z1, HR Z1, Pace Z1, RPE 1) to ENDURANCE (Power Z2, HR Z2, Pace Z2, RPE 2–3) for 10 min. Then perform 4 × 10s strides.
4 MILE LSD ENDURANCE RUN		**MS**: Run 4 mi at your Low ENDURANCE (Power Z2, HR Z2, Pace Z2, RPE 2–3) pace. **CD**: Jog 10 min

TUESDAY (PM)

PLANNED METRICS		
DURATION	00:25:00	**WU**: Jog for 10 min building from Active Recovery (Power Z1, HR Z1, Pace Z1, RPE 1) building to Endurance (Power Z2, HR Z2, Pace Z2, RPE 2–3).
DISTANCE	N/A	
TSS	8	**MS1**: Perform 2 sets of the following with 1–2 min rest between each set: 1. Front plank x 1 min. During this one minute, perform 30 reps of isometric squeezes of all core muscles. Immediately after … 2. Press into a child's pose for 30 seconds. Then … 3. Perform 15 reps of the bird dog on each side from all fours. Then … 4. Perform 30 reps of pilates roll ups from flat back
CORE AND HIP ROUTINE - PILATES STYLE		**MS2**: Perform 2 sets x 10 reps on each side of the following Pilates hip routine with 1–2 min rest between each set: 1. Point your toes & kick powerfully up & flex to slow down pulse with shorter ROM as above 2. Circle clockwise stopping at 12 o'clock circle counter clockwise stopping at 12 o'clock 3. Kick pointed toe forward & flex slow kick back to the start position 4. Kick forward flexed & slow point toe back to the start position **CD**: Perform 5–10 min of static stretching

WEDNESDAY (AM)

PLANNED METRICS		
DURATION	01:25:00	**WU**: Perform 5 mins of dynamic warm up: 1. Leg swings - 10–20 per leg 2. Marches - 10–15 per leg 3. Leg side swings - 10–20 per leg
DISTANCE	Various	
TSS	78	Build WU pace from ACTIVE RECOVERY (Power Z1, HR Z1, Pace Z1, RPE 1) to ENDURANCE (Power Z2, HR Z2, Pace Z2, RPE 2–3) for 10 min. Then perform 4 × 10s strides.
40 MIN LOW TEMPO RUN AND ENDURANCE		**MS1**: Tempo run: 40' Low TEMPO (Power Z3, HR Z3, Pace Z3, RPE 3–4). **MS2**: Run another 30' at ENDURANCE (Power Z2, HR Z2, Pace Z2, RPE 2–3). **CD**: Jog for 10 min ACTIVE RECOVERY (Power Z1, HR Z1, Pace Z1, RPE 1)

THURSDAY (AM)

PLANNED METRICS		
DURATION	00:35:00	**WU**: Perform 5 mins of dynamic warm up: 1. Leg swings - 10–20 per leg 2. Marches - 10–15 per leg 3. Leg side swings - 10–20 per leg
DISTANCE	3.5 mi	
TSS	35	Build WU pace from ACTIVE RECOVERY (Power Z1, HR Z1, Pace Z1, RPE 1) to ENDURANCE (Power Z2, HR Z2, Pace Z2, RPE 2–3) for 10 min. Then perform 4 × 10s strides.
3 MILE LSD ENDURANCE RUN		**MS**: Run 3 mi at your Low ENDURANCE (Power Z2, HR Z2, Pace Z2, RPE 2–3) pace. **CD**: Jog 10 min

FRIDAY (AM)

PLANNED METRICS		Strength Protocol - Week 1
DURATION	00:45:00	**Goal**: Endurance / Adaptation **Intensity**: 60% of 1 RM
DISTANCE	N/A	**Exercises**:
TSS	25	**Strength**:
STRENGTH WORK - WEEK 1		1. Bench Press (3 × 20) 2. Lateral Pull Down (3 × 20) 3. Seated Row (3 × 20) 4. Tricep Pulldown (3 × 20) 5. Bicep Curl (3 × 20) 6. Leg Press (3 × 30) 7. Leg Extension (3 × 20) 8. Leg Curl (3 × 20) 9. Calf Raises (3 × 20) 10. Back Extension (3 × 20) 11. Ab Curl (3 × 20) 12. Leg Tucked Rotation (3 × 20)

SATURDAY (AM)

PLANNED METRICS		**WU**: Perform 5 mins of dynamic warm up:
DURATION	00:50:00	1. Leg swings - 10–20 per leg 2. Marches - 10–15 per leg
DISTANCE	4.5	3. Leg side swings - 10–20 per leg
TSS	50	Build WU pace from ACTIVE RECOVERY (Power Z1, HR Z1, Pace Z1, RPE 1) to ENDURANCE (Power Z2, HR Z2, Pace Z2, RPE 2–3) for 10 min. Then perform 4 × 10s strides.
4 MILE ENDURANCE RUN		**MS**: Run 4 mi at your ENDURANCE (Power Z2, HR Z2, Pace Z2, RPE 2–3) pace. **CD**: Jog 10 min

SUNDAY (AM)

PLANNED METRICS		
DURATION	02:10:00	**WU**: Perform 5 mins of dynamic warm up: 1. Leg swings - 10–20 per leg 2. Marches - 10–15 per leg 3. Leg side swings - 10–20 per leg
DISTANCE	13.5	
TSS	97	Build WU pace from ACTIVE RECOVERY (Power Z1, HR Z1, Pace Z1, RPE 1) to ENDURANCE (Power Z2, HR Z2, Pace Z2, RPE 2–3) for 10 min. Then perform 4 × 10s strides.
13 MILE LSD ENDURANCE RUN		**MS**: Run 13 mi at your Low ENDURANCE (Power Z2, HR Z2, Pace Z2, RPE 2–3) pace. **CD**: Jog 10 min

WEEK #6

Training Focus: Base 2 - Week 2

MONDAY (AM)

PLANNED METRICS		
DURATION		Actively focus on recovery today: 1) avoid unneccessary physical exertion, 2) watch nutrition closely (healthy carbs, lean protein, and good fats), 3) stretch, and 4) drink when thirsty. Other common recovery aids include massage, napping, elevating legs, floating in water, and listening to music.
DISTANCE		
TSS		
DAY OFF		

TUESDAY (AM)

PLANNED METRICS		
DURATION	00:50:00	**WU**: Perform 5 mins of dynamic warm up: 1. Leg swings - 10–20 per leg 2. Marches - 10–15 per leg 3. Leg side swings - 10–20 per leg
DISTANCE	4.5	
TSS	50	Build WU pace from ACTIVE RECOVERY (Power Z1, HR Z1, Pace Z1, RPE 1) to ENDURANCE (Power Z2, HR Z2, Pace Z2, RPE 2–3) for 10 min. Then perform 4 × 10s strides.
4 MILE ENDURANCE RUN		**MS**: Run 4 mi at your ENDURANCE (Power Z2, HR Z2, Pace Z2, RPE 2–3) pace. **CD**: Jog 10 min

TUESDAY (PM)

PLANNED METRICS	
DURATION	00:25:00
DISTANCE	N/A
TSS	8

LOWER BODY STRENGTH + HIP ROUTINE #1

WU: 1. Jog for 10 min building from Active Recovery (Power Z1, HR Z1, Pace Z1, RPE 1) building to Endurance (Power Z2, HR Z2, Pace Z2, RPE 2–3).

2. Perform 15 reps per leg:
   a. knee hugs
   b. straight leg military march
   c. walking pigeon

MS: Lower Body & Core Strength:
12–15 reps of each
1. stability ball hamstring pull ins
2. ball transfer from hands to feet
3. top of the ball foot march
4. reverse crunch
5. low back/ glute & ham raise
6. single leg dead lift moderate weight dumb bell
7. side step up to box w/ moderate wt dumb bell pilates hip series 10 each without resting leg to floor until completion:
8. front circles with tow pointed quad firm
9. back circles with tow pointed quad firm
10. leg raise (controlled and slow) hold at the top after 10 for 10 sec then 10 fast pulses

CD: Static stretch for 10 min.

WEDNESDAY

PLANNED METRICS	
DURATION	01:00:00
DISTANCE	8.5
TSS	70

8 MI - 1 MI TEMPO INTERVALS

WU: Perform 5 mins of dynamic warm up:
1. Leg swings - 10–20 per leg
2. Marches - 10–15 per leg
3. Leg side swings - 10–20 per leg

Build WU pace from Active Recovery (Power Z1, HR Z1, Pace Z1, RPE 1) to Endurance (Power Z2, HR Z2, Pace Z2, RPE 2–3) for 10 min. Then perform 4 × 10s strides.

MS: For this 8 mi run, perform 4 × 1mi Tempo (Power Z3, HR Z3, Pace Z3, RPE 3–4) efforts with 1 mile "recovery" at Endurance (Power Z2, HR Z2, Pace Z2, RPE 2–3).

If the finish the balance of the run at Endurance (Power Z2, HR Z2, Pace Z2, RPE 2–3).

CD: Jog 10 min at Active Recovery (Power Z1, HR Z1, Pace Z1, RPE 1)

THURSDAY

PLANNED METRICS		
DURATION	00:30:00	**WU**: Perform 5 mins of dynamic warm up: 1. Leg swings - 10–20 per leg 2. Marches - 10–15 per leg 3. Leg side swings - 10–20 per leg
DISTANCE	Various	
TSS	25	Build WU pace from ACTIVE RECOVERY (Power Z1, HR Z1, Pace Z1, RPE 1–2) to ENDURANCE (Power Z2, HR Z2, Pace Z2, RPE 2–3) for 10 min. **MS**: Complete this 20 minute run. Build into the run VERY easy. Walk for the first 5 minutes, start a steady, Low ENDURANCE Z2 (Power Z2, HR Z2, Pace Z2, RPE 2–3) jog and at the 10 minute mark, complete 4 × 10 second "pick ups" gradually building into your 10k/THRESHOLD (Power Z4, HR Z4, Pace Z4, RPE 5–6). by the end of the 20s. 40s EASY Low ENDURANCE Z2 (Power Z2, HR Z2, Pace Z2, RPE 2–3) jog between. Run the final 6 minutes at low ENDURANCE Z2 (Power Z2, HR Z2, Pace Z2, RPE 2–3) jog.
20 MINUTE RUN WITH 4 × 10S PICKUPS		**CD**: Walk for 5–10 min. Perform static stretching as necessary.

FRIDAY

PLANNED METRICS		
DURATION	00:45:00	Strength Protocol - Week 2 **Goal**: Endurance / Adaptation **Intensity**: 60% of 1 RM
DISTANCE	N/A	**Exercises**:
TSS	25	**Strength**: 1. Bench Press (3 × 20) 2. Lateral Pull Down (3 × 20) 3. Seated Row (3 × 20) 4. Tricep Pulldown (3 × 20) 5. Bicep Curl (3 × 20) 6. Leg Press (3 × 30) 7. Leg Extension (3 × 20) 8. Leg Curl (3 × 20) 9. Calf Raises (3 × 20) 10. Back Extension (3 × 20)
STRENGTH WORK - WEEK 2		11. Ab Curl (3 × 20) 12. Leg Tucked Rotation (3 × 20)

SATURDAY

PLANNED METRICS		
DURATION	00:52:00	**WU**: Perform 5 mins of dynamic warm up: 1. Leg swings - 10–20 per leg 2. Marches - 10–15 per leg 3. Leg side swings - 10–20 per leg Build WU pace from ACTIVE RECOVERY (Power Z1, HR Z1, Pace Z1, RPE 1) to ENDURANCE (Power Z2, HR Z2, Pace Z2, RPE 2–3) for 10 min. Then perform 4 × 10s strides. **MS**: Run 4 mi at your Low ENDURANCE (Power Z2, HR Z2, Pace Z2, RPE 2–3) pace. **CD**: Jog 10 min
DISTANCE	4.5	
TSS	42	
4 MILE LSD ENDURANCE RUN		

SUNDAY

PLANNED METRICS		
DURATION	02:10:00	**WU**: Perform 5 mins of dynamic warm up: 1. Leg swings - 10–20 per leg 2. Marches - 10–15 per leg 3. Leg side swings - 10–20 per leg Build WU pace from ACTIVE RECOVERY (Power Z1, HR Z1, Pace Z1, RPE 1) to ENDURANCE (Power Z2, HR Z2, Pace Z2, RPE 2–3) for 10 min. Then perform 4 × 10s strides. **MS**: Run 13 mi at your Low ENDURANCE (Power Z2, HR Z2, Pace Z2, RPE 2–3) pace. **CD**: Jog 10 min
DISTANCE	13.5	
TSS	97	
13 MILE LSD ENDURANCE RUN		

WEEK #7

Training Focus: Base 2 - Week 3

MONDAY (AM)

PLANNED METRICS		
DURATION		Actively focus on recovery today: 1) avoid unneccessary physical exertion, 2) watch nutrition closely (healthy carbs, lean protein, and good fats), 3) stretch, and 4) drink when thirsty. Other common recovery aids include massage, napping, elevating legs, floating in water, and listening to music.
DISTANCE		
TSS		
DAY OFF		

TUESDAY (AM)

PLANNED METRICS		
DURATION	00:45:00	**WU**: Perform 5 mins of dynamic warm up: 1. Leg swings - 10–20 per leg 2. Marches - 10–15 per leg 3. Leg side swings - 10–20 per leg
DISTANCE	5 mi	
TSS	50	Build WU pace from ACTIVE RECOVERY (Power Z1, HR Z1, Pace Z1, RPE 1) to ENDURANCE (Power Z2, HR Z2, Pace Z2, RPE 2–3) for 10 min. Then perform 4 × 10s strides.
4.5 MILE ENDURANCE RUN		**MS**: Run 4.5 mi at your ENDURANCE (Power Z2, HR Z2, Pace Z2, RPE 2–3) pace. **CD**: Jog 10 min

TUESDAY (PM)

PLANNED METRICS		
DURATION	00:25:00	**WU**: 1. Jog for 10 min building from Active Recovery (Power Z1, HR Z1, Pace Z1, RPE 1) building to Endurance (Power Z2, HR Z2, Pace Z2, RPE 2–3).
DISTANCE	N/A	2. Perform 15 reps per leg: a. knee hugs b. straight leg military march c. walking pigeon
TSS	8	
LOWER BODY STRENGTH + HIP ROUTINE #2		**MS**: Lower Body & Core Strength: 12–15 reps of each 1. stability ball hamstring pull ins 2. ball transfer from hands to feet 3. top of the ball foot march 4. reverse crunch 5. low back/ glute & ham raise 6. single leg dead lift moderate weight dumb bell 7. single leg wall squat. 8. 1 legged bosu ball balance - 15–20s / leg 9. 1 legged bosu ball squats **CD**: Static stretch for 10 min.

WEDNESDAY

PLANNED METRICS		
DURATION	00:45:00	**WU**: Perform 5 mins of dynamic warm up: 1. Leg swings - 10–20 per leg 2. Marches - 10–15 per leg 3. Leg side swings - 10–20 per leg
DISTANCE	6.5 mi	
TSS	70	Build WU pace from ACTIVE RECOVERY (Power Z1, HR Z1, Pace Z1, RPE 1) to ENDURANCE (Power Z2, HR Z2, Pace Z2, RPE 2–3) for 10 min. Then perform 4 × 10s strides.
		MS: 1.5 mile at low Endurance (Power Z2, HR Z2, Pace Z2, RPE 2–3). Then crank it to Tempo (Power Z3, HR Z3, Pace Z3, RPE 3–4) for 3 mi. Then back down to Endurance (Power Z2, HR Z2, Pace Z2, RPE 2–3) for 1.5 mi
ENDURANCE-TEMPO SANDWICH		**CD**: Jog for 10 min at Active Recovery (Power Z1, HR Z1, Pace Z1, RPE 1).

THURSDAY

PLANNED METRICS		
DURATION	00:35:00	**WU**: Perform 5 mins of dynamic warm up: 1. Leg swings - 10–20 per leg 2. Marches - 10–15 per leg 3. Leg side swings - 10–20 per leg
DISTANCE	3.5 mi	
TSS	35	Build WU pace from ACTIVE RECOVERY (Power Z1, HR Z1, Pace Z1, RPE 1) to ENDURANCE (Power Z2, HR Z2, Pace Z2, RPE 2–3) for 10 min. Then perform 4 × 10s strides.
		MS: Run 3 mi at your Low ENDURANCE (Power Z2, HR Z2, Pace Z2, RPE 2–3) pace.
3 MILE LSD ENDURANCE RUN		**CD**: Jog 10 min

FRIDAY

PLANNED METRICS		
DURATION	00:45:00	Strength Protocol - Week 3 **Goal**: Hypertrophy **Intensity**: 70% of 1 RM **Note**: 3d set should be performed until exhaustion. **Exercises**: **Strength**: 1. Bench Press (3 × 8–12) 2. Lateral Pull Down (3 × 8–12) 3. Seated Row (3 × 8–12) 4. Tricep Pulldown (3 × 8–12) 5. Bicep Curl (3 × 8–12) 6. Leg Press (3 × 8–12) 7. Leg Extension (3 × 8–12) 8. Leg Curl (3 × 8–12) 9. Calf Raises (3 × 8–12) 10. Back Extension (3 × 8–12) 11. Ab Curl (3 × 8–12) 12. Leg Tucked Rotation (3 × 8–12)
DISTANCE	N/A	
TSS	25	
STRENGTH WORK - WEEK 3		

SATURDAY

PLANNED METRICS		
DURATION	01:00:00	**WU**: Perform 5 mins of dynamic warm up: 1. Leg swings - 10–20 per leg 2. Marches - 10–15 per leg 3. Leg side swings - 10–20 per leg Build WU pace from ACTIVE RECOVERY (Power Z1, HR Z1, Pace Z1, RPE 1) to ENDURANCE (Power Z2, HR Z2, Pace Z2, RPE 2–3) for 10 min. Then perform 4 × 10s strides. **MS**: Mid ENDURANCE (Power Z2, HR Z2, Pace Z2, RPE 2–3) - keep pace steady throughout. On a treadmill or long climb, perform 5 × 5 mins hill repeats at 3% to 5% with 3 min recovery at 0% grade. Try to keep the same ENDURANCE (Power Z2, HR Z2, Pace Z2, RPE 2–3) throughout the workout. **CD**: 10 min at ACTIVE RECOVERY (Power Z1, HR Z1, Pace Z1, RPE 1)
DISTANCE	6.5 mi	
TSS	80	
LONG HILLS		

SUNDAY

PLANNED METRICS		
DURATION	02:10:00	**WU**: Perform 5 mins of dynamic warm up: 1. Leg swings - 10–20 per leg 2. Marches - 10–15 per leg 3. Leg side swings - 10–20 per leg Build WU pace from ACTIVE RECOVERY (Power Z1, HR Z1, Pace Z1, RPE 1) to ENDURANCE (Power Z2, HR Z2, Pace Z2, RPE 2–3) for 10 min. Then perform 4 × 10s strides. **MS**: Run 14 mi at your Low ENDURANCE (Power Z2, HR Z2, Pace Z2, RPE 2–3) pace. **CD**: Jog 10 min
DISTANCE	14.5	
TSS	106	
14 MILE LSD ENDURANCE RUN		

WEEK #8

Training Focus: Recovery and Test Week

MONDAY (AM)

PLANNED METRICS		
DURATION		Actively focus on recovery today: 1) avoid unneccessary physical exertion, 2) watch nutrition closely (healthy carbs, lean protein, and good fats), 3) stretch, and 4) drink when thirsty. Other common recovery aids include massage, napping, elevating legs, floating in water, and listening to music.
DISTANCE		
TSS		
DAY OFF		

TUESDAY (AM)

PLANNED METRICS		
DURATION	00:45:00	**WU**: Jog for 15 min at ACTIVE RECOVERY (Power Z1, HR Z1, Pace Z1, RPE 1), then Perform the following dynamic stretches: 1. Toe Touches - 2 × 15 per leg 2. Leg Tucks - 2 × 15 per leg **MS**: Jog at ACTIVE RECOVERY (Power Z1, HR Z1, Pace Z1, RPE 1) **CD**: Walk for 10 min or until your HR drops below 100 BPM.
DISTANCE	Various	
TSS	19	
RECOVERY - JOG 40 MIN		

WEDNESDAY

PLANNED METRICS	
DURATION	00:52:00
DISTANCE	4.5
TSS	42
4 MILE LSD ENDURANCE RUN	

WU: Perform 5 mins of dynamic warm up:

1. Leg swings - 10–20 per leg
2. Marches - 10–15 per leg
3. Leg side swings - 10–20 per leg

Build WU pace from ACTIVE RECOVERY (Power Z1, HR Z1, Pace Z1, RPE 1) to ENDURANCE (Power Z2, HR Z2, Pace Z2, RPE 2–3) for 10 min. Then perform 4 × 10s strides.

MS: Run 4 mi at your Low ENDURANCE (Power Z2, HR Z2, Pace Z2, RPE 2–3) pace.

CD: Jog 10 min

THURSDAY

PLANNED METRICS	
DURATION	00:30:00
DISTANCE	Various
TSS	25
20 MINUTE RUN WITH 4 × 10S PICKUPS	

WU: Perform 5 mins of dynamic warm up:

1. Leg swings - 10–20 per leg
2. Marches - 10–15 per leg
3. Leg side swings - 10–20 per leg

Build WU pace from ACTIVE RECOVERY (Power Z1, HR Z1, Pace Z1, RPE 1–2) to ENDURANCE (Power Z2, HR Z2, Pace Z2, RPE 2–3) for 10 min.

MS: Complete this 20 minute run. Build into the run VERY easy. Walk for the first 5 minutes, start a steady, Low ENDURANCE Z2 (Power Z2, HR Z2, Pace Z2, RPE 2–3) jog and at the 10 minute mark, complete 4 × 10 second "pick ups" gradually building into your 10k/THRESHOLD (Power Z4, HR Z4, Pace Z4, RPE 5–6). by the end of the 20s. 40s EASY Low ENDURANCE Z2 (Power Z2, HR Z2, Pace Z2, RPE 2–3) jog between.

Run the final 6 minutes at low ENDURANCE Z2 (Power Z2, HR Z2, Pace Z2, RPE 2–3) jog.

CD: Walk for 5–10 min. Perform static stretching as necessary.

FRIDAY

PLANNED METRICS		WU: Perform 5 mins of dynamic warm up:
DURATION	00:45:00	1. Leg swings - 10–20 per leg 2. Marches - 10–15 per leg 3. Leg side swings - 10–20 per leg
DISTANCE	5 km	
TSS	35	Build WU pace from Z1 to Z2 for 20 min. Then perform 4 × 10s strides.
CRITICAL RUN SPEED/RFTP TEST - 5 KM		------- **MS**: Run 5 km (3.1) as fast as you can. You can do this on a bike trail, track, or sidewalk. Try to find the most flat surface (no hills) as possible. However, do not do the test on a treadmill. Track you HR. The four metrics you are concerned with tracking is your running power, pace, and HR, and the time it took you to complete the 5 km. ------- **CD**: Jog in for 10 min until your HR comes down to about 100 BPM

SATURDAY

PLANNED METRICS		Strength Protocol - Week 4
DURATION	00:45:00	**Goal**: Hypertrophy **Intensity**: 90% of 1 RM
DISTANCE	N/A	**Note**: Last rep should performed until exhaustion.
TSS	25	**Exercises**: **Strength**:
STRENGTH WORK - WEEK 4		1. Bench Press (6 × 4–6) 2. Lateral Pull Down (6 × 4–6) 3. Seated Row (6 × 4–6) 4. Tricep Pulldown (6 × 4–6) 5. Bicep Curl (6 × 4–6) 6. Leg Press (6 × 4–6) 7. Leg Extension (6 × 4–6) 8. Leg Curl (6 × 4–6) 9. Calf Raises (6 × 4–6) 10. Back Extension (6 × 4–6) 11. Ab Curl (6 × 4–6) 12. Leg Tucked Rotation (6 × 4–6)

SUNDAY

PLANNED METRICS		
DURATION	01:25:00	**WU**: Perform 5 mins of dynamic warm up: 1. Leg swings - 10–20 per leg 2. Marches - 10–15 per leg 3. Leg side swings - 10–20 per leg
DISTANCE	10.5	Build WU pace from ACTIVE RECOVERY (Power Z1, HR Z1, Pace Z1, RPE 1) to ENDURANCE (Power Z2, HR Z2, Pace Z2, RPE 2–3) for 10 min. Then perform 4 × 10s strides.
TSS	60	**MS**: Run 10 mi at your Low ENDURANCE (Power Z2, HR Z2, Pace Z2, RPE 2–3) pace.
10 MILE LSD ENDURANCE RUN		**CD**: Jog 10 min

WEEK #9

Training Focus: Base 3 - Week 1

MONDAY (AM)

PLANNED METRICS		
DURATION		Actively focus on recovery today: 1) avoid unneccessary physical exertion, 2) watch nutrition closely (healthy carbs, lean protein, and good fats), 3) stretch, and 4) drink when thirsty. Other common recovery aids include massage, napping, elevating legs, floating in water, and listening to music.
DISTANCE		
TSS		
DAY OFF		

TUESDAY (AM)

PLANNED METRICS		
DURATION	00:45:00	**WU**: Perform 5 mins of dynamic warm up: 1. Leg swings - 10–20 per leg 2. Marches - 10–15 per leg 3. Leg side swings - 10–20 per leg
DISTANCE	5 mi	Build WU pace from ACTIVE RECOVERY (Power Z1, HR Z1, Pace Z1, RPE 1) to ENDURANCE (Power Z2, HR Z2, Pace Z2, RPE 2–3) for 10 min. Then perform 4 × 10s strides.
TSS	50	**MS**: Run 4.5 mi at your ENDURANCE (Power Z2, HR Z2, Pace Z2, RPE 2–3) pace.
4.5 MILE ENDURANCE RUN		**CD**: Jog 10 min

TUESDAY (PM)

PLANNED METRICS		
DURATION	025:00	
DISTANCE	N/A	
TSS	8	

CORE AND HIP ROUTINE - PILATES STYLE

WU: Jog for 10 min building from Active Recovery (Power Z1, HR Z1, Pace Z1, RPE 1) building to Endurance (Power Z2, HR Z2, Pace Z2, RPE 2–3).

MS1: Perform 2 sets of the following with 1–2 min rest between each set:

1. Front plank x 1 min. During this one minute, perform 30 reps of isometric squeezes of all core muscles. Immediately after …
2. Press into a child's pose for 30 seconds. Then …
3. Perform 15 reps of the bird dog on each side from all fours. Then …
4. Perform 30 reps of pilates roll ups from flat back

MS2: Perform 2 sets x 10 reps on each side of the following Pilates hip routine with 1–2 min rest between each set:

1. Point your toes & kick powerfully up & flex to slow down pulse with shorter ROM as above
2. Circle clockwise stopping at 12 o'clock circle counter clockwise stopping at 12 o'clock
3. Kick pointed toe forward & flex slow kick back to the start position
4. Kick forward flexed & slow point toe back to the start position

CD: Perform 5–10 min of static stretching

WEDNESDAY

PLANNED METRICS	
DURATION	01:00:00
DISTANCE	Various
TSS	65

YASSO INTERVALS

WU: Perform 5 mins of dynamic warm up:

1. Leg swings - 10–20 per leg
2. Marches - 10–15 per leg
3. Leg side swings - 10–20 per leg

Build WU pace from ACTIVE RECOVERY (Power Z1, HR Z1, Pace Z1, RPE 1) to ENDURANCE (Power Z2, HR Z2, Pace Z2, RPE 2–3) for 10 min. Then perform 4 × 10s strides.

MS: 4–6 × 800 m @ upper Tempo (Power Z3, HR Z3, Pace Z3, RPE 3–4) with 400 at Endurance (Power Z2, HR Z2, Pace Z2, RPE 2–3) between each 800.

CD: Jog or walk at Active Recovery (Power Z1, HR Z1, Pace Z1, RPE 1) for 15 min.

THURSDAY

PLANNED METRICS		
DURATION	00:52:00	**WU**: Perform 5 mins of dynamic warm up: 1. Leg swings - 10–20 per leg 2. Marches - 10–15 per leg 3. Leg side swings - 10–20 per leg Build WU pace from ACTIVE RECOVERY (Power Z1, HR Z1, Pace Z1, RPE 1) to ENDURANCE (Power Z2, HR Z2, Pace Z2, RPE 2–3) for 10 min. Then perform 4 × 10s strides. **MS**: Run 4 mi at your Low ENDURANCE (Power Z2, HR Z2, Pace Z2, RPE 2–3) pace. **CD**: Jog 10 min
DISTANCE	4.5	
TSS	42	
4 MILE LSD ENDURANCE RUN		

FRIDAY

PLANNED METRICS		
DURATION	00:45:00	Strength Protocol - Week 5 **Goal**: Hypertrophy **Intensity**: 75% of 1 RM **Note**: 1. 3d set should be performed until exhaustion. 2. Only 3 upper body sets. **Exercises**: **Strength**: 1. Bench Press (3 × 8–12) 2. Lateral Pull Down (3 × 8–12) 3. Seated Row (3 × 8–12) 4. Tricep Pulldown (3 × 8–12) 5. Bicep Curl (3 × 8–12) 6. Leg Press (3 × 8–12) 7. Leg Extension (3 × 8–12) 8. Leg Curl (3 × 8–12) 9. Calf Raises (3 × 8–12) 10. Back Extension (3 × 8–12) 11. Ab Curl (4 × 8–12) 12. Leg Tucked Rotation (4 × 8–12)
DISTANCE	N/A	
TSS	25	
STRENGTH WORK - WEEK 5		

SATURDAY

PLANNED METRICS		
DURATION	00:55:00	**WU**: Perform 5 mins of dynamic warm up: 1. Leg swings - 10–20 per leg 2. Leg Tucks - 10–15 per leg 3. Toe touches - 10–20 per leg
DISTANCE	5.0 mi	
TSS	60	Build WU pace from ACTIVE RECOVERY (Power Z1, HR Z1, Pace Z1, RPE 1) to ENDURANCE (Power Z2, HR Z2, Pace Z2, RPE 2–3) for 10 min. Then perform 4 × 10s strides. **MS**: Keep upper ENDURANCE (Power Z2, HR Z2, Pace Z2, RPE 2–3) throughout the MS. The effort will increase with hills. **Perform 10×**: 90 sec at 3%, then 90s back at 0% Run balance of time at ENDURANCE (Power Z2, HR Z2, Pace Z2, RPE 2–3).
HILLS, HILLS, HILLS!!!!!		**CD**: Jog at ACTIVE RECOVERY (Power Z1, HR Z1, Pace Z1, RPE 1) for 10 min.

SUNDAY

PLANNED METRICS		
DURATION	01:30:00	**WU**: Perform 5 mins of dynamic warm up: 1. Leg swings - 10–20 per leg 2. Marches - 10–15 per leg 3. Leg side swings - 10–20 per leg
DISTANCE	12.5 mi	
TSS	100	Build WU pace from ACTIVE RECOVERY (Power Z1, HR Z1, Pace Z1, RPE 1) to ENDURANCE (Power Z2, HR Z2, Pace Z2, RPE 2–3) for 10 min. Then perform 4 × 10s strides. **MS**: Run 12 mi at ENDURANCE (Power Z2, HR Z2, Pace Z2, RPE 2–3). Starting at mile 10, run 2 mi at TEMPO (Power Z3, HR Z3, Pace Z3, RPE 3–4).
12 MI WITH TEMPO		**CD**: Jog or walk for 10 min at ACTIVE RECOVERY (Power Z1, HR Z1, Pace Z1, RPE 1)

WEEK #10

Training Focus: Base 3 - Week 2

MONDAY (AM)

PLANNED METRICS		
DURATION		Actively focus on recovery today: 1) avoid unneccessary physical exertion, 2) watch nutrition closely (healthy carbs, lean protein, and good fats), 3) stretch, and 4) drink when thirsty. Other common recovery aids include massage, napping, elevating legs, floating in water, and listening to music.
DISTANCE		
TSS		
DAY OFF		

TUESDAY (AM)

PLANNED METRICS		
DURATION	00:45:00	**WU**: Perform 5 mins of dynamic warm up: 1. Leg swings - 10–20 per leg 2. Marches - 10–15 per leg 3. Leg side swings - 10–20 per leg Build WU pace from ACTIVE RECOVERY (Power Z1, HR Z1, Pace Z1, RPE 1) to ENDURANCE (Power Z2, HR Z2, Pace Z2, RPE 2–3) for 10 min. Then perform 4 × 10s strides. **MS**: Run 4.5 mi at your ENDURANCE (Power Z2, HR Z2, Pace Z2, RPE 2–3) pace. **CD**: Jog 10 min
DISTANCE	5 mi	
TSS	50	
4.5 MILE ENDURANCE RUN		

TUESDAY (PM)

PLANNED METRICS		
DURATION	00:25:00	
DISTANCE	N/A	
TSS	8	

LOWER BODY STRENGTH + HIP ROUTINE #1

WU: 1. Jog for 10 min building from Active Recovery (Power Z1, HR Z1, Pace Z1, RPE 1) building to Endurance (Power Z2, HR Z2, Pace Z2, RPE 2–3).

2. Perform 15 reps per leg:
   a. knee hugs
   b. straight leg military march
   c. walking pigeon

MS: Lower Body & Core Strength:
12–15 reps of each
1. stability ball hamstring pull ins
2. ball transfer from hands to feet
3. top of the ball foot march
4. reverse crunch
5. low back/ glute & ham raise
6. single leg dead lift moderate weight dumb bell
7. side step up to box w/ moderate wt dumb bell pilates hip series 10 each without resting leg to floor until completion:
8. front circles with tow pointed quad firm
9. back circles with tow pointed quad firm
10. leg raise (controlled and slow) hold at the top after 10 for 10 sec then 10 fast pulses

CD: Static stretch for 10 min.

WEDNESDAY

PLANNED METRICS	
DURATION	01:00:00
DISTANCE	8.5
TSS	70

8 MI - 1 MI TEMPO INTERVALS

WU: Perform 5 mins of dynamic warm up:
1. Leg swings - 10–20 per leg
2. Marches - 10–15 per leg
3. Leg side swings - 10–20 per leg

Build WU pace from Active Recovery (Power Z1, HR Z1, Pace Z1, RPE 1) to Endurance (Power Z2, HR Z2, Pace Z2, RPE 2–3) for 10 min. Then perform 4 × 10s strides.

MS: For this 8 mi run, perform 4 × 1mi Tempo (Power Z3, HR Z3, Pace Z3, RPE 3–4) efforts with 1 mile "recovery" at Endurance (Power Z2, HR Z2, Pace Z2, RPE 2–3).

If the finish the balance of the run at Endurance (Power Z2, HR Z2, Pace Z2, RPE 2–3).

CD: Jog 10 min at Active Recovery (Power Z1, HR Z1, Pace Z1, RPE 1)

THURSDAY

PLANNED METRICS		WU: Perform 5 mins of dynamic warm up: 1. Leg swings - 10–20 per leg 2. Marches - 10–15 per leg 3. Leg side swings - 10–20 per leg
DURATION	00:52:00	
DISTANCE	4.5	
TSS	42	Build WU pace from ACTIVE RECOVERY (Power Z1, HR Z1, Pace Z1, RPE 1) to ENDURANCE (Power Z2, HR Z2, Pace Z2, RPE 2–3) for 10 min. Then perform 4 × 10s strides. **MS**: Run 4 mi at your Low ENDURANCE (Power Z2, HR Z2, Pace Z2, RPE 2–3) pace. **CD**: Jog 10 min
4 MILE LSD ENDURANCE RUN		

FRIDAY

PLANNED METRICS		Strength Protocol - Week 6 **Goal**: Hypertrophy **Intensity**: 75% of 1 RM
DURATION	00:45:00	
DISTANCE	N/A	**Note**:
TSS	25	1. 3d set should be performed until exhaustion. 2. Only 3 upper body sets. **Exercises**: **Strength**: 1. Bench Press (3 × 8–12) 2. Lateral Pull Down (3 × 8–12) 3. Seated Row (3 × 8–12) 4. Tricep Pulldown (3 × 8–12) 5. Bicep Curl (3 × 8–12) 6. Leg Press (5 × 8–12) 7. Leg Extension (5 × 8–12) 8. Leg Curl (5 × 8–12) 9. Calf Raises (5 × 8–12) 10. Back Extension (3 × 8–12) 11. Ab Curl (5 × 8–12) 12. Leg Tucked Rotation (5 × 8–12)
STRENGTH WORK - WEEK 6		

SATURDAY

PLANNED METRICS		
DURATION	01:00:00	**WU**: 15 minutes working into ENDURANCE (Power Z2, HR Z2, Pace Z2, RPE 2–3). Perform 4 × 30 s strides during this time. ------- **MS**: 1. 10 min @ ENDURANCE (Power Z2, HR Z2, Pace Z2, RPE 2–3) 2. 10 min @ mid TEMPO (Power Z3, HR Z3, Pace Z3, RPE 3–4) 3. 10 min @ upper TEMPO (Power Z3, HR Z3, Pace Z3, RPE 3–4) 4. 15 min @ SST (Power Z3.5, HR Z3.5 ,Pace Z3.5, RPE 5.5) ------- **CD**: 10 minutes at ACTIVE ENDURANCE (Power Z1, HR Z1, Pace Z1, RPE Z1)
DISTANCE	Various	
TSS	70	
TEMPO RAMP 1 × 45		

SUNDAY

PLANNED METRICS		
DURATION	02:25:00	**WU**: Perform 5 mins of dynamic warm up: 1. Leg swings - 10–20 per leg 2. Marches - 10–15 per leg 3. Leg side swings - 10–20 per leg Build WU pace from ACTIVE RECOVERY (Power Z1, HR Z1, Pace Z1, RPE 1) to ENDURANCE (Power Z2, HR Z2, Pace Z2, RPE 2–3) for 10 min. Then perform 4 × 10s strides. **MS**: Run 15 mi at your Low ENDURANCE (Power Z2, HR Z2, Pace Z2, RPE 2–3) pace. **CD**: Jog 10 min
DISTANCE	15.5	
TSS	117	
15 MILE LSD ENDURANCE RUN		

WEEK #11

Training Focus: Base 3 - Week 3

MONDAY (AM)

PLANNED METRICS		Actively focus on recovery today: 1) avoid unneccessary physical exertion, 2) watch nutrition closely (healthy carbs, lean protein, and good fats), 3) stretch, and 4) drink when thirsty. Other common recovery aids include massage, napping, elevating legs, floating in water, and listening to music.
DURATION		
DISTANCE		
TSS		
DAY OFF		

TUESDAY (AM)

PLANNED METRICS		**WU**: Perform 5 mins of dynamic warm up: 1. Leg swings - 10–20 per leg 2. Marches - 10–15 per leg 3. Leg side swings - 10–20 per leg Build WU pace from ACTIVE RECOVERY (Power Z1, HR Z1, Pace Z1, RPE 1) to ENDURANCE (Power Z2, HR Z2, Pace Z2, RPE 2–3) for 10 min. Then perform 4 × 10s strides. **MS**: Run 4.5 mi at your ENDURANCE (Power Z2, HR Z2, Pace Z2, RPE 2–3) pace. **CD**: Jog 10 min
DURATION	00:45:00	
DISTANCE	5 mi	
TSS	50	
4.5 MILE ENDURANCE RUN		

TUESDAY (PM)

PLANNED METRICS		
DURATION	00:25:00	
DISTANCE	N/A	
TSS	8	

CORE AND HIP ROUTINE - PILATES STYLE

WU: Jog for 10 min building from Active Recovery (Power Z1, HR Z1, Pace Z1, RPE 1) building to Endurance (Power Z2, HR Z2, Pace Z2, RPE 2–3).

MS1: Perform 2 sets of the following with 1–2 min rest between each set:

1. Front plank × 1 min. During this one minute, perform 30 reps of isometric squeezes of all core muscles. Immediately after …
2. Press into a child's pose for 30 seconds. Then …
3. Perform 15 reps of the bird dog on each side from all fours. Then …
4. Perform 30 reps of pilates roll ups from flat back

MS2: Perform 2 sets × 10 reps on each side of the following Pilates hip routine with 1–2 min rest between each set:

1. Point your toes & kick powerfully up & flex to slow down pulse with shorter ROM as above
2. Circle clockwise stopping at 12 o'clock circle counter clockwise stopping at 12 o'clock
3. Kick pointed toe forward & flex slow kick back to the start position
4. Kick forward flexed & slow point toe back to the start position

CD: Perform 5–10 min of static stretching

WEDNESDAY

PLANNED METRICS	
DURATION	01:05:00
DISTANCE	Various
TSS	65

3 × 7 MIN TEMPO PACE INTERVALS WITH ENDURANCE

WU: Perform 5 mins of dynamic warm up:

1. Leg swings - 10–20 per leg
2. Marches - 10–15 per leg
3. Leg side swings - 10–20 per leg

Build WU pace from ACTIVE RECOVERY (Power Z1, HR Z1, Pace Z1, RPE 1) to ENDURANCE (Power Z2, HR Z2, Pace Z2, RPE 2–3) for 10 min. Then perform 4 × 10s strides.

MS1: Start main set run at mid ENDURANCE (Power Z2, HR Z2, Pace Z2, RPE 2–3). Once comfortable, complete 3 × 7 min intervals at upper TEMPO (Power Z3, HR Z3, Pace Z3, RPE 3–4). Recover for 5 min ENDURANCE (Power Z2, HR Z2, Pace Z2, RPE 2–3) in between each interval. Then move on to MS2.

MS2: Run 2 mile at ENDURANCE (Power Z2, HR Z2, Pace Z2, RPE 2–3)

CD: Jog at ACTIVE RECOVERY (Power Z1, HR Z1, Pace Z1, RPE 1) for 10 min or until HR comes below 100 BPM.

THURSDAY

PLANNED METRICS		
DURATION	00:52:00	**WU**: Perform 5 mins of dynamic warm up: 1. Leg swings - 10–20 per leg 2. Marches - 10–15 per leg 3. Leg side swings - 10–20 per leg
DISTANCE	4.5	
TSS	42	Build WU pace from ACTIVE RECOVERY (Power Z1, HR Z1, Pace Z1, RPE 1) to ENDURANCE (Power Z2, HR Z2, Pace Z2, RPE 2–3) for 10 min. Then perform 4 × 10s strides.
4 MILE LSD ENDURANCE RUN		**MS**: Run 4 mi at your Low ENDURANCE (Power Z2, HR Z2, Pace Z2, RPE 2–3) pace. **CD**: Jog 10 min

FRIDAY

PLANNED METRICS		
DURATION	00:45:00	Strength Protocol - Week 7 **Goal**: Hypertrophy **Intensity**: 90% of 1 RM
DISTANCE	N/A	**Note**:
TSS	25	1. 3d set should be performed until exhaustion. 2. Only 3 upper body sets.
STRENGTH WORK - WEEK 7		**Exercises**: **Strength**: 1. Bench Press (3 × 4–6) 2. Lateral Pull Down (3 × 4–6) 3. Seated Row (3 × 4–6) 4. Tricep Pulldown (3 × 4–6) 5. Bicep Curl (3 × 4–6) 6. Leg Press (6 × 4–6) 7. Leg Extension (6 × 4–6) 8. Leg Curl (6 × 4–6) 9. Calf Raises (6 × 4–6) 10. Back Extension (3 × 4–6) 11. Ab Curl (3 × 4–6) 12. Leg Tucked Rotation (6 × 4–6)

SATURDAY

PLANNED METRICS		WU: Perform 5 mins of dynamic warm up: 1. Leg swings - 10–20 per leg 2. Marches - 10–15 per leg 3. Leg side swings - 10–20 per leg
DURATION	01:10:00	
DISTANCE	Various	
TSS	54	Build WU pace from ACTIVE RECOVERY (Power Z1, HR Z1, Pace Z1, RPE 1) to ENDURANCE (Power Z2, HR Z2, Pace Z2, RPE 2–3) for 10 min. Then perform 4 × 10s strides. ---------- **MS**: Run 10–5-3–2-1 minutes at Tempo (Power Z3, HR Z3, Pace Z3, RPE 3–4) and jog equal amounts between each segment at Endurance (Power Z2, HR Z2, Pace Z2, RPE 2–3) ---------- **CD**: 10 minute cool down at (ACTIVE RECOVERY (Power Z1, HR Z1, Pace Z1, RPE 1)
FARTLEK: STEP DOWN INTERVALS (TEMPO)		

SUNDAY

PLANNED METRICS		WU: Perform 5 mins of dynamic warm up: 1. Leg swings - 10–20 per leg 2. Marches - 10–15 per leg 3. Leg side swings - 10–20 per leg
DURATION	02:25:00	
DISTANCE	15.5	
TSS	117	Build WU pace from ACTIVE RECOVERY (Power Z1, HR Z1, Pace Z1, RPE 1) to ENDURANCE (Power Z2, HR Z2, Pace Z2, RPE 2–3) for 10 min. Then perform 4 × 10s strides. **MS**: Run 15 mi at your Low ENDURANCE (Power Z2, HR Z2, Pace Z2, RPE 2–3) pace. **CD**: Jog 10 min
15 MILE LSD ENDURANCE RUN		

WEEK #12

Training Focus: Recovery and Test Week

MONDAY (AM)

PLANNED METRICS		Actively focus on recovery today: 1) avoid unneccessary physical exertion, 2) watch nutrition closely (healthy carbs, lean protein, and good fats), 3) stretch, and 4) drink when thirsty. Other common recovery aids include massage, napping, elevating legs, floating in water, and listening to music.
DURATION		
DISTANCE		
TSS		
DAY OFF		

TUESDAY (AM)

PLANNED METRICS		**WU**: Jog for 15 min at ACTIVE RECOVERY (Power Z1, HR Z1, Pace Z1, RPE 1), then Perform the following dynamic stretches: 1. Toe Touches - 2 × 15 per leg 2. Leg Tucks - 2 × 15 per leg
DURATION	00:45:00	
DISTANCE	Various	
TSS	19	
RECOVERY - JOG 40 MIN		**MS**: Jog at ACTIVE RECOVERY (Power Z1, HR Z1, Pace Z1, RPE 1) **CD**: Walk for 10 min or until your HR drops below 100 BPM.

WEDNESDAY

PLANNED METRICS		**WU**: Perform 5 mins of dynamic warm up: 1. Leg swings - 10–20 per leg 2. Marches - 10–15 per leg 3. Leg side swings - 10–20 per leg
DURATION	00:52:00	
DISTANCE	4.5	
TSS	42	
4 MILE LSD ENDURANCE RUN		Build WU pace from ACTIVE RECOVERY (Power Z1, HR Z1, Pace Z1, RPE 1) to ENDURANCE (Power Z2, HR Z2, Pace Z2, RPE 2–3) for 10 min. Then perform 4 × 10s strides. **MS**: Run 4 mi at your Low ENDURANCE (Power Z2, HR Z2, Pace Z2, RPE 2–3) pace. **CD**: Jog 10 min

THURSDAY

PLANNED METRICS		
DURATION	00:30:00	**WU**: Perform 5 mins of dynamic warm up: 1. Leg swings - 10–20 per leg 2. Marches - 10–15 per leg 3. Leg side swings - 10–20 per leg
DISTANCE	Various	
TSS	25	Build WU pace from ACTIVE RECOVERY (Power Z1, HR Z1, Pace Z1, RPE 1–2) to ENDURANCE (Power Z2, HR Z2, Pace Z2, RPE 2–3) for 10 min. **MS**: Complete this 20 minute run. Build into the run VERY easy. Walk for the first 5 minutes, start a steady, Low ENDURANCE Z2 (Power Z2, HR Z2, Pace Z2, RPE 2–3) jog and at the 10 minute mark, complete 4 × 10 second "pick ups" gradually building into your 10k/THRESHOLD (Power Z4, HR Z4, Pace Z4, RPE 5–6). by the end of the 20s. 40s EASY Low ENDURANCE Z2 (Power Z2, HR Z2, Pace Z2, RPE 2–3) jog between. Run the final 6 minutes at low ENDURANCE Z2 (Power Z2, HR Z2, Pace Z2, RPE 2–3) jog.
20 MINUTE RUN WITH 4 × 10S PICKUPS		**CD**: Walk for 5–10 min. Perform static stretching as necessary.

FRIDAY

PLANNED METRICS		
DURATION	00:45:00	**WU**: Perform 5 mins of dynamic warm up: 1. Leg swings - 10–20 per leg 2. Marches - 10–15 per leg 3. Leg side swings - 10–20 per leg
DISTANCE	5 km	
TSS	35	Build WU pace from Z1 to Z2 for 20 min. Then perform 4 × 10s strides. -------- **MS**: Run 5 km (3.1) as fast as you can. You can do this on a bike trail, track, or sidewalk. Try to find the most flat surface (no hills) as possible. However, do not do the test on a treadmill. Track you HR. The four metrics you are concerned with tracking is your running power, pace, and HR, and the time it took you to complete the 5 km. --------
CRITICAL RUN SPEED/RFTP TEST - 5 KM		**CD**: Jog in for 10 min until your HR comes down to about 100 BPM

SATURDAY

PLANNED METRICS		Strength Protocol - Week 4 **Goal**: Hypertrophy **Intensity**: 90% of 1 RM **Note**: Last rep should performed until exhaustion. **Exercises**: **Strength**: 1. Bench Press (6 × 4–6) 2. Lateral Pull Down (6 × 4–6) 3. Seated Row (6 × 4–6) 4. Tricep Pulldown (6 × 4–6) 5. Bicep Curl (6 × 4–6) 6. Leg Press (6 × 4–6) 7. Leg Extension (6 × 4–6) 8. Leg Curl (6 × 4–6) 9. Calf Raises (6 × 4–6) 10. Back Extension (6 × 4–6) 11. Ab Curl (6 × 4–6) 12. Leg Tucked Rotation (6 × 4–6)
DURATION	00:45:00	
DISTANCE	N/A	
TSS	25	
STRENGTH WORK - WEEK 4		

SUNDAY

PLANNED METRICS		**WU**: Perform 5 mins of dynamic warm up: 1. Leg swings - 10–20 per leg 2. Marches - 10–15 per leg 3. Leg side swings - 10–20 per leg Build WU pace from ACTIVE RECOVERY (Power Z1, HR Z1, Pace Z1, RPE 1) to ENDURANCE (Power Z2, HR Z2, Pace Z2, RPE 2–3) for 10 min. Then perform 4 × 10s strides. **MS**: Run 10 mi at your Low ENDURANCE (Power Z2, HR Z2, Pace Z2, RPE 2–3) pace. **CD**: Jog 10 min
DURATION	01:25:00	
DISTANCE	10.5	
TSS	60	
10 MILE LSD ENDURANCE RUN		

WEEK #13

Training Focus: Build 1 - Week 1

MONDAY (AM)

PLANNED METRICS		
DURATION		Actively focus on recovery today: 1) avoid unneccessary physical exertion, 2) watch nutrition closely (healthy carbs, lean protein, and good fats), 3) stretch, and 4) drink when thirsty. Other common recovery aids include massage, napping, elevating legs, floating in water, and listening to music.
DISTANCE		
TSS		
DAY OFF		

TUESDAY (AM)

PLANNED METRICS		
DURATION	00:45:00	**WU**: Perform 5 mins of dynamic warm up: 1. Leg swings - 10–20 per leg 2. Marches - 10–15 per leg 3. Leg side swings - 10–20 per leg Build WU pace from ACTIVE RECOVERY (Power Z1, HR Z1, Pace Z1, RPE 1) to ENDURANCE (Power Z2, HR Z2, Pace Z2, RPE 2–3) for 10 min. Then perform 4 × 10s strides. **MS**: Run 4.5 mi at your ENDURANCE (Power Z2, HR Z2, Pace Z2, RPE 2–3) pace. **CD**: Jog 10 min
DISTANCE	5 mi	
TSS	50	
4.5 MILE ENDURANCE RUN		

TUESDAY (PM)

PLANNED METRICS	
DURATION	00:25:00
DISTANCE	N/A
TSS	8

CORE AND HIP ROUTINE - PILATES STYLE

WU: Jog for 10 min building from Active Recovery (Power Z1, HR Z1, Pace Z1, RPE 1) building to Endurance (Power Z2, HR Z2, Pace Z2, RPE 2–3).

MS1: Perform 2 sets of the following with 1–2 min rest between each set:

1. Front plank × 1 min. During this one minute, perform 30 reps of isometric squeezes of all core muscles. Immediately after …
2. Press into a child's pose for 30 seconds. Then …
3. Perform 15 reps of the bird dog on each side from all fours. Then …
4. Perform 30 reps of pilates roll ups from flat back

MS2: Perform 2 sets × 10 reps on each side of the following Pilates hip routine with 1–2 min rest between each set:

1. Point your toes & kick powerfully up & flex to slow down pulse with shorter ROM as above
2. Circle clockwise stopping at 12 o'clock circle counter clockwise stopping at 12 o'clock
3. Kick pointed toe forward & flex slow kick back to the start position
4. Kick forward flexed & slow point toe back to the start position

CD: Perform 5–10 min of static stretching

WEDNESDAY

PLANNED METRICS	
DURATION	01:00:00
DISTANCE	8.5
TSS	70

8 MI - 1 MI TEMPO INTERVALS

WU: Perform 5 mins of dynamic warm up:

1. Leg swings - 10–20 per leg
2. Marches - 10–15 per leg
3. Leg side swings - 10–20 per leg

Build WU pace from Active Recovery (Power Z1, HR Z1, Pace Z1, RPE 1) to Endurance (Power Z2, HR Z2, Pace Z2, RPE 2–3) for 10 min. Then perform 4 × 10s strides.

MS: For this 8 mi run, perform 4 × 1mi Tempo (Power Z3, HR Z3, Pace Z3, RPE 3–4) efforts with 1 mile "recovery" at Endurance (Power Z2, HR Z2, Pace Z2, RPE 2–3).

If the finish the balance of the run at Endurance (Power Z2, HR Z2, Pace Z2, RPE 2–3).

CD: Jog 10 min at Active Recovery (Power Z1, HR Z1, Pace Z1, RPE 1)

THURSDAY

PLANNED METRICS		
DURATION	00:52:00	**WU**: Perform 5 mins of dynamic warm up: 1. Leg swings - 10–20 per leg 2. Marches - 10–15 per leg 3. Leg side swings - 10–20 per leg
DISTANCE	4.5	
TSS	42	Build WU pace from ACTIVE RECOVERY (Power Z1, HR Z1, Pace Z1, RPE 1) to ENDURANCE (Power Z2, HR Z2, Pace Z2, RPE 2–3) for 10 min. Then perform 4 × 10s strides.
4 MILE LSD ENDURANCE RUN		**MS**: Run 4 mi at your Low ENDURANCE (Power Z2, HR Z2, Pace Z2, RPE 2–3) pace. **CD**: Jog 10 min

FRIDAY

PLANNED METRICS		
DURATION	00:45:00	Strength Protocol - Week 9 **Goal**: Hypertrophy **Intensity**: 75% of 1 RM
DISTANCE	N/A	**Note**: 1. 3d set should be performed until exhaustion.
TSS	25	2. Only 3 upper body sets.
STRENGTH WORK - WEEK 9		**Exercises**: **Strength**: 1. Bench Press (3 × 8–12) 2. Lateral Pull Down (3 × 8–12) 3. Seated Row (3 × 8–12) 4. Tricep Pulldown (3 × 8–12) 5. Bicep Curl (3 × 8–12) 6. Leg Press (5 × 8–12) 7. Leg Extension (5 × 8–12) 8. Leg Curl (5 × 8–12) 9. Calf Raises (5 × 8–12) 10. Back Extension (3 × 8–12) 11. Ab Curl (3 × 8–12) 12. Leg Tucked Rotation (5 × 8–12)

SATURDAY

PLANNED METRICS		
DURATION	00:55:00	**WU**: Perform 5 mins of dynamic warm up: 1. Leg swings - 10–20 per leg 2. Marches - 10–15 per leg 3. Leg side swings - 10–20 per leg Build WU pace from ACTIVE RECOVERY (Power Z1, HR Z1, Pace Z1, RPE 1) to ENDURANCE (Power Z2, HR Z2, Pace Z2, RPE 2–3) for 10 min. Then perform 4 × 10s strides. **MS**: Run 5 mi at your Low ENDURANCE (Power Z2, HR Z2, Pace Z2, RPE 2–3) pace. **CD**: Jog 10 min
DISTANCE	5.5	
TSS	50	
5 MILE LSD ENDURANCE RUN		

SUNDAY

PLANNED METRICS		
DURATION	02:45:00	**WU**: Perform 5 mins of dynamic warm up: 1. Leg swings - 10–20 per leg 2. Marches - 10–15 per leg 3. Leg side swings - 10–20 per leg Build WU pace from ACTIVE RECOVERY (Power Z1, HR Z1, Pace Z1, RPE 1) to ENDURANCE (Power Z2, HR Z2, Pace Z2, RPE 2–3) for 10 min. Then perform 4 × 10s strides. **MS**: Run 16 mi at your Low ENDURANCE (Power Z2, HR Z2, Pace Z2, RPE 2–3) pace. **CD**: Jog 10 min
DISTANCE	16.5	
TSS	130	
16 MILE LSD ENDURANCE RUN		

WEEK #14

Training Focus: Build 1 - Week 2

MONDAY (AM)

PLANNED METRICS		
DURATION		Actively focus on recovery today: 1) avoid unneccessary physical exertion, 2) watch nutrition closely (healthy carbs, lean protein, and good fats), 3) stretch, and 4) drink when thirsty. Other common recovery aids include massage, napping, elevating legs, floating in water, and listening to music.
DISTANCE		
TSS		
DAY OFF		

TUESDAY (AM)

PLANNED METRICS		
DURATION	00:45:00	**WU**: Perform 5 mins of dynamic warm up: 1. Leg swings - 10–20 per leg 2. Marches - 10–15 per leg 3. Leg side swings - 10–20 per leg
DISTANCE	5 mi	
TSS	50	Build WU pace from ACTIVE RECOVERY (Power Z1, HR Z1, Pace Z1, RPE 1) to ENDURANCE (Power Z2, HR Z2, Pace Z2, RPE 2–3) for 10 min. Then perform 4 × 10s strides. **MS**: Run 4.5 mi at your ENDURANCE (Power Z2, HR Z2, Pace Z2, RPE 2–3) pace.
4.5 MILE ENDURANCE RUN		**CD**: Jog 10 min

TUESDAY (PM)

PLANNED METRICS		
DURATION	00:25:00	**WU**: 1. Jog for 10 min building from Active Recovery (Power Z1, HR Z1, Pace Z1, RPE 1) building to Endurance (Power Z2, HR Z2, Pace Z2, RPE 2–3).
DISTANCE	N/A	2. Perform 15 reps per leg: a. knee hugs b. straight leg military march c. walking pigeon
TSS	8	**MS**: Lower Body & Core Strength: 12–15 reps of each 1. stability ball hamstring pull ins 2. ball transfer from hands to feet 3. top of the ball foot march 4. reverse crunch 5. low back/ glute & ham raise 6. single leg dead lift moderate weight dumb bell 7. single leg wall squat. 8. 1 legged bosu ball balance - 15–20s / leg 9. 1 legged bosu ball squats
LOWER BODY STRENGTH + HIP ROUTINE #2		**CD**: Static stretch for 10 min.

WEDNESDAY

PLANNED METRICS	
DURATION	01:10:00
DISTANCE	Various
TSS	70
YASSO INTERVALS WITH ENDURANCE	

WU: Perform 5 mins of dynamic warm up:
1. Leg swings - 10–20 per leg
2. Marches - 10–15 per leg
3. Leg side swings - 10–20 per leg

Build WU pace from ACTIVE RECOVERY (Power Z1, HR Z1, Pace Z1, RPE 1) to ENDURANCE (Power Z2, HR Z2, Pace Z2, RPE 2–3) for 10 min. Then perform 4 × 10s strides.

MS1: 5–7 × 800 m @ upper Tempo (Power Z3, HR Z3, Pace Z3, RPE 3–4) with 400 at Endurance (Power Z2, HR Z2, Pace Z2, RPE 2–3) between each 800. Then move to MS2.

MS2: Run 4 mile at ENDURANCE (Power Z2, HR Z2, Pace Z2, RPE 2–3)

CD: Jog or walk at Active Recovery (Power Z1, HR Z1, Pace Z1, RPE 1) for 15 min.

THURSDAY

PLANNED METRICS	
DURATION	00:30:00
DISTANCE	Various
TSS	25
20 MINUTE RUN WITH 4 × 10S PICKUPS	

WU: Perform 5 mins of dynamic warm up:
1. Leg swings - 10–20 per leg
2. Marches - 10–15 per leg
3. Leg side swings - 10–20 per leg

Build WU pace from ACTIVE RECOVERY (Power Z1, HR Z1, Pace Z1, RPE 1–2) to ENDURANCE (Power Z2, HR Z2, Pace Z2, RPE 2–3) for 10 min.

MS: Complete this 20 minute run. Build into the run VERY easy. Walk for the first 5 minutes, start a steady, Low ENDURANCE Z2 (Power Z2, HR Z2, Pace Z2, RPE 2–3) jog and at the 10 minute mark, complete 4 × 10 second "pick ups" gradually building into your 10k/THRESHOLD (Power Z4, HR Z4, Pace Z4, RPE 5–6). by the end of the 20s. 40s EASY Low ENDURANCE Z2 (Power Z2, HR Z2, Pace Z2, RPE 2–3) jog between.

Run the final 6 minutes at low ENDURANCE Z2 (Power Z2, HR Z2, Pace Z2, RPE 2–3) jog.

CD: Walk for 5–10 min. Perform static stretching as necessary.

FRIDAY

PLANNED METRICS		
DURATION	00:45:00	
DISTANCE	N/A	
TSS	25	
STRENGTH WORK - WEEK 10		Strength Protocol - Week 10 **Goal**: Hypertrophy **Intensity**: 90% of 1 RM **Note**: 1. 3d set should be performed until exhaustion. 2. Only 3 upper body sets. **Exercises**: **Strength**: 1. Bench Press (3 × 4–6) 2. Lateral Pull Down (3 × 4–6) 3. Seated Row (3 × 4–6) 4. Tricep Pulldown (3 × 4–6) 5. Bicep Curl (3 × 4–6) 6. Leg Press (7 × 4–6) 7. Leg Extension (7 × 4–6) 8. Leg Curl (7 × 4–6) 9. Calf Raises (7 × 4–6) 10. Back Extension (3 × 4–6) 11. Ab Curl (3 × 4–6) 12. Leg Tucked Rotation (7 × 4–6)

SATURDAY

PLANNED METRICS		
DURATION	00:45:00	
DISTANCE	4.5 mi	
TSS	60	
LONG HILLS		**WU**: Perform 5 mins of dynamic warm up: 1. Leg swings - 10–20 per leg 2. Marches - 10–15 per leg 3. Leg side swings - 10–20 per leg Build WU pace from ACTIVE RECOVERY (Power Z1, HR Z1, Pace Z1, RPE 1) to ENDURANCE (Power Z2, HR Z2, Pace Z2, RPE 2–3) for 10 min. Then perform 4 × 10s strides. **MS**: Mid ENDURANCE (Power Z2, HR Z2, Pace Z2, RPE 2–3) - keep pace steady throughout. On a treadmill or long climb, perform 5 × 5 mins hill repeats at 3% to 5% with 3 min recovery at 0% grade. Try to keep the same ENDURANCE pace throughout the workout. **CD**: 10 min at ACTIVE RECOVERY (Power Z1, HR Z1, Pace Z1, RPE 1)

SUNDAY

PLANNED METRICS		WU: Perform 5 mins of dynamic warm up: 1. Leg swings - 10–20 per leg 2. Marches - 10–15 per leg 3. Leg side swings - 10–20 per leg Build WU pace from ACTIVE RECOVERY (Power Z1, HR Z1, Pace Z1, RPE 1) to ENDURANCE (Power Z2, HR Z2, Pace Z2, RPE 2–3) for 10 min. Then perform 4 × 10s strides. **MS**: Run 18 mi at your Low ENDURANCE (Power Z2, HR Z2, Pace Z2, RPE 2–3) pace. **CD**: Jog 10 min
DURATION	03:10:00	
DISTANCE	18.5 mi	
TSS	150	
18 MILE LSD ENDURANCE RUN		

WEEK #15

Training Focus: Build 1 - Week 3

MONDAY (AM)

PLANNED METRICS		Actively focus on recovery today: 1) avoid unneccessary physical exertion, 2) watch nutrition closely (healthy carbs, lean protein, and good fats), 3) stretch, and 4) drink when thirsty. Other common recovery aids include massage, napping, elevating legs, floating in water, and listening to music.
DURATION		
DISTANCE		
TSS		
DAY OFF		

TUESDAY (AM)

PLANNED METRICS		**WU**: Perform 5 mins of dynamic warm up: 1. Leg swings - 10–20 per leg 2. Marches - 10–15 per leg 3. Leg side swings - 10–20 per leg Build WU pace from ACTIVE RECOVERY (Power Z1, HR Z1, Pace Z1, RPE 1) to ENDURANCE (Power Z2, HR Z2, Pace Z2, RPE 2–3) for 10 min. Then perform 4 × 10s strides. **MS**: Run 5 mi at your ENDURANCE (Power Z2, HR Z2, Pace Z2, RPE 2–3) pace. **CD**: Jog 10 min
DURATION	00:45:00	
DISTANCE	5.5 mi	
TSS	50	
5 MILE ENDURANCE RUN		

TUESDAY (PM)

PLANNED METRICS		
DURATION	00:25:00	**Equipment**: 1 Loop resistance band.
DISTANCE	N/A	**WU**: 1. Jog for 10 min building from Active Recovery (Power Z1, HR Z1, Pace Z1, RPE 1) building to Endurance (Power Z2, HR Z2, Pace Z2, RPE 2–3).
TSS	8	2. Perform 15 reps per leg: a. knee hugs b. straight leg military march c. walking pigeon
		MS: Perform 3 rounds with 20s RI: 1. Abductor extensions (20–25/leg) 2. Adductor (20–25/leg) 3. Lateral Monster Walks (20 steps in each direction) 4. Good Mornings (20 per leg) 5. Hip Flexion (20 per leg)
HIP GIRDLE LOOP BAND WO#1		**CD**: 5 min of static stretching focusing on flexibility.

WEDNESDAY

PLANNED METRICS		
DURATION	01:25:00	**WU**: Perform 5 mins of dynamic warm up: 1. Leg swings - 10–20 per leg 2. Marches - 10–15 per leg
DISTANCE	Various	3. Leg side swings - 10–20 per leg
TSS	80	Build WU pace from ACTIVE RECOVERY (Power Z1, HR Z1, Pace Z1, RPE 1) to ENDURANCE (Power Z2, HR Z2, Pace Z2, RPE 2–3) for 10 min. Then perform 4 × 10s strides.
		MS1: Tempo run: 40' Low TEMPO (Power Z3, HR Z3, Pace Z3, RPE 3–4).
		MS2: Run another 30' at ENDURANCE (Power Z2, HR Z2, Pace Z2, RPE 2–3).
40 MIN LOW TEMPO RUN AND ENDURANCE		**CD**: Jog for 10 min ACTIVE RECOVERY (Power Z1, HR Z1, Pace Z1, RPE 1)

THURSDAY

PLANNED METRICS		WU: Perform 5 mins of dynamic warm up:
DURATION	00:52:00	1. Leg swings - 10–20 per leg 2. Marches - 10–15 per leg
DISTANCE	4.5	3. Leg side swings - 10–20 per leg
TSS	42	Build WU pace from ACTIVE RECOVERY (Power Z1, HR Z1, Pace Z1, RPE 1) to ENDURANCE (Power Z2, HR Z2, Pace Z2, RPE 2–3) for 10 min. Then perform 4 × 10s strides. **MS**: Run 4 mi at your Low ENDURANCE (Power Z2, HR Z2, Pace Z2, RPE 2–3) pace.
4 MILE LSD ENDURANCE RUN		**CD**: Jog 10 min

FRIDAY

PLANNED METRICS		Strength Protocol - Week 11
DURATION	00:45:00	**Goal**: Hypertrophy **Intensity**: 95+% of 1 RM
DISTANCE	N/A	**Note**:
TSS	25	1. 3d set should be performed until exhaustion. 2. Only 3 upper body sets.
STRENGTH WORK - WEEK 11		**Exercises**: **Strength**: 1. Bench Press (3 × 4–6) 2. Lateral Pull Down (3 × 4–6) 3. Seated Row (3 × 4–6) 4. Tricep Pulldown (3 × 4–6) 5. Bicep Curl (3 × 4–6) 6. Leg Press (8 × 4–6) 7. Leg Extension (8 × 4–6) 8. Leg Curl (8 × 4–6) 9. Calf Raises (7 × 4–6) 10. Back Extension (3 × 4–6) 11. Ab Curl (3 × 4–6) 12. Leg Tucked Rotation (8 × 4–6)

SATURDAY

PLANNED METRICS		
DURATION	00:55:00	**WU**: Perform 5 mins of dynamic warm up: 1. Leg swings - 10–20 per leg 2. Marches - 10–15 per leg 3. Leg side swings - 10–20 per leg
DISTANCE	5.5	
TSS	50	Build WU pace from ACTIVE RECOVERY (Power Z1, HR Z1, Pace Z1, RPE 1) to ENDURANCE (Power Z2, HR Z2, Pace Z2, RPE 2–3) for 10 min. Then perform 4 × 10s strides.
5 MILE LSD ENDURANCE RUN		**MS**: Run 5 mi at your Low ENDURANCE (Power Z2, HR Z2, Pace Z2, RPE 2–3) pace. **CD**: Jog 10 min

SUNDAY

PLANNED METRICS		
DURATION	03:10:00	**WU**: Perform 5 mins of dynamic warm up: 1. Leg swings - 10–20 per leg 2. Marches - 10–15 per leg 3. Leg side swings - 10–20 per leg
DISTANCE	18.5 mi	
TSS	150	Build WU pace from ACTIVE RECOVERY (Power Z1, HR Z1, Pace Z1, RPE 1) to ENDURANCE (Power Z2, HR Z2, Pace Z2, RPE 2–3) for 10 min. Then perform 4 × 10s strides.
18 MILE LSD ENDURANCE RUN		**MS**: Run 18 mi at your Low ENDURANCE (Power Z2, HR Z2, Pace Z2, RPE 2–3) pace. **CD**: Jog 10 min

WEEK #16

Training Focus: Recovery and Test Week

MONDAY (AM)

PLANNED METRICS		
DURATION		Actively focus on recovery today: 1) avoid unneccessary physical exertion, 2) watch nutrition closely (healthy carbs, lean protein, and good fats), 3) stretch, and 4) drink when thirsty. Other common recovery aids include massage, napping, elevating legs, floating in water, and listening to music.
DISTANCE		
TSS		
DAY OFF		

TUESDAY (AM)

PLANNED METRICS		
DURATION	00:45:00	**WU**: Jog for 15 min at ACTIVE RECOVERY (Power Z1, HR Z1, Pace Z1, RPE 1), then Perform the following dynamic stretches: 1. Toe Touches - 2 × 15 per leg 2. Leg Tucks - 2 × 15 per leg
DISTANCE	Various	
TSS	19	
RECOVERY - JOG 40 MIN		**MS**: Jog at ACTIVE RECOVERY (Power Z1, HR Z1, Pace Z1, RPE 1) **CD**: Walk for 10 min or until your HR drops below 100 BPM.

WEDNESDAY

PLANNED METRICS		
DURATION	00:52:00	**WU**: Perform 5 mins of dynamic warm up: 1. Leg swings - 10–20 per leg 2. Marches - 10–15 per leg 3. Leg side swings - 10–20 per leg
DISTANCE	4.5	
TSS	42	Build WU pace from ACTIVE RECOVERY (Power Z1, HR Z1, Pace Z1, RPE 1) to ENDURANCE (Power Z2, HR Z2, Pace Z2, RPE 2–3) for 10 min. Then perform 4 × 10s strides.
4 MILE LSD ENDURANCE RUN		**MS**: Run 4 mi at your Low ENDURANCE (Power Z2, HR Z2, Pace Z2, RPE 2–3) pace. **CD**: Jog 10 min

THURSDAY

PLANNED METRICS		
DURATION	00:30:00	**WU**: Perform 5 mins of dynamic warm up: 1. Leg swings - 10–20 per leg 2. Marches - 10–15 per leg 3. Leg side swings - 10–20 per leg
DISTANCE	Various	
TSS	25	Build WU pace from ACTIVE RECOVERY (Power Z1, HR Z1, Pace Z1, RPE 1–2) to ENDURANCE (Power Z2, HR Z2, Pace Z2, RPE 2–3) for 10 min. **MS**: Complete this 20 minute run. Build into the run VERY easy. Walk for the first 5 minutes, start a steady, Low ENDURANCE Z2 (Power Z2, HR Z2, Pace Z2, RPE 2–3) jog and at the 10 minute mark, complete 4 × 10 second "pick ups" gradually building into your 10k/THRESHOLD (Power Z4, HR Z4, Pace Z4, RPE 5–6). by the end of the 20s. 40s EASY Low ENDURANCE Z2 (Power Z2, HR Z2, Pace Z2, RPE 2–3) jog between. Run the final 6 minutes at low ENDURANCE Z2 (Power Z2, HR Z2, Pace Z2, RPE 2–3) jog.
20 MINUTE RUN WITH 4 × 10S PICKUPS		**CD**: Walk for 5–10 min. Perform static stretching as necessary.

FRIDAY

PLANNED METRICS		
DURATION	00:45:00	**WU**: Perform 5 mins of dynamic warm up: 1. Leg swings - 10–20 per leg 2. Marches - 10–15 per leg 3. Leg side swings - 10–20 per leg
DISTANCE	5 km	
TSS	35	Build WU pace from Z1 to Z2 for 20 min. Then perform 4 × 10s strides. -------- **MS**: Run 5 km (3.1) as fast as you can. You can do this on a bike trail, track, or sidewalk. Try to find the most flat surface (no hills) as possible. However, do not do the test on a treadmill. Track you HR. The four metrics you are concerned with tracking is your running power, pace, and HR, and the time it took you to complete the 5 km. --------
CRITICAL RUN SPEED/RFTP TEST - 5 KM		**CD**: Jog in for 10 min until your HR comes down to about 100 BPM

SATURDAY

PLANNED METRICS		Actively focus on recovery today: 1) avoid unneccessary physical exertion, 2) watch nutrition closely (healthy carbs, lean protein, and good fats), 3) stretch, and 4) drink when thirsty. Other common recovery aids include massage, napping, elevating legs, floating in water, and listening to music.
DURATION		
DISTANCE		
TSS		
DAY OFF		

SUNDAY

PLANNED METRICS		**WU**: Perform 5 mins of dynamic warm up: 1. Leg swings - 10–20 per leg 2. Marches - 10–15 per leg 3. Leg side swings - 10–20 per leg
DURATION	03:10:00	
DISTANCE	18.5 mi	
TSS	150	Build WU pace from ACTIVE RECOVERY (Power Z1, HR Z1, Pace Z1, RPE 1) to ENDURANCE (Power Z2, HR Z2, Pace Z2, RPE 2–3) for 10 min. Then perform 4 × 10s strides. **MS**: Run 18 mi at your Low ENDURANCE (Power Z2, HR Z2, Pace Z2, RPE 2–3) pace. **CD**: Jog 10 min
18 MILE LSD ENDURANCE RUN		

WEEK #17

Training Focus: Build 2 - Week 1

MONDAY (AM)

PLANNED METRICS		Actively focus on recovery today: 1) avoid unneccessary physical exertion, 2) watch nutrition closely (healthy carbs, lean protein, and good fats), 3) stretch, and 4) drink when thirsty. Other common recovery aids include massage, napping, elevating legs, floating in water, and listening to music.
DURATION		
DISTANCE		
TSS		
DAY OFF		

TUESDAY (AM)

PLANNED METRICS		
DURATION	00:45:00	**WU**: Perform 5 mins of dynamic warm up: 1. Leg swings - 10–20 per leg 2. Marches - 10–15 per leg 3. Leg side swings - 10–20 per leg Build WU pace from ACTIVE RECOVERY (Power Z1, HR Z1, Pace Z1, RPE 1) to ENDURANCE (Power Z2, HR Z2, Pace Z2, RPE 2–3) for 10 min. Then perform 4 × 10s strides. **MS**: Run 5 mi at your ENDURANCE (Power Z2, HR Z2, Pace Z2, RPE 2–3) pace. **CD**: Jog 10 min
DISTANCE	5.5 mi	
TSS	50	
5 MILE ENDURANCE RUN		

TUESDAY (PM)

PLANNED METRICS		
DURATION	00:25:00	**WU**: 1. Jog for 10 min building from Active Recovery (Power Z1, HR Z1, Pace Z1, RPE 1) building to Endurance (Power Z2, HR Z2, Pace Z2, RPE 2–3). 2. Perform 15 reps per leg: a. knee hugs b. straight leg military march c. walking pigeon **MS**: Lower Body & Core Strength: 12–15 reps of each 1. stability ball hamstring pull ins 2. ball transfer from hands to feet 3. top of the ball foot march 4. reverse crunch 5. low back/ glute & ham raise 6. single leg dead lift moderate weight dumb bell 7. side step up to box w/ moderate wt dumb bell pilates hip series 10 each without resting leg to floor until completion: 8. front circles with tow pointed quad firm 9. back circles with tow pointed quad firm 10. leg raise (controlled and slow) hold at the top after 10 for 10 sec then 10 fast pulses **CD**: Static stretch for 10 min.
DISTANCE	N/A	
TSS	8	
LOWER BODY STRENGTH + HIP ROUTINE #1		

WEDNESDAY

PLANNED METRICS		
DURATION	01:00:00	**WU**: Perform 5 mins of dynamic warm up: 1. Leg swings - 10–20 per leg 2. Marches - 10–15 per leg 3. Leg side swings - 10–20 per leg
DISTANCE	8.5	
TSS	70	Build WU pace from Active Recovery (Power Z1, HR Z1, Pace Z1, RPE 1) to Endurance (Power Z2, HR Z2, Pace Z2, RPE 2–3) for 10 min. Then perform 4 × 10s strides. **MS**: For this 8 mi run, perform 4 × 1mi Tempo (Power Z3, HR Z3, Pace Z3, RPE 3–4) efforts with 1 mile "recovery" at Endurance (Power Z2, HR Z2, Pace Z2, RPE 2–3). If the finish the balance of the run at Endurance (Power Z2, HR Z2, Pace Z2, RPE 2–3).
8 MI - 1 MI TEMPO INTERVALS		**CD**: Jog 10 min at Active Recovery (Power Z1, HR Z1, Pace Z1, RPE 1)

THURSDAY

PLANNED METRICS		
DURATION	00:52:00	**WU**: Perform 5 mins of dynamic warm up: 1. Leg swings - 10–20 per leg 2. Marches - 10–15 per leg 3. Leg side swings - 10–20 per leg
DISTANCE	4.5	
TSS	42	Build WU pace from ACTIVE RECOVERY (Power Z1, HR Z1, Pace Z1, RPE 1) to ENDURANCE (Power Z2, HR Z2, Pace Z2, RPE 2–3) for 10 min. Then perform 4 × 10s strides. **MS**: Run 4 mi at your Low ENDURANCE (Power Z2, HR Z2, Pace Z2, RPE 2–3) pace.
4 MILE LSD ENDURANCE RUN		**CD**: Jog 10 min

FRIDAY

PLANNED METRICS		Strength Protocol - Week 12 **Goal**: Hypertrophy **Intensity**: 70% of 1 RM **Note**: 1. 3d set should be performed until exhaustion. 2. Only 3 upper body sets. **Exercises**: **Strength**: 1. Bench Press (3 × 4–6) 2. Lateral Pull Down (3 × 4–6) 3. Seated Row (3 × 4–6) 4. Tricep Pulldown (3 × 4–6) 5. Bicep Curl (3 × 4–6) 6. Leg Press (4 × 4–6) 7. Leg Extension (4 × 4–6) 8. Leg Curl (8 × 4–6) 9. Calf Raises (4 × 4–6) 10. Back Extension (3 × 4–6) 11. Ab Curl (3 × 4–6) 12. Leg Tucked Rotation (4 × 4–6)
DURATION	00:45:00	
DISTANCE	N/A	
TSS	25	
STRENGTH WORK - WEEK 12		

SATURDAY

PLANNED METRICS		**WU**: Perform 5 mins of dynamic warm up: 1. Leg swings - 10–20 per leg 2. Marches - 10–15 per leg 3. Leg side swings - 10–20 per leg Build WU pace from ACTIVE RECOVERY (Power Z1, HR Z1, Pace Z1, RPE 1) to ENDURANCE (Power Z2, HR Z2, Pace Z2, RPE 2–3) for 10 min. Then perform 4 × 10s strides. **MS**: Run 5 mi at your ENDURANCE (Power Z2, HR Z2, Pace Z2, RPE 2–3) pace. **CD**: Jog 10 min
DURATION	00:45:00	
DISTANCE	5.5	
TSS	50	
5 MILE ENDURANCE RUN		

SUNDAY

PLANNED METRICS		WU: Perform 5 mins of dynamic warm up:
DURATION	03:40:00	1. Leg swings - 10–20 per leg 2. Marches - 10–15 per leg 3. Leg side swings - 10–20 per leg
DISTANCE	20.5 mi	
TSS	170	Build WU pace from ACTIVE RECOVERY (Power Z1, HR Z1, Pace Z1, RPE 1) to ENDURANCE (Power Z2, HR Z2, Pace Z2, RPE 2–3) for 10 min. Then perform 4 × 10s strides.
20 MILE LSD ENDURANCE RUN		**MS**: Run 20 mi at your Low ENDURANCE (Power Z2, HR Z2, Pace Z2, RPE 2–3) pace. **CD**: Jog 10 min

WEEK #18

Training Focus: Build 2 - Week 2

MONDAY (AM)

PLANNED METRICS		Actively focus on recovery today: 1) avoid unneccessary physical exertion, 2) watch nutrition closely (healthy carbs, lean protein, and good fats), 3) stretch, and 4) drink when thirsty. Other common recovery aids include massage, napping, elevating legs, floating in water, and listening to music.
DURATION		
DISTANCE		
TSS		
DAY OFF		

TUESDAY (AM)

PLANNED METRICS		WU: Perform 5 mins of dynamic warm up:
DURATION	00:52:00	1. Leg swings - 10–20 per leg 2. Marches - 10–15 per leg 3. Leg side swings - 10–20 per leg
DISTANCE	4.5	
TSS	42	Build WU pace from ACTIVE RECOVERY (Power Z1, HR Z1, Pace Z1, RPE 1) to ENDURANCE (Power Z2, HR Z2, Pace Z2, RPE 2–3) for 10 min. Then perform 4 × 10s strides.
4 MILE LSD ENDURANCE RUN		**MS**: Run 4 mi at your Low ENDURANCE (Power Z2, HR Z2, Pace Z2, RPE 2–3) pace. **CD**: Jog 10 min

TUESDAY (PM)

PLANNED METRICS	
DURATION	00:25:00
DISTANCE	N/A
TSS	8

LOWER BODY STRENGTH + HIP ROUTINE #2

WU: 1. Jog for 10 min building from Active Recovery (Power Z1, HR Z1, Pace Z1, RPE 1) building to Endurance (Power Z2, HR Z2, Pace Z2, RPE 2–3).

2. Perform 15 reps per leg:
   a. knee hugs
   b. straight leg military march
   c. walking pigeon

MS: Lower Body & Core Strength:
12–15 reps of each
1. stability ball hamstring pull ins
2. ball transfer from hands to feet
3. top of the ball foot march
4. reverse crunch
5. low back/ glute & ham raise
6. single leg dead lift moderate weight dumb bell
7. single leg wall squat.
8. 1 legged bosu ball balance - 15–20s / leg
9. 1 legged bosu ball squats

CD: Static stretch for 10 min.

WEDNESDAY

PLANNED METRICS	
DURATION	01:15:00
DISTANCE	10.5 mi
TSS	85

10 MI - 1 MI TEMPO INTERVALS

WU: Perform 5 mins of dynamic warm up:
1. Leg swings - 10–20 per leg
2. Marches - 10–15 per leg
3. Leg side swings - 10–20 per leg

Build WU pace from Active Recovery (Power Z1, HR Z1, Pace Z1, RPE 1) to Endurance (Power Z2, HR Z2, Pace Z2, RPE 2–3) for 10 min. Then perform 4 × 10s strides.

MS: For this 10 mi run, perform 5 × 1mi Tempo (Power Z3, HR Z3, Pace Z3, RPE 3–4) efforts with 1 mile "recovery" at Endurance (Power Z2, HR Z2, Pace Z2, RPE 2–3).

If the finish the balance of the run at Endurance (Power Z2, HR Z2, Pace Z2, RPE 2–3).

CD: Jog 10 min at Active Recovery (Power Z1, HR Z1, Pace Z1, RPE 1)

THURSDAY

PLANNED METRICS		WU: Perform 5 mins of dynamic warm up:
DURATION	00:52:00	1. Leg swings - 10–20 per leg 2. Marches - 10–15 per leg 3. Leg side swings - 10–20 per leg
DISTANCE	4.5	
TSS	42	Build WU pace from ACTIVE RECOVERY (Power Z1, HR Z1, Pace Z1, RPE 1) to ENDURANCE (Power Z2, HR Z2, Pace Z2, RPE 2–3) for 10 min. Then perform 4 × 10s strides.
4 MILE LSD ENDURANCE RUN		**MS**: Run 4 mi at your Low ENDURANCE (Power Z2, HR Z2, Pace Z2, RPE 2–3) pace. **CD**: Jog 10 min

FRIDAY

PLANNED METRICS		WU: 1. Jog for 10 min building from Active Recovery (Power Z1, HR Z1, Pace Z1, RPE 1) building to Endurance (Power Z2, HR Z2, Pace Z2, RPE 2–3).
DURATION	00:45:00	
DISTANCE	N/A	2. Perform 15 reps per leg: a. knee hugs b. straight leg military march c. walking pigeon
TSS	15	
LOWER BODY STRENGTH + HIP ROUTINE + UPPER BODY #3		**MS**: Lower Body & Core Strength: 12–15 reps of each 1. stability ball hamstring pull ins 2. ball transfer from hands to feet 3. top of the ball foot march 4. reverse crunch 5. low back/ glute & ham raise 6. single leg dead lift moderate weight dumb bell 7. side step up to box w/ moderate wt dumb bell pilates hip series 10 each without resting leg to floor until completion: 8. leg raise (controlled and slow) hold at the top after 10 for 10 sec then 10 fast pulses 9. kicks - front/ front back long 10. kicks - back/ back/ front long 11. Bench Press - 2 × 15 - 18 repetitions at 65% of your 1 rep max 12. Dumbbell Pullovers - 2 × 15 - 18 repetitions 13. Dumbell Lateral Raises - 2 × 15 - 18 repetitions **CD**: Static stretch for 10 min.

SATURDAY

PLANNED METRICS		
DURATION	00:52:00	**WU**: Perform 5 mins of dynamic warm up: 1. Leg swings - 10–20 per leg 2. Marches - 10–15 per leg 3. Leg side swings - 10–20 per leg
DISTANCE	4.5	
TSS	42	Build WU pace from ACTIVE RECOVERY (Power Z1, HR Z1, Pace Z1, RPE 1) to ENDURANCE (Power Z2, HR Z2, Pace Z2, RPE 2–3) for 10 min. Then perform 4x10s strides.
4 MILE LSD ENDURANCE RUN		**MS**: Run 4 mi at your Low ENDURANCE (Power Z2, HR Z2, Pace Z2, RPE 2–3) pace. **CD**: Jog 10 min

SUNDAY

PLANNED METRICS		
DURATION	02:45:00	**WU**: Perform 5 mins of dynamic warm up: 1. Leg swings - 10–20 per leg 2. Marches - 10–15 per leg 3. Leg side swings - 10–20 per leg
DISTANCE	16.5	
TSS	130	Build WU pace from ACTIVE RECOVERY (Power Z1, HR Z1, Pace Z1, RPE 1) to ENDURANCE (Power Z2, HR Z2, Pace Z2, RPE 2–3) for 10 min. Then perform 4x10s strides.
16 MILE LSD ENDURANCE RUN		**MS**: Run 16 mi at your Low ENDURANCE (Power Z2, HR Z2, Pace Z2, RPE 2–3) pace. **CD**: Jog 10 min

WEEK #19

Training Focus: Build 2 - Week 3

MONDAY (AM)

PLANNED METRICS		
DURATION		Actively focus on recovery today: 1) avoid unneccessary physical exertion, 2) watch nutrition closely (healthy carbs, lean protein, and good fats), 3) stretch, and 4) drink when thirsty. Other common recovery aids include massage, napping, elevating legs, floating in water, and listening to music.
DISTANCE		
TSS		
DAY OFF		

TUESDAY (AM)

PLANNED METRICS	
DURATION	00:52:00
DISTANCE	4.5
TSS	42

4 MILE LSD ENDURANCE RUN

WU: Perform 5 mins of dynamic warm up:
1. Leg swings - 10–20 per leg
2. Marches - 10–15 per leg
3. Leg side swings - 10–20 per leg

Build WU pace from ACTIVE RECOVERY (Power Z1, HR Z1, Pace Z1, RPE 1) to ENDURANCE (Power Z2, HR Z2, Pace Z2, RPE 2–3) for 10 min. Then perform 4 × 10s strides.

MS: Run 4 mi at your Low ENDURANCE (Power Z2, HR Z2, Pace Z2, RPE 2–3) pace.

CD: Jog 10 min

TUESDAY (PM)

PLANNED METRICS	
DURATION	00:25:00
DISTANCE	N/A
TSS	8

CORE AND HIP ROUTINE - PILATES STYLE

WU: Jog for 10 min building from Active Recovery (Power Z1, HR Z1, Pace Z1, RPE 1) building to Endurance (Power Z2, HR Z2, Pace Z2, RPE 2–3).

MS1: Perform 2 sets of the following with 1–2 min rest between each set:
1. Front plank × 1 min. During this one minute, perform 30 reps of isometric squeezes of all core muscles. Immediately after …
2. Press into a child's pose for 30 seconds. Then …
3. Perform 15 reps of the bird dog on each side from all fours. Then …
4. Perform 30 reps of pilates roll ups from flat back

MS2: Perform 2 sets x 10 reps on each side of the following Pilates hip routine with 1–2 min rest between each set:
1. Point your toes & kick powerfully up & flex to slow down pulse with shorter ROM as above
2. Circle clockwise stopping at 12 o'clock circle counter clockwise stopping at 12 o'clock
3. Kick pointed toe forward & flex slow kick back to the start position
4. Kick forward flexed & slow point toe back to the start position

CD: Perform 5–10 min of static stretching

WEDNESDAY

PLANNED METRICS		
DURATION	01:10:00	**WU**: Perform 5 mins of dynamic warm up: 1. Leg swings - 10–20 per leg 2. Marches - 10–15 per leg 3. Leg side swings - 10–20 per leg
DISTANCE	Various	
TSS	80	Build WU pace from ACTIVE RECOVERY (Power Z1, HR Z1, Pace Z1, RPE 1) to ENDURANCE (Power Z2, HR Z2, Pace Z2, RPE 2–3) for 10 min. Then perform 4 × 10s strides. **MS**: 5–7 × 800 m @ upper Tempo (Power Z3, HR Z3, Pace Z3, RPE 3–4) with 400 at Endurance (Power Z2, HR Z2, Pace Z2, RPE 2–3) between each 800. Then move to MS2. **MS2**: Run 4 mile at ENDURANCE (Power Z2, HR Z2, Pace Z2, RPE 2–3)
YASSO INTERVALS WITH ENDURANCE		**CD**: Jog or walk at Active Recovery (Power Z1, HR Z1, Pace Z1, RPE 1) for 15 min.

THURSDAY

PLANNED METRICS		
DURATION	00:30:00	**WU**: Perform 5 mins of dynamic warm up: 1. Leg swings - 10–20 per leg 2. Marches - 10–15 per leg 3. Leg side swings - 10–20 per leg
DISTANCE	Various	
TSS	25	Build WU pace from ACTIVE RECOVERY (Power Z1, HR Z1, Pace Z1, RPE 1–2) to ENDURANCE (Power Z2, HR Z2, Pace Z2, RPE 2–3) for 10 min. **MS**: Complete this 20 minute run. Build into the run VERY easy. Walk for the first 5 minutes, start a steady, Low ENDURANCE Z2 (Power Z2, HR Z2, Pace Z2, RPE 2–3) jog and at the 10 minute mark, complete 4x10 second "pick ups" gradually building into your 10k/THRESHOLD (Power Z4, HR Z4, Pace Z4, RPE 5–6). by the end of the 20s. 40s EASY Low ENDURANCE Z2 (Power Z2, HR Z2, Pace Z2, RPE 2–3) jog between. Run the final 6 minutes at low ENDURANCE Z2 (Power Z2, HR Z2, Pace Z2, RPE 2–3) jog.
20 MINUTE RUN WITH 4 × 10S PICKUPS		**CD**: Walk for 5–10 min. Perform static stretching as necessary.

FRIDAY

PLANNED METRICS		Actively focus on recovery today: 1) avoid unneccessary physical exertion, 2) watch nutrition closely (healthy carbs, lean protein, and good fats), 3) stretch, and 4) drink when thirsty. Other common recovery aids include massage, napping, elevating legs, floating in water, and listening to music.
DURATION		
DISTANCE		
TSS		
DAY OFF		

SATURDAY

PLANNED METRICS		**WU**: Perform 5 mins of dynamic warm up: 1. Leg swings - 10–20 per leg 2. Marches - 10–15 per leg 3. Leg side swings - 10–20 per leg Build WU pace from ACTIVE RECOVERY (Power Z1, HR Z1, Pace Z1, RPE 1) to ENDURANCE (Power Z2, HR Z2, Pace Z2, RPE 2–3) for 10 min. Then perform 4x10s strides. **MS**: Run 4 mi at your Low ENDURANCE (Power Z2, HR Z2, Pace Z2, RPE 2–3) pace. **CD**: Jog 10 min
DURATION	00:52:00	
DISTANCE	4.5	
TSS	42	
4 MILE LSD ENDURANCE RUN		

SUNDAY

PLANNED METRICS		**WU**: Perform 5 mins of dynamic warm up: 1. Leg swings - 10–20 per leg 2. Marches - 10–15 per leg 3. Leg side swings - 10–20 per leg Build WU pace from ACTIVE RECOVERY (Power Z1, HR Z1, Pace Z1, RPE 1) to ENDURANCE (Power Z2, HR Z2, Pace Z2, RPE 2–3) for 10 min. Then perform 4 × 10s strides. **MS**: Run 8 mi at your Low ENDURANCE (Power Z2, HR Z2, Pace Z2, RPE 2–3) pace. **CD**: Jog 10 min
DURATION	01:05:00	
DISTANCE	8.5	
TSS	90	
8 MILE LSD ENDURANCE RUN		

WEEK #20

Training Focus: Taper and Race Week!!

MONDAY

PLANNED METRICS		Actively focus on recovery today: 1) avoid unneccessary physical exertion, 2) watch nutrition closely (healthy carbs, lean protein, and good fats), 3) stretch, and 4) drink when thirsty. Other common recovery aids include massage, napping, elevating legs, floating in water, and listening to music.
DURATION		
DISTANCE		
TSS		
DAY OFF		

TUESDAY

PLANNED METRICS		**WU**: Perform 5 mins of dynamic warm up: 1. Leg swings - 10–20 per leg 2. Marches - 10–15 per leg 3. Leg side swings - 10–20 per leg
DURATION	00:52:00	
DISTANCE	4.5	
TSS	42	Build WU pace from ACTIVE RECOVERY (Power Z1, HR Z1, Pace Z1, RPE 1) to ENDURANCE (Power Z2, HR Z2, Pace Z2, RPE 2–3) for 10 min. Then perform 4 × 10s strides.
4 MILE LSD ENDURANCE RUN		**MS**: Run 4 mi at your Low ENDURANCE (Power Z2, HR Z2, Pace Z2, RPE 2–3) pace. **CD**: Jog 10 min

WEDNESDAY

PLANNED METRICS		
DURATION	00:30:00	**WU**: Perform 5 mins of dynamic warm up: 1. Leg swings - 10–20 per leg 2. Marches - 10–15 per leg 3. Leg side swings - 10–20 per leg Build WU pace from ACTIVE RECOVERY (Power Z1, HR Z1, Pace Z1, RPE 1–2) to ENDURANCE (Power Z2, HR Z2, Pace Z2, RPE 2–3) for 10 min. **MS**: Complete this 20 minute run. Build into the run VERY easy. Walk for the first 5 minutes, start a steady, Low ENDURANCE Z2 (Power Z2, HR Z2, Pace Z2, RPE 2–3) jog and at the 10 minute mark, complete 4x10 second "pick ups" gradually building into your 10k/THRESHOLD (Power Z4, HR Z4, Pace Z4, RPE 5–6). by the end of the 20s. 40s EASY Low ENDURANCE Z2 (Power Z2, HR Z2, Pace Z2, RPE 2–3) jog between. Run the final 6 minutes at low ENDURANCE Z2 (Power Z2, HR Z2, Pace Z2, RPE 2–3) jog. **CD**: Walk for 5–10 min. Perform static stretching as necessary.
DISTANCE	Various	
TSS	25	
20 MINUTE RUN WITH 4 × 10S PICKUPS		

THURSDAY

PLANNED METRICS		
DURATION		Actively focus on recovery today: 1) avoid unneccessary physical exertion, 2) watch nutrition closely (healthy carbs, lean protein, and good fats), 3) stretch, and 4) drink when thirsty. Other common recovery aids include massage, napping, elevating legs, floating in water, and listening to music.
DISTANCE		
TSS		
DAY OFF		

FRIDAY

PLANNED METRICS	
DURATION	00:30:00
DISTANCE	Various
TSS	25

20 MINUTE RUN WITH 4 × 10S PICKUPS

WU: Perform 5 mins of dynamic warm up:
1. Leg swings - 10–20 per leg
2. Marches - 10–15 per leg
3. Leg side swings - 10–20 per leg

Build WU pace from ACTIVE RECOVERY (Power Z1, HR Z1, Pace Z1, RPE 1–2) to ENDURANCE (Power Z2, HR Z2, Pace Z2, RPE 2–3) for 10 min.

MS: Complete this 20 minute run. Build into the run VERY easy. Walk for the first 5 minutes, start a steady, Low ENDURANCE Z2 (Power Z2, HR Z2, Pace Z2, RPE 2–3) jog and at the 10 minute mark, complete 4 × 10 second "pick ups" gradually building into your 10k/THRESHOLD (Power Z4, HR Z4, Pace Z4, RPE 5–6). by the end of the 20s. 40s EASY Low ENDURANCE Z2 (Power Z2, HR Z2, Pace Z2, RPE 2–3) jog between.

Run the final 6 minutes at low ENDURANCE Z2 (Power Z2, HR Z2, Pace Z2, RPE 2–3) jog.

CD: Walk for 5–10 min. Perform static stretching as necessary.

FRIDAY

PLANNED METRICS	
DURATION	00:30:00
DISTANCE	Various
TSS	25

20 MINUTE RUN WITH 4 × 10S PICKUPS

WU: Perform 5 mins of dynamic warm up:
1. Leg swings - 10-20 per leg
2. Marches - 10-15 per leg
3. Leg side swings - 10-20 per leg

Build WU pace from ACTIVE RECOVERY (Power Z1, HR Z1, Pace Z1, RPE 1-2) to ENDURANCE (Power Z2, HR Z2, Pace Z2, RPE 2-3) for 10 min.

MS: Complete this 20 minute run. Build into the run VERY easy. Walk for the first 5 minutes, start a steady, Low ENDURANCE Z2 (Power Z2, HR Z2, Pace Z2, RPE 2-3) jog and at the 10 minute mark, complete 4x10 second "pick ups" gradually building into your 10k/THRESHOLD (Power Z4, HR Z4, Pace Z4, RPE 5-6). by the end of the 20s. 40s EASY Low ENDURANCE Z2 (Power Z2, HR Z2, Pace Z2, RPE 2-3) jog between.

Run the final 6 minutes at low ENDURANCE Z2 (Power Z2, HR Z2, Pace Z2, RPE 2-3) jog.

CD: Walk for 5-10 min. Perform static stretching as necessary.

SATURDAY

PLANNED METRICS		WU: Jog for 15 min progressing from ACTIVE RECOVERY (Pace Z1, HR Z1, Power Z1, RPE 1-2) to ENDURANCE (Pace Z2, HR Z2, Power Z2, PRE 2-3). Towards the end of the WU, perform 4x60s of strides to fully open up your muscles.
DURATION	00:30:00	
DISTANCE	Various	
TSS	30	
		MS: 1. 3 × 3 minutes @ 90% of your Threshold pace (Pace Z3, HR Z3, Power Z3, RPE 4-5) with 6 minutes of recovery at ENDURANCE Pace (Pace Z2, HR Z2, Power Z2, PRE 2-3).
		2. 3x10s pick-ups with 3 min recovery at ENDURANCE Pace (Pace Z2, HR Z2, Power Z2, PRE 2-3) in between
PRIMER (PRE-RACE)		**CD**: 10 min at ACTIVE RECOVERY (Pace Z1, HR Z1, Power Z1, RPE 1-2

SUNDAY

PLANNED METRICS		Good luck! When you start, try to hold back for the first few miles before settling in to your goal race pace. Marathon running is about dosing out your energy properly.
DURATION	Various	
DISTANCE	26.4	
TSS	180	Be sure to walk and stretch immediately after you finish to reduce soreness and stiffness in the days to come. Also, eat something with 30 minutes of completing the race. This will help with recovery.
RACE DAY!!!		Most of all, have fun! You have done the work and are ready for race day!!!

Test Interpretation Notes

CSS Interpretation Notes

During this first week, you will perform 2 swim tests. With this information, you will be able to calculate your critical swim speed (very similar to your FTP on the bike) and create pacing zones to train different efforts. So, how do you do this? On day one, you will perform two time trials. The first will be a 400 m time and the second will be a 200 m time trial. On a completely separate day, you will perform test #2 which is a 1000 m time trial. During each of these tests, you will need to record two metrics, your total time and your stroke rate. With this information, you will be able to calculate your pacings.

Pacing calculation instructions:
CSS = (1000 m – 400 m – 200 m) / (T3 – T2 – T1)
Goal: Calculate your threshold pace.

Example:
CSS = (400 m – 200 m) / (368 – 180)

CSS = 200 / 188 = 1.06 m/s

Threshold Pace (CSS) = 100 m / 1.06 m/s = 94s or 1:34 min/100 m

Zones - % of CSS
Zone 1: 75–80%
Zone 2: 80–90%
Zone 3: 90–100%
Zone 4: 100%
Zone 5: 100–110%
Zone 6: 110+%

Critical Run Speed/rFTP Test Calculations

This week, you will perform 2 run tests (5 km and 10 km distances). The 5 km test is the test you will use to determine your running functional threshold power (rFTP) or your running threshold pace. The 10 km test is used to determine if the calculated training zones from the 5 km test are accurate.

Running Power (For Stryd, RunScribe, etc.)
5 km Test - rFTP

The general equation for rFTP is as follows:

rFTP = 5-kilometer NP x coefficient

Note: The coefficient ranges between 92–95%. This is dependent on your current physical condition. 92% is typically used for beginners while 95% is used with well-trained or seasoned athletes.

Example:
5-kilometer run test normalized power = 262 W

rFTP = 95% × 262 W = 250 W

Now that the rFTP has been calculated, the running power training/pacing zones can be established for your TrainingPeaks under your user settings.

Running Threshold Pace

5 km Test

Calculate your normalized pace (NGP) from the 5 km test. Enter this pace into your TrainingPeaks pacing for running. This will allow TrainingPeaks to calculate your customized running pacing zones.

Critical Run Speed/rFTP Test Interpretation and Zone/Pacing Calculation #2

The 10 km test is a confirmation of your zones calculated from the rFTP test. Your 10 km rFTP and pace should fall within the upper Z2 and/or mid-Z3 range.

If you 10 km pace does not fall into this range, you may want to consider performing the rFTP test again.

Swimming Key Terms

1. **Tarzan:** Swim freestyle with your head held completely out of the water; keep your face pointing forward and do not turn or rotate your neck to breathe. Arch back to keep your legs and feet near the surface of the water. Keep a strong kick and focus on keeping your hips up near the top of the water.
2. **2/3 Catch up:** Push off the wall in a streamline and start your stroke normally. Leave the opposite hand fully extended, even during the recovery. Allow the opposite arm to almost catch the extended arm. As your opposite arm almost touches hands with the extended arm, have the extended arm move into the catch phase. When the opposite arm that just entered the water is fully extended, leave it fully extended. Now, allow the arm that just entered the catch phase "catch" the extended arm. Continually repeat these actions.
3. **Shark Fin:** Place a pull buoy between your legs (or without) and start your swim as you normally would. As your arm goes through the follow-through phase, slap the top of the buoy that is above the water. Continue your swim stroke as you normally would. If you perform this drill without a buoy, touch the top of your buttocks as if the buoy was present.
4. **Scull:** Kicking on your stomach, put your hands out in front of you with palms facing the bottom of the pool. Press your palms outward with the little finger toward the surface, then rotate your hand and press inward with the thumb up. Feel your body slightly lift as you move your hands in and out, keep your kick going.
5. **Fist:** Swim as you normally would. Instead of having an open hand, swim with a closed fist. Ensure you perform every aspect of the swim stroke.
6. **Golf:** During the first length (whether it is 50 m, 25 yds, or 23 yds) count the number of strokes it takes you to complete one length. On the next length, try to complete the same distance with less strokes. Keep going lower and lower ... just like in a game of golf! For example, if it takes you 34 strokes to do one 50 m length, try to complete the same distance in 33 strokes. This will force you to focus on the catch phase and generate more force and propulsion.

CPSIA information can be obtained
at www.ICGtesting.com
Printed in the USA
LVHW060512221021
701130LV00002B/4

9 781793 532